William Harrison Ainsworth

Mervyn Clithero

ISBN/EAN: 9783337191214

Printed in Europe, USA, Canada, Australia, Japan

Cover: Foto ©ninafisch / pixelio.de

More available books at **www.hansebooks.com**

William Harrison Ainsworth

Mervyn Clithero

MERVYN CLITHEROE

BY

WILLIAM HARRISON AINSWORTH

WITH ILLUSTRATIONS BY HABLOT K. BROWNE

LONDON
GEORGE ROUTLEDGE & SONS, LIMITED
BROADWAY, LUDGATE HILL
GLASGOW, MANCHESTER AND NEW YORK

INSCRIBED

TO

MY CONTEMPORARIES

AT THE

MANCHESTER SCHOOL.

CONTENTS.

BOOK THE FIRST.

CHAP		PAGE
I.	Showing how, although I lose my best friend just as I begin life, I am fortunate enough to find another friend, together with a good home	1
II.	An account of my schooldays, schoolfellows, and schoolmasters—Mr. Abel Cane proves that he IS able to cane—Dr. Lonsdale adopts a different mode of tuition—John Brideoake—a Bunker's Hill hero—a boy drowned	8
III.	Containing an account of my great-uncle, John Mobberley, his old dame, and his farm at Marston	19
IV.	Malpas and I attempt to cross Marston Mere during a hard frost—an adventure on the ice	28
V.	Consequences of the adventure on the ice	33
VI.	In which I ride round Marston Mere; meet with some gipsies in a strange place; and take part at the Twelfth Night merry-making in Farmer Shakeshaft's barn	41
VII.	Showing how my Uncle Mobberley and I were very painfully surprised on our return home	55
VIII.	A glance at Cottonborough—Apphia Brideoake	60

CHAP.		PAGE
IX.—Introduces a benevolent physician and a decayed gentlewoman		65
X.—A visit to the butler's pantry—A dinner-party at the anchorite's—Dr. Bray and Mr. Cuthbert Spring		73
XI.—I lose my uncle Mobberley, and believe myself heir to his property		89
XII.—A nocturnal alarm		97
XIII.—In which my uncle's will is read, and I experience the truth of the proverb, that "there's many a slip 'twixt cup and lip"		99
XIV.—I again encounter Peninnah		110
XV.—I meet Phaleg at midnight in Marston churchyard, and my uncle Mobberley's ghost appears to us		114

BOOK THE SECOND.

I.—In which it is probable that I shall forfeit the reader's good opinion, as I display sad want of temper, and great ingratitude; and give my enemies the advantage over me		129
II.—From which it will appear there is some truth in the saying that the absent are always wronged		139
III.—Despite Mr. Spring's advice I make a scene, and do not improve my position		142
IV.—Recounting my first hostile meeting, and, it is to be hoped, my last		154
V.—I renew my acquaintance with Phaleg		161
VI.—A summer morning in Dunton Park—sad intelligence		166
VII.—I am introduced to an eccentric elderly gentleman, familiarly styled Old Hazy; who, though no conjuror himself, is much addicted to necromantic lore, and has a very enchanting niece		174

CONTENTS. vii

CHAP.	PAGE
VIII.—Of the mysterious bell-ringing at Owlarton Grange	184
IX.—How we passed the rest of the evening at Owlarton Grange	193
X.—In which I fancy that I solve the mystery of the extraordinary bell-ringing	198
XI.—I obtain an insight into John Brideoake's heart	205
XII.—The legend of Owlarton Grange—My adventure in the haunted chamber	216
XIII.—Wherein old Hazy endeavours to persuade me that I have been deluded by an evil spirit	225
XIV.—Love in a maze	230
XV.—What happened in the orchard of the mill in Weverham Glen	235

BOOK THE THIRD.

I.—How the two wizards of Owlarton Grange raised a spirit which they did not expect	251
II.—Miss Hazilrigge takes me into her confidence	257
III.—Revelations	262
IV.—I give a rustic fête at the mill	270
V.—In which I appear in a new character	289
VI.—Showing what success attended the stratagem	292
VII.—I am worsted, and driven ingloriously from the field	297
VIII.—Mr. Comberbach has gloomy forebodings	300
IX.—In which John Brideoake is made acquainted with his family history by Doctor Foam	302
X.—John and I revisit our old school, and pass a few hours in the Chetham Library—Ill tidings	307
XI.—Delamere Forest	309
XII.—The turf-cutter's hut	315
XIII.—The chase across the morass	321
XIV.—The search for the body	323

CHAP.	PAGE
XV.—THE EXAMINATION BEFORE THE MAGISTRATES	329
XVI.—THE THAUMATURGUS AGAIN APPEARS ON THE SCENE	339
XVII.—FORTUNE AT LAST FAVOURS ME	346
XVIII.—THE STEEPLE-CHASE	353
XIX.—ONCE MORE AT THE GRAVE	362
XX.—AT HOME AT THE ANCHORITE'S	365

LIST OF PLATES.

	PAGE
FRONTISPIECE	
VIGNETTE TITLE	
A BUNKER'S HILL HERO	17
WHO SHOT THE CAT?	27
MY ADVENTURE WITH THE GIPSIES	47
TWELFTH NIGHT MERRY-MAKING IN FARMER SHAKESHAFT'S BARN	54
THE BENEVOLENT PHYSICIAN	73
THE DINNER-PARTY AT THE ANCHORITE'S	83
A NOCTURNAL ALARM	98
MY UNCLE MOBBERLEY'S WILL IS READ	104
MY ALTERCATION WITH MALPAS SALE	149
THE DUEL ON CRABTREE-GREEN	160
I RECEIVE SAD INTELLIGENCE FROM NED CULCHETH	168
THE MYSTERIOUS BELL-RINGING AT OWLARTON GRANGE	192
THE LEGEND OF OWLARTON GRANGE	218
MY ADVENTURE IN THE HAUNTED CHAMBER	220
THE STRANGER AT THE GRAVE	254
THE CONJURORS INTERRUPTED	256
I FIND POWNALL IN CONFERENCE WITH THE GIPSIES	268
THE RUSTIC FÊTE AT THE MILL	276
THE DEED OF SETTLEMENT	297
THE MEETING IN DELAMERE FOREST	316
THE EXAMINATION BEFORE THE MAGISTRATES	333
DEATH OF MALPAS SALE	359

BOOK THE FIRST.

LIFE AND ADVENTURES

OF

MERVYN CLITHEROE.

CHAPTER I.

SHOWING HOW, ALTHOUGH I LOSE MY BEST FRIEND JUST AS I BEGIN LIFE, I AM FORTUNATE ENOUGH TO FIND ANOTHER FRIEND, TOGETHER WITH A GOOD HOME.

I AM the only son, by his first marriage, of Captain Charles Clitheroe, of Clitheroe, in Lancashire. My mother's maiden name was Clara Leyburne. She was an orphan, and was brought up by a benevolent lady, a near relation of her own, Mrs. Mervyn, after whom I was named. She was only seventeen when she was united to my father, and extremely beautiful. I have but an indistinct recollection of her, but remember she had very dark eyes and very dark hair, and an expression of countenance which I thought angelic. I also remember she talked to me a great deal about my papa, and showed me his picture, telling me how tall and handsome he was, and hoping I should grow up like him. He was a long way off, fighting in India, she said, and she didn't think she should ever see him again, and the thought made her extremely unhappy. She told me I must never be a soldier, as, when I went away to the wars, I should make those who loved me unhappy. I promised I would not; and on this she pressed me to her bosom, and wept over me; and I wept too for company. She had always looked pale and thin, but she now began to look paler and thinner, and even I noticed the change. Sometimes, casting wistful looks at me, she would say, "What will become of you, Mervyn, if I leave you?" I told her she mustn't leave me; but she shook her head despondingly, and said, "Alas! I cannot help it." Soon after this she became very ill, and kept her bed, where I was often taken to see her; and very pretty she looked, though quite white, like a sheet. At such times she would kiss me, and cry over me. One day, when the nurse was carrying me out of the room, she desired her to bring me back, and, raising herself with difficulty, for she was extremely feeble, she placed her hands on my head, and said, "God bless you, my dear Mervyn! Don't forget mamma when she is gone. Never desert those who love you, dear. Good-by, my dearest child." And, kissing me tenderly, she sank back on the pillow quite exhausted. So Jane, the nurse, hurried me out of the room, for I had begun to cry bitterly.

On that night a circumstance took place for which I could never account, but it has remained graven on my memory, and I pledge myself as to its actual occurrence. I had been put to bed, and was very restless, for there was an unusual agitation and disturbance in the house, and I thought Jane would never come to me. I heard the clock strike several times, and at last it struck one, and soon after that she did make her appearance. I asked her what made her so late, but she didn't answer me; and, seeing I was regarding her inquisitively, for I thought she was crying, she bade me, in a broken voice, go to sleep. I tried to do so, but couldn't; and when Jane got into bed she felt very cold, and wept audibly.

I didn't like to speak to her, and was, besides, occupied by my own thoughts, which ran involuntarily on my poor mother, and on what she said about leaving me. Just when Jane became more composed, and seemed to be dropping asleep, I distinctly heard three knocks! Yes, three dull, heavy knocks, as if struck with the poker against the back of the fireplace in my mother's room, which was next to mine.

"Good gracious! what's that?" exclaimed Jane, starting up in bed. "Did you hear anything, Master Mervyn?"

"To be sure," I replied; "I heard the knocks plain enough. It must be mamma—she wants something. Go to her, Jane."

But, to my surprise, Jane, though ordinarily ready to obey the slightest summons from my mother, did not move, but looked petrified with terror.

"What can it be?" she ejaculated, at length. "There's no one in the room."

"No one!" I cried, in alarm. "Is mamma gone, then? Has she really left me?"

"Yes—no," stammered Jane.

"I'll go and see myself," I said. "I'm sure she wants something."

"No, no; you mustn't go, dear," cried Jane, detaining me. "Your mamma is there, but she wants nothing now, poor thing! Besides, you can't get in. The door's locked. Don't you see the key there, near the lamp?"

I couldn't conceive why she had locked poor mamma in her room, and thought it very unkind of her to stay in bed when she was summoned, and begged hard to be allowed to go myself, though I don't think I could have unlocked the door if she had let me try. But at last I was persuaded to be quiet, and fell asleep.

My first inquiries, next morning, were after mamma, and whether the door was unlocked; and I implored so earnestly to see her, that at last Jane consented.

"You mustn't make a noise if you go, dear," she said.

Jane opened the door of the adjoining room very softly, and entered with noiseless footsteps.

"Is mamma asleep?" I asked.

"Yes, dear,—sound asleep," Jane replied, in a low tone.

The room appeared dark, for the window-blinds were down, and there was a deathlike stillness about it that frightened me. I looked at Jane, and she seemed frightened too.

The white curtains were drawn closely round the bed. I had never seen them so before. Jane opened them, and showed me mamma, apparently fast asleep, and looking paler and prettier than ever. Her dark hair was parted smoothly over her marble forehead, and an angelic smile, which has haunted me ever since, hovered about her parted lips. One arm, very white and very thin, lay out of the covering. Jane held me down to kiss mamma's cheek. Its icy coldness startled me, and made me cry out.

Jane snatched me away, and, as she closed the door, I said—for I was very much troubled—"I hope mamma will waken soon."

"Alas! dear," she replied, "she will never waken more."

My mother was buried in the churchyard of Marston, a small village in Cheshire, where an uncle of my father's resided, and a fitter resting-place for so gentle a creature could not have been chosen. Often and often have I lingered by that grave, and have thought of its once lovely tenant—of her brief, reproachless career—of her devotion to my father, whose long absence broke her heart—of her tenderness to me. Many a bitter tear have I shed there, and many a lamentation uttered; but I never sought it without being cheered and comforted as if by a mother's love.

My mother was only twenty-three when she died, and I was not five years old at the time. As yet I had never seen my father, nor did I see him for years afterwards. My mother was in an interesting condition when he quitted England with his regiment, and was to follow him; but he wrote to say she had better not come out for some months; and when that time expired, he enjoined further delay. Eventually, he directed her to remain at home altogether, and take care of the boy she had brought him, adding, that he should soon be able to obtain a long furlough, and would join her in England.

Though heartbroken at the prolonged separation, my poor mother could not disobey her husband's injunctions. Feeling she could not have acted in like manner towards him, she began to fear his affections must be estranged; and the distress occasioned by this idea ended in undermining her already delicate health. But she never complained, nor would she allow any intelligence of her illness to be conveyed to my father. Indeed, only three days after her death, and before she was laid in her grave, a letter arrived from him, stating that he had at length obtained a furlough, and trusted to be with her before the expiration of three months. He spoke in ardent terms of the rapturous delight it would afford him to clasp his darling wife again to his bosom, and behold his little boy, of whom she had written him such charming accounts. If this letter had arrived a month sooner, the physician who attended my mother in her last illness afterwards told me, her life might possibly have been saved. But hope had been utterly extinguished.

Of course the sad tidings were immediately conveyed to my father, and, as he was totally unprepared for them, the shock must have been terrible. How severely he reproached himself, and how bitterly he lamented the loss he had sustained, was evident from his letters on this melancholy occasion. But he gave up all present idea of returning to England, and, making the needful remittances, willingly committed me to the care of Mrs. Mervyn, who had offered to take charge of me.

I was too young to feel deeply the irreparable loss I had sustained, and, as Mrs. Mervyn was very kind to me, and her house exceedingly comfortable, I soon became quite reconciled and happy. Mrs. Mervyn, for, though a spinster, she had taken brevet rank, was an elderly lady of a most charitable disposition, living at a very pretty place called the Anchorite's, about three miles from the great manufacturing town of Cottonborough, in Lancashire. She was the descendant of a stanch Jacobite family — her great-grandfather, Ambrose Mervyn, having, in November, 1715, joined the insurgent army at Penrith, and marched with it to Preston, where, on the surrender of the town to the government generals, he was taken, and, having been particularly zealous in promoting the cause of the Chevalier Saint George, aiding it with funds and followers, was executed, and his head set upon a pike in the market-place at Cottonborough. His son, Stuart Mervyn, who was a boy at the time of this catastrophe, came to a similar end, for in 1745 he was one of the most zealous supporters of the Young Chevalier during his progress through Lancashire, and received a French commission. The memory of these unfortunate persons was warmly cherished by Mrs. Mervyn, who regarded them as martyrs. Their portraits were placed in her bedroom, and this circumstance made me afraid to enter the chamber, thinking it impossible such troubled spirits could rest in their graves. Ambrose Mervyn in particular used to inspire me with intense awe, for he was represented as a swarthy, stern-looking fellow, with great searching black eyes, which seemed to follow me about.

Mrs. Mervyn used frequently to talk to me about her Jacobite predecessors; and, though ordinarily very calm in manner, grew quite excited by the theme, and launched forth into such glowing and enthusiastic descriptions of Prince Charles Edward, that I almost wished he was alive still, that I might fight for him like the two brave Mervyns. But her account of their executions shook my desire to be a rebel. She showed me a couple of prints representing the terrible scenes; pointing out in one of them little Stuart, who appeared to be taking an eternal farewell of his father, before the latter submitted himself to the ghastly apparatus of death; and she told me how Ambrose had then enjoined his son never to forsake the good cause, which dying command was implicitly obeyed, as I have related. I am afraid I unintentionally shocked Mrs. Mervyn's feelings a good deal, by inquiring what became of their heads, and whether she had them preserved in a box.

"No, my dear Mervyn," she replied, very gravely; "they are both deposited with the mutilated trunks in our family vault in the Old Church. You may read the inscription on the monument."

Mrs. Mervyn was always richly dressed in black, and with remarkable precision and care. She had a grave and somewhat austere aspect, which belied the extreme kindliness of her nature, and but rarely smiled. Nothing strongly excited her, except some matter connected with the bygone Jacobite cause.

Her predilections were exhibited even in her household, almost every member of which came of a Jacobite stock. Her old butler, Mr. Comberbach, numbered two unfortunate adherents to the good cause in his pedigree—imprimis, a great-grandsire, a barber, whose head was barbarously cut off in 1716, and set upon his own pole, as an example to all his brethren of the razor and strap not to meddle with affairs of state; and, secondly, a grandsire, who having dressed the Prince's peruke during his stay in Cottonborough, afterwards joined the regiment raised by Colonel Townley, with the intention of avenging his father's death; but he paid the penalty of his rashness—and a second barber's head was brought to the block. This similarity of fate between their respective ancestors, formed a link between the mistress and the butler, and consequently Mr. Comberbach was much favoured, and became a very important personage in the establishment at the Anchorite's. But he was far more blinded and intolerant than his mistress; the spirit of the old barbers burnt within his breast; and he was sometimes rather disloyal in his expressions touching the Hanoverian dynasty. Among his relics he preserved the family powder-puff which had been exercised on the princely peruke, and the basin from which the august chin had been lathered, and which I told him resembled Mambrino's helmet. When a little exhilarated, which was not unfrequently the case, he would sing old Jacobite songs, and take off a glass to the memory of the last of the unfortunate house of Stuart. But, notwithstanding his love of good cheer, like his mistress he observed the anniversaries of certain terrible events as rigorous fast-days, and put on mourning as she did. In fact, the house was very dismal altogether on these occasions, and I was glad when they were over; for Mrs. Mervyn moved about like a shade, and would eat nothing, and Mr. Comberbach stalked after her like a grim attendant ghost, and would eat nothing too; and, what was worse, would scarcely let me eat anything; while all the rest of the servants followed, or pretended to follow, their example. It was mainly owing to the butler's exertions that Mrs. Mervyn was so well supplied with Jacobites. He found out Mrs. Chadwick, the housekeeper,—a lineal descendant of a tallow-chandler, whose zeal being inflamed, like one of his own candles, by the Young Chevalier's arrival in Cottonborough, was afterwards very suddenly snuffed out. He likewise discovered the cook, Molly Bailey, whose great-uncle had kept the Dog Inn when Lord George Murray, the Prince's secretary, was quartered there, and who possessed some old receipts of dishes that his Highness was known to be fond of, and was, moreover, so skilful in her art, that she was worthy to have been his cook, if he had ever come to the throne, and she had lived in his days. He engaged Hudson, the coachman, who affirmed that his grandfather was the first person that came to the assistance of Sergeant Dickson, when he took the town of Cottonborough, attended only by a drummer and a sutlerwench, and afterwards joined him as a recruit. And Mr. Comberbach likewise unearthed Banks, the gardener, who declared he was a Jacobite every inch; for his "forefaythers" had kept the little inn at Didsbury, where the Jacobite Club used to meet, and drink the "King over the water." All the rest had some pretences or other of a like nature to Mrs. Mervyn's consideration, and she never investigated their claims too narrowly, but rested content with the butler's assurance of their eligibility. In short, we were all Jacobites, and the common folks nicknamed our place of abode "Jacobite's Hall."

And in case I should appear to be a very unworthy member of a house whose party feelings were so decided, but luckily so harmless, I may mention that I had as much right as anybody to call myself a Jacobite, and could boast, like some of them, of having had an ancestor hanged, seeing that my maternal great-grandfather, John Leyburne, was tried at Liverpool at the sanguinary assizes held there in 1716, for his adherence to the Chevalier Saint George, and afterwards executed at Garstang, near which place he had resided.

I easily found out that my father was no great favourite with Mrs. Mervyn. She had never approved of the match, and thought his conduct towards his wife wholly inexcusable. Indeed, and with some justice, she laid my mother's early death at his door. Three years later on, when news came from India that he had married again, and, having exchanged into another regiment just sent out, did not mean to return for some time, she declared she was not at all surprised at his proceedings. "He never estimated poor Clara at her true value," she said—"never understood her quiet and deep affection. Alas! poor girl, she is now entirely forgotten, and her place supplied by some other thoughtless young creature sent out on speculation for a husband. Well, whoever she may be, for I know nothing of her beyond her name, Bertha Honeywood, she has got no great prize, and it is to be hoped may be better treated than her predecessor. Captain Clitheroe seems not only to have forgotten his first wife, but all belonging to her," she added, looking hard at me; "it is well that some one was attached to poor orphan Clara, and for her sake will watch over the child she has left behind her."

Mrs. Mervyn had been always kind to me, but after this news she became even kinder than before. Remittances for my maintenance and education were regularly received from my father, but he expressed no interest whatever concerning me, and entered into no explanations as to his future intentions respecting me.

The Anchorite's was situated at the foot of a woody eminence overlooking the Vale of the Ater, on whose banks it stood. It derived its appellation from an old religious cell, the ruins of which could still be traced in the garden. A shady walk beneath a row of elms led to the brink of the Ater, and on the greensward and slopes were many old trees, probably contemporary with the retreat, and in especial an ancient yew, which must have numbered centuries when the hermit built his cell. Through openings in the grove sheltering the house might be caught glimpses, about three miles off, of the smoke-canopied town of Cottonborough, whose mills had already invaded some of the neighbouring heights commanding the circuitous windings of the river. Though not large, the house was commodious; comprehending a good sombre-looking dining-room, wainscoted with oak, and full of dusky oak furniture; a fine old oak staircase, highly polished; and an admirable library, full of old books. A deeply-embayed window, with stone mullion frames, looked from the library into the garden, and adjoining it was a small octagonal chamber, like an oratory, with windows full of stained glass, emblazoned with the arms of various Lancashire families.

Mrs. Mervyn was very hospitable, but her invitations were chiefly confined to clergymen, and a day seldom passed that one or two reverend gentlemen did not dine with her; and, as these excellent members of society are not supposed to despise the good things of the world, and the dinners at the Anchorite's were unexceptionable, a refusal was seldom experienced. Mrs. Mervyn had some fine old plate, and on state occasions the sideboard and table blazed with it, but ordinarily her dinners were more comfortable than showy. A clergyman always sat at the foot of the table, and, on the high days just alluded to, perhaps a bishop, or the warden of the Collegiate Church, an archdeacon, or some eminent clerical dignitary, would support her on the right and left. I have already said that she possessed a capital cook in Molly Bailey, whose Prestonpans cutlets, Hanoverian calf's head with Nonjuror sauce, baked Derwentwater pike with Brunswick pudding inside, Charles Edward's jugged hare, Earl of Mar's game pie, and Sacheverell puffs, were much enjoyed, notwithstanding their designations. Mr. Comberbach took care that the cellar should be well stocked with the finest old port and Madeira (champagne or hock were never given), and as Mrs. Mervyn never stinted her wine, while the reverend gentleman who sat at the bottom of the table was fully aware of her hospitable wishes, and carefully seconded them himself, her guests were always plentifully supplied. The Rev. Barton Lever, the divine in question, was a fellow of the Collegiate Church, and a very estimable, excellent man, a sound scholar, a lover of black-letter books, fond of antiquarian researches, and no mean poet. He officiated as Mrs. Mervyn's almoner, recommended worthy objects for her bounty, and distributed, unostentatiously, as she desired, the large sums devoted by her to charitable uses.

Thus, though in effect an orphan, for my father seemed to care so little about me, that I might almost as well have been without him, I had a very kind friend and a very good home; and I had, besides, some other kind friends and relatives, whom I shall hereafter introduce to the reader.

I must postpone further description of Mrs. Mervyn till I arrive at the period of my life when I was old enough to understand more fully the excellences of her character, and was permitted to take part at her hospitable entertainments, and make acquaintance with her guests. Several years must be passed over with the mere mention of their flight. In a word, I may say that the days of my childhood were happy, but dull, for I had few playmates. I was like a boy brought up in a monastery, or like Rasselas in the Happy Valley; for, though I had the run of the house and the garden, I was not permitted to stray beyond their precincts. Thus, I envied those who had more freedom than I had, and longed for the time when I should be sent to a public school. I had excellent private instruction, but I yearned for the company of other boys; and at last, when I was nearly twelve years old, Mrs. Mervyn reluctantly yielded to my wishes, and sent me to the Cottonborough Free Grammar School.

But, alas! the gratification of the wish was followed by immediate repentance and regret. Hitherto, I had not been conscious of my own happiness. The knowledge came too late. I would now willingly have gone back to my quiet life and easy studies at the Anchorite's, but very shame prevented me.

CHAPTER II.

AN ACCOUNT OF MY SCHOOLDAYS, SCHOOLFELLOWS, AND SCHOOLMASTERS—MR. ABEL CANE PROVES THAT HE *IS* ABLE TO CANE—DR. LONSDALE ADOPTS A DIFFERENT MODE OF TUITION—JOHN BRIDEOAKE—A BUNKER'S HILL HERO—A BOY DROWNED.

Founded by a benevolent bishop, in the early part of the sixteenth century, well endowed, and subsequently enriched by a great number of exhibitions and scholarships, the Cottonborough Free Grammar School has always maintained a high reputation for sound classical instruction, and though not ranking with Eton or Harrow as a fashionable place of education, from the circumstance of its being situated in a large manufacturing town, which has deterred some persons of good family from sending their sons to it, it has turned out many excellent scholars, who have cut a figure at the universities, and distinguished themselves afterwards in the various walks of life.

I cannot say much in praise of the architectural beauty of the school; for, if truth must be spoken, it was exceedingly ugly; and, though a very old foundation, the building was comparatively modern, and did not date back, from the period of which I write, more than twenty or thirty years. It was raised on a high sandstone bank overlooking the little river Ink, not far from its confluence with the Ater; and viewed on this side, in connexion with the old and embrowned walls adjoining it, its appearance was not unpicturesque—certainly more pleasing than when viewed from the crowded and noisy thoroughfare by which it was approached. It was a large, dingy, and smoke-begrimed brick building, with copings of stone, and had so many windows that it looked like a lantern. In front, between the angles of the pointed roof, was placed a stone effigy of the bird of wisdom, which seemed to gaze down at us with its great goggle eyes as we passed by, as if muttering, "Enter this academic abode over which I preside, and welcome, but you'll never come out as clever as I." What the school wanted in antiquity was supplied by a venerable pile contiguous to it, which, in remote times, had been part of the collegiate establishment of the Old Church of Cottonborough; but, in the reign of James I., falling into the hands of a wealthy and munificent merchant of the place, it was by him devoted to the foundation of an hospital for the maintenance and education of a certain number of poor lads, and to the creation, for public use and benefit, of a large and admirable library within its walls. This was the Blue-Coat Hospital and Library, for which Cottonborough has reason to be grateful.

Adjoining our modern iron rails was a venerable stone gateway, with an arched entrance opening upon the broad playground of the Blue-Coat Hospital, which as far surpassed anything we possessed, as its college-like halls and refectories exceeded our formal school in beauty; while the blank black walls of another part of the structure, composed of a stone so soft and friable that it seemed to absorb every particle of smoke that approached it, formed a little court in front of our door of entrance, and the flight of stone steps conducting to it. The school was divided into two rooms, each occupying a whole floor, and the lower school, in those days a very confined, dirty-looking place, utterly unworthy of such an establishment, was reached by a flight of steps descending from the little court I have described. But happily I knew nothing, from personal experience, of this dark and dismal hole, being introduced at once to the upper school, which, if it had no other merit, was airy and spacious enough. There were four fireplaces and four tables, those at either extremity being assigned to the head master and the second master, and the others to the two ushers. Each master had two classes, so that there were eight in all. The walls were whitewashed, and, like the flat roof, without any decoration whatever, unless the oak wainscoting at the back of the boys' benches, which surrounded the whole schoolroom, can be so considered. These benches, the desks in front of them, and the panels behind, were of the hardest oak; and it was well they were so, for they had to resist the ravages of a thousand knives. In some places they were further secured with clamps of iron. Everybody cut his name on the desks or wainscot, like the captives in state prisons in the olden time, and amongst these mementoes I suppose I have somewhere left mine. I know that while once carving it on the leads of the Collegiate Church I nearly carved off my forefinger. The place was not so light as might be conceived from the multitude of windows, for they were never cleaned, and the panes of glass were yellow and almost tawny from the reeky atmosphere.

On entering the school, the buzz of so many tongues was prodigious, and almost took away the power of thought or study; but after a while one got used to it, and the noise did not affect you in the least. When the din rose to too high a pitch, loud cries of "Silence, you boys!" would be heard, accompanied by the rapping of a cane on the table, or the dreadful sounds of a punishment would produce a partial lull; and then might be heard the deep sonorous voice of the *archi-didasculus*, Dr. Lonsdale, mouthing out a passage from Æschylus or Aristophanes, rumbling away like distant thunder, or the sharp, high-pitched voice of the *hypo-didasculus*, Mr. Cane. We began the day's work betimes, and prayers were read both at morn and at eventide. On winter evenings, when the school was lighted up by tapers, the twinkling light of which fell upon the boys as they knelt at prayer, while no sound was heard but that proceeding from the reader of the devotional exercises, I used to think the scene striking enough. But it was gone in a moment.

No sooner were prayers over, than everybody seized his hat and books; boxes were hastily clapped-to; tapers extinguished; the hurried trampling of departing footsteps succeeded—and all vanished like a dream.

The Rev. Abel Cane, under whose care I was first placed, was a sound, classical scholar, but a severe disciplinarian. He was one of those who believe that a knowledge of Latin and Greek can be driven into a boy, and that his capacity may be sharpened by frequent punishment. Under this impression he was constantly thrashing us. In his drawer he had several canes of various lengths, and of various degrees of thickness, tied with tatching-end to prevent them from splitting, and for all these he found employment. While calling us round for punishment he got as red in the gills as a turkey-cock, and occasionally rose up to give greater effect to the blows. Some boys were so frightened that they couldn't learn their tasks at all, and others so reckless of the punishment which they knew must ensue, whether or not, that they intentionally neglected them. I have seen boys with "blood blisters," as they called them, on their hands, and others with weals on their backs, but I do not recollect that the castigation did them any good, but the very reverse. But our preceptor had other ingenious modes of torture. He would make us stand in the middle of the school for a whole day, and even longer—sometimes on one leg—and the effect of balancing in this posture, with a heavy dictionary in hand, and a Virgil under the arm, was ludicrous enough, though rather perplexing. It must not be imagined that I escaped the cane. I had enough of it, and to spare, both on shoulders and hands. Notwithstanding our dread of him, we used to play Mr. Cane a great many tricks. We notched his canes so that they split when he used them; put gravel into the keyhole of his drawer; mingled soot with his ink; threw fulminating balls under his feet; and even meditated blowing him up with gunpowder. An adventurous youth essayed the effect of a burning-glass on his ear, but was instantly detected, and called round for punishment. Another tried to throw the rays from a bit of looking-glass into his eye, and shared the same fate. With all his discipline, if our dreaded master were called out of school for a few minutes, the greatest row would commence. The boys sitting at either end of the form would place their feet against the edge of the desks, and squeeze up those between them so unmercifully that they roared again. Books, volleys of peas from tin cases, and other missiles, were discharged at the occupants of the opposite forms; and the miserable fellows in the middle of the school became marks for their comrades, and returned the aggression in the best way they could. These disturbances were, of course, witnessed by the ushers, but they rarely mentioned them; and Dr. Lonsdale was too far off to hear what was going on, and I don't think he altogether approved of the second master's severity. To a new boy, it was dreadful to hear Mr. Cane cry out to some offender, "*Come round, you stoo-oo-pid ass-s-s!*" hissing like a serpent as he uttered the final word of scorn; dreadful to witness the writhings of the victim as he underwent castigation; still more dreadful to hear the words addressed to himself, intensified as they were by the furious looks that accompanied them. In some cases, Mr. Cane drove all the capacity they possessed out of the boys' heads. There was one poor little fellow, Devereux Frogg, whose wits could never be stimulated. Poor Devereux! how I pitied him, and tried to help him, and cram him—but it was of no use. When we went up he was so frightened that all went out of his head, and the daily drubbing ensued. And there were others like him. Mr. Cane was a fresh-complexioned man, with good features, and a handsome aquiline nose; he was scrupulously neat in his attire, and wore a long gold watch-chain, which he twirled about when walking, or when excited; and he had a habit of thinking aloud. What strange contradictions of character some persons offer. Out of school, Mr. Cane was very amiable and good-tempered, fond of music, and cultivated a taste for poetry. I hated him cordially then; but I learnt to like him afterwards, and now I lament in him the lost friend.

Dr. Lonsdale's plan of tuition was very different from that of Mr. Cane. His was the *suaviter in modo*, rather than the *fortiter in re*. He aspired to make his pupils gentlemen as well as good scholars. He never used the cane, but his rebuke was greatly dreaded, and his quiet, sarcastic remarks on a mispronunciation or a vulgarism effectually prevented their repetition. Dignified in manner and deportment, and ever preserving an air of grave courtesy, it would have been impossible to take a liberty with him, and it was never attempted. Dr. Lonsdale was a spare man, with large thoughtful features, and a fine expansive forehead, powdered at the top. He looked like a bishop, and ought to have been one. His voice was peculiarly solemn, and it was quite a treat to hear him read prayers. Under him the boys began to give themselves the airs of young men, wore well-cut coats and well-fitting boots, were very particular about their neck-cloths and about the fashion of their hair, and, above all, wore gloves —refinements never dreamed of in the lower forms, where, sooth to say, we were sad slovens.

But I must return there for the present, for I am not yet out of Mr. Cane's clutches. Of course, in a Free School like ours, there were boys of all sorts and all grades, and we got on together pretty well, some herding with one set, some with another; but there was one poor lad, named John Brideoake, with whom, when he first came, none would associate. He was so shabbily attired that we considered ourselves disgraced by his companionship, and made him sit outside the desk amongst the boxes. He was very timid and humble, and submitted to our ill-usage without a murmur. He was rather a small boy, apparently stunted in his growth, and looked very thin and emaciated, as if, in addition to being poorly clad, he was half starved.

I am sorry to say we jeered him both about his shabby clothes and his hungry looks, and would not let him rest even when driven from us, but tormented him in various ways, plucking his hair, and fastening him to the seat with cobbler's wax. We wouldn't lend him a book if he wanted it; nor answer him if he ventured to speak to us; nor let him come near the fire, though he was perishing of cold; and, of course, he wouldn't have been allowed to play with us, if he had desired to do so; but this he never attempted, but went straight home to his mother, who, we were informed, was in very poor circumstances indeed. He worked hard at his lessons, and, though when he first came he was somewhat behindhand, he soon bid fair to outstrip us all. I must say this for Mr. Cane, that he behaved kindly to the poor fellow; took his part against us, rebuked us for our pride, and punished us severely whenever he perceived us tormenting him. This, however, did not serve the lad, but made us use him still more unmercifully. But he never told of us, and for this we secretly respected him. In spite of all these distractions, John Brideoake made great progress, and rose in the class, so that we were obliged to admit him amongst us. Still, he was not *of* us. He was now just below me, but of course I did not notice him, for, indeed, I was one of the most determined of his opponents. One day, while up before Mr. Cane, I was construing some lines out of Terence, and was at fault for a word, when Brideoake whispered it to me, though he could have taken me down if he had spoken aloud.

This I thought great presumption on his part, and, as soon as the lesson was over, I said to him, angrily,

"Take care you never presume to prompt me again, Brideoake. I won't stand it."

"Very well," he replied, meekly.

In spite of this, he tried again the next day, but I would not attend to him, and he went above me. In a week from that time he was at the head of the class. Now we hated him worse than ever, and formed all sorts of combinations against him; but his mildness of manner defeated them all. He would not quarrel with us; but his superior ability was so evident, that Mr. Cane recommended him for promotion to the class above us. We pretended to be glad, and complimented him ironically; but he bore his triumph very meekly, and I think, after all, was sorry to leave us.

His example did me some good. Not liking to be outdone, I worked so hard that in six weeks I was promoted too, and got away from Mr. Cane and his cane.

During this interval a change had taken place in my opinions respecting John Brideoake. I felt I had ill-used him, and done him injustice, and I determined to make an apology. At first my pride revolted against the step, but I soon conquered the feeling. When I found myself again beside Brideoake he looked quite pleased to see me, but he didn't venture to congratulate me. Quite touched by his manner, I held out my hand to him, and he took it very warmly and gratefully. The tears were in his eyes, for he was softhearted as a girl, and extremely susceptible of kindness, of which he had experienced so little; for the boys in the new class were just as haughty and reserved towards him as we had been.

"Brideoake," I said, "I have behaved very ill to you, but I am heartily ashamed of myself, and beg you to forgive me. You never resented my conduct, as you might have done; and I'm very glad of it now, because I hope we may be good friends in future."

"I don't require any apology, Clitheroe," he answered; "you have only to say we are friends, to efface all recollection of past unkindness from my mind. Before this, I could not tell you how much

I regarded you, nor how grieved I was that you disliked me, or I am sure you would not have acted so. I have borne all annoyances—though some have been hard enough to bear—without repining, and, indeed, have felt endurance to be part of my lot; but I hoped one day to gain the good opinion of my schoolfellows, and chiefly yours, Clitheroe. The day has arrived. You have held out your hand to me, and promised me your friendship. I am quite happy."

These words of his cut me to the heart. I wondered how I could have behaved so unkindly to him, and I replied, with much emotion, "You may not blame me, Brideoake, but I severely blame myself. I ought to have known better, and to have recognised in you the merits you really possess, which are far greater than those of any other boy with whom I am acquainted. I shall always respect you, and others shall learn to respect you as I do. If any one attempts to molest you, he shall quarrel with me."

"Nay, nay, Clitheroe," he said; "that would distress me. Be my friend, but do not espouse my quarrels. I could not bear you to be involved in disputes on my account. My wish is to offend no one. Say what you please of me to the others, but let them act as they think proper."

"They shall learn what a generous-hearted, good fellow you are, Brideoake, and then not one of them but will be as proud of your friendship as I am."

And so it proved. I spoke of him in such enthusiastic terms, that instead of shunning him, the boys made up to him, and his gentle and unoffending manners caused him to be beloved by everybody. Besides, he was such an uncommonly clever fellow, that we began to regard him as a prodigy. He made nothing of the most difficult passages in Lucretius or Juvenal; wrote Latin verses with great facility; and his English compositions were much lauded. He was so good-natured and obliging, that we all applied to him when in difficulties; and he would at any time write a theme, or throw off a copy of Latin verses for an idle fellow, during breakfast time.

As we were now constantly together, John Brideoake acquainted me with his history—at least, with as much of it as he himself knew, for he was not very accurately informed on the subject. His father was a gentleman's son, who had resided somewhere in Northumberland, but having married against the consent of his family, had been disowned by them, and, after struggling ineffectually against a series of calamities, had died, leaving a widow almost penniless, and burdened with two children—himself and a daughter named Apphia. His mother, he said, was the best of women, but exceedingly proud, and, notwithstanding the extremities to which she had been reduced, would neither apply for assistance to her husband's relatives, nor to her own, with whom she had also quarrelled. She had determined to bring up her son as a gentleman, no matter what privations she underwent for the purpose, and designed him for the Church. Her straitened means forbade the accomplishment of the scheme in any other way except the one she had adopted. John Brideoake hoped to gain one of the best exhibitions connected with the school, which would help to defray his expenses at Cambridge, whither he meant to go.

I was so much interested in the description of his mother and his little sister Apphia, that I begged him to introduce me to them. He coloured up when I made the request, and said he must first ask his mother's consent. The next day he told me she was very much obliged, but she was unable to receive me.

"You will excuse her, Clitheroe," he said; "but I have told you she is extremely proud, and, to speak truth, she is ashamed of our lodgings. We are too poor to receive visitors. Better days may come, when we shall be delighted to welcome you."

I pressed him no further.

Opposite the school was a shop much frequented by us all. Its owner was an odd character, by name John Leigh. He had served in the early American war, and had lost his right arm at the famous battle of Bunker's Hill. John was a gruff old fellow, not over civil or obliging, but there were peculiarities about him that made us like him, in spite of his crustiness. He had large, heavy features, and a bulky person. He dressed in a pepper-and-salt coat, of ancient make, which looked as if there were more salt than pepper in the mixture, knee-breeches, not unfrequently besprinkled with flour, and wore buckles in his shoes. His right sleeve was fastened to his breast. His grey hair was taken back from his face, and tied in a thick, clubbed pigtail behind. John Leigh knew his customers well: to some boys he would give unlimited credit, to others none at all. Indeed, it was a matter of boast with many a lad, and argued well for his resources, if "he had good tick at John's." John's sweetmeats were excellent; at least we thought so, and we devoured far too many of his macaroons, queen's cakes, and jumbals, to say nothing of tarts, when fruit was in season, and the daily consumption of hot rolls and butter. John Leigh's shop was our constant resort. We lounged about it, sat upon the counter or the potato-bins (for John was a general dealer), or the corner of the flour or meal-chests, or in the great pair of scales, or wherever we could find a seat, and discussed the politics of the school, and other matters. Even during school-hours we would run across there, and rumours of our goings-on would reach the masters' ears, and search would occasionally be made for us. I recollect an incident of this sort, which occurred while I was under Mr. Cane. Some half-dozen of us were comfortably seated on John's counter, munching away at a pound of macaroons before us, when we perceived Cane issue from the gate, evidently marching in the direction of the shop. In an instant we all disappeared; some of us diving under the counter, and others hiding where they could. Shortly after, when Cane entered, no one was to be seen except John, close beside whose bulky legs I and two others were lying *perdus*.

"I thought some of the boys were here, John?" said Mr. Cane, sharply, and glancing round the place.

"I see none on 'em, sir," replied John, in a somewhat surly tone.

"That's not a direct answer, John," rejoined the pedagogue, peremptorily. "There are six of my boys out of school—Lathom, Hilton, Frogg, Simpson, Hyde, and Clitheroe. Has any one of them, or have all, been here?"

"I never answers no questions about the young gentlemen as frequents my shop," said John, doggedly.

"Then I conclude they have been here," observed Mr. Cane.

Upon this, we pinched John's fat legs rather severely, for we thought he might have done something better than this to get us out of the scrape. The pain made him roar out most lustily.

"What's the matter, John?" asked Mr. Cane, who was going out of the shop.

"A sudden seizure, sir, that's all," returned John; "but you mustn't go for to imagine, from anything I've said, that the young gentlemen has been here, sir. It's my rule never to speak about 'em, and I should have given you the same answer whether or no."

"Equivocation, you fancy, is not falsehood, I see, John; but give me leave to observe that your standard of morality is rather low. I shall draw my own conclusions," said Mr. Cane, turning away, and muttering to himself, "I'm sure they have been here."

Upon which we pinched John's great calves again, and the veteran angrily ejaculated,

"Come, I shan't stand this any longer."

"Ha! What's that? Did I hear aright?" demanded Mr. Cane, stopping short. "The man has been drinking," he muttered.

"Be quiet, I say, or I'll bundle you out o' th' shop," roared John.

"You'll do WHAT?" almost screamed Mr. Cane, coming up to him, with a countenance full of fury, and twirling his watch-chain as if he would fling it at John's head. "Did you address those disrespectful—those impertinent observations to me, man?"

We were so delighted at this mistake, that we nearly betrayed ourselves, and with difficulty stifled our laughter.

"They warn't addressed to you, sir," returned John.

"Then to whom were they addressed?" pursued Mr. Cane. "You affirm no one else is here. I see no one. John—John, I am afraid you are fuddled."

"Fuddled—I fuddled? I'd have you to know, Mr. Cane, that I never touches a drop in the morning; and the young gentlemen will bear witness to my sobriety."

"What young gentlemen?" demanded Cane.

Here we slightly admonished John again.

"The young rascals, I mean," he roared, stamping with rage and pain. "I wish they were all at the devil,—and you at their back," he added, to Mr. Cane, forgetting himself in the blindness of his wrath.

"It is evident you are not yourself, John," said the preceptor; "that is the only excuse I can make for you. At some more fitting moment I shall endeavour to reason you out of the sinful and pernicious course you are pursuing. Drink in the morning. Faugh! John."

With this he departed, muttering to himself, and was scarcely out of hearing than we jumped up, and saluted John with a roar of laughter worthy of Homer's heroes. But the hero of Bunker's Hill did not join in the Homeric merriment. His legs had been pinched black and blue, as if by wicked elves; and he had been told he was fuddled! Fuddled, forsooth! He who had never drunk anything to speak of since he left Boston. He wished he had never taken the shop, never seen the school, never dealt with any of us. He would go away, that he would. His exasperation rose to the highest pitch when he discovered that Hyde, who was a very mischievous lad, while lying behind the counter, had taken the opportunity of rubbing out the scores chalked upon a board placed there. On making this discovery, John seized the offender, held him between his legs, pummelled him soundly with his one arm, and only released him on his promise to pay the whole score, which was pretty heavy in amount. We then ran back to school, and our morning's amusement was concluded with a sound caning.

Notwithstanding John's indignant declaration, he showed no disposition to abandon his shop, and no particular objection to the continuance of our custom. He soon forgot his grievances, or rather they were effaced by new ones, for we were perpetually playing him tricks. We wanted him to tell us how he lost his arm ; but he always seemed shy of the subject, till one afternoon, when he was in good humour, and a good lot of us were assembled together, helping ourselves to cakes and confectionary, we thought we might get it out of him, and made the attempt accordingly.

"You'll be a soldier like your father, I suppose, Clitheroe?" observed Simpson.

"No, I won't," I replied.

"You're afraid of losing an arm, like John Leigh?" remarked Hyde.

"Perhaps I am," I answered. "But John seems scarcely to miss his limb. Hand me some figs, old fellow. And now, suppose you tell us how you got rid of your fin ?"

"Ay, ay, tell us all about it, John," the others chorused.

"Well," he replied, "it's a long story altogether, but I'll cut it as short as I can." (We signified our approval, and he went on.) "The Battle of Bunker's Hill, you must know, was fought many years ago, almost afore your fathers was thought of, young gentlemen, on the 17th of June, 1775 ; and though I oughtn't to speak disrespectfully of my commanding officers, yet I must say it was their fault entirely that we didn't give them Yankees twice the drubbing we did give 'em, as you shall hear. Well, the troubles had just begun in Americay, which ended in the great war, and a large body of troops had been collected by the Provincial Congress of Massachusetts; British blood had been spilt by the colonists at the fight of Lexington ; and Boston, of which General Gage was governor, was blockaded ; and a pity it was we hadn't some one more competent and determined than Gage for a governor, as the first outbreak might have been checked, and no more mischief done. Well, war to extremities was resolved on by our government, and more troops was sent over under the command of Major-General Howe, including some companies of grenadiers, amongst whom I was, and we landed at Boston towards the end of May. The time was now come when we might have read them saucy Yankees a lesson, and given them such a dressing, as Mr. Cane sometimes gives you misbehaved boys——"

"Don't be personal, John," Simpson cried.

"Howsomever, our generals took it mighty easy, and seemed resolved to let 'em go any lengths afore they'd fire a gun to stop 'em. Well, you must know, Boston's a very fine city, and is built on a peninsula connected with the mainland by a narrow neck, which was strongly fortified by old Gage. Opposite Boston, and only separated from it by a narrow channel, called Charles River, about as wide as the Thames at Lunnun, and now crossed, I believe, by a bridge, but quite open in my time, is another peninsula, on which stands the suburb of Charlestown, and at the back of it there rises a commanding height, completely overlooking Boston, called Bunker's Hill."

And thinking his description might be rendered more intelligible by some illustration, John took up a board, and rearing it against the counter, drew a few sketches upon it with a piece of chalk. This he performed very dexterously, considering he had to do it with his left hand.

"This here's Boston, you see, young gentlemen, and that there's Boston Neck, where we was stationed, and where our officers did nothing, as somebody said, ' but twist their tails and powder their heads;' and here's Boston Bay, where our men-of-war and transports was lying; and here's all the little islands—Noddle Island, and Hog Island, and Spectacle Island, and a great many more, where we used to have skirmishes with the Yankees; and now, look you, here's Charlestown, and Bunker's Hill above it. Well, these heights, Bunker's Hill and Breed's Hill, could be easily approached at the back by Charlestown Neck; and though, as I've said, they completely commanded Boston, they were wholly neglected by our generals; but they warn't neglected by our sharp-witted foes, for, early one fine summer morning—it were the 17th of June afore-mentioned—we was wakened out of our slumbers by a brisk cannonading from the *Lively* ship of war, and, rubbing our eyes, we seed that the Yankees, during the night, had contrived to throw up a redoubt on Bunker's Hill, and complete a breastwork nearly to its foot."

"And did no one discover or disturb their operations?" I inquired.

"Not a soul," John replied, "though the bay was full of shipping, and our fortifications was close at hand. Well, this was too much even for old Gage to stand; so he opens upon 'em a battery from Copp's Hill, in Boston, and finding this do little or no good, he despatches Howe and Pigot, with ten companies of light infantry, and the like number of grenadiers, to try and dislodge the stubborn Yankees. We landed at Moreton's Point, which lies at the foot of Bunker's Hill, and right in front of the entrenchments, though we might just as easily, and far more safely, have taken the enemy in the rear, and gone up by Charlestown Neck. Howsomever, our generals judged otherwise, and it was our business to go where they led. But somehow they didn't like the look of things, so we waited for further reinforcements, and the delay gave the enemy an opportunity of improving his defensive operations, while he also received considerable reinforcements. It was a sweltering hot day, and we was almost ready to sink under the weight we carried, for, besides our knapsacks, cartouche-boxes, and firelocks, we was encumbered with three days' provision. Well, at last the word was given, and severe work it was to climb the hill-sides, under that blazing sun, and to scale the walls and fences by which it was intersected. We was formed in two lines, the light infantry on the right, being led by Howe, and the grenadiers on the left, by Pigot. Our wing was first assailed by a body of militiamen, who had posted themselves in some adjoining houses, but we soon put a stop to this by setting fire to their places of shelter, and, as the habitations was altogether of wood, the conflagration spread with wonderful rapidity, and the whole of Charlestown was soon in flames. It was an awful sight, and the smoke of the burning buildings added to our annoyances. Well, we continued to toil up the hill, till we got close up to their entrenchments, when the Yankees, who had let us approach almost undisturbed, opened upon us a most dreadful and destructive fire. Our line was broken in several places, and for some moments Howe was left almost alone. It seemed as if we should have the worst of it, when, luckily, General Clinton crosses Charles River, rallies the flying men, charges the Yankees at the point of the bayonet, forces 'em from their works, and drives 'em down Charlestown Neck. Ah! well, it was a hard-fought fight, and a badly-fought fight, too; for if we had been properly led, we should have licked 'em in no time."

"But you've told us nothing about your arm, John?" I said.

"Haven't I?" he rejoined; "well, I left it on Bunker's Hill anyhow, for it was carried off close to the showldher in the first attack, and though thus disabled I didn't leave the ranks, but got the stump bandaged up, and made shift to hold my firelock in my left hand, until, as we gained the redoubt, I received a blow on the head from a Yankee, who fought with a clubbed musket, which stretched me on the ground, and left me for dead on the field. Howsomever, here I am, hale and hearty, though minus an arm. And that's all about it."

"And here come Mr. Cane and the Doctor," I cried, "so we must be off to school. Thank you, John, for the story."

But we were not John's only customers, though his best. He also had dealings, in a small way, with the Bluecoat boys, and when they couldn't get out, they would summon him by thumping against their iron-studded doors, and screaming out, "John Leigh! a penn'orth o' barley-sugar!" until the article required was put under the gate to them. With these lads we had repeated quarrels, and they would sometimes issue forth in a swarm from the wicket in their gateway, and take by surprise a party of our lesser boys, who were playing at marbles or other games, and give them a drubbing before they could be rescued by their bigger and stronger comrades. On the approach of danger, the Bluecoat boys would retreat through the sallyport, and close it against the superior force. Well was it, on these occasions, for our little fellows, if there were any loungers in John Leigh's to respond to their cries for aid. Now and then, we prevented the wicket from being closed, and, pursuing the invaders into their own territories, a general conflict would take place upon the broad playground, reinforcements continually arriving on both sides, until the battle was decided, which it generally was in our favour. These fights presented a curious spectacle, owing to the strange costume of our antagonists, who were sturdy little rogues, and exhibited a good deal of pluck.

Towards the end of that half year, a gloom was thrown upon the school by a melancholy incident. During the warm weather we were wont to bathe in the Ater, the place selected being a deep pool, into which we could plunge from an overhanging sandstone rock. Of course, this spot was only available to swimmers, but I was amongst the number, and being fond of the water, soon became very expert, and was considered a first-rate diver. But it is not of myself I am about to speak, but of poor Simpson, whom I have incidentally mentioned. He, too, was accounted an excellent swimmer. One luckless day I parted with him before breakfast, and he was then in high spirits, and wanted me to have a swim in the Ater. I told him I hadn't time, but would go the next morning. "Tomorrow, come never," he replied, with a laugh, little thinking how truly he spoke. Others were easily persuaded to accompany him. We had scarcely assembled, an hour afterwards, when a report came that Simpson was drowned. We could scarcely believe it, but it turned out too true. He had been seized with cramp, as was supposed, and had sunk suddenly, in sight of his companions. The body had not yet been found. Never shall I forget the shock occasioned by this intelligence. A profound and mournful silence took place of the universal din, and we could distinctly hear the voices of the masters consulting together. The boys spoke in anxious whispers, and smiles had fled even from the most thoughtless countenance. All felt the sudden loss, for Simpson was generally liked; and I felt it most of all, for he was my great friend. The school was immediately dismissed, but no one went to play. All went sadly and slowly home.

CHAPTER III.

CONTAINING AN ACCOUNT OF MY GREAT-UNCLE, JOHN MOBBERLEY, HIS OLD DAME, AND HIS FARM AT MARSTON.

MOST of my holidays were passed with my father's uncle, John Mobberley, of Marston, in Cheshire. Old John was a farmer, on a very extensive scale, and possessed some pastures which produced the richest cheeses in the county, and his cheeses made him the richest man, except the squire, in Marston. A farmer of the old school was John,—old-fashioned in the management of his land, of his crops, of his cattle,—old-fashioned likewise in his habits, manners, and attire. He wore a blue coat, which looked as if it had been cut out by some village snip about thirty years back in the last century, ornamented with plain, flat, white buttons, as dull as old pewter; a waistcoat to match, with large flapped pockets; knee breeches, grey worsted stockings, and shoes, fastened by great plated buckles. His low-crowned hat was looped up at the sides.

In the days of his robust manhood, as I have heard, John Mobberley was a stout, upright fellow, and could go through as much hard work as any man, but now Time had laid a heavy hand upon him, had bent his back, and shrunk up his limbs within his clothes. When walking, he required the support of a staff; and, besides being afflicted with the rheumatic pains generally attendant upon old age, had partially lost the sight of his right eye, which he kept covered up with a great black patch, while the remaining orb was red and blear, giving a somewhat formidable and fiery character to his physiognomy. His nose and chin were large and prominent, and, as he had lost all his teeth, frequently met together as he mumbled his food, while from the same cause his speech was not altogether intelligible. In manner he was somewhat testy, like most old fellows who have got large pockets with plenty of cash in them. But, notwithstanding this, he was a good fellow in the main, and was very much liked and respected. As may be imagined, his age and habits, as well as tastes, wholly unfitted him for society, and hence his only resource was a weekly visit to the Nag's Head, a little public-house in the village of Marston, which lay about half a mile from his own dwelling, where there was a bowling-green, at which he would sometimes take a hand, and where a seat was reserved for him by the cosy fireside. To this snug little house some of the better inhabitants of the village would repair to spell over the county paper, and gossip over a cheerful glass. Once a week, about three or four o'clock in the afternoon, according to the season, old John Mobberley would seize his staff, and after scanning the farmyard with his only available eye, to ascertain that the coast was clear, would steal through the side garden, and make the best of his way across the fields to the village. These stolen visits to the Nag's Head would have been prevented altogether by his good old dame if she had had the power, and she did check their too frequent occurrence, being well aware of the excesses attending them, and of the pernicious effect they had upon her husband's health. But in spite of all remonstrances, go old John would, once a week, though stealthily as I have described, and as if ashamed of himself. Once arrived at the little inn, all his misgivings vanished. He was warmly welcomed by the stout host and buxom hostess, the best seat near the fire was given him, his pipe lighted, and a glass of cold gin-and-water prepared for him.

Old John was very happy as long as his senses lasted, chirruped over his cups, treated his old cronies, and many a one would drop in, apparently by accident, told his old jests, and talked of his farm and his concerns as if he had been by his own fireside: indeed, he talked a great deal more at the Nag's Head than he ever did at home, where he was generally morose and taciturn.

Of course, in the inebriate condition to which he was invariably reduced on these occasions, it would have been utterly impossible for him to get home unassisted, and Sam Massey, one of the farming men, was usually sent to fetch him. One night I accompanied Sam on the errand. I had never seen my uncle in such a state before, and must confess I was surprised and shocked at his appearance. He was roaring out and gesticulating like a Bedlamite. On seeing me, whom he had not expected, he ordered a glass of gin-and-water to be given me, and another to Sam, while he drained that which stood before him. After this, and many futile attempts to keep steady on his seat, and to utter a few coherent sentences, he was persuaded, chiefly by the hostess, who seemed to exercise some influence over him, to go home. We had fine work with him in the fields, for he kicked the horn lantern, which I carried, into a clump of hazel trees, and while Sam was searching for it, he broke away from me, and started off at a pace which, in soberer moments, he certainly could not have equalled, and, before we could overtake him, fell headlong into a pond. We got him out as quickly as we could, and he sustained no further damage than such as was occasioned by the ducking. But the accident made him somewhat more careful for the next few weeks.

My aunt Mobberley presented an advantageous contrast to her husband in personal appearance; for though past eighty, while he was nearly ten years younger, she had preserved some traces of the comeliness which had distinguished her youth and maturer years. She was tall and perfectly upright, and though her features were deeply furrowed with wrinkles, they still retained a pleasing expression. Her eyesight was unimpaired, and her teeth tolerably good. Her hair was still abundant, and merely grizzled, whereas her husband's scanty locks were silvery white. She was in full possession of all her faculties, and, considering her great age, very active, busying herself about her household concerns, and superintending the dairy, which was still an object of great solicitude and interest to her. But the cheeses, which, during more than half a century, had been made by her own hand, were now manufactured by her niece, Hannah Massey, a stout damsel, who was fully equal to the important task assigned her, and whose tongue and limbs were never idle. Under Hannah's care the Marston cheese lost none of its high reputation.

The rest of the household comprised Hannah's younger sister Martha, a fresh-complexioned lass of fifteen, and her two brothers, Sam and Peter, the latter of whom was a great raw-boned fellow, and a tremendous bruiser. He was very fond of wakes and fairs, and required a good deal of looking after on the part of his elder sister. Besides these, there was the superintendent of the farm, William Weever, between whom and Hannah Massey an engagement of marriage subsisted, which was to be ratified at some period, early or late, as chance might dictate, when any change to warrant it might take place in the family. The proposed match met with the entire approval of the old couple, and my aunt only wished it to be postponed until after her death.

Nethercrofts—for so my uncle Mobberley's habitation was designated—was nothing more than a farm-house, with large cow-houses (shippons, in the dialect of the county), and other outbuildings attached to it. A few rooms had been added at the back, but a farm-house it remained to the end. The walls were whitewashed, the roof thatched. Within, the entire centre of the house was occupied by a spacious apartment, with a low roof encumbered by projecting rafters, from which hung hams and sides of bacon. Also, a bread-flake full of oat cakes. Also, Sam Massey's sword, which he used to wear when he went out with the North Cheshire Yeomanry, in which corps he served as my uncle's substitute. Also, a couple of horse-pistols, belonging to the said Sam, and a long disused duck-gun, with a wormeaten stock. The windows had small diamond panes, the floor was flagged, and the fireplace had a wide-mouthed chimney, and deep comfortable corners, furnished with wooden benches on either side. Over the fire hung a great black kettle, and not far from it a bake-stone.

The house-place—for so the room was called—looked extremely comfortable, with its white walls, its clean sanded floor, its dresser, its old oak chests, and its old clock, which stood quietly ticking in the corner. Near one of the windows was a long, high-backed sofa, the seat and cushions of which were covered with patchwork. Here my aunt Mobberley used generally to sit, and, when not employed, read her Bible, or some other good book, with her favourite white tom-cat at her feet—a huge animal, very gentle with her, but very spiteful to every one else, and to me in particular. My uncle's old arm-chair and spittoon were placed near the fire, with a little table close at hand, for the convenience of his pipe and tobacco-box; while, upon the hearth, Talbot, the retriever, would stretch his lazy length, as often as permitted.

In reviewing my visits to Nethercrofts, I seem to fix on the happiest period of my life. I liked the old farm-house; I liked the life I led; I had no distasteful tasks to fulfil—no Mr. Cane to apprehend; I was constantly out in the open air, constantly engaged in exercise. If this was not very intellectual employment, at least it was very healthful; and though rather delicate when at the Anchorite's, and confined all day in a public school, and in the evening by tasks, here, with plenty of exercise, and nothing on my mind, I became extremely robust, and got a fresh glowing colour in my cheeks. At one time I was a great angler, and thought of nothing else but rods, lines, tackle, and baits. I used to troll for jack, and catch perch and carp in the mere which lay in the valley about a mile from Nethercrofts; and would set drum-nets for tench, and night-lines for eels in my uncle's ponds. Such was the mania that possessed me, that I used occasionally to dream of catching pike as big as sharks. I longed for the time when I should be able to throw a fly and take the speckled trout in some mountain stream. My conversation turned wholly upon fishing; and I was thrown into ecstasies by hearing of any piscine preserves, and treasured the place in my memory. I have since learnt to dislike the angler's art, and, so far from thinking it a "gentle" sport, am of opinion that it is a very cruel pastime: but I had no such scruples of sensibility then. If I gained nothing else by the pursuit, at all events I acquired a love of Nature. I beheld her beauties under many a varied aspect—at morn and eve, amid showers as well as sunshine. I noted the pursuits of the feathered creation with interest, and listened attentively to their different songs and cries. To raise the wild duck or startle the coot from among the water-flags and bulrushes fringing the banks of the mere—to watch the heron, with outstretched legs, and head between the shoulders, wing his low and heavy flight across the water, and descend in some sheltered nook, to devour his prey undisturbed—to hear the bittern's booming cry—to see the long-billed curlew or the plover—the redshank and the sandpiper—and, above all, the kingfisher—these were delights and studies to me then.

Connected with these ornithological tastes, though not exactly with fishing, was my anxiety to possess an owl. One of these curious birds tenanted a barn at Nethercrofts. It was a great white owl, and I had often been startled by his screech, and marked with wonder his ghostly flight. Sam and I contrived to surprise him in his haunt, perched on a rafter festooned with dusty cobwebs at the top of the barn, and just when we had made sure of him, he dashed right in our faces, knocked Sam off the ladder, and escaped. On relating the circumstance to my uncle, to my surprise he was very angry, and peremptorily forbade us to molest the owl, or, as Sam called it, the bullart, in future. I am sorry to say I resolved to disobey him, for

I longed more than ever to obtain possession of the bird; but Sam, to whom I communicated my secret desires, did not dare to help me, and tried to dissuade me from making the attempt. But I would not be reasoned out of it, and succeeded in catching the owl, though, as it proved in the end, I had better not have meddled with him.

I have already mentioned that my uncle Mobberley was accounted very rich;—what the extent of his wealth might be I didn't know, but I felt sure it must be very great, for people always spoke of him as a man who had made his thousands. Whatever it was, his expenditure was so small that his money must have been constantly increasing. He had few relations on his own side, the nearest being my father and Dr. Sale, the vicar of Marston, both of whom stood to him in the same degree of affinity, being his nephews. His wife had a great many relations, none of whom were in very flourishing circumstances, and some of them had given him a good deal of trouble, but of these latterly he took no notice. One whole family, however—the Masseys, who were the children of a farmer whose wife had died before her eldest daughter, Hannah, had come of age, and who had himself followed her to the grave within a year—had found a home at Nethercrofts. They were not allowed to eat the bread of idleness, but were all employed about the house and farm in various capacities, and received good wages, as any other persons so engaged might have done. Naturally enough, some of these poor folks hungered for a legacy; but it was clearly understood that my uncle, though he did not mean to overlook his wife's relations altogether, intended to leave the bulk of his property on his own side, and in his own way. The old fellow had a good deal of pride about him; and though he had not himself led the life of a gentleman, he determined that his successor should, and he would leave him the means of doing so. He made no secret of his intentions; and as his worthy dame had brought him nothing beyond the active services which had helped him to save the fortune he thus meant to bequeath, she quite assented to his plans. Having no children of his own, my uncle looked about him for an heir, and eventually selected me.

"I like Mervyn," he said to my aunt; "he is a handsome, promising lad. His father, Captain Clitheroe, can't do much for him, especially since he has married again, and has got other children. The lad has the air of a gentleman, and I'll make a gentleman of him."

From this date I was understood to be adopted by my uncle Mobberley, and every one considered me a lucky dog. No doubt I had many enemies in consequence, and among the bitterest of them (though I was not aware of his enmity at the time) was Malpas Sale, the vicar's only son. For my own part, I was too young to think much upon the matter, and certainly evinced no improper sense of the preference shown me. I never sought to curry favour with my uncle, but always conducted myself in a very independent way towards him; and I have reason to think he liked me the better for it. There was nothing like servility in my nature, and I could not stoop to such an abject course, whatever I might have gained by it.

Lest my uncle's apparent neglect of the Sales might seem to justify Malpas's secret animosity towards me, I must explain how matters stood in that quarter. Some thirty years ago, when the Rev.

Wrigley Sale, then newly entered of the Church, and a very handsome young man, became tutor to the sons of Mr. Vernon, of Fitton Park, a proud Cheshire squire of large landed possessions, to whom Marston, its mere, and a considerable portion of the country adjoining it belonged, he exemplified in his own conduct how dangerous propinquity to a charming object may prove; for he speedily fell over head and ears in love with Lydia, the squire's youngest daughter. His passion was requited, and an engagement took place between them; but when the squire heard of it he was highly incensed, and turned the tutor out of doors. The young lady was disconsolate, her lover in despair. At this juncture, John Mobberley, with whom, after his expulsion from the hall, Sale sought refuge, came forward, and offered to settle 5000*l.* on the young lady if Mr. Vernon would consent to her marriage with his nephew. Moved by this consideration, and by his daughter's tears, the squire at length yielded; the money was paid down, and the young couple united. Thereafter, Wrigley Sale moved in the best society in the county; kept a good nag, hunted with all the neighbouring squires (for most country clergymen with good livings were fox-hunters in those days), dined with them, and drank with them; and as this mode of living led him into expenses far beyond his means, he was obliged to have recourse to John Mobberley, from whom, at different times, he managed to borrow a couple of thousand pounds, for which he gave his bond. A few years afterwards Sale's position was greatly improved. His father-in-law, the squire, with whom the advowson rested, presented him with the valuable living of Marston when it became vacant; and he had now twelve hundred a year, and a capital residence. Still, he did not pay back the money he had borrowed from John Mobberley, nor was he ever dunned for it by the old trump, as he called him, who told him he would leave him the bond when he died, but he must expect nothing more from him. With this arrangement Dr. Sale (for he had now obtained his doctor's degree) was well content. Not so, however, his son Malpas—as will appear in the course of this history.

As may be easily imagined, John Mobberley, who pretended to be nothing more than a plain farmer, never supposed himself upon any terms of equality with Dr. Sale's aristocratic connexions and friends, and he declined all invitations to meet any of them at the vicarage. For this the vicar was not sorry, as he began to feel ashamed of an old uncle, trump though he might be, who had amassed a fortune by selling cheeses; but his wife, who could not forget old John's generosity to her, and who was too conscious of her own proud descent and high connexions to think herself degraded by associating with a worthy farmer, regretted the old man's absence. She often called at Nethercrofts—often took Dr. Sale with her when he would not have gone of his own accord; but John Mobberley rarely passed the gates of the vicarage. Of course, when staying at Marston, I went there when I chose; but though I liked Mrs. Sale extremely, the vicar was a great deal too proud and pompous to please me.

Malpas Sale and I were very intimate. He was three years older than I, and much taller; very handsome, but effeminate-looking, with small features, as delicate as those of a woman; very small hands and feet; an exceedingly pale, almost sickly, complexion; and large dark eyes, which, though shaded by long silken lashes, and ordinarily soft in expression, would sometimes emit fierce and sinister glances. He had fine black hair, which hung in wavy curls about his face.

Malpas used often to come over to Nethercrofts, and we went fishing and shooting together, for I had already begun to handle a gun, and was a tolerable shot. I liked him well enough, but I never felt any great regard for him, his manner not being calculated to inspire affection, for he had a strong tendency to sneer, and his jests were always sarcastic. His laughter had more of derision than enjoyment about it. Nevertheless, he could be very amusing when he chose, and on the whole was a pleasant companion.

But when it became known that my uncle meant to make me his heir, his manner changed. He came to Nethercrofts as usual, but appeared to shun me, and when we met seemed resolved to pick a quarrel with me. I was equally resolved he should not, and seldom made any reply to the bitter and provoking things he said to me; but I could not always command my temper, and on one occasion an outbreak took place which ended in a fight between us. We were alone together in the barn, when he began, as usual, to jeer me about some trifling matter, and finding his remarks produce no effect, he proceeded to taunt me with being my uncle's favourite, insinuating that I had used unworthy means to become so. This was more than I could bear; and I told him in plain terms he was uttering falsehoods.

"You think yourself sure of old Mobb's money," he said; "and give yourself airs in consequence; but if the old cheesemonger knew as much about you as I do, what mischievous tricks you play, and how you turn him and the old woman into ridicule behind their backs, he wouldn't leave you a shilling."

"How dare you make such shameful assertions, Malpas?" I cried, reddening with passion; "so far from ridiculing my uncle, to whom I am so much indebted, and whom you so impertinently nickname old Mobb, I have always checked your sneers at the odd ways, as you term them, of him and my aunt. But I comprehend the motive of your anger. You are disappointed because you are not so great a favourite as I am, and vent your spleen upon me, who have done nothing to offend you."

"But you *have* offended me, and, what is more, you have injured me," Malpas rejoined. "You have told lies about me to old Mobb, and have alienated his regard from me. Before you came, *I* was the favourite, and should have continued so, and been his heir, but for your underhand practices."

So, then, the secret is fairly out, I thought; and I could not help laughing at the way in which he had betrayed himself. This exasperated him more than the bitterest retort I could have made.

"Take care of yourself, my lad," he cried; "the game is not all your own yet. Consummate hypocrite as you are, I will unmask you, and display you in your true colours to my uncle."

"You have displayed yourself in your true colours to me, Malpas," I rejoined, "and they are not over-creditable to you. But you say I have told lies about you to my uncle. This I positively deny. I have said nothing to your disadvantage to him or to any one. As to underhand practices, you ought to be ashamed of entertaining such unworthy suspicions; but I suppose you judge of me by yourself. You have also called me a hypocrite; and unless you retract the word——"

"What will you do, my young cock?" he interrupted, crowing like chanticleer, and enchanted that he had roused me at last. "We shall see—for I shan't retract a syllable. Now then, what'll you do?"

My answer was a blow, which knocked him from his perch. When he got up, his pale cheeks had turned absolutely green with rage.

"We'll soon settle this," he cried. "Come out into the croft."

I followed him out as he rushed through a side door. We went behind a haystack, and our jackets were off in a moment. He attacked me before I was quite ready for him, and fought in a very unmanly way, more like an infuriated animal than a human being, tearing my cheeks with his long nails, kicking me severely on the shins, and biting my hands like a wild cat when we closed. To put a stop to this, I gave him a tap on the nose, which drew his claret plentifully, and sent him reeling backwards. I thought he had got enough, for he stood still and took up his jacket, as if searching for a handkerchief to stanch the blood. But he brought out a knife instead, and was opening it, when I knocked it from his grasp, and set my foot upon it. Thus disarmed, and finding himself no match for me—for though the younger and the lesser lad of the two, I was the stronger and the more active—he began to cry, and declared in a very abject manner that he yielded.

"Do you retract what you have said about me?" I demanded, scornfully.

"I do," he replied.

"And you won't call my uncle 'old Mobb,' or 'the cheesemonger,' any more?"

He promised he wouldn't; and I extended him the hand bearing the blue impression of his teeth. He took it with evident repugnance.

Just then we became aware of the presence of a third party, and perceived my uncle a short distance off, leaning on his staff.

"Halloa! what's the matter?" the old man cried, between the intervals of a violent fit of coughing; "fighting, eh? (Ugh, ugh.) You ought to be ashamed of yourselves. (Ugh, ugh.) Two young gentlemen, and disgrace yourselves in this way. What would Madam Sale say, Malpas, if she could see thee now, with that bleeding nose? (Ugh, ugh.) And what would Madam Mervyn say to thy scratched face, eh, boy? (Ugh—ugh—ugh.)"

"The quarrel wasn't of my seeking, uncle," Malpas hastily replied. "I didn't begin it. He struck me first."

"Thou saidst something to provoke him, no doubt," rejoined my uncle. "Thou'rt older than he, and ought to know better."

"Allow me to explain, uncle," I said.

"No, sir, I don't want any explanations," interrupted the old man. "I don't want to know the cause of the dispute. I only want to prevent its repetition. I won't hear either of ye. (Ugh, ugh.)

You're both in the wrong, and it's immaterial to me who is the most to blame. (Ugh, ugh.) Shake hands and be friends, and let's hear no more about it. Go to the pump and wash the stains from your faces. (Ugh, ugh.)"

As we set off to obey the injunction, leaving him expectorating freely after this lengthy harangue, Malpas observed to me,

"You'll not say anything about the knife to old Mobb, Mervyn?"

"I'll give you another thrashing, if you call him that name again," I replied. "Recollect how largely your father is indebted to him, and hold your peace."

This effectually silenced him.

After this occurrence, Malpas was very civil to me, and we became better friends than we had been for some time previously. He was also very attentive to my uncle, and I thought, if any one could be accused of trying to curry favour with the old man, it was he, and not I. However, I did not concern myself about his proceedings, and my uncle showed no increased regard for him. I thought, however, from hints let drop occasionally by the old man, that he had got some notions into his head respecting me which he had not previously entertained. Somehow or other, he found out that I had caught the owl, and was very cross with me for disobeying him. Then Talbot was lamed, and it was said that I had beaten him with a heavy stick, though I was much too fond of him to beat him at all. The great boar had lost his curly tail, and the appendage being unaccountably found in my pocket, it proved a great *bore* to me. But the climax was put to my offences by one of such an aggravated nature, that it threw me into disgrace. My aunt's favourite tom-cat was shot, and it was supposed—nay, proved—that I had done the ruthless deed. Poor Tom, who was fond of exercising his claws, had certainly scratched me rather severely, and it was said I had breathed vengeance against him. No such thing. The next morning master Tom was missing, and after vainly calling to him, he was at last found by Malpas in the garden, with half an ounce of shot in his head. Never shall I forget my poor old aunt's distress at the sight of her favourite, held up before her by the heels like a great jack-hare by Malpas.

"Zounds and fury!—who killed the cat?" cried my uncle, coughing terribly.

"Ay, who indeed?" said my aunt;—"poor pussy!"

"My goodness! here's a pretty piece of work!" screamed Hannah Massey, rushing out of the dairy. "Who can have done it?"

All eyes were directed to me, and, though I was perfectly innocent, I looked and felt like a culprit.

"It must be this young imp of the devil. He's always in mischief," cried my uncle, shaking his stick menacingly at me. "Where's Sam Massey? He'll tell us something about it."

Sam was accordingly called, and, being questioned, was obliged to admit that I had taken out my gun on the previous evening, and that he had heard one or two reports apparently at the back of the house. This was enough. In vain I declared I had only fired once, at a rabbit, and had missed it. My assertions were disbelieved. I was pronounced guilty of taking the life of the cat by violence and with malice aforethought, and incurred the angry denunciations of my uncle, and, what was far worse to bear, the tearful reproaches of my aunt, who mourned the death of her favourite.

This incident unquestionably shook me in my uncle's good opinion, and auguries, very unfavourable to my ultimate succession to the property, were drawn from it by interested parties; and Malpas was considered now to have the better chance. But whatever the old man's secret intentions might be, he did not publish them to the world at Nethercrofts, and everybody was left to doubt and speculation.

Soon after this I was summoned back to the Anchorite's, and to school; and several months elapsed before I again visited my uncle.

CHAPTER IV.

MALPAS AND I ATTEMPT TO CROSS MARSTON MERE DURING A HARD FROST—AN ADVENTURE ON THE ICE.

THE Christmas holidays had commenced, and I went over to Marston. I hoped my uncle had forgotten all my transgressions, real or supposed, and it seemed he had, for he received me with as much kindness as heretofore. My aunt was not quite so gracious. I was sorry to find her grown a great deal more feeble; and it was clear she couldn't last much longer. She had got a new tabby cat; but she told me, with tears in her eyes, that she didn't love him half so well as poor Tom.

Malpas, who was an Etonian, had come home likewise, and never allowed a day to pass without paying a visit to Nethercrofts, chiefly under pretence of joining me in my amusements, but secretly, I believe, with the view of gaining the good graces of my uncle, in which he fancied he had made considerable progress.

It was a winter of unusual severity; and though the cold pinched the old folks sadly, it did us lads a world of good. The blood spun through my veins, and my spirits were so elastic, that I could scarcely contain myself for delight. I had taken to skating, and, like all my other pursuits, devoted myself to it with ardour. I used to be off to the mere at six in the morning—almost before it was light; and oh! how I enjoyed the exercise,—what rosy cheeks I had,—and what an appetite for breakfast! No tea and toast, nor any such effeminate luxuries then, but a good jorum of boiled milk and bread, or wholesome meal pottage. And as to the coarse viands at dinner, how I relished them!—how I devoured the pickled pork and peas-pudding, or the salt beef and cabbage, and huge slice of suet-dumpling sweetened with treacle.

Well, the frost increased in intensity; and after the lapse of a fortnight, Marston Mere was frozen over—a circumstance almost without precedent, and such as had not occurred within my uncle's recollection, and he had known it for seventy years. The opportunity was not to be lost, so Malpas and I resolved to cross the mere —an exploit which, as far as we knew, had never been achieved or even attempted. We said nothing of our intentions to any one, for fear of being prevented, but set out one day before breakfast in high glee. It was a dull, grey morning, with woolly clouds threatening snow: and, as the ground did not feel quite so hard and crisp as it had done, Malpas thought the frost must be giving way. I was afraid so too, and fancied, if we had delayed our exploit to another day, it might have been too late. I had taken my gun with me in expectation of picking up a snipe or a wild-duck as we went along. Descending a narrow lane, bordered with hazels and alders, we soon reached the edge of the mere, whose broad expanse was entirely sheeted with ice. Crowning a high bank on the left stood the venerable church of Marston, a beautiful and picturesque object; and close adjoining it, amid a grove of ancestral trees, now stripped of their leafy honours, but with many a rook's nest discernible amid their branches, stood the vicarage. At the foot of the lawn, which came down to the mere, was a boat-house, with its tiny craft frozen fast in the water. Beyond this the banks rose still higher and more abruptly, and their sides were clothed with brushwood and timber. Still further they dipped gently down, and the view was bounded by the thick dark woods of Dunton Park, which shrouded the residence of the Earl of Amounderness. The fairest object in this part of the prospect was Dunton Church, which stood on a gentle hill about a mile north of the mere. It was an old pile with a square tower, like that of Marston, and I know not to which church the palm of beauty ought to be assigned. It was pleasant in summer-time to float on the mere, and hear the bells of both fanes ring out in merry rivalry. Those of Marston were deepest, Dunton's sweetest in tone. On the right of Dunton the view was terminated by the dark and distant range of Lancashire hills. My glances, however, were not cast in this direction, but towards the tower of Marston Church, the summit of which was lighted up by a straggling sunbeam. I thought of my mother, and fancied her eye might be upon me.

My reflections were put to flight by a flight of wild-fowl. I fired amongst them, and brought down a couple of fine ducks, and, having bagged them, we commenced our attempt. The southern extremity of the mere, where we were, was the widest, and the point we intended to make for—a cottage on the low banks, belonging to Ned Culcheth, one of Squire Vernon's keepers—might be about a mile off, in a direct line. At first, the ice was strong enough, and we trampled down the flags and bulrushes as they appeared above the surface; but after we had got two or three hundred yards, and were above deep water, it certainly looked thinner, and was very blue and clear. As we knew there were many springs in the mere, we kept a sharp look-out for all such dangerous places; and, indeed, they were pointed out to us by the water-fowl, which assembled at the spots in search of the fish that swarmed there to breathe. By this time I had encumbered myself with another duck, and having advanced for a quarter of a mile without accident and without alarm, we were in high spirits at our progress, and made sure of accomplishing the rest of the distance.

While loading my gun, after an unsuccessful shot, we stopped for a moment to look around us. It was a fine winterly scene: ice— ice—everywhere, spreading out in a vast unbroken sheet, smooth, shining like a mirror, and as slippery too. Just then the clock of Marston Church struck seven, in an unusually solemn manner I thought; and we went on, running and sliding over the glassy surface. All at once we became aware that the ice was bending unpleasantly beneath us, and we looked at each other uneasily. Forcing a laugh, I began to repeat the schoolboy rhymes—

"If it bends, it'll bear,
If it cracks, it'll swear,
If it breaks————"

"Hold your tongue!" interrupted Malpas. "Why the devil do you mention such a thing as breaking now? I wish we were safely back again. What a fool I was to come with you at all!"

He was here interrupted in his turn by a most terrific crack, beginning just beneath his feet, passing under mine, and sweeping on with an awful noise to an immense distance. Malpas and I stared at each other aghast, uncertain whether to advance or retreat.

We were now about midway from either shore, and therefore it seemed immaterial which course was adopted. Malpas was for turning back; but he had scarcely moved a foot in that direction, when another crack, louder and more appalling than the first, took place beneath him, and water sprang from between the fissures. Starting back with a cry of terror, he speeded off in the course we had originally pursued. We trod as lightly and moved as swiftly as we could, stepping on the points of our feet. The distance between us and the shore seemed interminable. The ice seemed fairly giving way, and cracked and groaned most fearfully. On looking back, I saw that the surface not fifty yards behind us was covered with water. I now gave myself up for lost, and thought of my mother, hoping I should be buried beside her, if my body was ever found, in Marston Churchyard.

Malpas, who was not encumbered with a gun and a bag of wild-ducks, and who, besides, had a very light pair of heels, got considerably in advance, and thinking I might safely follow where he went, I shaped my course accordingly. But I soon found this to be an error, for the ice, which bent beneath him and cracked, would hardly sustain me, and more than once gave way altogether, so that my escapes from destruction seemed almost miraculous. For some time, my attention had been so intently directed to my own precarious situation, that I had not dared to glance towards the shore; but now looking in that direction, with a thrill of delight I discovered that I was much nearer it than I expected—scarcely more than a hundred yards off, while the ice had become much firmer. But where was Malpas? Had he already reached the bank? I could nowhere perceive him. A vague apprehension crossed me that he had sunk through the ice; and my fears were instantly afterwards confirmed by remarking his cap only a few yards before me. At a glance I saw what had happened. In his haste, he had incautiously approached a spring, and had fallen through the thin covering of ice. The sound of his immersion had been drowned in the loud cracks and explosions. All selfish considerations were lost in the thought of saving him, and twenty rash plans—any of which would have cost me my own life—occurred to me. I approached as near as I dared to the hole. Nothing was to be discerned of him. The ice was as transparent as crystal, and I looked eagerly around for any object beneath it. The next moment I distinguished Malpas under the glassy barrier, with his hands outstretched, and his eyes open and fixed on me. Never shall I forget their expression. I sprang to where he was, pointed in the direction of the aperture, and signed to him to move towards it. He understood me, and with a last effort struggled thither, and got his head above the ice. But the frail support broke beneath his hold, and he sank again. I uttered a cry of despair. But the next moment he reappeared; and, having thrown myself flat on the ice, I managed to lay my gun across the hole, and he caught hold of the barrel. But I saw that he was so much exhausted, that unless he could be immediately extricated he must unquestionably perish; and I therefore approached still nearer, though at the greatest personal risk, until I could grasp his hand, and then, bidding him second my efforts, I exerted all the strength I possessed, and succeeded in dragging him out of the hole.

I was so overjoyed by his deliverance, that I felt disposed to fall on my knees and offer up thanks to Heaven for it; but there was something in his look that checked me.

Seeing he was too much exhausted to move, I laid hold of him and dragged him along the surface of the ice, which, fortunately, was very smooth, so that I had little difficulty in the job, for he himself was as helpless as a sack. When I got him to land he was quite insensible, and I was very much frightened, scarcely knowing what to do. However, Ned Culcheth's cottage was close by; so I hurried thither, and fortunately finding the keeper within, he came out at once, and by his help and that of his wife, Malpas was quickly transported to the little habitation, where he was wrapped in warm blankets, and some hot spirits and water poured down his throat; after which he began to revive. At first he didn't seem to know what had happened, nor where he was; but when his dark eye lighted on me as I sat by the pallet on which he was laid, all seemed to flash upon him, and an uneasy expression crossed his face.

"Weel, Master Malpas, how dun you find yourself, sir," inquired Ned. "You'n had a narrow squeak for your life, and if it hadn't been for Master Marvyn here, yo'd ha' been food for th' fishes by this time. You owe your life to him."

"It's a debt I shall never be able to pay," Malpas rejoined, turning away as if in pain, and averting his gaze from us.

The keeper shook his head.

"I dunna like that lad," he muttered between his teeth. "There's summut naw reet about him"

With this he left the room; and, after a little time, as Malpas did not speak, I fancied he must be asleep, and got up to leave too, but just as I was passing through the door I glanced towards the bed, and beheld his eyes fixed upon me, with an expression of absolute hate. I was stepping back to him, but he motioned me off, saying, impatiently and pettishly,

"I don't want you. Shut the door. I'm trying to go to sleep, and your presence disturbs me."

So I left him, and stepping outside the cottage found Ned, who had been to fetch my gun and the ducks which I had left on the ice.

"Why you're one o' t' warst poachers abowt Marston, Master Marvyn," Ned cried, "and I dunna know what t' Squoire would say if he seed you wi' these dooks. Howsomedever, we won't say nowt about it. Hang that chap inside; I canna 'bide him. Take care he dunna do you an ill turn. You'n thrown a chance away. If I'd been i' your place, when his head was once fairly under water, I'd ha' letten him be. No one could ha' blamed you, and he'd ha' done you no more hurt."

"But I should have blamed myself, Culcheth," I rejoined, somewhat severely, for I was much displeased with the freedom he took; "or rather, I should never have forgiven myself, if I had acted in the way you suggest. I would rather suffer any wrong than commit the heinous crime of allowing a fellow-creature to perish, when I could render him aid, even granting he were my enemy at the time, and, which I can scarcely believe, should continue an enemy afterwards."

"Weel, them's Christian sentiments, I must say," returned the keeper, rather abashed; "and I am glad any one can be found to act up to 'em, but you're young i' th' warld yet, and dunna know human natur—the worst part on it I mean, for it's not all bad—Lord forbid! When you'n lived as long as I have, you'n find that wi' some folk every kindness you show 'em is worse than an injury inflicted."

I put an end to the discussion, for I thought nothing would be gained by pursuing it further; and we entered the cottage, where a clean cloth had been spread upon the table, and a plain, but ample and very good breakfast had been prepared by the keeper's wife, consisting of fried eggs and bacon, toasted oat-cakes, butter, cheese, and a large basin of new milk. To these good things I did ample justice, for I was as hungry as a famished wolf.

Sissy Culcheth was a young and very pretty Welsh woman, and wore a man's hat, which was extremely becoming to her. Her countenance was redolent of health and good humour, and her cherry lips were ever sundered by smiles, as if to show her white teeth, while a pretty dimple was constantly displaying itself in her blooming cheeks. She was particularly clean in her person and attire; and as I looked round the cottage, which in all its arrangements and details showed evidence of her neatness and taste, I thought Ned must be a very happy fellow with such a tidy and pretty helpmate. In return for the excellent meal she had provided me with, I offered her the wild ducks I had shot, and she appeared much obliged by the present; but Ned laughed, and said, "Nah, nah; it would be like bringin' coals to Newcastle, to give her the dooks."

Before I sat down to breakfast, Sissy peeped into the room where Malpas lay, and finding him asleep, did not disturb him; but now that nearly two hours had elapsed, and his clothes were quite dried, she went again, and almost instantly returned, with a look of alarm, saying he was sitting up in bed, talking very wildly and incoherently, and, she feared, must be in a high fever. Ned and I instantly flew to the room, and found her apprehensions verified. On seeing us, he sprang out of bed, and seized me by the throat; and it required all Ned's strength to get him back again, and hold him down. In a little time the paroxysm passed, and a shivering-fit ensued; and as it was evident immediate assistance must be obtained, Ned said my Christian charity must be put in practice once more, and I must run for Simon Pownall, the village barber-surgeon, and he would keep watch over Master Malpas meanwhile, to prevent mischief. He added, that I had better call at the vicarage, and let Dr. Sale know how matters stood. This was not a very pleasant task, but there was no help for it, and I set off as fast as I could to Marston.

CHAPTER V.

CONSEQUENCES OF THE ADVENTURE ON THE ICE.

SIMON POWNALL, the barber-surgeon of Marston, was a strange, conceited little fellow, with whom I was well acquainted, for he shaved my uncle Mobberley three times a week, brought him mixtures for his cough, lotions for his sore eye, and powders for his rheumatism. He was the greatest gossip in the village, and knew every one's affairs far better than they knew them themselves. There were no secrets, he declared, in any family round the place with which he was not acquainted. His practice had put him in possession of queer matters, if he chose to disclose them; "but ' mum ' 's the word with me," he said; "professional men never betray their patients." Simon, moreover, was of a very meddlesome turn, and liked to push his nose—and it was very long and sharp—into everything, and to give advice without being asked for it; and as, from one cause or another, he was very much feared, people took care to be on good terms with him. He had plenty of employment with shaving and tooth-drawing, blistering men and bleeding cattle, attending the farmers' wives in their confinements, and physicking their sons and daughters. He powdered the vicar's hair, and quacked him for his gout and other ailments; was very skilful in reducing a fracture; and, indeed, in his own opinion, was very skilful at everything. In short, he was a clever little empiric, with a smattering of most things, and knew how to make the most of the little he possessed. Though a great egotist, he generally managed to drop the personal pronoun when speaking of himself. His shop was close to the Nag's Head, somewhat retired from the road, with a comfortable bench in front, a gallipot and a red rag in the window, and a blue and white striped pole projecting from the door.

When I rushed in, in breathless haste, Simon was operating on the chin of a farmer, and, startled by the noise, he exclaimed, on seeing me,

"Something wrong at Nethercrofts, eh? Be bound it's the old dame. Never recovered the loss of her cat. Been in a low way ever since—sinking—sinking—gradually sinking. Tried to support her. Got her a fine tabby. No use. Ah! ah! poor soul—knew it would come to this."

"But there's nothing the matter with her!" I cried. "My aunt's not worse than usual."

"Oh, la! then it's the old man!" Pownall ejaculated. "What ails him? Shaved him yesterday. Cough troublesome; rheumatiz ditto. Well enough, though, to go to the Nag's Head in the afternoon, and drink his gin-and-water as usual. Sudden attack, eh?"

Having now quite recovered my breath, I stopped his guess-work by explaining what had really happened, and in what way his ser-

D

vices were required. On hearing that Malpas and I had crossed the mere, he lifted up his hands in amazement; so did his apprentice, Cheetham Quick, who was almost as queer a character as his master; and so also did Tom Shakeshaft, the farmer, who had waited quietly all this while with his broad good-natured face covered with lather.

"Oh, la! wonder you're here to tell the tale!" Pownall cried, after this general expression of astonishment. "Risks young folks run, to be sure. Wouldn't have done it for twenty pounds; would you, Master Shakeshaft?" (A grunt of assent from the farmer.) "Off immediately—that is, as soon as you're finished, Master Shakeshaft. Take care of the shop, Chetham."

And, having cleared the jolly farmer's cheeks and chin of their stubble, he put a case of lancets, some bandages, and a few other matters into his pocket, and, leaving Chetham Quick to conduct his business in his absence, hurried off to the keeper's cottage, while I repaired to the vicarage, very doubtful as to the reception I should meet with.

The vicarage was a thoroughly comfortable residence. Trust your well-beneficed parsons for taking care of themselves, and making all snug about them. I was ushered into the study, whither the doctor had retired after a substantial breakfast, the remains of which I saw on the sideboard as I passed the dining-room. Dr. Sale was a pompous, portly personage, with a rosy, handsome countenance, set off by well-powdered hair, and boasting a goodly protuberance of stomach, sustained by many a fat haunch of venison from Fitton Park, which was now in the possession of his wife's brother, to whom in former days he had been tutor. Dr. Sale suffered from gout, and as his weight and corpulency prevented him from taking as much exercise as he required, his temper suffered likewise. He looked much surprised at my visit, and when I told him, as briefly as I could, what had occurred, he flew into a towering passion, and, ringing the bell furiously, bade the man desire Mrs. Sale to come to him immediately. He then rated me soundly, as if I had been the sole cause of the accident.

Before I could offer any further explanation, Mrs. Sale entered. She was still very handsome, possessing a tall, graceful figure, and an unmistakable air of high breeding in manner and deportment. Her son greatly resembled her in point of features, but in no other respect, for she was an excellent person, and very amiable.

"Good morning, Mervyn. What is the matter, Dr. Sale?" she inquired, calmly.

"The matter is this, Mrs. Sale," replied the vicar. "Malpas, at the instance of this hair-brained boy, and in company with him, has been crossing the mere—you know it is frozen over, Mrs. Sale: was ever such an act of insanity committed?—and he has fallen through the ice, and is now lying, more than half-drowned, at Ned Culcheth's cottage. Is not that the sum of it, eh, sirrah?" he bellowed to me.

"Good gracious! is this possible?" exclaimed Mrs. Sale, sinking upon a chair, and looking as if she would faint away.

"It is not so bad as you represent, sir," I replied, hastening to relieve the lady's anxiety. "Malpas is, no doubt, in a feverish state, caused by the immersion, but I trust he will soon be better. I did not persuade him, as you assert, Dr. Sale, to undertake the feat which so nearly proved fatal to both of us; but I may say this—though, if you had not taxed me so unjustly, I should not have mentioned it—that but for my exertions in helping him out of the water, he would be there now."

Mrs. Sale instantly rose and embraced me. "So you have preserved his life? You were always a brave boy, Mervyn."

"God bless my soul! so you pulled him out, eh?" cried the vicar. "Good boy—brave boy, but very rash to cross the mere—very wrong—many springs in it—which never freeze—dreadfully dangerous. And so Malpas is not in danger? Well, that's a comfort—a very great comfort. You'll go to him directly, Mrs. Sale, and take Mr. Vawdrey with you. I daren't venture out this dreadfully cold morning, for you know I'm taking colchicum, and the gout would inevitably fly to my stomach, and then the consequences might be worse to me than the ducking to Malpas." So saying, he stirred up the fire, and took up a position before it, spreading out the ample skirts of his black coat. "You had better lose no time, Lydia. Mervyn tells me that Simon Pownall is gone to the boy, but, if necessary, you can send over to Knutsford for Dr. Lamb."

"I will do all that is requisite, Dr. Sale," replied the lady. "It is needless to take Mr. Vawdrey. Mervyn will accompany me. I will be ready in a moment, my dear."

So we set out together.

On arriving at the keeper's cottage, we found Malpas in the hands of the little barber-surgeon, who had breathed a vein, and administered a soothing draught, and the patient was now perfectly tranquil, and doing so well, that Pownall declared he would answer for his perfect recovery in twenty-four hours if he were not disturbed. But for the intervention of Sissy Culcheth, who thought it would be a thousand pities to disfigure so handsome a young gentleman, Malpas would have been robbed of the flowing locks, of which he was so vain, by the scissors of the barber-surgeon; and for this Sissy received the thanks of Mrs. Sale, who was dismayed to hear that such a dreadful notion had been for a moment entertained.

Having satisfied herself that her son was doing as well as represented, and that her presence only disturbed him, Mrs. Sale took leave, committing him to the care of the keeper and his wife, and promising them a handsome reward for the inconvenience to which they were put. Ned, I could see, would have been right glad to get rid of the intruder, but Sissy smilingly undertook the charge, and said, in her pleasant Welch tones, "An' please you, matam, I shall pe a fery coot nurses to him."

"What a pretty, well-behaved young woman Sissy Culcheth is; and how clean she keeps her house. I declare, we haven't whiter linen at the vicarage," Mrs. Sale observed, as we walked along. "Ned Culcheth has not been long married. He brought his wife from some place in Caernarvonshire. I have often noticed her at church, but never spoke to her before. A very pretty young person indeed!"

Mrs. Sale then inquired into all particulars concerning the accident, and I related them, I hope, with becoming modesty. She could not thank me sufficiently for rescuing her son.

When we got back to the vicarage, Dr. Sale was so pleased with the account we brought of Malpas, that he invited me to dine with him, saying there would be giblet-soup, a fine roast turkey, and minced pies. "Boys always like minced pies," he added, with a chuckling laugh. "And you shall have a glass of port—SUCH PORT!—ten years older than yourself, you dog—ho! ho! ho!"

Mrs. Sale urged me likewise, and said she would walk over with me to Nethercrofts, and ask my uncle's permission.

"Pray do, my dear," said the vicar, who was now all blandness and smiles, "and I shall be happy to see the old gentleman too, if he will come. But there's little chance of it, I fear."

"I wish, indeed, he would come," Mrs. Sale observed, with a sigh. "No one ought to be a more welcome guest at the vicarage than Mr. Mobberley, for, without him, we might never have possessed it."

"Quite true, Lydia, quite true," Dr. Sale returned. "But if a man won't dine with you when you ask him, the fault is generally considered to rest with him, not you. I should be glad to show Mr. Mobberley more attention if he would let me; but, you'll allow, it would scarcely be consistent with my cloth to join him at the Nag's Head. But go with Mervyn, and invite him; press him; say what you please, my love—only bring him, that's all."

"I will try," Mrs. Sale replied; "but I despair of success."

And the vicar seemed to be of her opinion, for he chuckled immensely at the answer.

I was very glad of the proposed arrangement, for I hoped it would save me from the "rowing" I anticipated from my uncle, when he came to learn how my morning had been spent; and I therefore seconded it very warmly. So Mrs. Sale and I set out once more. Marston was a straggling little place, consisting for the most part of detached dwellings, with small gardens beside them, full of damascene plum-trees and elders. The prettiest part of it was near the vicarage, the lower garden-gates of which opened at the foot of a hill; the ascent being lined with picturesquely-disposed cottages, intermingled with shrubs and trees. At the top of the hill, the road turned off on the left to the church, and the rest of the village straggled on in a straight line for about a quarter of a mile. The shortest way to Nethercrofts was across the fields, but Mrs. Sale preferred the road, and so well did her agreeable conversation beguile the distance, that I did not care how far we went about. As we passed along, it was delightful to observe the respect with which she was everywhere treated; but her affability and kindness fully entitled her to it. The news of Malpas's accident had spread about like wildfire—very likely owing to that gossiping Chetham Quick, whom we met running about—and frequent inquiries were addressed to her respecting her son.

On our arrival, my uncle would have conducted Mrs. Sale to a little parlour, which was assigned to the better order of his guests, but she would not hear of it; told him she much preferred the house-place, and sat down on the sofa beside my aunt, whose hand she took very affectionately, and made many inquiries after her health. The old dame gave but a poor account of herself, but was delighted to see her visitor, and so was my uncle, for her presence diffused unwonted cheerfulness throughout the dwelling. It was surprising how much at home Mrs. Sale made herself, how easy the old folks seemed with her, and how well she adapted herself to their habits and feelings. There was not the least condescension on her part, not the slightest departure from her usual good breeding, and yet she managed all this without difficulty. I could not have had a better advocate with my uncle. She narrated the adventure on the mere, and applauded my conduct so highly, that the old gentleman, instead of being angry, looked quite pleased with me.

"Dost hear what Madam Sale says, Phœbe?" he observed to my aunt.

"Ay, ay," she replied, "Mervyn's a mettlesome young spark, I reckon. But I hope he won't kill any more cats."

The force of this allusion being explained to Mrs. Sale, she again undertook my defence, and asked whether I would declare upon my honour that I was not guilty of poor Tom's death.

"Upon my honour I am not," I said.

"Then you must believe him—you must acquit him, Mrs. Mobberley," Mrs. Sale observed.

"Ay, ay, the lad wouldn't say as much as that if he *had* done it," remarked my uncle.

"I don't think he would," said my aunt. "But somebody must have shot the poor creature—I can partly guess who it was now. And then there was the owl."

"I certainly did catch the owl, aunt, but I let him go afterwards."

"And the boar's tail, what dost say to that, boy, eh?"

"Never mind the boar's tail, my dear Mrs. Mobberley," Mrs. Sale interposed, laughing. "There—I'm sure you've quite forgiven him. He's a brave, generous boy, and I shall always look upon him as the preserver of my son."

Thus, if Malpas had managed to get me into disgrace, as I sometimes suspected, his mother was the cause of my restoration to favour, for from this time my aunt fully forgave me.

Though strongly urged, my uncle could not be prevailed upon to dine at the vicarage, but he willingly allowed me to go; and I escorted Mrs. Sale home again. Intelligence, meanwhile, had been brought by Simon Pownall that Malpas was going on so favourably, that no more uneasiness need be entertained about him; and this made his mother quite happy. We had a capital dinner; Mr. Vawdrey, the curate and Malpas's private tutor, being the only guest beside myself. I did full justice to the roast turkey and the minced pies, but I did not appreciate the old port as much as it deserved, and was glad to leave the two churchmen to the enjoyment of a second bottle, and join Mrs. Sale in the drawing-room.

Next morning I went over to the keeper's cottage to see after Malpas, and found him nearly well, and seated by the fireside, on a rocking-chair, with pretty Sissy Culcheth opposite him, plying her spinning-wheel. Ned, I found, had gone out early to shoot. Malpas pretended to be very glad to see me, and thanked me, with apparent warmth, for the important service I had rendered him the day before. Sissy chimed in, too, and was louder in my praises than seemed agreeable to Malpas, for he checked her with a frown, and said:

"Well, you've talked enough about it, at all events, Sissy."

"I suppose you'll return to the Vicarage presently, Malpas?" I remarked.

"I'm very comfortable where I am," he replied; "besides, I don't feel quite strong enough to move."

"Well, you look so," I said.

"Pless your 'eart, Master Mirfyn, you mustn't trust to his looks at all," Sissy interposed; "he's so weak still, look you, tat he was forced to lean upon me all the ways to the chairs; and he couldn't eat any preckfasts, though I made him a fery nice one."

"Well, he ought to get well soon, you take such good care of him, Sissy," I remarked; "though I dare say he'll be sorry to be out of your hands."

"I tare say he'll pe fery glat to get away," Sissy replied. "Why should a young gentlemans wish to stay in a poor cottage like this?"

"Why, because he has such a nice nurse," I replied. "It's worth while getting a ducking to be so tended."

"Thank you, Master Mirfyn. You're fery complimentary, look you," Sissy returned, blushing, and glancing furtively at Malpas, who didn't look over-pleased at our conversation.

It was, perhaps, just as well that at this juncture Simon Pownall presented himself.

"Aha! out of bed, eh?" he exclaimed, on perceiving his patient. "Knew how it would be—soon set you to rights. Pulse feeble, but good—all danger over—must keep quiet to-day, though. Brought you a draught. Wine-glass here, Sissy—tonic—restore appetite—quicken pulse—two hours hence, another glass—Sissy will administer it—nice nurse—mustn't fall in love with her, though," with a knowing wink—"husband jealous—mum's the word with me."

Sissy was all confusion at this speech; and Malpas, who looked very angry, exclaimed:

"None of your ridiculous insinuations, Pownall. Can't one be attended by a pretty young woman without falling in love with her?"

"Don't know," the barber-surgeon replied. "Complaint catching."

The fair object of these remarks now looked really distressed.

"Look you, Master Malpas, you must go home, sir. You can't stay here, after these pat 'ords."

"There, you see what you've done with your infernal nonsense, Pownall," Malpas cried. "I've a good mind to throw the phial at your head, you stupid, meddling old ass."

The barber-surgeon burst into a loud laugh.

"All a joke—meant no harm," he said. "Didn't think it could be taken amiss, or wouldn't have said it. Like a little bit of fun—thought it *was* fun."

"Then you find out your mistake," Malpas rejoined, sharply.

"Do—and apologise," Pownall returned. "Think no more of it, Sissy. Heard the news, eh? Bessy Birch, the miller's daughter, has gone off with a bagman from Cottonborough. Know it for a fact. Not the first sweetheart she has had—could tell—but mum's the word with me."

"Oh, pless us! pretty Pessy Pirch gone off with a packman! An' her fathers tat was so fery font of her, too, poor ting! What'll happen next, I wonder!"

"You had better make yourself scarce, Pownall, if you have nothing but this stuff to talk about," Malpas cried.

"Difficult to give satisfaction it seems. Try again. Heard of the Twelfth Night merry-making in Tom Shakeshaft's barn, of course? Twelfth-cake—spiced ale—fiddling—dancing—all kinds of fun and frolic. All the young folks of Marston—and some of the old ones, too—will be there; and amongst the latter your humble servant, who hasn't quite lost his agility yet. Down the middle! up the middle! fol-der-iddle-ido." And singing, and snapping his fingers, he cut several lively capers round the room, to our infinite amusement.

"Of course you're going, Sissy?" I asked.

"'Teet and I can't tell, Master Mirfyn," she replied. "I should like it fery much, look you, but I ton't know whether my hurbants will let me go, and tat's the truth."

"Let you! he must—he shall," Pownall cried. "The merry-making would be nothing without Sissy Culcheth. And here he comes, at the very moment he's wanted. Put it to him at once."

"So please you, sir, ton't; it'll only make him cross."

Ned entered with four or five dogs at his heels: an old pointer, a water-spaniel, a terrier, and a couple of fine bloodhounds, answering to the sounding names of John of Gaunt and Hugh Lupus. Having made his four-footed companions lie down, deposited his double-barrelled gun, and taken some game out of his bag, he approached us. If a manly frame, supported by strong thews and sinews, is to go for anything, Ned was no unsuitable mate for pretty Sissy. He was about thirty-five, and by no means a bad-looking fellow, though perhaps too much of a Rufus for some people's tastes, for his poll was a perfect forest of red hair, and his great bushy red whiskers covered his cheeks and met under his chin. Ned was upwards of six feet in height, and very powerfully built, with broad shoulders and a wide deep chest; and his athletic frame was well displayed in his velveteen shooting-jacket, and leathern leggings, coming high up on the thigh.

"Weel, Master Pownall, han yo quite cured th' young gentleman?" he asked.

"Not quite, Ned," the barber-surgeon replied, "but he'll be himself again to-morrow. Can't perform merracles, Ned."

"Hum!" the keeper muttered.

"Talking of Tom Shakeshaft's Twelfth Night hopping just as you came in, Ned," Pownall pursued. "Mean to take Sissy, of course?"

"No I dunnat, and that's flat."

"Sorry for it. Know what folks will say—but mum's the word with me."

"Ah!—what wun they say?"

"Mum's the word with me."

"What'n they say, I say?"

"Why, that you're a jealous oaf, since you want to know."

"Jealous! me jealous! Ha! ha! Weel, then, I wun go, if only to show 'em I'm not."

What coaxing ways Sissy had. I saw her take Ned's hand, and look at him so persuasively there was no resisting her. But the cunning barber-surgeon thought it was his doing entirely.

"Knew how to do it, you see," Pownall whispered Sissy, with a wink. "Took him on the right side. Down the middle! up the middle! fol-der-iddle-ido." But this time his capers were suddenly cut short by Lupus and Gaunt and the rest, who threatened to fly at him, and Ned had to bring out his whip to make them lie down.

Order being once more restored, the barber-surgeon said:

"Tom Shakeshaft has left the management of the affair to me. Sure to go off weil in consequence. Must have the Fool Plough and Sword Dance. Ought to be on Plough Monday, as you know, but will do just as well on Twelfth Night. Only three days too soon. You'll play the Fool, Ned, eh?"

"Dang'd if I do."

"Dang'd if you don't, and see who's right. Chetham Quick, my 'prentice, shall play Old Bessie. Honour us with your presence, young gentlemen?—invite you both in Tom Shakeshaft's name."

"Oh! I'll go, if I'm well enough," Malpas said.

"And so will I," I added, "provided my uncle has no objection."

"Answer for him—make him go too," Pownall said, with a laugh.

"Oh! if the gentlefolk be goin', I must cry off," Ned observed.

"An' why so, look you?" Sissy inquired.

"Ay, why so, indeed?" Pownall cried. "People *will* talk, then. But mum's the word with me."

"Besides, you promised just now, and you never preck your 'orts, Ned."

Ah, Ned, my good fellow! you will never be able to resist those soft looks and coaxing ways. Nor could he; for he replied, with a yielding laugh,

"Weel, a promise is a promise. Yo' han me there, lass, and I'll e'en play the fool, too, since Mester Pownall wishes it."

Satisfied with accomplishing his object, the barber-surgeon told Malpas he should pay him a final visit in the morning, after which he might return to the vicarage as soon as he pleased. Pownall then took leave, and I accompanied him. On the way to the village we met Mrs. Sale, to whom the barber-surgeon gave a very satisfactory account of her son.

"I'm pleased with all you tell me, Pownall, but I shall go on and see him, since he is not to come home till to-morrow," she said. "Won't you walk back with me, Mervyn?"

I could not refuse—and, indeed, I had no desire to do so—and therefore retraced my steps with her. What was our surprise, when we came within a hundred yards of the cottage, to perceive Malpas walking slowly towards us. We hurried to meet him.

"Why, my dear, this is very imprudent—very imprudent indeed," the lady cried. "Simon Pownall told me you oughtn't to move till to-morrow. Why have you run this risk?"

"That Rufus of a keeper is such a brute, I can't stand him,"

Malpas replied. "He says the rudest things to his wife and to me; and because I replied—would you believe it?—he has ordered me—*me!*—to leave the house."

"I'm sorry to hear it!" Mrs. Sale cried; "and Sissy such a nice creature. Ah! here she is!"

As she spoke, Sissy came up, with her apron to her eyes, and sobbing violently.

"So please you, Master Malpas—do come back, sir! My husbants is fery sorry for what he said, look you, sir—he's hasty. Do come back, sir."

Malpas looked as if he would have complied, but his mother interposed:

"No, my dear, since you have ventured out, you had better go home. Where would be the use of returning? You have been very kind to him, I'm sure, Sissy; and I'm greatly indebted to you; but I'm quite distressed there should be any unpleasantness between you and your husband; and I hope my son has not been the cause of it. I will go with you and arrange it, for I cannot bear differences between married people. Mervyn, my dear, give Malpas your arm, and walk home with him. Come, Sissy, no more tears."

And as Mrs. Sale went to the cottage with the keeper's wife, Malpas and I proceeded slowly to the vicarage. I asked him what was the cause of the disturbance, and he replied:

"Oh! Rufus is infernally jealous, that's all."

"Well, don't give him cause, Malpas," I said.

"I—pshaw!" he exclaimed, contemptuously.

And he then continued silent till we reached the vicarage, where I left him.

I was afterwards happy to learn from Mrs. Sale that all differences were made up between the couple; while I was subsequently informed by Ned himself that he and his wife had been very handsomely rewarded for the trouble they had been put to in regard to Malpas, who, I may mention, did not suffer in the least from quitting the house so suddenly, but was perfectly well next day, and able to come over to Nethercrofts and join me in my sports.

CHAPTER VI.

IN WHICH I RIDE ROUND MARSTON MERE; MEET WITH SOME GIPSIES IN A STRANGE PLACE; AND TAKE PART AT THE TWELFTH NIGHT MERRY-MAKING IN FARMER SHAKESHAFT'S BARN.

And plenty of sport, out-door and in-door, too, we had, for it was holiday time at Marston, and all the lads of the village were enjoying themselves in various recreative exercises and games suitable to the season. There were battles with snowballs in the fields; football, and bat and ball on the ice; wrestling and nine-pins in the barns; and hot-cockles, hunt the slipper, blindman's-buff, puss in the corner, and other romping games within doors at night. Marston was a very primitive place, and Christmas was kept well at it. The old church was decked with evergreens, and the windows of the farm-houses were stuck full of holly and ivy, while a bunch of mistletoe was hung in the middle of the house-place; the great yule log blazed on the hearth, and merry parties assembled round it to eat minced pies or plum porridge, drain the well-spiced bowl of elder wine, and disport themselves afterwards at some boisterous game. The mummers, too, came round in their tinsel finery and ribands, ranted, and struck their lathen swords upon the floor, and executed their dances. So that, though the season was severe, the cold was well fenced off by wholesome exercise and mirthful pastime. But the crowning piece of festivity was to be the Twelfth Night merry-making given by Farmer Shakeshaft; at which I anticipated no little amusement, and to which even Malpas seemed to look forward with interest; probably because he hoped to meet Sissy Culcheth there. As to Simon Pownall, he did nothing but talk about the great event; and he not only induced the vicar and his lady and Mr. Vawdrey to promise that they would look in for a short time at the proceedings, but even prevailed upon my uncle Mobberley to give a similar promise.

However, we were two or three days from it yet, though, in the mean time, as I have shown, there was no lack of amusement. My uncle, very good-naturedly, allowed me to go to some of the rustic parties I have mentioned (always sending Sam Massey with me, though I could have dispensed with the attention), and very amusing I found them. And many a comely maiden did I meet at them, too; for Marston had its full share of female beauty. Our return home, which, I am sorry to say, was sometimes later than was supposed, did not disturb my uncle, for I slept at some distance from him, and in a part of the house allotted to the men.

And here I may as well complete the survey, which I previously commenced, of the premises. I have described the large and comfortable house-place where my uncle and aunt usually sat. Adjoining it was a snug little parlour, where company was received, containing some old-fashioned furniture, and a few scriptural pictures on the walls, and but seldom used. On the other side, a short passage led to the room where the men had their meals, which was provided with a narrow oak table and benches of the like substantial material. A door at one end of the house-place opened upon the women's apartments, and another door led to the old people's chamber, which occupied the ground-floor of the more modern part of the building. Above it was a bed-chamber once allotted to me; but as to gain it I had to pass through my uncle's room, I preferred, as I have just stated, a different part of the house, where the men slept, and which was gained by the help of a narrow ladder-like staircase ascending from the back kitchen or washhouse, and communicating with a large room having a roof like that of a barn, crossed by great beams, so that a man had to stoop in passing under them, though I could still do so with ease. Here were three beds, of one of which I had taken possession, while the furthest was occupied by William Weever and Peter

Massey, and in the middle bed slept my friend Sam. A mingled odour of apples and cheese pervaded the place; and no wonder, for close adjoining was the room where the cheeses were deposited in long rows of three or four deep, while near it was a store-closet, filled with the produce of the orchard. But I didn't mind this at all. On the contrary, I thought the cheesy smell rather agreeable, and decidedly wholesome. Just below was the dairy, where Hannah reigned supreme, and where she was always to be seen with her helpmates filling milk-pans, scouring pails, churning butter, or pressing curds into a mould; while the whole place rang with her shrill tones. Outside the door was the pump, with a large array of clean white milk-pails beside it. In front of the dwelling was the farmyard, a large quadrangular area, filled with heaps of litter, surrounded on three sides by shippons, stables, barns, and piggeries; and on the fourth by an orchard, full of old damascene plum-trees, with stems as green as the mantle of the ditch that divided the orchard from the meadows. In fact, I suspect the drainage of the place must have been rather imperfect, for not only had a large black pool collected near the pigsties, but the gates and palings, as well as the fruit-trees, were painted in bright green by the hand of Nature. The garden lay at the back of the house, and, though small, was pretty; and, besides possessing a couple of clipped yew-trees, was defended on the north by one of the finest holly hedges in the county. In a sunny corner was a row of beehives. Adjoining the garden was a paddock, or croft, scattered over with old apple-trees and pear-trees, and occupied at one end by numerous stacks of hay and straw, with a dovecot amongst them.

But garden and grounds were now bound up by the rigorous hand of winter. The farmyard was full of snow; the poultry and pigeons had some difficulty in obtaining a living; and as to the poor ducks and geese, they were quite disconsolate, while the tracks of the cart-wheels threw up masses that looked like great lumps of sugared plum-cake. The old plum-trees in the orchard appeared frostbitten, like starved old men, and on the weather side were white with snow. The pools and ditches were caked over with chocolate-coloured ice; the thatched roof of the house had its coat of congealed and sparkling snow, and from the wide eaves icicles depended like stalactites; the beehives were gone, and nothing was green except the ivy on the wall and the long holly hedge, and they were in the fulness of their beauty. As the old song says:—

> "Holly hath birdies, a full fair flock—
> The nightingale, the popinjay, the gentle lavcrock.
> Good ivy, what birdies hast thou?
> None but the howlet, that cries 'How! how!'"

Though there were no nightingales that I am aware of, plenty of blackbirds and thrushes resorted to the holly hedge to appease their hunger on the red berries; and I dare say my favourite owl came to the ivy-bush for its black fruit, though I never saw him, nor heard his "how! how!" To my thinking, the old place never looked so well nor so cheery as at this wintry season; and on a clear bright day, when the sun shone upon its snowy roof, I thought it positively beautiful.

On such a morning as this—on Twelfth Day, for which I had longed so much—I went to the stable with Sam Massey to saddle my pony and take a ride round the mere. I had announced my intention the evening before to Malpas, and asked him to accompany me, but he declined, saying he would ride out and meet me as I came back, a mile or two out of Marston. My pony was soon ready, and, as I had not ridden him much of late, owing to the frosty weather, he was very frisky, and Sam bade me mind what I was about, or I might miss the hopping that night. I told him never to fear, and, touching Taffy with the whip, dashed out of the farmyard. The roads were very slippery, and justified Sam's caution; but my pony was clever and careful, and being "sharpened," as they have it at Marston, kept his feet well. Taffy was a rough little fellow, with a shaggy mane and long tail, but came of good Welsh mountain stock, and had recently been given me by kind, good Mrs. Mervyn to ride between the Anchorite's and school.

A blithe and joyous morning it was, and I was in high spirits, and sang and shouted from mere exuberance of happiness. Ah! days of our youth! how happy are we then, if we only knew it! Then we ride merrily on, with no black Care seated behind us. Many a rosy-cheeked, bright-eyed damsel, roused by the clatter of my pony's heels, came forth to look at me, and as I gave to each a passing salutation, adding a hope that I should meet her at the merry-making at night, in every instance the response was in the affirmative. So thinks I to myself thinks I, "What a large party we shall have."

Taking the right bank of the mere first—Marston lying on the left —I proceeded at a gallant pace up the slippery hill, and down the still more slippery descent; passed deep snowdrifts that had buried whole hedges, and now folded beautifully over them; crossed runnels turned to ice; and paused to look at an old picturesque mill, whose water-wheel was stopped, and overhung with icicles, and when the miller came forth my gaiety prompted me to ask him after his daughter Bessy, whom I knew to be a pretty girl. He shook his head, and went back into the mill without a word; and Simon Pownall's story rushing upon my recollection, I blamed myself for my indiscretion.

Again I rode on: now looking at the wide expanse of the ice-bound mere, and pluming myself upon having crossed it, yet thinking nothing should tempt me to do so again; now glancing at some black old tree, half-clad in snowy drapery, or holly, bowed down by the weight upon its leaves; until having mounted the gentle acclivity on which Dunton Church was situated, I halted near its reverend walls. Hence, in spring time, the view was exquisite. Then it looked, as now, as if the whole country were covered with snow, but from a different cause, the white vesture being occasioned by the bloom of the damascene plum-trees with which the numerous orchards abounded, and the blossom of the sloe, or the bullace in the hedges. At such a season the mere would gleam like a sheet of silver, mirroring the bright sky above it. Now its surface sparkled in places, but in others was seamed, roughened, and covered with snow, like a frozen ocean. Suddenly, a merry peal of bells arose in the distance, and I knew it came from Marston Church, which stood directly opposite me, across the mere. How pleasantly those bells sounded; and yet, somehow, they awakened a train of half-melancholy reflections, as a pensive thought will intrude in the midst of deepest joy. But my reverie was speedily disturbed by a deafening crash overhead, and the jackdaws flew screaming away from the church tower. The challenge of Marston had been answered by the ringers of Dunton, and loudly and exultingly did the peals of the latter resound.

But the din was rather too much for me, so I hastened away, and presently entered Dunton Park, through which the road passed. These sylvan domains of the Earl of Amounderness boasted much noble timber; and many a sweeping vista, lined by magnificent though leafless trees, now opened before me. Beneath the lordly beech-trees the ground was thickly strewn with red sere leaves, which contrasted strongly with the snow in the brake beyond them. The dappled denizens of the forest might be seen herding together in some favoured patches which had escaped the drift; hares, emboldened by hunger, dashed from out the covert, and passed by regardless of my presence; and pheasants, tamed by the severity of the season, fed like barn-door fowls on grain placed for them by the keepers.

Having cleared the park, and left it nearly a mile behind, I descended a gentle hill, and approached a secluded spot, where, many years ago, a robbery had been committed by a noted highwayman. Since then, however, the road had been slightly turned, and a deep ravine, overshadowed by brushwood, through which it had formerly passed, avoided. Just as I reached the brink of this hollow, a lad suddenly started forward, and, planting himself right in my path, screamed and flung his arms in the air, and so startled Taffy that I was nearly thrown from his back. Notwithstanding the severity of the weather, the lad was half-naked, and evidently, from his tawny skin and cast of features, of gipsy origin. I bade him get out of the way; but he uttered a wild and peculiar cry, which was instantly answered by a crushing amongst the brushwood, caused by a fierce-looking man, who presently emerged from it, and springing upon me with a bound, seized hold of my bridle, and dragged Taffy towards the edge of the ravine. I resisted as well as I could, and tried to make him leave go by cutting at his hands. But he snatched the whip from me with an oath, and gave it to the lad, who scutched the pony behind, and made him go on.

"Where are you taking me to? What are you going to do?" I cried, greatly terrified, and unable to conceive what was about to happen.

"You'll larn presently," the man replied, with a savage grin. And he forced Taffy down the slippery sides of the hollow; and if the pony had not been as sure-footed as a goat of his own native hills, he must have fallen. As it was, he slided down for some yards. I would have jumped off if I could, but the gipsy held me fast. On reaching the bottom, I became aware that the ravine was inhabited, and perceived at a little distance a low shed, protected from the weather by a sloping roof of dried gorse, and having wattled sides. The snow had been carefully cleared away around it, and in this space a turf fire was burning, and heating a caldron suspended above it from a cross-sticks. In summer this ravine must have been beautiful as well as secluded; but now it had a savage and almost fearful aspect, more fitted to the lair of a wild beast than the haunt of man. Black and gnarled roots of trees protruded from the sides, looking hideous from the congealed snow around, and the shoots of ice hanging from them. So strange and fantastic were some of the tricks played by the spirits of frost and snow, that the hollow had almost the appearance of an icy cavern; and at the further end, where the boughs overhead were thick, making an arch impervious to the sun in summer, the snow had lodged in masses, and then freezing, formed a roof from which long icicles depended, giving the whole place the semblance of a grotto, with a pavement of "thick-ribbed ice," caused by the accumulations of a half-frozen rivulet that tried to force its way through it.

I was so much alarmed that I called loudly for help; but the gipsy bade me hold my tongue or he would silence me for ever. At the cry, a woman and a girl issued from the tent. The former was not so dark as the man, who was excessively swarthy, but she was very handsome, with coal-black hair, and fine black eyes; and the girl, who might be twelve years old, promised to be very like her. I felt some assurance of safety when I saw them, more especially when the woman, advancing towards me, seemed to scrutinise my features, in spite of the man's orders to her to go back.

"What do you mean to do with him, Phaleg?" she asked.

"Give him a winding-sheet of snow, Peninnah," the gipsy replied, with a ferocious look at me that thrilled to my very marrow; "he'll sleep soundly under it, and no one will ever find him till it melts."

"You won't let him do it?—you won't let him murder me?" I cried, appealing to Peninnah, who looked as if she had some touch of compassion about her.

"No—no; don't be afraid, my little gentleman; he's only joking," she replied. "It's a queer way he has with him. He shan't harm a hair of your pretty head. You don't mean it—do you, Phaleg?"

The man contradicted her with a muttered oath, and a savage scowl at me.

"He wants to buy your pony—that's it—eh, Phaleg? Our old donkey died last week."

"Mayhap he'll give us the pony?" Phaleg said, with a grin.

"No, I won't," I replied, endeavouring to appear unconcerned, though I was terribly frightened; "I'll neither give it you, nor sell it. So pray let me go."

But the man seemed in no humour to consent to my departure, and I began to fear he would put his threats into execution, and I considered what I could do to obtain help. A few words passed between the pair in an under tone; but I caught what the woman said in conclusion.

"You shan't lay a finger upon him, I tell you," she continued, in a tone of authority, "no matter who bids you, nor what you may get. So go to the shed and take Rue with you."

"Well, you always will have your own way, Ninnah," Phaleg replied, as he sullenly obeyed her, and left us alone together.

"And quite right I should have it, when I'm tied to such a headstrong, violent fool as thee," she muttered, looking after him with contempt. "And now, my pretty little gentleman, let me tell you

your fortin. But first you must cross my hand with a lucky half-crown. I knows you've got one."

As I willingly complied with her request, she looked into my palm, and appeared to study its lines intently. At last she spoke:

"Plenty of adventure for you, my pretty little gentleman; many an up, many a down—many a difficulty, many a danger—before you comes to your own There's a good deal of love in your hand, my merry little gentleman, but a good many crosses. All won't go smooth where your heart's consarned, so you musn't expect it. You'll find many friends, and some enemies—some bitter enemies—ay, you've got one now, secretly trying to work your ruin. You ought to have a large fortune, my little gentleman, but there seems summat in the way of it, and I fear it won't come to you. But keep up your heart; you've a bright eye and a merry look, and riches doesn't bring happiness—at least, good folks say so, though I'm of a contrairy opinion myself, and should like to roll in wealth. And now I'll tell you how you may know my words to be true. You've lost your mother, and haven't never seen your father."

"How do you know that?" I asked.

"As I know all else about you—from the lines on you hand. And they tell me," said she, in a serious and almost solemn tone that lent force to her words, "that before many hours are over, you'll receive a sudden and painful shock."

I inquired what she meant, but she replied she could tell me no more, when some object rolled down the bank, and was almost buried in the avalanche of snow that attended its rapid course. It turned out to be the gipsy lad. He was pursued by a bloodhound, which dashed down the brake after him, and which no doubt would have seized him and lacerated him dreadfully, but for the intervention of his father, who, hearing the noise, rushed out of the tent to his assistance, armed with a stake, with which he kept the hound off.

"This is Ned Culcheth's dog," exclaimed Phaleg. "Is he at hand, Obed?"

"Ay, daddy," the lad replied, "and there's the young gentry cove with him."

"What young gentry cove?" inquired Peninnah.

"Young Sale."

"Curse you, hold your tongue," interrupted Phaleg, "and give the young gentleman his whip—d'ye hear?"

"You now see I was right," observed Peninnah; "that hound would have discovered all."

"Devil take his baying. I've a good mind to settle him," cried Phaleg, raising the stake.

But at this moment Ned Culcheth dashed down the ravine, with a double-barrelled gun on his shoulder, and followed by his other bloodhound, as well as by Malpas, who, it afterwards appeared, had tied his horse to a tree at the top of the bank. Both expressed great surprise at seeing me, while Ned called off the hounds, which showed a strong disposition to attack the gipsies. As Malpas came up, I fancied I detected a glance of intelligence between him and Phaleg.

"Why, Mervyn, who the deuce would have thought of finding you here?" he cried. "I was riding along to meet you as I promised last evening, and wondering where you could be loitering, when just as I crossed the bridge over the Rollin, I overtook our friend Rufus here, and was chatting with him, when old Gaunt started off, and gave chase to this little black rascal, who dived into the hollow to avoid him."

"And if I'd obeyed your orders and ca'd Gaunt back, Master Malpas," Ned remarked, "we should nother ha' found Master Mervyn, nor unkennelled these foxes. Howsomever, they shanna ha' a chance of robbing hen-roostes, smoking pheasants, and snaring hares hereabouts any longer. I've long been on their trail, and at last have lected on their harbour, and now I gies 'em notice to quit, and without delay, for if I finds 'em here again we'n see what Lupus and Gaunt can make on 'em."

"Nay, let them be, Ned," interposed Malpas; "I dare say the poor people do no harm. Besides, you must be uncharitable indeed to begrudge them shelter in such a place as this. Ough!" he added, with a shudder, "I'd as soon live in an ice-house, or be sent to Siberia."

"Uncharitable or not, they shan tramp," Ned returned; "and as to doing no harm, they're nowt but a parcel o'thieves and wagabones. Nothin's safe from 'em; they pisons pigs, lames cattle, nets fishponds, and snares game. No harm! Ask your uncle, Squoire Vernon, what he thinks on 'em."

"I will speak to him myself about them, Ned. I shall see him tomorrow," Malpas said, authoritatively. "Till then you will not disturb them."

"Varry weel, sir; as yo' please," Ned replied; "but yo'n find th' squoire's of my way of thinking, if so be he hasna altered his mind."

"I must say they scarcely deserve my intercession, especially the woman, who looks as if she wasn't to be trusted," Malpas observed; "but I have always had a liking to gipsies."

"And so have I till to-day," I remarked.

"Why, they hanna ill-treated you; they hanna attempted to rob you?" demanded Ned.

I was about to make some reply, when Malpas hastily interposed.

"I suppose you came here to have your fortune told, and the woman hasn't laid it on thick enough, eh?" he said.

"She told me a good many things; and, amongst others, that I 'ad a secret enemy," I replied, looking hard at him.

"Oh! she told you that; and you believe her, I suppose?" he rejoined, with a forced laugh, and glancing significantly at Peninnah; while Phaleg also looked disconcerted and angry. Malpas, indeed, seemed disposed to address some menaces to the gipsy-woman, but her looks apparently checked him, and he cried out to me, "Well, we've wasted time enough here. Come along, Mervyn."

He then went off, and, nodding to Peninnah, to whom I felt very grateful for having rescued me from her husband's clutches, I contrived to scale the bank without dismounting. Ned, who was not very gracious in his adieux, brought up the rear with Gaunt and Lupus. On gaining the road, we found Malpas unfastening his horse, and he said to me,

"I've a good mind to ask those gipsy folk to Tom Shakeshaft's hopping to-night; it would be rare fun."

"But Shakeshaft mayn't like it," I said.

"What does that signify? Simon Pownall will manage it. I'll do it, by Jove! Take care of my tit for a moment till I come back."

And, throwing the bridle to me, he disappeared down the brake. But he didn't return quite so soon as I expected; and thinking I heard voices in dispute below, I asked Ned if we should go down and see what was the matter.

"Na, na," he replied, with a peculiar smile; "dunna yo' be afeard—he'll come to no hurt. He's among friends. Didna it strike yo' that he seemed to know them warmint, Master Mervyn?"

"It did, Ned."

"Weel, he's a queer chap, and I hope he may come to good."

At this moment Malpas reappeared, and, springing on his horse, exclaimed, with a laugh, "Well, I've settled it all. They're coming."

"A nice party we shall have," I thought, echoing my previous rumination.

"Comin', be they!" growled Ned. "We shan see what Master Shakeshaft win say to it. I know what I would."

Malpas let the remark pass without notice, and we soon afterwards quitted the keeper, and rode on quickly towards Marston.

When we came to where the little lane turned off to Ned's dwelling, Malpas apparently found the attraction irresistible, and proposed that we should call on Sissy. I assented. Apprised of our approach by the sound of our horses' feet, Sissy came to the door, and greeted us in her clear musical voice. To be sure, how pretty she looked in her broad-brimmed hat, and how well it contrasted with her blooming cheeks, and light sunny tresses with a golden glint in them, braided in front, and gathered in a large roll behind. And then what a trim waist she had, and how well her blue tight-fitting bodice set it off; and what small hands and feet! Sissy was certainly a little inclined to coquetry, probably because she had had so many admirers before Ned won her from them. With an arch smile she told us that if we wanted her "husbants" he was from home, and mightn't return for an hour. Malpas said he knew that, but he had called to see her, and her alone; and then he laughed and paid her some highflown compliments, which heightened the roses in her cheeks.

"If you want to please me, Sissy," I said, "you'll go in that becoming hat to the merry-making to-night."

"You're fery easily pleased, then, Master Mirfyn, look you. Put since you wish it, I will wear the hats. What a peautiful ponies you've got."

"I'm glad you like him, Sissy," I rejoined; "but it's no wonder for he's from your own country."

"You ton't say he's Wales?" she replied, putting her arms roun Taffy's neck, and patting his shaggy head. "There are no ponies li our Welsh ponies, look you."

"And no peauties like your Welsh peauties, look you," Malpas joined, mimicking her tones, and glancing at her with so much ard that Sissy hastily retreated, and closed the door in our faces.

I told him he had offended her, but he laughed and said no wom was ever offended by a compliment.

F

So we rode off; when, just as we got to the end of the lane, who should we meet but Rufus, as Malpas called him, striding along at a great pace, with Gaunt and Lupus at his heels. On beholding us, the keeper knew where we had been, and looked "so confoundedly glum," as Malpas observed, that we thought it advisable to hurry on without a word; nor did we again draw the rein till we reached the barber-surgeon's shop, where I left my companion, who wanted to speak to Simon about the gipsies, and made the best of my way to Nethercrofts.

The day seemed unusually long to others as well as to me, but night arrived at last, and about eight o'clock—for we kept better hours in Marston than they do at some places—a large party of us prepared to set out. My aunt had been unusually cheerful that day, and when my uncle displayed some wavering in his purpose of going, she confirmed it, by saying it would be better for him than a night at the Nag's Head. As all the household were invited, Susan Sparkes, a decent old body, was engaged to attend upon my aunt, and a near neighbour, Dame Hutchinson, whose rheumatism prevented her from taking any part in the village festivities, came to spend the evening with her. A fire was therefore lighted in the little parlour, the curtains were closely drawn to keep out the cold, the best china tea-things were brought out, and everything was made nice and comfortable for the good old gossips.

"Well, good night, and God bless thee, John," my aunt said to my uncle, as I helped him on with his great-coat, preparatory to starting. "I wish I were young enough to go wi' thee, as I did fifty-five year ago, to some such hopping, before thou and I wert man and wife. Good lack-a-day! we were a bonny couple then, and could dance, too, with the best of 'em. 'Odds life! neighbour Hutchi'son, you wouldn't know Phœbe Massey in the poor withered thing before you. Would she, John?"

"I shouldn't," he replied, gruffly.

"Well, that's plain-spoken, man, I must say. It's odd how my thoughts are running on the days of my youth. Dost remember when we first met near Marston Mere, John?—and how thou didst use to come courting me o' nights?—and how I let thee in at the dairy? Ah! those were happy days. But I see Mervyn wants to be off, and I won't detain him with these dreams of past times, though my head's full of 'em, and I could ramble on for an hour. There, give me a kiss, my own old man, for the sake of bygone times."

My uncle seemed pleased at the request, and complied; and, putting my arms round my aunt's neck, I said I must have a kiss too; after which we quitted the room, the good old dame bestowing another blessing on us both.

So we set out in very good spirits. My uncle and I, and Sam Massey, on whose arm the old man leant, led the way; Hannah and William Weever, dressed out in their best, came a few paces behind; and Martha and Peter brought up the rear. We did not require a lantern, for the moon shone so brightly that it was almost as light as day. On reaching the village, we found all the folks coming forth, bent on the same errand as ourselves, and most of them very merry. My uncle complained bitterly of the cold, though he was well wrapped up, and would fain have entered the

Nag's Head, but Simon Pownall, who came up as he paused, told him the house was shut up for the night; for the host and hostess were among Tom Shakeshaft's guests; so he went on, rather grumblingly. Quitting the road for a short distance, we approached the dwelling of our entertainer, and while crossing the large farmyard, at the end of which stood the barn, were greeted by the enlivening strains of a fiddle issuing from it.

Considerable preparations had been made for the entertainment, which was of a thoroughly rural character, and there was plenty of amusement, though of a rather boisterous kind. The place of reception was capable of accommodating a large crowd; and a large crowd was already assembled in it. It was not very brilliantly lighted up, to be sure, and the floor was of hard clay; but what did that matter. I have since seen many a splendid ball-room with chalked floors, and blazing with wax-lights, where there was not half so much real enjoyment. Of course, everything had been cleared away for the company; and wooden benches and stools were ranged round the space. A few chairs were set apart for the great folks. Light was afforded from two old copper branches suspended from the great cross rafters, and from tin sconces stuck against the walls. At one end was a table, where spiced elder wine and hot ale and cakes were served,—and where there was a large twelfth-cake. The sides of the barn and even the rafters were plentifully decorated with evergreens, and from the central beam hung a large bough of mistletoe, and constant laughter was going on as some swain dragged his blushing sweetheart beneath it, and snatched a kiss from her rosy lips. A fiddle, a fife, and a bassoon constituted the band. I looked about for Sissy Culcheth, and was not long in discovering her. She wore her hat, as she had promised. Ned was with her, and though he seemed very proud of her, it was easy to perceive, by his quick glances, that he did not like too much attention to be shown her; while poor Sissy, from natural gaiety and liveliness, not to say coquettishness, was constantly attracting it. This became evident to all when Malpas made his appearance. Comporting himself with considerable insolence to the hinds around, Malpas marched up to Sissy, and, taking her from her husband, ordered the musicians to strike up a jig, and whisked her about in a way that was highly displeasing to Ned, who watched them with great impatience. Aware that the keeper could put little constraint upon himself, and fearful lest some mischief might ensue, I went up to him; and it was well I did, for at this moment the whirl of the jig brought his wife and Malpas under the mistletoe-bough, when the latter very imprudently snatched a kiss from her cherry lips. Ned would certainly have done him some hurt, if I and Pownall, who happened to be near, had not restrained him. Sissy, who was a good deal embarrassed, almost immediately afterwards quitted Malpas, and came up to her husband; but he turned sullenly away, and there was a good deal of tittering among the bystanders, and some not very complimentary remarks among the female portion of them, who disliked Sissy for her good looks. I came to her rescue, and following Ned she soon succeeded, by her coaxing ways, in restoring him to good humour.

E 2

By this time, Dr. and Mrs. Sale, and Mr. Vawdrey, had joined the assemblage, and seemed much amused with what was going forward. The vicar was unwontedly condescending, and his lady affable as usual. They were accommodated with chairs, raised a little from the ground, so that they could command the whole scene; and my uncle Mobberley was placed on Mrs. Sale's right, and Mr. Vawdrey near the vicar. I also noticed Phaleg the gipsy, and Peninnah, and little Rue among the throng. Peninnah had a yellow handkerchief bound over her raven hair, and was otherwise rather gaudily dressed, as was Rue; and Phaleg had donned his holiday clothes, and did not appear quite so ruffian-like as in the morning. Their appearance amid the crowd was picturesque enough, but they were generally looked upon as black sheep, and avoided.

Just then Simon Pownall, mounting on a bench, announced that the twelfth-cake was about to be divided, and invited all to come to the table for a slice. And he repeated the lines:

"Now, now, the mirth comes,
With the cake full of plums,
Where BEAN is King of the sport here.
Beside, you must know,
The PEA also
Must revel as Queen of the court here."

The order was eagerly obeyed, and great was the pressure that ensued. The arrangements were entrusted to Simon, who, assisted by Chetham Quick, distributed the cake; and by some accident the Bean fell to me, and the Pea to Sissy; consequently, we were Queen and King, and were hailed as such amid the shouts and laughter of the company. Ned looked pleased enough, for somehow he didn't appear to be jealous of me; but now Malpas became angry in his turn, and I heard him swear at Pownall for not giving him the bean. The barber-surgeon shrugged his shoulders, and declared he meant to do so, but it was all the fault of that stupid Chetham, to whom he had entrusted the distribution of the cake. And, indeed, the surmise proved to be correct, for Chetham presently nudged me, and, with a sniggering laugh, whispered in my ear, "You owe all this to me. I knew what master was after, so I changed the slices of plum-cake, and gave yours to Malpas. He! he! he!"

My first business was to present my queen to the state party, and they all looked very much pleased with her, Mrs. Sale complimenting her on her good looks, and congratulating me on my good fortune. I then ordered the musicians to strike up a country-dance, and taking our places at the head of it, we were soon actively engaged. My pretty little partner danced uncommonly well, and with so much spirit, that I was quite sorry to find myself at the bottom of the dance. But the life and soul of it was Simon Pownall. He had a jest for everybody, and made everybody do his or her best. When he got to the top it was quite wonderful to see the capers he cut — how he cantered down the middle, and galloped back again. And but little inferior to him was Chetham Quick, whose lithe limbs were thrown about in a surprising manner. He was quite his master's double, and imitated all his flourishes. In the course of the dance

I found myself under the mistletoe with Sissy, but I did not dare to repeat Malpas's experiment, more especially as the jealous Rufus was standing by, when to my great surprise he said, with a laugh, " Dunna be bashful. Kings is privileged. Yo'n more right than the jackanapes who tuk the liberty afore you."

" Right, Ned," cried Chetham Quick, who was skipping by at that moment, and overheard him. " It's part of the royal prerogative—he! he! Suitable to the occasion—Twelfth Night, or What you Will—Shakspeare—ahem!"

So I readily took advantage of the suggestion, and gave her a hearty kiss; and if Ned had wanted to annoy Malpas, who witnessed the proceeding, he could not have adopted a better expedient, as the looks of the latter showed plainly enough.

As Malpas seemed inclined to interrupt the mirth of the evening by ill-humour, I determined to plague him. So I caused it to be announced, through the medium of Simon Pownall, that I should assign partners to all the women for the next dance, and I gave Malpas to Peninnah. He was obliged to obey the mandate, though he did so with a very ill grace. In the dance after that, the queen chose partners for the men, and then Malpas made sure she would select him; but no such thing, she gave her hand to Chetham Quick, and assigned little Rue to her disappointed admirer, who, however, flatly refused compliance, and for this act of *lèse majesté* I adjudged that he should salute the oldest and ugliest woman present. But this he also refused. Ned and Chetham now disappeared to prepare for the Plough Dance.

After partaking of some refreshments, of which, after our violent exercise, we stood in need, our master of the ceremonies, Simon Pownall, now called out to us to make way for the Fool Plough; whereupon the whole of the company drew up in lines, and the barn-doors being thrown wide open, a dozen men entered, clothed in clean white woollen shirts, ornamented with ribands, tied in roses, on the sleeve and breast, and with caps decked with tinsel on their heads, and tin swords by their sides. These mummers were yoked to a plough, likewise decked with ribands, which they dragged into the middle of the barn. They were attended by an old woman with a tall sugar-loaf hat, and an immense nose and chin, like those of Mother Goose in the pantomime. The old beldame supported her apparently tottering limbs with a crutch-handled staff, with which she dealt about blows, right and left, hitting the toes of the spectators, and poking their ribs. This character was sustained by Chetham Quick, and very well he played it, to judge by the shouts of laughter he elicited. By the side of Old Bessie was an equally grotesque figure, clothed in a dress partly composed of a cow's hide, and partly of the skins of various animals, with a long tail dangling behind, and a fox-skin cap, with lappets, on the head. This was the Fool. Over his shoulder he carried a ploughman's whip, with which he urged on the team, and a cow's horn served him for a bugle, from which he ever and anon produced unearthly sounds. Notwithstanding the disguise, there was no difficulty in recognising Ned Culcheth as the wearer of it. The entrance of the mummers was welcomed by shouts of laughter from the whole assemblage, and the hilarious plaudits increased as they drew up in the middle of the barn, and, unyoking themselves from the plough, prepared for the dance. The spectators then formed a ring round them. Chairs, on an elevated position, had been provided for Sissy and myself, who, as king and queen, were entitled to superior accommodation, and we therefore looked on at our ease. The musicians now struck up a lively air, and the dance began, the mummers first forming two lines, then advancing towards each other, rattling their swords together, as if in mimic warfare; retreating; advancing again, and placing all their points upon the plough; forming a rose; next a four-square rose; then bounding over each other's heads, laying down their swords, joining hands, and dancing round Old Bessie and the Fool, who remained near the plough, dancing very funnily by themselves. A general clapping of hands showed how well this dance was liked by the company, and the mummers were brought by Simon Pownall to be presented to the king and queen.

All went on very well till it came to the turn of the Fool. Just as he made his obeisance, which Simon took care should be low enough, Malpas suddenly leaped upon his back, and throwing him on the ground, set his foot on his neck, while the prostrate man was prevented from rising by Phaleg, who held him by the shoulders. Malpas then seized the Fool by the tail, and tugged so lustily at it, that it came off altogether; and then, and not till then, did Ned disengage himself from the gipsy's gripe. Exasperated by the laughter and shouts of the assemblage, Ned seized the ploughman's whip, and before he could be prevented, laid it soundly across Phaleg's shoulders, ending with a severe cut at Malpas. Phaleg was not a man to put up calmly with the treatment he had experienced, and in his turn he assailed Ned; but he was put out of the way in a trice by a stunning blow from the huge fist of the keeper. Malpas was furious, as he might well be, and vowed he would be revenged, and, though Sissy herself entreated him to stay, he quitted the party in high dudgeon. Luckily, before this incident, Dr. and Mrs. Sale had retired, for I should have been really sorry if the latter had witnessed it. When his passion had subsided, Ned seemed heartily ashamed of himself, and scarcely dared to face his wife, who was as cross with him as such a pretty creature could be. However, I contrived to make peace between them. Good humour being once more restored, we had some merry gambols, and then another country-dance, and with this the entertainment concluded, for it was eleven o'clock, and, as I have previously observed, we kept good hours at Marston.

My uncle Mobberley remained to the last, and would have stayed longer, if there had been any excuse for doing so, for he was very well amused. Early in the evening a bowl of gin-punch had been made for him by Tom Shakeshaft, and it proved to be so good that even the vicar and the curate condescended to share it with him. When they departed, which they did with Mrs. Sale at ten o'clock, pipes were produced, the bowl was replenished, and a party of my uncle's old Nag's Head cronies collected round him, to help him to discuss it. Very merry they all were, as merry as us younger folk, and when the party broke up they had got through a third bowl.

You may be sure that when eleven o'clock struck, which was pro-

claimed to us by the inexorable Pownall, the usual valedictory ceremonies observed on such occasions were not neglected. There were a great many tender last words, a great deal of kissing under the misletoe, a great deal of squeezing of hands, a great deal of whispering, and a great many arrangements made about seeing young damsels safely home across the fields. And Simon Pownall afterwards informed me that some half a dozen happy marriages were the result of Tom Shakeshaft's Twelfth night merry-making.

Well, at length we all separated, some going one way, and some another, while we shaped our course towards Nethercrofts, my uncle, who was in a high state of elevation, marching between Sam Massey and Pownall, the latter having volunteered to go home with him.

I ought to have mentioned that, just as I had quitted the barn, Peninnah passed me and whispered, in a boding tone:

"Recollect what I said this morning."

CHAPTER VII.

SHOWING HOW MY UNCLE MOBBERLEY AND I WERE VERY PAINFULLY SURPRISED ON OUR RETURN HOME.

A DEEP, prolonged howl startled us as we entered the little orchard.

"What's that?" my uncle cried, stopping.

"It's Talbot!" I exclaimed. "He has got shut out, and is howling to be let in."

"Don't like it," Pownall observed to me, in an under tone—"bodes no good."

The shadow of a large bird flitted past, and a hoarse croak was heard overhead.

"Worse and worse," the barber-surgeon muttered. "Night-crow. A death will soon follow."

I shuddered at these prognostications, for the dismal sounds, I confess, awakened a superstitious feeling of dread in my own breast. And I likewise thought of the gipsy's boding words. Otherwise there seemed nothing to fear. The night was spiritually beautiful and tranquil, with myriads of stars paving the deep vault above. The farmhouse glittered in its case of snow, and the hoar plum-trees around us looked as if laden with diamonds, like the gardens in some Arabian story of enchantment. Talbot now came up to us with his tail between his legs, looking at us with wistful eyes, howling mournfully. I tried to silence him, but ineffectually.

"He would tell us something, if he could, poor fellow," I thought.

A tap at the back door near the dairy procured us admittance, and we entered the house-place. A good fire was blazing on the hearth, and a table was set before it, on which were some cold viands and bread. All looked snug and comfortable—but my aunt was not to be seen.

"Phœbe—where art thou, Phœbe?" my uncle cried out. "Gone to bed—eh? I never knew her do so before."

"Nah—nah—mester, hoo wouldna go to bed, and yo' out," old Susan replied. "Dame Hutchi'son went whoam at ten o'clock, that's two hours ago, for it's just on the stroke of twalve now. Yo' be'n late whoam to-neet, mester, boh I reckon yo'n been enjoying yoursel', and when folks does that, time flees without their knowin' it."

"Oh! ay, I recollect, she's in the parlour," said my uncle, taking off his great-coat. And he called out, "Phœbe! Phœbe! I'm come home."

"Maybe hoo's asleep," the old woman remarked. "I hanna been near her sin Dame Hutchi'son went, for hoo took up her Bible, and towd me to leave her, and set out supper; and when I'd done that I set me down i' your chair, mester, and took a nap mysel', an' I didna waken up till I heerd yo' at th' dooer—that's the truth. Boh I'll go an' see efter her."

"No, I'll go and see myself," my uncle said, staggering towards the door, and opening it.

Pownall and I followed him, and it was well we did so.

"Well, Phœbe, lass," he cried, "I'm late home to-night, but it's Christmas time, and Twelfth Night, and we've had a rare merry-making at Tom Shakeshaft's. I wish thou hadst been there, to see the fun, old lass, that I do. It put me in mind of the old times thou wert talking about. And I thought of thee, old woman, when I saw that young thing, Sissy Culcheth, skipping about. She's a bonny lass that; but, bless thy old heart, thou wert once as bonny thyself, and turned all the lads' heads, and mine among 'em—ha! ha! Come, now I'm in the humour to talk of our young days, when I went to court thee, and brought thee to Nethercrofts, and thou won't give me a word in answer. What's the matter wi' thee? Art asleep—eh?"

And then, as if he had all at once become sensible of some terrible calamity, he uttered a loud cry, that alarmed the whole house.

Pownall caught the old man in his arms, or he must otherwise have fallen to the ground.

My poor aunt was gone.

Her end must have been easy indeed, for she was leaning back in the chair as if asleep, and nothing indicated that the parting of the spirit from its earthly tenement had been attended even with a struggle. Her life had been breathed out like a sigh. The Bible was open before her, as if she had leaned back to meditate on what she had read, and so expired.

A candle, long unsnuffed, stood upon the table. She must have been dead more than an hour, Pownall said. I was greatly shocked, and felt stunned, as if by a violent blow.

The shock completely sobered my uncle; and as he was now fully sensible of the loss he had sustained, it was piteous to witness his distress and hear his self-reproaches. We all stood by mournfully and in silence, for we respected his grief.

After awhile he arose from the seat in which Pownall had placed him, and, taking the cold hand of his wife, pressed it to his lips.

"How little did I think when I left thee, my poor Phœbe," he ejaculated, "that I should never see thee more alive—thou that hast been my partner for more than fifty years!—and better partner man never had, truer wife, or worthier woman. I knew it must come to this at last,—that we must separate; but I hoped to have gone before thee; for what shall I do without thee? Thou didst always guide me right; didst always speak truth to me; wert always what a wife should be. And I have been revelling while thou wert dying." A convulsive sob heaved his breast and choked his utterance; but, recovering himself, he added, "Well, thou art only gone before me, for I know I shall soon follow thee. Farewell! true heart and virtuous woman; thou hast been, indeed, to me a jewel above all price." Having said thus much, he sat down, and covering his face with his hands, wept aloud.

It was a deeply-affecting scene. I believe no eye was dry, and I am sure mine were not, for I cried bitterly.

At length my uncle recovered himself sufficiently to give directions to those about him relative to the removal of the body. He spoke very kindly to me, and said:

"Ah! Mervyn, thou hast lost a good friend in thy poor aunt. But comfort thyself, lad. Thou hadst her last blessing as well as I; and it will profit thee, as the blessings of the righteous ever do."

After this, Simon Pownall prevailed upon him to retire, undertaking to see all his directions fully carried out, and promising to stay till morning. And very well it was that he did so, for without his aid I believe my uncle would have died that night. His moans could be heard throughout the house.

The poor old man was terribly prostrated, and when he appeared next day a great change was visible in him. But he now bore the weight of his grief with manly resignation. There were no more outbursts of sorrow. The flood-gates had been opened; the torrent had gushed forth; nothing but the deep, black void was left. The vicar and his wife came early to condole with him, and from Mrs. Sale he really did seem to derive comfort. His tears again flowed as she spoke of his wife, but they were not tears of anguish and reproach, such as he had shed the night before. Malpas also presented himself, and so overacted his feigned grief, that I am sure my uncle saw through it.

Some old customs were observed, such as watching by the body, and placing a pewter plate upon it, filled with salt; and, on the day of the funeral, arvil-bread and burnt wine were distributed amongst the mourners. My uncle attended the sad ceremonial, and supported himself well through it. The burial service was read by Dr. Sale, and a large crowd of the villagers was assembled on the occasion, and one might read the esteem in which my aunt had been held in their dejected countenances. Snow was falling thickly at the time, and the pall of the coffin was white with it. To me the scene was doubly sad, for the grave adjoined my mother's, and my thoughts were running upon her as well as upon the kind relative I had lost. The coffin was lowered down; and as I looked at my uncle, with his venerable head bowed upon his breast, and his scanty locks exposed to the snow, I thought there was warrant for what he said to the sexton and his assistant—"Ye need scarcely trouble yourselves to fill up that grave, lads, for ye'll soon have another to put into it."

But my uncle was a strong-minded man, and though he felt my

aunt's loss keenly—perhaps more keenly than he showed it—he would not give way to grief, but bore up against it resolutely, and after a week's struggle, during which it appeared doubtful whether he would ever be himself again, obtained the mastery, and resumed his former habits. But he missed his old partner at every turn; and when any question of household concern was put to him which she would have answered, he looked well-nigh bewildered. Sometimes he would glance towards the sofa on which she had sat, as if about to address her, and then, turning back quickly, would mutter, "Oh! I forgot—she's gone."

He never again entered the room where she died.

But he thought he might be suddenly taken off, and displayed great anxiety as to the settlement of his worldly affairs, frequently talking them over with Simon Pownall, who, since my aunt's death, became his sole adviser. He sent for Mr. Gripper, of Knutsford, an attorney, and made a new will; and whether Pownall was aware or not of the disposition he had made of his property, and that it was in my favour, I cannot say, but he now treated me with great obsequiousness.

On the day after Mr. Gripper's visit, my uncle called me into his bedroom, where he now sometimes sat, and pointing out a drawer in an old bureau near the bed, said:

"Thou'lt find my will there, Mervyn. I'm glad thou hadst thy aunt's blessing, my dear. It strengthend me in my purpose. A good woman, my dear,—a truly good woman, who never did wrong in her life. There are few such left behind her. The best thing I can wish for thee is, that thou mayest meet with some one like her; and that thou mayst live as happily with thy wife as I have done with mine. Ah! but it's hard to part with a friend of five-and-fifty years' standing. My will is there, I say. Thou'lt know all about its contents one of these days,—mayhap, sooner than thou think'st for."

And, as if afraid of exhibiting any further emotion, he signed to me to leave him.

Of course, an end was put to all our Christmas festivities, and to amusement of every kind, and the house was for a time so changed that I would fain have returned to the Anchorite's, but I could not leave my uncle in his affliction. However, he got better, as I have related; and as the time for my departure was close at hand, I announced it to him. He seemed loath to part with me, but did not remonstrate, as he knew I must go back to school.

I went over to take leave of Ned Culcheth and his pretty wife, and only found the latter at home. I learnt from her that they had been waylaid and attacked by Phaleg, on their way home from the merrymaking, but that her husband had beaten off his assailant; and that since then many depredations had been committed upon their outdoor property, and Ned suspected the gipsy, but had not been able, as yet, to bring any of the offences home to him, for he and his family had left their haunt in the ravine and disappeared, though Ned was convinced they were still in the neighbourhood, and was active in his search for them. I asked her if she had seen much of Malpas of late, and she blushed and said:

"A great teal too much, look you, Master Mirfyn. He quite haunts the place."

"Well, take care of yourself, Sissy," I replied. "You've got a good husband. Don't throw him away."

"You give me fery coot atfices, Master Mirfyn. Put ton't be afraid. I love my husbants tearly."

"But you don't dislike other people's admiration, Sissy. Well, good-by! I hope to find you looking prettier than ever when I come back."

I had seen little of Malpas. Since Mr. Gripper's visit, he had scarcely been once at Nethercroft's; and probably, having received some information from Simon Pownall, which had dispelled his hopes, he thought it needless longer to play the hypocrite. My uncle did not miss him, and rarely inquired after him.

I called at the vicarage on my way home, and here also found only the lady within. She spoke to me much about my uncle; said she thought him declining fast; and was very sorry I was obliged to leave him. Though she had too much delicacy to allude to my prospect of inheriting his property, I could plainly see she had heard the report. I was sorry to hear from her that Malpas was not to go to Eton that half year. He did not feel very strong, she said, but was to read at home with Mr. Vawdrey. As I rose to depart, she desired her love to Mrs. Mervyn, whom she often visited; and bade me a very kindly adieu, hoping to see much of me hereafter.

Malpas came next morning to say good-by—most likely at the instance of his mother—and Simon Pownall came with him. I was very much depressed in spirits towards the last, and began to think I ought not to leave my uncle; and if he had asked me to stay then, I should have complied. But he did not. My things had been sent off the night before by the carrier, and Taffy was saddled and waiting for me at the door. I had bidden farewell to Hannah and Martha, and was in tears when I came to my uncle, who shook me very kindly by the hand, and said:

"Whether I shall be spared till thou com'st back at Easter, Mervyn, or whether thou'lt be sent for sooner, Heaven only knows; but if I'm gone, thou'lt be master here—that's all."

My uncle had never announced his intentions so openly before, and the effect on the auditors was somewhat curious. Malpas bit his quivering lips till the blood sprang from them, and glanced angrily askance at Simon Pownall, who made me a cringing bow; while those of the household who were present appeared to be pleased, though most of them were interested parties. But my uncle didn't give them time to make any observations, for he hurried me off, saying:

"And now, good-by, and God bless thee, Mervyn. Be a good lad."

Malpas never offered to shake hands with me, but went out at the back door, with a countenance of unconcealed rage and mortification. The rest followed me, vieing with each other in attentions; and the sycophantic Simon even held my stirrup, wished me a pleasant journey, and with a significant look, for which I longed to lay the whip across his shoulders, whispered:

"Hope you may be soon 'sent for,' as the old man said—knew **all** about it—but mum's the word wit̄ ne."

CHAPTER VIII.

A GLANCE AT COTTONBOROUGH—APPHIA BRIDEOAKE.

A WONDROUS town is Cottonborough! Vast—populous—ugly—sombre. Full of toiling slaves, pallid from close confinement and heated air. Full of squalor, vice, misery: yet also full of wealth and all its concomitants—luxury, splendour, enjoyment. A city of coal and iron—a city of the factory and the forge—a city where greater fortunes are amassed, and more quickly, than in any other in the wide world. But how—and at what expense? Ask yon crew of careworn men, wan women, and sickly children, and they will tell you. Look at yon mighty structure, many-windowed, tall-chimneyed, vomiting forth clouds of smoke, to darken and poison the wholesome air. Listen to the clangor and the whirl of the stupendous and complicated machinery within. Count the hundreds of pale creatures that issue forth from it at meal-times. Mark them well, and say if such employment be healthy. Yet these poor souls earn thrice the wages of the labourer at the plough, and therefore they eagerly pursue their baneful task-work. Night comes; the mighty mill is brilliantly lighted up, and the gleam from its countless windows is seen afar, looking like an illuminated palace. Come nearer, and you may hear the clangour and the whirl still going on, and note the steady beat of the huge engine, that, like the heart of a giant, puts all in motion; and you may see the white faces flitting past, and young girls and boys still toiling on, sweltering beneath the glaring gas that consumes the vital air. The owner of that mill, and the worker of that vast machinery of flesh and blood, iron and steam—for all are mere machines with him—is rich, and will soon be richer—richer than many a prince. And he will strain the money-getting principle to the utmost, for the power has been given him. And there are a thousand such in Cottonborough. There Mammon has set up his altars: there his ardent votaries are surest of reward. Ugly and black is Cottonborough, shrouded by smoke, tasteless in architecture, boasting little antiquity, and less of picturesque situation; yet not devoid of a character strongly impressive, arising from magnitude, dense population, thronged streets, where the heavy waggon with its bales of goods takes place of the carriage, vast warehouses, and a spacious and busy 'Change—the resort of the wealthiest merchants of the realm. Active and energetic are its inhabitants, enterprising, spirited, with but one thought—one motive—one aim, and one end—MONEY. Prosperous is Cottonborough—prosperous beyond all other cities—and long may it continue so; for, with all its ugliness, and all its faults—and they are many—I love it well.

Some such thoughts crossed me as I approached the large and smoky town, though, doubtless, as I now record them, they have got mixed up with impressions subsequently received. And it is only right to add, that, of late years, considerable ameliorations have been made by the millowners, and the hours of labour limited, from which causes the health, condition, and morals of the persons employed, especially the girls and children, have been materially improved. But I could not then help contrasting the careworn countenances and emaciated frames of the fustian-jackets I now encountered, with the cheerful, ruddy visages, and hardy limbs of the country people I had left; and I thought how infinitely preferable was the condition of the latter. The women, too, and the young girls—how different were those sallow faces, bleached like their own calico, from the rosy-cheeked, brown-armed damsels of Marston!

I passed through the far-spreading suburbs, consisting for the most part of long rows of mean-looking habitations of red brick, with occasional bare spaces, which had once been fields, and still retaining a few consumptive bushes of thorn to show where hedges had grown, but otherwise caked over with cinders, or receptacles for rubbish; I passed by many public-houses; several Methodist chapels; an ugly, formal church, part brick, part stone—(a magnificent Roman Catholic temple has since been erected in the same neighbourhood); more rows of red brick houses, but of a better description, and neater, with low iron rails in front to fence them from the road, and bright brass plates on the doors; huge mills, whose smoke was blackening the air, and blotting out the sun; little streams that ran like frothing ink, and into which the mills and dye-works discharged their steaming and livid waters; and, crossing a bridge over a river, into which all these inky currents poured, I entered the town.

All looked dark, dirty, and disagreeable. When I left Marston—and even a few miles off—the sun was shining brightly; but now, imperfectly distinguished through the canopy of smoke, the luminary looked like a great red ball,—as it does through a London November fog. The streets were almost ankle-deep in black sludge, and where the frost had maintained its power, the snow had become the colour of soot. The very houses seemed to wear an unusually dingy aspect, as if the black snow had melted into them, and stained them of its own hue. The fog and smoke appeared to have got down everybody's throat, for almost all the people I met were coughing, and I myself felt affected by the reeky atmosphere, to an extent that made my eyes smart with water. I would have got on faster if I could, but my course was impeded by ponderous waggons laden with heavy bales of cotton, carts, hand-carts, and numerous other vehicles, and I was compelled to proceed at a slow pace through the long thoroughfare, intersecting the town from south to north. The eye found little pleasurable to rest on, but much that was disagreeable and even distressing; and the ear constantly caught the sharp click of the patten, and the clamp of the wooden clog: clogs are much worn in Cottonborough.

Amid the crowd, which was constantly increasing, as the tide poured in towards the centre of the town, there were many haggard faces that told of want and disease, many miserable, famished children, without shoes and stockings, trampling through the mire. Then there were the sots at the doors of the public-houses, with the recruiting-sergeant amongst them, holding out his lures, by which some of them were sure to be caught. Then came another wide thoroughfare, leading to the quays along the banks of the Ater, and to a bridge connecting Cottonborough with its sister town of Spinnyford; but my way not being along it, I passed by a large butcher's shambles, held under a low roof, approached by low brick archways, and delightfully inconvenient; by a great coaching-house, with several stage-coaches before it; by a long range of warehouses, with here and there an old black and white chequered house among them (mementoes of other days, and looking quite beautiful amid so much architectural uniformity, not to say deformity); by another bridge leading to Spinnyford; and leaving the Square and the Exchange, and several other public places unvisited, I descended the eminence on which the fine old Collegiate Church is situated, crossed the Ink, and was right glad some quarter of an hour afterwards to find myself under the roof of the sequestered Anchorite's.

How glad Mrs. Mervyn was to see me! and how much I had to tell her about my poor aunt Mobberley, and about Mrs. Sale, and about everything! And how well she thought my mourning fitted me! And when she had done with me, what a deal Mr. Comberbach and Mrs. Chadwick made of me! And what a nice little dinner Molly Bailey gave us!—how pleasantly Mr. Barton Lever talked!—how well the old Madeira tasted—Mr. Lever made me take a second glass—and how glad I was to get back to my own bed at night! I quite hugged the pillow with delight.

But not quite so pleasant was my return to school, for I had been so used to freedom of late, that I felt the restraint rather irksome at first. But I was delighted to meet my old schoolfellows again, and had plenty to tell them, while on their part they had much to relate to me. We had long confabs at John Leigh's, which might be called the school-club; and the consumption of cakes, and tarts, and "pop," as the ginger-beer was called, went on as swimmingly as our Bunker's Hill hero could desire.

I have not yet mentioned John Brideoake, though he was more pleased to see me than any of the others, and though he was foremost in my own regard, but for that very reason have left him apart, for I shall now have a good deal to say about him. John continued to work as hard as ever, but he looked so ill that I was sure the mind was preying upon the body, and I also felt sure he had not nourishment enough, and sometimes suspected, from his faintness, that he went without breakfast altogether, though he said he took his morning's meal before he left home at six o'clock; but this I accidentally found out was rarely more than a crust of bread and a cup of water. On making this discovery, I devised a scheme for helping him which should not wound his feelings. Not having time to return to the Anchorite's during the hour allowed for breakfast, I used to have a basin of milk and a hot roll or two in a little parlour at the back of John Leigh's shop, and I asked Brideoake to share the meal with me, assuring him there was enough for both of us. He was very diffident, but I overcame his modest scruples, and nothing could exceed the heartfelt satisfaction I experienced at his enjoyment of the meal, and the good it evidently did him. He thanked me again and again, and apologised for eating too much; but his hunger was too real and unmistakable not to show how much privation he endured.

Bridcoake repaired daily to the public library, attached to the Blue-Coat Hospital, to read during the intervals of school hours. The reading-room was most congenial to study. Antique, with a coved and groined ceiling, deeply-embayed windows filled with painted glass, which threw a mellow and subdued light around, walls wainscoted with black oak, a high, carved mantelpiece, above which hung the portrait of the munificent founder, an austere-looking man, "frosty but kindly, like a lusty winter," chairs of ancient make, with leathern seats and backs, old oak tables, and quaint old reading-desks in nooks —such was the room, and such its furniture.

In the deep recess of an oriel window projecting from the centre of the chamber sat the pale young student, working with intensity of zeal. Having in a short space mastered the task-work of the day, he would plunge into writers with whom we had no concern; would acquaint himself with the natural history of Pliny, or take up the Annals of Tacitus, the Institutes of Quintilian, or the Offices of Cicero; would dip into the Thebaid and Achilleid of the wordy and turgid Statius, or test the pure latinity of the later poets, Ausonius and Claudian, by the *Mosella* and other idylls of the one, and the *Proserpina* of the other. Neither did he neglect the Greek historians, dramatists, and philosophers, and meditated often upon the precepts of the divine Plato. Sometimes he would consult the Fathers, and pore over Origen, Lactantius, and Chrysostom. The only apprehension was, lest he should sink under his labours—his slight and delicate frame seeming wholly inadequate to sustain the spirit burning within it, while neither due rest nor support were afforded. But no personal consideration could check his ardour, and he worked on like one determined to win the race or perish in the effort. I have sat for hours with him in the college library, and have been surprised at his zeal, and the extent of information he acquired. He read with great rapidity, and his memory was so extraordinarily retentive, that he never forgot what he read, however hastily.

Convinced from his appearance that his health was giving way, I spoke to him earnestly on the subject, but remonstrances were in vain. I was therefore scarcely surprised, though deeply distressed, when he did not make his appearance as usual, and was fully prepared for the intelligence which was brought to Dr. Lonsdale two days afterwards, that he was very ill, and unable to attend school. On receiving this message, which appeared to make him uneasy, the doctor called to me, and bade me make further inquiries of the messenger, who was at the door. I went there, and found a little girl outside, whom I knew at once must be Bridcoake's sister, Apphia.

She was a child of extraordinary beauty. Her features were of the most pefect regularity, lighted up by eyes of the tenderest blue, and her complexion was as soft as the tint of an opening damask-rose; her limbs were slight, but very gracefully formed; and long fair ringlets hung about her shoulders. But there was a canker in the rose—the worm was there—and the bloom, now so delicate and fugitive, would soon, I feared, be altogether effaced by sadness and want.

"I presume you are Apphia Brideoake?" I said. "I am very sorry to hear your brother is unwell. I hope it is nothing serious?"

"I hope not," she replied, heaving a deep sigh, while tears filled her eyes. "I hope not—for he is everything to us. We don't know what is the matter with him, but he is so faint and weak that he can't get up; and his mind slightly wanders at times. He complains that he can't read; for when he takes up a book the letters dance and skip before him, and he can't make out a word."

"Who attends him?" I inquired, anxiously.

"Only mamma," she replied. "We can't afford a doctor. Besides, he says he wouldn't take anything if it were given him. A little cup of broth was all that passed his lips yesterday. He had a very restless night, mamma says, for she sat up with him; and I don't think he is any better to-day."

"He must have advice without delay," I said. "Where do you live, Apphia? for although John Brideoake is my intimate friend, whom I love as a brother, I have never been made acquainted with his dwelling. But now I must know it."

"You are his friend, Mervyn Clitheroe, I suppose?" she inquired, fixing her eyes full upon me. And, on my replying in the affirmative, she blushed slightly, and continued: "I thought so the moment I saw you. John described you exactly. But I must go. Mamma will wonder why I stayed so long."

"Not before you have answered my question, Apphia," I rejoined. "Nay, do not hesitate. Under any other circumstances I would not intrude, but now your brother's life may be at stake."

"Well, I will tell you," she replied; "for I am sure you mean so kindly that mamma cannot be offended, and even if she is, I must bear her displeasure. Our lodgings are in Preston-court, in Friar's-gate—the last house on the right; and the upper story," she added, blushing deeply.

"Don't be ashamed, Apphia," I said, taking her hand. "Poverty is no crime, and if John is spared he will make a good home for you; of that I'm certain. And now good-by. Try to cheer your mamma, and tell her I will obtain medical advice for your brother in the course of the morning."

And the little child, looking gratefully at me, hastened away.

On re-entering the school I told Dr. Lonsdale what I had heard, and I saw he shared in my apprehensions as to the dangerous condition of John Brideoake, in whom, as being one of the most promising of his pupils, he took a warm interest. He immediately wrote a note, and told me to take it at once to Dr. Foam, his particular friend, who, besides being the most eminent physician in the town, was a very humane man, and would attend to the case without fee or reward. I had intended mentioning the matter to Mrs. Mervyn, but this did just as well, and I accordingly repaired to the residence of the physician, which was in one of the principal streets of Cottonborough.

CHAPTER IX.

INTRODUCES A BENEVOLENT PHYSICIAN AND A DECAYED GENTLEWOMAN.

DR. FOAM was a stout little man, with a head like an old piece of polished ivory—so perfectly bald, that I do not think there was a single hair upon it. His eyes were deeply sunk in their sockets, and his chin almost buried in the ample folds of a cravat. He wore a black coat, drab knee-breeches, and brown top-boots. The room smelt terribly of tobacco, as if he had just been smoking. His voice was extraordinarily husky, and he wheezed very much as he spoke; but his manner was affable, and he made me feel easy with him directly. Inquiring after Mrs. Mervyn, he launched out into praises of her, and spoke of her admirable library. I thought he had a good library of his own, as I glanced round the walls, which were covered with well-filled book-shelves; and, noticing the glance, he told me every room in the house was equally full of books, but still he was always adding to the collection; "though where I'm to put them all I don't know," he continued, with a smile, "and that reminds me that I've a sale to attend at Tomlinson's to-day. There are several works I have marked (putting a catalogue into his pocket) which I mean to purchase if I can, for there are other collectors besides myself in Cottonborough, and I am often outbidden now. Tell Mrs. Mervyn, with my compliments, that I shall avail myself one of these days of her obliging offer to show me some of her manuscript treasures—her Jacobite memorials. And now as to this poor lad—this John Brideoake. Brideoake," he repeated—"a north country name. I'm a Northumbrian myself. You've written down the address, my young friend—ay, Preston-court, Friar's-gate—sad hole it must be. Wretchedly poor you say, and the lad a good scholar. Dr. Lonsdale says his best pupil—a hard student—a second Picus de Mirandola. Ah! we must preserve him. A miracle of erudition must not be nipped in the bud. I will be there in an hour, and will see what can be done for him. Don't forget my message to Mrs. Mervyn."

I promised him I would not; thanked him for his kind intentions towards John Brideoake; and left him with a lightened heart.

I next flew to my poor friend's abode, and soon reached the narrow court where it was situated. I went straight to the house, and having passed through the lower rooms, tenanted by two different families, ascended a narrow, steep staircase, and reached a door, against which I tapped. It was instantly opened for me by Apphia, who greeted me sadly, and said, "John is worse." I cast my eyes round the room, and saw that the walls were almost bare, and that it was nearly destitute of the needful articles of furniture, two or three rickety chairs and a deal table forming the sum total, while a small shelf contained a scanty supply of crockery. The

F

whole place bore marks of extreme poverty, even to the miserable fire, on which a small pan was set. Some of John's school-books were lying on the mantelshelf, near a tin candlestick. Apphia was employed at some needlework, and had a basket before her. I had scarcely completed my survey, when an inner door opened, and Mrs. Brideoake came forth.

I was greatly surprised by her appearance, for, though worn and sorrow-stricken, there were still traces of great beauty in her countenance, coupled with an expression of pride wholly unsubdued, while her deportment was almost commanding. She was dressed in faded black; but, in spite of her poor attire, it was perceptible at once that she was a lady. There was none of the gentleness about her that characterised both her children. She was made of sterner stuff. In her looks and in her manner it could be seen that all she had endured had not crushed her spirit, and that, probably, she would see her children perish from want, and perish likewise herself, rather than abate a jot of her independence. So, at least, I thought when I beheld her.

She thanked me for the interest I had taken in her son; but when I mentioned that Dr. Foam was coming in a short time to pay him a visit professionally, she appeared much annoyed and disconcerted, and a slight flush, almost of shame, overspread her pale features.

"Dr. Foam! I had rather it had been any one else," she exclaimed.

"He is a very kind, humane man, ma'am," I observed.

"So the world reputes him, and, no doubt, with justice; for it does not speak too favourably of any one," she rejoined. "I have known the doctor under different circumstances, and at a time when I did not anticipate the sad reverses I have since experienced, and then liked him greatly. It will be a trial to me to see him now; but it cannot be helped, and I must submit. I will go and prepare my son."

"May I not see him?" I inquired, hastily.

"Not yet," she answered, in a tone that did not admit of dispute. "Not till Dr. Foam has been here. If he permits it, you shall." And she returned to the room whence she had come, and I presently heard John's feeble accents, as if in expostulation with her.

Suddenly a sharp cry pierced our ears, and Mrs. Brideoake, in a voice of great alarm, called to Apphia to bring a cup of water quickly. I could not restrain myself, but rushed into the room likewise, and beheld John, stretched on a miserable pallet. I thought him dead; and his mother thought so too, for she was kneeling beside him, clasping her hands in bitterest anguish.

"He is gone!" she ejaculated, despairingly. "I have lost him—my only hope—my only support! He who was so good, so persevering, so clever, so wise—he who could have repaired our fallen fortunes, and reinstated me in my lost position—he is gone—gone for ever! Heaven, in its mercy, take me too, for I have nothing left to live for."

As she uttered this outburst of selfish sorrow, my heart bled for poor little Apphia, who was weeping and trembling beside her.

Meanwhile, I had taken John's arm, and feeling the returning pulsation, calmed Mrs. Brideoake's frantic transports, by assuring her that her son was not yet lost to her. I sprinkled his face with water, and in a few moments he opened his eyes. Their gaze alighted on me.

"Ah!" he murmured, faintly. "Dear Mervyn here! I have seen him—I shall die content."

"You are not going to die yet, John," I replied. "Be of good heart. You have many years in store for you. You must live for your mother and sister."

He looked at them ruefully.

"I have prayed fervently to Heaven to spare me for them," he said.

"And the prayer will be granted, rest assured," I replied. "Doctor Foam is coming to see you. He will be here presently. But your mother thinks it may do you harm to talk to me. So I will go into the next room to await the doctor's arrival."

Pressing his hand, I withdrew, and, at a sign from her mother, Apphia followed me.

The poor child appeared almost broken-hearted; and I was so much touched by her looks, that I took her little hand in mine, and tried to cheer her.

"You must not dwell upon what escaped your mother in her affliction, Apphia," I said. "She scarcely knew what she uttered."

"I suppose not," she replied; "but she loves John better than me, because he is to make us rich again, if he lives, poor fellow. Have you any brothers and sisters; and does your mamma make any distinction between them and you? Does she love you as well as the others?"

"Alas! Apphia," I said, scarcely able to repress my emotion, "I have no mamma; she died when I was a little child; but I remember she was very fond of me. I have some half-brothers and sisters, for my papa has married again, but I have never seen them—nor, indeed, him. They are in India."

"Pray forgive me for asking the question. I fear I have occasioned you pain," she said.

"No, Apphia; I always like to think and talk of my dear mother," I rejoined. "Some day I will tell you all I know about her, and you will be pleased to hear how good and beautiful she was. And now dry your eyes, and don't imagine yourself friendless, for even if you were to lose John, I will be a brother to you."

Apphia then sat down, and attempted to resume her needlework, but in vain. The tears coursed down her pretty cheeks. I would have cheered her if I could, but I had exhausted all my stock of comfort, and now felt inclined to weep with her, for my sympathies were powerfully awakened in her behalf.

At length a knock was heard at the door, and Dr. Foam was admitted. He was puffing and blowing from the exertion of mounting the steep stairs, when Mrs. Brideoake came from the inner room. On seeing her, he gave a start, and looked as if he could scarcely believe his eyes.

"Bless my soul! Can it be?" he exclaimed.

"It is the person you suppose, Dr. Foam," she replied, receiving him with as much stiffness and dignity as if she herself had sent for him, and intended to fee him handsomely. "You perceive to what I am reduced. I must beg you to consider me as what I am—Mrs. Brideoake, a poor widow—not what I was—nor what I may be," she added, with a sigh.

"I will observe your instructions, madam," replied the doctor, with a deferential bow.

"I ought to apologise for being the means of bringing you to such a wretched place, Dr. Foam," she said, offering him a rickety chair, on which he seemed unwilling to trust his bulky person. "I wonder you, who have all the wealthy families in Cottonborough as patients, would condescend to visit such poor people as we are."

"Tut, tut, madam!" the doctor cried. "I came to visit your son, because I was asked to do so by Dr. Lonsdale; but I would have come just as readily—nay, far more readily—if you had sent for me yourself. I have many poor patients as well as many rich ones; and as I take more from some than I ought, I balance the account by attending the others gratis. I care nothing about the apartments, except that I lament you should be obliged to occupy them. But I must say I take it unkindly in you, madam, not to send for me,—if only for the sake of former times."

"I entreat you not to refer to those times, doctor," Mrs. Brideoake said, coldly.

"I only did so to show the claim you had upon my services," the physician rejoined. "But come, madam," he added, rising, "I have now recovered the breath I had lost in mounting your staircase. Show me to your son."

"I must again apologise for the room, doctor——"

"Pooh! pooh! no more apologies, madam," cried the physician, impatiently. "Let's see the lad."

And they entered the room, closing the door after them, and leaving Apphia and me in a state of breathless anxiety as to the result of the examination.

Some time elapsed, which seemed much longer to us than it was really, before they came forth again; and when they did so, I augured well from the physician's cheerful looks. Doctor Foam seized a chair, and popping down in it rather hastily, it gave way beneath him, and he was prostrated on the floor. I flew to his assistance, and as he got up he laughed very heartily at the accident, checking Mrs. Brideoake's apologies, and telling her there was no harm done except to the chair, which he would mend with a new one. Not liking to trust himself to another equally crazy concern, he continued standing, and Apphia went up to him timidly, and asked him how he found her brother.

"I am glad I can relieve your mind respecting him, my dear," he replied, patting her head. "And yours too, youngster. John will get better, but time will be required for his entire recovery. He has greatly overworked himself, and his frame is in a most debilitated condition. If he had been allowed to go on as he is now, fever would have supervened, and have speedily taken him off. But there are no really dangerous symptoms about him; and what I most feared, consumption, has not declared itself; and I trust, under Providence, to be able to ward off its insidious attacks. As I have intimated, two or three months of repose of mind and body, of entire cessation from study, of freedom from all anxiety, will be required to reinstate him completely. He must have better air, better diet, and better rooms."

"But, my good sir, where is the money for these things to come from?" Mrs. Brideoake exclaimed.

"Out of my pocket, madam."

"I am equally indebted to you, doctor, but I cannot accept your assistance."

"Cannot! But, madam, I tell you, you MUST. Without the aids I have mentioned I won't undertake to cure your son. If he remains here another week he will die, madam. D'ye understand me now?"

"I must submit to the will of Providence," Mrs. Brideoake replied. "Your professional aid I am willing to receive, doctor, but not your money. That I must positively decline. As you well know, I need not be here now if I would bow my neck."

"Much better if you would bow it," I heard Doctor Foam mutter.

He looked hard at her, but he saw no further arguments would prevail. It was an anxious moment both to me and Apphia; and I was very indignant with Mrs. Brideoake, for I feared she would sacrifice her son to her false notions of pride. At last the doctor's countenance brightened up.

"I have hit upon a plan which I think will overcome all your scruples, madam," he said. "I can appreciate, though I cannot approve of, your motives for declining pecuniary assistance from me, which, after all, would have been no obligation on your part whatever, because your son could repay me when he becomes a rich man; and he will assuredly be rich one of these days, if he lives. But, as I was saying, my plan will obviate every difficulty. I am acquainted with an excellent lady, whose whim—and a most amiable whim it is—is to render help without being cognisant of the names of those she assists, while the persons aided are kept in equal ignorance of their benefactress. Will you consent to be indebted to her for a time—only for a time, madam?"

Mrs. Brideoake appeared to hesitate. Little Apphia approached her, and taking her hand, looked up in her face in a manner so earnest and supplicating, that it could not be resisted.

"Well, for John's sake, and his sake only, I consent," Mrs. Brideoake said; "for I would not willingly be indebted to any human being, and that you may believe, doctor. But you are not deceiving me about the lady—indeed, I am sure you are not—you are too much of a gentleman for that, and have shown that you understand my feelings too well. I leave all in your hands."

"Delighted to hear it, madam," returned Doctor Foam, gleefully. "You will attend strictly to my directions respecting your son. Give him the medicine, which will be sent in by the apothecary, and a glass of the wine, which will be sent in by myself, and which you'll find the best medicine after all. Don't stint it, madam, for I shall send you a good supply, and some good wholesome nutritious food, which will be equally efficacious. I wish you good morning, Mrs.—ah! let me see—Brideoake. Yes, that's it. I shall see you again in the course of the day, Mrs. Brideoake, and trust to find John improved. Come, young sir," he added to me.

I was much surprised that Dr. Foam, who appeared so well acquainted with the lady, should hesitate about her name, and I reflected upon the matter as I followed him out of the room.

A small, old-fashioned yellow chariot, like a post-chaise, with a pair of old horses attached to it, and an old coachman on the box, was waiting at the entrance of the court, and the doctor begged me to get into it, telling the man to drive home. During the ride thither, he questioned me particularly as to Mrs. Brideoake's circumstances. I told him all I knew, and he said, "It is a sad case. The poor lady has borne up with great fortitude; and so, indeed, have they all. But she is most to be pitied, for she is as proud as Lucifer; and what humiliation and misery must she not have endured! Hers has been mental torture, while the poor young things have only been half-starved. However, that's bad enough."

I thought so too, and by no means agreed with him that they were less to be pitied than their mother, whose inordinate pride appeared to be the sole cause of their misery. And as I felt sure there was some mystery in the case, which the doctor could unravel if he liked, I tried to bring him to the point.

"You have asked me a good many questions, doctor,—will you allow me to ask you one in return? I observed, when you were taking leave of Mrs. Brideoake, that you hesitated about her name, as if it did not come naturally to you. Is it assumed? If so, I do not believe her son can be aware of the circumstance."

Doctor Foam looked a little puzzled, but at length said, "Do not ask me that question, my young friend, for I am not at liberty to answer it. And as to John, I must beg of you not to mention to him any suspicions which my inadvertence may have roused in your mind. They would only disturb him, and do no good whatever. You are his friend, I know, and will attend to my caution."

I assured him I would, and soon after this we reached his house, and alighted. I went with him into the study, where he wrote out a prescription, and, ringing the bell, gave orders to the servant to get it made up, and take it, without loss of time, as directed, with a basket of provisions, which he specified, and another of wine, to the same address. "And here," he added, "let this easy-chair be taken to the same place, and one of my flannel dressing-gowns. D'ye hear?"

The servant having departed to execute his behests, he turned to me and said, "I must now tell you to whom I mean to apply for the relief of this poor lady. It is, as you see, a case of peculiar delicacy and difficulty, in which I am not allowed to interfere personally. Your relative Mrs. Mervyn's purse is always open, while her eyes are closed towards the object of her bounty. The channels in which her benevolence flows are only known to those who claim it. I shall apply to her; and I hope there will be no impropriety in the step."

"I guessed whom you referred to, doctor, when you proposed your plan to Mrs. Brideoake," I replied, "and I felt sure no one could be found more willing to assist her than Mrs. Mervyn, while neither the poor lady nor her children need ever be made aware to whom they are indebted."

"Well, then, since you agree with me in opinion, my young friend, we will go to the Anchorite's at once. I am not fond of begging— and wish I had been allowed to have my own way—but there is no help for it in this case."

We then got into the old chariot again, and, having stopped for a few minutes at the auction-rooms in the Exchange, where the doctor handed in the catalogue, with the books marked in it which he wished to purchase, we drove to the Anchorite's.

Mrs. Mervyn was at home, and received the doctor very courteously, and he immediately entered upon the object of his visit, concluding by stating, that he had been emboldened to make the request, not only by his knowledge of her most charitable disposition, but because he was aware of her strong feelings towards the Jacobite cause.

"I am not permitted to disclose the name of the lady for whom I venture to solicit your assistance, madam," he said; "neither, perhaps, would you desire to know it; but when I tell you that she belongs to one of those unfortunate families in the north of England, who suffered in the Rising of '15, I am sure I have said enough to enlist your strongest sympathies in her behalf."

"You have, indeed, doctor," Mrs. Mervyn replied, the tears springing to her eyes; "and I shall be indeed happy if you will point out a way in which I can be useful to her—not now, but hereafter." As she said this, she unlocked a coffer, and, taking out a roll of banknotes, gave them to the physician, adding, "I very rarely wish to know whom I am fortunate enough to be able to serve, but in this instance I must say my curiosity is aroused, and, if not disagreeable to her, I should be truly happy to make the lady's acquaintance."

I was so delighted that I felt disposed to tell her at once, but the doctor checked me by a look.

"I am truly grieved that I cannot comply with your request, madam," he replied; "but the lady is singularly proud, and if she discovered——"

"She would discover nothing from me," Mrs Mervyn interrupted.

"I do not for a moment imagine it, madam. But I fear it must be delayed—there are reasons——"

"Very well, doctor, I shall urge you no further. But I must repeat the hope that you will not hesitate to apply to me again. I am always ready in such cases, and more particularly in one where my feelings are deeply interested, like the present."

"The sum you have given is more than ample to meet any present emergency," said the doctor, who had glanced at the amount of the notes. "And now, like all solicitants who have obtained their suit, I must make my bow. On some future occasion I will crave permission to examine your library and its manuscript treasures."

"Come and examine it to-morrow, and dine with me afterwards," said Mrs. Mervyn. "I happen to have a little dinner party, to which you will be a great acquisition."

"I see only one objection to the arrangement, madam—I expect Dr. Bray on a visit to me—and he arrives to-day."

"Pray bring him with you," Mrs. Mervyn said; "I shall be delighted to see Dr. Bray, of whom I have heard so much."

"You will find him a little eccentric in manners, and perhaps rather too *Johnsonian* in his talk, madam," Dr. Foam said.

"Never mind that," she replied. "Mervyn will like to see so celebrated a person, so he shall dine with us too. I shall expect you and your learned friend, doctor."

The physician bowed.

"I think I must take this young gentleman back with me," he said; "he will like to see a family, in which he is interested, made happy."

"As you please, Dr. Foam," she replied; "and though I am not permitted to know who my Jacobite friends are, I am glad Mervyn is more fortunate."

"You will know them some day, I am sure, my dear Mrs. Mervyn, and like them as I do," I replied, for 1 was overjoyed at her conduct, and not only loved her dearly, but felt quite proud of her.

The doctor walked through the garden, on the way to the carriage, and promised himself a great treat, on some occasion, in examining Mrs. Mervyn's hothouses and greenhouses.

As we drove back again to town, I told him that I thought good accommodation for the family might be obtained at Marston, and added, that I knew of a cottage (I was thinking of Ned Culcheth's) which I was sure would suit them exactly. The doctor said a better spot could not be selected. Marston was remarkably salubrious, and he would recommend it to Mrs. Brideoake. It was then agreed that I should ride over on the day but one following, as I could not miss the dinner on the morrow, and engage the lodgings.

Arrived once more at Preston-court, we climbed the steep staircase, and were speedily admitted by little Apphia, who smiled as she beheld us, and we saw at once the change that had been effected. The provisions supplied by the doctor's care were spread on the table, and had evidently been partaken of by mother and daughter; perhaps the first hearty meal they had enjoyed for months. A bottle of old Madeira was opened, and its fragrance perfumed the apartment. But the chief object of attraction was the invalid himself, who was seated in the easy-chair sent by the doctor, and wrapped in the worthy man's flannel dressing-gown. He looked very wan and feeble, but his eye dwelt with gratitude on Dr. Foam and on me.

The physician felt his pulse, and said he was going on capitally. "He will be none the worse for another glass of Madeira," he added, pouring it out, and handing it to him.

As John, with trembling hand, conveyed the generous wine to his

lips, Dr. Foam turned to Mrs. Brideoake, and, taking the bank-notes from his pocket-book, placed them in her hands.

"The lady I mentioned to you, madam," he said, "has commissioned me to present you with this sum of money. It will, I hope, fully meet the present exigency, and be the means of restoring your son to you in health. A cottage at Marston, in Cheshire, will be engaged for you, and in a few days John will be strong enough, I trust, to be conveyed thither."

For the first time Mrs. Brideoake's pride was shaken, and she seemed completely overcome by emotion.

"Oh, sir!" she ejaculated, "I cannot thank you as I ought."

"You must not thank me, madam," he replied; "you must thank your own unknown friend."

"I do—I do," she rejoined; "but you have been the instrument, doctor. The blessings of a poor widow will requite you!"

"What, you want to thank me too, eh?" said the doctor, turning to little Apphia, who had crept up to him. "You must let me see the roses which you will pick up at Marston."

"That I will, sir,—I will bring you plenty," replied Apphia, taking the words literally.

Meanwhile, I had approached John, and said a few words to him, when the doctor, who had now discharged his commission, fearing the invalid might be over-excited, put a stop to our further conversation, and, beckoning me to follow him, I was obliged to obey the summons.

CHAPTER X.

A VISIT TO THE BUTLER'S PANTRY—A DINNER PARTY AT THE ANCHORITE'S—DR. BRAY AND MR. CUTHBERT SPRING.

WHEN any secret information is required, servants are sure to furnish it, and what Mrs. Mervyn could not have learnt from me respecting the objects of her bounty, she had already obtained from Mr. Comberbach, as I discovered on my return home in the evening. Our butler was in the pantry cleaning plate, preparatory to the dinner on the following day, and as I chanced to pass the door he requested me to step in for a moment.

The pantry was quite a chamber of horrors, the walls being covered with prints representing the tragical fate of the persons composing our butler's martyrology. Nowhere else could be seen such a direful collection of hangings and decapitations; and I wondered what pleasure Mr. Comberbach could have in contemplating them. The scaffold on Tower Hill was repeated at least a dozen times, the prominent figures being Kilmarnock, Balmerino, Lovat, and Charles Ratcliffe,

Lord Derwentwater's brother. There was the execution on Kennington Common of the unfortunate Jemmy Dawson, whose fate Shenstone has so pathetically bewailed, and the Carlisle and Cottonborough tragedies. Interspersed among these were several broadside ballads, or "Laments," headed with cuts as appalling as the prints. On the mantelshelf were a couple of skulls, looking very yellow and grim, and asserted by our butler to be those of his luckless progenitors. A waggish friend told him he must have lost his own head when he put the others there. Then there were the powder-puff and brass basin belonging to the owners of the skulls; and the comfortable arm-chair now occupied by our butler had once stood, he affirmed, in the shop of the valorous shavers, who went before him, in Old Mill Gate.

Our butler was a very respectable looking man, fat and florid, but not unwieldy; and he not only knew how to decant a bottle of old port, but to discuss it too, if opportunity offered. In age, he was hard upon sixty, and was very particular as to his dress. Indeed, when fully rigged out, he looked as grand as a lord, for he wore a sky-blue coat with gilt buttons, a white waistcoat, with a satin under-waistcoat of the royal Stuart tartan (so arranged as to look like the riband of an order of knighthood), knee-breeches, and black silk stockings of a very fine web. Our butler was not a little vain of his large calves and small feet; and, as became the descendant of a line of barbers, he wore powder in his hair. Fastened to his under-waistcoat, and so placed as to have the appearance of a decoration, was an immense brooch, surrounded by mock brilliants, containing a miniature of Prince Charles Edward.

"Pray, Master Mervyn," Mr. Comberbach said, as he rubbed away at a large two-handled silver cup, "may I inquire after Master John Brideoake?" And seeing me stare at the question, he winked knowingly, and continued: "Nay, you needn't make no secret of it with us, sir. We knows it all." (Our butler had a way of mixing himself up with his mistress in his observations.) "We knows whom you and Dr. Foam wisited to-day; and I'll tell you how we comes for to know it. The doctor's coachman, old Andrew Beatson, is a crony of mine; so, says I to him, as I takes him a pot of our mild October to the garden gate, where the carriage was a-standing, 'So, Andrew,' says I, 'you've brought home Master Mervyn—from school, eh?' Says he to me, a-blowin' off the froth, 'My sarvice to you, Mr. Cummerbaych.' (Thus our butler pronounced his own name.) 'No, sir, we comes from Preston-court, i' Friar's-gate.' 'Preston-court!' says I. 'That's a queer place, Andrew! What could young master be doing there?' 'Why, a poor lad is ill, as lives there,' says he; 'one John Brideoake—a schoolfellow of hisn—and he got the doctor to wisit him—that's it.' 'Oh! that's it?' says I; 'thank you, Andrew.' 'Nay, thank *you*, Mr. Cummerbaych,' says he; 'you've a werry good tap here. I don't care how often I tries it.' So, hoping to see him soon again, I wishes him good day, and when missis arterwards inquires whether I knows if you have any friend at school as is unwell, and as comes of a Jackeybite fam'ly I sees it all at once, and, says I, 'Yes, mem; John Brideoake, whom he and the doctor have been to wisit this morning, afore they comed here. *His* fam'ly is Jackeybite, mem.' "

"How do you know that, Mr. Comberbach?" I asked.

"How do I know it?" our butler replied, with a cunning smile. "Never you mind that, sir." And, putting the cover on the silver cup, and holding it aloft by both handles, he exclaimed, "Historikil plate this, sir—the werry flagon out of which the young Prince drank when he brexfarsted here, on his march to Cottonborough, as you've oftentimes heerd missis relate. I reverences this cup, and could kiss it, only I should spile its polish. Ah! Master Mervyn, what a pity them good old times can't come over again! How I should like to have waited at table at that 'ere famous brexfarst; I'd have played my grandfather's part, and shouted,—'Live Charles Ed'ard, and down with the 'Lector of Hanover!' "

And in his excitement he knocked off the cover of the cup, which, in its fall, upset the box of red plate powder, scattering its contents over his apron and lower garments. As soon as matters were put to rights, and I had done laughing, I asked him what Mrs. Mervyn said when he told her about John Brideoake.

"Why, let me see. She said, says she, 'I'm almost sorry I axed you the question, Mr. Cummerbaych; for, to tell you the truth, I scarcely expected an answer.' Then, says I, 'Ma'am, if you had only given me a hint, I wouldn't have answered it.' But I seed she wanted to hear more, so I tells her all I knew—and that wasn't much. And now, Master Mervyn, may I ask you who these Brideoakes is? We don't recollect the name,—and we knows all the old Jackeybite fam'lies. We knows the Tyldesleys, the Daltons, the Hiltons, the Sandersons, the Heskeths, the Standishes, and the Shuttleworths; but we never heerd tell of the Brideoakes—never."

"I can give you no information, Mr. Comberbach."

"You're a werry discreet young gentleman, I must say," he rejoined, with a look of some annoyance; "but allow me to observe, in my missis's name, that there is no occasion for myst'ry in this case, our object being to sarve the fam'ly. You're aware of our attachment to the Good Cause, and how ready we are to aid those who suffered for it?"

"Oh, yes, I'm aware of all that, Mr. Comberbach; but I really know no more than you do yourself."

Our butler shook his head, and smiled incredulously. Taking another piece of plate out of the great chest which was standing open before him, he fell vigorously to work upon it with the polishing leather, chanting the while an old Jacobite ballad:

> "MacIntosh is a soldier brave,
> And of his friends he took his leave,
> Unto Northumberland he drew,
> And marched along with a jovial crew.
>   With a fa la la ra da ra da.
>
> "My Lord Derwentwater he did say
> Five hundred guineas he would lay,
> To fight the Militia, if they would stay,
> But they all proved cowards, and ran away.
>   With a fa la, &c.

> "The Earl of Mar did vow and swear,
> If that proud Preston he came near,
> Before the Right should starve, and the Wrong should stand,
> He would drive them into some foreign land.
>   With a fa la, &c.
>
> " MacIntosh is a valiant soldier,
> He carried a musket on his shoulder.
> ' Cock your pistols, draw your rapper,
> Damn you, Forster, for you're a traitor.'
>   With a fa la," &c.

Leaving him singing, I went up-stairs to Mrs. Mervyn; and though, after what I had heard in the pantry, I expected to be questioned by her, she made no allusion whatever to the Brideoakes.

On returning from school next day, in anticipation of the dinner party at which I was allowed to assist, I found our butler and two hired waiters in the hall. Mr. Comberbach was arrayed in all his finery, with his plaid satin under-waistcoat very skilfully displayed, and his large brooch glittering like a star upon his breast.

"Well, sir," he said, with a smirk, "they're come, sir."

"Who're come?" I exclaimed, almost expecting him to mention the Brideoakes, upon whom my own thoughts were running.

"Dr. Foam and his friend, Dr. Bray, sir. Lor' bless us, Master Mervyn, it's a parfit pleasure to see a man like that. He's none of your every-day humdrum parsons, as wears a black coat and white choker like other folks—not he! He's full dress, band and cassock, shorts and silks, and a wig, sir,—ay, sir, *sich* a wig! I tuk him for a bishop when I sees his full-bob, and he tuk me for a lord when he beholds my brooch. And werry respectful bows we makes each other, till at last Dr. Foam kindly undeceives us. I warn't displeased at the mistake a bit, nor were Dr. Bray; for, says he, ' You are premature, my good friend—whatever I may be when the Whigs comes in, I'm not a bishop yet.' ' You'll be a bishop afore I'm helewated to the peerage, doctor,' says I ; ' but I thought the Wigs must be comed in,' I adds, eyeing his bob-major. ' Aha!' cries he, laughing, ' you can joke, eh? jackanapes!' ' Jackeybite, sir,' says I—' we're all Jackeybites here.' And he laughs ready to split his fat sides and walks off, for he sees he's no match for me at a rippertee."

And our butler grinned and winked at the two waiters, who nodded their heads and grinned in return, as much as to say they entirely agreed in the estimate he formed of his own powers.

" They're up-stairs in the library," Mr. Comberbach said.

On this hint I went thither, and found Dr. Foam examining some thick folio volumes of manuscript Jacobite correspondence, which were generally locked up in the bookcase, but had no doubt been laid out for him by Mrs. Mervyn. He was so deeply engaged, that he did not remark my entrance, but continued reading letter after letter.

At last he closed the volume, exclaiming, "Very strange! very strange indeed!" And then observing me, he added, "Ah! my young friend, I didn't know you were here. My exclamation was occasioned by a very curious discovery which I have just made in glancing through this Jacobite correspondence. I have chanced upon some letters which show that a friendly intercourse subsisted between the main branch of the family which your worthy relative so kindly aided, and the unfortunate Ambrose Mervyn. Not having yet had time to go through the whole of the correspondence, I cannot say precisely how it ended. But I must borrow the volume from Mrs. Mervyn, to examine the letters at my leisure. I dare say she will trust me with it. And now I see you fancy you will be able to make out the secret; but though I have furnished you with a clue to it, you will not; for the real names are not given, and portions of the correspondence being in cypher, you won't be a bit the wiser if you search. Thus much I may tell you. The people you are interested in come of a very good family, and have more title to your regard than I was aware of. If upon investigating the matter I find my conjectures correct, I may perhaps consider it my duty to acquaint Mrs. Mervyn with my accidental discovery. But I shall say nothing at present. A propos of the Brideoakes, I am glad to be able to report to you that John is decidedly better. I have now no fears of him. Of course, you go to Marston to arrange about the lodgings to-morrow? And now let me present you to Dr. Bray."

A feeling of awe came over me as we approached the formidable personage in question. Dr. Bray was seated in an arm-chair, in the little octagonal room opening out of the library, and was poring over a volume, which I knew to be Salmasius's Commentary on the Hellenic language. He was short and corpulent, with rather hard features, charged with a sort of bull-dog expression, and, though Mr. Comberbach had prepared me for his full clerical suit of black, his band and cassock, my ideas had not come up to his full-blown cauliflower wig. It was portentous. I did not wonder that our butler had taken him for a bishop, for he certainly had the air of one; but I *did* wonder that the rascal ventured to treat him with familiarity. *I* could never have done so. Dr. Bray looked up at me from beneath his shaggy grey eyebrows, and grunted out, "Salve, puer!"

"Salve, doctor eruditissime," I replied, bowing respectfully.

"Humph! Well, boy, so you are at the Cottonborough grammar-school, I understand, and a fairly reputed school it is, though Dr. Lonsdale spoils you all because he does not flog you. 'Lumbos dolare virgis,' is my maxim. I always use the birch freely, and find it of wonderful efficacy. It quickens the circulation, and sharpens the intellect. No boy can get on well unless he is well birched."

"Mr. Cane is apparently of your opinion, sir," I replied, timidly.

"And, sir, let me tell you, Mr. Cane is right, and Dr. Lonsdale wrong. Severity is wholesome—wholesome as a bitter potion. Infantiam delitiis solvimus. Dr. Lonsdale is all honey—and I tell you it won't do, sir. If you have any classical knowledge at all, you owe it to Mr. Cane."

"He certainly did not spare me, sir," I answered, quaking.

"And quite right, I say again. Whatever punishment you received must have been richly deserved. Sir, I honour Mr. Cane. A good flogging is like exercise to the body, it gives you an appetite for study."

As he said this, he put on such a terrible countenance, that I hastily retired into the library, almost apprehensive lest he should try whether a good flogging would give me an appetite for dinner. Probably he was only jesting though; for I noticed a smile cross his cynical features as he glanced at Dr. Foam, who appeared greatly amused. Whether jesting or not, I was glad when the first dinner-bell rang, giving me an excuse for beating a retreat, and I left the two classical seniors talking about Vossius and Scaliger, Bellendenus and Warburton, Bentley and Porson.

About half an hour afterwards, on coming down stairs, I met Mr. Barton Lever, and was glad of his support as I entered the drawing-room. Dr. Bray was seated in an easy-chair next to Mrs. Mervyn, and I suppose they had been discussing the lady's favourite topic, for Dr. Foam observed to her, "I begin to think, madam, that you will make Dr. Bray a convert to your Jacobite opinions."

"Nay, sir, I am of Mrs. Mervyn's opinions already; for though I will not say what I might have felt, or how I might have acted at the time of the Risings of '15 or '45, my sympathies are always for the unfortunate, and I now therefore lean towards the Jacobites."

"I scarcely expected so much from you, Dr. Bray," Mrs. Mervyn said, looking much gratified.

"He must have little bravery in his nature, madam, who could triumph over a fallen cause; and I am not so prejudiced as to be incapable of admiring loyalty and devotion, even when employed against my own party. Many pleasing portraits adorn your walls, madam. Probably, they are those of your ancestry."

"They are so, Dr. Bray," she replied. "This martial figure, in the steel breastplate and plumed cap, and leaning on his cane, with the war-horse behind him, is Montacute Mervyn, a staunch cavalier, who fought at Edge-hill, Marston Moor, and Naseby. On either side are his two sons, one of whom was a judge, and the other a general. I descend from the soldier, Pierrepoint Mervyn, who served under James II., and attended him during his exile at St. Germains. Some of the ladies of our line were much admired as beauties in their days. My great-grandmother, whom you see there, was considered to be very lovely."

"The wife of Ambrose Mervyn, I suppose. She was a Widdrington, I think?" Dr. Foam remarked.

Mrs. Mervyn replied in the affirmative, and, as the doctor went up to examine the portrait, which was that of a very beautiful woman, in the costume of Queen Anne's day, I looked at it too, and was then struck by a certain resemblance which it seemed to bear to Mrs. Brideoake; so much so, that I almost expected to hear Dr. Foam make a remark to that effect; but whatever he might think, he kept his opinion to himself.

"But, my dear lady," Dr. Bray observed, "there are two other portraits which you have omitted to particularise, though they strike me more than all the rest. They are likenesses, I should say, of a father and son—homines spectatissimæ fidei—very loyal-hearted, determined men."

"You have judged correctly, and characterised them justly, Dr. Bray," Mrs. Mervyn replied, with some emotion. "Both were distinguished for the qualities you mention, and were, in the words of the poet,

'True as the dial to the sun,
Although it be not shone upon.'

Both suffered for their loyalty."

These were the portraits of Ambrose and Stuart Mervyn, which had been recently removed to the place they now occupied.

Very opportunely, at this moment, some arrivals took place, the first of which were Colonel and Mrs. Harbottle. The colonel was a very stout, short man, with a face quite as red as his coat, and snow-white hair. He commanded a regiment of heavy dragoons then quartered at Cottonborough. His lady was a little inclined to *embonpoint*, but still very handsome, with a brilliant complexion, remarkably fine eyes, and a casket of pearls in her mouth which were constantly offered to general inspection. She was twenty years at least younger than the colonel, and they formed a curious contrast, for she was the taller of the two by the head. Mrs. Harbottle was related, though not very nearly, to Mrs. Mervyn, and they were great friends. On the present occasion the colonel's lady was dressed in black velvet, which suited her full, stately figure exactly, and set off her white arms and beautifully rounded shoulders to admiration. The Harbottles were accompanied by their oldest daughter, Rosetta—a good-humoured, lively girl of eighteen, who had neither mamma's figure nor mamma's features, being round-faced, fat, and dumpy; but she had a fresh complexion, and good eyes, which did some execution, though, as she disliked boys, they rarely strayed towards me. When Mrs. Harbottle was presented to Dr. Bray, he seemed greatly struck by her, for I heard him observe in a loud whisper to Dr. Foam: "Sir,—a gorgeous woman —domina venustate eximiâ—quite a Juno, sir." Though very complaisant to her, the doctor was distant and dignified with the colonel, who seemed as glad to get away from him as I had been; making way for two new comers, whose reception by the great man was no less frigid and ceremonious. The first of these, the Rev. Mr. D'Ewes, was tall and thin, and distinguishable for a claret-coloured complexion, an aquiline nose, and a very well made light-brown wig. His thumbs were generally stuck in the arm-holes of his waistcoat, and he moved about his fingers as a seal uses its flappers, often whistling as he talked. The next was the Rev. Hardicanute Freckleton, a large man, rather pompous, inclined to grandiloquence, and fond of a quotation. Mr. D'Ewes and Mr. Freckleton, having made their bows to the "lion," stepped aside, when another lady was presented—Mrs. Addington, a young and handsome widow, with raven hair, and eyes of oriental size and splendour; and, lastly, a gentleman was introduced, whose appearance I hailed with the greatest satisfaction.

A more agreeable person than Cuthbert Spring could not easily be found. What Mr. Freckleton applied to him, during his presentation to Dr. Bray, was richly deserved:

"A merrier man
Within the limits of becoming mirth,
I never spent an hour's talk withal."

He had great vivacity of manner, unflagging spirits, perfect good humour; was as ready to take a joke as to make one; and his droll stories were inexhaustible. I was much attached to him, and he took an interest in me, for he had been my father's schoolfellow and intimate friend, and was chosen groomsman on the occasion of my father's marriage. Mr. Spring had some reason to recollect the circumstance, for in riding home from the wedding he broke his arm. But Cuthbert was no less remarkable for soundness of judgment than for good spirits. He was always ready to advise or to serve a friend, and, as he had more friends than any man in Cottonborough, this was no joke. Sometimes his counting-house was besieged, and it was with difficulty that admission could be obtained to him. What with public meetings, and private business, scarcely a moment of his time was unemployed. He had all sorts of charities connected with the town to dispense; widows without end to advise about their jointures; and spinsters to counsel as to their marriage settlements. In the highest circles it has been said that a matrimonial alliance cannot take place without a certain great duke being consulted; and in Cottonborough, on these occasions, Cuthbert Spring played the part of the great duke. He was sometimes referred to before the family solicitor. A young gentleman about to propose was sure to apply to Cuthbert; while ten to one but the papa would repair to the same quarter to inquire into the said young gentleman's eligibility. Thus, in many cases, Cuthbert was consulted by both parties, and always gave his advice so judiciously and dexterously, that he accomplished the most difficult of all tasks, offending neither if he did not please both. He was everybody's trustee; everybody's executor; everybody's friend; and nobody's enemy—not even his own. Cuthbert was a confirmed old bachelor, of good fortune and good family—hospitable, but unostentatious. Rather under than above the ordinary height, he had large handsome features, so mobile that they took any expression he chose while relating a story; and as he abominated the modern practice of clothing the cheeks with whisker and beard, there was nothing to interfere with their effect. His brow was lofty and ample, and his bright, merry blue eye "begot occasion for his wit." His manner was singularly prepossessing, and he had much of the courtesy of the old school, without its formality, as in his attire he was precise, without foppery. He lost nothing of his stature, but stood remarkably upright.

The ordeal of presentation over, Cuthbert Spring shook me very cordially by the hand, and set off at score as usual: "There ought to be a great deal of wisdom under that wig; though on the principle of good wine needing no bush, a man should hardly hang out a sign to let us know how learned he is. But some folks judge by the outside merely. Well, thank Heaven! pigtails, powder, and periwigs are gone out. I once wore a pigtail myself, but never could manage a wig. Did I ever tell you about Dr. Peacock's wig? No. I will then. Dr. Peacock was very particular—particular about his dress—particular about his eating—particular about his acquaintance—and particularly particular about his wigs, for he had two, one of which was daily powdered and dressed for him by Stoby, the perruquier. You should have seen him strut about with his wig and cane. Well, there were two maiden ladies—sisters—young I won't call them, for they weren't so exactly—but they had charms enough for the doctor, whose wig they very much admired. He was supposed to be paying his addresses to one of them, though *which* was not exactly settled, for both claimed him. Exactly opposite their residence was a shop kept by a widow, who *was* young, and extremely lively and captivating; and for these reasons, I suppose, and because she attracted the young sparks of the town, the two old maids disliked her. Amongst the pretty widow's admirers was my friend Pilcher Phipps, who, being fond of a practical joke, determined to play off one at Dr. Peacock's expense. So being aware of the arrangement with the hairdresser, he goes there one evening, just before dusk, and hires the doctor's full-bottomed wig, and clapping it on, and wrapping himself in a cloak, pretends to sneak into the pretty widow's shop, taking care that the two old maids, who were generally on the watch at that hour, should see him. This trick he repeated on three occasions, and always with success, for the lively little widow good-naturedly favoured the joke. Perhaps she bore no great good-will towards her opposite neighbours, and thought them prudish and envious. After the third evening, the two old maids could stand it no longer, and when the doctor presented himself, in happy unconsciousness, and in the offending wig, they burst like furies upon him, wondering how he dared to show himself in a respectable house, after his improper conduct. He besought an explanation, but they would give him none; till at last they cried, looking daggers, 'Your wig, doctor! We blush to name it—but it has betrayed your proceedings.' 'My proceedings, ladies!' he exclaimed, in utter astonishment at the charge. 'Dear me! is there anything wrong about my wig? It was only dressed last night.' 'We know that, doctor;' and they added, with fearful emphasis, *'and we also know who dressed it.'* 'Really, ladies, I can't see any harm in that.' 'You can't see any harm in it,' they both screamed—'and you have the effrontery to tell us so to our faces. Leave the house instantly, sir, and never let us see either your face or your wig again.' So the doctor was summarily dismissed, and after this mishap, which caused much laughter at his expense, he very wisely took to the covering with which nature had provided his head."

During the narration of this story, a group had gathered round Cuthbert Spring, all of whom laughed heartily at its close, and I have no doubt he would have followed it with another equally diverting, if dinner had not been announced; on which he offered his arm to Mrs. Addington, who was standing near him, and we all went down stairs, Mr. Barton Lever taking Mrs. Harbottle, Mr. D'Ewes Rosetta, and Mrs. Mervyn, of course, consigning herself to the care of Dr. Bray, while I brought up the rear. We were just a dozen—a number which the room could comfortably accommodate. Dr. Bray was placed on Mrs. Mervyn's right hand, and the colonel on her left; but the arrangements of the table were somewhat disturbed by the doctor, who insisted upon Mrs. Harbottle sitting beside him. This being accomplished to his satisfaction, he said grace in a very sonorous voice, and we all took our seats, mine being between Cuthbert Spring and Mr. Freckleton.

G

"A very comfortable dining-room, madam," Dr. Bray observed to Mrs. Mervyn, looking round with satisfaction. "I like your old oak panels, I like your carved sideboard, and I like your old plate. Nothing like an old house. I am reminded of one of our ancient collegiate halls."

"Royal Stuart turtle, or Hanoverian mock?" Mr. Comberbach interposed, offering a choice of soup to Dr. Bray.

"Give me the first, if it be real turtle, sirrah," the doctor rejoined. And speedily emptying his plate, he added: "Nay, it is so good, that I care not if I pay court a second time to the Stuart."

"Very glad to hear it, doctor," Mrs. Mervyn said. "Allow me to recommend a glass of cold punch."

"Made after Lord Widdrington's receipt," our butler said, handing a glass.

"What! the nobleman who was attainted in 1716?" Dr. Bray exclaimed. "I remember he was fond of good living, and carried a bottle of strong soup with him in his march. His punch, therefore, may be better than his politics. Let me taste it. In good truth, it has merit." And, turning to Mrs. Harbottle, he added: "You should not omit to taste this Jacobite mixture, madam."

"I'm afraid it would be too potent for me, doctor."

"Nay, madam; we must strive against our enemies to overcome them. Taste it. Another glass, Mr. Comberbach, and one for Mrs. Harbottle."

"It is a pity you did not bring Mrs. Bray with you to Cottonborough, doctor," Mrs. Mervyn remarked.

"In a forced march, madam, I always leave the heavy baggage behind," the doctor returned.

"Are we to infer that you have run away from your wife, doctor?" Mrs. Harbottle asked, with a laugh.

"Not exactly, madam," he replied, with a glance at her. "But there are occasions when one's wife is quite as well out of the way."

"Indeed, doctor, I don't understand you."

Some fine Ribble salmon, with Townley sauce, was now handed round, and met with universal commendation; and Dr. Bray thought it so good, that he said to Mrs. Mervyn: "Madam, I never expected to admire anything that originated with the crack-brained gentleman, qui temerè et sæpe dejeravit, after whom this sauce is called, but I suppose he picked up the receipt when he served under Louis XIV., and fought under the Duke of Berwick, at Philipsburg."

"It may be so, doctor; but in any case, I am glad you like it," Mrs. Mervyn replied.

At our part of the table we were merry enough, thanks to Cuthbert Spring, who, during the interval of the courses, related another anecdote of his friend Pilcher Phipps, and gave us, this time, an excellent idea of the original of the story, who, from his representation, must have been a little, weasen-faced, high-shouldered man, with a very odd squeaking voice. "Pilcher," Cuthbert commenced, "had a great horror of dentists—most of us have—but as he was tormented by a raging tooth, it became absolutely necessary to call one in, so, after many qualms, he decided upon undergoing the operation in his own counting-house. But when the tooth-drawer came—from fright, I

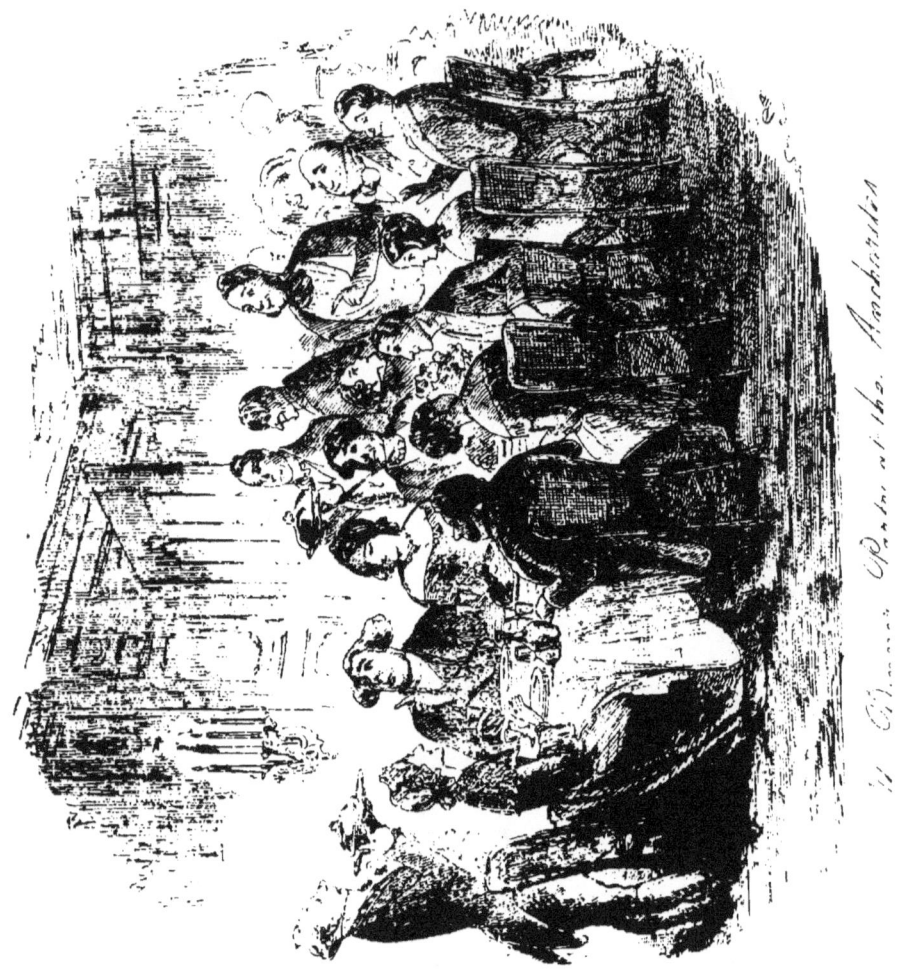

suppose—the pain entirely subsided. What was to be done? He couldn't send back the man empty-handed. He must pay him his guinea. Luckily, Pilcher had a ready wit, and luckily also for the expedient that occurred to him he had a partner, a good, simple, easy, unsuspecting soul, named Sutton, upon whom it was easy to play a trick. Mr. Sutton was immediately summoned, and, on his appearance, Pilcher said, in a whining, hypocritical tone, 'Oh! Mr. Sutton, here's Mr. Faulkner come to extract your tooth.' 'My tooth!' cried the poor man, staring in alarm at the dentist, who was getting his implements ready. 'But it doesn't ache. It's as sound as a rock, and as fast as a church. Who sent for him?' 'I did, Mr. Sutton, because I was sure you'd never have courage to do so yourself. I did it from the best of motives, and entirely out of regard for your convenience, for I knew your tooth had been aching, and was sure to ache again, very likely at a time that would be particularly inconvenient to you. The races are coming on, you know, and you've many other engagements besides—so I felt I shouldn't be acting the part of a friend, if I allowed you to run the risk of such an annoyance. But sit down without more ado. It'll be over in a second.' There was no help for it, so poor Sutton resigned himself to his fate, while the crafty Pilcher hurried out of the room, laughing in his sleeve at the success of his stratagem."

An awkward interruption here took place. Our butler, somehow or other in passing, contrived to hook the large button at his wrist into the curls of Mr. D'Ewes's wig; and, in plucking his hand away too hastily, he laid bare the poor gentleman's naked poll. What Mr D'Ewes's feelings must have been I do not pretend to say. But Mr. Comberbach made matters worse; for, in his fright and confusion, espying Dr. Foam's bald head, and imagining it to be the one he had robbed of its covering, he clapped the hot wig upon it, and pulled it carefully down, before he found out his mistake. Up started the doctor, swearing lustily. Up started, also, Mr. D'Ewes, not swearing, but tremendously wroth; and several minutes elapsed before all could be put to rights. Our butler's apologies and regrets were then accepted, and the dinner was allowed to proceed.

As dish after dish was handed round, and loudly named by Mr. Comberbach, Dr. Bray, who was not prepared for such a strange nomenclature, pricked up his ears. The Gladsmuir cutlets seemed to tickle his fancy, and also to tickle his palate, for he asked for a second supply; and the fillets of rabbits, *à la Chevalier de Johnstone*, did not displease him; but when at length a large raised pie was placed before him, he thought fit to feign great displeasure.

"Madam," he said to Mrs. Mervyn, in a solemn tone, and with great apparent gravity, "I have partaken of many dishes, the names of which were obnoxious to my ears, but I have tolerated them.— nay, more, I have eaten them with relish. I have not raised the voice of reproof against calf's head with Nonjuror Sauce, because I must admit the sauce so named to be meritorious; but I decidedly object, madam, to the Cardinal of York's pie. P. C. may be marked on it, as the girls used to mark their pincushions in the Pretender's times, but that does not appease me. Mr. Comberbach, take away this pie."

"Take it away, sir?" our butler inquired in astonishment. "You are not aware how good it is, sir. It's our cook's *shay doover*."

"That may be," the doctor sternly rejoined, "but I cannot allow it to remain. There are limits even to toleration. Remove it, I say."

"When you goes to Rum, you should do as the Rummuns does, sir; and when you dines with a Jackeybite lady, you should make up your mouth to Jackeybite fare," our butler observed, with more than his customary assurance, for he was highly offended.

Dr. Bray had some ado to preserve his countenance at this sally, but he managed to repeat his injunction with some semblance of gravity.

But when Mr. Comberbach took up the silver dish on which the pie was placed, such an outcry arose from the other guests, that he held it suspended over the head of his mistress.

"Is it really going?" I said to Cuthbert Spring.

"Upon my soul I don't know!" he replied, rising from his seat. "Come, come, this is carrying the joke too far. I meant to have some of that pie myself."

"And so did I," Mr. D'Ewes cried. "I know its excellence of old."

"So did we all," Mr. Freckleton added:

——"The pie—the pie's the thing,
Wherein we'll catch the conscience of the king."

"And upon *my* conscience, ladies and gentlemen, it's a pie worthy of a king—and of the right line too," our butler exclaimed.

On this there was a loud laugh, during which Mrs. Mervyn interposed.

"Really, Dr. Bray, I must insist upon being mistress in my own house. Some of my guests wish to taste that pie, and I beg it may be replaced on the table."

"On the condition only that its heterodox designation be dropped, will I consent, madam," the apparently inflexible doctor replied. "If the letters P. C. be reversed, they may signify Cold Pie. Call it by that name, and my objections vanish."

"What's in a name?" cried Mr. Freckleton:

——"That which we call a rose,
By any other name would smell as sweet."

"Thank you, Mr. Freckleton," Mrs. Mervyn said. "Put the cold pie on the table, Mr. Comberbach. I dare say it will eat just as well under its new name."

"It ought to do, ma'am, for it has been *well doctor'd*," our facetious butler remarked.

Instead of being offended by this piece of impertinence, Dr. Bray laughed heartily, making it evident he had been merely jesting throughout. The pie was set down, but before he could remove the crust, and plunge his spoon into its savoury contents, Cuthbert Spring called out in a loud voice, "Mr. Comberbach, be so good as to hand the obnoxious pasty round. We won't trouble Dr. Bray to help us to it."

Our butler did not require a second order, but carried off the dish to Mr. Spring, who, putting a large portion on his plate, whispered to his neighbours to do the like. We obeyed, and the rest of the party, divining his intentions, followed his example, so that when the pie came back to Dr. Bray, who had watched its progress with some anxiety, it was entirely empty.

"P. C. stands for pie-crust, as well as cold pie, sir," our butler said; "there's plenty of that left, though not much of the Cardinal Prince's good stuff."

Dr. Bray had the good sense not to be offended; and he invited Cuthbert Spring to take a glass of Madeira with him, saying:

"And be sure that, the next time I meet with the Cardinal of York's pasty—I mean cold pie—I shan't send it to you till I've helped myself."

"Sorry you should have been disappointed on the present occasion, doctor. Allow me to send you some of this hare, which is roasted to perfection. You never tasted a boiled hare, perhaps? Nor I. But I'll tell you a story of one. Counsellor Leech was a large man, with an appetite in proportion—a great *bon vivant*, who liked a bit of the best, especially if it could be had at a friend's expense; but of all good things he preferred a roast hare. And he liked it done to a *hair*—well basted, and well froth'd. 'When a man sends one a hare,' he would say, in his big, round voice, ' he ought always to send with it a pound of butter and a quart of cream, or the present is no present at all.' So well known among his circle of acquaintance were his tastes in this respect, that it became a matter of course with them to ask a friend to eat a hare and meet Counsellor Leech. And few could escape the infliction, for he invariably contrived to find out when and where a hare was sent; and on making the discovery, never failed to invite himself to partake of it. Among his acquaintance was Mr. Oldcastle, who determined to put a stop to the practice so far as he himself was concerned; and having received a hamper of game, he thought the opportunity had arrived, for he made sure Leech would hear of its arrival. And so it turned out, for three days afterwards the counsellor popped upon him as he was coming from 'Change, crying out, ' Well, Oldcastle—when do you mean to cook that hare?' 'To-day.' 'Oh, then I'll come and dine with you. Make no stranger of me. Only the hare, mind.' 'You won't object to a woodcock afterwards?' 'Why, no, provided it only flies through the kitchen. Mind that. But give strict orders about the hare. Your cook dresses it well, I know. Bid her not spare the cream and butter—baste it well—froth it well—that's the grand secret. A sharp six, eh? I'll be punctual.' And as the clock struck the hour he knocked at Mr. Oldcastle's door. He was in high glee, and rubbed his hands in ecstatic anticipation of the feast. Presently dinner was announced. A plain boiled sole to begin with. He could trifle with that till better things came. But why not try the sole? His patience was rewarded at last. The principal dish was put upon the table; the cover was raised; when—oh! horror of horrors! in place of the richly-embrowned, well-dressed dish he expected, he beheld a ragged, scraggy, unsightly, utterly uneatable object. The hare was trussed for roasting, but it was BOILED. ' Boiled hare! Whoever heard of such a barbarous proceeding? The cook must be mad, or drunk.'

'I ordered it so,' Mr. Oldcastle calmly replied. 'Let me help you?' 'No, thank you. I'll wait for the woodcock.' And he fumed and fretted till the new dish appeared. 'What's this?' he cried, as the servant uncovered it. 'Boiled woodcock! You must have taken leave of your senses, Oldcastle.' 'A mistake, certainly,' the host replied; 'I told the cook to let the bird merely fly through the kitchen, in compliance with your request; but I suppose it must have dropped into the pot by the way. Try it.' But the counsellor declined, and making an excuse, got away as soon as he could; nor did he ever afterwards volunteer to eat roast hare with his friends. And now, Dr. Bray, let me recommend you a glass of port wine. Counsellor Leech declared it was the correct thing, and he was a judge. Red wine with red meat."

"Well, madam," Dr. Bray observed, after grace had been said and the cloth removed (for Mrs. Mervyn was too proud of her darkly-polished table to keep it covered), "whatever other merits the Jacobites may have possessed—and I will deny them none here—they must have had excellent cookery, and that is much to say for them."

"Much, sir!" Doctor Foam rejoined. "It is everything. I should always be of High-Church and Tory principles in the matter of good living."

"No one but a Tory deserves port like this," Colonel Harbottle cried, smacking his lips. "Admirable indeed!—bright as a ruby. And look at the bee's-wing! You beat us hollow, Mrs. Mervyn. We have no such wine at our mess. Would we had fifty dozen of it."

"It is, indeed, superlatively good—'vinum vetustate edentulum,'" Dr. Bray said, emptying his glass. "I never drank better—perhaps not so good. This increases my respect for the Jacobites; and I am clearly of opinion that, out of compliment to our hostess, of whose hospitality we have partaken, and whose feelings we appreciate, though we may not share them, we ought to drink to the memory of the unfortunate house of Stuart." And he filled a brimmer.

Mrs. Mervyn looked much gratified as the toast was drunk, and so did Mr. Comberbach, who now appeared to regard the doctor as a convert to his own opinions.

"You have many family recollections, no doubt, madam, connected with the Young Pretender's—I beg pardon, the young Prince's—visit to Cottonborough?" Dr. Bray observed.

"A great many," Mrs. Mervyn replied. "The Prince breakfasted in this very room!"

"Indeed, madam!" Dr. Bray exclaimed. "I was not aware of it."

"Yes, indeed, doctor. I have often heard my father relate the circumstance; for, though a mere child at the time, he recollected it perfectly. It was on the 29th of November, 1745; and the main body of the Prince's forces had marched from Wigan to Cottonborough, where preparations were made for his reception. My grandfather placed his house at the Prince's disposal, but it was thought advisable that he should be in the town; and, therefore, Mr. Dickenson's house, in Market-street-lane, was chosen. My grandfather had joined the Prince on the march into England; and when a halt was made at Preston, he rode on to procure all the aid he could. About ten o'clock in the morning, Prince Charles Edward, accompanied by M. d'Eguilles, and attended by a body of Highlanders, arrived here, and was received by my grandfather at the gates with as much ceremony as if he had been crowned monarch of the realms. The Prince was very affable, and said, with a most engaging smile, 'I wish, Mr. Mervyn, that we had many such loyal servants as you in this county. In that case my father would soon be master of his dominions again.' 'Fear nothing, Prince,' my grandfather replied; 'Lancashire is full of loyal men.' And taking my father by the hand, who, as I have said, was but a child then, he continued: 'I devote this boy to your restoration. If I fall he will supply my place.' On this the child kissed the Prince's hand, which was graciously extended to him; while the latter said, 'I trust I shall be able to requite your devotion, sir. The Mervyns have always been a loyal race; and, if I ever mount the throne, your son shall find I have not forgotten his father's devotion, nor that of his grandfather, which was sealed with his blood.' The Prince then entered the house with M. d'Eguilles, and was ushered into this very room, where a substantial repast was prepared for them, and where my grandfather waited upon his Highness. While that was going forward, Colonel Townley and Lord George Murray arrived. The colonel came in booted and spurred, and, dashing his hat upon the table, swore—for, I am sorry to say, he generally swore very profanely—that the Cottonborough folks had deceived him,—and that many of them were rank Hanoverians. 'But we'll send all the wrongheads to the devil!' he cried. Seeing the Prince look a little downcast at what Colonel Townley had said, my father observed, that 'his Highness had only to show himself in the town, and thousands would flock round his standard.' On this the colonel laughed, and, swearing a great oath, hoped it might prove true. The Prince then filled a flagon with wine, and, putting it to his lips, drank to my grandfather, and told him to pledge him; and as my father had come into the room at the time, his Highness said the boy must pledge him too. And he did so. You may be quite sure I set great store on the cup which has been so honoured, Dr. Bray."

"Here it is, sir," our butler interposed, bringing forward the two-handled drinking-cup for the doctor's inspection.

"And how did the Prince look on the occasion?" Mrs. Addington inquired.

"Remarkably well, my father said," Mrs. Mervyn replied. "He wore a Highland dress and sash, and a blue bonnet with a white rose in it."

"And a grey peruke which my grandfather dressed," Mr. Comberbach added.

"Very true," Mrs. Mervyn replied; "but I fear I have wearied you with my Jacobite recollections, Dr. Bray. Do me the favour to pass the wine."

"Perhaps you may have heard, madam," the doctor said, "that it is my custom to smoke a pipe after dinner. You look shocked—but it is so—and wherever I go, I am indulged. The finest ladies of my acquaintance, and the most delicate, permit it. Even royalty respects my weakness, and the Duke of Wessex himself not only tolerates my pipe, but smokes with me. I see I have your consent, and, having obtained it, I care not who else may object. He who desiderates the society of Dr. Bray must take him as he is. Mr. Comberbach, bring me a pipe and tobacco."

Though greatly scandalised, our butler went out, and soon afterwards returned with the articles in question.

"And now, madam," said the doctor to Mrs. Harbottle, when he had filled his pipe, " you shall light it for me. It is a favour I always accord to the handsomest woman in the room."

"Well, doctor, after the pretty compliment you have paid me, I shall not disoblige you," Mrs. Harbottle rejoined, applying the match. And seeing Dr. Bray preparing to exhale a volume of smoke, she got up hastily, crying, "Mrs. Mervyn, I really must make my escape, for I cannot bear the smell of that dreadful weed."

"Nor I," Mrs. Addington cried. And all the ladies got up and hurried out of the room as fast as they could, followed by the laughter of Dr. Bray.

An inveterate smoker like his friend, Dr. Foam took a pipe, and so did Colonel Harbottle, and all three puffed away so lustily, that the room was presently in a state of semi-obscurity. Dr. Bray seemed in elysium, and though he presented a very odd and incongruous appearance in his canonicals while thus employed, his conversation was so amusing, and he started so many subjects, displaying such ingenuity of argument, such wit, and such learning, that all were entertained by him. The fine old port contented the non-smokers, and the smokers were supplied by Mr. Comberbach with a bowl of cold Widdrington punch, which seemed to give them great satisfaction. I went up-stairs long before the rest, and all the ladies declared I smelt so dreadfully of smoke, that they couldn't endure me.

"What will it be, my dear Mrs. Mervyn, when the rest come upstairs," Mrs. Addington observed. "Really this is an odious practice in Dr. Bray. I wonder people can endure him."

"I wonder so, too," Mrs. Mervyn replied; "and I have bought my experience rather dearly. Our old Jacobite gentlemen would never have been guilty of such conduct in a lady's house."

And when the gentlemen did make their appearance, they brought with them an atmosphere of tobacco so dreadfully pungent, that it gave Mrs. Addington and Mrs. Harbottle a violent fit of coughing.

"This is really too bad of you, Harbottle," the latter said.

"My dear, what would you have me do?" the colonel replied, upon whom the combined influences of the punch and tobacco had made some impression. "Consider the great Dr. Bray."

"Consider a fiddlestick. The great Dr. Bray is no excuse for your making yourself disagreeable. Don't approach me. Mervyn, give me that bottle of *eau de Cologne.*" And, after sprinkling some over her husband, she scattered the rest about the room.

It was a great relief to Mrs. Mervyn when, on the departure of her guests, the windows could be thrown open, and a purer air admitted.

I must not omit to mention that Dr. Foam carried off with him the volume of Jacobite correspondence.

CHAPTER XI.

I LOSE MY UNCLE MOBBERLEY, AND BELIEVE MYSELF HEIR TO HIS PROPERTY.

I ROSE betimes next morning, and, mounting Taffy, set out for Marston. On reaching the heights of Dunton I first caugthsight of the mere, gleaming in the valley. Even at that distance I could detect a boat, like a speck, on its smooth surface. I tried to make out Nethercrofts, but though I knew where it lay, it was hidden from me by intervening objects. Riding on through the park, I passed the edge of the ravine where my adventure with the gipsies had occurred, and this set my thoughts running upon Phaleg, when just as I approached a high bank overlooking the road, I chanced to raise my eyes, and detected a black, hairy visage protruded over the edge of the bank. It was instantly withdrawn, but I knew it to be that of the gipsy, and was sorry to find he was still prowling about the country.

My chief business being at the keeper's cottage, I went there first, and, tying Taffy to the gate, entered the dwelling. Sissy was busy about some household employment at the back of the premises, but, hearing me, she came out, and bade me heartily welcome. Having explained my errand to her, she said:

"Why, look you, Master Mirfyn, I shall be fery glad to accommodate your friends, and to nurse the poor sick young gentlemans—profided my husbants has no objections. There are three of them, you say,—a laty, and her daughters, and sons—that's three. Well, we can put the two laties into our own rooms—that's the best—and give the poor sick young gentlemans the other beds, and Ned and I can make shift somewheres. Ay, that'll do. And then there's the little parlours for the laties, where they'll be all alone by themselves."

"Yes, that'll do nicely, Sissy, if Ned approves of the plan, for, as you say, he must be consulted before anything is decided on. But I don't think he'll have any objection, for they are nice, quiet people; and I'm sure you'll like my poor friend John Brideoake, and take as much care of him as you did of Malpas—perhaps more."

As I said this, not without intention, Sissy blushed very deeply, and hung down her head.

"I wish you wouldn't mention him, Master Mirfyn," she said, at length. "He has been the cause of much troubles to me and my husbants."

"I'm sorry to hear it, Sissy; but you may remember my caution at parting. It was in reference to him that I gave it."

"Pless my 'eart, here comes Ned," Sissy cried, opening the window, and pointing out a boat, which was rapidly nearing the shore. We went out to meet the keeper, and almost as soon as we reached the landing-place he leaped ashore, and squeezed my hand with his horny fist. Gaunt and Lupus, and the rest of his four-footed companions, scrambled out of the boat after him. Ned had got plenty of fish, and offered me a fine jack, if I liked to take it to Nethercrofts. I then explained the object of my visit, and was particularly careful to describe the family to him. When he had heard me out, he exclaimed,

"Weel, an' what does Sissy say to it?"

She told him she was quite agreeable.

"If that's the case, so am I," he replied; "though we want no company to make our house merry. Dun us, lass?"

"But this is a charity, and we may do coot, Ned."

"True," he rejoined; "and therefore I say 'Yea,' wi' a' my heart. An' we'n get a' ready for 'em."

So the thing was fully settled to my great delight. Ned appeared so glad to see me, that I stayed with him longer than I intended, and even partook of some of the newly-caught fish, which Sissy would insist upon broiling for me, and which proved excellent. Thinking the keeper should be made acquainted with Phaleg's propinquity, I told him that I had certainly seen the gipsy that morning.

"Then the rascal's comed back again," Ned cried, "for I scoured the whole country round after him, and made sure I had driven him away. I know the spot reet weel where yo' seed him. It's just above the Claylands, and there's a thick copse behind it. I'll hunt him up this very day; and woe betide him if I catch him."

Soon after this I took my leave, and Ned walked by my side down the lane. Just as we were parting, he said:

"Dunna yo' leave your uncle o'ermuch. He's gettin' owd an' dotin'. There's folk as would gladly stand i' your shoon, and wudna care what they did to get into 'em. Tak' a friend's advice, and keep near him. He's weel worth tenting."

Before I got to Nethercrofts I received a second caution.

While mounting the ascent leading to the village, I thought Tally went a little lame, and on examination, finding he had lost a shoe, I stopped at the smithy to get him another. Amongst the odd characters of Marston was the smith, Job Greaseby, a big brawny old fellow, between sixty and seventy, who had once possessed prodigious strength. Of an afternoon Job was a constant visitant at the Nag's Head, but in the morning he might be seen with a leathern apron on, his shirt unfastened so as to expose his ruddy chest, covered with a grizzly pile, and muscular arms bared to the shoulder, directing his men, and sometimes lending them assistance.

The smithy was full of cart-horses, and all the hands employed, so that I should have tarried for some time if Job himself had not undertaken the task.

"I'll make a shoe for your pony, Master Mervyn," he said, "and that's more nor I would do for one of Squire Vernon's hunters. Well, I'm glad to see you, young gentleman. Your uncle has been fretting about you, and fancies you don't want to come near him. I hope you mean to stay now. It were only last night he were talking of you at the Nag."

"Then my uncle goes to the public-house as much as usual, eh, Job?"

"He goes theere more nor usual, an' drinks more nor's good for him. He says he does it to drive away care; but that's not th' way, for though drink may make a mon merry for t' moment, he's worse than ever next day. That's my maxim. Ah! he's never been reetly hissel' sin' th' poor owd ooman's death," Job cried, taking the iron from the fire, and beating it on the anvil; "'as sparks fly uppard, so mon is born to misery,' as t' preacher says, and then he's quenched like this," plunging the hissing iron into the water. Having nailed the shoe on, he put his large hand on the pommel of my saddle, and, leaning towards me, said, in a low tone, "Simon Pownall's a great deal at Nethercrofts now. He allus taks t' owd mon whoam fro' t' Nag, when he's not able to tak' care o' hissel'; and there's no owd missus to look after him. Now, we a' know what t' owd mon intends, and who's to be his heir, for he makes no secret on it; but there's no saying what he may be got to do when he's i' licker."

I told Job I was much obliged to him, and would certainly come over and stay at Nethercrofts very shortly.

"Weel, dunna delay it too long," Job said; "and I tell ye what I'll do meantime. I'll go whoam wi' t' owd chap mysel', to prevent mischief."

On arriving at Nethercrofts, my uncle was delighted to see me, but I noticed a great change in him; he was much more infirm than before, and more querulous. He had just been shaved and put to rights by Simon Pownall, who was present at our meeting, and was as fawning and servile to me as ever, though he evidently wished me far enough. The old gentleman inquired whether I was going to stay, and seemed much pleased when I told him I should certainly return for that purpose in a few days; but my reply did not appear to give equal satisfaction to Simon Pownall.

In the course of the afternoon, while taking a survey of the premises, and strolling through the croft, Simon Pownall came after me, and entered into conversation.

"Nice farm, Nethercrofts, eh?" he observed, with a disagreeable grin. "Well stocked. What do you think your uncle will leave? Upwards of two thousand a year in land and money. Good sum —eh?"

There was a familiarity in his tone that I didn't like, and I showed it by not answering the remark.

"Two thousand a year is no bad thing, and he who gets it may think himself well off."

"What do you mean, Pownall?"

The barber-surgeon tapped his long sharp nose significantly.

"The old man has made two wills already, but he may make a third. Old folks are whimsical. Understand. 'Mum''s the word with me."

"What are you driving at?" I said, sharply. "Come to the point."

Pownall again tapped his beak.

"The old man is a mere child in my hands. Does as I bid him. It rests with me, therefore, whether he makes a new will or not. Understand now—eh?"

"Perfectly—I perfectly understand you, Pownall. You mean to

insinuate that you can induce my uncle to leave you his **property,** if you choose."

"Oh, no! that wouldn't be honest," he cried.

"Honest!" I exclaimed, contemptuously. "That consideration isn't likely to deter you."

Pownall did not seem offended, but sniggered as if I had said a good thing. After glancing round to ascertain that he could not be overheard, he said: "It must be worth something to be *quite sure* of two thousand a year. How much should you say, sir?"

"I haven't given it a thought."

"Then do, and let me know. Only think if it all went to some one else whom you don't like. How mortifying if all these broad acres—that snug farm-house—and all the money snugly lodged in the Cottonborough banks and in the funds, were to slip through your fingers, and go elsewhere. Think of that, and consider what it would be worth to secure the whole. Another person would give a good sum, but 'mum''s the word with me." He paused for a moment, and then added, "Make me your friend, and the whole's yours."

"Never," I replied. "I reject your dishonourable proposal. Not to purchase thrice Nethercrofts would I consent to anything so base. I have listened to you only for the purpose of fathoming your black designs; but my uncle shall know the rascal he has to deal with."

Still Pownall remained unmoved. "Try him," he cried, with a smile. "See what you can do with him. And when you fail, as you will — when you understand my power — come back to me. Always open to an offer. Rather serve you than another. But must knock down to the best bidder."

And he went away laughing, leaving me almost petrified at his assurance, and not a little uneasy, for I was convinced his influence over my uncle must be immense, or he would not venture to act thus. And so I found it; for the old man turned a deaf ear to my hints, and said, "A very good man, Simon. Since I lost thy poor aunt, I can't do without him. He's my right hand."

"But are you sure, uncle, that he always advises you rightly?"

"Quite sure on't, lad. What silly notions hast thou got into thy head?"

Finding him in no humour to listen to me, I thought it better to postpone my disclosures to a more favourable opportunity, and soon afterwards took my departure.

In passing through Cottonborough I called at Preston-court to acquaint Mrs. Brideoake with the arrangements I had made for the accommodation of herself and her family at the keeper's cottage at Marston, with which she was extremely well satisfied. I did not see John, but she told me he was improving gradually, and Dr. Foam thought he might be moved in a couple of days, and had engaged a carriage for their conveyance. This visit paid, I went home.

During the evening I explained to Mrs. Mervyn the necessity that existed of my going over to Nethercrofts, telling her I feared my uncle was in the hands of a very designing person. She approved of my resolution, though she almost feared, she said "that my youth and inexperience would not be of much avail against such cunning and roguery. However, you are a quick boy, my dear," she added, "and it is much better to be on the spot, for there is no saying what a person of your uncle's age and habits may do. It is very unfortunate that he is in the hands of such a knave as you describe Pownall to be, especially as the old gentleman has so much to leave; and it is, indeed, melancholy to think, that as age and infirmities creep upon us, and we are less able to protect ourselves, we become a prey to such wretches. I wish I could be of any service to you, but that is out of the question; and I cannot very well write to Mrs. Sale, for it is a delicate matter, though I am sure she would prevent any improper conduct. She wrote in the highest terms of you to me, and I am sure has your real interest at heart. You may perfectly trust her, though it may appear against her own interest. Heaven bless you! my dear boy This is a very important matter to you; but you must not be too sanguine, in case of disappointment. I will write to Dr. Lonsdale to explain your absence from school."

Owing to some arrangements I had to make, I did not start until late next day, and it was quite dark when I entered Marston. As I passed the smithy, which cast a ruddy and pleasant glow across the road, I saw Job standing near the forge, and hailed him. He told me he was just going over to the Nag's Head, where my uncle had been for the last two hours, and I begged him not to say he had seen me, as I did not want Simon Pownall to be made aware of my return. He promised me he wouldn't, and I then rode on to the farm-house. About two hours after my arrival, I heard a noise in the orchard, occasioned by my uncle and his attendants, and could tell from the scuffling and the tones of his voice that the old man was very tipsy. He was accompanied by Simon Pownall and Chetham Quick, and, practised dissembler as he was, the barber-surgeon could not conceal his vexation at finding me there to receive them. I am sure, from his manner, that he intended to put his plan into execution that night, but my presence deterred him. My uncle ordered some hot water and spirits, but Hannah and I told him he had had enough, and between us we persuaded him to go to bed, while the baffled Pownall was compelled to take his departure empty-handed.

Next day the poor old man was very ill, and could only take a little gruel. He got up, but didn't leave his own room, and, what was very unusual with him, had a fire lighted in it. I meant to remonstrate with him, for it was evident he was abridging the little left to him of life. Simon Pownall made his appearance in the course of the morning, and was going at once into my uncle's room; but Hannah stopped him, saying the old gentleman must not be disturbed. So Simon went out, but his manner awakening my suspicions, I kept watch upon him, and found he had gone into the little garden, and placed himself in such a position as to overlook my uncle's proceedings, which could be easily done, the room being on the ground floor. He continued in this attitude for some minutes, intently observing what was going forward, and unconscious that he was watched in his turn.

But I was called away from my post of observation by my uncle, and promptly obeying the summons, I found him seated by the fire, on which some half-consumed parchments were hissing and crackling. He bade me push them further into the flames, and as I obeyed him, I perceived that one of them was a bond from Dr. Wrigley Sale for 4000*l*. There were other securities, the destruction of which the old man seemed to watch with satisfaction.

"I don't want anybody to be plagued after my death," he said, "and when I am gone, thou'lt tell Dr. Sale thou didst see his bonds destroyed. There are more papers," he continued, pointing to a heap on the bed,—"put them in the fire too,—not too many at a time,—not too many."

They were old memoranda, faded and discoloured by age; but at last I came to something of more modern appearance. It was a packet tied with a piece of black tape, sealed, and endorsed thus: "𝕿𝖍𝖊 𝕷𝖆𝖘𝖙 𝖂𝖎𝖑𝖑 𝖆𝖓𝖉 𝕿𝖊𝖘𝖙𝖆𝖒𝖊𝖓𝖙 𝖔𝖋 𝕵𝖔𝖍𝖓 𝕸𝖔𝖇𝖇𝖊𝖗𝖑𝖊𝖞."

I took it up, but immediately laid it down again, saying to my uncle:

"I suppose I mustn't burn that?"

The old man, who had been very much abstracted during this operation, with his eye fixed on a note in his poor wife's writing, looked at me, and, hastily snatching the packet from me, exclaimed:

"No, no; thou mustn't burn that, lad; that's my will." But after examining it for a moment, he added: "No; it's not my last will. I forgot. But my memory's so bad I can recollect nothing now. There's the right will."

And he pointed to another packet, exactly similar to the one I had taken up, and similarly endorsed, lying on the shelf of the open bureau.

But, as if to satisfy himself, he got up and examined it, and then muttering, "Ay, ay, it's all right," carefully locked the bureau, adding to me: "Now all's safe, and there can be no mistake; put t'other will down. We'll burn it presently. There, lay it on the bed with the other papers."

The bureau, I may remark, stood in a corner of the fireplace, and the room being small, the bed was not far from the window, which was partly open.

The note which my uncle had been examining related to the sale of some cheeses, and thinking it of importance, he desired me to take it to Hannah, and I left the room for that purpose, shutting the door after me. She was in the dairy, and kept me a few minutes to clean her hands before she would touch the paper, but when she had examined it, she said it was of no consequence—"she knew all about it—it had been settled long ago." As I passed through the house-place on my return, Simon Pownall came in from the door leading from the garden. He looked rather confused, but I took no notice of him, and went to my uncle. The old man had thrown a great heap of papers on the fire, which were burning slowly. Not seeing the will where I had left it, I asked him if he had destroyed it, and he said he supposed he had, with the other papers. He then inquired whether Simon Pownall was in the house, and, on my replying in the affirmative, he desired me to call him.

The barber-surgeon glanced at the grate as he came in, and said:
"Making a clearance—eh, sir? Somebody'll be the better for it."
"You'll be the better for it yourself, Simon, for now you owe me nothing. There's your quittance in full."
"Much obleeged to you, sir," Simon replied, obsequiously.
"But I've not forgotten you besides, as you'll find. I've left you a hundred pounds. My will is there, Simon, locked up in that bureau. You know what I mean to do with my money."
"Pretty nearly, sir," Simon replied, looking hard at me.

My uncle then took up the poker to raise the smouldering heap of papers, and let the air in among them. As the pile blazed up, and the ashes flew up the chimney, he laughed childishly.

This business got through, the old man tottered into the house-place, and sat down in his accustomed chair. A weight appeared to be taken from his mind. Pownall gave him a mixture for his cough, which was so troublesome at times that I thought he would be suffocated. He retired early that night, but would not let anybody sit up with him; and about four o'clock in the morning Hannah was aroused by a noise in his chamber, and hastening thither found him in the last struggles.

He expired with his wife's name on his lips.

Hannah took possession of his keys, and when Simon Pownall came, and seemed disposed to assume the management of the house, she let him know pretty sharply he should do no such thing; so, after fidgeting about for some time, the barber-surgeon went away, saying he should despatch his apprentice to Knutsford to let Mr. Gripper know that the old man was dead, with a request to him to come over on the morrow to read the will.

Here, then, was a novel situation in which to be placed. My uncle was dead. Was I really his heir?—master of the house—and owner of 2000*l.* a year? Everybody seemed to consider me so—and I considered myself so.

I did my best to repress them, but I hope I may be pardoned if I confess that, in spite of myself, feelings of exultation would arise in my breast, and I indulged in a thousand extravagant fancies natural to a boy of my age, who finds himself, as he supposes, master of a large fortune. I resolved to live at Nethercrofts, but to enlarge and improve the house, keep hounds and hunters, shoot and fish, and, in short, lead the life of a country gentleman. Ned Culcheth should be my head keeper, and I would double his present wages, whatever they were. Every one of my dependents should experience my bounty, and there should be no stint to my hospitality. I couldn't make up my mind as to what I would do for John Brideoake; but as to Apphia, when she should be old enough, I was quite determined to marry her. At one time I resolved to leave school directly; but, on second thoughts, I decided on going there again, just to let the boys see what a fine fellow I had become; and I pictured myself walking into John Leigh's shop, telling him how rich I was, and treating the whole school. My head was quite turned, and I am sorry to say I thought but little of my poor uncle.

Later in the day I received a very kind note from Mrs. Sale, condoling with me on the sad event which had just occurred, begging me to make the vicarage my home, and to come to them as soon as I liked. I thankfully acknowledged the invitation, but declined it.

A strange world we live in. In the evening, preparations were made for a supper—a "lyke wake" Hannah called it—and several neighbours and gossips dropped in. There was old Mrs. Hutchinson, old Susan Sparkes, Tom Travice, the undertaker (on the look-out for the job), Job Greaseby, Dick Dobson, the parish clerk, Simon Pownall, and Chetham Quick. The latter having just returned from Knutsford, brought word that Mr. Gripper would come over next morning at eleven o'clock to read the will. Simon Pownall also informed us that he had left a message to that effect at the vicarage, and had caused notice to be sent to all parties supposed to be interested, so that he had no doubt everybody would be assembled at the hour appointed. We all sat down to supper, and no one would have taken us for a set of mourners. At first I felt very sad; but mirth is contagious, and by-and-by, as the cans of ale went round, I became as merry and uproarious as the rest. They called me the "Young Squire," placed me at the head of the table, in my uncle's chair, said they were right glad the old man's money had been so well bestowed, and drank my health with a shout. And *then* I thought of him whose place I was usurping, and bitterly reproached myself. However, the feeling quickly passed away. Our mirth was somewhat dashed by Simon Pownall, who, when supper was over, and spirits and water were introduced, related a terrific ghost story. He alarmed us all so much, that Sam Massey and William Weever, who had intended watching by my uncle during the night, immediately declared they wouldn't do it—"not that they were afraid—only they wouldn't"

"And quite right too," said Pownall, chuckling.

"I don't approve of 'watching;' it's a Popish practice, and inconsistent with our Church," the parish clerk observed, gravely.

"Rank Popery," Pownall rejoined. "Glad to hear you say so, Mr. Dobson. *I* wouldn't do it."

"Nor I," Tom Travice, the undertaker, said. "And I speaks from experience."

Pownall then told us another ghost story, more dreadful than the first, and seemed to take a malicious pleasure in the terror he inspired. For my part, I began to fear my uncle would walk in amongst us. Even old Talbot seemed affected, for he refused the drumstick of a fowl which I offered him, though I had seen him take a piece of cheese from Pownall just before the latter began the story, and, creeping under the sofa, the poor old dog remained there during the rest of the evening. Soon after this the party broke up, everybody, except Pownall, renewing their congratulations to me as they went away.

CHAPTER XII.

A NOCTURNAL ALARM.

It had been arranged that I should henceforth occupy the room above that where my poor uncle was lying, and a bed in it had been prepared for my reception; but I confess the barber-surgeon's ghost stories had produced such an effect upon me, that I decided on retaining my old quarters until after the funeral.

When we retired to rest, the men, who had drunk pretty freely, were soon locked in slumber; but feeling no disposition to sleep, I did not even take off my clothes, and sitting down on the edge of the bed, gave free course to my reflections, which were painful enough, for I now severely blamed myself for my levity and folly, and felt utterly unworthy of my uncle's kindness.

In such ruminations hour after hour passed by, and the clock below had just struck one, when I heard a strange kind of noise, apparently proceeding from below, and, being greatly startled, listened for its recurrence with a palpitating heart. But the men snored loudly, and not being able to make out anything clearly, I crept cautiously down stairs, and peeped into the house-place. There were no shutters to the windows, and, the curtains being partially drawn aside, the moonlight streamed in, shining upon the table, which was still standing in the middle of the room, covered with the remains of the supper. But I could see nothing to occasion alarm, and only heard the chirping of the crickets on the hearth and the ticking of the old clock.

Thinking I had been deceived, I was preparing to return, when I distinctly heard footsteps in my uncle's room. It was a dead, dull sound, as if some one were walking about without shoes, or in list slippers. My first impulse was to try and rouse Talbot, who was now sleeping on the hearth, but though I shook him he would not move.

Meantime, my ears were strained to catch the slightest repetition of the sound. For a few seconds all had been still. Then I heard the footsteps again, followed by a noise like the falling of a hammer, or some implement. On this I called out loudly, but the men were too sound asleep to hear me. Hannah, however, whose bedroom adjoined that of my uncle, opened her door, and asked what was the matter. I told her that robbers were in the house; whereupon she hastily retreated and bolted her door, while I ran up-stairs, and with some difficulty aroused the men, who were all very much astonished and alarmed.

During the time occupied by them in huddling on their clothes, I got my gun, which was reared in a corner near my bed, and, loading it, put in a good charge of swan shot. We then went down stairs together, but when I explained to the men that the noise proceeded from my uncle's room, they shook their heads mysteriously, and declined entering it.

"We shan see nowt there belongin' to this warld," Will Weever said.

"Weil, I'll go in, if no one else will," I cried, cocking my gun. On this, Sam plucked up his courage, and, taking down his yeomanry sword, drew it from the scabbard, while Will Weever armed himself with the disabled duck gun, and Peter, unhooking the horse-pistols, grasped the barrel of one in either hand, holding up its brass-mounted butt-end in readiness for action.

In this state we advanced to the door.

After a moment's breathless pause, during which Hannah's head was again popped out, the door was thrown open by Will Weever, and Sam, with the drawn sabre in his hand, sprang into the room. I was close at his heels, and the others followed us. We expected something dreadful, but the only dreadful thing we beheld was the dead man, upon whose rigid features the wan moonlight fell, through the small panes of the uncurtained window.

Sam looked at me, and shook his head; but I declared, whatever he might think, that I had heard footsteps and other noises in the room, and nothing would convince me to the contrary. On this, careful search was made throughout the chamber, and also in the room above, but no one was found, nor was anything discovered to indicate that a robber had been there, for all appeared to be in the precise state in which it was left in the evening. The window was next examined. There were no shutters to it, and though there were iron bars outside, they afforded little protection, being so wide apart, that a slight person might easily get between them. However, there was nothing to prove that such had been the case.

Still, I was not satisfied, and insisted upon the men going with me round the premises, to ascertain that no one was lurking about. Before doing so, I again endeavoured to rouse Talbot; but though I pushed him with my foot, he neither growled nor stirred.

"What can be the matter with the dog?" I cried. "He seems quite stupified."

"He's afeard—that's it," Will Weever replied, shaking his head. "Them dumb creeturs sometimes knows more nor a Christin; an' Talbot may see t' owd mon walking about, or mayhap sittin' in his arm-cheer, though we cannot."

Though this explanation was not entirely satisfactory to me, I accepted it, and we went forth. Our search was fruitless until we came to the garden, where I detected the figure of a man hiding behind a wall, and recognised it at once as that of Phaleg. Levelling my gun, I called to him to surrender. To our surprise, the gipsy came forward, saying he had something worth knowing to tell us, but I must lower my gun, and promise not to harm him. I replied I would make no terms with him, but if he attempted to run away, or offered any resistance, I would certainly shoot him. He laughed, and said:

"Yo'n repent it, when it's too late."

And, without another word, he sprang back, and cleared the wall at a bound. The movement was so sudden, and took me so much by surprise, that he was gone before I could pull the trigger; but I instantly ran up to the wall, and, descrying him running across the croft, fired at him. I had not taken any precise aim, but I am sure I hit him, for he uttered a loud cry, and we afterwards found traces of blood near the spot; while such was the gipsy's fright that he actually knocked down a gate in his haste.

Being now satisfied that I had discovered the cause of the alarm, I returned with my companions to the house, and watch was kept till daylight; but nothing more occurred. Phaleg, it appeared, had visited the hen-roosts, but we could not discover that he had carried off anything. No footmarks could be traced on the gravel walk under the garden window, nor on the little flower-beds adjoining it, and all the household still continued to regard the noises I had heard as supernatural.

CHAPTER XIII.

IN WHICH MY UNCLE'S WILL IS READ, AND I EXPERIENCE THE TRUTH OF THE PROVERB, THAT "THERE'S MANY A SLIP 'TWIXT CUP AND LIP."

SIMON POWNALL came early in the morning, and when told of the nocturnal disturbances, he shook his head gravely, and said he knew what they were. The old man couldn't rest till his will was read. But when Pownall heard about the gipsy, his countenance changed, and he wished I had shot the villain dead. What could bring him there, and a corpse lying in the house? Had the reprobate no conscience? He hoped to see him hanged, and speedily too.

Not having had a wink of sleep during the night, I felt greatly fatigued, as well as harassed in mind, but endeavoured to prepare myself for the important business of the day.

At ten o'clock precisely Mr. Gripper rode into the yard, and dismounted at the door. In outward appearance he resembled a farmer more than a man of law, for he had a broad ruddy face, and a large person; and though, out of respect for the occasion, he had substituted black upper garments for the green riding-coat and striped waistcoat which he usually wore, he still retained his corduroy knees and buff gaiters. He had a nose shaped like the ace of clubs, on which rested a pair of heavy plated spectacles. He was attended by his clerk, a seedy-looking personage, with a pasty face and a snub nose. Mr. Gripper did not think it necessary to assume even a show of grief. On the contrary, he was particularly cheerful, shook me warmly by the hand, and congratulated me very heartily. His shabby-looking clerk, whose name was Elkanah Catchpool, did not presume to shake hands, still less congratulate me, but he made me several ducks with his bullet head as his master introduced me in the following terms:

"In this young gentleman, Elkanah, you behold Mr. Mobberley's heir. This is Master, I should say *Mister* Mervyn Clitheroe, Elkanah—a very good-looking young gentleman, as you perceive, Elkanah, and worthy of his good fortune." Then, turning to me, he added, "Ah! we are not all equally fortunate, my dear young sir. We haven't all rich uncles to provide for us."

"No, sir; indeed I wish we had," Elkanah said, again ducking his bullet head. And he looked so miserably poor, that thinking a guinea would do him good, I resolved to give him one before he went away.

We all three sat down to breakfast, and Elkanah ate voraciously, bolting huge mouthfuls in such a way that I expected he would choke himself. Indeed, he did once get black in the face, and I had to thump his back to set him right. During the repast, Mr. Gripper was continually turning to me, talking about my property, offering various suggestions for its improvement, and at last he told me in plain terms he would find me a steward if I desired it, and the executors consented. I said I was very much obliged to him for the offer, but I had made up my mind to employ William Weever in that capacity, and to keep the whole household just as my uncle had left it. He said my determination showed great good feeling, and had no doubt my suggestions would be attended to, but all arrangements must be referred to Mr. Evan Evans, of the firm of Evans, Owen, and Jones, bankers of Cottonborough, and Mr. Cuthbert Spring, of the same place, merchant, who were appointed trustees and executors under my uncle's will; and he added, that having sent over a messenger expressly the night before to these two gentlemen, stating the object for which they were required, he expected their attendance that morning.

This intelligence was satisfactory to me, though I was quite unprepared for it. I was aware that my uncle knew Cuthbert Spring, and esteemed him highly. I was not surprised, therefore, at the trust reposed in that gentleman; and, on my own part, I was well pleased to have the advantage of such able and friendly advice in the management of the property. Of Mr. Evans I knew nothing except by report. The banking-house to which he belonged was one of the first in Cottonborough.

Breakfast over, Mr. Gripper got up and said,

"Now, Elkanah, we'll proceed to business. Be so good as to step with me, Mr. Mervyn. You know where the will is placed."

The keys being brought by Hannah, we went to my uncle's room. The bureau was unlocked, and the will found lying just where I had seen it. Mr. Gripper took it up, and glanced at the indorsement.

"Halloa! how's this?" he cried.

And opening all the drawers, he peered into them, but without discovering what he sought.

"Zounds! this cannot be it, surely."

"That is my uncle's will, sir, if you are looking for it," I observed.

"He showed it to me himself the day before he died, when he destroyed his papers."

"Oh!—papers, eh? Did he destroy many?"

"Oh! yes, sir; a great many—all his bonds and securities, for he said no one should be troubled after his death; and he particularly charged me to tell Dr. Sale that I had seen his bonds destroyed. I believe my uncle burnt one of his wills."

"Whew!" Mr. Gripper whistled. "That explains it. Changed his mind at the last, I suppose. You say you *believe* he burnt his will. Are you quite sure of it? Mind what you say. It concerns you."

"I didn't see him actually throw it on the fire," I replied, "but I believe I saw it partly consumed. And he told me himself he had destroyed it."

"That's enough," Mr. Gripper said, rather shortly.

For some time after we returned to the house-place Mr. Gripper seemed lost in reflection. His manner towards me became quite altered, and Elkanah, who took his cue from his master, was so far from being humble or obsequious, or even civil, that I determined to withhold the guinea I had designed for him.

By-and-by the expectant legatees began to assemble. There was Harry Heygate, an old farmer, and his two sons. Roger and Ralph, relatives of my aunt's, who had walked over from Dunton; and Adam Worthington and his wife and daughter from Knutsford, likewise relatives on Mrs. Mobberley's side, and some other folks with whom I was wholly unacquainted. Besides these there was Tom Shakeshaft, Simon Pownall, and Chetham Quick, Job Greaseby, Dick Dobson, the parish clerk, and Grimes Earthy, the sexton; and lastly came Dr. and Mrs. Sale, with Malpas. Dr. Sale looked very serious, but he was uncommonly affable to me, almost treating me with respect; Mrs. Sale was kind and considerate as usual, and shed tears as she spoke of my uncle; but as to Malpas, he made it apparent that he came solely on compulsion. I was so disgusted by his unfeeling behaviour, that I would not notice him. Mr. Gripper, I observed, was extraordinarily civil to the Sales, particularly to Malpas, who, however, made a very poor return indeed for his attentions, snubbing him rudely, and turning off as if he would go away.

"You had better stay, my dear young gentleman, indeed you had," Mr. Gripper remarked, with some significance. "Do. You won't regret it."

"Oh! very well, if you wish it, certainly," replied Malpas, shrugging his shoulders. "But what the devil are you waiting for? Why can't you read the will without more ado?"

"We are waiting for the executors, Mr. Evan Evans and Mr. Cuthbert Spring," the attorney replied. "I expect them here every moment, for I appointed eleven o'clock, and it's now a quarter past," he added, consulting his watch. "We cannot open the will till they arrive. A little patience, my good young sir. We have the whole day before us."

"Well, it's a great bore," Malpas cried.

"I'm sorry you find it so, but it cannot be helped," Mr. Gripper replied.

Another quarter of an hour elapsed, and still no executors arrived. Mr. Gripper looked at his watch every five minutes, and began to grow fidgety. I heard him ask Elkanah, in a whisper, if he was sure the messenger had started overnight for Cottonborough, and the clerk replied that he was quite sure of it. The interval was certainly very tedious, for no one knew what to talk about. Outside there was a considerable hubbub, for the farm-yard was full of inquisitive folks from Marston and the neighbourhood, and they were talking and laughing loudly. The cows were lowing in the shippons, and old Talbot, who was now quite lively, was barking loudly at the strangers. In doors we were quiet enough. The poor relatives endeavoured to appear unconcerned, but could not conceal their anxiety. They gathered together in little groups, and I could tell from their glances, which were frequently directed towards me, and with no friendly expression, that I was the chief object of their conversation; and that they regarded me as an interloper, who had no business there, but had artfully contrived to rob them of their rights. Indeed, I was the centre of general observation and remark, and felt so uncomfortable in consequence, that I would willingly have retired, if I could have done so without impropriety.

Keeping aloof from the rest, Malpas flung himself upon the sofa, where he sat, looking the picture of insolent impatience, tapping his neat little boots with a cane, and grumbling audibly. At last, unable to stand it longer, he got up with a gesture of ennui, and was really about to withdraw, when Simon Pownall, who had been hanging about the sofa for some time, stopped him. My attention was attracted, and I caught what passed.

"Heard what Mr. Gripper said, sir. Better stay," the barber-surgeon observed.

"What for?" Malpas demanded, with a sneer. "Only to learn how much that upstart fool has got. No, thankee—I'm off."

"Wait five minutes. Only five. Can't give my reasons now for asking you. Find 'em out in time. 'Mum' 's the word with me."

"You know it's all up with me, and only want to keep me here to have a laugh at my expense, you mischievous rascal. But I'll disappoint you."

And he tried to tear himself away, but Pownall detained him by the button.

"Sit down, my dear—pray," Mrs. Sale interposed.

And as Malpas reluctantly complied, I heard Pownall say to him, "Must have a word with you, after the will is read."

"Must! indeed!" Malpas exclaimed—"suppose I won't."

"Yes, you will," Pownall rejoined, with his abominable cunning grin. "'Cos why? It'll be to your own advantage. Understand. 'Mum' 's the word with me."

At this moment great excitement was occasioned among the assemblage, by the announcement that a post-chaise had driven up to the garden-gate, bringing the long-looked-for executors. Mr. Gripper went to meet them, and in a minute or two afterwards ushered them into the house. Mr. Evan Evans was a middle-aged man, with pleasing features, and his bald head glistened like a piece of marble. He was very deaf and carried an ear-trumpet. Cuthbert Spring looked grave, as befitted the occasion, but I could detect a merry twinkle in the corner of his eye, as he shook hands with me, and said, in an under tone,—" Well, young squire, your fortune's made, I'm told. I didn't expect we should meet again so soon, and under such circumstances. I hope you'll do credit to your good uncle's preference."

" I hope I shall," I replied. And as my conduct on the previous night flashed across my recollection, I thought I had begun but badly. However, I resolved to act very differently in future, and neither to countenance nor permit such proceedings as had then taken place.

Mr. Evan Evans likewise shook hands with me, and after he had apologised to the assembly generally for being so much behind his time, alleging that he had been detained by unavoidable engagements, we all adjourned to the little parlour, where chairs had been placed; and while the principals ranged themselves round the table, Mr. Gripper took his seat, and proceeded to open the will. Next to him sat his clerk Elkanah. Deeply interested as I was, I could not help scrutinising the countenances of the assemblage. Some of the poorer relatives, who stood humbly in the doorway, mixed with the household, looked painfully anxious; indeed, almost everybody had a serious air except Malpas, who was leaning with his back against the mantelpiece, and Simon Pownall, who stood close beside him.

Mr. Gripper adjusted his spectacles, and giving a preliminary cough, all eyes were immediately fixed upon him, except those of Simon Pownall, which I felt were maliciously riveted on me.

" Before I commence," Mr. Gripper sententiously observed, " I may remark that my late respected friend and client, Mr. Mobberley, whose will I am about to read, considerately—very considerately I may say—thought proper to destroy several bonds and securities which he held for various sums lent by him to different parties, most of whom being here present, may consider themselves thereby fully released from their liabilities; but I think it right to observe that such discharges must be considered in the light of legacies."

Mr. Evan Evans, who had held his trumpet to his ear to catch the purport of this speech, exchanged glances with his co-executor.

I took advantage of the pause to whisper to Dr. Sale that I had seen his bonds destroyed by my uncle.

The doctor looked considerably relieved, and said, " Very kind in the old gentleman, indeed."

Some of the other interested parties did not express equal satisfaction, but, on the contrary, groaned audibly.

Mr. Gripper proceeded:

" With regard to what I have to lay before you, I may observe, *in limine*, that, in the course of my practice, I have prepared two wills for my late respected friend and client; one during the lifetime of his excellent wife, and about the time when she had the misfortune to lose a favourite cat (glancing at me), disposing of his property in a particular manner (glancing at Malpas, who returned a look of angry impatience); and another immediately after Mrs. Mobberley's death, entirely altering the disposition of his property (another glance at me) —as regards the person chiefly concerned, though, in other respects, the second will was a mere transcript of the first. One of those wills Mr. Mobberley destroyed on the day preceding his death. It is not for me to remark upon the conduct of my respected friend and client, which an interested party might no doubt consider to be the caprice of old age. It is sufficient for me to state the fact. Without further preamble, I shall therefore proceed to read the will, which, as the only one left, is necessarily the only one that can be acted upon."

Unfolding the document, he then began to read it. But just at this moment there was some confusion at the door, which caused him to stop. Silence being restored, Mr. Gripper went on.

Slowly and calmly he read the will, as if it was no matter to anybody.

Every countenance, however, changed, and looks and gestures of the utmost surprise were interchanged, as it was announced that the person nominated by the testator as his heir, and to whom the bulk of his property was left, was no other than—MALPAS SALE.

Scarcely able to believe what I heard, I interrupted Mr. Gripper, exclaiming:

"Have you read the name aright, sir?"

I saw Pownall's malicious eyes fixed on me, enjoying my confusion.

Malpas, if possible, was still more surprised than myself. He endeavoured to maintain a semblance of composure, and to appear unconcerned, but his flushed cheek and nervously-excited frame betrayed his extraordinary agitation. In a voice of forced calmness, he inquired:

"Are you in earnest, sir?"

"Mr. Malpas Sale," Mr. Gripper replied, with great gravity, but, at the same time, extreme suavity of manner, "I announced to you, and to every one present, that one of your uncle's wills was destroyed. That was the later will, by which Mr. Mervyn Clitheroe was declared to be his heir. But the instrument I hold in my hand must now be acted upon, and by it you take the property."

"Huzza!" Malpas shouted, unable to conceal his satisfaction.

"Malpas, my boy, I sincerely congratulate you," Dr. Sale cried, getting up and shaking his son's hand. "You are a lucky fellow. This is more than I expected."

"Dr. Sale, I entreat; consider who is present, and his disappointment," Mrs. Sale interposed.

"True, my dear," the doctor replied. "Such expressions of satisfaction are unbefitting a serious occasion like the present. I feel it. However, there's some excuse, you must own."

By this time I had in some degree recovered from the confusion

into which I had been thrown, and dashing aside the tears, which, in spite of my efforts to repress them, started to my eyes, I addressed myself to the executors, both of whom appeared perfectly astounded at the unexpected turn that affairs had taken. Cuthbert Spring looked much concerned.

"It is impossible this can be right, gentlemen," I said. "There must be some trickery or fraud, by which my uncle's intentions in regard to me are frustrated. As far as I can, I protest against the will now brought forward, and call upon you, and upon every one here present, to bear witness that I do so. It is *not* my uncle's *last* will; nor ought it to be considered as his *will* at all, for it is totally at variance with his own expressed declarations to me, made within a few hours of his death."

There were confused murmurs among the assemblage at this speech; some of the speakers being for me, but the majority were against me. Mr. Gripper took upon him to reply:

"What you assert, young gentleman, may very well be," he said, gravely. "Your uncle possibly intended to leave you the property, but unluckily for you he destroyed the instrument by which his intentions might have been carried out."

"But I do not believe that he *did* destroy it," I rejoined.

"State your grounds for that opinion," said Mr. Evan Evans, who had listened to me through his ear-trumpet. "Can you produce the other will, or tell us where to find it?"

"I am sorry I cannot," I replied. "But my reasons for believing the will is not destroyed are these: on the day before his death I assisted my uncle to burn a quantity of old papers, amongst which was the document now brought forward by Mr. Gripper."

"Do you mean to tell us that you saw your uncle burn the identical instrument which I hold in my hands?" the attorney remarked, jocosely. "If so, how came it to be restored, in its present uninjured state, to the bureau, where I found it?"

"That I cannot tell," I replied. "I only know it was placed on the bed, ready to be destroyed, while the right will was deposited in the bureau. Of that I am quite sure."

"Well, gentlemen," Mr. Gripper said, with a half-smile, "shall we proceed—or have these observations any weight with you?"

"A moment, if you please, sir," Cuthbert Spring cried. "You say, Mervyn, that one will was laid upon the bed, with other papers, for the purpose of being destroyed. How do you know it was the first will, and not the last?"

"Because my attention was called to the circumstance by my uncle. He told me it was the first will."

"And you afterwards saw that will—whichever it might be—burnt?"

"No; I was sent out of the room for a few minutes, and on my return my uncle told me he had destroyed it."

"Then you did not see it thrown on the fire?"

"I did not."

" Nor partly consumed ?"

" I am not sure. I had left it on the bed, as I have stated, and when I came back it was gone. There were several papers burning on the fire, and my uncle said it was among them."

" The matter is easily explained, gentlemen," Mr. Gripper interposed; " one will has been mistaken for the other; and the last has been accidentally destroyed. That is quite clear."

" I fear so," Mr. Evan Evans said, laying down his ear-trumpet.

" No such thing," I cried. " I am positive of the correctness of what I have stated. My uncle examined the packet in the bureau, and convinced himself that it contained his last will, before he decided on committing the other to the flames. He was extremely particular in what he did, and apprehensive lest a mistake should occur."

" This is certainly singular," Cuthbert Spring said. " Shall we postpone the reading of this document till further investigations can be made ?"

" I scarcely see the necessity of doing so," Mr. Evan Evans replied. " The matter seems clear to me."

" It may be made still clearer, if you choose, gentlemen," Simon Pownall said, stepping forward.

" How so ?" Cuthbert Spring asked.

" What do you know about it, friend ?" Mr. Evan Evans inquired, again putting his trumpet to his ear.

" A great deal. Saw him burn it."

" What! were you in the room, man ?" Cuthbert Spring cried, sharply.

" No; in the garden. Could see him quite plainly, though. Knew what he was about. When Master Mervyn left the room, the old man got up, unlocked his bureau, took out a packet, and tossed it into th' fire, putting t'other, which was lying on the bed, in its place."

" Impossible !" I exclaimed.

" Oh! no, it's quite possible," the barber-surgeon rejoined, with a grin,—" for there it is."

There was no denying that; and as everything seemed against me, I was obliged to sit down.

" What took you to the garden, man ?" Cuthbert Spring inquired.

" Curiosity," Pownall replied. " Always like to know what's going on. Took a peep, that was all, sir."

" Are you satisfied now, gentlemen ?" Mr. Gripper asked.

Cuthbert Spring had nothing more to say, and Mr. Evan Evans replied, " We are."

Upon this the attorney proceeded with the reading of the will.

With the exception of some legacies, the entire property was left to Malpas, in trust, to be paid over to him when he came of age; but this event was deferred until his twenty-fifth birthday—an arrangement which somewhat damped his previous satisfaction, though his spirits again rose when he heard that 500*l.* per annum was to be allowed him in the interim.

My uncle had not quite forgotten me. He bequeathed me 1000*l.*, coupled with an injunction against killing cats, which showed under what feeling the legacy was left. Five hundred pounds were also left to Hannah Massey, provided she married William Weever, and 500*l.* each to the executors. Simon Pownall and Job Greaseby, likewise, came in for 100*l.* each. I forget the rest of the legacies, but they were not much.

When he had done reading the will, Mr. Gripper arose, and, walking into the house-place, the rest followed him there, with the exception of Cuthbert Spring, who remained behind with me.

"I am very sorry for you, my dear boy," Cuthbert said. "It is a bitter pill, but it must be swallowed. And, after all, it is, perhaps, just as well that this fortune should not have come to you, for you will now be compelled to work, and may in the end be better off in all respects than you would have been otherwise. Depend upon it, what a man gains by his own exertions has a twofold value."

"I should not care for what has occurred, if I did not feel that I have been defrauded of my rights—most likely by the contrivance of Simon Pownall. He is a designing knave, and I am sure the statement he made was utterly false."

"Yet it appears to be borne out," Cuthbert Spring replied; "and I fear the real explanation of the fatal mistake is, that poor Mr. Mobberley did not know what he was about. Such is my conviction. Was Pownall trusted by your uncle?"

"So much so, unluckily, that the rascal tried to induce the old gentleman to make a will in his own favour; and failing in that, he has resorted to other underhand measures, of which the result is now apparent. Why, there he is!"

"What! your uncle?" Cuthbert exclaimed.

"No—Pownall," I replied, pointing to the window, close to which was the malicious countenance of the barber-surgeon.

On seeing he was observed, he retreated.

"I hope he has overheard what I said of him," I remarked.

"Listeners never hear any good of themselves, that's certain; and he is a strangely prying fellow," Cuthbert rejoined. "Come, let us go into the other room. Don't be cast down. There are always people malicious enough to rejoice in the mortifications of others. Don't gratify them."

"I won't," I replied, firmly.

And we went into the house-place, where the party were partaking of biscuit and wine, and I heard much coarse jesting at my expense, which even my presence did not restrain. It was a relief to me to find that Mrs. Sale was gone. After a little private conference with Mr. Gripper, to whom they gave certain instructions, the two executors departed; Cuthbert Spring telling me he would watch strictly over my interests, and if anything came to light which might benefit me, he would not fail to take instant advantage of it.

As soon as the executors were gone, Simon Pownall, who had kept out of the way till then, reappeared, and approaching Malpas, who was chatting and laughing with his father, signified that he wanted a word in private with him.

On this Malpas went with him into the little parlour, where they were closeted together for some time.

When Malpas came out he looked so much perturbed, that his father asked him what was the matter.

"Oh, nothing," he replied.

I could not resist the impulse that prompted me to go up to him, and say, "So, Pownall has told you how he managed it,—and has bargained for his reward, eh?"

Malpas stared at me, quite confounded, and turned excessively pale.

"I don't understand what you mean," he stammered out.

"Yes, you do," I replied, speaking with great vehemence; "you understand me well enough, for I can read in your looks what has passed between you and that villain. He has changed the wills—I know he has. What do you give him for the job?"

"Really, Mervyn," Dr. Sale interposed, "I cannot allow this intemperate, this improper language to be addressed to my son. I can make every allowance for your disappointment, and the bitter feelings it must naturally engender; but your passion carries you too far, and you must not bring serious charges like these against a respectable man—a highly respectable man—like Simon Pownall—a man whom I myself have known for many years, and who, during the whole of that long period, has conducted himself with the utmost propriety, and borne a character above reproach or suspicion."

"Entirely above suspicion, Dr. Sale," the barber-surgeon cried, advancing. "Hold my head as high as any man. What has Master Mervyn to say against me?"

"Better leave him alone, Simon," Dr. Sale said, with bland dignity.

"Oh! let the fool go on," added Malpas, who had now recovered his audacity, "he'll only get deeper in the mire."

I was so enraged, that I felt inclined to knock him down, but my loss of temper had already given my opponents such evident advantage over me, that I tried to calm myself; but it was no easy task.

"Let me ask Simon Pownall one question?" I cried.

"Twenty, if you please, sir," the barber-surgeon replied, readily, and with a self-satisfied grin, as much as to say, "You'll find yourself no match for me."

"Did you not offer to make all sure for me with my uncle if I would pay you a large sum of money?"

"Decidedly not. No motive for doing so. Believed you his heir."

"Of course you did, Simon," Dr. Sale observed; "so did we all."

"Ay, we all believed it," the assemblage chorused.

"Any more questions?" Pownall said. "Clever young man, Mr. Gripper?" winking at that gentleman.

"Remarkably clever," the attorney replied, with a smile. "Ought to go to the bar."

"Will go to the bar, perhaps," Simon said, facetiously

"It was foolish in me to put any questions to you at all, Pownall," I cried, "for I might have known that a man who would make such a nefarious proposal as you did to me, would not hesitate to deny it. What I intend to ask shall be asked elsewhere, and in a different manner."

"Look to yourself, Master Pownall," the attorney observed, jocosely. "Mr. Mervyn decidedly means to prosecute you."

"Quite welcome," the barber-surgeon replied. "Meantime,—let me ask *him* a question. It shall be a poser."

"Does it relate to the will?" Mr. Gripper said.

"It does," Pownall rejoined. "Attention, gentlemen. Si—lénce! Now, sir," addressing me, "no equivocation—direct answer—WHO SHOT THE CAT?"

"Ay, ay—who shot the cat?" several voices repeated, amid the general laughter of the party.

Stung by this insult, I seized hold of Pownall's long nose, and tweaked it so severely that I speedily changed his note; but when Malpas advanced to the rescue, I quitted my hold of the barber-surgeon's proboscis, and dealt my younger opponent a blow, which drove him with considerable force against his father's fat paunch, and caused him to trample on the reverend gentleman's gouty toes, eliciting as many oaths from the doctor as he had breath left to utter. In the scuffle that ensued, old Talbot came to my assistance, and, snapping right and left, cleared a passage for me to the door, where Elkanah Catchpool attempted to oppose my egress, but seeing the dog approach open-mouthed, the scoundrelly clerk turned tail and fled, and I had the satisfaction of seeing him chased round the farm-yard, and finally deposited in the black pool near the pigsties, into which he soused in his efforts to escape.

How I got there I scarcely know, but I found myself beside my mother's grave. There I burst into tears—there, after a while, I found consolation. A gentle voice seemed to whisper peace to my troubled breast. I no longer burnt with anger, nor meditated revenge. The last twenty-four hours had wrought a great change in my character, and had given me thoughts beyond my years. I had imagined myself possessed of a large fortune, which, suddenly as it came, was wrested from me. I had indulged in dreams of the future, which had vanished as quickly as they rose. My momentary elation had been followed by bitter disappointment. I hoped what I had gone through might be a wholesome lesson to me, and, as I stood there, I felt it would be so.

"Perhaps it is for the best," I cried. And a voice from the grave seemed to repeat my words—"Yes, it is for the best. This is but a trial."

But the trial was severe; and how much I regretted that I had no mother's tender bosom whereon to repose my throbbing head after the conflict.

CHAPTER XIV.

I AGAIN ENCOUNTER PENINNAH.

I STAYED by the grave more than an hour, when I heard the gate opened, and distinguished the voices of Dr. Sale and Simon Pownall, and not wishing to be discovered by them, I leaped the low wall that bounded the churchyard on the side of the mere, and making my way down the steep descent, and through the narrow copse skirting the water, sat down on the stump of an old tree to meditate.

While thus musing, I perceived Ned Culcheth rowing his boat, in a very leisurely manner, across the mere, and remarking also that a little girl was seated near him, it struck me that the latter must be Apphia Brideoake. And so it turned out; for, as Ned drew nearer, I could distinguish her features distinctly. And she also caught sight of me at the same moment, and stood up in the boat, waving her hand to me in recognition. On this, Ned pulled vigorously towards me, and in a few minutes afterwards I had sprung on board, and was seated by Apphia's side, making inquiries about John and her mother.

She told me they had arrived on the previous night, and were quite delighted with the cottage I had chosen for them. It was so clean and comfortable, and airy—so unlike the lodgings they had quitted. John was better—much better—but, being fatigued with the journey, he had not yet left his room. Apphia was in raptures with Sissy, and spoke of her good looks and good-nature with childish admiration; while Sissy, from Ned's account, was equally charmed with her, and couldn't make enough of her.

"Hoo would ha'e me tak little miss out i' my boat when I comed back fro' Nethercrofts," he said.

"And if he hadn't done so I shouldn't have met you, dear Mervyn," Apphia cried.

This was unanswerable, and I could only say how much obliged I felt to Sissy for her attention; but I added, to the keeper:

"You've heard what has happened, then?"

"I tarried i' th' farm-yard till a' were known, and then I comed away," he replied. "There's been foul play somewhere."

"Little doubt of it, Ned. But what can't be cured must be endured."

"True. But, mayhap, this *can* be cured. However, we munnot talk on't now. There's little missy wonderin' what we mean."

"What is it, dear Mervyn?" Apphia asked, fixing her large blue eyes inquiringly upon me.

"I have been building castles in the air, and they have melted away," I replied.

"That's rather above my comprehension," she rejoined; "but I can see it is something that distresses you, and therefore I'm sorry for it."

"Land us for a moment near Throstlenest-lane, Ned," I cried, anxious to change the subject; "there's a bank in it which is generally covered with primroses and violets at this time of year, and I should like to send a nosegay to the invalid. You will take it to him, Apphia?"

"Oh! that I will," she answered, joyously.

The keeper readily complied, and we soon stepped ashore. As I expected, we found plenty of violets, and the banks were literally starred with primroses. How full of delight was Apphia as she culled a little nosegay for her brother! How like a sylph she looked as she flew from spot to spot, or paused in her task to listen, enraptured, to the songs of the birds from the adjoining copses! When I had first beheld her I thought her an exquisitely beautiful child, but her beauty inspired uneasiness, for it appeared transient as a fitful bloom upon the cheek. Now health seemed reviving, and strong hope was held out that her nascent charms would be brought to maturity. I watched her with the greatest interest. What witchery was there in her every look and every movement! What transports of delight she exhibited when the thrilling notes of the throstle reached her ear! How she clapped her little hands, and ran herself out of breath, in mounting the steep acclivity!

"Where did the lane lead to?" she inquired. I told her to Nethercrofts. "Oh! how much she should like to see the farm-house!—Was it far off?" And then, seeing me look grave at the inquiry, she begged pardon for making it.

"Apphia," I said, "you shall now hear what has happened. My uncle is dead, and Nethercrofts and the lands belonging to it, which I expected would be mine, have gone to another. I have reason to think I have not been fairly dealt with, and shall make every effort to obtain my rights, but I doubt whether I shall succeed."

"That depends upon yourself, my pretty little gentleman," a voice cried. "If you go the right way to work, you will—not otherwise."

"Who spoke?" Apphia said, in a low tone, with a look of surprise mixed with alarm. "I see no one."

"Neither do I," I answered, gazing round; "but I know the voice. It is that of Peninnah, the gipsy-woman."

"You're right, my pretty gentleman—it is," Peninnah cried, coming from behind some bushes, which had screened her from our view.

Apphia clung to me with alarm as the gipsy-woman advanced towards us.

"Don't be frightened," I said; "she shan't injure you."

"I don't wish to injure her," Peninnah rejoined, "and I don't wish to injure you, my pretty gentleman, though you've hurt my husband, and tried to take his life. I bear you no malice. If I wanted to do you a mischief," she added, with a look that made Apphia tremble in my arms, "you would soon find out whether I had the power or not. But I don't—and I don't blame you for shooting at Phaleg, though he was going to do you a good turn at the time. But how should you know that? You weren't likely to trust him."

"No, indeed," I replied. "And I scarcely know whether I ought to trust you. But I will. What have you got to say?"

"I can't tell it now," she rejoined; "neither can I tell it without Phaleg's consent, and I'm not sure he'll give it. Indeed, I'm certain he won't, unless you make it worth his while."

"What will make it worth his while?" I asked.

"That's for him to settle—not me," she answered. "He bears you no love, you may be sure, my pretty gentleman, and wouldn't let me make terms with you, nor even speak with you, if he could help it. However, I don't mind him."

"What am I to do, then? What do you recommend?" I asked.

Peninnah cast down her eyes to reflect. And during the momentary pause, Apphia whispered something to me, but I did not catch its import.

"A month hence you shall know," the gipsy-woman said, at length.

"A month hence! that's a long time," I exclaimed.

"You may thank yourself for the delay," she rejoined; "you've wounded Phaleg, and he won't be quite well till that time."

"Oh! then, I'm to have an interview with him, eh? Where is he?"

"You don't expect me to tell you that? But I'll tell you where to find him. In a month's time he'll be all right, as I've said. This is Friday. On Friday month, at midnight, be in Marston Church-yard, at the back of the church, near the mere. You shall meet him there. I'll answer for your safety."

"Why appoint such an hour and place?" I asked, feeling Apphia shudder, while a tremor ran through my own frame.

"Because it will suit Phaleg. I've no other reason. You'll come?"

"I don't know," I replied, hesitating.

"Oh, no, don't promise—don't go, dear Mervyn," Apphia entreated.

The gipsy-woman looked hard at her.

"You're very fond of him," she said, with a cunning smile. "Are you his sister? You're pretty—but you're not like him."

"I'm not his sister," Apphia answered, with a slight blush; "but I don't want him to run into danger."

"Oh, bless your tender little heart! he won't do that," Peninnah rejoined. "He'll come; for I've seen him in real danger afore now, and I know he's one as isn't easily frightened. He'll run no risk now; and, as I said afore, if he goes the right way to work, he'll larn summat to his advantage—ay, greatly to his advantage."

"Well, I'll keep the appointment," I said. "But you must tell me which is the 'right way' you speak of."

"You'll easily find that out. Mind, you must come alone; and mustn't mention the meeting to a single soul. Can you keep a secret, my pretty miss? You look as if you could."

"I can, if I choose," Apphia replied.

"Then you *must* choose and do so now, for it consarns him more than it does me or mine. Let me look at your hand, my little dear."

Apphia, however, was very unwilling to comply, but at last, at my request, she held it out.

"Are you going to tell her her fortune?" I asked, after the gipsy had attentively studied the lines on the small palm for some minutes.

"I want to satisfy myself on some points," Peninnah answered. "She ought to be born to good luck and high places, but misfort'n and poverty have been her portion hitherto. That I can see. You may fancy I'm deceivin' of you in what I'm agoin' to say, but I'm bless'd if I am. Her future happiness will mainly depend on what takes place on that Friday night I've mentioned."

"Ah! you want to induce me to go," I cried.

"If I do, it's for your own good—as well as for hers," she rejoined. "And now I've done. Recollect my caution. Alone, and at midnight, in the churchyard."

"On this day four weeks. I will be there," I returned.

And Peninnah stepped behind the bushes, while Apphia and I retraced our steps towards the boat. As we went on, the little girl remarked:

"You did not take any notice when I whispered to you that some one was watching us."

"I did not—because I did not hear what you said," I replied. "Was it her husband—Phaleg? But why do I ask, when you don't know him."

"The man didn't look like a gipsy. I could only see him indistinctly, for he tried to conceal himself behind the hedge."

"Should you know him if you saw him again, Apphia?"

"I think so, but am not quite sure."

As we were speaking, Ned Culcheth, who I thought had been in the boat, jumped down the bank and joined us.

"Have you seen any one about, Ned?" I asked.

"Only Ninnah, the gipsy," he replied; "I seed her talkin' wi' you; an' I heerd what she said, too. I mean to be i' th' churchyard that neet os weel os you."

"Then it was Ned you saw, Apphia?" I cried.

"No, it wasn't," she answered; "it was a much shorter man, and much older; a man with a very long nose."

"Then it was Simon Pownall, I'll be bound," I cried; "he must have seen me leave the churchyard, and has kept me in view, and dogged me about, ever since. It's just like him. The rascal has the longest nose in Marston, and pokes it into everything—but I gave it good pulling this morning."

I was not sorry that Ned had overheard what had passed between me and the gipsy-woman, because I could now talk the matter over with him without any breach of confidence; but I was very much vexed that Pownall (if it indeed were he, as I could scarcely doubt) should have been a listener likewise; and I determined to concert

I

measures with Ned, between this and the appointed meeting, to defeat any mischievous designs the prying rascal might form.

I did not embark again, but took leave of Apphia, promising to call and see them all at the cottage next day; and having watched the boat pursue its course across the mere, I turned back, and proceeded slowly to Nethercrofts.

CHAPTER XV.

I MEET PHALEG AT MIDNIGHT IN MARSTON CHURCHYARD, AND MY UNCLE MOBBERLEY'S GHOST APPEARS TO US.

A MONTH had passed by, and the Friday had arrived on the night of which I was to meet Phaleg. I was all anxiety for the interview, as I felt it might be of importance to me, and had fully prepared for it; but, before detailing the strange events of that night, I must briefly relate what had occurred in the interval.

I was still staying at Nethercrofts, for, in compliance with the directions of the executors, no change whatever had been made in the establishment; and William Weever and his wife (for he and Hannah were already united), to whom the management of the house and farm was entrusted, were very kind to me, and expressed great concern at my disappointment. I believed them to be sincere, and felt their kindness much. Malpas had not been near the place since the day on which the will was read, and I had only seen him once— at the funeral, on which occasion he acted as chief mourner. *Acted*, I may say, in every sense; for his pretended grief was disgusting, not only to me, but to the greater part of the numerous assemblage of mourners. He carried a fine cambric pocket-handkerchief in his hand, which he constantly applied to his eyes, and when the coffin was lowered into the earth, and the poor old man was once more laid beside his wife—from whom he had only been a few months separated—he gave utterance to a loud groan. I could hardly restrain myself; but I did. When all was over, we confronted each other, and I gave him a look which told him plainly what I thought of him. He turned away, pretending to wipe the tears from his eyes, and again groaned loudly. Unable to stand it longer, I snatched the handkerchief from him, and threw it into the grave, crying out,

"Away with this mockery of sorrow! You shall not insult the dead longer."

Malpas made no reply, but retreated a step or two, while his father advanced towards me, with a countenance charged with frowns. The thunder burst in this way:

"Sir, your behaviour is scandalous. Talk about insulting the dead, indeed! I should like to know who has exhibited most indecorum—

most insensibility on this sad and solemn occasion—you or my son? If you felt as you ought, you would blush for what you have done; but I fear there is little shame in your composition. But though you have disgraced yourself by your conduct, sir, you have unintentionally done my son a service. You have shown how unworthy you are to be your uncle's heir. You have proved how rightly and wisely the excellent old man acted in cutting you off from his property at the last moment. It is well that his money has gone from you, sir, for you would have made bad use of it. This is the second occasion on which you have shown how ungovernable is your temper, and how little regard you have for the decencies of life, or the duties of a Christian. Nothing appears to restrain you. But be warned in time, or you will bring disgrace on all connected with you. You will come to be hanged, sir. That you may amend your ways is the worst I desire for you. Go home, sir, and reflect on what you have done."

So saying, and leaving me a good deal abashed by his reprimand, which I felt to be, in some degree, deserved, the doctor withdrew with his son. He was right in stating that I had done myself an injury by yielding to the impulse of passion, though I had some cause for it; for my conduct operated greatly to my disadvantage in the opinion of the bystanders. Amongst those who were loudest in censuring me was Simon Pownall, and he found many to agree with him. I went home in no enviable frame of mind.

After this, I should certainly have returned to the Anchorite's, but I had two inducements to remain at Nethercrofts which overcame all my objections to continue in the neighbourhood of the Sales: one was my desire to meet Phaleg, and learn what he had to disclose, and the other was the propinquity of the Brideoakes, with whom I passed the greater part of each day. I had written to Mrs. Mervyn, telling her how unluckily for me things had turned out, and had received a very kind and consolatory letter from her in return. She told me that Cuthbert Spring had called upon her, and acquainted her with all the circumstances of the case. She offered no opinion of her own as to the possibility of fraud being practised in regard to the will, but said that Cuthbert Spring had expressed his conviction, in which his co-executor concurred, that the destruction of the document which would have been advantageous to me was purely accidental. "Under these circumstances, my dear Mervyn," she wrote, "there is nothing for it but submission. Your loss is to be regretted, certainly, as every loss must be, but I shall be sorry if it occasions bad feeling between you and Malpas. Had you been the gainer by the *accident*, for such, in compliance with Mr. Cuthbert Spring's opinion, I must call it, I believe—nay, I am sure—you would have acted very differently towards him from what he is likely to act to you. But that is no reason why you should display resentment. You are not without friends, and you do not want a home, so, though you have not gained what you expected, and no doubt feel some annoyance in consequence, you will soon get over it, and are not, indeed, much to be pitied. I suppose you will come home after the funeral."

Such were the terms of her letter. Not wishing to return for the reasons I have stated, I therefore wrote to beg she would allow me to remain a month where I was, and she kindly complied with the request.

I have said that I spent the greater part of my time with the Bridconakes, and I had now not only the companionship of little Apphia, but of John, who had become so much stronger that he was able to take short walks with us, and, if the days were fine, to pass a few hours upon the mere. Ned's occupations did not allow him always to go with us, but he let us have his boat when we pleased, and as I could manage the oars pretty nearly as well as himself, I used to row the two young folks about. There was scarcely a nook of the lake that we did not visit; and wherever there was anything to be seen on the banks, Apphia and I landed, leaving the invalid on board. Three weeks had transformed the little girl into a new creature. She was now full of health and spirits, and blithe as a bird on a spring morning. Her brother's recovery was much slower in progress, but he gradually and surely made way, and towards the end of the month I no longer entertained any apprehensions for him. All his ardour and thirst for knowledge returned, and, if he had been allowed his own way, he would have resumed his studies as unremittingly as ever. But this being entirely counter to Dr. Foam's orders, all books were kept out of his way by his mother. He was a strange boy, John Bridconake; and I now became confirmed in my opinion that he would become a remarkable man. He would sit for an hour together in the back of the boat, completely abstracted from the scene around him, undisturbed by the lively chattering of his sister, and almost unconscious that he was alone, if we left him when we landed. At such times he was taxing his memory to the utmost, recalling passages in the books that were denied him, and forcing his brain to work, though such toil was strictly interdicted. When this process of study was over, his countenance would light up, and he would become as gleeful as Apphia herself—would watch the shadow of the boat as it cleaved the water—would pluck a bulrush in the reedy shallows, and use it as a fairy lance against some imaginary opponent—would expatiate in rapturous and eloquent terms on the beauty of all around him, viewing the scene as a painter might have viewed it, and describing it like a poet. I listened to him, on these occasions, with wonder; and even Apphia hung mute upon his words. Neither of us had ever heard him talk so before, for he sometimes spoke as one inspired.

I have not mentioned Mrs. Bridconake hitherto, though I saw her daily, of course, for I cannot say that I liked her, nor that she improved upon acquaintance. I began to feel the same awe for her that her children entertained. She was the haughtiest woman, and the most absolute, I ever met with. John and Apphia were accustomed to obey her implicitly in everything, and she exercised complete tyranny over them. Even John's strong mind was subdued by her And now that I was so much with them, and, as it were, a member of the family, she treated me in the same manner. I had naturally acquainted her with the disappointment I had experienced, and, instead of sympathising with me, she blamed me for allowing myself to be outmanœuvred. Malpas, she said, had shown himself the cleverer of the two. Success, with her, however obtained, always commanded applause; failure found no excuse, and only met with contempt. I wondered she maintained such opinions, considering the reverses which she herself had experienced; but so it was; and argument with her was out of the question, for she never allowed the slightest contradiction. To Ned Culcheth and his wife she was extremely condescending, and they thought her a perfect lady, as indeed she was, though a very proud and disagreeable one; but with her children and with me she was imperious and exacting. She frequently questioned me about the Sales—particularly Mrs. Sale —of whom I was glad to be able to speak in high terms. The warmth of my praises excited Mrs. Brideoake's derision, and I could see I had sunk in her estimation as a poor-spirited fellow.

It so happened that Mrs. Sale heard that a family was staying at the keeper's cottage—indeed, she saw them all at church—and, making inquiries about them from Sissy, she intimated her intention of calling upon Mrs. Brideoake. When this was communicated to the proud lady, she said,

"I hope she won't give herself the trouble. I won't receive her. No one shall intrude on me."

Poor Sissy did not dare to remonstrate, but she thought it better to make some excuse to Mrs. Sale, and consequently the visit was not paid. In justice to this excellent lady, I am bound to say that she did her best to bring about a reconciliation between me and Malpas, but I declined all overtures, and on two or three occasions when she came over to Nethercrofts expressly to see me, I am ashamed to say I kept out of her way.

But, as I have said, the long-expected Friday had arrived, and even the very night was come, on which I was to have the mysterious interview with Phaleg. Apphia had often tried, in her childish way, to dissuade me from keeping the appointment, by representing the danger I should incur; but I was proof against her remonstrances. Independently of all other considerations, there was a romantic character about the affair, exactly in accordance with my own notions of an adventure. Whatever the risk might be, I was resolved to run it. Not a word relative to the meeting had been mentioned to John either by myself or Apphia, for we would not violate the confidence reposed in our secrecy. But, as Ned Culcheth had become aware of the circumstance, the case was different with him. My only real apprehension was in regard to Simon Pownall, and if I had encountered Peninnah in the interim, I would have got her to change the place of rendezvous, so as to thwart any designs the rascal might have formed; but she had either left the neighbourhood, or kept out of my way, for I saw nothing of her. The only plan to be adopted under the circumstances was the one suggested by Ned, to the effect that he, Culcloth, should keep watch over the barber-surgeon's dwelling during the whole of the evening, and if he perceived him come forth, should follow him, and prevent any interruption on his part. After due consideration this was agreed to. It might appear that I should have some difficulty in leaving Nethercrofts late at night without explaining my errand; but I gave myself little concern on this point. I had known the men slip out too often during my poor uncle's lifetime, not to feel quite sure I could manage matters in the same way.

Oh! how slowly—how very slowly time passed that evening. I could settle to nothing—could think of nothing but the meeting. At nine o'clock the men went to bed, but pretending to be deeply interested in a book, I remained down stairs. After a while, when all was quiet, I extinguished my light, and threw myself on the sofa, in anxious expectation of the hour for starting. I did not dare to sleep, nor, indeed, do I think I could have slept, even if certain of awakening at the right moment. I counted the minutes by the ticking of the old clock, and thought it went slower than usual. At last, to my great relief, it struck eleven. Then I arose and moved noiselessly across the house-place. But, quietly as I proceeded, I roused Talbot, who had been slumbering, as usual, on the hearth. I had taken off my shoes, and left them near the back door with my gun, which was loaded. The bolt was gently withdrawn, the latch raised, and I stood in the farm-yard. Talbot had come out, too; for though I would rather have been without him, I could not send him back without making a noise, which would have betrayed me. Having carefully closed the door, and put on my shoes, I shouldered my gun, and set off with the old dog at my heels, congratulating myself upon the success which had hitherto attended my movements.

The moon was in her last quarter, and every now and then was visible through drifting clouds, shedding a ghostly glimmer around; but generally speaking it was profoundly dark. It was also extremely cold, and I walked fast to keep my blood in circulation. My way lay across the fields, and for some distance the path skirted a hedge, in which grew many large trees. While speeding along, I fancied I heard footsteps behind me, and looked back in some trepidation; but though my eyes were by this time accustomed to the gloom, I could discern nothing except a pollard elm a few yards off. I then stopped for a moment, but as no one came on, I proceeded in my course, and as I did so I again heard the footsteps. They might be merely echoes of my own, for as I once more halted the sound suddenly ceased. Still I felt uneasy, and an undefinable terror began to steal over me. There was a sense of loneliness in those fields at that hour such as I had never before experienced, and I was now glad of the companionship of old Talbot, who kept very close to me. If any one were following me, I thought it must be Phaleg, who might have watched me come out; but if so, why did he not declare himself? The cold had become excessive, in consequence of the mists arising from the marshy grounds adjoining the mere, and these vapours added to the obscurity. I was often in danger of falling into a ditch; and, in spite of all my efforts, I could not keep my teeth from chattering. While getting over a stile, I fancied I perceived a shadowy figure behind me, and strained my eyes to penetrate the gloom that shrouded it. All at once, the moon burst from behind a rack of clouds, and the figure seemed to take the form of my uncle Mobberley, but the next moment the moon was again hidden, and it melted from view.

I was dreadfully frightened, I must confess, as any one else, I suppose, would have been in my situation, and for some minutes remained fixed where I was, gazing into the vacancy, and resolved to address the spirit if it appeared again. But it declined to gratify me in this respect; and, somewhat reassured, I proceeded on my way.

Had I received a warning from the grave? Did my dead uncle intend to take part in the interview? I asked myself these questions, but felt unable to answer them. Again, had not my own distempered imagination conjured up the phantom? I inclined to the latter opinion, but the evidence of my senses was against it. I had certainly seen a figure in all respects resembling my uncle, and fancy could not have cheated me into the belief. Old Talbot seemed to have no doubts on the subject, for he had slunk off to a distance, and trembled and whined as I approached him. I would have turned back, but it was now too late; and, moreover, I did not like passing the spot where the phantom had appeared. The churchyard was close at hand, and I felt impelled to enter it.

It may seem strange that I had scarcely set foot within the hallowed precincts than my courage returned. Though I was now disturbing the repose of those who lay beneath the flags and rounded hillocks, and at an hour

"When churchyards yawn, and graves give up their dead,"

I felt none of the superstitious fears which had beset me in the lonesome fields.

I stood still, and listened. As I did so, the butt-end of my gun came in contact with a large stone, covering the entrance to a vault, and a hollow clangour was returned. There was no other sound. All was hushed as death itself. Yes, after a while there was a cry from the church tower, and a great white, ghostly object flitted past me; but it caused me no alarm, for I knew it was only an owl.

The church itself, though close at hand, showed like a huge, heavy black mass: buttress, window, and porch were undistinguishable. The dusky outline of roof and tower was alone preserved.

It required some knowledge of the gloomy locality to shape my course towards the back of the church; but possessing this, I moved on without hesitation. More than once I stumbled over a low headstone, and on each occasion I fancied that mocking laughter succeeded my fall. But it might be only the echoes of the spot. Presently a black jagged object appeared before me. It was a yew-tree, and I then knew precisely where I was, for this tree grew at the back of the church, and close to my uncle's grave. I again came to a pause, and awaited some signal to announce Phaleg's approach.

But I was before my time, and at least a quarter of an hour elapsed before the church clock struck twelve. The solemn sounds had scarcely ceased vibrating through the air, when a figure emerged from the gloom, and a voice, which I recognised as that of Phaleg, exclaimed,

"Hist! where are you?"

"Here," I replied, stepping towards him.

"I see you now. How infernally dark it is. Are you alone?"

"I am."

"That's right; for, if not, you'd have heerd nothing from me. But how's this? You've got a gun with you, and a dog."

"The gun is only to protect myself, and the dog won't harm you unless you molest me. You needn't be afraid of either."

"Afeared!" he echoed, with a fierce laugh. "Afeared of a stripling like you! No, I'm not much afeared, my joker. And if it warn't that I've promised my wife not to harm you, and that I expects to make a good sum by you, I'd pay you off for the mischief you did me a month ago, in spite of dog and gun."

"I suppose you didn't come here merely to threaten me," I rejoined. "What have you got to disclose?"

"Come nearer," he returned; "I don't like talkin' too loud. Them folks below might overhear us," he added, with a chuckle that made me shudder.

"No; keep off!" I cried, presenting my gun. "I won't trust you."

On this the gipsy swore a great oath, and he brandished a tremendous bludgeon with which he was armed; so I kept my finger on the trigger, ready to pull it if he made any attack upon me. Talbot barked at him furiously.

"Keep the dog quiet, curse you!" he cried; "you'll rouse the neighbourhood. Well, then, to make short work of it, I've a secret to sell you."

"I imagined so," I replied. "What do you want for it?"

"A thousand pounds—not a farden less. It would be cheap to you at two thousand, but I won't drive a hard bargain. I'm tired of this wagabond life, and that sum would set me up respectable."

"How do I know your secret is worth it?"

"I'll soon make it plain to you," he replied, in a cunning tone. "You know the valley of your uncle Mobberley's property. You know you've lost it as things now stand. S'pose I finds the missin' will, and puts you in possession?"

"If you do, the money's yours," I replied.

"Is it a bargain?"

"It is."

As I was trembling with anxiety for the revelations that were to ensue, a hollow groan, apparently issuing from the depths of an adjoining grave, broke on our startled hearing, and Talbot, who was standing near me, howled and ran off.

"What the devil's that?" my companion ejaculated, in tones that bespoke his terror.

Another hollow groan responded to the exclamation, and the moon bursting forth at the same moment, revealed the ghostly figure of my uncle Mobberley beneath the yew-tree.

He appeared to be standing near the edge of an open grave, into which it was fortunate I had not tumbled, for I had not hitherto observed it.

His habiliments were those he had worn in life; and he was leaning upon his crutch-handled stick, with the black patch drawn over his death-like features. We both gazed at the apparition in mute terror. I would have spoken, but my tongue refused its office.

But the ghost did not require to be addressed first. Contrary to the usage of spirits, it spoke, after shaking its shadowy arm menacingly at Phaleg. The voice seemed changed, and was deeper than my uncle's, before he shuffled off his mortal coil.

"What are you doing here?" he cried, with ghostly gruffness, "abusing the lad's patience with idle tales. Am I to be disturbed in my grave by a gipsy rascal like you? I have disinherited him, and he knows it. I have burnt my will, and given my property to one who'll take care of it."

"That's a lie, old chap," replied Phaleg, who had regained his confidence, having probably begun to smell a rat. "I can tell a very different tale."

"You may tell it where you please," the ghost rejoined, "but no one will believe you. You'll be hanged, rascal."

"Not afore I brings a greater rogue than myself to the gallows."

"The world is come to a pretty pass, when honest men's characters can be sworn away," the ghost said. "I'm well out of it."

"Ay, that you are; and I advise you to go back to your coffin. It's the fittest place for you," the gipsy returned, with a brutal laugh.

The ghost groaned dismally.

"Groan away," Phaleg continued; "you won't frighten me. The devil, your master, couldn't. Change your tone, Mister Ghost."

Apparently, the ghost thought the suggestion worth attending to, for it replied, rather more mildly,

"You've come here on a fool's errand."

"I don't think so," Phaleg returned, in a jeering voice. "I can do business here quite as well as elsewhere—mayhap better. I didn't expect the pleasure o' your company; but I'm glad to see you, nevertheless, an' quite prepared for you. Ghosts seems to have bad mem'ries—no wonder, all things considered—an' yours want's jogging. You made a slight mistake just now, when you towd your nevvey you'd burnt your will. I can prove the contrairy. But I don't want to take you unawares. Have you any objections to my tellin' him where to find it?"

"Let him go home," the ghost rejoined, significantly.

"Nay—nay, that'll never do," Phaleg said. "I cannot take all this trouble for nuffin."

"Nor I," I cried, having drawn my own conclusions from their discourse. "I don't mean to stir hence; and I'll take good care that you, Phaleg, don't stir either, till I've obtained the information you promised me."

"You hear how the little bantam-cock crows?" Phaleg exclaimed, with a laugh; "there'll be a reg'lar fight for it, that's sartin, if I disappoints him."

"That there will," I said, resolutely; "and I'm armed, as you know."

"Now, Mister Ghost," the gipsy said, "you see how matters stands. Shall I stick to him, or come over to you? You'll rest more comfortabler in your grave, I dare say, if I keeps your secret; but if I does, I must have better terms than he offers. So make up your mind quick."

"You shall have anything you please,—only get rid of him," the ghost cried.

"Now, young gen'l'man," Phaleg said, "you perceives as how your uncle an' me has come to an understandin'? The best thing you can do, therefore, is to make yourself scarce as quickly as you can. No talkin'—mind."

"'Mum' must be the word," the ghost cried.

"You have betrayed yourself, Pownall," I rejoined. "I suspected who it was from the first. You are a couple of precious rascals; but you'll find that, boy as I am, I'm a match for both of you. Phaleg, you are my prisoner."

"Your prisoner—ho! ho! Come, I likes that."

"Yes, my prisoner—unless you do as I bid you. And first, I order you to seize and secure Simon Pownall."

"Why, look you, my lad, I could easily do what you tells me, but I don't see how it would answer my purpose."

"It wouldn't," the barber-surgeon cried. "Stand by me, and we'll soon dispose of him."

Notwithstanding my bravado, I was much alarmed, for I felt I was in the power of these miscreants; and though I might shoot one of them, I should probably be mastered by the other. Having selected Phaleg, as the most dangerous of the two, I determined to make him my mark; but little time was allowed me for consideration, for almost before I could raise my gun, which I had previously lowered, the gipsy hurled his bludgeon with tremendous force at my head. Luckily, I avoided the blow by stooping, and I heard the missile take effect upon Simon Pownall, who was in a line with me, and who, giving vent to a groan very different from those he had uttered before, fell backwards into the grave; at least, I judged so by the sound. However, I was in great confusion, for unfortunately as I thought, but fortunately as it turned out, my gun went off as I stooped down. With a fearful oath Phaleg rushed upon me, threatening to finish me; and probably he might have done so, but at that moment the deep baying of a bloodhound was heard, accompanied by the voice of Ned Culcheth, cheering him on.

In spite of the threats of the gipsy, I shouted for aid at the top of my voice, and was instantly answered by the keeper. Phaleg had caught me by the throat, as the only means of silencing me, but he was now obliged to leave go, and dashing me, half-strangled, upon the ground, he leaped the churchyard wall, and disappeared.

He had not been gone more than a second, when Gaunt and Lupus pounced upon me, setting their heavy paws on my prostrate body, and growling horribly. Though I felt their dreadful jaws close to my face, I managed to cry out, and the keeper coming up at the same time, and quickly comprehending my situation, called them off before any harm could be done to me. As soon as I could find breath, I explained to him what had occurred. In return, he told me he had watched by Pownall's house throughout the whole evening, but, not seeing the barber-surgeon go out, he concluded all was right so far as he was concerned. Still, he had not quitted his post until some ten minutes after midnight, when he proceeded towards the churchyard, to see whether I required any assistance, and on hearing the discharge of the gun, he had hastened in the direction of the sound.

As we both of us agreed that Simon Pownall was safe enough in the grave into which he had fallen, we determined to pursue the gipsy without further delay; on which Ned immediately put his bloodhounds on the scent, and as they leaped the churchyard wall, we followed on their track.

Down the declivity we dashed, led on by the voices of the hounds, for it was too dark to keep them in view. Through the thick copse skirting the mere—along its reedy marge—we ran at a headlong pace, until we came to the little boat-house. Here the hounds were at fault, and bayed angrily.

"Can he have taken a boat?" Ned cried. "Dang him, he has. He has broken the chain, and got off."

"But we can follow him; there's another boat," I exclaimed.

"Ay, ay," Ned replied; "an' we shan catch him, for we han got the swifter craft of the two."

"Lose no time, then," I cried, unable to control my impatience, and helping him to unfasten the boat.

In another instant we were ready; the hounds were on board, and Ned grasped the oars. Before plunging the latter into the water, he paused to listen for some sounds to guide him in the direction of the fugitive. We could hear nothing, owing to the mutterings of the dogs, and could see nothing upon the darkling surface of the mere, which seemed to blend insensibly with the gloom; and if we struck out in the wrong direction, we should probably lose him altogether, when fortunately, a momentary burst of moonlight pointed the gipsy out to us, a good way off, pulling right across the mere.

"Hurrah! now then we have him, to a dead sartinty," Ned cried, giving way instantly, and plying his oars with the utmost vigour.

I didn't feel quite so certain that we should come up with him, notwithstanding the keeper's exertions; but if we saw where he landed, we could not fail to run him down with the hounds. To keep him in view, however, was no easy matter, for, the gleam of light having been instantly withdrawn, it was now dark as pitch. In spite of all our efforts to silence them, the hounds would not cease baying; and, consequently, though we could hear nothing of him, our movements must be made known to the fugitive, and help him to avoid us. Of this we were fully aware; and though I steered the boat as well as I could, I was in great uncertainty. How anxiously I watched for another gleam! At last it came, and then we found that, instead of being ahead, as we supposed, the gipsy had doubled upon us, and was rowing back towards the point from which he had started. The head of our boat was instantly turned, and we gave him chase.

"We must mind what we're about, Ned, or he'll give us the slip yet," I cried, "and I wouldn't lose him—no, not for a thousand pounds."

"Never fear, sir," the keeper replied, pulling away with lusty strokes.

Again, all was darkness and uncertainty. My eyes were strained to catch the slightest glimpse of the other boat, and my ears open for any sound, however faint.

"I think he has turned again, Ned," I exclaimed. "Rest on your oars for a moment, and listen."

The keeper complied, and the next instant got up, and, seizing the two hounds by the throat, so tightly as almost to throttle them, he said in a whisper to me:

"He's comin' direct towards us. Howd your tongues, wun ye—ye dang'd tell-tale brutes."

Ned was right. In his attempt to escape, the cunning fox had run right into our jaws. The darkness which had hitherto favoured him, now helped us in our turn, and he did not descry us till he was within twenty yards of our boat. Uttering a fearful oath, he made an effort to turn; but it was now too late. On seeing his prey within reach, Ned instantly set free the hounds, snatched up the oars, and, with a loud shout, in which I joined, dashed at him. Phaleg, I suppose, finding he could not escape, awaited us, and in a minute we were beside him. I thought we should have overset his boat, for we struck against it with great force.

"Wun yo' yield quietly?" Ned thundered.

"You'd best let me alone," the gipsy rejoined, fiercely.

"Take care o' the oars," Ned cried to me. "Here, Lupus—here, Gaunt—at him, lads!"

The savage hounds were as fully prepared for the attack as their master, and sprang after him into the other boat, yelling dreadfully. The contest was unequal, but Phaleg was desperate, and not disposed to yield tamely. He had unshipped an oar, and before Ned could seize him, he struck the keeper such a violent blow on the head, that I thought he had killed him. The poor fellow lost his footing, and fell overboard. But though he had thus liberated himself from one foe, Phaleg had two others, yet more formidable, to contend with. It was terrific to hear the yells of the bloodhounds, and the cries and imprecations of the gipsy. I thought they would tear him in pieces. He shouted to me to keep them off, promising to tell me all if I did so, but I had not the power of compliance. Besides, my attention was engrossed by poor Ned, who had just strength left to keep himself afloat in the water, and I tried to get him into the boat before he should sink altogether from exhaustion, for a stream of blood was running down his face from the wound in his head. In this I succeeded, and was just in time, for no sooner had I managed to help him on board, than with a loud groan he fell back insensible.

Almost at the same moment the struggle between the gipsy and the bloodhounds ceased. I thought they had got him down, but breaking from them at the expense of his skin, as was afterwards shown by the blood-stained condition of his assailants' jaws, he sprang over the side of the boat, and swam off. I called to him, but he disregarded my cries; and as we were almost in the middle of the mere, I thought it impossible he could reach the shore, and therefore gave him up for lost.

My attention was now directed to Ned. He had begun to breathe again, and in a few minutes, recovering speech, begged me to take him home, as he thought he must be severely injured. I examined his wound as well as I could, and finding the blood had ceased to flow, I bade him not be afraid, for I thought he was more stunned than really hurt, his skull being a pretty hard one; and after tying a handkerchief round his head, and placing him in the stern of the boat, I took up the oars and rowed in what I supposed to be the direction of his cottage. Of course, Gaunt and Lupus were with us, for when their prey had escaped from them, after exhibiting their vexation in a long howl, they returned to me, and were now crouching at their master's feet.

As I could not shape my course very accurately, owing to the darkness, nearly an hour elapsed before I reached Ned's dwelling, and by that time my predictions in regard to the nature of the injury he had received were fully verified, for he was able to step ashore without assistance; and he declared he should not say a word about it to Sissy till the morning, as he made no doubt he should be all right then. Unfastening the door, he begged me to come in with him, and stay till daylight. I acceded to the proposal; and Ned having thrown off some of his wet garments, and wrapped himself in an old great-coat, we seated ourselves by the fireside, with the dogs at our feet, and were soon fast asleep.

The bright sunshine awoke me, and, rubbing my eyes, I beheld a ghastly object. It was Ned, whose red locks were matted with congulated blood. Sissy came down at the same moment, and screamed at the sight of her husband. The cry roused him, and, perceiving his wife, he became conscious of his condition, and dispelled her terrors by a hearty laugh. Telling her he would soon clear off the bloody stains, he proceeded to the pump, while I related to her what had occurred. The instant he came back they were folded in each other's arms, and I left them together, and proceeded to Nethercrofts.

On the way thither I passed through the churchyard, and examined the grave into which Simon Pownall had fallen, in the hope of finding him there still; but he was gone. The events of that night did not tend to elucidate the mystery of my uncle Mobberley's will, nor help me to its discovery. Simon Pownall denied all knowledge of the circumstances, protesting that he had never left his home that night, as he could prove on the testimony of his apprentice, Chetham Quick. But I was quite certain it was he who had played the ghost, for I ascertained that he had contrived to possess himself of my uncle's wearing apparel, together with his hat and stick.

Nothing was heard of Phaleg; and his body not being found in the mere, the probability was, that, notwithstanding his lacerations from the bloodhounds, he had managed to swim ashore.

A few days afterwards I returned to the Anchorite's.

BOOK THE SECOND.

BOOK THE SECOND.

CHAPTER I.

IN WHICH IT IS PROBABLE THAT I SHALL FORFEIT THE READER'S GOOD OPINION, AS I DISPLAY SAD WANT OF TEMPER, AND GREAT INGRATITUDE; AND GIVE MY ENEMIES THE ADVANTAGE OVER ME.

I SHALL now resume the story of my life at an epoch of its greatest interest to myself, namely, when I had just turned Twenty-One.

Though I had entered upon man's estate, I still possessed a very youthful appearance, and I have seen the upper lip of many a bewitching Andalusian dame more darkly feathered than mine was at the period in question. Some people told me I was handsome, and my tailor (excellent authority, it must be admitted) extolled the symmetry of my figure, and urged me to go into the Life Guards. But these flattering comments did not turn my head. Thus much I may say for myself, and I hope without vanity: I excelled in all manly exercises; I could run, swim, or leap as well as most young men of my day; and I had never met with a horse that I should have hesitated to mount. My habits were so active, and I was endowed with a frame so vigorous, that I scarcely knew what it was to feel fatigue. I was a hard rider, fond of shooting, and of all field sports, and had stalked deer in the Highlands, and speared the wild-boar in the woods of Germany. No one could enjoy better health than I did, and the only time I was ever laid up was owing to an accident, as I shall presently relate. To complete my personal description, I may refer to the passport which I obtained on going abroad, and where I find the following items in my *signalement*:—" Hair, dark brown, and worn long; eyebrows, arched; eyes, blue; forehead, open; nose, straight; mouth, small; chin, round; visage, oval; complexion, rosy; beard, none; height, five feet eleven inches." As these particulars were meant to convey some idea of me to foreign authorities, they may possibly serve the same purpose to the reader.

It may seem, from what I have just stated, that I was more sedulous in cultivating the body than the mind. But such was not altogether the case. It is true that I did not work so hard as I might have done while I was at Cambridge, but I gained the Seatonian prize and Sir William Browne's medal, and these distinctions were enough for my then ambition. Had I been less fond of boating, riding, and other sports, and had not idled away so much time, I might have won honours. As it was, I took a respectable degree.

On quitting Cambridge, I spent a few weeks at the Anchorite's, and then set out on a lengthened continental tour. I remained abroad more than a year, and during the time visited several of the principal cities of Europe. While I was absent, some circumstances occurred which exercised a considerable influence over my future career; but, before I proceed to recount them, let me show how I stood in reference to Mrs. Mervyn.

In a previous portion of my history I have mentioned that my kind relative took charge of my education, sending me to college, paying all my expenses there, and when I left Cambridge, making me a handsome allowance. It had been her wish that I should go into the Church, but feeling no special vocation for the holy office, I could not with propriety accede to her wishes. My own predilections were for the army; but here Mrs. Mervyn was strenuously opposed to me, declaring that my poor mother had expressed a hope on her death-bed that her boy might never be a soldier. This I could not contradict, as I full well remembered that she had said the same thing to myself, and had even made me promise never to follow in my father's footsteps. So medicine and law alone were left, and as I was averse to both, it seemed not improbable that I should have no profession at all.

However, my prospects, on entering life, seemed fair enough. It is true that I did not derive much assistance from my father, who was still in India; but I had every reason to suppose that Mrs. Mervyn would continue to befriend me. The thousand pounds bequeathed me by my uncle Mobberley was untouched. And here, having alluded to my father, let me mention that he was now Colonel of the 1st Regiment of Bombay Light Cavalry, stationed at Neemuch; and held, besides, some other appointments. But his second wife was a very extravagant woman, and having a large family by her, and fancying I was provided for, he did not trouble himself much about me. He had wished me to enter the army, and to join some regiment going out to India; but understanding that Mrs. Mervyn was opposed to the step, he no longer pressed it.

"You have experienced such unbounded liberality and kindness from your excellent relative," he wrote to me, "that her wishes must be law to you. I have never seen you, my dear boy, and should like to look upon your face—your portrait tells me it is like your mother's —before I close my eyes. But as good Mrs. Mervyn has an objection to our noble service, and desires to retain you near her, by all means stay. I will never interfere with her. Whatever profession you may choose, if you take after your father, you will always be a soldier at heart. So, receive my blessing, and may you prosper!"

And now a word as to some others of the reader's acquaintance. And first of John Brideoake. When mention was last made of him,

John was staying, for the recovery of his health, at Ned Culcheth's cottage, at Marston Mere, in Cheshire. The poor boy got better, and returned to the Cottonborough Free Grammar School, but having overtasked his brain, he was never able to work so hard as he had previously done. He obtained a Somerset scholarship from our I. G. S., and matriculated at Cambridge at the same time as myself. We were both at St. John's College, but he was only a sizer. No doubt, if John had been able to study hard, he would have greatly distinguished himself, but severe application was strictly prohibited by Dr. Foam. He made a final effort, but was nearly sinking under it, and had a renewal of the attack under which he had laboured at an earlier period, only recovering sufficiently to take his degree. This bitter disappointment cast a deep gloom over him. He became melancholy and despondent, and seemed to have lost all relish for life. Another unhappy consequence attended his want of success. His mother, who had built her hopes upon him, and had fully persuaded herself that he would be a senior wrangler, was astounded and angry at his failure, and never forgave him. He ought to have died rather than give in, she said; and he *would* have died most assuredly, Dr. Foam declared, if he had persisted in his efforts. His mind was incapable of further strain. John Brideoake took holy orders, and became curate to the Rev. Dr. Foljambe, vicar of Weverham, near Delamere Forest, in Cheshire. A tranquil life, well suited to his tastes, here awaited him, but he saw little of his mother and sister. Mrs. Brideoake appeared to have lost all affection for him, and besides, she had other schemes in view, with which he might have interfered. But of these anon.

Before proceeding, I must remind the reader, who may, perhaps, have forgotten the circumstance, that Dr. Foam, when dining with Mrs. Mervyn, borrowed a volume of Jacobite correspondence from her. The correspondence related chiefly to the Rising of '15, and most of the letters were in cypher; but the doctor, being familiar with the characters, was able to make out their import. While examining these documents he made some discoveries relative to Mrs. Brideoake's family, which he thought it necessary to communicate to Mrs. Mervyn, and thenceforward the kind-hearted lady took an extraordinary interest in the widow and her children. But Mrs. Brideoake's pride presented for some time an obstacle to the full development of my relative's generous intentions towards her.

By Mrs. Mervyn's instrumentality, and at her cost, Apphia was sent to an excellent school at Dunton, in Cheshire—a pretty village, which I have heretofore described as about three miles north of Marston Mere. A cottage near the school was also taken for Mrs. Brideoake.

It may almost seem incredible, after such favours had been showered upon her, that Mrs. Brideoake should be loth to make the personal acquaintance of her benefactress; but nearly three years elapsed before they met, and during the whole of this time Mrs. Mervyn never ceased to extend her bounty both to mother **and daughter.**

At last, the way was paved to an intimacy by Apphia. The now blooming girl of sixteen was taken by Dr. Foam to call on Mrs. Mervyn, and the latter was so pleased with her, that she insisted upon her passing a few weeks at the Anchorite's. Mrs. Brideoake reluctantly assented to this arrangement; but she might not have displayed so much hesitation if she could have foreseen its results.

Apphia's amiable disposition and winning manners produced such a favourable impression upon her kind hostess, that the latter declared she could never part with her. So she sent for Dr. Foam, and telling him it was indispensable to her happiness that mother and daughter should live with her, charged him with a message to that effect to Mrs. Brideoake. The worthy doctor seemed apprehensive that he should not discharge his mission very satisfactorily, but he succeeded beyond his expectations. Whatever arguments he employed with Mrs. Brideoake, they prevailed. She consented to become Mrs. Mervyn's guest for an indefinite period; and thenceforth she and her daughter were regularly installed at the Anchorite's.

Every consideration was shown them. They had their own apartments, and Mrs. Brideoake was not expected to appear, unless she chose to do so, when there was company in the house. The influence of her strong mind over Mrs. Mervyn's gentler nature soon became apparent. Whether this influence was for good or ill, will be seen hereafter. Suffice it that ere a year was over Mrs. Brideoake had acquired a complete ascendancy over her protectress.

As to Apphia, Mrs. Mervyn became more and more strongly attached to her, and her affection in this instance was fully requited. Ever since she had come to reside at the Anchorite's, Apphia had the advantage of a daily governess, and of the best instructors that Cottonborough could provide. At eighteen her education was pronounced complete, and it would have been difficult to meet with a more accomplished girl. The promise of beauty held out by the child was more than fulfilled by the young woman. Her figure was tall and slight, and her features were of the rarest order of beauty, but their prevailing expression was pensive rather than gay, probably the result of early anxiety. The candour, simplicity, and sweetness of her character might be read in her open countenance; and her smile evidently came from the heart. Her eyes were of a clear, tender blue, and serene as a summer sky; her complexion exquisitely delicate; and her fair hair was braided over a brow as white as marble. Such was Apphia Brideoake at eighteen. Those who were fond of meddling with other people's concerns began to talk of Mrs. Mervyn's great attachment to her, and some of them even went so far as to say that it was quite certain the old lady would leave all her property to her new favourite. So she might, for anything I should urge to the contrary.

Apphia and I were like brother and sister, and I think she was quite as fond of me as of her own brother John. I am quite sure if I had had a sister I could not have loved her better than I loved Apphia. The innocent intercourse of young persons of opposite sexes has a delight that no other commerce of friendship can bestow; and the happiest moments of my early life were those spent in this sweet girl's society. I even derived improvement from it; for, though younger than myself, she was wise beyond her years, and capable of giving me good counsel; while the evenness of her temper frequently offered a wholesome check to my headstrong impetuosity. A hasty temper, indeed, was my failing; as the reader will find out as I proceed, if he has not found it out already. Apphia soon discovered this fault in me, and tried to correct it. Knowing that I was quick to acknowledge an error, she did not despair of my amendment. Her nature was the kindliest imaginable. Considerate to all; utterly free from selfishness; she had not a particle of the pride that beset her mother. Humility rather was her attribute.

I used often to go over to Dunton to call on Mrs. Brideoake at her cottage, and I must confess that my chief inducement for these visits was the hope of meeting my charming little playmate. Many a stroll have we taken in the adjacent park, with John for a companion, and we have even rambled on as far as Marston Mere. Ah! those were blissful hours!—not to be recalled without a sigh.

Apphia was no longer a child when she came to reside at the Anchorite's, and some little change, as might naturally be expected, took place in her manner towards me. Amiable and obliging as ever, she was rather more distant. No longer did we run hand-in-hand together as we had been wont to run in Dunton Park. No longer had we any little confidences. Our feelings, I dare say, were just the same, but we put more constraint upon them. Each time that I returned from Cambridge during the vacations, I remarked that Apphia's reserve towards me increased. I once questioned her about it, and she replied that she had as much regard for me as ever, but we were no longer children. So I was bound to be satisfied. Whether any feeling, warmer than friendship, had sprung up in our breasts, I cannot positively assert; but perhaps the conviction of a secret sentiment of the kind may have produced the growing restraint I have noticed on Apphia's part. That I looked upon her in the light of a future wife is certain, though I never consulted her on the subject; but I fully determined, when I returned from my continental tour, to propose to her in form. Our parting, on the occasion of my setting out on this tour, served to precipitate matters. While exchanging our adieux, she exhibited such unwonted tenderness, and seemed so sorry to lose me, that I do not think I could have torn myself away at all, if her mother had not cut short the interview. But before we were thus separated, I had extorted from her the confession that she loved me, with a pledge that she would be mine; while I, in my turn, vowed to wed no other.

But I must leave this pleasant theme, and turn to one who was a good deal mixed up with my early history, and with whom I was fated frequently to come in contact—I mean, Malpas Sale.

I could never do away with the conviction that Malpas had defrauded me of the property I ought to have inherited from my uncle Mobberley, and though he made many friendly overtures to me, I always rejected them. He had now grown into a remarkably handsome young man. His features were finely chiselled; his complexion of almost feminine delicacy; and he wore a superabundance of black curling hair. I have elsewhere mentioned that he was three years older than myself—being now twenty-four. It might be prejudice on my part, but I thought, notwithstanding his good looks, that he had a sinister expression. There is no denying, however, that he had easy, prepossessing manners, and an air of good breeding and distinction. Perhaps, he might be a little of a coxcomb—at least, I thought him so. He had been a fellow-commoner at Trinity College, Cambridge, where, during his residence, he lived like the young noblemen and other youths of large expectations with whom he consorted; kept several horses, gave expensive entertainments, and spent a great deal of money—much more than the five hundred a year allowed him by our uncle Mobberley's will. It will be remembered that he was not to come into the whole of that property, which was estimated at 2000*l.* per annum, until he attained the age of twenty-five. Malpas used to grumble a good deal about this arrangement, and wondered what the old man could have been thinking of to keep him so long out of his money.

Malpas was my senior by about two years at Cambridge, so that when I became a member of the University, he belonged to another set, who looked down upon us freshmen. Moreover, as a fellow-commoner, he had better society than I could expect to obtain; but, on my arrival, he called upon me, and proffered me all sorts of attentions; but, as I have said, I declined them. I distrusted even his civilities. Strange to say, he would not be offended by my rudeness. Though I avoided him as much as possible, we not unfrequently met; for, being of the same college, we had necessarily some mutual acquaintances, and rather than make a row, I endeavoured to control my dislike. It was difficult, too, to quarrel with him; he was so confoundedly civil and obliging.

How he obtained his degree was matter of surprise to every one who knew the sort of life he led; but he had excellent abilities, and was remarkably quick when he chose to apply, so that in an inconceivably short space of time he mastered what it took others months to learn. Besides, he was well crammed. He told his friends afterwards that he expected to be plucked, and he found that such a result had been anticipated by them. This made his triumph the greater.

He left the University deeply in debt; but what of that? His creditors felt secure. In four years (he was then twenty-one) he would come of age, and they would be paid in full. Meanwhile, they received full interest on their claims. Malpas gave himself little concern about them. His business was pleasure; and as reflection on the state of his affairs would have interfered with his amusements, he took care not to trouble himself on that score.

Malpas's next step was to purchase a commission in the Second Life Guards. As may be supposed, what with his present position, his 2000*l.* per annum in expectancy, his good manners, and his handsome person, he was very popular, and was invited everywhere. This sort of life lasted for two or three years, during which he launched into all sorts of fashionable extravagances; but at the end of that time supplies were not to be so easily obtained, and he became what is vulgarly styled rather "hard up." Still, as in fifteen months he would come into his property, he thought the executors would readily make him an advance.

With this design he came down to Cottonborough, and had an interview with the two trustees under our uncle Mobberley's will—Mr. Evan Evans, and Cuthbert Spring. He wanted 10,000*l*., but finding them disinclined to accede to the request, he lowered his demands, and said he would be content with half the amount. This was likewise refused. Cuthbert Spring, who subsequently gave me full particulars of the interview, told me that when Malpas pressed them still further, he said to him, very decidedly,

"We are interdicted by the will from making you any advance at all, Mr. Sale, and we grieve that you have exceeded your annual allowance of 500*l*., which we think amply sufficient for your requirements. We sincerely trust that you will not seek to raise money on the property you expect to acquire, as you can only do so at great disadvantage, since the lenders of the money will incur considerable risk."

"How so?" Malpas demanded. "In little more than a twelvemonth the property must be mine, and I can then deal with it as I please. It is not a very long minority."

"Granted," Cuthbert Spring replied; "but life is uncertain, and it is possible you may never attain the age of twenty-five, as required by your uncle's will. It is also just possible—I do not say probable—that the other will may turn up during the interval."

On hearing this remark, Cuthbert Spring told me that Malpas became excessively pale, but, quickly recovering himself, he forced a laugh, and said,

"I do not think that very likely, Mr. Spring."

"Neither do I," the other rejoined; "but the fear of such an occurrence may deter a money-lender, or make him very extortionate in his demands."

Malpas was not put out of countenance by the remark. Assuming an air of indifference, he said,

"Well, gentlemen, if such is your decision, I must bow to it. I shall do the best I can elsewhere, for money I must have." And so he left them.

Failing in this quarter, Malpas had recourse to his father; but he could not help him. Dr. Sale had provided him with funds to purchase his commission, and had no more money to spare, for though he had a living of twelve hundred a year, he saved nothing out of it. However, since his son's necessities were urgent, he bestirred himself, and thinking Mrs. Mervyn likely to aid him in the emergency, applied to her. He made out the best case he could for Malpas, glossed over all his indiscretions and extravagances, said that he had been led into expenses by keeping high company, and, in a word, made every excuse he could devise for the dashing young Guardsman. Malpas, he said, in conclusion, was now fully sensible of his folly, and determined to turn over a new leaf. Mrs. Sale, who accompanied her husband, spoke to the same effect, and her genuine maternal pleading had more weight with Mrs. Mervyn than the doctor's plausible arguments. The good lady would not give an immediate answer, but required a day or two for consideration. Her manner, however, convinced Dr. Sale that he had gained his point. And he was right in the conclusion. When he again waited upon her, Mrs. Mervyn informed him that she was willing to lend his son 2000*l*. till such time as he should come of age: only stipulating that he, Dr. Sale, should become security for the repayment of the amount. Of course no objection could be made to this proposal by the vicar, and he joyfully acceded to it.

I was abroad when the arrangement took place, but Mrs. Mervyn communicated it to me, and I confess I felt greatly displeased by the intelligence. All the animosity which had continued to rankle in my breast against Malpas was revived, and, while in this state of irritation, I wrote a letter to my benefactress, which I have since felt to be highly improper, and which I had soon good reason to regret. I told her she had a perfect right to do as she pleased with her money, but I thought she might have employed it more profitably than by throwing it away upon a reckless prodigal like Malpas Sale.

My surprise may be conceived when, about a month afterwards, I received a letter from Mrs. Mervyn, informing me that she was perfectly satisfied that in lending money to Malpas Sale she was dealing with a man of honour, and consequently she had not the slightest feeling of insecurity as to the repayment of the 2000*l*. More than this, the loan was only for one year. She added, that I seemed to have formed a very unjust opinion of Malpas, and she could not subscribe to it.

What made this letter more galling was, that it was enclosed in another from Malpas himself, couched in terms of most provoking civility, and complaining that I had done him great injustice, but he forgave me, as I had some grounds for my enmity towards him; but he advised me, if I regarded my own interest, not to attempt to dictate to Mrs. Mervyn in future.

My first impulse on receiving these letters was to hurry back to England—I was then sojourning at Rome—and it would have been well if I had done so. But I contented myself with writing—and I am sorry to say more intemperately than before. In fact, I could not control my feelings. To this fresh ebullition of anger, Mrs. Mervyn sent a very short reply, stating that she was not very well, and as she did not like a correspondence of this kind, she had deputed Dr. Sale to write to me.

Accordingly, the next post brought me a stiff, formal letter from the vicar, reminding me of the obligations I was under to my benefactress, and hinting (as I have since learnt he had no authority for doing), that if I did not lay aside the tone I had adopted, my allowance would be discontinued.

I was never, as the reader knows, of a very patient turn, and this was too much for my endurance. I did not perceive the snare set for me, but at once fell into it. Acting again on the impulse of the moment, I despatched an angry missive to Mrs. Mervyn, saying that as she had found new friends whom she preferred to one who had hitherto held the chief place in her regards, it was natural she should wish to get rid of the latter; and that with the deepest sense of gratitude for past favours, I must decline to accept more for the future. In sending off this most injudicious, and I will now say (for I cannot attempt to exculpate myself), most ungrateful letter, I could not have taken a step more serviceable to my enemies. It gave them an advantage over me of which they were not slow to profit. Prudence would have counselled very different measures, to say nothing of better motives. Want of temper was the cause of all this mischief.

An opportunity of setting myself right was afforded me by Mrs. Mervyn herself; but I neglected it. She wrote to say that I had quite misunderstood her, that her sentiments of affection for me were entirely unchanged, and she hoped I should think better of the determination which I seemed to have formed.

To this I replied, that I was glad to receive the assurance of her unabated regard, but after what had passed, I could no longer consent to be a dependent upon her bounty. Again want of temper. But I fancied it a mere display of independence.

This unpleasant correspondence was closed by a brief note from Mrs. Mervyn. It was to this effect: "You have been hasty, but I excuse you. It is the fault of the temperament you have inherited from your father. You will think differently ere long. No more till I see you."

My vexation was not lessened when I learnt, as I did from Cuthbert Spring, to whom I wrote, that Malpas had obtained a footing at the Anchorite's, which for some reason or other he seemed most anxious to maintain.

"Perhaps I may be able to throw some light upon his motives," Cuthbert wrote. "We shall see. But remember, it will be merely conjecture. You are aware of the loan which Mrs. M., at the pressing instance of Dr. and Mrs. S., has been induced to make him. If I had been consulted, she should never have complied with their solicitations; but let this pass. I cannot be always at her elbow, and the wisest and best of women will sometimes err. I suspect—mind, this is only suspicion—that Mrs. B. advised her to lend the money. Mrs. B., you know, is now omnipotent at the A——'s, and she seems to have taken a great fancy to M. S. Whether the wily lady may have any ulterior views in respect to him, I cannot say. But this is anticipating. Let me go on. Right or wrong, the loan was accorded, and a few days after the money was advanced, M. S. called to thank Mrs. M. for the favour done him. You know he can be most agreeable—indeed, I may use a stronger term, and say, fascinating—when he chooses; and on this occasion he exerted himself to the utmost to please. It was very well you were not there, or your ire would infallibly have been excited. Mrs. M. was delighted with him—and not she alone, but Mrs. B., who rarely finds visitors to her taste, honoured him with her approval. He was asked to come again, and eagerly availed himself of the invitation. So well did he play his cards, that in less than a week he had got the run of the house, and is now always a welcome guest—welcome, as I have said, to the hostess, welcome to the hostess's right hand, welcome—no, perhaps it would be too much to say he is welcome to the young lady. So, you see, you have a rival. But, to be serious. Shall I tell you what I think? I am of opinion, then, that Mrs. B. would not dislike to have M. S. for a son-in-law. What qualities she can discern in him to make such a connexion desirable, I cannot guess; but, in hazarding the assertion, I do not believe I am far wide of the truth. M. S. may be a suitor to A. B. She is certainly a girl well calculated to inspire a great passion. He pays her marked attention; but I won't say that his attentions are agreeable to her —indeed, I even fancy the contrary. A report has been spread about here of late, that A. B. is to be Mrs. M.'s heiress. Well founded or not, this report may have had some influence on the suitor, and it would not surprise me to hear that he had proposed for her hand. Thus I have endeavoured to give you an idea as to how matters stand at the A——'s, and you will judge whether you ought to expedite your return."

Here was matter, indeed, to make me pause and reflect. New gall was added to my bitterness, and pangs of jealousy heightened my rage. I could not believe for a moment that Apphia, whom I regarded as my affianced bride, would listen to the addresses of this coxcomb; but her mother might interpose her authority. Mrs. Brideoake's will was law with her children—that I knew. There was the danger.

And Malpas! how I execrated him. Ever in my path!—not content with robbing me of my inheritance, the villain was now endeavouring to deprive me of one dearer to me than any earthly treasure. And I—fool that I was!—had left the stage clear to him and his machinations. Nay, I had played into his hands. But I must repair the error I had committed without delay. I must drive the enemy from the vantage-ground which I had foolishly allowed him to occupy. I must return at once.

This resolve taken, my preparations were quickly made, and I set off from Rome, burning with anxiety to reach England. But all my impatience, all my exertions, availed me little. I experienced a sad check. The carriage in which I travelled was upset, and the injuries I received by the accident detained me a month on the journey.

What was passing, meantime, at the Anchorite's?

CHAPTER II.

FROM WHICH IT WILL APPEAR THERE IS SOME TRUTH IN THE SAYING, THAT THE ABSENT ARE ALWAYS WRONGED.

THE unlucky accident I have mentioned, occurred between Martigny and St. Maurice; but after a detention of some hours at a small inn at the latter place, where my bruises were examined, and such remedies as were at hand applied, I was transported to Villeneuve on Lake Leman, and thence by steamer to Geneva.

No bones were broken, but I had received many severe contusions about the head and body, and it was at first feared there might be internal injury, but luckily this did not prove to be the case. However, I was so much shaken, that nearly three weeks elapsed before I could leave my room at the Hôtel de l'Ecu, and another week was required for my complete reinstatement.

I then set off for Paris. Day and night I travelled on. How I counted the hours, and flew on faster than the horses that bore me. Apphia's image was with me during the whole journey—sometimes cheering me, but more frequently filling me with uneasiness. I dreaded losing her more than life itself.

Since I left Rome, now more than a month ago, I had heard nothing from the Anchorite's. How, indeed, could I have heard, since I had written to no one! None of my friends knew where I was, or what had befallen me. For nearly a fortnight after my accident I was incapable of holding a pen, and as I got better I felt disinclined to write. Anything I might address to Mrs. Mervyn I feared would be misinterpreted; and what could I say to Apphia? How could I put her upon her guard against Malpas? To suppose she would lend a favourable ear to his suit would be to insult her. Time enough to set matters right on my return.

After a brief halt at Paris, I started for London; and from London I set off, on the night of my arrival, on the box of the fastest coach running to Cottonborough. The journey was quickly made, but not half quickly enough for my impatience. Evening was approaching as we came in sight of the huge manufacturing town, distant about six miles, and distinguishable by its numberless mills, with their tall chimneys darkening the air with clouds of smoke. Before we reached the town, rain came on; not a smart shower, but a sort of Scotch mist, which, mingling with the murky atmosphere, threatened to choke me. Everything wore a cheerless air; and a sense of coming ill filled me with despondency. After some delays, the coach drove up to the Palace Inn. I descended, got out my luggage, secured a bedroom, and having despatched a note to Mrs. Mervyn to announce my arrival and say I would present myself to her at noon next day, I set out to call on my friend, Cuthbert Spring.

I found him at home, and alone. He appeared very glad to see me, but not a little surprised, and inquired where in the world I sprang from?

I answered that the last place I had sprung from was a coach-box, and proceeded to give him a hasty account of what had befallen me. I saw he looked rather grave and perplexed, and conjectured that he had some disagreeable intelligence to communicate; but whatever it might be, he seemed anxious to postpone it, and telling me he was just going to sit down to dinner, begged I would join him at the repast.

I willingly assented, and, during the meal, he confined himself to general topics, talking chiefly of my travels. He rallied me upon my foreign appearance, and jestingly declared that I must have stolen my moustache from some Spanish señorita; inquired what were the last fashions in Rome and Naples?—where I had seen the prettiest girls?—and so forth; but, on the whole, I thought him less lively than usual, and it was a relief to me when the servant withdrew, and we were left alone.

He then unburdened himself in this wise:

"I wish, my dear fellow, from the bottom of my heart, that you had returned a month ago. That accident near Martigny was most untoward. Your enemies must have bribed the postilion to upset you. Great changes, as you are aware, have occurred at the Anchorite's, and I grieve to have to tell you that good Mrs. Mervyn's health is very much on the decline. Dr. Foam gives very poor accounts of her. I am afraid you have caused her considerable anxiety. She was much hurt by your letters, and there were those at hand to heighten the annoyance, and keep it alive."

"I confess I have been greatly to blame," I exclaimed, full of self-reproach. "But I will atone for my error. Mrs. Mervyn, I am sure, will forgive me."

"Perhaps she may. But I cannot disguise from you that there are difficulties in the way of a reconciliation with her—great difficulties, as you will find. Mrs. Brideoake is not very favourably disposed towards you."

"There you surprise me. Mrs. Brideoake is the last person who ought to be unfriendly to me."

"Granted—but so it is. Then there are the Sales. You cannot expect them to study your interests."

"Hang the Sales!" I exclaimed. "I should like to kick the vicar and his son out of the house."

"I dare say you would," he replied, with a half smile; "but I advise you not to try the experiment, or you won't mend your position. Why, my good fellow, you are as hot-headed as your father, and he was the most irascible man I ever knew. Your sole chance of setting yourself right with Mrs. Mervyn depends upon prudence. Make a scene, and all will be up with you."

"You give me very good advice, and I hope I may be able to follow it," I replied. "But now, Mr. Spring, let me ask you a question?"

And I looked hard at him, hoping he would understand my meaning.

He evidently did so, for he slightly coughed, rubbed his chin, and begged me to fill my glass.

I complied, and, after raising it to my lips, summoned up resolution to remark :

"You have spoken of Mrs. Brideoake; but you have said nothing about her daughter?"

"Ah! I see now what you would be at. Well, it's all settled."

"Settled!" I exclaimed, starting. "What do you mean? What is settled?"

"Why the marriage, to be sure. I told you in my letter that Malpas Sale was a suitor to the young lady, and he ended, as I anticipated, by proposing to her."

"But she refused him?"

He shook his head, and looked grave.

"I am sorry to say she did nothing of the kind. She accepted him."

I sprang to my feet, with an explosion of rage.

"If what you tell me is true, my hopes are blasted, my happiness destroyed for ever," I cried.

"Come, come, my young friend," he said, kindly, "I understand your feelings, and sincerely sympathise with you in your disappointment. The blow is sharp; but you must bear it like a man."

"I will—I will," I replied, in a broken voice. "But the shock is so unexpected that it quite overcomes me. There is no doubt as to the correctness of your information?"

"None whatever. I won't give you any false hopes. The affair was only arranged three days ago, so if your return had not been delayed by that unlucky accident, you would have been in time to prevent it. The marriage, however, will not take place immediately, but is to be deferred till Malpas comes of age. I hope it may not take place at all."

Having said thus much, he tried to offer me some further consolation; but, finding his efforts unavailing, he desisted, and we both remained silent for some minutes.

As I could not master my emotion, I felt I ought no longer to trespass upon his patience.

"Excuse me, my good friend, if I quit you abruptly," I said; "but in my present frame of mind I should only distress you by remaining. I will call upon you to-morrow, after I have been to the Anchorite's—after I have seen *her*. I shall then be more composed."

"I trust so," he rejoined, in a tone of sincere commiseration. "The meeting will be painful, but get it over as soon as you can. Above all, as I said before, don't make a scene—it will do no good, and may cause you further mischief."

I made no answer, but wrung his hand; and rushing out of the room in a state bordering on distraction, made my way to the inn.

CHAPTER III.

DESPITE MR. SPRING'S ADVICE I MAKE A SCENE, AND DO NOT IMPROVE MY POSITION.

I PASSED a sleepless night, and arose jaded and greatly depressed. If I had been enduring bodily torture instead of mental anguish, I could not have suffered more acutely. I felt so supremely miserable, that my worst enemies might have pitied me. My haggard looks quite startled me, as I regarded myself in the glass. This nervous prostration, which threatened wholly to unfit me for the ordeal I had to undergo, must be overcome; so I went forth to try the effect of air and exercise.

It was early morning, and the bustle of the day had not begun, but the pavements were thronged by troops of pale-faced men, young women, and sickly-looking children of both sexes, flocking to their unwholesome employment in the cotton-mills. The thunder of the engine announced that work had already commenced—if, indeed, it had ever ceased—in these enormous structures; and jets of gas lighting up the interior, showed the rollers, cylinders, and flying wheels of the spinning machines pursuing their course. The sight had no attractions for me, and hurrying on, I soon found myself in the country. Though Cottonborough is an ugly town, black as smoke can make it, and with scarcely a picturesque feature about it, except in its ancient houses, its environs are agreeable and diversified, and the direction I had taken led me towards a range of hills of no great height, but commanding pleasant prospects. My object, however, was not to contemplate scenery, but to regain my composure. The morning was fine, with a keen, invigorating air, which served to refresh me; and persevering in violent exercise till I had succeeded in shaking off all feeling of depression, I returned with nerves firmly braced. In my anticipated interview with Apphia, I was resolved to exhibit no outward trace of emotion, however my heart might be wrung, but to maintain throughout it a cold and impassive demeanour.

Noon was at hand, and I drove out to the house I had always hitherto regarded as a home. Would it be a home to me any longer? That was a question which would be speedily decided; but so doubtful was I of the reception I should meet with, that I did not take my luggage with me.

My heart throbbed violently as I approached the familiar dwelling. Little did I think, on quitting it a year ago, how I should return. But brief space was allowed me for the indulgence of such sentimental reflections, for a circumstance occurred that completely changed my train of thought. A carriage passed me, which I at once recognised as belonging to Dr. Sale, and I thought the coachman grinned impudently as he perceived me. The saucy rascal knew me well enough, but did not think fit to touch his hat. The vicar—and probably his son—had evidently just been set down at the Anchorite's. Perhaps they had been summoned by tidings of my return. So much the better. I felt eager to confront them. If I had experienced any renewal of my late nervous sensations, this would have effectually cured me.

I descended at the garden gate, and rang the bell. No one came. After a little while, I rang again, more loudly than before. Presently the door was opened by a strange man-servant, with a surly expression of countenance, and he seemed disinclined to admit me; but, without waiting for his permission, I passed him haughtily by, and marched towards the house, on the steps of which I encountered Mr. Comberbach.

The portly butler appeared stouter and redder than usual, but I could easily perceive that the extra ruddiness of his countenance proceeded from embarrassment at my presence. He was, indeed, greatly confused, and stammered and hesitated in a very unusual manner as he spoke to me. He glanced at the surly-looking man-servant, who had followed me, as if rebuking him for letting me in, and the other muttered something about not being able to help it. Mr. Comberbach, I saw, did not mean to admit me, but being resolved to go in, I pushed him by as I had done the other servant, and entered the hall.

"Stay a moment, sir—stay a moment, if you please!" he exclaimed, stepping after me. "You mustn't go in. It's against orders."

"Against whose orders?" I demanded, sternly. "Mrs. Mervyn's?"

"No, no," he faltered; "not hers—Mrs. Brideoake's."

"Mrs. Brideoake!" I exclaimed. "Is she mistress of the house?"

"Something like it, sir," he replied, glancing uneasily round, as if afraid of being overheard. "But pray don't put any more questions to me, for all conversation with you is interdicted."

"Again by Mrs. Brideoake?" I demanded.

"By that lady," he answered.

"Tell your new mistress then," I said, raising my voice, in the hope that it might catch the ear of a listener, if there should be one nigh, "that I have no intention of going till I have seen Mrs. Mervyn."

"Impossible, sir—you can't do it—upon my honour you can't. Now, do obleege me, sir, by retiring, or I shall be under the very disagreeable necessity of—of——"

My fierce looks, I suppose, alarmed him, for the rest of the sentence expired upon his lips.

"Show me to Mrs. Mervyn at once," I cried, authoritatively.

"I daren't do it, sir—it's as much as my place is worth."

"Then I will go to her room," I rejoined, proceeding towards the staircase. "Mrs. Brideoake shall not prevent me from seeing her."

"You mustn't do it, sir," the butler cried, rushing after me in a state of great excitement. "Missis is dangerously ill, I assure you, sir. Any agitation might be the death of her."

"But I shall not agitate her," I replied; "I only desire to offer her some explanation, which she will be pleased to receive."

"Do it by letter, sir—do it by letter—that'll be the best way. I'll take care she gets it," he said, in a low tone, and winking significantly. "Address it to me. You understand."

"Yes, I understand," I rejoined, "but I don't choose to adopt such an expedient. Now answer me without equivocation. Has Mrs. Mervyn received my letter acquainting her with my intention of presenting myself this morning? Your tell-tale looks show that my suspicions are correct. She has not. Go to her at once, and announce my arrival. Say I entreat permission to see her."

"But Dr. Sale is with her, sir."

"What does that signify? Do as I bid you. Yet stay. Is Miss Brideoake within?"

"Yes, sir, she is within; but you can't see her. Against orders, as I observed before. Possibly you may not be aware——"

"Peace, fellow!" I cried, cutting him short. "Let Miss Brideoake know I am here. If she refuses to see me, well and good. When you have delivered my message to both ladies, you will find me in the library."

And disregarding his opposition, I marched up-stairs, and entered the room I had mentioned. It was empty, and I flung myself into a chair.

While I was thus seated, wondering what would happen, but determined not to be baffled in my object, an inner door opened, and Apphia Brideoake stood before me.

I instantly arose, and should have sprung towards her, but deep sense of wrong withheld me. She looked exceedingly pale and anxious, and as I regarded her fixedly, I thought her countenance bore traces of suffering. As she advanced towards me, I made her a cold salutation, but did not put out my hand.

She was the first to speak, and there was an indescribable sadness in her accents, as well as in her regards.

"Are we indeed strangers, Mervyn," she said, "that you greet me thus?" Then pausing for a moment, but receiving no answer, she continued, with a sigh, "Well, I suppose it must be so. I saw you approach the house—I heard your voice—and could not resist the impulse that prompted me to come to you: though now I feel I was wrong in doing so. I ought not to have disobeyed my mother's injunctions."

"I am glad you have given me an opportunity of offering you my congratulations, Miss Brideoake," I rejoined, bitterly. "May you be happy in the union you are about to form!"

"You do not wish me happiness, Mervyn. You cannot wish it

me. I neither expect it, nor deserve it. I only desire your pity and forgiveness."

Her words, and the tone in which they were pronounced, touched me to the heart. I felt my courage fast deserting me. But I tried hard not to give way.

"You should have both, if you stood in need of them," I rejoined, with somewhat less bitterness than before; "but I cannot see that either are called for. I will not affront you by supposing you would wed without affection; and, if you love, what occasion can there be for pity?"

"Oh, Mervyn!" she exclaimed, in a supplicating voice that quite overcame me, "do not taunt me thus! It is ungenerous of you. You have occasioned me so much misery, that you ought to compassionate rather than reproach me. If I have broken faith with you, it is your own fault."

My courage vanished in an instant, and I trembled to learn what would be laid to my charge.

"My fault?" I ejaculated, gazing at her as if my soul was in the inquiry. "Mine!"

"Listen to me, Mervyn,—dear Mervyn,—calmly, if you can,—and you shall know all. Then blame me if you choose; but I think you will not. I now feel I was in error in regard to you, and the sad consequences of the pledge I have given are before me. But it cannot be recalled."

After pausing for a moment, as if overpowered by emotion, she went on: "The hurried promises of unchangeable affection that passed between us on the eve of your departure are fresh as ever in my memory, and can never be effaced from it;—but I thought you no longer loved me."

"Oh, Apphia!" I exclaimed, reproachfully, but yet tenderly, for my heart was now quite melted. "How could you think so?"

"You never wrote to me; and after a while I began to conclude that other objects had banished me from your recollection."

"You were never absent from my thoughts!" I cried. "You are connected with every place I have visited. I never beheld a beautiful scene without thinking of you, and wishing we could have viewed it together. With what impatience and delight did I look forward to a meeting after our long separation! But if I dwell upon these thoughts I shall go mad. You say you never heard from me. How can that be—if wrong has not been done us? I wrote you several letters, to which I received no reply. Your silence was strange—but I had no misgiving. My letters must have been intercepted—I can easily guess by whom."

"They never reached me," she replied, sadly. "Hence this unhappy misunderstanding. But I did not know how serious it would prove. Attentions were paid me by Malpas Sale—marked attentions. I discouraged him as much as possible, and when he appealed to my mother, I acquainted her with my promise to you, and told her my affections were engaged. She was very angry, chided me, and said it

L

was a silly promise and could not be kept—you had evidently forgotten me. And so, indeed, it seemed, since you never answered the two letters I addressed to you at Rome, and which I am sure were sent, for I took the precaution to post them myself."

"When were those letters sent?" I cried, almost breathless with emotion.

"More than a month ago. I told you how I was circumstanced. I implored you, if you still loved me, and held to your promise, to return at once—or at all events, to write. But as you came not, and no answer arrived, I could not gainsay what was told me—that you no longer cared for me. But I held out till hope entirely forsook me,— and then—only then— yielded to my mother's commands."

I felt stunned as by a heavy blow, and some time elapsed before I could find utterance.

"A cruel hand has been at work here, Apphia," I said; "but I forbear to point it out. Fate also has been against us. Your letters missed me. Before they could arrive at Rome I had started for England. Ill luck pursued me on my journey; and a severe accident detained me for three weeks at Geneva. More than once I was on the point of writing to you, but my evil genius prevented me. Little did I think how much unhappiness a few words of explanation would have saved us!"

I stopped in alarm at Apphia's looks. She became deathly pale, and would have fallen, if I had not caught her in my arms. Ere long she recovered, and gently disengaged herself from my hold.

"This must not be," she said, gently. "You have spoken truly, Mervyn. Fate is against us, and it is useless to struggle against its decrees."

"Oh! say not so, Apphia," I cried. "Do not condemn me to despair. You are not bound by a pledge given in error. My claims are prior to those of any other. Our engagement has never been cancelled. Your mother has no right to compel you to a marriage which must be fraught with misery. I know her imperious nature. I know she has ever exacted strictest obedience to her behests from you and from your brother. But parental authority has its limits, and she has overstepped them. Besides," and I hesitated, though I felt I must speak out plainly, "she has not dealt fairly with you— nor with me. You are justified in resisting her commands."

"Hush!" Apphia whispered, in affright—"she is here."

I turned and saw who was beside us.

A great change had taken place in Mrs. Brideoake's appearance since I last described her. There was no emaciation in figure or features now. On the contrary, she could boast a certain fulness of person deemed indispensable to majesty. And majestic she was beyond a doubt. She looked younger than she did in the days of her misfortune; and might well have been termed handsome, for her lineaments were noble, but arrogant and imperious in expression. Her hair was still black as jet; and her attire rich, though of sombre colour.

There she stood, close beside us; with her brow charged with frowns, and her eagle eye fixed upon me.

"So, Mr. Mervyn Clitheroe," she said, sternly—"so, sir, you are traducing me to my daughter, and trying to make her disobedient. Luckily, she knows her duty better. But how comes it," she added, in a strange, low, impressive tone to Apphia, "that I find you here?" And then, without waiting for an answer, she raised her arm imperiously, and pointed to the door.

"A moment, mother," Apphia said, with an imploring look.

But Mrs. Brideoake was inexorable, and the poor girl, casting a piteous glance at me, withdrew.

My blood boiled in my veins, and I could not help telling Mrs. Brideoake that her treatment of her daughter was unwarrantable.

"I am the best judge of what is fitting for my daughter, sir," she replied, disdainfully, "and rest assured that I, at least, will not submit to your dictation. All intimacy between you and Apphia is at an end. Rely upon it, she will not disobey me a second time. And now, Mr. Mervyn Clitheroe," she continued, in a sarcastic tone, "you who are so ready to censure others—what have you to say in defence of your own conduct? Are you acting like a high-spirited gentleman? I scarcely think so. You force yourself into a house, where you are aware you are no longer welcome, in spite of the efforts of the servants to prevent you. You attempt to prejudice my daughter against me, and to alienate her affections from one to whom she has plighted her faith. You will fail, sir, I tell you—you will fail. Nor, so far as Mrs. Mervyn is concerned, will you gain anything by the intrusion. She will not see you. She is deeply offended with you—and, according to my view of the case, justly offended."

"Are you sure, madam, that Mrs. Mervyn knows I am here?" I observed, haughtily, for her taunts stung me to the quick. "I will never believe she will refuse me an opportunity of exculpating myself."

"Believe, or not, as you please," she replied, indifferently. "Mrs. Mervyn is acting under my advice, and as I have the care of her, I shall not permit an interview which might be attended with mischief. Her medical advisers enjoin the strictest quietude. But you may say anything you please to me, and I will take a fitting opportunity of repeating your explanations to her."

"No doubt, madam," I replied, "and with such additions or suppressions as you may deem desirable. Tell Mrs. Mervyn, then, since I am not allowed to see her, that I have never swerved from my devotion to her, and shall never cease to feel unbounded gratitude for her kindnesses. My indignation was roused because I felt she was duped by a trickster, and I wrote in stronger terms than I ought, perhaps, to have employed. But no disrespect was intended to her. I am incapable of any other feelings towards Mrs. Mervyn except those of attachment and respect. My anger was directed against Malpas Sale, of whose arts you yourself are the dupe."

"Mr. Malpas Sale is just in time to thank you for the character you give him," Mrs. Brideoake replied, with a contemptuous smile at me, as the door opened, and Malpas entered the room.

He was attired in a dark-blue military-looking surtout, braided and frogged, and had a cap and a silver-handled whip in his hand. The only recognition he condescended to bestow upon me was a supercilious look, which added fuel to my wrath.

"And pray what has Mr. Mervyn Clitheroe been good enough to say of me?" he remarked, addressing Mrs. Brideoake, and displaying his white teeth.

"He says that Mrs. Mervyn and I are the dupes of a trickster. You will readily guess to whom he makes allusion."

"I will use a stronger term, if necessary," I observed.

"Ha! ha!" Malpas replied, laughing scornfully. "No wonder Mr. Mervyn Clitheroe should say malicious things of me, since he finds himself completely cut out. If I do not notice his contemptible insinuations now," he added, with a glance at me, "it is because this is not precisely the moment to do so. He need not fear they will be forgotten. But how is our dear invalid? Is she visible?"

"To *you*—yes," Mrs. Brideoake answered, with marked emphasis. "You will find Mrs. Mervyn in her room. Your father is with her."

This insult was more than I could bear. My blood mounted to my temples, and a mist gathered before my eyes. Malpas admitted, and I denied the privilege! He was stepping lightly and gaily towards the inner door, with a smile on his curling lip and a glance of triumph in his eye, when I sprang suddenly forward, and checked his progress.

"You shall not pass this way. You shall not enter her room," I cried.

"You imagine you can prevent me, do you, sir?" he said, derisively.

"I do."

"A word, Mr. Mervyn Clitheroe. Let me appeal to your sense of decorum. One would think you must see the gross impropriety of making a disturbance in a sick lady's house. Mrs. Mervyn is in a highly nervous state. Excitement may be fatal to her."

"So I have already told him," Mrs. Brideoake remarked.

I might have listened to what they said, but there was something in Malpas's manner that added to my provocation.

"Nobody can grieve for Mrs. Mervyn's condition more than I do," I said to him; "but you shall not pass."

"You see how obstinate he is, Mrs. Brideoake," Malpas observed, shrugging his shoulders. "Nothing will serve his turn but a scene. I take you to witness that I have shown him every possible forbearance."

"More than he deserves, I must say," she rejoined. "If he hopes to gain anything by this unseemly conduct he will find himself mistaken. The servants shall show him to the door."

And she approached the bell and rang it violently.

"Now, sir," Malpas said, laying aside his mocking air, and assuming an insolent tone of authority, " stand aside!"

I laughed contemptuously.

" Then, by Heaven! I will make you."

He raised the whip, but in an instant I had snatched it from his grasp, while with the other hand I seized him by the collar of his braided coat.

" It is not the first time I have chastised you," I cried, furiously.

And I was about to apply the whip, when the inner door suddenly opened, and Mrs. Mervyn, supported by Dr. Sale, and followed by Apphia, tottered into the room. At the same time Mr. Comberbach and the surly-looking man-servant, summoned in all haste by Mrs. Brideoake's vigorous application to the bell, rushed in from the opposite door, and stood staring at us in astonishment.

On seeing me thus engaged with Malpas, Mrs. Mervyn uttered a feeble cry, and Dr. Sale, surrendering her to Apphia, hurried forward to separate us, discharging a volley of angry exclamations against me. Poor Apphia, who was quite as much agitated as Mrs. Mervyn, could only render her very indifferent assistance.

The sight of my offended relative restored me to reason, and I relinquished my hold of Malpas, who lost not a moment in turning the occurrence to my disadvantage; and indeed it must be owned that I had given him ample opportunity of damaging me without any departure from the truth. I saw by his gestures to Mrs. Mervyn that he was throwing the whole blame upon me.

She was greatly aged—more than I should have thought it possible she could be in a year's time;—her once upright figure was bowed; and her movements betokened extreme debility. I could not notice these sad changes in one so dear to me, and to whom I owed so much, without infinite concern; and if Cuthbert Spring's supposition proved to be correct, and my conduct had caused her anxiety enough to undermine her health, I ought never to be free from self-reproach. She was wrapped in a loose dressing-gown; a carelessness of attire, in itself indicative of change, for she had heretofore been remarkably precise in point of dress.

Apphia and Malpas led her to an easy-chair, into which she sank as if the exertion had been too much for her. I should have tendered my assistance, but Dr. Sale interposed and waved me off, and I could not approach her without creating fresh confusion. She regarded me, I thought, more in sorrow than in anger, but did not address me; and indeed her feeble accents could scarcely have been heard above the din caused by Dr. Sale. After gazing at me for a short time, she covered her face with her hands, and sobbed aloud.

Oh, Heavens! what I endured at that moment.

All at once, Dr. Sale's torrent of objurgations ceased. Not from any want of supply; but a glance from Mrs. Brideoake told him he was rather overdoing it. He contented himself, therefore, with glaring furiously at me, and seemed inclined to order the servants to turn me out. Mrs. Brideoake however, conceiving the presence of the menials to be no longer necessary, signed to them to leave the room; whereupon Mr. Comberbach and his companion rather reluctantly departed—possibly to solace themselves by listening at the door.

"If you have a spark of good feeling left, you will instantly withdraw," Mrs. Brideoake said to me. "You see how you distress her."

So completely was I subdued and self-abased, that I should have obeyed, if, at the moment, Mrs. Mervyn had not uncovered her face, and turned her tear-dimmed eyes towards me. I thought she was relenting, but I could not be sure, for she presently fell to sobbing again. Still the look was sufficient to rivet me to the spot.

Dr. Sale now thought it behoved him to interfere.

"I really cannot permit this," he said to me. "You must go, sir —you *must*. I never witnessed such total want of decency in the whole course of my life."

"I will go at once, if Mrs. Mervyn desires it," I replied, hoping to obtain a word from her.

"Very artfully observed, sir, but it will not serve your turn. Mrs. Mervyn will not be entrapped into conversation with you," Mrs. Brideoake sharply remarked. "You may gather from her silence what her wishes must be."

"Let her intimate as much by a sign, and I will no longer trouble her with my presence," I said.

I saw Apphia bend towards Mrs. Mervyn. I could not catch her words, but I felt sure she was pleading for me. And so it proved.

"Yes, yes, you are quite right, my child," Mrs. Mervyn said to her. "He must not go without a word from me, though it will cost me much to utter it. Mervyn Clitheroe," she continued, regarding me steadfastly, and addressing me in a voice with nothing harsh in it, but which yet sounded in my ears like a death-sentence, "you were once very dear to me—very dear indeed—as well for your poor mother's sake as for your own. That I can no longer regard you with the same affection as heretofore is no fault of mine. The change in me has been occasioned by your own conduct. I will not reproach you; but it is due to myself to tell you that you have caused me much unhappiness—far more than I have experienced at any previous period of my life. Those who have been with me know how greatly I have suffered."

"We do, indeed, my dear madam," Mrs. Brideoake observed, in a tone of well-feigned sympathy; "and our hearts have bled for you. Ingratitude is hard to endure, and you have felt all the sharpness of its sting."

"Not all its sharpness, madam," I said, looking at her.

"But a balm may be found for the wound," Apphia murmured, heedless of her mother's menacing glance.

"The wound is nearly healed, my child," Mrs. Mervyn remarked. "I must not open it anew."

"Of course not, dear madam," Dr. Sale cried. "You would do wrong to expose yourself to like danger again."

A retort rose to my lips, but I checked it, and looked earnestly at Mrs. Mervyn, as if awaiting the close of my sentence. It came.

"I will not say what I have looked forward to from you," the good lady pursued, sorrowfully rather than reproachfully. "All that is past and gone. But you may believe that I have been grievously disappointed."

"Will you not give him a further trial, dear Mrs. Mervyn?" Apphia implored. "Look how repentant—how sorrowful he appears. I am sure he will never offend you again."

"How do you know that?" Malpas cried, sharply. "Has he not just shown that his temper is utterly uncontrollable? He thought he was to have his own way entirely here, and gave himself the airs of lord and master; but finding it won't do, he now alters his tone."

"It is false," I cried; "I have had no such thought."

"Did I not say so?" Malpas cried, jeeringly. "You see he cannot control his temper now."

"I will not allow false statements respecting me to be uttered, without giving them instant contradiction," I said. "Oh, madam!" I cried to Mrs. Mervyn, "you cannot believe me the ingrate I am represented? You, who have always treated me kindly, will not be unjust to me now? Grant me a few moments in private? What I have to say is for your ear alone."

"Oh, yes, dear Mrs. Mervyn, do grant his request?" Apphia implored.

As she spoke, she sedulously avoided her mother's ireful glance.

"On no account, madam," Mrs. Brideoake said, advancing towards her, and pushing her daughter aside. "Your feelings must not be worked upon thus. Pray let me put an end to this painful interview? It would be a relief if this intemperate young man would take his departure—never to return."

"Oh, mother, you are too harsh—far too harsh!" Apphia ejaculated, bursting into tears.

"Come to me, my child," Mrs. Mervyn cried, embracing her tenderly as she obeyed. "I cannot do as you would have me, for I am not equal to further excitement. But let me finish what I have begun. Mervyn Clitheroe, I am of opinion—an opinion deliberately formed, and supported by those on whose judgment I rely—that we should not meet again—until certain impressions are entirely effaced. But though I shall not see you," she continued, in a voice in which rising tenderness struggled against the attempt at firmness, "I shall always feel the warmest interest in your welfare, and rejoice in your success. Your friend, Mr. Cuthbert Spring, will inform you that arrangements have been made for the continuance of your allowance, and will explain to you how it is to be paid. If at any time you require more, you have only to apply to me through him."

"Nobly done, and like yourself, I must say, Mrs. Mervyn," Dr. Sale exclaimed. "You are acting in a spirit of forgiveness and generosity almost without parallel. Mr. Mervyn Clitheroe ought to feel deeply beholden to you."

I took no notice of the vicar's remark, but addressed myself, with such composure as I could command, to Mrs. Mervyn.

"I hope you will not think me insensible to your great kindness, dear Mrs. Mervyn," I said, "nor impute it to unwillingness on my part to accept a favour from you—I have accepted far too many to have any such scruples—if I, in all thankfulness, decline your proffered bounty. All I desire is to be reconciled to you, and to atone for the errors I have inadvertently committed."

She was evidently much moved. After looking wistfully at me for a moment, she held out her hand. I sprang forward and pressed it eagerly to my lips.

"You forgive me, dear Mrs. Mervyn—you forgive me?" I exclaimed, passionately.

Before she could answer, Mrs. Brideoake had interposed.

"Do not give way to this weakness, madam," she said, "or the peace of mind you have just regained will be jeopardised. You have done all that kindness, generosity, and good feeling can prompt; and if Mr. Mervyn Clitheroe declines your offer, it cannot be helped. Perhaps a little reflection may make him change his mind."

I let the insinuation pass without remark.

"In any emergency, you have me to apply to; and do not hesitate, dear Mervyn. Let that be understood," my relative said, kindly, and pressing my hand as she spoke. "And now, my dear, I think you had better go. Take my forgiveness!—take my blessing!"

I could only reply by a few exclamations of liveliest gratitude.

"No more, my dear—no more," Mrs. Mervyn rejoined. "You shall hear from me, and perhaps—— But I will not raise expectations that I may not be able to fulfil. For the present, farewell."

"Farewell, my best and dearest friend!" I cried. "You send me away comparatively happy."

As I slowly drew back, Mrs. Mervyn again put her handkerchief to her eyes. At the same time, I saw a look pass between Mrs. Brideoake and Dr. Sale, which, if I interpreted it aright, meant that I should never set foot in the house again. They both saluted me coldly as I passed them.

I had not ventured to glance at Apphia, but before I left the room my eyes sought her out. She was standing as if transfixed; but perceiving me halt, she flew towards me, before any one could prevent her.

"Farewell! for ever, dear Mervyn!" she cried, clasping my hand almost convulsively. "We shall meet no more."

"Farewell!" I rejoined. "Since you discard me, we must henceforth be strangers. I resign you to him you have preferred."

And I relinquished her to Malpas, who had flown to ring the bell, and now came quickly up, with ill-disguised rage in his looks. He took her away, but his glances proclaimed he had an account to settle with me. I was glad of it; and I let him understand by a look that I was as eager for a meeting as he could be.

While this was passing, Mrs. Mervyn, alarmed by the slight cry which Apphia had uttered, was anxiously inquiring what was the matter? But Mrs. Brideoake appeased her by saying it was only the silly child bidding me adieu.

I heard nothing more, for the door was suddenly thrown open by Mr. Comberbach, and I went out.

As I descended the stairs, the butler thought fit to apologise for his reception of me, and hoped I clearly understood that it was not his fault. He had received positive orders (he did not venture to say by whom) not to admit me.

"I made a decent show of resistance," he said, with a half smile, "but I'm glad you didn't take me at my word, but would come in. It's a blessed piece of luck that you saw the dear old lady, for if you'd gone away without doing so, you'd never have had another chance. Miss Apphia managed it, I'll be bound. Ah! Mr. Mervyn, things are strangely altered here since you went abroad. It's not like the same house. But I'm sure our good old lady still loves you dearly at the bottom of her heart. Molly Bailey thinks so too. Old Molly is now more of a nurse than cook, and constantly with our missis. Mind what I say, Mr. Mervyn, if you can get an opportunity of seein' the old lady now and then, all will come round again. You may count upon my services. A letter addressed to me, as I said before, will be sure to reach—Molly Bailey will give it to her—you understand. But don't trust that crusty-faced chap, Fabyan Lowe. He'll play double, and report all you do to a certain lady—you understand."

"I am much obliged to you, Mr. Comberbach," I replied. "I began to fear the whole house had turned against me, but I am glad to find I have some friends left in it. Do me this favour. Tell Mr. Malpas Sale, if he has any communication to make to me, that I am staying at the Palace Inn."

"I won't fail to deliver the message to him," the butler replied; "and I beg you to believe that you have a trusty friend in your humble servant, Tobias Cummerbaych."

I again thanked him, and passed quickly through the hall, where I found the sour-looking Fabyan Lowe in attendance. He eyed me, I thought, rather malignantly. Mr. Comberbach accompanied me to the garden gate, and made me an obsequious bow as he put up the steps for me and closed the coach door, bidding the driver be remarkably careful how he took me to the Palace Inn.

CHAPTER IV.

RECOUNTING MY FIRST HOSTILE MEETING, AND, IT IS TO BE HOPED, MY LAST.

My first business, on arriving at the inn, was to engage a private room, and as I could not go out, for I felt certain I should soon receive a hostile message from Malpas, I despatched a note to Cuthbert Spring, acquainting him with my quarrel, and begging him to act as my second in case I should require his aid. An answer came from him almost immediately, expressing his great regret that his services should be needed in such an affair, but adding, that of course I might depend upon him.

By-and-by, the waiter entered to inform me that Colonel Harbottle was without, and begged to speak with me. I desired the man to show him in, and the next moment the fat little colonel made his appearance. His round, rosy, good-humoured features wore a rather serious expression, which I was at no loss to interpret; but while the waiter was present nothing but common civilities passed between us. I offered him a chair, and he sat down.

"You will guess the object of my visit," Colonel Harbottle said, as soon as we were alone, "and I need scarcely assure you that the office I have undertaken is anything but agreeable to me. Indeed, I would have refused it, if I had not hoped to be able to bring the quarrel to a pacific termination. With this motive in view, I hope, my dear Mr. Mervyn Clitheroe, that you will excuse me, as an old acquaintance, for saying that I think an apology is due from you to Mr. Malpas Sale—and furthermore, that it will not discredit you to offer him one. The expression employed by you towards him was highly opprobrious and offensive, and such as no man of honour could pass unnoticed. It must be retracted. This done, I am persuaded——"

"Your efforts are well meant, Colonel Harbottle," I interrupted, somewhat haughtily, "and I fully appreciate them. But they are quite thrown away. I will not retract a word I have said in reference to Mr. Malpas Sale, neither will I offer him the slightest apology. That is my answer."

"I am afraid a meeting must take place, then, sir," the colonel rejoined, rising from his seat; "but it is a pity—a great pity!"

"There is no possibility of settling the matter otherwise, colonel," I said, in a tone calculated to put an end to discussion. "I must refer you for all arrangements to my friend, Mr. Cuthbert Spring."

"Very well, sir—very well," the colonel rejoined, blowing his nose with a sound like a trumpet. "You could not be in better hands than in those of Mr. Spring. I will go to him at once; and as, unfortunately, the affair cannot be accommodated, I may as well mention that my principal would desire the meeting to take place with as little delay as possible."

"The sooner the better," I replied. "This evening, if you will. I have no desire to let the quarrel grow cold by sleeping upon it."

"To-morrow morning would be better, and more *en règle*." Colonel Harbottle said. "But since you are both impatient, I will not balk your humour, unless Mr. Cuthbert Spring sees objections to the arrangement which do not occur to me. Let us consult the almanack, as the man says in the play. Ay, here it is. The moon is nearly at the full, and rises at ten o'clock, so there will be light enough after that hour, if the weather holds fine."

"Oh, we shall see each other plainly enough for our purpose, I make no doubt, colonel," I replied, with a grim smile. "Let the appointment be for eleven o'clock. The ground you will choose."

"Give yourself no concern about that, sir," Colonel Harbottle rejoined. "You may trust Mr. Spring and myself to find a convenient spot. He is an old hand at these affairs, as well as myself." And with a military salute he took his departure.

I was now left alone to my reflections, and they were agitating enough, as may be supposed. But I had no uneasiness. Intense hatred of Malpas, and thirst for vengeance, overwhelmed every other consideration, and I felt a savage satisfaction in dwelling upon the approaching combat. I would not spare my foe. Still, fortune might decide against me; so, after pacing to and fro within the room for some time, I sat down to write two letters, which were only to be delivered in the event of my falling in the duel.

The first was addressed to my father, and in it I took a solemn farewell of him. We should never meet on earth, but I trusted we might meet in heaven. I had never tarnished his name, but should die as became a soldier's son.

The second letter was to Mrs. Mervyn. It was longer than the one to my father, for I had more to say to her. I spoke of the love and reverence I had ever borne her, and of my gratitude, which would never cease but with life. I entreated her always to think kindly of me, and to put the best construction she could upon my failings. As there was no one to whom I was so largely indebted as to her, so no one was so fully entitled to the little I could leave as herself. I therefore drew a draft in her favour upon my bankers for the 1000*l*. left me by my uncle Mobberley, and which constituted my sole property, and enclosed it in my letter.

Just as I had sealed my second letter, Cuthbert Spring was ushered into the room.

He regarded me with a serio-comical expression of countenance peculiar to him, and gave utterance to a low whistle.

"Here's a pretty kettle of fish!" he exclaimed, as he took a seat; "but it's just what might be expected. The peace wasn't likely to be kept if two such fire-eaters as you and Malpas chanced to meet. I ought to take you to task severely for not attending to my counsel; but you wouldn't listen to me if I did, so I'll confine myself to the matter in hand. To begin then: all preliminaries have been settled between Colonel Harbottle and myself. You are to meet an hour before midnight at Crabtree-green, near the Raven's Clough."

"I know the place well," I observed; "it lies between Dunton Park and the river Rollin, a little to the right of the Chester road. A retired spot, and suitable for the purpose; but why need we go so far?"

"For a very good reason," he replied. "Your adversary is obliged to return to the vicarage at Marston with his father, and cannot make any excuses for absenting himself without awakening Dr. Sale's suspicions. Indeed, the doctor is exceedingly distrustful as it is, and insists on his son accompanying him. Under these circumstances I could not offer any objection to the arrangement."

"Certainly not," I cried, in a tone that almost startled him. "I would not have any obstacles thrown in the way of the encounter."

"You are bent on mischief, I perceive," he remarked, drily, "and mean to kill your man. Humph! I have been engaged as second—never as principal, I am happy to say—in half a dozen duels, and have arranged double that number of quarrels, but not one out of the six combatants killed his adversary, though they all came well out of the field."

"That was lucky for both sides," I rejoined, perceiving the drift of his remark. "But tell me, Mr. Spring—Malpas is considered a good shot, is he not?"

"A dead shot," he answered. "But you are not much his inferior in point of skill, I fancy."

"Not much, I flatter myself. I am not in practice just now, but I used to be able to split a bullet on the edge of a knife at twenty paces—or hit a Spanish dollar at double the distance."

"Egad, there'll be sanguinary work, then, if you don't cool down. Of course such a fiery spark as you are must be provided with duelling pistols. If not, I can furnish you with a pair."

I thanked him, and told him I had a case of pistols.

"I could have sworn it," he replied, with a droll look. "You wouldn't be Charles Clitheroe's son if you travelled without them. I don't mean to set up your gallant father as an example to you in this particular, but he was one of the six combatants I have alluded to. In fact, he was the first person I had the honour to take into the field."

"And possibly I may be the last," I observed, in a nonchalant tone.

"That you undoubtedly will be if any mishap befals you. And this brings me to another point," he said, glancing at the letters on the table. "Have you any instructions to give me in regard to these letters?"

"I have only to beg you to take charge of them," I replied. "If I fall, you will kindly cause them to be sent as addressed."

And placing them in his hands, I explained their purport to him. He seemed at first disposed to offer some objections to the draft I had enclosed to Mrs. Mervyn; but he presently altered his opinion, and expressed approval of the step. It would, at all events, put the sincerity of my gratitude beyond question, he said.

"As to the letters," he continued, putting them by carefully, "you may rest easy they shall be delivered, if circumstances require it; but I trust I shall have to return them to you."

Saying which, he warmly squeezed my hand.

"I don't like to ask any questions of a painful nature," he observed, after a pause; "but I suppose you saw Apphia Brideoake this morning?"

I told him I had done so, and had ascertained that my letters written to her from the Continent had been kept back. He looked very grave on receiving this piece of information, but made no comment upon it, simply saying we must talk it over hereafter.

Hereafter! I could not help echoing with a sigh.

"I will not charge you with any message to Apphia," I said, in a melancholy tone, "but if I fall, my last thoughts are sure to be of her."

"Pshaw! you mustn't be despondent," Cuthbert Spring cried, putting on a more lively air. "You are not the first man who has lost his lady-love—I was jilted myself in my younger days—and if you come out of this duel with the credit I anticipate, you will find no difficulty in filling up the void in your heart. Plenty of pretty girls are to be found. But I must now leave you for a short time, as I have some arrangements of my own to make. I will take care that Mr. Rushton, the surgeon, is in attendance. A post-chaise shall be in readiness in an hour. We will drive to Dunton, and dine quietly at the Stamford Arms. This will be better for you than remaining in this noisy inn, and we shall only have a mile or two to go to the place of rendezvous."

I quite approved of the plan he proposed, and he took his departure. I occupied the interval of his absence in making such further preparations as I deemed necessary.

At the time appointed, Cuthbert Spring returned, and informed me that the chaise was at the door; whereupon I took up my cloak, in which I had enveloped the green baize bag containing my pistol-case, and declining the waiter's offer of assistance, marched forth with my friend.

We were soon rattling over the granite-paved streets of Cottonborough, and forcing our way through the strings of waggons and carts, all laden with bales of the staple merchandise of the place. Ere long, we gained the Chester road. Not that we were even then in the open country, for rows of low brick habitations, with little gardens in front, lined the way for miles. At last, we came upon well-cultivated fields, skirted by tall poplars, but I took little note of any object we passed, being absorbed in reflection, and my companion, reading, perhaps, what was passing in my breast, did not disturb me. Suddenly, I was aroused, as from a troubled dream, by finding we had arrived at Dunton.

The Stamford Arms, where we alighted, was a comfortable country inn of the good old kind—now sadly too rare—and noted for its excellent cookery, its old port wine, and its well-kept bowling-green. It had been much frequented in former days by rollicking Cheshire squires. We were shown into a pleasant room on the ground floor, with windows looking upon the bowling-green, and walls adorned with pictures of hunters celebrated in the county. In due time a nice little dinner was served. My companion did full justice to the good cheer, and, all things considered, seemed in excellent spirits. I am convinced he did not dislike the excitement of the affair. For my own part, whatever my secret sensations might be, I managed to preserve a tolerably cheerful exterior. After dinner, our host brought us a bottle of the famous old port, and appeared very proud of its brilliancy and bee's-wing. I contented myself with a single glass, which I took to please the landlord; but Cuthbert Spring, who smacked his lips over the wine, and declared it to be in superb condition, would have had me drink a pint to steady my nerves.

It was a delicious evening, with a clear atmosphere and cloudless sky, that gave us assurance of a fine night. We sat with the windows wide open, and enticed forth by the beauty of the evening, I left my friend to enjoy his wine alone; continuing to walk backwards and forwards on the smooth velvet sod, until a sudden burst of radiance falling upon me through a break in the trees that sheltered the garden, told me the moon had arisen. For some time before this I had heard voices proceeding from the room I had quitted, and returning thither, I found Mr. Rushton, the surgeon, conversing with Cuthbert Spring. He shook hands with me as I entered, but made no allusion to the affair on which we were engaged. Soon afterwards, a waiter came in to say the chaise was ready, and we all prepared to depart. Mr. Rushton's private carriage was waiting for him at the door, and it was arranged that he should follow us.

While I was getting into the chaise, having previously deposited the pistol-case within it, Cuthbert Spring approached the postilion, and gave him some directions inaudible to the bystanders. The man touched his hat in token of acquiescence, and the next moment my friend was by my side, the steps were put up, the whip cracked, and we set off along the Chester road. The sound of other wheels informed us that the surgeon was close behind.

It was a lovely night, almost as bright as day. The road we were pursuing ran along high ground, and the wide vale below was steeped in moonlight. Some three miles off I could discern the shimmering expanse of Marston Mere, with the old church tower just above it. As we approached Dunton Park, and passed through part of it, its noble woods and long sweeping glades derived wonderful effect from the medium through which they were viewed. In places, the road was completely overshadowed by enormous beech-trees, which flourished vigorously in the sandy soil, and quite intercepted the moonbeams by their thick foliage.

We were mounting a slight ascent, where one side of the road, being comparatively free from timber, admitted the full radiance of the moon, while the other was cast into deep shade by a thick grove of black pines; when I noticed two dark figures standing on a high sand-bank, under the shadow of the sombre trees. Even in that imperfect light, I could tell that they were gipsies, and I pointed them out to Cuthbert Spring. Both of the men were armed with bludgeons. I could not help watching their movements, and when we came close upon them I thought I recognised the swarthy lineaments of my old acquaintance Phaleg, who, it would appear, had returned to his former haunts; while in the lithe young man by his side I had no doubt that I beheld Phaleg's son Obed. My face was turned towards them, and as the moon lighted up my features, I am sure Phaleg knew me, for he bent eagerly forward, and pointed me out to his son. If the gipsies meditated an attack, they abandoned the design on seeing the other carriage approach; but they looked after us, as if half disposed to follow. They were soon, however, out of sight, owing to a turn in the road, and I thought no more about them.

A rapid descent brought us to the foot of a hill, and in a few minutes more we had reached the entrance of a narrow lane, about a bow-shot from the little stone bridge crossing the Rollin. Here we alighted, and leaving the postilion in care of the chaise, proceeded on foot towards the place of rendezvous, which was not very far off. Mr. Rushton followed more leisurely.

Crabtree-green was a small common, bounded on the left by the river Rollin, which flowed in so deep a channel as to be altogether invisible, unless on a near approach to its banks. On the right, the green was edged by a woody dingle, called the Raven's Clough. About midway in the common, and a few yards in front of the clough, stood a remarkable tree, forming a most picturesque object in the landscape. It was an ancient oak, scathed by lightning, and reduced almost to a hollow trunk; but it had still some vitality left in its upper limbs, and flung abroad its two mighty arms like an old Druid in the act of prophecy. In this fantastic-looking tree a pair of ravens used to build, and were never allowed to be molested. At the further end of the green was a small cottage—the only tenement adjoining it; and in the enclosure near the cottage, grew an old crab-tree, which lent its name to the spot.

We were first in the field. Cuthbert Spring looked at his watch, and said it wanted five minutes to eleven—in five minutes more they would be here.

While he went to select a favourable piece of ground, I walked towards the banks of the river, and remained gazing at its current as it flowed tranquilly by. More than half the stream was in deep shade, and looked black as ink, but just beneath me the circling eddies glittered brightly in the moonlight. The serene beauty of the night had gradually softened my heart, and, as I looked down on that quiet stream, the thirst of vengeance, which had hitherto consumed me, subsided, and I felt reluctant to take the life of him who had so deeply injured me.

Hearing sounds as of persons approaching along the lane leading to the green, I returned to Cuthbert Spring, whom I found on a perfectly bare piece of ground, about fifty yards in front of the scathed oak. Mr. Rushton was standing by himself, a little way off, nearer the cottage, with a case of instruments under his arm.

The next moment, Colonel Harbottle and Malpas Sale were seen advancing, and as they drew near they both saluted us ceremoniously, and we returned the greeting in the same formal manner. Colonel Harbottle then took Mr. Spring aside, and conferred with him for a few moments.

While this was passing, I glanced at Malpas, who stood opposite to me in a careless attitude. The moon was shining full upon us, and it might be the effect of its pallid light, but I thought his features looked ghastly.

Presently, the seconds returned, and Colonel Harbottle approaching me, inquired in a very courteous manner if there was any possibility of the matter being accommodated. I answered sternly in the negative, and as I spoke Malpas cast a sharp look at me. He then stood erect, with compressed lip, and knitted brow.

The seconds now retired, and the pistols were loaded. This done, the distance was measured; we were respectively placed; and the weapons were delivered to us. It was arranged that the signal to fire should be a white handkerchief waved by Colonel Harbottle.

Once more the seconds withdrew. Just then, two ravens flew over our heads, croaking hoarsely and angrily, evidently disturbed from their roost in the scathed oak-tree. I could not help glancing at them, and, in doing so, perceived that another couple of ravens had put the legitimate occupants of the old oak-tree to flight. The younger gipsy, Obed, it seemed, had climbed the antique tree, and taken up his station on one of its mighty arms. Phaleg himself was standing beneath, leaning against the massive trunk, and watching us composedly. I should have drawn the attention of the seconds to these unlicensed intruders, but ere I could do so Colonel Harbottle coughed loudly to call attention. On the instant I became fixed, with my eye upon my antagonist, yet watching for the signal. It was a trying moment, and I could scarcely draw breath. But I never swerved from the resolution I had formed while gazing at the river.

The handkerchief was waved, and we both fired at the same moment. I am certain I could have killed my adversary; but I had no such intention. I raised my arm aloft, and discharged my pistol into the air.

The seconds ran towards us, making anxious inquiries, accompanied by Mr. Rushton, who had drawn near before the encounter took place.

I was hit. A sharp knock, just above the right elbow, had quite numbed my arm, and the pistol dropped from my grasp.

CHAPTER V.

I RENEW MY ACQUAINTANCE WITH PHALEG.

Both the seconds seemed greatly relieved by the assurance I was able to give them that I was not much hurt, and having seen me fire into the air, they declared that the duel was at an end. Leaving me in the hands of the surgeon, Colonel Harbottle went to confer with his principal, while Mr. Rushton commenced an examination of my arm, and finding I could not take off my coat, he instantly slit up the sleeve, and then discovered a severe contusion just above the elbow, where the ball had struck me. Owing to my arm being raised at the moment of receiving the shot, the ball had glanced off without doing much damage except to the muscles, which it had battered and benumbed, and then running along, had lodged itself in my dress, behind the shoulder. The surgeon took it from my shirt, and laughingly presented it to me, at the same time giving me the comfortable assurance that the hurt would be well in a few days, though my arm might probably continue stiff for a somewhat longer period.

At this juncture, Colonel Harbottle and Malpas came up.

"I am rejoiced to hear such a good report of you, Mr. Mervyn Clitheroe," the colonel said, with great politeness, "and so, I am quite sure, is my principal. After the magnanimity you have displayed, it would have been matter of deep regret to him, as well as to all engaged in this affair, if any ill consequences had resulted from his shot. This, sir, I beg you to believe. And now that the quarrel is adjusted, and you have so gallantly received your adversary's fire (which I trust I may construe into a tacit admission that you were somewhat hasty in your expressions concerning him), let me hope that a reconciliation may take place between you and my friend. It will gratify me extremely to see you shake hands together before we quit the field."

Cuthbert Spring was about to make an observation, but I checked him, and addressing Colonel Harbottle with some warmth, said: "You are entirely mistaken in concluding, that because I did not choose to make Mr. Malpas Sale my mark, I admit that I was in the wrong. No such thing, sir. I regret the occasion of the quarrel; but my opinion of Mr. Malpas Sale is unchanged, and I do not mean to retract anything I have said of him."

"I am sorry to hear it," Colonel Harbottle rejoined, rather nettled. It is scarcely what I expected from you."

A flush had spread over Malpas's face while I was speaking, and

M

it was with evident discomposure that he now remarked: "I should have been quite willing to shake hands with Mr. Mervyn Clitheroe had he been so inclined; but since he rejects all friendly advances, and refuses to place me upon an equality with himself in a meeting like the present, I trust he will give no further license to his tongue."

"Softly, sir—softly," Cuthbert Spring interposed. "My principal has offered you full satisfaction, and you ought to be content. Colonel Harbottle, I am sure, must be of my opinion."

"I am, sir," the colonel rejoined. "We can ask no more than we have obtained. Still, I may be permitted to observe——"

"Nay, colonel, you must perceive that nothing can be gained by prolonging this discussion," Cuthbert Spring interrupted. "I must positively put a stop to it."

"I have done," Colonel Harbottle rejoined. "In taking leave, I can only repeat my regret that we are no nearer a settlement than when we began. It is no compliment to Mr. Mervyn Clitheroe, but the simple expression of truth, to say that he has conducted himself throughout the affair like a man of honour. Good night, gentlemen." Whereupon he and Malpas formally saluted us, and withdrew.

They had not, however, proceeded far, when they were brought to a halt. Two dark figures were seen hurrying towards them. I had been so completely engrossed by what had occurred during the last ten minutes, that I had taken no note of the pair of gipsies; and I should have expected them to disappear when their curiosity was gratified, rather than to come forward in this manner.

"Halloa! who the deuce are you?—what d'ye want?" Colonel Harbottle exclaimed, facing them.

"I wants a word wi' his honour, Capt'n Sale, afore he goes," Phaleg replied. "He knows Phaleg, the gipsy. I did a little job for him some years ago. His honour will recollect it, I dar say," he added, with some significance.

"His honour has no desire to recollect his boyish follies," Malpas replied, evidently annoyed by the interruption. "What are you doing here at this time of night, fellow?"

"Nay, I might put that question to your honour," Phaleg rejoined, drily, "but I needn't ax when my eyes and ears ha' gied me information. If gen'l'folk chooses to settle their quarrels wi' pistols or swords, Ize nivir interfere wi' um—not I. I likes the sport too well."

"You had better be off to your tent, wherever it may be pitched," Malpas rejoined. "And here, you shan't go empty-handed." he added, giving him a piece of gold, as I conceived the coin to be from the eagerness with which the gipsy took it.

"Thank your honour!" Phaleg cried. "Obed and me will drink your honour's health, an' wishin' you better luck next time."

"I can't have better luck than to come off scot free myself, and hit my adversary," Malpas rejoined, with a laugh.

"Yea, you might have better luck nor that," Phaleg replied.

"I don't understand you, fellow." Malpas rejoined, sternly. "Hark ye, sirrah, if you value your safety, you won't remain in this neighbourhood. Once before you made it too hot for you, and you may do so again, and not get off so easily."

"Bless your honour, capt'n, I've nowt to fear. I've left off poachin' this many a day. I be an honest tinker now by trade, and so be my son Obed."

"Yes, we both of us be tinkers, at your honour's sarvice," Obed chimed in.

"I be noways afeard to show myself i' broad dayleet," Phaleg said, "and if your honour win only let me know when I can wait upon you at the vicarage, I win ca' and tell you summat you may be pleased to larn."

"Hang you for an importunate rascal!" Malpas cried, impatiently. "Call to-morrow morning if you will, but don't keep me any longer now. I owe you a thousand apologies for detaining you thus, colonel," he added, turning away. And taking his friend's arm, they marched quickly off the ground.

While the conversation just described took place between the gipsy and Malpas, the surgeon was engaged in dressing my bruised arm, and he applied some strong stimulant to the injured part that made it smart excessively. Mr. Rushton had bound up my arm, and was making a sling with a silk handkerchief to support it, when Phaleg came and planted himself right in front of me, with his thick bludgeon under his arm, and an impudent grin on his swarthy face.

"How d'ye like the feel of cold lead, mester?" he asked, perceiving me wince a little with the pain. "Uncommon pleasant—ben't it? You once put half a charge of swan-shot into me, and every devil's pellet—each on 'em as big as a pea—had to be picked out. That wad ha' made you grind your teeth, and kick out a bit. I'm not sorry to see you writhe i' your turn."

"I tell you what, you insolent scoundrel," Cuthbert Spring cried, "you'll have another taste of cold lead yourself, that may do your business effectually, if you and your comrade don't be off pretty quickly."

"Me and my son be doin' no harm to nobody," Phaleg rejoined, in a tone of surly defiance; "and we've as much right to be here as you, or anybody. I shan't stir; and I advise you not to molest me, or mayhap you'll get the warst on't."

Armed as he was, Phaleg did seem an awkward customer, and his son, though a lighter weight, appeared well able to support him. For the last few moments I had been considering what course to pursue. If I had been able to use my right arm, I would have seized the rascal without hesitation; but though the odds were in our favour, I doubted whether we could master the pair of ruffians. Cuthbert Spring had threatened to use the pistols, but Phaleg knew well enough that the weapons were not loaded. It might be as well, therefore, to temporise. Moreover, I called to mind the mysterious conversation I had had with the elder gipsy in Marston Churchyard some years ago, and resolved to try whether anything could be extracted from him.

M 2

"No harm shall be done you, Phaleg, if you keep quiet," I observed, in a tone calculated, as I thought, to appease him. "Give heed to what I'm about to say to you. You once offered to sell me a secret. Are you still willing to dispose of it, or have you made a better bargain elsewhere?"

"Oh! you're on that tack, eh?" the gipsy cried, in a jeering tone, and with an insolent grimace. "You intend goin' roundabout, I perceive; but I'll come to the pint at once, like a plain-spoken chap as I be. Now, gie good heed to me, young mester. Twice I meant kindly by you, and both times you sarved me an ill turn. I've sworn not to forgie you. When I met you that night i' Marston kirkyard, I would ha' dealt fairly with you; but you and that infernal keeper hunted me like an otter i' th' mere, and weel-nigh drownded me, besides tearin' my flesh to bits wi' your great hounds. I *have* a secret as 'ud make a man on you—a *gen'l'man*. But," he added, with a savage look, while his black eyes blazed with vindictive malice, "I'd not sell it you for twice—ay, thrice as much as I axed then."

Cuthbert Spring and the surgeon, as may well be supposed, stared in astonishment at what they heard, and the former took out a powder-flask and made a hasty attempt to load one of the pistols. But Phaleg was upon him in a twinkling.

"Put that by!" he cried, with a deep oath, and brandishing his bludgeon as he spoke, "or Ize do ye a mischief."

"Hold hard, Phaleg!" I exclaimed, grasping his arm with the hand I could still employ. "I will engage that my friend shall not meddle with you. Leave him alone," I added to Cuthbert Spring—"he's dangerous."

"Ay, I *be* daungerous," Phaleg cried, shaking off my hold, "as he'll find, and you too, if you tries me."

"What does the fellow want?" Mr. Spring demanded, uneasily. "Are we to be robbed and maltreated, and offer no resistance?"

"Fair words, mester, or we shall come to blows," Phaleg rejoined, in a menacing voice. "You'll nother be robbed nor moltrayted by me or my son. We be tinkers, as I telled his honour, Capt'n Sale, just now, and arns an honest livelihood. I want nowt from you nor onybody else; but I expects civil usage, and I'll *have* it," he added, with another deep oath. "There, now you knows my mind. And he"—(pointing to me)—"knows it too; and he onderstands by this time what he have lost by playin' cross wi' me."

Without another word he turned away, and motioning to his son, they ran towards the Raven's Clough, and plunged down its woody banks.

Before they had reached the covert, Cuthbert Spring inquired why I had let them go? I replied that the attempt to detain them would have been attended with great risk, and that it would be idle now to follow them, and Mr. Rushton concurred with me in opinion. "But don't suppose," I said to Mr. Spring, "that I have done with the rascal. I mean to have another interview with him before long. He must hide pretty closely if he hopes to baffle my search for him."

In a few minutes more all preparations were made for our departure, and we quitted the field. The incident that had just occurred formed the subject of our discourse as we walked along. Cuthbert Spring thought that immediate information should be given to the police at Dunton about Phaleg, but I dissuaded him from taking the step, as I had a scheme of my own for dealing with the gipsy.

Before we reached the spot where the carriages had been left, my bruised arm began to give me great pain; and after getting into the chaise, the motion of the vehicle increased my anguish so much that I determined to stop at Dunton, and pass the night at the Stamford Arms. Thither accordingly we drove, and the hour being now late, we had to knock up the house. However, I soon gained admittance, and on beholding me with my sleeve ripped up, and my arm in a sling, the landlord immediately divined what had happened. Indeed, he now owned that he had previously suspected my intentions. He promised that a comfortable bed should be prepared for me directly.

Cuthbert Spring did not alight, but said he would come over to me on the morrow, and bring my luggage from the Palace Inn at Cottonborough, as I might feel disposed to recruit myself by a few quiet days at Dunton. In taking leave of me, he said in a tone of great kindness, and not altogether void of emotion, " I told you you would come out of this affair with credit to yourself,—and you have done so. I fully appreciate the motives which, I am sure, induced you to fire into the air. You acted nobly. Here are the letters you entrusted to my charge," he added, delivering them to me. " I am truly happy in having to return them."

With this, he drew back in the chaise to make room for Mr. Rushton, who took a place beside him, for the sake of companionship on the road; and having ordered the other carriage to follow, both gentlemen bade me good night, and drove off.

Previously to his departure, the surgeon had given me a phial, the contents of which he directed me to apply to my bruised arm; adding, with a laugh, that he felt sure I should not require any further attendance on his part. The village apothecary would suffice, he said, if I needed further aid.

Shortly afterwards, I sought my couch. The landlord aided me to disrobe, and would gladly have learnt some particulars of the duel, but I did not gratify his curiosity. It will be readily conceived that I did not sleep much that night.

CHAPTER VI.

A SUMMER MORNING IN DUNTON PARK.—SAD INTELLIGENCE.

My arm was very stiff next morning, but, the pain having in a great degree abated, I did not think it needful to call in the village surgeon. Having converted a black silk neckerchief into a decent-looking sling to support my injured limb, and put on a cool over-coat and a broad-leaved brown hat to shade me from the sun, I sallied forth, with the intention of proceeding to Marston. Before starting, I took care to order dinner for seven o'clock; giving particular directions about a bottle of the wonderful old port for Mr. Spring.

It was a tempting day for a walk; rather warm, but a pleasant breeze tempered the heat. For some little distance, the road was the same as that which I had taken on the previous night; but with different feelings I now pursued it! Nerve oneself as one may, the thought of an approaching conflict, the issue of which may be fatal, is anything but agreeable. I was glad the duel was over—and without bloodshed. I had sustained a trifling injury, but it gave me no concern; whereas, if I had shot Malpas, I might ever afterwards have been a prey to remorse. Certainly, I should not have enjoyed the bright sunshine and the lovely prospect of wood, vale, and lake, as much as I now enjoyed them. Occasionally a saddening thought connected with Apphia would intrude itself, overshadowing me like a dark cloud; but the exhilarating influences I have described soon enabled me to chase it away.

On reaching Dunton Park, instead of proceeding along the highway, I leaped the moss-grown pales, and shaped my course through the thickest parts of its magnificent woods. How tranquillising is the deep stillness of an ancient grove on a summer's day! How favourable is such a spot for contemplation! Ever and anon I sat down beneath the ample shade of some gigantic tree, and indulged in a pleasing reverie. A herd of fallow deer, a chance squirrel, rabbits, and a few songsters of the grove were the only living objects in view. If I reclined thus like Jaques, my meditations were neither moody nor misanthropic. Though I looked upon myself as an injured man, my feelings towards my fellows were far from unkindly. My desire was to mix more with the world, and form fresh friendships, for I felt convinced that happiness can always be found if the right way of seeking it is only taken.

While I was thus musing, the sudden flight of the herd of deer which had been couching beneath the shade of some evergreen oaks on the skirts of the wood, the cries of a jay and the chattering of magpies, made me aware that an intruder was at hand; and I presently saw a keeper, habited in a velveteen jacket and leather leggings, ride out of the covert. The man was mounted on a strong, shaggy-looking pony, which he appeared to guide entirely by voice, for he never touched the reins—his hands being occupied by a rifle, which he rested upon the saddle. He was accompanied by a coal-black bloodhound, and after galloping for a few minutes after the flying herd, by the help of the hound he singled out a fine buck and then suddenly halting, leaped to the ground, levelled, and fired. The deer fell with a single bound, being apparently hit between the horns. The keeper then placed the carcase of the noble animal upon the back of the pony, and secured it from falling by tying cords to the legs.

While watching the man during this operation, I became convinced that it must be Ned Culcheth. Those broad shoulders and athletic frame—those six feet of stature—those tremendous whiskers and forest of red hair—those manly features and that bold deportment, could belong to none but Ned. But how came he—one of Mr. Vernon's keepers—to be shooting a buck in the domains of Lord Amounderness? Be this as it might—entertaining no doubt as to the identity of the personage with Ned—I went to the borders of the grove and hailed him. My voice arrested him just as he was setting off. He knew me directly, and hurried towards me—the hound keeping close at his heels, and the pony, with its load, trotting after him, like a dog of a larger breed, and halting when he halted.

A very cordial greeting passed between us, for I had a great liking for the honest fellow. I had not seen him for three or four years, and now that I scanned his features more closely, I perceived that he was much changed. Anxiety was visible in his open countenance, and a frost seemed to have settled upon the tips of his glowing whiskers. I began to fear something had gone wrong with him. In explanation of his presence in Dunton Park, he told me that he was now in the service of its noble owner; and while imparting this piece of information, he heaved a deep sigh. However, he made an effort to appear cheerful, and cried:

"Why, you be grown quite a man, I declare, Mester Mervyn—and a fine man, too, as ever I clapped eyes on. But what be the matter wi' your arm?—not broken, I hope, sir?"

"Oh! a mere nothing, Ned—an accidental shot, that's all."

"A pistol-shot, maybe?" Ned rejoined, with a sly look. "I did hear as how there war some shootin' on Crabtree-green last night, and it wouldn't surprise me to larn that you got hit there—by accident, of course, sir."

I turned off the question with a laugh, and directing my attention to the hound, remarked, while patting the animal's head, "What a noble hound you have got, Ned!—a Saint Hubert—eh?"

"A Saint Hubert he be, sir," Ned replied. "He comes from the forest of the Ardenues, they tells me, and be one of the true race from Saint Hubert's Abbey. He were sent to Squire Vernon fro' foreign parts, and the squire gied him to me; and a better gift he couldn't have bestowed—for Hubert—I calls him Hubert, sir,—hasn't his match."

"A perfect hound, Ned, I'll warrant him," I replied, regarding him with a sportsman's admiration—"he bears about him all the marks of keen scent, great swiftness, and extraordinary force and endurance. When I first beheld him just now, I called to mind an old distich by a huntsman of Lorraine, which might be engraved on his collar:

> 'My name came first from holy Hubert's race,
> Souyllard my sire, a hound of singular grace.'

I congratulate you on the possession of such a hound, Ned. But it is time to inquire after the other occupants of your kennel. How are my old friends and your faithful companions, Gaunt and Lupus?"

"Lupus be dead more nor a year ago," the keeper replied; "but poor owd Gaunt be still livin', though too stiff for work, so I leaves him at home to tend the house."

"A trusty watch-dog I'm sure, old as he is," I rejoined. "But I have been sadly remiss, Ned. I ought to have asked long ago after sweet Sissy? How is your darling little wife?"

I never was more startled in my life. I thought the strong man would have dropped. He shook as if an ague had seized him, and staggered towards a tree, against which he leaned for support.

Suspecting I had harmed his master, Hubert glared at me with his deep-set red orbs, while his lips curled fiercely. For my own part, I was exceedingly distressed. But I had never heard of poor Sissy's death. And that Ned must have lost her I now felt certain, from the emotion he displayed.

I thought it best to let him be—and, indeed, I did not know how to comfort him. Sissy had always been a great favourite of mine, and it was sad to think that so fair a flower should be cut off thus prematurely.

At length, Ned made an effort to rouse himself, and throwing back his head as if to ease his labouring breast, he came slowly towards me. I took his hand, and looked kindly into his haggard countenance.

"I have been abroad for some time, Ned, and am only just returned," I said. "I was not aware of the heavy loss you have sustained, or I wouldn't have said anything to distress you."

"Ay, ay, it be a heavy loss, sure enough—heavier a'most than I can bear," Ned groaned. "Mine were once a happy home—no man's more so. Sissy made a palace of my humble dwelling—leastways I thought it so. When I cum'd home tired and jaded after a long day's work, her smiles and cheerful words set me right at once. You ha' been i' my cottage often, sir, and know whether she kept it tidy or not. There wasn't a cleaner cottage in the county—that I'll uphold. And as to the missis herself—but I won't speak about her. You know what she were."

"I do, Ned. She was the prettiest woman of her class I ever beheld—and as good as she was pretty."

"Hold, sir!" he cried, with a look I shall never forget. Don't say a word about her goodness. It were her misfortune that she were so pratty. Better she had been the plainest lass i' Cheshire than turn her beauty to ill account."

"I dare not ask for an explanation of your words, Ned," I replied, inexpressibly shocked; "but I hope I mistake their meaning. At all events, let me implore you to think kindly of the dead."

"Sissy ben't dead, sir," he rejoined, with a stern look. "Would she were! Then I could truly lament her. She have betrayed me—she have left me. But she ben't dead—no—she ben't dead," he repeated, with a fearful shudder.

Hubert uttered a low growl, and again glared fiercely at me.

I hardly knew what to say to the poor keeper, for his deep affliction quite unmanned me, but at length I addressed him thus:—"If any one else, but yourself, had told me this, Ned, I would have flatly contradicted the statement. Even now I can scarcely believe it. If Sissy has proved false, I shall lose my faith in all the rest of her sex."

"I wish I could doubt it myself, sir," he replied. "But it be only too true. Heaven knows I dearly loved her — better than life! I thought of nothin' but her; and couldn't do enough to please her. She had only to ax an' have. so far as my poor means went; and as to failin' i' constancy to her, I could as soon ha' failed in duty to my Maker. But," he added, with intense bitterness, "I suppose I warn't handsome enough for her—I warn't fine gen'l'man enough—I couldn't talk softly enough."

"And she left you, then, for some one who styled himself a gentleman, Ned?" I demanded. "Am I to understand you so?"

"Ay," he replied, "she left me who valleyed her more than silver and gowd—more than a' the treasures on airth—f..' one who only took her for an hour's pastime, and then cast her off. I don't know what black art he used to wean her affections fro' me—for I think her love were mine once—I don't know whether she struggled against his snares—but she fell into 'em, and left me. And this I can say for myself, sir—and say it wi' truth—she left as fond and faithful a husband as ever woman had."

And he sat down, and covered his face with his great freckled hands, utterly unable to control his grief. When men like Ned Culcheth weep, it is a sorry sight.

Hubert uttered a mournful howl, and laid his large black head upon his master's lap.

I looked on much distressed—utterly unable to offer the poor fellow consolation.

"You'n excuse me, sir," Ned said, constraining himself at length. "I'm not often i' this way, but the sight o' you, and the way you spoke of her, brought a' back again. I mind the time when you used to come to our cottage when it were the abode of wedded happiness and love. Now there be no Sissy at the door to look out and welcome me—no cheerful hearth wi' Sissy sittin' smilin' beside it to gladden me—no Sissy to put her arms round my neck and kiss me. But I be a lone, deserted, broken-hearted man."

"Not so bad as that, I trust, Ned. Don't think of Sissy any more. She doesn't deserve to be held in your regard."

But he seemed to have a pleasure in opening his wounds anew; for, without heeding me, he took a locket from his bosom and pressed it to his lips.

"You recollect her beautiful hair," he said, with a tenderness that almost overcame me, "how it used to glint like gowd i' the sunshine. This bauble contains a lock of it. It be a' I ha' left on her. I have tried to throw it away, but it clings to my heart, and win stick there, I fancy, till that heart ceases to beat."

And kissing the locket again, he replaced it softly in his bosom, and then sprang to his feet.

"You must give me full particulars of this unhappy affair, Ned, on some future occasion, when you are calmer. But if it will not distress you too much to dwell upon the subject now, I should wish to know when Sissy's flight took place, and what led to it?"

"She left me about four months ago," he replied, "and if you must know what led to the step, I think it were a quarrel betwixt us. But I couldn't see a handsome, dashin' young gent'l'man al'ays danglin' after her, and not feel jealous. Besides, folks jeered me about it. He used to row her out i' my boat on th' mere. When I heer'd o' this—for I hadn't seen it—I determined to put a stop to it—and one e'en I came upon 'em by surprise, just as they landed. You may believe, sir, when my blood were up, that I didn't use much civil speech to the young spark. I forbade him to come near my cottage, and commanded my foolish wife never to speak to him again. Bitter words passed between me and Sissy, and I sat by myself a' that night, half distracted, yet never dreamin' of the misery in store for me. Ere day dawned, I went forth to a distant cover, without biddin' Sissy good-by—the first time I had ever done such a thing sin' we were wedded—and when I got back at noon, there were no one to greet me—no meal ready—she were gone. She had quitted the house at night without my bein' aware on't."

"But she went alone?"

"Oh! he were there to help her—trust him for that. She got through the window and joined him. It were a mercy I didn't hear 'em, or I should ha' shot 'em both on the spot. So help me, I should, sir! I were nearly shootin' myself when I found it out."

"You are certain she didn't go alone, Ned?"

"Quite sartin. Things spoke for themselves when I cum'd to examine 'em. But it were so contrived that I couldn't bring it home to him; and when I taxed him wi' robbin' me of my wife, he point blank denied it; and endeavoured to lay the weight of the black deed on another man's showthers."

"But did you make no search for your wife, Ned?"

"Sarch,—yes, sir. I sarched for her high and low—far an' near, but could gain no tidings whatever on her—and to this blessed day I ha' learnt nothing."

I reflected for a short time, and then said, "It doesn't appear, from what you tell me, Ned, that you have any clear proof of your wife's infidelity. She may have fled with the tempter, and left him immediately afterwards, and yet have dreaded to return to you. But, however I may try to exonerate Sissy, I will not attempt to defend the villain who has sought to ensnare her. If it be as I suspect, and I had known as much as I do now, I would not have spared him when I had him within pistol-shot last night."

"What!" Ned exclaimed, "did you fight a duel wi' Capt'n Sale last night?"

"Then it is as I suspected, Ned. He is the person who has wronged you."

"Ay, he be the villain who have destroyed my happiness," Ned rejoined, fiercely. "I would give ten years o' my life to stand opposite him i' fair fight. I would send a bullet through his black heart. But though he wouldn't scruple to injure me, he won't gie me satisfaction."

"No, no, Ned," I replied, bitterly; "the laws of honour won't compel a gentleman to give satisfaction to one of your condition. Don't think it."

"And you ca' such laws as those, laws of honour, sir?" Ned cried, with furious scorn. "Because I be a poor man, have I no sense of injury? Is not my wife as much to me as the gen'l'man's wife be to him? And if the gen'l'man wrongs me so deeply that nothing but the gen'l'man's blood can wash out the stain, am I to be denied that satisfaction which would be open to the gen'l'man's equal? If those be your laws of honour, sir, I shan't respect them. I bide my time," he muttered, in a stern tone, and with a sombre look, "and will find my own mode of redress. Woe be to him!—woe be to him, I say, if he once gets into my clutches!"

"Patience, Ned—patience!" I exclaimed. "Dismiss these violent notions, and act like a just and prudent man. The laws of honour, I agree with you, ought to bind all classes alike; and if a man is not too proud to injure another, his rank ought not to screen him from the consequences of the act. If such a person refuses satisfaction to his inferior, he ought to be stamped with dishonour. But this cannot be, and therefore it is idle to discuss the question. Attend to what I am about to say to you. Malpas Sale has injured me only a degree less than he has injured you. We will make common cause against him. Prove to me beyond question that he lured your wife from you—that she eloped with him. Prove that they were seen together after her flight. Discover her retreat, so that she may be produced, if we find occasion. Do this, and I will ensure you ample redress."

"But how be I to obtain such proofs as you require, sir?" Ned rejoined, looking quite confused. "How be I to discover Sissy's retreat? Capt'n Sale—curses upon him!—and she ha' never been seen together, that I can larn, sin' she left me. I ha' taxed him wi' it as I tell'd you afore; but he denies the charge a'together, and declares I'm mista'en i' the man. I'm sorely perplexed i' my mind Capt'n Sale were at the vicarage on the day after the elopement, for I seed him myself; and he ca'd his sarvant man to prove that he had not been out the night afore. He treated the matter quite lightly, and said if Sissy had eloped at all, it must have been wi' Simon Pownall."

"With Simon Pownall!—ridiculous!"

"Ridic'lous, indeed, sir! I towd him he couldn't impose upon me by such a falsity. But when I began to make inquiries, things seemed to bear out his assertions. A' the folk i' Marston believed then, and believes to this day, that Simon were the offender."

"But where is Simon Pownall?" I exclaimed. "Cannot he be found?"

"No, sir, he cannot. He disappeared at the same time as poor Sissy, and has never been heer'd on sin'; and that's what confirms folks' suspicions. I ought also to mention one circumstance, that weighs wi' others, though it doesn't weigh much wi' me—Simon were seen, and spoken with, i' the lane leadin' to my cottage, at an hour when all honest folks should be a-bed, on the night of the elopement."

"Tut!—that was part of the plan. The knave took care to be seen. Simon Pownall was a tool in the affair, I make no doubt; but not the principal. You have been far too slack, Ned. You must not rest till you find Pownall, and discover your wife's retreat."

"Point out the way, sir, and I'll set about it at once."

"You are a woodman, Ned, and will understand the advice I am about to give you. If you sought for a hart in a forest, you would look for his slot, and follow him up by it. Do the same now. A few slight footprints, which have hitherto escaped your notice, will lead you to Pownall's lair, and enable you to unharbour him. But you must devote yourself wholly and solely, and with all your energies, to the task."

"I will, sir," Ned replied, firmly. "Your words ha' put new mettle into me. Hitherto, I ha' been too slack—I feel it now—but then I ha' been wofully cast down, and have had none to counsel me. Hencefor'rard, you shan't complain o' my want o' zeal. I once thought Sissy might ha' gone to her family at Llanberis, i' Carnarvonsheere—and I wrote to 'em for tidings on her—but, alas! they could gie me none. She had never been nigh 'em."

"It is a sad affair, Ned, and strange as sad—but we must unravel the mystery. You shall have all the assistance I can render you—money, if you want it. But what's the matter with Hubert? He seems disturbed."

"He hears, or scents something, sir," Ned replied, noticing the warning attitude of the hound. "More ears ha' been listenin' to us than we counted on. We'll soon find out the spy. Hyke, Hubert! to him, lad!"

As he uttered the words, the hound bounded off, as if unleashed, towards a bed of fern, from out of which, at the same moment, sprang the younger gipsy, Obed.

But the spy only fled to a short distance, and then, turning round, laughed derisively at us.

He had taken precautions, as speedily appeared, to secure himself from the attack of the hound; and he must have possessed all the stealthy wiliness of a savage of the backwoods of America, for he had managed, during our converse, to creep up behind the pony, and cut a large piece of flesh from the neck of the deer.

Hubert was caught in the trap set for him. He sprang with a few mighty bounds to the spot where the lump of deer's flesh had been thrown down by the gipsy, and began to devour it greedily, and not all his master's threats could make him stir.

Pointing with a blood-stained wood-knife to the deluded hound, Obed mimicked the challenge of a cock-pheasant, cut a caper, and then took to his heels at full speed. Ned ran after him, after vainly trying to tear Hubert away from his repast, but I felt quite sure the agile gipsy would give him the slip. And so it proved. In a few minutes the keeper reappeared, alone and out of breath. The fugitive had escaped.

By this time Hubert had gorged himself with the deer's flesh, and approached his master with a very abject and contrite air. Ned would have chastised him severely with his dog-whip; but I interfered to save him. Conscious that he deserved punishment, the hound looked up wistfully in the keeper's face, as if eager to repair his error.

"If I were to put him upon that pryin' young warmint's scent now," Ned observed, "he would hunt him down fast enough. But I have other matters to see to. I mun tak' up this buck to th' house; and then I'll try and get the steward to speak wi' his lordship, who luckily be down here just now, to let me off for a month. Even if I lose my place I'll do nowt else but attend to this job."

While Ned was chasing the gipsy, I had been considering what could have brought the young rascal into the park, and I arrived at the conclusion that he must have been watching me.

"Harkye, Ned," I said, "beware of these gipsies. They are capable of doing you a mischief, and I shrewdly suspect they are in the pay of our enemy. It is strange that Phaleg should be again in this neighbourhood. I saw him and his son on Crabtree-green last night. They seem to dog me about."

"Do they?" Ned cried. "Then I'll dog *them*. Leave 'em to me. I ben't a bit afeared on 'em. Where be ye stayin', sir—i' Marston?"

"At the Stamford Arms at Dunton. If not there, I shall be in the neighbourhood."

"You shall hear fro' me, or see me, as soon as I've owt to communicate," Ned rejoined. "I'll find Sissy or die. And now fare ye weel, sir, and Heaven bless you!"

Whereupon he warmly grasped the hand I extended to him, and strode away, followed by the pony and Hubert, taking his course down a long glade sweeping in the direction of Amounderness House.

CHAPTER VII.

I AM INTRODUCED TO AN ECCENTRIC ELDERLY GENTLEMAN, FAMILIARLY STYLED OLD HAZY; WHO, THOUGH NO CONJURER HIMSELF, IS MUCH ADDICTED TO NECROMANTIC LORE, AND HAS A VERY ENCHANTING NIECE.

Poor Ned! I pitied him from the bottom of my heart. His wound, I feared, would prove incurable.

And poor Sissy! I pitied her too—though she might not deserve commiseration. I could not think of her without a pang. Her image rose before me as I had seen her last—a model of rustic beauty, coquettish, captivating, not unconscious of her charms, and rather fond of admiration, yet devoted to her husband, whose love was wholly hers. And she had fallen—alas! alas!

Years ago I had been filled with vague apprehensions that Malpas was secretly indulging dishonourable love for her, and had grieved that she should trifle with him so much—but I had not foreseen the lamentable consequences that were to follow. Even now I could scarcely believe her guilty.

I had preached patience to Ned Culcheth, but I felt none myself. My hatred of Malpas was rekindled in all its intensity—if possible, heightened. I should have reproached myself with sparing him, but that a greater and more complete revenge seemed to be in my power. I would crush him utterly. But to accomplish this effectually, I must curb the impetuosity that prompted me to take immediate steps against him. I must go cautiously to work, and not precipitate matters, as I had recently done. I must draw the nets slowly round him and leave him no loophole to escape. Thus did I reason with myself; but I confess that if I had encountered Malpas at the moment, all my prudential resolves would have flown to the winds, and passion alone have swayed me. Luckily, I was not exposed to the temptation.

Full of wrathful and vindictive emotions, I set off at a rapid pace to Marston, and did not halt till I reached the churchyard and stood beside my mother's grave.

Often in earlier days and in moments of trouble had I come to this spot, and had ever found relief. Consolation was not denied me now. The clouds that had gathered round me began to disperse; and as a mother's endearing smiles and words chase away childish grief, so my troubles were sensibly alleviated.

Quitting this hallowed spot, I approached the low stone wall at the back of the churchyard, and gazed over the tops of the trees growing at the foot of the eminence on which the sacred fabric was reared.

Little as Marston Mere, which now lay before me, would bear comparison with other lakes, world-renowned for beauty, which I had recently visited, it had charms of its own, arising from old associations, which endeared it to me, and rendered it more attractive in my eyes than even classic Como or lovely Lugano. I now beheld it in perfect repose. Unruffled by a breath, its surface reflected every object on its banks,—trees, church-tower, boat-house,—as distinctly as a mirror. Tall black stakes, to which fishing-nets were fastened, dotted out the shallows on the right, and nearer the strand, in the same direction, stood a group of cattle cooling themselves in the water. Golden lights were thrown upon the trees by the westering sun, and a stream of radiance ran along the edge of a low copse on the left. Between this copse and the majestic woods of Dunton, crowning the distant heights, floated a thin summer haze, giving them a slumberous beauty. I looked on for some time entranced, following the shores of the lake, on either side, to the remotest point. Sweet Marston Mere, scene of my earliest pleasures, how dear was it to me! How often had I rowed upon its waters, or plunged into their pellucid depths! How often had I fished from its banks, or roused the wild duck from its reeds only to fall beneath my gun! My perilous exploit in crossing its frozen surface with Malpas Sale, occurred to me—and the midnight chase with Ned Culcheth of Phaleg, the gipsy. Poor Ned's cottage was plainly discernible from where I stood, but I sedulously avoided looking at it.

It required an effort to tear myself away from this enchanting scene, but I could not gaze at it for ever, so I crossed the churchyard, and, avoiding the vicarage, passed through a small gate, and took a path which I knew would bring me out near Simon Pownall's former habitation in the upper part of the village. In a few minutes I reached the barber-surgeon's shop, and the only external change I perceived in it was the substitution of Chetham Quick's name for that of Pownall. The apprentice had succeeded his master, and, in doing so, aped his master's peculiarities, and even personal appearance, to such an extent that he might almost have been taken for him. As I entered the shop, Chetham was sharpening a razor, and, on seeing me, he exhibited momentary surprise and perhaps alarm; but being by no means destitute of self-possession, he as quickly recovered himself, and cocking up his impudent nose, regarded me with a saucy, consequential air. He declared he knew nothing whatever of his late master, but his private opinion was that he was gone to America with Sissy Culcheth. At the time of Simon's sudden disappearance, more than a year's salary was due to him, and he had seized upon the contents of the shop as part payment of the debt, and set up in his master's place. Could he do anything for me? Could he cut my hair—shave me—or trim my whiskers? Could he bleed me,—or dress my arm—he had a sovereign remedy for a bruise?—He was rattling on in this way, when I suddenly checked his loquacity, by observing with some sternness that I didn't believe a word he had just told me—that I felt quite sure his master was *not* gone to America—and equally sure that Sissy had *not* eloped with his master—but that both were kept designedly out of the way, and he knew it. While saying this, I eyed him fixedly, but though he grew a thought paler, he did not move a muscle. He replied in a saucy tone that he was sorry I doubted his word, but he had given me all the information in his power, and if I was not satisfied I had better inquire elsewhere. Upon which he began sharpening the razor anew, and I left the shop.

My next visit was to Job Greaseby's smithy. Old Job did not recollect me at first, but as soon as he made out who I was, he evinced his delight by griping my hand—my left hand, luckily—as he would have griped a pair of pincers. I put the same question to him that I had done to Chetham Quick. Job shook his grey head, and said it was a thousand pities Sissy was gone, and with such a "feaw owd reprobate" as Simon Pownall. He did not blame her as much as most folks did, but he was very sorry for her husband, who was as worthy a chap as ever breathed, and had always treated her kindly. This was all I could extract from honest Job. He either suspected no one else, or kept his suspicions to himself.

I made no further inquiries in the village, but walked across the fields to Nethercrofts, where I fortunately found both William Weever and his wife at home. William had still got the management of the farm, and appeared to thrive on his stewardship. He and Hannah looked very well-to-do and comfortable. Neither of them had grown thinner. The old farm-house was but little changed since my uncle Mobberley's time. The old articles of furniture occupied their customary places, and I was glad to hear the old clock ticking still. Notwithstanding my remonstrances, I was shown into the parlour, and Hannah would fain have brought me some refreshments, but I would only take a cup of milk. I soon brought up the subject of Sissy's elopement, but I learnt nothing new. They both believed that Simon Pownall was the offender, and pitied her taste. William Weever was disposed to be as charitable as Job Greaseby, but his wife would not hear a word in Sissy's defence. She had always been a vain, good-for-nothing hussy, and Hannah wasn't a bit surprised at her conduct. Poor Ned was well rid of her, if he could only think so. It was a pity he couldn't see his wife with other people's eyes.

Failing in obtaining any further information, I rose to depart, promising the good couple to pay them another visit very shortly, as I intended to remain for a little time in the neighbourhood.

I had a pleasant walk back to Dunton, varying the route by keeping on the side of the mere, opposite to that by which I had come to Marston.

As I approached the Stamford Arms, I perceived, under the shade of a large tree in front of the inn, an old-fashioned barouche, with a pair of very fat horses attached to it, a remarkably stout coachman in an antiquated livery on the box, and a couple of ladies seated inside it; while just within the porch of the hostel there stood a singular-looking old gentleman, engaged in earnest discourse with Cuthbert Spring.

This old gentleman, whom I recognised at once, for I had seen him before, was Mr. Norbury Radcliffe Hazilrigge, of Owlarton Grange, near Delamere Forest—a very worthy person, but rather eccentric—of whom I had heard a great deal from various friends—amongst others, from John Brideoake, who was curate at Mr. Hazilrigge's parish church of Weverham, and who had described the old gentleman in his letters,—but I had never been introduced to him, and was very glad of the opportunity that now offered of forming his acquaintance.

Mr. Hazilrigge was between sixty and seventy, but had still a hale look, and though very odd in manner and grotesque in attire, had decidedly the air of a gentleman. In person he was rather comical, being short and punchy, while his round shoulders tended to diminish his stature. On the ridge of his large hooked nose rested a pair of massive silver spectacles, through which glimmered eyes the most extraordinary I ever beheld — large, light-blue, projecting, but dim. In a word, the old gentleman was moon-eyed. He wore his hair in powder, brushed back from the forehead, and tied behind in a long and respectable pigtail. His attire, of the formal cut of George the Third's day, might have been made about the beginning of the present century, or the end of the last, and consisted of a long blue coat, cut away at the breast and skirts, and having flat, gilt buttons, a red waistcoat, buckskins, boots with brown tops looped up behind, a large plaited frill to his shirt, and a padded cravat tied with immense bows. A broad-brimmed, low-crowned beaver, specially noticeable for its deep hat-band and buckle, and a gold-headed cane, completed his appointments.

Mr. Hazilrigge was so much engrossed by what he was saying to Cuthbert Spring, that he did not notice my approach until I was close beside him. He then turned round, and, adjusting his spectacles, looked me full in the face. His manner was so odd, and the expression of his countenance so droll as he regarded me thus, that I could scarcely help laughing at him.

"Why, this is he, Mr. Spring!" he exclaimed—"this is the young duellist!—I'm sure of it."

"You are right, Mr. Hazilrigge," Cuthbert Spring rejoined; "this is my young friend of whom we have just been speaking—Mr. Mervyn Clitheroe. Allow me to introduce him to you."

"Delighted to know you, sir," the old gentleman said, returning my salute. "You behaved very well in that affair last night with young Sale—very well indeed, upon my honour. But you'll never guess, Mr. Clitheroe, what brought me to Dunton to-day—will he, Cuthbert?—ha! ha!"

"No, I don't think he will," Mr. Spring rejoined, winking at me.

"I can't pretend to guess what business may have brought you here, Mr. Hazilrigge," I observed. "But it is a fortunate circumstance for me, since it has procured me the pleasure of your acquaintance."

The old gentleman made me a low bow.

N

"Sir, you are extremely complimentary," he said. "I won't keep you longer in suspense. Know, then, that a dream brought me here."

"A dream!" I ejaculated, with difficulty preserving my gravity.

"Yes, sir," he answered. "I dreamed that the old yew-tree in the churchyard yonder, with the bench round it, was struck by lightning and withered. This I dreamed last night—three times, sir—and I resolved to drive over this morning, and ascertain, from personal inspection, whether the yew-tree had really sustained any damage from the fiery element. I found it fair and flourishing. Now the learned Artemidorus, in his treatise *De Somniorum Interpretatione*, tells us that to dream of thunder signifies jars, quarrels, fierce debates, and contentions. And again, Anselmus Julianus, in his *Art and Judgment of Dreams*, says that a burnt or withered tree denotes vexation, fear, displeasure, and grief. Therefore, mine was a bad dream every way—a very bad dream, sir."

"Not so, sir," I rejoined, willing to humour him, and yet set him at ease. "To the great oneirocritical authorities you have brought forward, I will oppose the opinion of the oracular Apomazar, who declares that a burnt yew-tree presages the destruction of an enemy."

"Does Apomazar say so, Mr. Clitheroe?" he cried, staring at me with his purblind orbs. "Does he indeed? Apomazar is a wise man —a very wise man—*plus sapit quàm Thales*. You greatly relieve my mind. I am not aware that I have an enemy—but no matter."

"You forget your other dream about cleaving logs, Mr. Hazilrigge," Cuthbert Spring interposed. "What does that portend?"

"The visit of a stranger to the house of the dreamer, according to Artemidorus," the old gentleman answered.

"There Artemidorus is in the right, Mr. Hazilrigge," I rejoined, laughing. "*I* am the stranger, and will pay you a visit at Owlarton Grange whenever you choose to invite me."

"That is already settled," Cuthbert Spring observed. "The invitation has been given and accepted. I answered for you, as I felt sure a visit to Owlarton Grange would be highly agreeable to you. We are going to dine with my worthy friend to-morrow, and spend a few days with him."

I expressed my entire satisfaction at the arrangement.

"Mr. Spring ought to tell you that mine is a haunted house, sir," Mr. Hazilrigge said, looking at me through his spectacles.

"So much the better," I rejoined. "I have long desired to stay in a haunted house; and must beg you, as a particular favour, to put me into the ghost's room."

"Tut! you don't know what a request you are preferring," Cuthbert Spring cried. "You won't sleep a wink. I have tried the experiment once, and don't desire to try it again."

"Well, well, there are other rooms at the grange if the ghost's room shouldn't suit Mr. Clitheroe," Mr. Hazilrigge said. "He shall have his choice. We will do our best to amuse you, sir. Weverham Glen is accounted picturesque by sight-seers, and you may explore Delamere Forest, noted as the scene of several of the predictions of our famous old Cheshire prophet, Robert Nixon."

"No want of attractions, sir," I rejoined. "But one of the greatest pleasures to me will be the opportunity of seeing my dear friend—almost brother—John Brideoake, who lives near you."

"John Brideoake is constantly with us," Mr. Hazilrigge rejoined. "I have the greatest regard for him, and so has my sister. He has often talked of you, Mr. Clitheroe, and has wondered when you would return from the Continent. Poor Brideoake! I fear he has some secret sorrow. He never complains, but he looks unhappy, and his state of health gives my sister much uneasiness. You shall meet him at dinner to-morrow. But come, sir, let me make you personally known to my sister, Miss Hazilrigge, and my niece, Ora Doveton. They know you already by description."

With this, he conducted me to the barouche, and presented me in form to its occupants. Both ladies received me very graciously; but I was wholly unprepared for so much beauty as I discovered in Ora Doveton,—having only directed a casual glance towards her as I previously passed the carriage.

Miss Doveton evidently remarked my surprise, and enjoyed it. A sparkling brunette, about nineteen, with a rich bloom under the olive skin, splendid black eyes, dark pencilled brows and long silken eyelashes, magnificent black hair, teeth like pearls, and lips of the brightest coral. Such was Ora Doveton. The contour of her face was exquisite. Her manner had a peculiar witchery and grace, well suited to the southern style of her beauty; and her black silk attire and lace might have been worn by an Andalusian damsel.

I have described the niece first, because I confess that her beauty quite dazzled me, and left me very little power of noticing the aunt. But Miss Hazilrigge merited more attention than I paid her. Full fifteen years younger than her brother, she was still good looking, and had a very amiable expression. She wore her own grey hair, which suited the fresh tint of her comely features extremely well. A certain family likeness existed between her and her brother, but she was evidently shrewd and sensible, and quite as much matter-of-fact in her notions as he appeared to be the reverse.

Both ladies expressed great satisfaction on hearing that I was about to pay Owlarton Grange a visit; but Ora Doveton assured me with a smile, which rather contradicted her words, that I should find the place dreadfully dull. Her countenance wore an extremely arch expression when she spoke of the singular errand on which her uncle had come to Dunton, and she did not appear to share in his belief in dreams. I soon found out that gravity formed no part of Ora's composition. She was the merriest creature imaginable, and her high spirits carried everything before them. We were upon intimate terms directly. She rallied me upon my wounded arm, and the cause of the duel, of which she had heard—and I became so much interested by her sprightly talk, and so much enthralled by the magic of the beautiful eyes bent down upon me, that I felt quite annoyed when Mr. Hazilrigge ordered a tall old footman in an antiquated livery (Finch by name) to let down the steps, and got into the carriage.

The old gentleman then bade us good-by,—hoping to see us on the morrow,—the ladies smiled adieu—Ora's smile completed her conquest—and the stout coachman put his fat cattle in motion.

"Well, what do you think of Old Hazy?" Cuthbert Spring asked, as we entered the inn, and repaired to the room opening upon the bowling-green, where the table was spread for dinner.

"I think him very diverting," I rejoined. "He seems to have the organ of credulity rather extensively developed."

"He is the most credulous person alive," Mr. Spring returned, "and but for his excellent sister would be the dupe of any artful impostor who might choose to practise upon him. You heard on what an absurd errand he came here to-day—a dream! ha! ha!—but he is always on some wildgoose-chase or another—always finding a mare's-nest. Every nook and cranny of the old fellow's head is stuffed full of tales of hobgoblins, spectres, wood-demons, gnomes, elves, and fairies; and he reads nothing but books of necromancy, witchcraft, and judicial astrology. You will have a treat, if he shows you his library. But, notwithstanding his whims and eccentricities, Old Hazy is an excellent, estimable person."

"Amongst his numerous merits, not the least, in my opinion," I remarked, "is the possession of a very charming niece."

"Faith! you may say so. There isn't such a pair of black eyes as Ora Doveton's in the county. Why, zounds! at your age I should have fallen head-over-heels in love with her at first sight. And mark what I say, Mervyn,—beauty isn't Ora's only recommendation. She will be her uncle's heiress. Old Hazy is rich. He has no other nephews or nieces—no other near relations that I know of, except his sister; so Owlarton Grange and all belonging to it must be Ora's. There's a look-out for you, my boy."

I smiled, but not caring to acknowledge the interest I had begun to feel for Ora, I spoke of Miss Hazilrigge and the singular contrast she presented to her brother, and soon afterwards dinner was served, and we sat down to it. After the removal of the cloth, and while we were discussing a bottle of the delectable port, our conversation turned upon Owlarton Grange, and the report of its being haunted. I laughingly inquired under what form the ghost appeared?

"I am not aware that the phantom has ever revealed itself to mortal gaze," Mr. Spring replied; "but I have *heard* it, as you may possibly do, since you mean to occupy the haunted room. Owlarton Grange, as you will find, is a very curious old house—one of those quaint black and white, timber and plaster structures which I have heard you admire—and abounds in dark galleries, oddly-shaped rooms, bay-windows full of stained glass, wide staircases, narrow staircases, and out-of-the-way mouldy passages. Ghosts must be partial to such a dwelling, so no wonder one has found its way there. The grange has been in possession of the Hazilrigge family for more than two centuries, and connected with it is the remnant of a still older edifice, once appertaining to the Monastery of St. Mary, Vale Royal. But to come back to the haunted room. I won't describe it—for it will soon come under your own observation—except to say that it is spacious, with a low ceiling crossed by great oak beams, and has black oak panels, a singular old portrait, and a fantastic-looking old tester bed, with strangely carved pillars, and hangings of faded tapestry. I am not superstitious, but when I saw this bed, I felt very little inclination to occupy it. However, since there was no help, in due time I laid my head upon the pillow. Whether I had dropped off to sleep I cannot say, but I was suddenly roused by an extraordinary knock—a dull, dead, but distinct sound, as if caused by a heavy blow struck against the inner side of the wall, just below the room. I listened intently, and in another minute the knock was repeated. I counted five distinct blows—and then the sound ceased."

"Did you not arise and try to ascertain whence the sound proceeded?" I inquired.

"I had extinguished my taper, and thick curtains were drawn before the large bay-window, so that I was in profound darkness. I confess that I felt considerable trepidation. After an interval of ten minutes the mysterious sound was renewed—knock!—knock!—knock!—as if the blows had been deliberately dealt by the hand of a giant. Each blow seemed to approach nearer—and the last sounded as if struck against a closet door, which I expected would burst open, and some terrible intruder stalk in. These mysterious knocks must have commenced about midnight, and they continued at intervals, as I have described, for nearly two hours."

Cuthbert Spring had more than once replenished his glass during the progress of this story, and he now thought that its length entitled him to a second bottle of port, but having had enough, I left him to its enjoyment, and strolled out upon the bowling-green to breathe the evening air. Not to pollute the sweet atmosphere with the odour of tobacco be it understood, for I abominate the practice of smoking, and never indulge in it. While pacing to and fro, I reviewed the various incidents of the day, and though my meeting with Ned Culcheth, and the story of his wrongs had left a very painful impression upon me, yet I found myself chiefly dwelling upon a more recent occurrence. My susceptibilities seemed to be roused anew. I began to persuade myself that, by encouraging my admiration of Ora, I might succeed in forgetting Apphia. Undoubtedly there did not seem to be so great a blank in my heart as there had been in the morning. As I gazed up at the stars in the clear vault above me, I thought of orbs that rivalled them in brilliancy. Yes, yes,—I fear Apphia was in a fair way of being supplanted by the beautiful and bewitching brunette.

By-and-by, Cuthbert Spring joined me. He was in a merry mood, and soon brought up the subject of Old Hazy's charming niece, and now I did not discourage him. It was just the hour to talk of a pretty girl, and I felt disposed to unbosom myself, and own that I was half captivated, but a certain bashfulness restrained me. However, I said quite enough to convince him that I was slightly hit.

After partaking of a cup of tea in the open air, we retired early to our chambers, and my arm being much easier, I made up that night for my previous want of rest.

I arose next morning in better spirits than I had known for many a day. Could it be the anticipation of seeing the charming Ora Doveton that made me feel so joyous? I cannot precisely answer the question, but I think she must have had something to do with my good spirits. When we met at breakfast, Cuthbert Spring congratulated me on my improved appearance, and told me I looked more like my former self. He could perceive, he said, that I had been dreaming of something more agreeable than blighted yew-trees—perhaps, of a pair of fine black eyes, which was especially lucky, if the fine black eyes seemed to ogle you—according to Artemidorus. My personal comfort was increased by the amended condition of my arm, which now gave me much less inconvenience, and promised soon to be useful again. Moreover, the fine weather continued, and everything held out a pleasurable prospect. So no wonder I felt gay.

Cuthbert Spring left me to my own devices until four o'clock, at which time it was agreed that we should start for Owlarton Grange. If the arrangement had been left to me, I should have set out at once—for I was impatient to be off—but my friend had letters to write, and of course his convenience must be consulted.

Not finding much to amuse me in-doors, I sallied forth, and proceeded to the churchyard to look at the ancient yew-tree which had served me as a medium of introduction to the charming Ora. It was a fine old tree, in perfect preservation, with a bench, capable of accommodating at least twenty people, encircling its mighty stem. Dunton Church, as I have heretofore stated, stands on an elevated ridge of land, overlooking the extensive vale of the Mersey, with the Lancashire hills bounding the view on the north, while on the south, or Cheshire side, the prospect is even more diversified and beautiful. I had seated myself on the bench beneath the yew-tree, and was trying to discover some landmark to indicate the position of Owlarton Grange, when the noise caused by the shutting of a gate at the bottom of the churchyard made me aware of some one's approach. It was Ned Culcheth. He was accompanied by Hubert, and had come over to inform me that a month's leave of absence had been granted him by Lord Amounderness. He had heard something overnight which he thought would furnish him with a clue to Simon Pownall's retreat. A person very like Simon had been seen a few days ago at Knutsford with Chetham Quick. Chetham, therefore, as I had suspected, was most probably in secret communication with his old master. That Chetham must be in league with Captain Sale, Ned thought quite certain, for soon after my visit to the barber's shop on the day before, Chetham had run down to the vicarage to inform the captain of the circumstance. Phaleg had also been to the vicarage. This was the sum of Ned's intelligence. It was not much, but by closely watching Chetham he felt sure he should soon learn more. I agreed with him that he was now upon the right scent, and likely soon to unearth the old fox, but

I advised him to use the utmost caution in his proceedings, as no doubt he would be watched in his turn. I then told him of my proposed visit to Owlarton Grange, and that I should probably remain there for three or four days. Ned said he would come over to the Grange, if he had any tidings to give me, and he then left me—taking my best wishes with him—and made his way out of the churchyard, with Hubert at his heels.

The rest of the morning passed rather slowly, and was unmarked by any incident, but at four o'clock a yellow rattler, as Mr. Spring termed the post-chaise, came to the door, and we started on our expedition. Our road lay through a fair and fertile district, abounding in comfortable homesteads, orchards, barns, cow-houses, stacks of corn, hay, and beans, and other evidences of the prosperous condition of the cultivators of the soil. Nowhere in England is there better farming than in this part of Cheshire; nowhere are such cheeses made — a fact which alone would prove the extraordinary fatness of the land. But it was not merely the comfortable farm-house and its appurtenances that we beheld. In the course of our drive we passed by many an ancestral hall and lordly mansion, enriched with the accessories of wood and water—for without a mere a Cheshire park would be incomplete. Some of these domains were of vast extent, and calculated to give exalted notions of the territorial importance of their possessors. The Cheshire squires may well be proud. But by far the most picturesque scene we beheld was towards the end of the drive, and as my companion had not prepared me for it, I was quite taken by surprise. Emerging from a thick wood, through which the road was cut, we came suddenly upon a most romantic glen, hemmed in on either side by rocks some sixty feet in height, seemingly rent asunder, and spanned by a giddy-looking stone bridge, such as might be thrown across an Alpine ravine. Beneath this bridge dashed a rapid stream, which, falling over ledges of rock, formed a cascade, and then taking its way down the glen, the bottom of which was covered with well-grown timber, reached a point where its waters were dammed, in order that they might turn the wheels of a most picturesque-looking mill, causing them to spread out into a miniature lake. In some places the rocks were naked and precipitous; in others, where less steep, their sides were clothed with shrubs and evergreens. On the further side of the glen, and overhanging it, stood a venerable fabric, with a fine square tower, and I learnt to my surprise that this was Weverham Church, of which John Brideoake was curate. John did not live in the village, but his cottage was pointed out to me amongst a clump of trees behind the church. Most assuredly I should have called there, had I not expected to meet him at dinner. We were now within a couple of miles of Owlarton Grange, and my heart began to beat with pleasurable anticipation. The last mile was rather trying to our horses, being up a deep sandy lane, but having waded slowly through it, we came to firm ground, and entered a long avenue of stately sycamores at the end of which we descried the old hall.

CHAPTER VIII.

OF THE MYSTERIOUS BELL-RINGING AT OWLARTON GRANGE.

On a nearer approach, I was struck with the lonesome look of the place. It had an air of gloom about it that filled me with superstitious fancies. How could Ora dwell there, and retain such high spirits? A stagnant moat, covered with duckweed and flags, and with its edges overgrown with rushes, surrounded the house and the quaintly-cut parterres in front of it. This moat was crossed by a stone bridge, on either side of which grew a sombre pine. There was no lodge, but on the further side of the bridge stood a tall arched gateway of red brick, with stone copings and large stone shields, on which were sculptured the arms of the family. Over a smaller gate on the right was a demi-wyvern carved in stone. A brick wall, about four feet high, with iron rails on the top, skirted the garden, and extended as far as some small outbuildings. The house itself was a very fair specimen of an old Cheshire timber-framed hall. According to dates preserved in different parts of the edifice, which I afterwards saw, it must have been built in the reign of James I., when a great portion of the ancient grange was probably demolished. Cuthbert Spring's description of the place was sufficiently accurate, though its exterior was more picturesque than he had led me to anticipate. From a narrow centre sprang two small projections; and beyond these advanced, far out, a couple of broad wings, constituting altogether a frontage of great beauty. In each of the wings and lesser projections were large transom windows, with stained glass in the small octagonal leaden frames. All the timber of the hall was painted black, and the plaster white, with quatrefoils in the squares, producing a very charming and fanciful effect. Sharp gables terminated each point of the roof.

Our summons at the gateway-bell was speedily answered by Finch, the old footman, and a stout, respectable-looking butler of remarkably sedate aspect, whom Cuthbert Spring addressed as Mr. Ponder. The gates being thrown open, we drove on to the porch, and, alighting there, made but a step into a spacious entrance-hall, hung round with old buff coats, hunting horns, battle-axes, and pikes. Here Mr. Hazilrigge came forth to bid us welcome.

The old gentleman seemed enchanted to see me. I had evidently won his heart by my solution of his dream, but he told me, with a very solemn look, that he was sure some misfortune awaited him, for the yard-clock had struck thirteen at midnight, and old blind Mungo, the superannuated house-dog, had howled throughout the night. Moreover, Mrs. Duncalf, the cook, had complained that the kitchen fire would only burn on one side of the grate. This I could not but admit was a very bad sign, portending that the meat would be only half roasted, and I recommended an immediate and vigorous application of the poker, in order to dispel the charm. To my infinite regret, Mr. Hazilrigge next informed me that John Brideoake was too unwell to leave home on that day. He sent his love to me, and hoped I would come over and see him on the morrow. How grieved I then felt that I had not called on him as I passed through Weverham. But where was Ora? I was just going to inquire after the ladies, when my host moved an adjournment to the library, and I followed him, hoping to find them there; but the chamber was vacant, and I learnt that it was a sanctum sanctorum which none of womankind were allowed to invade. I also remarked, as the old gentleman closed the door, that Cuthbert Spring had vanished, and I soon discovered the reason of his declining to accompany us.

The library was well furnished with musty volumes. But just then I was in no humour for examining black-letter tomes, and would far rather have encountered the black eyes that had bewitched me. However, there was no escape, so, groaning internally, I seated myself in the chair offered me by Old Hazy, and listened, as attentively as I could, while he took down some of his treasures, and descanted upon them. He propounded the magical oracles of Zoroaster—half fascinated me by the wondrous narratives of Frommannus and Leonard Vair—cited Delancre, Delrio, Cardan, Torreblanca, John Baptist Porta, Psellus, Pererius, Doctor Dee, and other writers on occult philosophy—recounted the history of the three possessed Virgins in Flanders, the Princess of the Sorcerers in Provence, and Martha Brossier—discoursed on the Clavicula Salamonis and the Euchiridion of Pope Leo—flagellated demons and sorcerers with the lashes of Bodinus—revealed the confessions of witches by the help of Binsfeldius—and stunned me with the Malleus Maleficorum.

While listening to him, I felt as if I myself were in a magic circle from which there was no escape. At last he took down a large mystic folio, bound in black vellum, and full of blood-red characters and conjurations, and, telling me it was the Grimoire, was about to exhibit to my stupified gaze the veritable sign-manual of the Prince of Darkness, when, luckily, the rumbling of a gong announced that it was time to dress for dinner, and I was liberated from a purgatory of more than an hour's duration. My delight was excessive as we returned to the entrance-hall, and, fancying there was no immediate prospect of seeing Ora, I willingly accepted my host's offer to conduct me to the haunted room, which had been prepared for me, in accordance with my request.

Passing through an arched opening in a richly-carved screen of dark oak, Mr. Hazilrigge then led the way to a magnificent staircase of the same lustrous material, with massive and elaborately-carved handrails and balusters. Tall posts at each angle supported the family crest—a demi-wyvern—together with a carved shield with armorial bearings. Light was afforded by large transom windows, glowing with rich dyes. As I commenced ascending the staircase, the sound of light musical laughter reached my ears, and looking up at an open gallery above, I beheld Ora Doveton. Yes—there stood the charmer in the prettiest attitude possible, between the pillars, with one small hand resting upon the low balustrade in front of her. No portrait in Old Hazy's gallery could be better framed—no frame could contain more exquisite portrait. My gaze must have expressed the admiration I felt, for an added colour rose to her cheeks. Close behind her stood her aunt and Cuthbert Spring. On our joining the party, Miss Hazilrigge chided her brother for detaining me so long in the library, but Ora, with a sly glance, said she thought I must be just as fond of necromantic lore as her uncle, since his books seemed to have more attraction for me than their society. Good-natured Mr. Hazilrigge came to my rescue at once, declaring if anybody was to blame he was; but, finding my tastes congenial to his own, he had seized the earliest opportunity of displaying his treasures to me, and was happy to state that I fully understood and appreciated them. Ora must not suppose that conversation with a silly girl was half so attractive as discourse with departed sages, to a young gentleman of my reflective turn. He had seldom met with so patient a listener as I had proved, and he hoped I should pass many equally profitable hours with him in his study. All his recondite stores should be laid open to me. My fair tormentress heard him quietly to an end, looking all the while archly at me, but she then broke into a fit of merriment, which was only checked by her uncle ordering her to go and prepare for dinner, while he carried me off—much to my chagrin—down the long, dark corridor. Cuthbert Spring accompanied us, but Ora tripped off with her aunt in the opposite direction, and we had just reached the door of the chamber assigned to me, when her jocund laugh was heard again, as if she thought I was about to undergo a second ordeal. Looking round, I just caught a glimpse of her mirthful countenance ere she disappeared.

Cuthbert Spring left me at the door, saying, with a shrug of the shoulders, that he had had quite enough of that chamber. Mr. Hazilrigge himself only just entered the room, and after looking round to see that all was comfortable, and inquiring whether I wanted anything, proffered to send his valet, Rivers, to assist me in my toilet, and departed.

I looked round with curiosity, not unmixed with a little superstitious dread. The room was spacious and gloomy, owing to the sombre character of the furniture, and the dark oak panels. Opposite the antique tester bed, with its stiff, faded hangings, described by Cuthbert Spring, was a large bay-window filled with painted glass, now glowing with the radiance of the setting sun, and casting its rich dyes on the polished oak floor. Over the carved mantelpiece hung the portrait of an old man in a nightcap wig, and a long loose coat of reddish brown cloth wrapped round his attenuated limbs. The features of the personage thus represented were spare and sharp, with a nose like a hawk's beak. He wore spectacles, by the aid of which he was examining an account-book. Behind him stood an attendant in a square-cut coat and long-flapped waistcoat, with a sinister expression of countenance. This was the only picture in the room, and it strongly arrested my attention.

I was examining it when Rivers entered. He was a young man, and an importation from town, and rattled away all the time he was helping me to dress. Rivers did not think it possible he could remain in his place, for though he had no objections to make to his master or Miss Hazilrigge, or to any one else, yet such strange things had happened in the house of late—such alarming noises had been heard—that he couldn't stay in it. I questioned him as to the kind of noises he meant, but he glanced round in trepidation, and said, in a low tone, "I daren't speak in this room, sir, lest the ghost should overhear me. But you'll find it out. Between ourselves, I don't think you'll stop here long. Nobody does, sir." And with this consolatory remark—his services being no longer required—he left me.

Seating myself on an old fauteuil covered with faded Utrecht velvet, I again began to examine the remarkable picture I have mentioned, and might have been occupied in this way for two or three minutes, when the door suddenly opened, and Rivers bounced into the room. Seeing that he looked startled, I asked him what was the matter.

"Pray what may be your pleasure, sir?" he said.

"I want nothing," I returned. "I didn't ring."

He eyed me rather incredulously, but, without making any further remark, bowed and departed.

But he had not been gone more than a couple of minutes when he reappeared.

"This time you must have rung, sir," he observed. "There can be no mistake, for I watched the bell. Excuse me for remarking, sir, that nothing disturbs my master so much as the loud ringing of chamber-bells, or, indeed, any other bells, and he hopes his guests will kindly consider him in this particular."

"Your master may rely upon it I will not disturb him," I rejoined, "but no bell has been rung by me. I have not quitted this chair since you were last here."

Rivers looked at me again, shrugged his shoulders, and departed.

I thought his conduct very odd, but I was still more surprised when he once more burst into the room.

"Now, sir!" he exclaimed, "I am certain of it."

"Certain of what?" I rejoined, almost laughing in his face. "Certain that I rang the bell?"

"Yes, sir,—yes!—and very loudly too! Mr. Ponder, the butler, and old Finch, the footman, heard it as well as me—and watched it."

"This is very extraordinary," I remarked.

"Very extraordinary indeed!" he rejoined, "if you didn't ring the bell, sir. But perhaps it's a joke, sir?"

I looked angrily at him, but at this moment the sedate-looking tler came in, having previously tapped at the door.

"Beg pardon, sir, but the bell has been rung again—since Rivers went up."

"Well, at least he can bear witness that I have not rung it," I said.

"Certainly, sir—there's no denying it," the valet replied, staring with surprise.

"Is there not a possibility of mistake as to the bell?" I asked.

"None whatever, sir," Mr. Ponder answered. "We all know the bell belonging to this room well enough. It hasn't rung for many a long day—not since Mr. Cuthbert Spring slept in the room."

Here there was another tap at the door, and old Finch, the footman, entered.

"It be goin' again," Finch said, "and I be come to see whatever be the matter."

We all exchanged glances of astonishment, but no explanation could be given.

"This is very strange—very unaccountable," I remarked.

"Ours is a very strange house, sir, and very odd things happen in it," Mr. Ponder rejoined, gravely. "But let me beg you not to mention the circumstance to my master. It would put him out exceedingly, and he would have no rest during the whole evening. If we hear any more ringing, we shall conclude that we needn't answer the summons. Dinner will be served directly, sir."

Upon this, he quitted the room with the two other servants, and I soon afterwards found my way to the drawing-room, in which all the party, with one important exception, had assembled. Of course, having been cautioned by the butler, I said nothing of the strange circumstance that had just taken place to Mr. Hazilrigge. Soon afterwards, Ora entered, looking ravishing in a dark evening dress, which set off the graces of her exquisite person to the utmost advantage. With a sly smile she asked how I liked the haunted chamber — whether my courage had evaporated—and whether I had heard any supernatural sounds? Not for worlds would she sleep in that room, she declared. She would not even enter it in broad daylight. Had I noticed the portraits of the miser and his wicked servant—old Clotten Hazilrigge and Jotham Shocklach? Before I could reply to these inquiries, the bell at the garden gate rang loudly, attracting general attention.

"Eh day! who can that be?" Mr. Hazilrigge exclaimed. "I expect no one. Perhaps it may be John Brideoake, after all. I hope so."

"Mr. Brideoake would never ring in that manner," Ora remarked. "But whoever it is, he is just in time for dinner."

We waited a little in expectation, but no one was announced. Presently the bell rang again more loudly than before.

"Very strange the servants shouldn't go to the door," Mr. Hazilrigge cried, impatiently. "What can be the matter with them?"

Here there was another peal from the bell, louder and longer than any that had preceded it—a peal to disturb the whole house. Exclamations of astonishment burst from all the party. Who can it be?—what can it mean?

The tremendous peal had scarcely ceased when Mr. Ponder entered the room, and with an imperturbable manner, as if nothing had happened, and in a very quiet tone, announced that dinner was served.

"Dinner!" Mr. Hazilrigge exclaimed. "I thought you were going to announce half a dozen unexpected guests. Pray who has been ringing the door-bell?"

"The door-bell, sir?" Mr. Ponder exclaimed. "I beg your pardon, sir—did you say the door-bell?"

"To be sure I did! Would you try to persuade me you didn't hear it? There it goes again—there! do you hear it now, sir?"

"Oh yes, sir, I hear it," Mr. Ponder replied, quietly.

"Zounds! Ponder, you're enough to provoke a saint with your imperturbability! Will nothing move you? If you *do* hear it, why don't you answer it?—why don't you go to the door?"

"I *have* been to the door, sir," Mr. Ponder replied, without moving a muscle. "And I saw—no one."

"You don't mean to say that the bell has been ringing of its own accord, Ponder?" Mr. Hazilrigge cried.

"It seems very like it, sir," the butler answered.

"A hoax!—a manifest hoax!" Cuthbert Spring exclaimed.

"I don't see how that can be, sir," the tranquil Ponder rejoined. "Rivers and Finch are stationed near the gate. Apparently, the bell has made up its mind to ring, and it *will* ring in spite of us."

As he said this, there was an almost imperceptible smile about the butler's placid features. Suspecting a hoax, and eager to detect it, I begged Mr. Hazilrigge to excuse me, and rushed forth.

I have already described the position and appearance of the gateway to the hall. It was to the side gate, reserved for foot passengers, that the bell, which had disturbed us by its peals, was affixed. It was sheltered from the weather by a little wooden penthouse, but was otherwise fully exposed to view. It was ringing violently as I approached, and continued to do so for a minute or two after my arrival, when it ceased. Rivers and Finch were watching it narrowly, and both declared they could not account for its extraordinary agitation. The bell-pull was outside, but no one was there to touch it. I went out upon the bridge, and looked along the wall skirting the moat, but no one was visible. There was still light enough to enable me to distinguish clearly any object within that range. Failing to make any discovery, after remaining on the spot for a few minutes, I returned to the house, followed by the two servants, speculating on the mysterious occurrence. But scarcely had we gained the porch when the provoking clamour commenced again, and we all three rushed back, quick as lightning. In an instant I was out of the gate—but not a soul could be seen.

Again the bell ceased, and again we retraced our steps, with a like result, for the ringing recommenced. But this time we left the bell to indulge its mysterious vagaries unobserved, and entered the house.

The whole party were assembled in the hall, awaiting our return, and hoping we should be able to offer some elucidation of the mystery, but we could give none. Mr. Hazilrigge took off his spectacles, rubbed them with his pocket-handkerchief, as if he thought that would enable him to see more clearly into the matter. Ora Doveton laughed heartily, and thought it an excellent joke; while Cuthbert Spring suggested that we should let the bell ring till it was tired, and go to dinner. Mr. Hazilrigge assented, and we then repaired to the dining-room—a large room panelled with oak, like most of the other apartments, and full of antique furniture—where a very comfortable meal was served, and we were allowed to enjoy it in peace—contrary, I must own, to my expectation, for I feared some fresh interruption would occur. In spite of the reported half-burning fire, the saddle of mutton was roasted to perfection. Moreover, word was brought that at last the garden-bell had ceased its clamour, and this news increased the general satisfaction. During dinner our host entertained us with relations of divers preternatural occurrences, and quite monopolised the talk, compelling Ora and myself, as we sat at opposite sides of the table, to discourse by glances—a mode of conversation in which we soon became adepts.

Dinner was over, and Mr. Hazilrigge's stock of wonderful narratives was far from exhausted. He was just beginning to tell us a marvellous story from Johannes Tritenhemius, when Mr. Ponder made his appearance with a fresh jug of claret. Eyeing the butler in some displeasure, for he did not like to be interrupted, Mr. Hazilrigge pointed to the decanter before him, which was half full, and said that more wine was not wanted at present.

Mr. Ponder looked as cool as the claret he had just brought, and while placing the bottle on the table, quietly observed, "You rang, sir."

"Your pardon!" Mr. Hazilrigge exclaimed; "I did *not* ring."

"Oh! then I must have been mistaken," the latter rejoined, respectfully. "I am really very sorry, sir—very." And he left the room with the quietest footstep imaginable.

"What can Ponder mean, I wonder?" Mr. Hazilrigge ejaculated. "I never knew him make such a mistake before. He must be bewildered by the bell-ringing out of doors."

"I hope the bells in-doors are not going to follow the example set them outside," Cuthbert Spring remarked. "This looks like it."

He might have foreseen what was about to occur. Scarcely were the words uttered when there arose the strangest noise imaginable, as if all the bells in the house had gone mad. Tingle! tingle!—crash! Jingle! jingle!—louder crash! Brangle! brangle!—grand crash! —But I despair of giving any idea of the discordant din by words. Simultaneously we rose from our places. Miss Hazilrigge looked alarmed, but Ora Doveton burst into a fit of laughter. As to Old Hazy, he got excessively red in the face, and appeared half-suffocated by passion.

"Take it easily, my good friend," Cuthbert Spring said to him— "no use being angry at a trifle."

"'Sdeath! do you call this disturbance a trifle? It will drive me frantic if it goes on. Ha!—I see it all. This is the dire calamity portended by my dream of the blasted yew-tree, the clock striking thirteen at midnight, the howling of Mungo, and the half-burning kitchen fire."

At this juncture, Mr. Ponder returned. Amidst the extraordinary uproar he maintained his unperturbed manner, and approaching his master, said quietly, "Do you hear anything, sir?"

"Do you suppose I am deaf, sir?" Mr. Hazilrigge rejoined, with a tremendous explosion of rage. "I wish I were, for then I might escape this infernal clatter. What's the meaning of it, sir? Why don't you put a stop to it?"

"Perhaps you will come and look at the bells, sir," Mr. Ponder replied, quietly, "and then you may suggest something."

"Yes, yes, come along! we'll all go!" Cuthbert Spring cried.

Upon this, we should all have hurried out of the room, but the deliberate butler would allow no such exhibition of impatience, but calmly led us to the scene of disturbance.

In order to render the mysterious circumstance about to be described comprehensible, I must premise that behind the great staircase stood a massive oak screen, separating the entrance-hall from the back part of the house. Richly carved, and of great beauty, this screen contained two arched entrances to a passage communicating with the butler's pantry, housekeeper's room, servants' hall, and kitchen. This passage, called "the Screens," from the timber partitions of which it was formed, was long and gloomy,—it might be about six feet wide and fourteen high,—and had a conventual appearance, owing to the number of cell-like doors, with low arches, opening out of it. Half way down it a flight of steep stone steps, protected by a little wicket, conducted to the cellars, and at the further end stood the buttery hatch.

Commencing at a point nearly opposite the entrance to the cellar-steps, and against the slightly-projecting cornice of the oak screen on the right side of the passage, hung thirty bells in a row. I am sure of the number, for I subsequently counted them. All these bells were pealing as we entered "the Screens." The effect was at once ludicrous and appalling. The noise was furious, stunning—almost terrifying. The bells seemed to be under some extraordinary influence, and were so violently agitated that the spiral flexible irons supporting them were constantly dashed against the ceiling. I expected the whole row would tumble to the ground. The wires were also jerked with great force. The whole household were collected on the spot. Near the kitchen door was huddled together a group of women-servants, headed by the fat cook, and a pretty-looking lady's-maid, who called Ora mistress. Most of these, however, would have taken to flight, if astonishment and terror had not detained them. The men-servants, stationed in front of the female part of the establishment, tried to put a bolder face upon the matter, but were evidently little less alarmed, and the only one amongst them who appeared calm was Mr. Ponder. Not so Mr. Hazilrigge. The unearthly clangour exasperated him almost to frenzy. Every nerve in his body seemed to vibrate in unison with the infuriated bells. He stamped, shook his hands, and raved like a madman. His sister endeavoured to lead him away; but he would not stir. The louder the bells rang, the more frantically did he gesticulate at them.

All at once, and as if by magic, the bells stopped. The sudden cessation of the noise, though a relief, was startling. No one made a remark for a moment, but we consulted each other by our looks. Ora Doveton, who had treated the matter with ridicule while at a distance, could scarcely be persuaded to remain, when she beheld the diabolical bells in motion. Now that they were silent, she regained her courage, and began to smile again, though rather timorously.

Cuthbert Spring declared it was a hoax—a most unpardonable hoax—though he could offer no explanation as to how the trick was managed.

Emboldened by the cessation of the terrifying peals, the women-servants now ventured to come forward, and planted themselves beneath the row of bells the better to examine them; but they were sent screaming away in an instant, as the wire was observed to make and the foremost bell began to tinkle. Its lead was soon followed by a second—a third—and so on, till the whole row was again in motion. Then ensued another concert as astounding as the first; and during its continuance Mr. Hazilrigge was thrown into transports of fury as outrageous as those he had previously exhibited; but no entreaties of his sister, or of Cuthbert Spring, could move him from the spot. After continuing to peal in this violent manner for full five minutes, the bells again stopped. The sound did not die away by degrees, but appeared at its loudest, when it was checked with startling suddenness.

Amid the silence that prevailed, Mr. Hazilrigge shouted to the butler to bring him some implement to cut the wires.

Mr. Ponder displayed great promptitude in executing his master's orders. He disappeared for a moment, and then returned with a pair of pruning-shears with long handles. At the same time, old Finch brought a step-ladder, and Rivers another lighted candle. Seizing the shears impatiently, Mr. Hazilrigge caused the ladder to be placed just under the bells, and aided by the butler, who held a light for him, mounted the steps.

"This will stop it, I think," he exclaimed, looking round triumphantly. "This will stop it," he repeated, applying the points of the shears to the wires.

But before he could bring the sharp edges to bear, the diabolical bells fired forth a volley with the suddenness and force of an electric shock. Not singly this time, but all together. The bell which was nearest to Old Hazy's face seemed actually to hit him on the nose. Certainly his spectacles were knocked off and broken in their fall. So startled was he by the sudden shock, that he lost his balance, and must have been precipitated to the floor, if Mr. Ponder had not fortunately caught him before he fell. Screams arose from the women-servants, and one of the housemaids, in trying to beat a hasty retreat into the kitchen, lost her footing, and two others, together with the fat cook, tumbled over her. The men, in rushing to their assistance, made matters worse, for three of them were stretched upon the ground. Nor did the ladies display very great presence of mind. Ora Doveton uttered a cry on seeing her uncle's danger, and clung to me for support; while poor Miss Hazilrigge, frightened almost out of her wits, positively fell into Cuthbert Spring's arms.

During all this confusion the bells pealed on furiously as ever, and as if deriding Old Hazy's futile attempt to check their clangour.

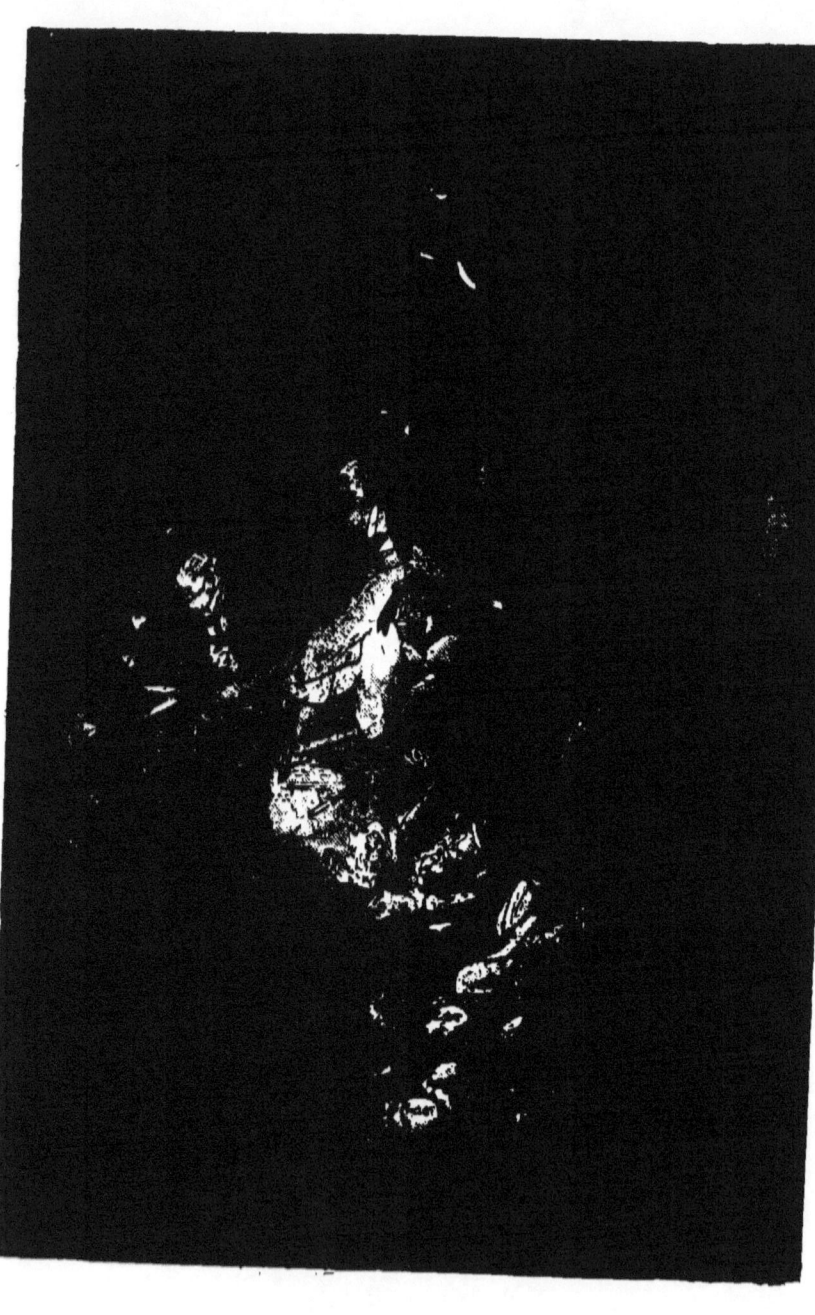

CHAPTER IX.

HOW WE PASSED THE REST OF THE EVENING AT OWLARTON GRANGE.

THE bells still pealed furiously. It was now a continuous grand crash.

"Will nobody stop this infernal clamour?" Mr. Hazilrigge cried, despairingly.

"I should like to know how it is to be done?" Cuthbert Spring said. "The ladies are nearly stunned, and I shall be deaf as a post for a month to come."

"It can't be stopped, sir," Mr. Ponder observed, in a solemn tone. "Those bells are rung by no mortal hand."

"You think so, Ponder!" Mr. Hazilrigge exclaimed, staring at him. "You think so—eh?"

"I am perfectly sure of it, sir," the butler answered.

Not entirely coinciding with Mr. Ponder in opinion, I left Ora, and quickly mounting the step-ladder, which had not been removed since Old Hazy's misadventure, I seized one of the bells and held it firmly, so as to prevent further oscillation.

On first touching it, I fancied I experienced a slight electric shock, but whether the sensation was really so produced, or by the violent action of the bell, I could not determine. While detained in my grasp the bell shook very perceptibly, and when released, it began to ring as furiously as before.

After trying the same experiment on the two adjoining bells with precisely the same result, I desired Ponder to hand me the shears, in order that I might sever the wires, but he seemed disinclined to obey me, expressing his firm conviction that I should only do mischief; and Mr. Hazilrigge also begging me earnestly to desist, I reluctantly came down from the step-ladder.

"Ponder is quite right, Mr. Clitheroe," Old Hazy said. "If you provoke the mischievous sprites, who are evidently here at work, they may occasion me infinitely greater annoyance. They may pinch me grievously while I am in bed—squat down heavily upon my chest, so as to check my breathing, and prevent all power of motion—pluck off my nightcap, or the bedclothes, and give me my death from cold: all which things are related by Robert de Triez in his *Ruses, Finesses et Impostures des Esprits Malins.* Or the sprites may do other mischief, as described by Le Loyer in his treatise *Des Spectres*—such as upsetting pots, platters, tables, and trenchers, and tumbling them down stairs—removing doors from their hinges—and causing strange rumbling noises. No, no, Mr. Clitheroe, it won't do to enter into a contest with invisible foes. You see they have already broken my spectacles—a mischievous freak that I don't remember to have met with either in Robert de Triez or Le Loyer."

Undoubtedly the old gentleman's observations were enough to disturb any one's gravity, but chancing to detect a furtive smile on the butler's usually immovable countenance, I fixed my regards keenly upon him as I addressed Mr. Hazilrigge.

"I am no believer in *esprits malins*, sir," I said, "in spite of the well-authenticated relations of such veracious writers as Robert de Triez and Le Loyer; and extraordinary as this bell-ringing may appear, I have no doubt that the trick could be easily performed by some designing person, well acquainted with the premises, and aided by a confederate."

"You look at me, sir," Mr. Ponder observed, very calmly, but with an air of offended dignity, "as if you suspect that I have a hand in the trick, as you are pleased to term it, but which I venture to affirm is no trick at all. I should be ill deserving of the confidence which my master reposes in me, if I could attempt to deceive him—or allow him to be deceived in any way. My master, I am sure, will do me the justice to say that he entertains a favourable opinion of me."

"So I do!—so I do!" the old gentleman cried. "I entertain the highest opinion of you, Ponder." Then turning to me he added. "A trustier servant does not exist than Ponder, Mr. Clitheroe. He is my right hand."

"Take care he doesn't get the upper hand of you, my good friend," Cuthbert Spring muttered.

The butler either did not hear the remark or did not choose to notice it, but bowed profoundly in acknowledgment of his master's commendations.

"Well, Mr. Ponder," I said, "I will frankly confess that a momentary suspicion of you did cross me, but I am now persuaded that I did you injustice. But pray don't take offence at my asking if all the household were assembled here just now?"

"All, sir—male and female."

"There are no visitors to the servants in the house?" I continued. "Excuse the question, but you will perceive its necessity."

"The inquiry is very proper, sir," Mr. Ponder replied. "We have no visitors this evening in the kitchen."

"And you suspect no one?"

"No one whatever, sir. I have already stated my belief as to the cause of the disturbance."

"I am not as yet acquainted with this house, but Mr. Spring, in describing it to me, stated that a portion of the old monastic grange closely adjoins it. Is that ancient fragment a ruin?"

"A ruin, no!" Mr. Hazilrigge cried. "It is a very comfortable farm-house, inhabited by my bailiff, Stephen Blackden, and his family. And very quiet, respectable folks they are."

"Have you any suspicion of Blackden?" I continued, addressing Ponder.

The butler looked surprised by the inquiry.

"Lord bless you! no sir," he cried. "Stephen Blackden, as my master well knows, is the last man to play mischievous tricks."

"The very last man," Old Hazy chimed in. "Stephen Blackden is the quietest and most inoffensive person breathing."

"Now you call my attention to the farm-house, sir," Ponder cried, as if an idea had suddenly struck him, "perhaps I ought to mention that a certain Dr. Hooker sometimes lodges there; and I believe he is there now. But he is a man of very retiring habits—quite a philosopher, sir. My master knows him very well."

"Oh yes! I know Dr. Hooker," Mr. Hazilrigge said, rather hastily, as he did not like the subject. "He often stays with Blackden."

Before I could institute any further inquiries concerning this Dr. Hooker, I was interrupted by Cuthbert Spring, who having been all this time embarrassed by the charge of both ladies, neither of whom had entirely recovered from her fright, called out to me to lend Ora an arm, as she and Miss Hazilrigge had had quite enough of it, and wished to retire.

Of course I instantly complied. It struck me at the moment that Cuthbert was rather anxious to get rid of Ora in order to devote himself exclusively to her aunt.

Just as we were quitting the "Screens," the bells left off pealing. And with this cessation of their clatter, I may mention, the disturbance wholly ceased.

Cuthbert Spring as well as myself would fain have remained with the ladies, but our host would have us back to the claret, and we were obliged therefore to accompany him to the dining-room.

As may be supposed, the conversation turned chiefly upon the mysterious occurrences of the evening, and on my inquiring from Mr. Hazilrigge whether the bells had ever rung in this extraordinary manner before, he replied, that they had not done so in his time, but he thought he had heard that similar disturbances took place in his grandfather's days; at which period, it was, he added, that the grange was first reported to be haunted.

This led the old gentleman into a discourse upon nocturnal noises, which threatened to be interminable, illustrated as it was by a variety of stories culled from his favourite authorities — Becker's *World Bewitched*, Paul Grilland, Pierre Massé, Taillepied, and Thiræus *De Locis Infestis:* until at last, Cuthbert Spring's patience being fairly exhausted, for the claret had been long since finished, and our host was too much engrossed by his narrations to think of ordering another bottle,—he voted that we should adjourn to the drawing-room, and I joyfully seconded the movement.

By this time, the ladies had got over their alarm, and Ora was as

o 2

lively as ever; but her aunt had another strange incident to relate, to which she particularly called my attention.

Mr. Pouder, she said, had just been in to inform them that he and old Finch had made a strict search of the house, and while standing in the corridor they had both distinctly heard the sound of footsteps within the haunted chamber. They listened for a few minutes before they could muster up courage to enter the room, but on doing so, it was perfectly empty.

"Mere fancy!" I exclaimed. "Their imaginations were heated by what has recently occurred. If they really *did* hear footsteps in the chamber, the sounds must have been caused by some living person, and I shall make a point of carefully searching the room before I retire to rest."

"Search as much as you please, you won't find anybody," Mr. Hazilrigge remarked. "It was more than fancy."

Apprehensive of a fresh batch of supernatural stories from our host, Cuthbert Spring here interposed, and begged Ora to favour us with a song. She willingly complied, and, proceeding to the piano, charmed me with some gay French canzonets. During a pause in the singing, I spoke of John Brideoake's fondness for vocal music, upon which Ora volunteered to give me his favourite song—one of the most pathetic of Moore's Irish Melodies—which she executed with great feeling and tenderness, and, while listening to it, I thought that such strains must have touched John to the heart.

After expressing my admiration, I chanced to say, "By-the-by, you have not told me how you like my friend, Brideoake?"

The abruptness of the question brought the colour to her cheeks.

"He is a great favourite of my aunt," she replied, somewhat evasively.

"But not equally so with you?" I rejoined. "I am very sorry for it."

"Oh! no, I don't mean that. I respect Mr. Brideoake greatly, and may have liked him a little once, but I am very capricious, as you will find when you know me better."

A strange thought crossed me. Why it came into my head I cannot tell, but I fancied poor John might have been captivated by this bewitching girl, and his passion treated with disdain. The notion gave me a pang, and I would have questioned Ora further, but she struck up a a sprightly sequidilla, which transported me in a moment to the banks of the Guadalquivir. What with music and mirthful chat the time flew by almost too quickly, and the moment for separation for the night arrived much sooner than I desired.

The signal for dispersion was accidentally given by our host, who, while indulging in a nap in an easy-chair, suddenly started up, vociferating, "There they go again! ring! ring! ring!—Will nobody stop those confounded bells?"

We assured him that he had only been dreaming, but he persisted in asserting that he had heard the bells, and would not be convinced that they had not actually recommenced their diabolical concert, until he had summoned Ponder, who respectfully assured him that the mischievous sprites had entirely left off their vagaries. Hereupon the ladies prepared to retire, and as Ora bade me good night, she said she expected I should have something surprising to relate at breakfast. A rather tender parting, as it appeared to me, took place between Cuthbert Spring and Miss Hazilrigge, as the old bachelor gallantly attended the elderly spinster to the door, and gave her a flat candlestick.

We did not remain long after them, and indeed, as we ascended the great staircase, I heard the echoes of Ora's jocund laughter resounding from above, but I was not indulged with another glimpse of her witching countenance, for ere we reached the corridor she had vanished.

Having bade good night to my host and Cuthbert Spring, I entered the haunted chamber, and closed the door.

My feelings were very different, I confess, from those which I had experienced when viewing the chamber by broad daylight. It now seemed far gloomier than it had appeared then, and the sombre bed-hangings looked perfectly funereal.

I stole a glance at the singular picture over the mantelpiece, but I quickly withdrew my gaze, for it seemed as if the features of the sinister-looking figure in the background were instinct with life, and that the personage represented frowned at me. Ashamed of this weakness, I marched boldly towards the picture, and, holding up the light, gazed steadily at it. The effect was instantly dispelled. I could see nothing but the dull canvas.

While thus occupied I fancied I heard a slight rustling sound behind me, and turned sharply round, but I could perceive nothing. The noise had appeared to come from that part of the room where the bed stood, and stepping in that direction, I looked behind its stiff hangings, and examined every part of the cumbrous piece of furniture which could by possibility screen an intruder. No one was there.

Not content with this scrutiny, I next commenced an investigation of the whole room. An old black walnut wardrobe, of the same date as the bed, attracted my attention, and opening it, I found only a few of my own habiliments hanging inside it. Heavy curtains were stretched across the deep bay-window. These I drew aside, and let in a flood of moonlight. My investigations, though very strictly conducted, not being rewarded by any discovery, I persuaded myself that I had been deceived by overwrought fancy.

However, it was some time before I could prevail upon myself to take possession of the antique bed, and several hours fled by ere I became lost to consciousness.

CHAPTER X.

IN WHICH I FANCY THAT I SOLVE THE MYSTERY OF THE EXTRAORDINARY BELL-RINGING.

On again opening my eyes I was glad to perceive the sun shining brightly through the large bay-window. Everything looked so cheerful now that I could not help laughing at the fears I had experienced overnight. But I must have slept unusually soundly, and to a much later hour than was my custom, for, on consulting my watch, I found it was near nine o'clock—a discovery that caused me to quit my stately couch without a moment's delay.

My toilette being expeditiously made, I went down stairs, but before joining the party at breakfast, I resolved to have a word with Stephen Blackden's philosophic lodger, Dr. Hooker.

With this design I sallied forth into the garden, and made my way to the back of the hall, where I found the old monastic grange; or rather a very substantial and comfortable-looking habitation, which had been constructed out of the ancient materials. It was a picturesque-looking structure, being partly overgrown with ivy, and harmonised very well with the hall, which it closely adjoined. In fact, the two fabrics touched.

The occupants of the farm-house were Stephen Blackden, his wife, a couple of grown-up daughters, and his son—a sharp-looking lad between thirteen and fourteen, to whom I addressed myself on entering the farm-yard.

On inquiry from this youth, I learnt that Dr. Hooker had left them early that morning, and on asking which room he had occupied, the lad pointed it out to me, and I saw at once from its situation that it must be in close connexion with the hall. I then expressed a desire to see the room. Evidently much surprised at the request, the lad replied that he didn't know whether I could see it, but he would ask his mother, for his father was not within.

On this he went into the house, and presently afterwards Dame Blackden came out to me, followed by her two daughters, rustic lasses, not without some pretension to good looks. Dame Blackden was a decent-looking woman, but appeared rather confused, and said she was sorry she couldn't oblige me by a sight of the room, as her husband had locked it up, and taken the key.

Not quite crediting this story, I inquired when she expected Dr. Hooker to return, and she answered that he might be back in two or three days, or even sooner—she couldn't say exactly.

While talking to her, I noticed a long ladder reared against the building, and thinking it might aid me in my investigations, I bade young Blackden help me to place it near the window which he had pointed out as belonging to Dr. Hooker's room, in order that I might look in.

The lad became very red, and appeared extremely unwilling to obey me, and his mother shook her head at him as if to negative the order; but, as I repeated the injunction more authoritatively, he was forced to comply, and by our joint efforts the ladder being soon placed by the side of the window, I began to scale it.

But quick as were my own movements, I have reason to suspect that the movements of some other party were yet more expeditious. While we were shifting the ladder, one of the young women hastily withdrew, and I am almost certain that I heard a tap at the door of the room I was about to reconnoitre, coupled with a word or two of caution from a female voice in a low key. These sounds were instantaneously followed by a slight stir, as if some one had got up and cautiously closed a door; but at this moment I had reached the window, and was able to gaze through its small leaden-framed panes into the chamber.

Unluckily, the window was fastened inside, and white dimity curtains being drawn partially across it, I could not make out the objects within very distinctly. But it appeared pretty evident, from sundry slight circumstances warranting such an inference, that some one had just quitted the room.

That Dr. Hooker must be sometimes engaged in scientific experiments was evident from the number of machines that I beheld; amongst others, there was a powerful galvanic battery, with its trough, plates, glasses, and wires complete.

On beholding this battery, I felt sure that I had detected the secret of the mysterious disturbance of the previous night, as by means of connecting wires all the bells about the place could be easily set in motion by the apparatus. There were other instruments in the room, the use of which I did not so well understand; but everything tended to show that Dr. Hooker must be an ingenious personage.

On the table lay some books, which, if I had seen them in Mr. Hazilrigge's sanctum, I might have taken for treatises on divination and magic; and I am by no means certain, after all, that these volumes did not come from the old gentleman's library. Besides these there was a large piece of white cloth stamped with black mystical figures, evidently derived from Cornelius Agrippa, the Clavicula Salamonis, and Dr. Dee. There was not much furniture in the room; a small bed in one corner, a little clothes-press, a table, and a couple of chairs, constituted the sum total of it; but the rest of the space was almost entirely encumbered by the various machines I have mentioned.

In the hasty survey which I took, I tried in vain to discover a door communicating with the hall. I could perceive none; neither could I detect by what means the occupant of the room had effected so hasty a retreat.

Having finished my scrutiny, I descended the ladder, and made a few apparently careless observations on what I had seen to Dame Blackden and her son, who had been watching me inquisitively from below. I remarked that Doctor Hooker must be a very learned man; and she replied that he was quite a conjuror, and knew almost as much as the old Squire himself. Indeed, he and the old Squire often put their heads together, and when they did something extraordinary was sure to come of it. This I told her I could readily believe, and added that I should be glad of an opportunity of consulting the sagacious Dr. Hooker. Satisfied with the discovery I had made, I then left her and returned to the garden.

The path which I now pursued led me by the side of the hall, and against this portion of the building a large pear-tree was trained. Remarking that the bell-wires were carried along beneath the branches of the pear-tree, I thought it not improbable that about this point a junction with the wires of the galvanic battery migth have been effected. But I did not attempt further investigation.

How particular bells—such as the bell at the entrance gate, and the bell belonging to the haunted chamber—had been rung I could not so easily explain, but entertaining no doubt whatever that electricity was the agent by which the trick had been performed, in order to satisfy myself fully on the point, I proceeded to the low wall which I have described as skirting the inner bank of the moat, and, after careful scrutiny, I detected a wire running along it so close to the ground as to be wholly undiscernible except upon careful examination. I next traced the course of this wire along the wall until within a few feet of the entrance-gate, where it had evidently been cut off, though no doubt during the extraordinary ringing its junction with the gate bell was complete.

The mystery seemed thus satisfactorily solved. But I determined to keep my discovery to myself for the present, in order to see whether any fresh attempt at disturbance should be made at night, in which case I would put an instantaneous stop to it.

I then entered the house, and repairing to the dining-room, found the party assembled and breakfast nearly over.

Excepting Mr. Hazilrigge, who made no remark on the subject, everybody was convinced that I had seen the ghost; and Ora, while assisting me to a cup of coffee, fixed her dark eyes inquiringly upon me, and besought me to satisfy her curiosity without delay. She was dying to know what I had heard, or seen.

Mr. Spring declared that I generally rose with the lark, and he could only account for my being so late by the supposition that I must have been kept awake more than half the night by a lengthened ghostly confabulation.

Miss Hazilrigge came next. Rivers, the valet, she had been told by Ponder, had knocked twice at my door and received no answer, and on the third occasion he had entered the room and found me fast asleep —upon which he had considerately withdrawn. This sudden change in my habits proved that something extraordinary must have happened, and I was bound to give them an explanation.

Paying little attention to the raillery of the elderly couple, I told Ora that I was sorry I could not give a distinct answer to her inquiries. The events of the night appeared like a dream to me—a reply not at all satisfactory to my charming catechiser, who insisted upon a relation of my dreams, and pressed me so hard, that at last I was obliged to say that, whatever had happened to me (and she might tax her imagination to any extent she pleased), my lips were hermetically sealed. If I knew anything I could not disclose it. Mr. Hazilrigge declared that I was quite right. If the ghost had admitted me to its confidence, I was bound in honour not to betray it. Such was the opinion of Melancthon and Ludovicus Vives, confirmed by Le Loyer. As there was no disputing authorities like these, Ora ceased to importune me, but she looked a little piqued.

Luckily a turn was given to the conversation by Cuthbert Spring, who inquired from our host whether any discovery had been made as to how the bells were rung overnight. Mr. Hazilrigge shook his head, and replied that the mysterious affair was still as great a mystery as ever.

"I think I can unravel it," I said, with a smile.

Everybody looked at me in surprise.

"You don't pretend to say that you have found out how the trick was performed—for trick it was, I maintain?" Cuthbert Spring cried.

"I have detected the juggler who played it," I rejoined; "that must suffice for the present."

"You have!" Mr. Hazilrigge exclaimed, starting to his feet. "Who is it? Tell me at once, Mr. Clitheroe. If it should be one of my servants who has dared to practise on me thus—even Ponder himself —he shall be instantly sent about his business."

"Rest easy on that score, sir," I rejoined. "It is not Mr. Ponder, nor any of your servants, that you need suspect. I will point out the real author of the trick to you by-and-by, and then you can deal with him as you think fit."

"Hum!" Mr. Hazilrigge ejaculated. "I fancy I know whom you allude to. But it's not he!—it's not he!"

"More concealments?" Cuthbert Spring cried. "Are we to be kept in the dark for ever?"

"Very tantalising, I must say," Miss Hazilrigge cried.

"Very unfair!" Ora added. "Mr. Clitheroe will entirely forfeit my good opinion if he goes on in this way."

"I hope not," I replied; "as far as I am concerned, I have no desire to make any mystery of the matter, and if Mr. Hazilrigge desires it, I will name the person I mean."

"Better not," the old gentleman interposed, hastily. "As soon as you have finished breakfast, Mr. Clitheroe, we will adjourn to my sanctum, and confer upon the matter."

"I shall be at your service in a moment," I replied, trying to make up for lost time by proceeding rapidly with my meal.

"Dear heart! brother, you are in a great hurry. You won't allow Mr. Clitheroe to make half a breakfast," Miss Hazilrigge said.

"Step to the side-table and carve him a slice of ham, I beg of you—our hams are excellent, Mr. Clitheroe. Perhaps you would prefer pigeon-pie—the eggs and the cutlets are cold, I am afraid, so I won't recommend them—but do take a little marmalade. Brother, brother—a slice of ham instantly for Mr. Clitheroe."

"Don't hurry me, sister," the old gentleman replied, testily; "Mr. Clitheroe prefers intellectual food to gross diet like this. I want to show him my copy of Père Jacques d'Autum's *L'Incrédulité savante et la Crédulité ignorante, au sujet des Magiciens et Sorciers.*"

"I am doing extremely well," I observed, attacking the grilled leg of a chicken; "but I will trouble Miss Doveton for another cup of coffee."

"Ora! Ora! attend to your duty, child," the good-natured lady cried. "More coffee to Mr. Clitheroe, and plenty of cream."

"I should compassionate Mr. Clitheroe for his poor breakfast, if he were more communicative," Ora said, with a smile. "Perhaps he will condescend to tell us what he intends doing this morning?"

"In the first place, I mean to walk over to Weverham to see my dear old friend, John Brideoake," I replied.

"Dear heart a day! Ora," Miss Hazilrigge exclaimed, "you have upset the coffee-cup, I declare. I never knew you so careless before. One would think that the mention of Mr. Brideoake's name agitated you."

The observation was made in jest, but it almost appeared to be called for, for my eyes being fixed upon Ora at the moment, I perceived the colour mount to her cheek, and I asked myself, with some internal misgiving, what it could mean?

"My aunt and I propose driving to Delamere Forest to see the Headless Cross, spoken of in Nixon's prophecies," Ora said, "and Oak Mere, and the Hind's Well, and Sevenlowes, and Swan's Well, and Castle Cob, and some other curious spots, and we thought you might feel inclined to accompany us."

"Nothing would afford me greater pleasure than such a drive," I replied; "but I should be wanting in friendship if I delayed another hour to call on John Brideoake—especially after learning that he is unwell, and has expressed a desire to see me."

"Oh! he wishes to see you! I didn't understand that," Ora remarked.

"To be sure he does, and very naturally," Miss Hazilrigge said. "Go to him by all means, Mr. Clitheroe, and don't mind us in the least. We will take another drive into the forest to-morrow, or next day. Mr. Spring will oblige us with his company to-day."

"I shall be enchanted," Cuthbert rejoined, gallantly; "and I think Mervyn ought not to delay his visit to his friend."

"I never chanced to see Apphia Brideoake," Ora remarked, with a sly glance at me. "I am told she is very beautiful. Is it so, Mr. Clitheroe?"

"Dear heart, child! what a question to ask!" Miss Hazilrigge cried. "Don't you know——?" and she suddenly stopped.

"Know what, aunt?" Ora inquired, with affected simplicity. "Oh yes!—now I recollect. How very stupid of me! The duel was about her, to be sure! Pray excuse me, Mr. Clitheroe. But since I have been silly enough to put such a question, perhaps you won't mind answering it. Is she at all like her brother? Is she very beautiful?"

It will be easily imagined that these questions caused me considerable embarrassment, and rather interfered with the progress of my breakfast. However, I managed to reply that I didn't think there was any great resemblance between the brother and sister, but that Apphia unquestionably was very beautiful.

"That I can vouch for," Cuthbert Spring remarked; "and she is exceedingly amiable and accomplished as well. If I had not models of perfection before me," he proceeded, glancing from aunt to niece, "I should say she was without a peer. At all events, she is a great deal too good and too charming for the person for whom she is designed."

"Mr. Malpas Sale, is it not?" Ora cried, laughing at the extravagance of Cuthbert's compliments. "I have never seen him, but I am told he is excessively good-looking. I suppose I mustn't ask your opinion of him, Mr. Clitheroe?"

"Certainly not, my dear," Miss Hazilrigge interposed, quickly. "How can you think of such a thing? By-the-by, Mr. Spring," she continued, "can you tell me who the Brideoakes are? I don't know Mrs. Brideoake, but from the airs I am told she gives herself, she ought to be somebody. Who was she, and whence does she come—eh?"

"I'm sorry I cannot answer your questions," Cuthbert Spring rejoined. "The only person originally acquainted with Mrs. Brideoake, Dr. Foam, always observes a discreet silence concerning her; but I presume he imparted any information he possesses to Mrs. Mervyn before the intimacy commenced between the two ladies—an intimacy which you are aware has resulted in Mrs. Brideoake becoming virtually mistress of the Anchorite's."

"Very odd!—very odd, indeed!" Mr. Hazilrigge exclaimed, looking up. "And you, also, are unable to enlighten us as to this proud lady's family—eh, Mr. Clitheroe?"

"Entirely so, sir," I replied. "And what is more extraordinary still, I believe John Brideoake to be as much in the dark as myself. He has often told me that his mother can never be prevailed upon to speak to him of his father, but always checks his inquiries on the subject."

"I fancied, from what I could pick up from him, that Brideoake was rather imperfectly acquainted with his genealogy," the old gentleman said; "and you now account for his ignorance. But why should the mother withhold knowledge from her son to which he is entitled?"

"I cannot answer for Mrs. Brideoake—neither can John," I replied. "She has her own rule of conduct, and will allow no interference with it."

"Where nothing is positively known, all must be matter of mere conjecture," Cuthbert Spring remarked; "but I have always fancied that Mrs. Brideoake belongs to a good old Jacobite family, crushed by the Rebellion of '45. This would account for the interest that Mrs. Mervyn, whose predilections for the Stuarts are notorious, takes in her."

"It accounts for it partly, but not entirely," I replied. "My relative must have some particular interest in Mrs. Brideoake, or she would not have devoted herself to her so warmly. Of that I am certain. It almost seems to me that she has discovered a relation in Mrs. Brideoake."

"A connexion by marriage possibly," Cuthbert Spring replied. "After all, it may turn out that Brideoake is an assumed name."

"Nonsense! Mr. Spring. I cannot think that," Miss Hazilrigge cried.

"While you are about it, you may as well try to make out that Mrs. Brideoake is of a noble family," Mr. Hazilrigge said. "There were several such attainted in '15 and '45, and she may belong to one of them."

"And why not?" Mr. Spring cried, laughing. "Many a random shaft has hit the mark. But, as I said just now, all this is mere conjecture. Mrs. Brideoake may be of noble origin—and if hereditary nobility were universally characterised by arrogance and haughty bearing, I should have no doubt about it. She may also be related by marriage to Mrs. Mervyn, and I think I can discern how the connexion may have arisen——but," he added, checking himself, "it is idle to speculate further, since we cannot, by possibility, arrive at the truth."

Ora, who had been listening with almost as much attention as myself to the foregoing conversation, now observed:

"You have been making out a delightfully romantic history for John Brideoake. If he should turn out to be grandson of some attainted Jacobite peer, and the title be restored! Wouldn't that be enchanting, aunt!"

"Poh! you silly creature! No such good fortune is likely to attend the poor fellow," Miss Hazilrigge rejoined.

"Romantic as the idea may be of John Brideoake's restoration to the forfeited honours of his ancestors, I fear there is very little chance of such a consummation," Cuthbert Spring observed, with a smile. "Even supposing him to be in reality what we have imagined him to be in jest, where are the estates to come from to support a title?"

"Ay, where indeed?" Mr. Hazilrigge exclaimed. "He is as poor as a rat."

"Still, a title is a title, brother," Miss Hazilrigge said.

"And a very fine thing, too, aunt," Ora remarked; "and if John Brideoake were only to become a lord, he might marry some rich heiress, and so repair his fortunes."

"In that view of the case, I trust he may get a title," Cuthbert Spring remarked with a smile. "One thing is quite certain, that before the projected marriage takes place between Malpas Sale and Apphia, positive explanations as to who the Brideoakes really are must take place."

"I should think the Sales are already well informed on that point, Mr. Spring," Miss Hazilrigge said. "The vicar would naturally make all inquiries; and his son, from what I hear of him, has a keen eye to his own interests."

Seeing that I had done breakfast, Mr. Hazilrigge now rose, and again proposed an adjournment to his sanctum to examine his Père Jacques d'Autum; but I excused myself on the plea of extreme anxiety to see my friend, and Miss Hazilrigge coming to my aid, I happily escaped the infliction.

Not long afterwards I set out on my expedition, and the ladies having put on garden-bonnets in the interim, volunteered to accompany me to the end of the long avenue; on arriving at which point Miss Hazilrigge showed me a path across the fields leading to Weverham, telling me it was the shortest and pleasantest road.

Ere we separated, it was arranged that, after taking their drive, the ladies should call for me at John Brideoake's cottage, and bring me home in the carriage, and Miss Hazilrigge trusted that my friend would be well enough to dine with them on that day, and she charged me to invite him. No company were expected, and he would therefore be perfectly quiet.

CHAPTER XI.

I OBTAIN AN INSIGHT INTO JOHN BRIDEOAKE'S HEART.

I FOUND John Brideoake's little domicile without difficulty, having carefully noted its position in passing through Weverham on the previous day.

A pretty ornamental cottage; small, but commodious enough for its occupant, with a thatched roof, a rustic porch overgrown with honeysuckles and other creepers, and whitewashed walls covered with a profusion of roses. In front, a trimly-kept garden with dainty flowerbeds, and a grass-plot planted with standard roses. John must have become excessively fond of roses, for he had them in every variety, and the plants appeared to be well tended. There was a cheerful look about the little habitation that delighted me, and I lingered in the garden, admiring its beauty and arrangement, before I advanced to the porch.

Suddenly I heard my name pronounced by a well-known voice, and John himself, issuing from an arbour where he had been reading, hastened towards me, and with an exclamation of delight flung his arms round my neck.

My poor friend! he was sadly changed, and my heart sank within me as I gazed at him.

If he could have stood erect, John would have been above the average height, but his slender frame was prematurely bent, and his movements betokened extreme debility. He was so thin, that his clothes hung loosely about him; and his looks altogether were calculated to inspire the most serious apprehensions. But in spite of their emaciation his features were handsome—I might almost say beautiful; and his eyes were large and lustrous—too lustrous, indeed, when viewed in connexion with his pallid cheeks with the ominous red spot upon them.

While regarding him wistfully I could scarcely repress my emotion, and I found it wholly impossible to give utterance to the expressions of joy which a meeting with him must otherwise have prompted. My poor friend had no such misgivings in regard to me, but seemed unfeignedly delighted to see me, and the affectionate warmth of his greeting, while it endeared him still more to me, increased, if possible, my anxiety for him.

Still keeping his arm over my shoulder, he led me into his cottage, and opening the door of a little room, which he called his study, ushered me into it.

A pleasant room, looking upon the garden, embowered with roses, and furnished with book-shelves laden with the works of divines and writers on ecclesiastical history. Amongst them I distinguished South, Strype, Stillingfleet, Tillotson, and Sherlock. On the table lay a large annotated Bible, with book-marks placed in it, writing materials, and a half-finished manuscript sermon. I told John, as I took a chair, that he had a delightful abode, and I thought he must now lead a truly happy life.

"As happy a life as I can ever expect to lead, dear Mervyn," he replied. "My desires are few, and my great object is to do all the good I can. I am of some little use to my parishioners, and if more strength were granted me I might do yet more for them. As it is, I persuade myself that I have gained their love, and they listen to my counsels. I have healed some differences—have brought several erring sheep back to the fold—and I would fain believe that I have been the humble instrument of rescuing one soul at least from perdition."

"That you discharge the duties of your sacred calling to the fullest extent of your power, I cannot for a moment doubt, dear John," I replied, "and fortunate it is for those amongst whom you are thrown that they have such a pastor and friend. But you must take care of yourself, and not tax your energies too far. The country about you is very beautiful—indeed I hardly know a more picturesque district—but are you quite sure that the place is healthy?—does it agree with you?"

"If I suffer, dear Mervyn," he replied, "it is not from any ill effects caused by the air of the place, but by latent disease, which I have reason to fear is consuming me. I am quite as well here as I should be elsewhere—perhaps better. Indeed, I should not be so well elsewhere, for then I should be anxious about my little flock. No, Mervyn, the end with me cannot be far off, and I trust to be permitted to breathe my last amongst those whom my precepts and example may benefit. I shall not be able to accomplish half the work I would fain perform, but while power is granted me I will never abandon it."

Recalling the singular conversation we had had about my friend during breakfast that morning, I said,

"But were circumstances suddenly to change your position, John, would you still desire to stay here?"

"There is little likelihood of my position being changed," he replied; "but thus much I will say, that even under altered circumstances, if any choice were left me, I would remain here. As I have told you, I am strongly attached to my flock, and it would pain me to separate from them."

"I understand and respect the feeling," I replied. "You have found a home here amongst strangers which you could not meet with amidst your own family."

"It is quite true, Mervyn," he said, sadly. "My mother, as you are aware, has cast me from her, and without any just cause, as I verily believe, on my part, treats me as if I had deeply offended her. I have disappointed her—though that can scarcely be imputed to me as a fault, since my strength failed me in the task—but I myself am more deeply disappointed than she can ever be. It is a deplorable thing, to imagine a mother without love for her children; but on reviewing my life calmly, I am forced to come to the conclusion that she never loved—in the full sense of maternal love—either myself or Apphia."

"A saddening reflection indeed, John," I replied; "but as you have said so much, I will not hesitate to go further, and declare my conviction that your mother will not scruple to sacrifice the happiness of her children in order to carry out her own designs. She is about to force Apphia into a match which must be productive of wretchedness to her. The marriage must be averted, if possible. Ill will come of it. You know that I would never malign even an enemy, and will believe me when I assert that Malpas Sale is in all respects unworthy to be your sister's husband."

"You are incapable, I am sure, of asserting anything you do not fully believe, Mervyn; but in this instance you are influenced by feelings that may warp your judgment. You have long entertained a dislike to Malpas, and latterly your dislike has deepened into animosity. You can, therefore, scarcely be accounted a fair judge."

"Perhaps not, John; but I advance nothing that I am not prepared to prove. I did not dislike Malpas formerly without cause—neither is it without good cause that I hate him now. I have been wronged —deeply wronged—and must have reparation."

"But not in the way you propose, Mervyn," he replied, with gentle gravity. "I grieve to hear you profess sentiments so totally at variance with those which Christianity inculcates, and by which alone your conduct ought to be governed. Forgiveness may be hard to practise, but, trust me, it is the only way to efface the sense of injury. I speak to you, Mervyn, because I love you as a brother, and loving you thus dearly, I cannot be blind to your faults. You have many excellent—nay, admirable qualities—you are generous, enthusiastic, warm-hearted, loyal—but you are also impetuous, quick in anger, disposed to be resentful. It is the latter tendency, more than any other, that I desire to see corrected; because it wars most with your present happiness, and may endanger your future weal. I do not say that you are unforgiving—far from it— such conduct would be incompatible with the generosity of your nature. But your wrath, easily kindled, does not soon die out, and you believe yourself bound by laws of honour to obtain satisfaction for wrongs, sometimes imaginary, but even if real, not to be thus repaired. Leave vengeance in His hands, who alone is able to repay."

Gentle and kindly-intended as was John's reproof, it somewhat chafed me, and I answered, I fear, rather impatiently,

"I am quite sure you are right, John, but I should play the hypocrite were I to admit that I shall act as you would have me act. Believing Malpas Sale to be a villain, I do not mean to rest till I have unmasked and punished him."

"Malpas may be as bad as you represent him, though I hope not. But grant that he is so, do not you, Mervyn, commit a fault as grave as any you reprobate. Leave others to decide the question. You cannot act both as accuser and judge."

"Act as judge yourself, then, John, and decide between us. Has Malpas not robbed me of my fortune? Has he not snatched from me your sister, whom I loved better than life? These are the wrongs that goad me to call down punishment upon his head. You, John —pure and virtuous yourself—can scarcely believe in the misdeeds of others. In addition to the injuries he has done me, enough to warrant the most terrible reprisals on my part, Malpas has carried desolation into a once happy family—has destroyed the happiness of a fond husband—taken away from him his wife——"

"Hold! Mervyn," John interrupted. "This last charge, at all events, falls to the ground. I am aware of the unhappy case to which you refer, and I am persuaded that Malpas was not the author of the wrong then committed."

"You believe, then, that Simon Pownall was the destroyer of Ned Culcheth's peace?" I cried.

"I do," he answered. "I have means of knowing the truth of this lamentable case, and I believe it to be as I have stated."

"You are imposed upon, John," I said.

"Alas! not so," he replied, sadly but firmly. "It is you, Mervyn, who are blinded by prejudice. May you, one day, see the truth clearly—and not, as now, through a glass darkly!"

He spoke with so much earnestness and conviction that I was staggered; but a moment's reflection brought me back to my original opinion.

"Poor Sissy's avowal alone shall satisfy me," I cried.

"If that will suffice, perhaps it may be obtained," he returned.

"How?" I exclaimed, startled. "Do you know where she is?"

"I am not at liberty to answer any questions on the subject," he said. "There is only one person to whom I can reveal anything that has been divulged to me. To Sissy's unhappy husband I may possibly speak—but to no other."

"Then do speak to him, John, I adjure you; and perhaps, through your intervention, something of peace may be restored to his breast. At all events, he may be brought to a better frame of mind."

"Send him to me, and I will do all that in me lies to help him," the young curate said, fervently. "But do not raise your hopes too highly," he continued, with an expression of great sadness. "Poor Ned has had a severe trial; but the worst is not yet over. Question me no further, I pray of you. Let us change this painful theme."

"So be it," I replied, reluctantly. "Let us return to a matter in which I myself am personally interested. Will you not oppose your sister's marriage with Malpas?"

"I do not conceive that I should be warranted in opposing it—neither do I think that any opposition on my part would be availing. I have already remonstrated with my mother, and have angered her so much against me by doing so, that she will neither write to me herself, nor suffer Apphia to write to me. I am unwilling to widen the breach. My mother, with all her faults of temper, is still my mother, and I owe her a son's obedience."

"But, by the same rule, your sister is your sister, and as a brother you are bound to save her from certain misery."

"If I saw the matter with your eyes, I might act differently, Mervyn. But Apphia seems reconciled to the match. You know my weaknesses, and I could not, therefore, disguise them from you, even if so disposed. Naturally timid, in my mother's presence I lose all my self-possession, and I could no more dispute with her than I could wrestle with an athlete. She has always been accustomed to exact obedience from me and Apphia, and neither of us have ever disputed her control."

"I know it, John—but if your sister's happiness depended upon your resolution, would you not throw off this unfortunate weakness?—for such, in truth, I esteem it."

"I must first feel that the effort is needed. It might be fatal to me. I am equal to little now."

"Forgive me, John, if I put a question to you, which has its origin in no idle curiosity, but in sincere interest in yourself. Your mother's proud deportment has excited surprise, and I have been asked what there is to justify her haughtiness—in a word, whether she belongs to some family of good lineage. I could offer no information, for I have none to give."

"Neither can I afford you any information, Mervyn, being in utter ignorance as to my mother's family. Such a statement might appear incredible to any one except yourself, who know

P

my mother, and are aware of the extraordinary reserve of her character. What may be her motives for casting an impenetrable veil over her family history I pretend not to divine. But she has done so from my earliest years, and could never be induced for a moment to withdraw it. All I know relative to my father is that he died before my mother gave birth to Apphia, and that the marriage, either on one side or the other—but probably my mother's—had offended her connexions so deeply, that they disowned her altogether, and she was consequently plunged into the greatest distress. At that period we all suffered much, and my proud mother most of all. She forbade us then ever to speak of her relations—ever to inquire after them—and I religiously obeyed her. Apphia, indeed, has questioned her repeatedly in my hearing, but has always been sharply checked for her curiosity. So little do I know about myself, Mervyn, that I am by no means sure that the name I bear is my rightful name. Enough!—it will serve to be inscribed upon my tombstone."

Profound emotion kept me silent for a short space. At last I said,

"But if you are indifferent to your parentage, John, I am not. Have you any objection to my instituting inquiries for you?"

"I would rather you did not. I should gain nothing by learning a secret which my mother has sedulously kept from me. What boots it, Mervyn, who I am? I am alone in the world—or nearly alone. Heaven knows that I seek to honour and love my mother, and strive to obey her! Heaven knows, also, that I dearly love my sister, though I am not permitted to behold her, or to profit by her love! I have no kinsman; and except yourself, my friend and brother, I have none to care for me—none to sympathise with me, or to share my sorrows."

He bowed his head, and we were again silent.

"Yet do not think that I repine," he continued, more cheerfully. "While I can be useful in my limited sphere, I ought to be content."

"Long as I have known you, John," I exclaimed, regarding him with admiration, "I never fully understood you till now."

"You overrate me, my dear friend," he replied, kindly. "Suffering has made me a better man. By constantly fixing my thoughts on Heaven, I have been able to shake off the ties of earth. Yet when I had emancipated myself from thraldom, and conquered, as I deemed, all my worldly feelings and passions, I was again for awhile enslaved."

I thought this a fitting opportunity for putting a question I had meditated; and I inquired if his heart had ever been touched?

He would not hide the truth from me, but answered, though with some bashfulness,

"Yes, I was foolish enough to indulge for a time a hopeless passion. Before becoming aware of it, I had swallowed the intoxicating potion, and, under its influence, I lost my customary self-control. I loved madly—yes, madly is the word — for what but madness could it be in me to aspire even in thought to a young and lovely heiress?"

"Did you ever declare your passion, John?" I said, regarding him earnestly.

"Never in words," he replied, an almost maidenly blush suffusing his pale cheek. "I should not have dared to give utterance to my feelings."

"Speak to me without reserve, John, for you know you are speaking to a brother. Did she—did the object of your regard seem to encourage your suit? Tell me the exact impression produced upon you by her manner?"

"My impression, then, is, Mervyn, that she perceived she had made my heart captive, and merely encouraged me for her amusement. When she found she had gone too far, she made me clearly understand that she was indifferent to me. Alas! it was then too late for me. The arrow was shot which will rankle in my breast so long as sensibility lasts within it."

"My poor friend!" I exclaimed, with deep sympathy. "But you may find some other person to whom you can transfer your love."

"Love like mine, Mervyn, cannot be transferred," he replied, mournfully. "My heart is not susceptible of a second impression."

"You have not confided to me the name of the syren who has bewitched you, John, but I guessed it from the first. And I admit that her beauty is quite sufficient to account for the influence she has gained over you—nay more, I will own to you, my dear friend, that I was well-nigh falling into the same snare myself."

"You!" he exclaimed, quickly, and putting his hand to his heart as if to repress a pang, while a hot flush sprang to his cheek. Then suddenly recovering himself, he added, "Forgive me, Mervyn, for the selfish feeling which crossed me for a moment. Why should you not love Ora Doveton? Why should my senseless passion, which ought never to have been indulged, prevent you from winning her regard—from claiming her hand? Let no thought of me stand between you and her. If you love her, it will be my fondest aspiration that you may win her. I had, indeed, hoped that another union might have brought us more closely together—might have made us really brothers, as we are in regard—but that hope is crushed. Whether Ora is as well calculated to make you happy as Apphia, cannot now be considered. You have lost the one, may you gain the other!"

"I fully appreciate the unheard-of generosity of your motives, John," I said. "But I have no reason to believe that Ora has thought seriously about me for a moment. Nay, now that I am better acquainted with her character than I was at first, I cannot help suspecting that she has been trifling with me in the same heartless manner that she trifled with you. But I am still able to stop."

"But why should you stop?" John cried. "Not from consideration to me—for I am out of the question. Besides, it would be idle to institute any comparison between us. Though merely coquetting with me, Ora could scarcely be otherwise than sincere with you, formed as you are to please. No—no—our cases are widely different. Success awaits you, though failure has attended me."

I regarded him in astonishment, scarcely able to credit such self-abnegation, even in him.

"I should not be the true friend I am to you, John," I said, "if I were to yield to your generous solicitations. Not till I am assured that Ora has no regard for you, will I indulge another thought of her."

"Take the assurance from me," he said. "I am not likely to be deceived on such a point."

"I do not know that," I replied. "Your diffidence makes you despair where a bolder man might justly feel confident. Again, I say, I must ascertain from her own lips that Ora has dismissed all thoughts of you before I advance another step."

"You must do no such thing, Mervyn," John said, earnestly. "Promise me that you will never mention what has passed between us to Ora. I am ashamed of my folly and presumption. Do not expose me to ridicule. I have laid bare my heart to you as a brother. Respect its secrets."

"Calm yourself, dear John," I said. "Your wishes shall be obeyed. What is more, I believe you are right. Neither of us ought to think of Ora. What I have just learnt explains your absence yesterday. You shun a meeting with her."

"Till I am completely cured, I judge it safest not to meet her," he returned. "But in truth I did not feel equal to dining out yesterday—so the excuse was justifiable."

As we were talking, I perceived an old man, with a leathern bag slung across his shoulders, enter the garden, and march towards the cottage door.

"Whom have we here, John?" I asked.

"The postman," he replied. "His visits are rare here. I receive few letters. You have been my best correspondent."

Shortly afterwards a pretty little rustic-looking girl, about ten years of age, entered the room with a letter on a tray, and handing the missive to John, and dropping a curtsey to me, she retired.

"Apphia's handwriting!" John exclaimed, in surprise, after glancing at the superscription of the letter. "What can it mean? The poor girl must have written to me without our mother's knowledge?" He then paused, and his countenance lost the glad smile which had for a moment illumined it. "A presentiment crosses me that this is a messenger of ill tidings. Have you never felt, Mervyn, ere opening a letter, that you had a notion of its contents—and could tell whether it brought weal or wo?"

"I have experienced something of the sort, I confess. But I trust your present forebodings may not be verified."

"We will ascertain at once," he replied.

"Hold, John," I cried, rising. "I will quit you for a short time, in order that you may read your letter tranquilly. Apphia may write to you about many circumstances which might render my presence undesirable."

"I thank you for your consideration, dear Mervyn," he replied. "It may possibly be as you suggest. I will call you when I have read the letter."

Taking my hat, I stepped forth into the garden. After lingering near the flower-beds for a few minutes, finding that John did not summon me, I walked out into the highroad, which a little further on was completely overshaded by large trees, forming a natural avenue to the church—a structure of great beauty and antiquity, distant about three hundred yards. Between the church and my friend's dwelling several cottages intervened, and amongst others a small public-house. At the door of the latter stood a tall man, evidently making inquiries, and as he turned towards me I recognised Ned Culcheth. Indeed, I should have known Ned at once if I had seen Hubert, who now sprang over a hedge, and came bounding towards me.

On descrying me, the keeper hurried forward, and we soon met. He told me he had been to Owlarton Grange, and learning there that I had gone over to Weverham, he had followed me, and had just been inquiring at the public-house for Mr. Brideoake's dwelling. Ned added that he was sure he was now on Simon Pownall's track, and felt confident, ere long, of discovering the rascal's retreat. It would surprise me, he said, to learn that Simon must be somewhere in the neighbourhood of Weverham. He had picked up this piece of information by playing the spy upon Chetham Quick, and had managed to overhear a private conference between Chetham and the young gipsy, Obed;—the end of which was that Obed was engaged to convey a letter secretly to Pownall. The pair had not spoken of Pownall by his right name, but Ned was certain that their discourse referred to him.

Obed started on his mission before daybreak that morning, and Ned, who had never lost sight of him, followed him as closely as he judged prudent, making sure that the gipsy would guide him to Pownall's retreat. But the wary vagabond must have found out who was upon his heels, for on entering Weverham Glen he entirely disappeared, and after a couple of hours' fruitless search, aided by Hubert, Ned was obliged to quit the ravine. Obed, no doubt, had waded for some distance in the brook to destroy the scent, for the hound lost it on the banks. What became of him afterwards Ned could not discover.

Ned's scheme having thus failed, he had naturally gone on to Owlarton Grange to consult me. His relation was curious, and might have interested me more, if I had not been chiefly struck by the singular opportuneness of the poor fellow's arrival.

After debating with myself whether I should tell him what John Brideoake had intimated to me about Sissy, I arrived at the conclusion that any disclosure respecting her would come best from the young clergyman himself, and I therefore said,

"Well, at all events, whether you find Pownall or not, Ned, you have not come hither on a bootless errand. Mr. Brideoake can give you some intelligence of your wife. What it is, I know not, for he declined to communicate any particulars to me — saying they were for your ear alone; but I must prepare you for bad tidings, for such, I fear, they will prove."

"I have not lost her?" Ned said, halting and looking hard at me. "You don't mean to prepare me for that?"

"No—no," I replied; "your apprehensions of calamity far outstrip my meaning. I only judge, from Mr. Brideoake's manner, that he has something distressing to relate, and I deem it right to prepare you for it."

"Nothing more distressing can be in store for me than what has already occurred," Ned replied, marching by my side as I proceeded towards the cottage.

Before introducing the poor keeper, I thought it best to acquaint John with his unexpected arrival, and, leaving Ned and his hound in the garden, I entered the cottage alone.

I found my friend in a state of utter prostration, evidently occasioned by the perusal of his sister's letter.

"I am not the only sufferer in my family, Mervyn," he said. "Apphia appears to be equally unhappy. The view I took of her position, which I explained to you just now, is entirely changed by the details she gives me in this letter, which, as I supposed, is written without my mother's knowledge. I now agree with you that her marriage with Malpas ought never to take place. And yet to thwart my mother!—to disobey her—to incur her lasting displeasure—perhaps her malediction—it is frightful to think of it."

And his countenance proclaimed the terror and agitation to which his thoughts gave birth.

"Does Apphia urge you to interfere, John?" I cried. "I ask only that."

"She does, and of course I cannot refuse the appeal. But, as I have already told you, the effort will cost me my life."

"Courage! John, courage!" I exclaimed. "Rouse yourself and be a man. You shall have all the support I can give you. Though the difficulties of the task may appear insurmountable at first, they will dwindle into nothing if met firmly. But we will talk of this anon. I have another matter to bring before you now. There is a person at hand whose claims upon your attention are urgent, and ought not to be deferred."

And I then acquainted him with the unexpected arrival of Ned Culcheth, and entreated him to admit him.

"Assuredly I will see him," he replied, "though I would willingly have chosen another occasion—when my nerves might be more firmly strung—for an interview with the poor fellow. Where is he —in the garden?—bid him come to me, and I will speak to him at once. And I must beg you, dear Mervyn, to let me have some quarter of an hour's discourse with him in private. I will do my best to console him under his heavy affliction."

On this I stepped forth, and calling to Ned Culcheth, bade him go in. He at once obeyed, uncovering his glowing locks, and bowing his tall head as he crossed the little threshold. I kept Hubert with me, and taking the hound into the arbour, sat down to meditate.

Many minutes had not elapsed when a startling noise was heard at the door of the cottage, as of some one rushing hurriedly forth, and Hubert, who was couched near me, sprang up, and dashed out of the arbour.

I followed, and was just in time to stop poor Ned, who was making his way wildly across the little parterres and grass-plot, regardless of the shrubs and flowers that he trampled beneath his feet.

His looks were fearfully haggard, and his demeanour desperate. Nevertheless, I ran up to him, and laying hold of his arm, arrested him forcibly.

"What are you about, Ned?" I cried.

"I am about to put an end to a wretched existence," he rejoined, in a voice scarcely human. "Stand off! and let me go."

"Never, for the fell purpose you are bent on, Ned," I exclaimed, still keeping fast hold of him. "What's the matter with you, man? Have you become suddenly demented?"

"Ay!" he replied, dashing his cap on the ground with a force and fierceness that made Hubert spring back in alarm, "you've said the word. I am demented. I've suffered enough," he continued, with a burst of anguish very painful, indeed, to hear. "I can bear no more. Let me die."

"Forbear, Ned!" I sternly and authoritatively exclaimed, for I felt this was the only way to deal with him. "By raising your hand against yourself to escape present misery, which *must* and *can* be borne, you will destroy all your hopes of hereafter. Your present paroxysm of grief will abate, and you will then view matters differently. Give heed to what the good young man you have just abruptly quitted may say to you. Go back to him,—go back at once, or you will for ever forfeit my esteem—and return to me when you are calmer."

Ned looked at me for a moment, wildly, almost savagely, but he gradually quailed beneath my steady gaze, groaned, let his head fall upon his breast, and, without a word, went back to John, who was standing beneath the porch anxiously watching us, and re-entered the cottage with him.

I returned to the arbour with Hubert, who seemed instinctively to comprehend that something was amiss with his master, for he whined and looked quite downcast.

A long interval occurred before Ned's footsteps were again heard. Hubert and I came forth to meet him. The poor fellow's heart had evidently been melted—his eyes were red with recent tears.

"I am calmer now, sir," he said, in a low tone, and with a look of humble **resignation**; "I will do whatever you and Mr. Brideoake bid me."

"Then you must remain with me here till to-morrow, my poor friend," John Brideoake said, issuing from the porch. "You know why I desire you to stay," he added, with a certain significance, "and what I would have you do."

"I do, sir," Ned replied; "and I hope Heaven will grant me strength to go through with it!"

At this juncture the sound o carriage wheels was heard in the distance, and Mr. Hazilrigge's barouche, with the ladies inside it, could be descried coming slowly along the road towards the cottage.

"Make my excuses to Miss Hazilrigge, Mervyn," John cried, hastily. "I cannot see her or Ora to-day. Come over to me to-morrow morning. I have much to say to you. This poor fellow," he added, pointing to Ned, "will remain with me. He will have need of preparation—and so shall I—for the painful task which we have to perform. Farewell, my dear friend!"

Signing to Ned Culcheth to come with him, John then retired, and Hubert followed them into the cottage.

I met the carriage at the gate, and made the best excuses I could for John. Both ladies displayed great interest concerning him, and I had some difficulty in preventing Miss Hazilrigge from getting out to see him. She felt sure she could be of service to him, she declared. Could she send him anything?—wine—chicken-broth—calves-foot jelly, or blanc-mange? I declined all for my friend. At last the steps were let down, and I got into the carriage, taking a place beside Cuthbert Spring.

We had not a very cheerful drive back to Owlarton Grange, for a gloom was cast over the party by the accounts I gave them of poor John's alarming state of health.

CHAPTER XII.

THE LEGEND OF OWLARTON GRANGE.—MY ADVENTURE IN THE HAUNTED CHAMBER.

Mr. Hazilrigge was out when we returned to the grange, and recent occurrences indisposing me for anything like light conversation, I at once withdrew to my own room, and continued there until the hour for dinner had arrived.

On descending, I found good, kind Miss Hazilrigge consulting with her brother about the propriety of having John Brideoake at the grange to be nursed, and the worthy old gentleman told her to do just as she pleased. She had his full consent to send for John at once, and nurse him as long as might be needful. I offered no objection, of course, though I felt almost certain that John would not accede to the arrangement. Cuthbert Spring expressed extraordinary sympathy for the invalid, and offered many suggestions for his benefit; but I could not help fancying that the interest he manifested was not entirely disinterested, but had its origin in a desire to please Miss Hazilrigge.

Ora's vivacity had completely deserted her, and I could scarcely recognise in her the lively girl of the day before. Very little conversation passed between us at dinner. This was more my own fault than hers, I suspect, for she was too quick not to perceive that my manner towards her was changed; neither could she be ignorant of the cause of the alteration. There was no longer any exchange of speaking glances between us, but on the contrary a growing coldness, which we both of us understood and felt, though neither cared to explain.

If there was any flirting that day, it was between Cuthbert Spring and Miss Hazilrigge, and I began to think it not unlikely that a match might be struck up between them. The ladies retired soon after dinner, for Ora complained of a severe headache.

Supernatural stories of course formed the staple of our conversation while discussing our claret. Our host inquired whether I had ever heard the legend connected with his house, and on my answering in the negative, and expressing a great desire to hear it, he was good enough to relate it to me.

"You have no doubt," he premised, "remarked a curious picture hanging over the mantelpiece in the haunted chamber?"

I replied in the affirmative, and that the picture had struck me forcibly.

"The principal personage represented is my great-grandfather, Clotten Hazilrigge, surnamed, from his parsimonious habits, the 'Miser.' The figure standing behind him is his much-trusted, but perfidious servant, Jotham Shocklach. Old Clotten little thought, when causing that portrait to be painted, that he would preserve the features of his murderer."

"The portraits are admirably painted," I observed, "and the artist must have caught the exact expression of the originals."

"He was too indifferently paid, I make no doubt, to flatter. Old Clotten looks like what he was, and Jotham has the air of an assassin. But to my story. Clotten Hazilrigge had one son, Leycester, with whom he quarrelled, on account of his alleged extravagance, though I really believe the young man gave him no just cause of complaint on that score. But the miser could not bear to part with money even to his only son. His wife—fortunately, perhaps, for her—died about three years after their marriage—tradition says of a broken heart, but this is beside the purpose. Clotten lived by himself at the grange, and his penurious habits increased as he grew older. He was morose, unsociable, tyrannical, and was disliked both by tenants and neighbours. He visited no one, invited no one, and would allow no one to enter the house except on matters of business. He discharged all his servants except Jotham Shocklach, and in him, who merited the trust so little, he reposed implicit confidence.

"Now it was well known that old Clotten had vast hoards of gold secreted in the house, and his steward often remonstrated with him on the danger he ran from robbers by keeping such large sums of money in his possession; but the miser despised the warnings: denying that he had any secret hoards, and declaring that if thieves broke into the house they would find nothing. And Jotham privately confirmed the assertion, for though he knew, he said, that his master must have a heap of treasure somewhere about the premises, he could never find out where it was secreted.

"But he did discover the hidden store at last. One night, it is supposed—for this must rest on conjecture—he entered his master's bed-chamber, and found, wide open, a narrow sliding door in the panels, of the existence of which he must have been previously unaware. Through this aperture he passed—stealthily, no doubt—and tracking a strait passage contrived in the thickness of the walls, arrived at a small chamber without a window, constructed for a priest's hiding-place, for our family once were Papists. Here he discovered old Clotten, with a huge chest full of money-bags before him.

"No eye beheld them, no tongue related the dark transaction, yet the state in which all was subsequently found showed clearly what took place. Old Clotten must have sprung from his hoards like a tiger, and have seized Jotham by the throat, for a piece of the villain's cravat was found in the miser's gripe. But Jotham was a strong man, and, no doubt, shook himself easily free. With a heavy mallet, which it is supposed he picked up in the priest's hiding-place, he dealt his master a fatal blow on the head, and then stuffing his pockets with gold, and taking as many money-bags as he could carry, hurried to the secret door.

"His horror and fright may be conceived on finding it closed. The lamp brought by his master had been crushed and extinguished in the death-struggle. It was found beneath the miser's body. In vain the murderous villain searched for the secret spring. In vain he tried to batter open the door with the mallet. It was of stout oak, and resisted his attempts. He was caught in a trap from which there was no escape. He would only be liberated to meet the shameful death he merited. Yet a worse fate awaited him in his self-contrived prison.

"Next day, some tradesfolk from Weverham came to the house, but finding none to answer them, they went away. This did not excite surprise, for the miser's habits were so eccentric that it was thought he might have gone forth with his servant; but when he did not return on the succeeding day, some alarm began to be felt. Still no one entered the house until the evening of the third day after the murder, when the steward and some of the villagers got in through a window, and, after searching about, went to the miser's bedroom. While there, they heard a faint knocking against the wall. Somebody must be shut up there, the steward cried—old Clotten, or Jotham—perhaps both. He called out, and the knocking was renewed, but very feebly. Then there was a groan, and all became silent. After some search, the secret door was discovered; the spring was touched, and it flew open.

"A terrible spectacle presented itself to the steward, who was the first to enter—Jotham Shocklach lying dead with the mallet in his hand. The wretch had only just expired. Bags of money were near him, and the floor of the narrow passage was strewn over with pieces

of gold. They dragged out the body of the murderer, and then, proceeding further, discovered his victim. All was now explained.

"After old Clotten's tragical end, my grandfather, of course, came into possession of the property, and caused the secret door to be nailed up. Notwithstanding this, the restless spirit of Jotham Shocklach disturbed the house. Mysterious knockings, groans, and other appalling sounds were heard in that room at dead of night. These nocturnal disturbances, however, had ceased for many years, and only began again about four months ago, when Cuthbert Spring occupied the haunted chamber."

Tea being announced soon after this recital, we obeyed the summons, and found Miss Hazilrigge alone, for Ora's headache having increased, she had retired for the night. As we could have no music, in consequence of Miss Doveton's indisposition, we sat down to a rubber of whist, and, in cutting for partners, Mr. Spring fell to Miss Hazilrigge's share—a circumstance that diverted them immensely. I felt so *distrait* that I scarcely knew what I was about, and it is surprising that I did not commit some unpardonable blunders. We did not play more than one game, which was won by the old bachelor and his partner, and then Miss Hazilrigge bade us good night, saying she must see how Ora was going on. As on the former occasion, Mr. Spring gallantly attended her to the door, where they had a few more "last words."

No further bell-ringing having taken place that night I deferred my solution of the mystery till the morrow, but I put a few more questions to our host relative to Dr. Hooker. From Old Hazy's description of the Doctor, he appeared to be well skilled in chiromancy, physiognomy, necromancy, natural and judicial astronomy, could cast nativities, interpret dreams, and do many other wonderful things besides. I dare say the old gentleman did not tell me half the delusions that had been practised upon him by the Doctor, but he told me quite enough to show me to what extent he had been duped. I tried in vain to open his eyes to the man's real character. He would not believe that he was a charlatan. The world, he said, always called the wisest men charlatans, but he knew better, and would never join in the senseless cry. Dr. Hooker had not overrated his influence over his dupe. When I affirmed that I was certain that Hooker had rung the bells, I rather raised than lowered him in the old gentleman's opinion, for he declared that such a feat could not have been accomplished except by supernatural aid; and this alone was sufficient to establish the Doctor's extraordinary powers. No, no; I must not attempt to depreciate such a man. I did not reveal what I knew of the galvanic battery and the electric wires—for I kept that disclosure for another occasion. Cuthbert Spring made no remarks about Dr. Hooker, for he was too well aware of Old Hazy's peculiarities to meddle with them.

Midnight had nearly arrived before our host released us.

Once more I was alone in the haunted chamber. Again I glanced at the portraits of the miser and his murderous servant, and, now that I was acquainted with the legend connected with the picture, it impressed me still more powerfully. In consequence, no doubt, of the story I had heard from Old Hazy, superstitious fancies crowded thickly upon me, and all my efforts to shake them off were unavailing. As on the previous night, I drew back the heavy curtain from before the deep bay-window, and allowed the moonlight to stream into the chamber. I took some precautions which I had not deemed needful on the former occasion. Taking my case of duelling-pistols from my portmanteau, I loaded the weapons, and laid them on the table. Then seating myself in an easy-chair, I determined to keep watch, but in spite of my resolutions of vigilance, sleep after awhile stole over my eyelids.

How long I slumbered I cannot say, but I was suddenly aroused by a strange and startling noise, which I at once recognised as the ghostly knocking described by Cuthbert Spring. I listened intently. After the lapse of about a minute there was another heavy blow as if dealt by a mallet—a third—a fourth—up to ten; with the same intervals between each.

The unearthly sounds seemed to proceed from the lower part of the wall on the left of the bed. But they did not appear to be stationary. On the contrary, the blows were dealt at various points inside the wainscot.

I am not ashamed to own that I felt appalled. My taper had burnt out, and the wan light of the moon, which must have been struggling with passing clouds, only served to make darkness visible. The further end of the chamber in which the bed stood was plunged in deep shade.

While peering into this obscurity I fancied I saw a figure standing near the bed. It was perfectly motionless, and scarcely distinguishable; but as far as I could make it out, the attire of the phantom—or semblance of attire—was like that worn by Jotham Shocklach, as represented in the portrait—while the features, as far as they could be discerned—were those of the murderous servant. Something like a thin shroud hung over the lower part of the figure, and in its right hand it held a mallet.

Terror completely transfixed me. I strove to speak—but my tongue clove to the roof of my mouth. My limbs refused their office, and I could not grasp my pistols. The figure remained motionless and stationary, half concealed by the dark drapery of the bed, from which it could scarcely be distinguished. As I gazed at it, for I could not withdraw my eyes, it began to glide slowly towards me. No sound that I could detect attended its progress.

My terror increased. At length the phantom came under the influence of a ray of moonlight streaming athwart the chamber, which lighted up its ghastly and cadaverous features. It then paused; and at that moment I recovered my firmness, for I felt convinced that I had to do with one of mortal mould. Starting to my feet, I demanded of the ghost, in tones that sounded hoarse and strange in my own ears,—who it was,—and what it wanted?

The apparition made no answer, but pointed to the door, as if enjoining my departure. But I did not move.

"You would fain persuade me," I cried, in a bolder tone than I could at first assume, "that you are the restless spirit of the murderer, Jotham Shocklach. But I know better. Unless I am much mistaken, we have met before, and this is not the first time I have seen you play the ghost."

The phantom was evidently much discomposed, and I felt satisfied that I was right in my conjecture.

"It is useless to attempt to impose upon me further," I cried, in a voice of thunder. "I know you, rascal. You are Dr. Hooker, alias Simon Pownall."

The ghost would have beaten a hasty retreat, but I snatched up a pistol.

"Attempt to stir," I exclaimed, levelling it at him, "and I will send you to join the miscreant whose likeness you have assumed."

Probably the ghost thought I should put my threat into execution, and seeing no chance of escape, dropped on its knees.

"Spare me!" it ejaculated in a piteous voice, which I instantly recognised as that of Simon Pownall—"spare me, and I will confess all."

"Ho! ho! So it is you, then, Pownall?" I cried.

"Why, yes; there's no use in denying it, since you've found me out."

"Well, get up," I cried, drawing near to him. "I don't want to take your life, or even harm you, unless you force me to do so by attempting to escape. You are my prisoner. You must answer to Mr. Hazilrigge for entering his house in this unlicensed manner; as well as passing yourself off upon him under a false name. I have been in search of you, but I little expected to find you here."

By this time, Simon, finding that I did not mean to injure him, had recovered some of his natural audacity.

"I can easily satisfy old Hazy," he replied. "He won't punish me."

"Don't make too sure of that, rascal," I returned. "Mr. Hazilrigge is credulous and good-humoured, but he will not allow such liberties as these to be taken with him with impunity. This is not the only trick you have played since my arrival at Owlarton Grange. You rang the bells better than you have played the ghost."

At this remark, Simon seemed entirely to forget the jeopardy in which he stood, and laughed long and heartily.

"A capital joke!—wasn't it, ?" he cried, with a fresh explosion of laughter.

"I don't quite appreciate the joke," I rejoined, sternly, "neither I think, will Mr. Hazilrigge, when he learns that the bells were rung by an electrical machine under your management. You will be prosecuted for the offence."

"You are mistaken, sir. Mr. Hazilrigge will treat the matter as a jest, and pass it by." The rascal spoke so confidently, that I felt staggered, and, perceiving it, he went on: "But let us leave this question of the bell-ringing and pass to your own concerns. What cause of complaint have you against me?"

"Dare you put such a question to me, sirrah, when you know how much mischief you have done me? The day of reckoning has been long postponed, but at last it has arrived, and I mean to have a settlement in full."

" You go the wrong way to work," he replied, in a tone of dogged defiance. "You will get nothing from me by threats. Adopt another course, and you will stand a better chance of gaining your object."

"I understand what you mean," I rejoined; "but I will make no terms with you. You fancy yourself secure, but you will be forced to give an account of your conduct—not to me only, but to another whom you have injured. You have hitherto contrived to hide yourself from poor Ned Culcheth, but you will now have to brave his just indignation. How will you answer him when he demands back his wife from you? Will you give her to him?"

"I cannot," he replied, sullenly.

"Then she has left you?" I cried.

"I will answer no questions about her," he replied. "If Ned believes she ran away with me, he is welcome to think so. I shan't contradict him. But he won't find her with me, and he won't learn from me where to find her—that I can promise him. But I will tell you, sir, since you seem to interest yourself in the matter, that it will be happier—far happier for Ned—never to see her again, than to see her as she is."

"What do you mean?" I exclaimed, startled by his words, which seemed to corroborate some fears that had been aroused within me by the obscure remarks of John Brideoake.

"I have said I will answer no more questions—and I mean to keep to my word," he returned.

The audacity of the man quite confounded me.

I considered what I should do with him. I could not let him go, and yet felt unwilling to disturb the house. Besides, the rascal's unconcern added to my perplexity, and I almost fancied there might be some sort of understanding between him and Mr. Hazilrigge, though I could hardly reconcile such a notion with my ideas of the old gentleman's sense of propriety. If he had employed Pownall for any purpose, it must have been because he was in total ignorance of the man's character.

At length, I asked my prisoner how he got into the room?

"I didn't come through the keyhole, though it looks like it," he replied, with a laugh. "But I've no objection to tell you, provided you promise to keep the information secret."

"I will give no such promise," I replied. "It is quite enough for me to be aware that there is a concealed entrance to the room to be able to find it out. I have merely to sound the walls to make the discovery."

"Something more than sounding the walls is required," Pownall rejoined; "but since you decline my offer, you must exercise your own ingenuity. May I ask what you intend to do with me? I presume you don't mean to keep me here all night?"

"I haven't quite decided," I replied; "but one thing is quite certain—you won't be allowed to depart."

"As you please, sir," he replied, in an indifferent tone. "But, methinks, you'll be tired of my company before I am of yours. I am by no means sorry to have an opportunity of a little confidential chat with you, as it may lead to a result advantageous to both of us."

"How so?" I cried.

"To begin—you will do well to make a friend of me."

"I am of a contrary opinion. But let me hear what advantage I am likely to gain by a partnership with a rogue and a traitor."

"Nay, if you employ such terms as those, we are not likely to come to any understanding," he rejoined, sharply. "It seems to me, that for so shrewd a young gentleman as you appear to be, you are singularly blind to your own interests."

"Why, yes, I happen to have notions on the score of honesty and straightforward conduct which appear highly absurd to you, Pownall, I make no doubt. But such as they are, I act up to my opinions. I am quite sure you could serve me materially if you would; but I am equally certain you won't."

"Why are you so certain of it, may I ask, sir?"

"Because, by doing so, you would incur the chance of a tolerably long term of penal servitude."

"That would not be very pleasant, I admit. But why take such a view of the case? The course I propose would accomplish your object, and bring no one into trouble—least of all, your humble servant."

"I see very plainly what you are driving at, Pownall," I rejoined, "and I am glad to learn that it is yet in your power to repair the mischief you have done."

"It is quite in my power to put you in possession of your uncle Mobberley's property, if you mean that," he replied.

"You confess it then, scoundrel," I cried—"you confess you stole the rightful will. You shall be compelled to produce it before a Court of Justice."

"Stop, sir," he rejoined. "You are getting on a leetle too fast. I may readily admit certain matters to you which I should be loth to admit if a third person were present; but as to compelling me to produce the will in a Court of Justice, you must first prove the existence of such a document, and next, that I have got it—neither of which you can easily do. For you may rely upon it that if any steps are taken against me, such as you threaten, the precious document in question will be destroyed. Now, sir, you will know how to act."

And he burst into a mocking laugh, which provoked me to such a degree that I felt inclined to brain him with the butt-end of the pistol.

"Come! come! my good young sir," he cried, checking his ill-timed hilarity, apprehensive, perhaps, of irritating me too much, "let us be reasonable. An affectation of stern morality may have great influence with some folks—with me it has none at all. I am apt to be sceptical when a man deliberately tells me that he will sacrifice his own interests for a point of principle. He takes me for a fool, but I know him to be a hypocrite. Now, you are a person of good sense—a little too hasty, perhaps—but shrewd enough when you choose to exercise your judgment properly. Look at the matter as it ought to be looked at. There is only one way in which you can ever gain your point—namely, by employing me."

"By buying you, in short."

"Well, by buying me, if you like the term. Of course, you can't expect to get a good thing for nothing, and won't grumble at paying for it."

"You are a cool hand, Simon!" I cried, with irrepressible disgust, "and persuade yourself that your criminality cannot be proved. You are deceived. There is a witness who can tell how you purloined that will, and I will obtain his evidence."

"No, you won't, sir," he rejoined, in a tone of defiance. "The man you allude to will never peach. He would rather bite off his tongue than utter a word to serve you, so bring him forward and welcome. Much good Phaleg will do you—ha! ha! But I am sure you must have had enough of my society, so I'll relieve you of it."

"Hardly so," I rejoined. "You will not quit this room, unless I consign you to some one who will detain you in safe custody till the morrow."

"It will be useless to ring," he observed, with a laugh. "All the servants are a-bed, and, even if they heard the bell, they wouldn't answer it. I will summon assistance for you, for I am as anxious to be gone as you can be to get rid of me."

And, before I could prevent him, he struck three heavy blows with his mallet, which he still held, upon the floor. While I was wondering what would ensue, a tap was heard at the door, and a voice which sounded like that of Mr. Hazilrigge inquired what was the matter?

Greatly surprised, I called to the old gentleman to come in—but after waiting for a moment, finding that my request was not attended to, I sprang to the door, opened it, and looked out.

No one was there that I could discern, for it was pitch-dark in the corridor. Neither did any one answer when I spoke. I did not think it possible that Pownall could have stirred without my hearing him; and not the slightest sound reached my ears. But when I turned, he was gone.

Highly provoked, I proceeded to search the room, hoping to detect a sliding panel or secret door through which he might have passed. But in vain.

CHAPTER XIII.

WHEREIN OLD HAZY ENDEAVOURS TO PERSUADE ME THAT I HAVE BEEN DELUDED BY AN EVIL SPIRIT.

THAT Simon Pownall would return to his own room in the Old Grange by some secret passage communicating with it, I nothing doubted; but that he would be found there in the morning appeared highly improbable. Unless, therefore, I intended to let him get off altogether I must effect his recapture without loss of time.

It was provoking in the extreme to be outwitted and derided by the rascal. Yet what could be done? To alarm the house and obtain the assistance of the servants seemed the only course to be pursued under the circumstances; but the objections to such a step were twofold. In the first place, I must necessarily create a great disturbance —and this I did not like to do. Secondly, it was almost certain that Old Hazy would prohibit any interference with his associate. The extraordinary audacity exhibited by Simon Pownall could only arise from confidence in the hold he had, by some means or other, obtained over the credulous old gentleman.

What was to be done? I asked myself again. Unable to answer the question satisfactorily, I at length made up my mind to abide patiently till the morrow. And so I retired to rest.

Sleep, though long in coming, visited me at last, and I had just opened my eyes in the morning when Mr. Ponder entered my room, and approaching the foot of my bed, observed, with more than his usual gravity of manner, "I am afraid, sir, you must have been a good deal disturbed last night."

I made no reply, and he continued:

"I feel assured that you must have had a visit from the ghost, sir. My bedroom is situated immediately above this chamber, and about one o'clock I heard the dreadful knocking quite distinctly. After that, I heard voices, as if a long conversation were taking place. Then came three startling knocks. And then all was still."

"If you heard this, Mr. Ponder, why on earth didn't you come down to me?" I demanded.

"Come down to you, sir!" he exclaimed. "Lord love you! I hadn't courage enough to get out of bed. I wouldn't have entered this room at that unearthly hour for fifty pounds—and that's more than my year's wages. On hearing the last three knocks I dived under the bed-clothes to shut the ghost from my sight in case it should rise through the floor."

"I did not suppose you were such a poltroon, Mr. Ponder."

"I am no coward in broad daylight, sir, but at dead of night, and in a haunted house like this—with supernatural objects swarming around you—it's a different matter altogether. I'm not ashamed to confess my fears.—But, save us! what's this?" he cried, starting back in affright. "As I'm a sinner, the ghost has left its mallet behind it!"

"Indeed!" I exclaimed; "I didn't notice it. Reach it to me, Ponder."

"I wouldn't touch it for the world!" he cried, recoiling.

"Why, surely you don't imagine there can be mischief in that wooden hammer," I observed, laughing. "It won't strike you."

"I don't know that," he answered, in great trepidation. "At any rate, I won't give it the chance. Can I be of any further use to you, sir?" he added, evidently anxious to depart.

I told him that I had a little commission which I wished him to execute for me; and on his promising prompt compliance, I bade him go to the old Grange, and ascertain whether Dr. Hooker was still there.

"Merely make the inquiry," I said, "without stating who sent you."

"I can satisfy you at once on the point, sir," he replied. "My master sent me with a message to the same gentleman more than an hour ago; and Stephen Blackden himself informed me that Doctor Hooker left at eight o'clock last night."

"Stephen Blackden must have misinformed you," I cried. "Doctor Hooker was here—in this very room—an hour after midnight."

"Here, sir!" Ponder ejaculated, staring at me. "Here!—in this room, an hour after midnight! Pray how did he get in?"

"That's more than I can explain. But here he was, most undoubtedly. And by your own account you must have heard him conversing with me. It was no ghost who visited me last night, Ponder, but a mortal like ourselves."

"I wish I had known that, sir," the butler replied; "I'd have been down with you in a trice. But you haven't told me in what manner the doctor disappeared."

"He vanished suddenly from my sight—that is all I can tell you. He may be hidden in the room now, for aught I know to the contrary!"

"Zounds! sir, I hope not. Mayhap he flew through the window. It wouldn't be a difficult feat for a conjuror—and folks say the doctor is one. I wonder my master likes the society of a man who, beyond all doubt, must be in league with Beelzebub."

"Is the doctor, as you style him, much with Mr. Hazilrigge?" I inquired.

"More than he should be, if I may presume to say so," Ponder replied. "He is often with my master in the library, and there they sit poring for hours over those abominable books of witchcraft and magic. I should like to see 'em all burnt; and so would Miss Hazilrigge, for I've heard her say so."

"I should rejoice in such an *auto da fe* myself," I rejoined. "I wish the Holy Inquisition could get hold of Doctor Hooker. Miss Hazilrigge, I am sure, cannot approve of such a person."

"Approve of him!—not she, sir. But my master has his fancies, and won't be interfered with by his sister, or by any one else Doctor Hooker has got an unaccountable influence over him. But perhaps I've said too much on this subject already, sir?"

And receiving no answer, for I had fallen into a reverie, the butler bowed respectfully, as was his wont, and retired.

As it was pretty certain now that Simon Pownall had decamped, I was forced to abandon all idea of recapturing him for the present. Before going down stairs, however, I took another and more rigorous survey of the room—examined the panels, and struck them here and there with the mallet which my nocturnal visitor had left behind, but could detect nothing to indicate a secret door. I specially directed my attention to that part of the chamber where the bed was placed; but the panels seemed just as solid here as elsewhere. Wherever it might be, the entrance was exceedingly well concealed, and completely baffled my researches.

After this, I went down stairs. Nothing worthy of note occurred at breakfast, except that Ora did not join the party. I made no allusion to my adventure overnight—reserving what I had to say for my host's private ear. Luckily, I was not questioned on the subject; Miss Hazilrigge and Cuthbert Spring being too much occupied with each other to trouble themselves about me or Old Hazy.

As we rose from table, I volunteered to accompany the old gentleman to his sanctum; but I half repented the step when, on ushering me into the room, he closed the door, and, forcing me into a chair, without allowing me to utter a word of remonstrance, hurried to the bookshelves, and taking down a little volume, exclaimed,

"I must show you this treasure, Mr. Clitheroe. It is a rare little treatise called the Antidemon of Macon, containing a true and particular relation of what a Demon said and did in the house of Father Perreaud. Let me read you a few passages from it. They are highly instructive, and well worth hearing, I assure you."

"I have no doubt of it, my good sir," I replied, impatiently. "But just now I have too much on my mind to attend to Father Perreaud. I want to open your eyes to the true character of the soi-disant Dr. Hooker, whom I must denounce as a charlatan—an impostor—and something worse."

"You denounced him yesterday," old Hazy rejoined, petulantly. "Why persist in assailing him? Doctor Dee was called a charlatan, an impostor, and something worse; and so were Paracelsus, Cornelius Agrippa, and the Alberts, Great and Little. There is hardly one amongst the professors of occult philosophy whose works load these shelves who has not been calumniated and reviled. But I shall ever protest against such injustice, Mr. Clitheroe. Here, in this sanctum, a true disciple of those glorious sages shall never be treated with opprobrium. Dr. Hooker is a second Doctor Dee. He is a true Thaumaturgus. As a physiognomist, he is equal to Taxil and Jean Indagine; in chiromancy, to Prætorius and Cocles; he can read the celestial influences as well as Father Francis; can cast a horoscope as well as Joseph de Tertiis; and pronounce a judgment upon a nativity as well as Fevrier and Ranzonius."

"He practises a great many more tricks than you are aware of, Mr. Hazilrigge," I rejoined. "I have discovered something about him that will astonish you. What do you think, sir?—last night, he personated the ghost of Jotham Shocklach."

"Ah! my good young sir," the old gentleman cried, regarding me with compassion, "you are deceived. You are unacquainted with the subtleties and devices of evil spirits. If the ghost of Jotham Shocklach did not actually appear to you—as is more than probable—it was an evil spirit in the guise of the defunct assassin—not Dr. Hooker."

"This is idle, sir," I cried, almost out of patience. "Suffer me to say that in this rascal, who personated the ghost of Jotham, and who calls himself Dr. Hooker, I discovered——"

"An evil spirit—I know it," Old Hazy exclaimed.

"No, sir; not an evil spirit, but a knave, who has cheated me, and duped you—and who continues to dupe you, sir."

Mr. Hazilrigge shook his head.

"A diabolical illusion, my good young friend. I can produce plenty of instances of the kind from Fathers Perreaud and Taillepied. Permit me to cite some of them."

"Pest take Fathers Perreaud and Taillepied!" I cried, impatiently. "Am I not to trust the evidence of my own eyes and my own ears?"

"Assuredly not, in a case of this kind. You ought to discredit all you see and hear. The plainer and more palpable the thing appears, the more certain is the delusion. Such is the opinion of Father Perreaud, and I will refer to him for some observations in support of my argument. Attend to what he says in his eighth chapter touching demoniacal illusions: 'It cannot be doubted that demons can charm the eyes and ears in such manner externally, putting between the eye and the ear, and the thing seen or heard, a body which produces the effect they desire.' And further on, he adds: 'Demons, who are beyond comparison more subtle than all the most subtle of men, can deceive and elude our senses by a thousand false and deceitful appearances. This they can do either immediately of themselves, or mediately by magicians and sorcerers.' You hear the opinion of this erudite man. In your case, the delusion has been practised immediately, that is, without intervention, by an evil spirit."

"Pshaw!" I cried, "I am dealing with the material world. I told you the other night, sir, that I have no belief in evil spirits."

"I am sorry to hear you confess so much after your recent experience. As to the existence of evil spirits, I must again refer to Father Perreaud. Observe how he closes his first discourse, which is directed against those who, like yourself, are perverse and sceptical. 'It ought to be sufficient for us, after what we have heard, drawn from the word of God and from experience, that we are assured, or ought to be so, that spirits of evil exist in great abundance.' I will give you the father's words in his own language: '*Qu'il y a vrayement et d'effet des diables et malins esprits, voire une grandissime et innombrable quantité!'*—*Une grandissime quantité!* Mark that!" he added, regarding me with an air of triumph.

I did not attempt to reply; feeling it was useless to reason with him. I merely observed, therefore, " I sincerely wish you could divest yourself of this strange opinion for a moment, sir. Why should not the person you call Dr. Hooker have found his way to my room?"

"For the best of all reasons—he was far away. No, no; trust me, Mr. Clitheroe, you have been deluded. Shall I give you another quotation from Father Perreaud?"

"On no account," I replied, hastily. "One more question, Mr. Hazilrigge, and I have done. Did you not overhear what was passing in my room last night?"

"I overhear what was passing!" he exclaimed.

"Yes. Were you not summoned by three blows of a mallet on the floor? Did you not knock at my door, and inquire what was the matter?"

"Ah, my good young friend!" he cried, shaking his head compassionately, "if anything could convince you, this ought to do so. Why, sir, I was fast asleep in bed, and if there was a knock at your door, as you assert, and a voice heard like mine, it must have been a diabolic delusion. Taillepied gives an infallible test whereby you may know whether a demon has appeared to you. 'If the person whose semblance the spirit puts on strives to tempt you, or counsels a wicked action, you may be assured that the spirit is evil.' Was it so in your case?"

"I must confess," I replied, unable to refrain from laughter, "that the rascal did give me evil counsel, and tried to incite me to wrong."

"An evil spirit, beyond all question. Dr. Hooker would never have acted so. No, no, the demon has assumed the doctor's shape in order to beguile you."

"Then you absolutely refuse to believe that it was Dr. Hooker who visited me last night?"

"Absolutely and entirely."

"And you likewise refuse to believe that I recognised in the soi-disant Hooker a knavish and runaway barber from Marston?"

"I entirely disbelieve it. You have been deluded by evil spirits, who, I grieve to say, abound in this house. Suffer me to read you a few passages from Thiræus *De locis infestis ob molestantes dæmoniorum et defunctorum spiritus.*"

But I had had quite enough While he was searching for his tiresome Thiræus; Boissier's *Recueil de Lettres au sujet des Malefices et du Sortilege;* Martinus de Arles; and some other works of a like nature, which he particularised, but the titles of which I now forget, I took to flight.

As soon as I got into the hall, I snatched up my hat and rushed out into the garden, where I soon regained my tranquillity.

CHAPTER XIV.

LOVE IN A MAZE.

TAKE it altogether, I have never seen a more perfect specimen of an old-fashioned garden than that of Owlarton Grange. I have said little about it hitherto, because I have waited for a favourable opportunity of describing it.

The garden was originally laid out more than a couple of centuries ago, and its general plan was still carefully maintained. Some few alterations had no doubt been made in certain parts, but they were so slight as not to interfere with the principal features. The broad terrace walks, with the smooth green slopes, the stone steps for the mimic waterfalls, the "pleached bowers,"

> Where honeysuckles, ripened by the sun,
> Forbid the sun to enter—

the mossy seats upon the slopes—all these were the same as heretofore. The garden-knots, moreover, were extremely quaint and curious, and no departure from their pristine shape was permitted. There you could see the cinque-foil, the trefoil, the fleur-de-lis, the fret, and other designs, that had charmed the loiterers in this Eden during the time of James I., still embroidering the parterres. The preservation of the garden in its integrity was chiefly owing to Miss Hazilrigge, who paid great attention to it, and allowed nothing to be disturbed. She abominated "landscape gardeners," and said they had spoiled many of the finest old places in England. The garden at Owlarton Grange thus continued intact. Its long dark green alleys of clipped yew-trees—its magnificent hedges of holly—its marvellous specimens of topiarian art, exhibited in groups of trees, trimmed and twisted into a variety of fantastical devices, some of which looked as if Ovid's Metamorphoses had been put into action upon the lawns—its statues—dial—fountains—maze—and mound, with summer-house on the top, overlooking the moat—all these formed the admiration of the neighbourhood, and would have made the garden of Owlarton Grange one of the "sights" of that part of Cheshire, if its owner would have allowed it to be shown.

As the hall would have been incomplete without its garden, so the garden would not have been perfect without the hall. One was an indispensable adjunct to the other. The picturesque old pile was seen to the greatest advantage from the smooth-shaven lawn; while the garden looked enchanting as the bowers of Armida when beheld from the house.

I was wandering about this delightful garden—admiring its

various objects of interest—now looking at a little fountain with a curious mechanical contrivance that caused a musical sound—now at a bay-tree, trimmed and twined into a representation of Daphne—now at a marble statue of Leda and the swan, weather-stained, and crusted with lichens—now pausing to look at the old hall, as it displayed itself under some new and picturesque aspect—when I perceived Ora hastening towards me across the lawn, and I instantly flew to meet her.

We walked together for some time, conversing upon indifferent topics, but I could perceive that she had something upon her mind, which she desired to mention, though she hesitated long ere coming to the point. At last she spoke of John Brideoake, and inquired, with some anxiety, whether I thought him alarmingly ill?

"I am indeed seriously apprehensive about him," I replied. "He is suffering in mind as well as in body."

"But, perhaps, some remedy might be found," she cried, quickly. "If your friend has a secret sorrow, no doubt he imparted it to you—and it may, possibly, be relieved. Don't you think so?"

I looked at her fixedly.

"If hope could be once more kindled in John's breast," I said, "he might perchance recover. At present, life is a blank to him. My poor friend has no secrets from me, Miss Doveton, and has laid bare his innermost heart to me. He has had the temerity to fix his affections on an object utterly unattainable, and is now paying the penalty of his folly."

"But why should he conclude that the object is unattainable?" Ora rejoined.

"Because he feels that it would be the height of presumption in him to think otherwise. How should he—a poor curate—dare to aspire to the hand of a young and lovely heiress?"

"Some men have aspired, and successfully, Mr. Clitheroe."

"Would you have him—the most modest of men—imitate the most audacious, Miss Doveton?" I exclaimed.

"I would have him get well—I would help to bring about his cure, if I could," she replied.

"A word from you will do it. You have only to make the experiment to see what a result will follow. Will you authorise me to give my friend a hope?"

"I cannot prevent you from saying anything you choose to him," she answered, smiling.

"That is hardly sufficient. You must promise that you will not contradict what I *do* say. Suppose I were to tell him that the fair being whom he thinks only laughed at him, takes a real interest in him, and grieves for the despairing state into which he has been thrown?"

"Enough! enough!" she interrupted. "No doubt you will say a great deal more than you ought to do—more than I shall ever authorise you to say. But at any rate, you *may* say that I sincerely hope he will get better."

"For your sake?" I said.

"You may add, 'for my sake,' if you think proper," she replied.

I uttered a joyful exclamation.

"If John is not too far gone already I will answer for his cure," I cried. "I am now bound for his cottage, and shall, indeed, be the bearer of good tidings."

"Do not go till you have seen my aunt," Ora said. "Perhaps she may drive over to Weverham in the course of the day, and if so I will accompany her."

"That will be a very kind act. It will do John an infinitude of good to see you. I will prepare him for the visit."

"Well, let us find my aunt," Ora cried, in a far more lively tone, for her spirits seemed to have wonderfully improved within the last few minutes, "and learn what she has to say about it. I have no doubt she will go, unless she has fixed some other plan with Mr. Spring. They are somewhere in the garden—very likely in the maze. I saw them straying in that direction just before I joined you."

To the maze accordingly we repaired.

On entering the leafy labyrinth, we could distinctly hear the voices of the elderly couple, though, of course, they were hidden by the tall ranges of privet.

Ora stopped for a moment, gave me an arch look, and put her finger to her lips to impose silence.

"Well, here we are, I declare, in the very centre of the maze," Cuthbert Spring exclaimed. "I should never be able to find my way back through all its intricate windings without guidance."

"I have a good mind to leave you, and let you try," the elderly spinster replied, with a laugh.

"Oh! no, don't, I entreat of you," Mr. Spring rejoined. "Nay, indeed, I must detain you. This is the most inviting spot imaginable for a tête-à-tête. Let us be seated upon this bench, which seems contrived for lovers. No fear of interruption here, my dear Miss Hazilrigge."

"I don't know that," she replied. "Ora and Mr. Clitheroe are in the garden. I saw them as we emerged from the *allée verte* just now."

"I did not observe them," Cuthbert returned. "And in truth I had no eyes save for the charming person at my side."

"A truce to compliments, Mr. Spring," the elderly spinster simpered. "You have paid me too many already."

"Not one more than you deserve, my dear Miss Hazilrigge," Cuthbert said. "Shall I tell you what the meanderings of this maze have put into my head?"

"Pray do, Mr. Spring," she answered. "I am curious to know what they have suggested to you."

"They have convinced me that I should find my way much more readily through the twists and turnings which I have yet to take in life if I had some one to direct me."

"You have got on very well hitherto without assistance, Mr. Spring," Miss Hazilrigge replied.

Here Ora could not repress her laughter.

"What was that, Mr. Spring?" the elderly spinster cried. "I am sure I heard something. I hope there are no listeners near us."

"Have no fear, my dear Miss Hazilrigge," Cuthbert cried, in a more impassioned tone than he had yet assumed—I almost fancied he must have thrown himself upon his knees. "This is the moment when my fate must be sealed. You have it in your power to make me the happiest of men. Speak and decide!"

"Dear heart a day! Mr. Spring," the lady rejoined, evidently quite in a flutter, "you have taken me quite by surprise. I don't know what to say, I am sure. Your proposal is very flattering, but it requires consideration. Before answering you positively, I think—nay, I am quite sure—that I ought to consult my brother."

"By all means, my dear Miss Hazilrigge. Very proper! very proper! But I am confident my friend Hazilrigge won't oppose your wishes, when he learns which way they tend. So, after all, the decision will rest with you. You do not bid me despair."

"A regular proposal, I declare!" Ora exclaimed. "Oh, aunt!"

"Who's that?" Miss Hazilrigge cried, in alarm. "I am sure it must be Ora. Where are you, child? What are you doing?"

"I am making my way to you aunt, through the maze, as fast as I can, with Mr. Clitheroe," Ora replied.

So saying, she hurried on, trying to repress her laughter, and the next moment we stood before the elderly pair of turtle-doves, both of whom, though they strove to put a good face upon the matter, looked excessively annoyed, as well they might, at the interruption.

"We were searching for you, aunt," Ora said. "Mr. Clitheroe is going to Weverham. I told him you would probably drive there in the course of the day. Have you any message for Mr. Brideoake?"

"Is that all?" Miss Hazilrigge cried, rather tartly. "There was no occasion to come to me on such a trivial matter. My message to Mr. Brideoake—which I beg Mr. Clitheroe will be good enough to deliver to his friend—is that my brother and myself hope that the dear young man will make arrangements to come and stay with us for a month. We can make him, perhaps, a little more comfortable than he is in his cottage, and he shall be well nursed."

"I will not fail to deliver your kind message to him," I replied, "and when you come, he will give you his answer."

"Nay, I will have no refusal," Miss Hazilrigge returned. "I mean to bring him away in the carriage."

"Be sure to tell him so," Ora subjoined. "And now, Mr. Clitheroe," she cried, with an arch look, "do not stir till I clap my hands, and then try to catch me. You must promise not to break through the fences, for that would not be fair."

She then disappeared, and in another moment I heard the signal given, accompanied by a merry laugh, and I set off after her—much to the relief, I am sure, of the elderly couple. But though I ran on and on, I must, somehow, have taken a wrong turn, and greatly to my surprise and annoyance found myself once more near the centre of the maze. Despairing of getting out unaided, I went into the little enclosure, where I found the elderly couple seated close together on the bench.

"What! you can't find your way out, Mr. Clitheroe?" Miss Hazilrigge said, rising. "The maze is very perplexing. I have known people puzzled by it for hours. Come! I will help you."

I glanced at my friend to let him know how sorry I was to interrupt him—but he took it very good humouredly, and Miss Hazilrigge preceding us, we were soon extricated from the labyrinth. Ora was standing outside, and appeared not a little diverted. Ever since she had taken me into her confidence—as I have just intimated—her former liveliness had completely returned to her; and she now looked as full of merriment and mischief as ever.

"Well, I must say, this maze is the most perplexing place I ever entered," Cuthbert Spring observed. "I would as soon attempt to unravel a tangled skein of thread as make my way out of it unassisted."

"You must always have my aunt for a guide, Mr. Spring," Ora observed, archly, "and then you will have no difficulty in tracking its meanderings—or in getting through any other twistings and turnings which you may have to take in life."

CHAPTER XV.

WHAT HAPPENED IN THE ORCHARD OF THE MILL IN WEVERHAM GLEN.

I HAD quitted my friends at the Grange, and was pursuing the pleasant path across the fields leading to Weverham, when I saw Ned Culcheth, with Hubert at his heels, coming towards me from the opposite direction. Even at a distance I could perceive that the poor fellow was labouring under great depression, and, on joining him, I found that the judgment I had formed was correct. He was scarcely able to open his lips, and we walked together, side by side, for some little time in silence. Arrived at a stile, I besought him to try and ease his breast of its cares.

"Of a truth, my breast does need lightening, sir," he replied, with a groan. "A feather's weight more of care would crush me. Ah! sir, what I have gone through since we parted yesterday no words of mine can tell."

Then after a pause, during which he struggled with his violent emotion, he added—"I have seen her, sir."

"Your wife!" I exclaimed, starting.

"Ay, sir—Sissy; and I almost wish I had *not* seen her. Oh! sir," he continued, with a despairing look, "there have been moments when, maddened by jealous passion, I have wished ill to Sissy—but never, never, sir—I take Heaven to witness!—never did I wish her ill like this!"

"You fill me with terrible apprehensions, Ned," I rejoined, regarding him anxiously. "Relieve me, if you can."

"I can scarcely bring myself to speak it," he rejoined, with an agonised look, " but it must out. Sissy is no longer herself, sir. I stood beside her and she did not know me. I spoke to her in the tenderest way I could—called her by her name, and told her I forgave her, as I did from the bottom of my heart—but she paid no heed to me. I tried to clasp her in my arms, and fold her to my breast, but she pushed me off with horror. Oh! sir, I shall never forget the look she gave me. It froze the very blood in my veins. Much as I love her—for I do love her still, in spite of all that has passed—I don't think I can have her to live with me again. I could have borne it better if she had known me—but this state drives me almost mad myself—and Mr. Brideoake gives me no hopes whatever of her recovery."

"How long has she been thus afflicted, Ned?" I inquired, after a pause.

"You shall hear the whole sad story, sir," he replied, "for I now feel able to tell it. On the day after she left my roof, she was brought, by a man who represented himself to be her husband, to the Plough at Weverham—the little inn at the door of which you saw me standing yesterday. There is no doubt from the description given of him by the landlady of the Plough that the man who brought Sissy was Simon Pownall. Well, Simon left her—saying he would fetch her on the morrow—but he never returned. When she first arrived at the Plough, Sissy was ill and excited—but she soon got worse. On the second day, a brain fever came on, and she was at times quite lightheaded. Mrs. Vines, the landlady—a good, kind-hearted soul—did not know what to do with her guest. Ill as she was she could not turn her out of the house, and yet it was almost impossible to keep her. Poor Sissy would not give any account of herself, but declared she was a wretched, guilty thing, and only wished to die. Sorely put about and distressed, Mrs. Vines thought the best thing she could do was to consult the curate, and, on hearing her relation, Mr. Brideoake came down with her to see the unfortunate guest—and, to his surprise and grief, found that the poor sufferer was Sissy.

"Well, sir, as Mr. Brideoake told me yesterday, the poor creature, on seeing him, was terrified almost out of her senses—and supplicated him not to send her back to me, as I should certainly kill her—she knew I should. Her terror was so great, that the worthy young gentleman, believing that violence on my part was to be apprehended—though Heaven knows his fears were unjust—promised to screen her till my anger should pass away. And he kept his promise, as you know. Indeed, he would not disclose her retreat to me yesterday, until I had solemnly pledged my word not to harm her.

"But to proceed with my narration. After seeing Mr. Brideoake, Sissy got worse. The fever lasted for a week, and when it left her, her senses were gone—never more—as it seems, to return. She was removed to the mill in Weverham Glen, where a room was engaged for her by Mr. Brideoake, and where she has been ever since."

"And Mr. Brideoake has been at all charges for her, I suppose?"

"Heaven bless him for his kindness!—yes, sir. He watched over her during her illness, and prayed constantly by her side. That she is still living is mainly—if not entirely—owing to his care. If there is a good man on earth, it is Mr. Brideoake. I would go through fire and water to serve him. I have met two friends in him and you, sir—two such friends as a poor man like me seldom meets. But there is another point on which it is right I should speak to you, sir—painful though it be to me to mention it. It is Mr. Brideoake's firm opinion that Simon Pownall, and not Captain Sale, is the author of all this misery. Poor Sissy, he says, as good as confessed this to him, when he questioned her. She never mentioned the other at all—but spoke only of Simon."

"That does not convince me, Ned," I rejoined. "You may think me unwilling to acquit Mr. Sale—perhaps I am so—but I am persuaded he is the real offender. The truth will come out some day, and then you will find who is in the right."

"Well, I own that I incline to your opinion myself," he returned. "But it is strange that Sissy should make such a declaration."

"A good deal depends upon the way in which she was interrogated

Mr. Brideoake's suspicions of Malpas were not then aroused, and no doubt, in ascertaining the name of Simon Pownall, he thought he had elicited the whole truth. Moreover, Sissy herself might have wished to screen her betrayer."

"That's true," Ned replied, with a sombre look. "I didn't think of that. Mr. Brideoake preaches forgiveness to me, and I would willingly follow his counsels. But I find it hard to forgive injuries like these. When I think of Sissy—in her present woful state, and what has caused it—I must be more than man, or less than man, not to nourish vengeance against the author of the wrong."

I made no reply, for I could not contradict him.

After another pause, I said, "I suppose it is impossible now to btain any further information from poor Sissy?"

"Quite impossible, sir," he replied. "Poor soul! she can give no rational answer to any questions put to her. Yet she is very gentle and easily managed. The good folks at the mill are extremely kind to her. Master Mavis, the miller, and his dame treat her like one of the family, and their little daughter, Grace, is constantly with her. I hope you will come with me to see her, sir. Mr. Brideoake himself is at the mill, and waits your arrival there. He sent me to meet you and bring you to him."

Though I felt it would pain me exceedingly to behold poor Sissy in her present forlorn state, I could not refuse to accompany Ned, and so put myself under his guidance.

Our course, it appeared, lay to the right, for Ned struck off in that direction, and after crossing a few fields, we gained the high road, along which we proceeded for about a quarter of a mile, and then again diverging to the right, reached the edge of the rocky glen which I had seen on first approaching Weverham.

From these craggy heights which looked like the frowning battlements of a castle, nearly the whole of the glen was visible; beginning at the point where the alpine bridge was stretched across it, and where the rocks were highest and most precipitous, and terminating where the banks were much lower and further apart, and where the stream, checked by a dam, had expanded almost into a lake. The mill itself was situated at the widest part of this pool, and with its floodgate, bridge, and large water-wheels—formed an extremely picturesque feature in the scene. Adjoining the mill, and bounding the further side of the pool, was a large orchard, and in this pleasant place I saw three persons walking—a young woman, a little girl, and a man attired in black. I had no doubt who these persons were, and on consulting Ned by a glance, he answered my mute inquiry with a look that told me I was right in my conjecture.

Following my conductor down a zigzag path hewn in the rock, I soon gained the bottom of the ravine, and proceeding along a road, shaded by tall trees, and skirted by the brawling stream, we ere long reached the pool We next crossed a narrow bridge thrown over the rapid mill-race, and entered a yard, where Mavis and two of his men were busily employed in loading a cart with sacks of flour. Ned said a word to the miller, and the good man touched his dusty cap to me, and we passed on. A few steps more brought us to the door of the dwelling, which stood open, and Ned entering without ceremony, called out for Dame Mavis. At the summons, a fresh-complexioned, tidy little woman, of middle age, came out of an inner room, and seeing me dropped a curtsey, and bade me welcome. In reply to Ned's inquiries, Dame Mavis told us we should find Sissy in the orchard with Mr. Brideoake and her little daughter, and, as Ned knew the way thither, there would be no occasion for her to attend us; whereupon she retired.

Before entering the orchard, I paused at the gate to look at Sissy, and being partially concealed by the hedge, neither she nor her companion noticed me. She was not so much changed as I anticipated, and except from a certain flightiness of manner and a strange look about the eyes, I should not have deemed her mind to be affected. Though her attire was not arranged with the care she had once bestowed upon it, it was still neat; and it was evident, from the knots of ribands stuck upon her dress here and there, that her love of finery was not entirely effaced. Her long and beautiful tresses were unbound, and floated in disorder over her neck and shoulders, giving her rather a wild look. In manner she seemed extremely gentle. Her little attendant, Grace, who might be about seven or eight years old, had twined her a wreath of honeysuckles, and was in the act of placing the simple garland over her brows at the moment of my arrival. Delighted with the effect of the wreath when so disposed, little Grace clapped her hands with childish glee; and Sissy, no less pleased, cried out to the little girl, "Does it not suit me? Am I not pretty?—am I not pretty?"

"Indeed you are," little Grace replied. "You look very pretty in that wreath, Sissy."

Here John Brideoake interposed, and taking the wreath from Sissy's brows, gave it back to little Grace. The poor sufferer did not in any way oppose him, though she seemed sorry to lose the ornament.

"You must promise me to tie up your hair to-morrow, Sissy—will you not?" John said.

She assented with a motion of the head, and presently inquired, "Do I look better with my hair tied up?"

"Much better," John replied.

Upon this the poor thing instantly sat down upon the grass, and plucking off one of the bows of ribbon from her dress, was proceeding to gather together her luxuriant tresses, when John interrupted her, saying, "Not now, Sissy. Another time. Let us continue our walk. Come with me."

But at this moment an irrepressible groan burst from Ned, and the sound attracting Sissy's attention, she touched John's arm, and pointed in the direction where we stood. Finding I was discovered, I opened the gate, and entered the orchard; and as soon as he was able to control himself, Ned followed. I went up at once to Sissy, but on addressing her by name, and holding out my hand to her, she merely dropped me a bashful curtsey.

"Won't you shake hands with the gentleman, Sissy?" little Grace said to her.

Before complying, Sissy consulted John Brideoake by a look, and having obtained his permission, gave me her hand. As I held it for a moment it felt cold as marble.

"Do you not know me, Sissy?" I said, looking hard at her. "I am your old friend, Mervyn Clitheroe."

She shook her head, and exhibited no sign of recognition.

"Don't you remember our merry-making on Twelfth Night, in Farmer Shakeshaft's barn at Marston, Sissy?" I continued. "I was king on that night, and you were queen."

"I never was a queen, an' please you, sir," she replied. "I'm only a poor country girl—from Wales, sir."

"Yes, I know that," I rejoined; "but try if you can't recollect me."

She again shook her head, and said, "You're a pretty young gentlemans, sir, put I never saw you pefore."

"Oh, you are quite mistaken!" I rejoined. "You have often seen me with your husband, honest Ned Culcheth. Yonder he stands. Look at him."

"I haf no huspants, sir," she answered; adding, with a strange, half-terrified, mysterious look, "I must never be married."

"Indeed! why not?" I asked, willing to humour her.

"I've had my fortunes told, sir, by a plack gipsy oomans, an' she said I should make a pad wife—a fery pad wife—and pring sorrow an' shame on my huspants—so I must never marry—oh, no, I must never marry."

"But if your husband should be a good man, and a kind man, Sissy, he might forgive your faults, however great they might be, and take you back to him."

"Come this way, and I'll tell you something," Sissy cried, taking my hand, and leading me to a short distance. "I must whisper it in your ear, for no one must hear it—least of all, that tall mans yonder, who is watching us. What do you think the plack gipsy oomans told me? She said I should play my huspants false—and when he found me out he would kill me—and they would hang him for the plootty teet. So you see I must never marry.—Who is that tall mans, sir?" she continued, with a terrified look; "and why does he stare at me so? He frightens me. I've treamt of somebody like him."

"Are you sure you have only dreamed of him, Sissy? Perhaps you have seen him before. Think!"

"No, it was only a tream," she answered, after a pause, during which she vainly essayed to collect her scattered wits—"but I *did* tream that a man like him was my huspants. But he won't kill me because I treamt so, will he?"

"Make yourself easy, Sissy. Husband or not, the good fellow will never harm you. He forgives you."

"Forgives me—what for? What harm have I done him? Ask him to tell you."

"Why not ask him yourself, Sissy?"

"Because I am afraid of him," she replied, shuddering. "He means me mischief. I know he does. I can read it in his eyes."

"Come! you must shake off these groundless fears, Sissy. Let me call him to you. Ned!"

Thus summoned, the poor fellow sprang towards her instantly, but the sight of her distress arrested him.

"Oh! no; do not let him come near me!" she exclaimed, clinging to me with affright. "He will be the death of me—I know he will. Keep him off!—keep him off!"

I was obliged to motion Ned away, and he withdrew to a bank and sat down upon it, evidently very painfully affected.

John Brideoake and the little girl now joined us, and engaging Sissy in conversation, she soon regained her serenity, and at little Grace's request, sang me one of her native airs with so much sweetness and pathos, that I could not refuse it the tribute of my tears.

While poor Sissy was warbling her touching strains, Dame Mavis came into the orchard, and taking John Brideoake aside, said a few words to him which seemed to cause him infinite surprise. Signing to me that he would be back presently, he went away at once with Dame Mavis. Her song concluded, Sissy dropped me a curtsey, and taking little Grace's hand, walked with her towards the further end of the orchard, where they were hidden by the trees. Being thus in a measure left alone—for poor Ned still remained seated on the bank, with his face buried in his hands, and his faithful Hubert crouched at his feet—I walked down to the edge of the pool, and stood for a few minutes contemplating the beautiful scenery of the glen. All at once, I perceived a chariot about half a mile off coming rapidly along the road which Ned and I had just traversed. While watching the progress of this vehicle, and wondering whether it could be coming to the mill, I heard footsteps behind me, and turning, I almost started back with astonishment and delight on beholding Apphia coming towards me with John. She was in a riding-habit, and must have just dismounted from her horse. I bounded towards her with rapture; but my transports were instantly checked by the profound gloom of her looks—a gloom that was shared by her brother. Though kindly in her greeting, her manner towards me was constrained and cold.

"It is strange that we should meet here, Mervyn, in this unexpected manner," she said, "and at a juncture which may affect all my future life. Knowing how I am circumstanced, you will not be surprised to learn that I have come to claim my brother's protection. Ever since your visit to the Anchorite's, I have felt that I could not fulfil my contract with Malpas, but I lacked the courage to break it. Yesterday decided me. I came with my mother to the vicarage at Marston to spend a few days with the family with whom I was to be connected, and some circumstances occurred last evening—not worth detailing now—but which made me resolve to emancipate myself at once from a thraldom which I found insupportable. To accomplish my design, I was obliged to have recourse to artifice—

excusable, I trust, under the circumstances—and I solicited my mother's permission to ride over to Weverham this morning to see John—stipulating that I should only be attended by Dr. Sale's groom, and not accompanied by Malpas. Her consent was rather reluctantly given, but she at last yielded to my importunities. Before leaving, I entrusted a letter to one of the servants—to be delivered an hour after my departure—in which I acquainted my mother with my determination. On arriving at John's cottage, I learnt, to my great disappointment, that he was not within—but ascertaining that he was at the mill, I rode hither at once. All uneasiness is dissipated, since I have found him."

"But you are pursued!" I cried, pointing to the road on the further side of the mill-pool. "Yonder is Dr. Sale's carriage. No doubt your mother has likewise been to John's cottage, and has traced you here."

"Let her come. I will not return with her, unless John means to give me up."

"I will afford you an asylum," John replied; "but who shall say, in my infirm state of health, how long I may be able to offer it you?"

"Cannot I help you, Apphia?" I exclaimed. "You might give me rights, even more sacred than those of a brother, to aid you and protect you."

"I thank you from the bottom of my heart, Mervyn, for your devotion," she replied. "But, alas! I cannot profit by it. I have given a promise—a solemn promise to my mother—never to bestow my hand upon any one without her consent—and I am well assured she will never consent to my union with you."

"I had not foreseen this," John said, mournfully. "A hope was springing in my breast that I might see you both happy—but you have wholly crushed it, Apphia. I lament that you have uttered this rash promise—but having given it, you must, perforce, keep it."

"I do not think so," I rejoined, warmly. "Such a promise ought not to be exacted by a parent, and can never be binding on a child."

"If the child voluntarily chooses to place such an obligation upon her conscience, she must abide by it," John rejoined. "Apphia cannot be released, except by her mother."

"You are right, John," she replied. "I fear there will always be an insuperable bar between me and Mervyn. I must therefore look to you—and to you alone. And yet, perhaps, I ought not to place you in this position. You will have lasting differences with our mother, on my account."

"Do not consider me, Apphia," he said. "I would not offend our mother if I could help it—and I will strive to reason with her now. Failing my endeavours in this respect, my home is your home."

"I thank you, John," she replied, earnestly.

"Your decision is only just made in time," I cried, "for here comes Mrs. Brideoake."

As I spoke, the carriage drove up to the little bridge near the

R

mill. A footman immediately came down from the box, crossed the bridge, and returned the next moment with Mavis, who, doffing his cap, evidently told the occupants of the carriage that the persons they sought were there. On receiving this information, the steps were instantly lowered, and Malpas Sale and Mrs. Brideoake alighting, proceeded towards the mill.

"We will await their coming here, Apphia," John said to his sister. "You had better withdraw, Mervyn, for your presence might tend to complicate matters. Retire behind those palings," he added, pointing to the palisades of a gardener's shed. "You will then hear all that passes. I desire to have you for a witness. Should I need you, I will call you. Take Ned Culcheth with you. He would be in the way."

Feeling that no time must be lost, I ran towards Ned, and rousing him as well as I could from the state of apathy into which he had sunk, I half dragged him behind the palings which John had indicated, and which completely screened us from view.

We had only just gained this retreat, when I heard voices, and placing myself in a position that enabled me to see without being seen, I beheld Mrs. Brideoake, attended by Malpas, approach her son and daughter. John made a respectful salutation to his mother as she approached, taking off his hat as she drew near, and remaining uncovered during the whole of his interview with her. On her part, she treated him with the utmost coldness—did not shake hands with him—but eyed him with severe displeasure. As to Malpas and John they might have been utter strangers to each other, so distant was the manner in which their salutations were made.

Apphia took refuge behind her brother, and remained with her eyes fixed upon the ground.

"You are aware what brings me here, John," Mrs. Brideoake began, in a dictatorial tone, and as if determined to enforce obedience to her commands. "Apphia has left me in an extraordinary manner, and I am sure you will see the propriety of her immediate return to her duty."

"Apphia has fully explained her sentiments to me," John replied, in tones the gentleness of which contrasted strongly with his mother's haughty accents, "and I can therefore speak for her. She is quite willing to return to you, and to obey your behests as heretofore——"

"I am glad of it," Mrs. Brideoake interrupted. "No more need be said, then."

"Pardon me, mother, much remains to be said. That you desire my sister's happiness and worldly prosperity I do not doubt, and that in choosing a husband for her, you have chosen one who, in your own opinion, justifies your selection, I am ready to grant. But the heart cannot be controlled, and Apphia feels that to marry without love—in her case, at least—would be to marry to certain misery. She therefore—through me—beseeches you not to seek to force her inclinations, but to leave her the free exercise of her will;

and on this understanding she will willingly, cheerfully return to you. I also join my earnest entreaties to hers that you will accede to her request."

No supplication could be more gently, more respectfully preferred. But John's humility served only to heighten his mother's imperiousness of manner.

"I can make no terms with a disobedient child," she said. "I order Apphia to return to me. She will disobey at her peril."

"A word more, mother," John urged, in the same respectful manner as before. "Apphia is most unwilling to resist your mandates—believe me when I say it. Surely, surely, after what I have stated, you cannot wish to doom her to unhappiness? Neither after what he has heard, can the gentleman to whom she is affianced desire fulfilment of the contract."

"Since I am appealed to," Malpas said, "I must answer that I have placed myself entirely in Mrs. Brideoake's hands. I am naturally unwilling to surrender one to whom I am devotedly attached—and I shall not of my own accord break the contract I have entered into. But if Mrs. Brideoake desires it, I will forego all claim to her daughter's hand. Not otherwise. Indeed, I am at a loss to understand the meaning of this sudden change in Apphia's feelings towards me. She entered into this engagement deliberately—and as far as I am able to judge, voluntarily—but within the last week her sentiments seem totally altered, and she appears to regard me with aversion."

"The cause of the change is easily explained," Mrs. Brideoake said. "It is because by the return of Mervyn Clitheroe a foolish attachment, which she indulged in as a child, has been revived in her breast. But," she added, sternly, addressing Apphia, "let her mark me well, if she thwarts my inclinations, she may rest assured that, under no circumstances, and on no pretence, will I consent to her marriage with the object of her fancied regard. And you, John," she continued, turning to him, "who argue for her, let me point out to you the mischief you are doing, by combining with your undutiful sister against me. It is your fault if I am compelled to mention matters without due regard to delicacy. Listen to me with attention, and you will see how little of a brother's regard for a sister's welfare there is in your opposition to me. My dear friend, Mrs. Mervyn," she continued, slowly and emphatically, "has executed a deed, by which she settles one half of her large property—and a large property it is, being upwards of 4000*l.* a year—upon Apphia—on her marriage."

"On her marriage with Malpas Sale—and no other?" John asked, quickly.

"On her marriage with Malpas Sale, and no other," Mrs. Brideoake repeated, deliberately. "Malpas is the person specified in the settlement, which would become null and void in the event of Apphia's union with—say Mervyn Clitheroe. The marriage is appointed for Malpas's next birthday, when he will be twenty-five, and will consequently attain his majority, according to the terms of his uncle Mobberley's will. At the same time, he will come into 2000*l.* a year—so that the fortunes of bride and bridegroom will be fairly balanced."

"Having heard this statement, which I can confirm," Malpas said, "Mr. Brideoake will no doubt give it due consideration."

"It merits consideration, indeed," John replied, after a moment's pause. "You had better take time for reflection, Apphia."

"I require none," his sister replied, firmly. "I decide at once. No pecuniary consideration shall induce me to enter into this marriage, and I am sure it was not with any design of forcing my inclinations, that kind, excellent Mrs. Mervyn acted thus generously towards me. Having no claim upon her bounty—no expectations from her—I do not now feel disappointed; but I am not less grateful for her kindness, though I cannot accept the gift with its conditions."

"And this is your decision, Apphia?" her mother cried, severely. "You had better pursue the course recommended you by your brother, and reflect. Bear in mind that you will not only forfeit this large property—but my love and protection—my love and protection," she sternly repeated.

"I cannot help it, mother," Apphia answered, meekly. "I shall strive to bear your displeasure, hoping that time may soften it."

"Be not mistaken—time will never soften it," Mrs. Brideoake cried, furiously. "Have I reared you—have I toiled for you—have I paved your way to fortune—ungrateful, disobedient child, only to find you turn upon me thus? But tremble! Your ingratitude and disobedience warrant me in invoking condign punishment upon your head."

And as she spoke she raised her arm, as if about to pronounce a malediction. Affrighted at the gesture, Apphia flung herself at her feet, and clasped her knees.

But Mrs. Brideoake was held in check by one who had never before asserted supremacy over her. For the first time in his life her son turned a menacing and indignant look upon her, and she gazed upon him, as all who beheld him did, in astonishment and awe.

John seemed endowed with superhuman power, and drawing up his tall figure to its full height, he regarded his mother with eyes that flashed with lightning.

"Forbear, mother!" he exclaimed, stretching out his hand towards her. "In my sacred character, which you are bound to respect, I command you to desist! You have no just cause of offence against your daughter. She has ever been dutiful towards you, and if she now rebels against your authority, it is because you exact too much. Heaven has not ears for invocations like yours, and if you call down curses upon your child, be assured they will recoil on your own head. Rise up, Apphia, rise up, and come to me. I have made every effort to soften our mother's obdurate heart; but in vain. She casts you off, my poor child. Be it so. I receive you. If there should be remorse and repentance for this day's unhappy proceedings, they will not rest with us."

Mrs. Brideoake, who had appeared quite confounded by her son's address, now made an effort to retrieve the ground she had lost.

"John, John—you ought not to take part with her, but with me," she cried. "You share her disobedience."

"Peace! mother, and let us part," John replied. "I will never reproach you, though when you think of me hereafter, you may sometimes reproach yourself. Neither, I am sure, will Apphia reproach you, even if you refuse to make her happy by assenting to her union with the only man she can love. I would that we might part with you in a better frame of mind, and that you would leave your blessing with us."

"My blessing—never! ungrateful as you both are," she rejoined, with asperity. "You will both repent this step—bitterly repent it."

"It is to be hoped, for your own sake, that you may repent it, mother," John replied.

Mrs. Brideoake made a movement, as if to quit the spot.

"Nay, tarry a moment, my dear Mrs. Brideoake," Malpas said. "Let us have something like an amicable understanding if we can, ere we separate. I will not further press the fulfilment of the contract between myself and Apphia, but as she has alleged no stronger reason than change of mind for the avoidance of her solemn engagement, I will still venture to hope that, ere long, another change may occur, and I may be reinstated in her good opinion, which, for no fault of my own that I can discern, I appear to have forfeited. All I will beg, therefore, is to be permitted to visit her as a friend, and I will undertake not to renew my proposition unless it shall be agreeable to herself."

"The proposal appears reasonable," John rejoined. "What answer do you make, Apphia?"

But before she could reply, a soft and plaintive voice was heard singing a Welsh song, and little Grace and her companion were seen advancing along a path that led towards the party.

"It is Sissy Culcheth!—I am sure it is!" Apphia exclaimed.

As she spoke the song ceased, for poor Sissy, perceiving the party, hurried towards them. Her lap was full of wild-flowers, and she offered a branch of honeysuckle to Apphia.

I had kept my eye on Malpas. When the voice of the poor singer was heard he became pale as death, trembled, and would no doubt have taken to flight, if he could have framed a plausible excuse for his sudden departure. But when Sissy came up, he found his position intolerable, and was moving off, when John Brideoake caught hold of his arm, and detained him.

"Stay a moment, sir," John cried, sternly. "I am compelled to put some interrogations to you. You have just stated that my sister can allege no stronger reason for refusing to fulfil her contract with you, than change of mind. A plea seems now to be furnished her, which, if correct, cannot be resisted. A charge of the gravest character has been brought against you in reference to this distracted woman. Can you look the poor creature in the face, and declare solemnly, and as you will render a final account of your actions to Heaven, that you are not the cause of her present lamentable condition?"

"I trust not," Malpas replied, shuddering and averting his head.

"Look at her, I say," John continued, "and do not equivocate in your answer. Did you, or did you not, lure her from her husband's home?"

"These questions are only put to me for the purpose of enabling Apphia to break her engagement with me," Malpas said, trying to feign indignation, though his faltering tones showed how differently he was affected, "and they do not deserve to be answered. Enough for me to declare at once that all such assertions respecting me, by whomsoever made, are false and calumnious. The person with whom this unhappy woman left her home is Simon Pownall."

"If so, you cannot object to an ordeal which I will propose, with a view to test your innocence?" John said.

"What ordeal do you mean?" Malpas asked, in faltering tones.

"You shall see," John replied. "Here, Sissy," he cried, taking the hand of the poor creature, who was busily engaged in picking out a sprig of blooming eglantine from her bundle of flowers, "come this way. An old acquaintance wishes to see you. Look at him. Do you not know him—Mr. Malpas Sale?"

Poor Sissy, at first, had not heeded what was said to her, but continued to pursue her occupation. On hearing the name, however, which John repeated more than once, with marked and peculiar emphasis, she looked up, and fixing her eyes on Malpas, a fearful change came suddenly over her countenance.

"It is he! it is he!" she shrieked. "It is the pad man of my treams. It is he who is to take me from my huspants, and cause my death!"

Then, uttering a piercing scream, and placing her hands before her eyes as if to exclude some dreadful vision, she would have sunk to the ground, if Apphia had not supported her.

On hearing this cry, Ned, who had with difficulty restrained himself, rushed forth, and I followed him, for I feared from the expression of his countenance that he might do some desperate act.

Malpas seemed as if he would have gladly sunk into the earth when the vengeful husband stood before him.

"Look at me," Ned vociferated—"look at me, thou black-hearted, shaking villain. Dost know me? Dost know me, I say?"

Malpas made no answer, but turned to fly.

But the grasp of a giant was laid upon him. Seizing him by the shoulder, Ned plucked him round as easily as if he had been a child. They were again face to face.

"Well, what do you want with me?" Malpas faltered.

"Satisfaction!—that's what I want," Ned thundered—"satisfaction for the wrongs done me. And by the Heaven above us! I'll have it."

"What do you want satisfaction for, my good fellow?" Malpas said, trying to appease him. "I've done you no harm."

"Thou liest!" Ned cried. "Thou hast done me a wrong which nothing but blood can wipe out—and thy blood I'll have. I have tarried thus long for vengeance because I doubted thy guilt, but her cries have accused thee. Prepare thyself if thou canst—thy hour is come."

"Hear me, Ned," Malpas cried, seriously alarmed by the other's infuriated aspect. "I swear to you that I have not injured you as you suppose."

"Oaths like thine won't weigh with me," Ned cried. "Thy victim there gives thee the lie. Look at the wreck thou hast made, and ask thyself if I am likely to spare thee."

"This madman will do Mr. Sale a mischief," Mrs. Brideoake said. "Will nobody fly for assistance? Nay, then, I must go myself. There will be murder done. Help! help!"

And she ran screaming towards the mill.

"Come, Ned," I cried, "I feel for you deeply, as you know, but I cannot stand by and see outrage done."

"What! you, too, take his part, sir, eh?" Ned roared, blinded by fury. "I didn't expect it. But neither you nor Mr. Brideoake shall baulk my vengeance. Hubert will keep you both off. Tent 'em, lad!—tent 'em!"

And the fierce hound instantly displayed his glistening fangs, and seemed ready to spring at us.

"Now stand upon thy defence and we will fight, as man with man," Ned cried, releasing Malpas.

"No; I won't fight you, Ned," Malpas replied. "I'm no match for you."

"Thou thought'st thyself more than a match for me wi' yon poor fool, thou dastardly villain," Ned rejoined, with scornful fury. "But if thou won't fight, down on thy knees, confess thy guilt, and sue for mercy."

At this moment shouts were heard, and several persons were seen hurrying towards us from the mill.

"Sue for mercy to you, fellow—never!" Malpas cried, reassured by the sound.

But the words were scarcely out of his mouth when a tremendous blow in the face from Ned's clenched hand stretched him, bleeding, upon the ground. The enraged keeper knelt upon his prostrate body, and seizing him by the throat, would infallibly have strangled him, if I had not, at great personal hazard, come to the rescue. Aided by John Brideoake, who prevented Hubert from attacking me, I succeeded in compelling Ned to relinquish his death-gripe of Malpas. In another moment, Mavis, with three of his men, reached the scene of strife.

Mrs. Brideoake tried hard to have Ned seized, charging him with a murderous attack upon Malpas; but as soon as Mavis learnt from

John Brideoake and mysel how matters really stood, the worthy miller would not allow Ned to be touched—declaring that, under similar provocation, he should have acted in the same manner.

While Malpas, quite insensible from the crushing blow—enough to stun an ox—which he had received, was carried to the mill, Ned devoted himself to his wife, and, as she no longer repelled his advances, he pressed her to his bosom, and covered her with kisses. Poor Sissy appeared, in some degree, to have regained her faculties, for she murmured, as her husband strained her fondly to his breast, "If you mean to kill me, Ned, do it now."

"Kill thee, dear lass!" he exclaimed. "If I do kill thee, it shall be wi' kindness. I have got thee back at last, and nought shall part us more."

"And, Ned!—dear Ned!" she cried, "I have been foolish, and greatly to blame, but I am innocent—on my faith I am. Forgive me—oh, forgive me!"

"I forgive thee, dear, from the bottom of my heart," he replied; "and I fully believe what thou dost tell me. Oh! what a load is taken from my breast!"

Sissy gazed at him for a moment with inexpressible gratitude and affection, and flung her arms about his neck. They remained locked in each other's embrace for a few moments, when Sissy's hold relaxed, and she swooned away. The revulsion of feeling had been too much for her.

Ned bore her gently towards the mill, and we followed, in silence and in tears. While witnessing such a touching scene as was exhibited in the reconciliation of this poor couple, it was impossible to utter a word.

Mrs. Brideoake was already gone. She had left when Malpas was removed, without vouchsafing a word to either of her children.

END OF BOOK THE SECOND.

BOOK THE THIRD.

BOOK THE THIRD.

CHAPTER I.

HOW THE TWO WIZARDS OF OWLARTON GRANGE RAISED A SPIRIT THAT THEY DID NOT EXPECT.

ABOUT two months must be allowed to elapse ere I resume my narrative. No events of any importance had occurred to me during this interval. My affairs were pretty nearly in the same unsettled state as heretofore, and there seemed no immediate prospect of their amendment. I had made more than one unsuccessful attempt to obtain an interview with Mrs. Mervyn; and I had reason to believe that the letters which I addressed to her were never permitted to reach her—at all events, they were never answered. Neither Mr. Comberbach nor Molly Bailey, though both well enough disposed towards me, were able to lend me aid. Mrs. Bridconke still reigned supreme at the Anchorite's. As I was given to understand, she accounted for her daughter's absence by saying that Apphia was obliged to remain with her brother, whose feeble state of health required constant attendance, and, as no contradiction was given to the statement, Mrs. Mervyn probably believed it. But the poor lady—now almost entirely confined to her room—mourned for her absent favourite, and sighed for her return.

Malpas Sale had not been to the Anchorite's since his misadventure at the mill. Besides producing insensibility for several hours, the violent blow dealt by Ned's huge fist disfigured his features, and he was too personally vain to exhibit himself in public until his good looks were completely restored. By this time his leave of absence had expired, and he was obliged to join his regiment, which was stationed at Windsor. Before departing, he made an effort to obtain an interview with Apphia, but she declined to see him. He had previously written to her, professing undying love, and hoping still to be reinstated in her affections. Moreover, he utterly denied the accusations brought against him by Ned Culcheth, and solemnly protested that he had not seen Sissy from the time of her quitting her husband's roof until the luckless day at the mill.

This latter assertion, John Brideoake, who answered the letter for his sister, showed to be an evasion of the truth. It was now known, John said, by Sissy's confession, that Simon Pownall had been a mere instrument in the base plot, and Sissy was only saved from actual guilt by the agonies of suddenly-awakened conscience, which had thrown her into a fever, and for a while, as Malpas knew, had disturbed her intellects. John concluded his letter by saying that his sister must decline to hold any further intercourse with Mr. Sale.

To this communication Malpas sent a haughty rejoinder from Windsor—to the effect that "he should formally demand fulfilment of his marriage contract with Apphia at the time appointed; and as he had her mother's support, it would then be seen whether his just claim could be resisted." Here the correspondence ended.

Quitting Malpas, whom it is small pleasure for me at any time to mention, let me say that John's cottage—always delightful—was rendered doubly so by its new inmate. His roses seemed to gain in beauty and fragrance from her sedulous attention. And John's powers of serving his parishioners were materially increased by his sister's zeal and unremitting exertions. Much as the young curate was beloved, his sister bade fair to eclipse him in general regard. One result followed Apphia's instalation in her brother's abode, which, if there had been no other reason for it, would have made her advent fortunate. John's health improved—slightly, it is true; but improve it did. Whether he had less upon his mind—whether her presence cheered him—or that she took such good care of him—certain it is that the progress of disease was arrested, and confident hopes began to be entertained of his ultimate recovery. Moreover, John was hopeful about himself, and that was a good sign. If careful nursing could accomplish a cure, it must be owned that he had an excellent chance. Not only had he his sister to watch over him, but he had frequent visits from the ladies of Owlarton Grange. Scarcely a day passed on which Miss Hazilrigge and Ora failed to drive over to Weverham, bringing with them all sorts of nourishing things for the invalid.

Apphia and Ora took a liking to each other at once, and mutual regard soon ripened into warmest friendship. If good, kind Miss Hazilrigge, who was little behind her niece in regard for Apphia, could have had her own way, she would have had both John and his sister to stay with her at the Grange; but as this could not be, she contented herself with passing as much time as possible in their society. What degree of encouragement John had received from Ora, and whether there had been any "love passages" between them, I shall not at this moment pause to inquire. As regards myself and Apphia, I would be more explicit, but unluckily I have nothing to relate. Apphia treated me as a friend—nothing more. I was free to come and go to John's cottage as I pleased, and was always kindly welcomed by herself and brother. But I was given clearly to understand by the young lady that I must not assume the character of a suitor; and whatever constraint I was obliged to put upon myself, in order to comply, I never sought to violate her injunctions.

Thus matters stood with my friends at Weverham.

As at John's cottage, so at Owlarton Grange, I was always welcome. Old Hazy would have had me consider his house as my home —and Miss Hazilrigge insisted upon my taking her brother at his word. Cuthbert Spring had long since returned to Cottonborough— though he now and then came over to spend a day at the Grange. Whether any positive matrimonial engagement had been entered into between him and the elderly spinster, I am not prepared to say. No such announcement had been made; and Miss Hazilrigge was still Miss Hazilrigge.

Charmed with the beautiful situation of the mill, and liking both Dame Mavis and her husband, I took up my abode with them. My new quarters suited me extremely well, and enabled me to enjoy the society of my friends, both at Owlarton Grange and Weverham. I bought a serviceable horse from the miller, and rode about in every direction throughout the county—visiting some new scene on nearly every day. A couple of months thus passed by almost without my being aware of their flight. If not entirely happy, I was content. A more active life might have suited me better, but I felt that a time would come when I should have work enough—and I determined to enjoy my present leisure.

What had become of the Thaumaturgus, Doctor Hooker, since his disappearance from the old Grange, on the night when he played the ghost, I could not ascertain. Old Hazy did not like to be questioned about him, and took it in such high dudgeon if I ventured to disparage the Thaumaturgus in his hearing, that at last I ceased to allude to him. But I did not intend to let the rascal escape with impunity. I only bided my time.

Peace had once more returned to Ned Culcheth's humble dwelling. Sissy had sufficiently recovered to be able to attend to her household concerns, and strove to repay by duty and affection her husband's deep devotion to her. No more coquetry—no more frivolity now. She had received a severe lesson, and meant to profit by it for the rest of her life.

With this brief reference to most of the reader's acquaintances, I shall resume my story.

I had ridden over to Marston, in order to have a day's fishing in the mere—according to previous arrangement with Ned Culcheth. Very good sport we had, and caught a couple of jack, besides a basketful of perch and other fish. With this supply we returned to Ned's cottage, where some of the perch were fried for me by Sissy— constituting, with a roast fowl and a few rashers of bacon, a most excellent repast.

The shades of night had fallen when I rose to take leave of my humble but hospitable entertainers. I had left my horse at the Nag's Head in the village, and Ned offered to row me across the mere and land me at the foot of the church, which would save me a mile's walk; besides, as the night was extremely fine, with bright moonlight on the water, he thought I shou'd prefer that plan. I gladly accepted the proposal. Nothing could be more exquisite than the appearance of the mere as our little bark clove through its shining waters. Before us towered the old church amidst its trees — its square tower illumined by the silvery radiance. Leaning back in the boat, I did not address a word to Ned, who plied his oars in silence. In spite of the beauty and tranquillity of the scene, sad feelings stole over me. I thought of the dead — and of one who was as if dead to me: of my mother in her grave in the adjacent churchyard, and of my father, whom I had never seen, in India. Melancholy musings like these engrossed me, until the boat reached the strand, when I leaped ashore, and taking leave of Ned, climbed the hill, and entering the precincts of the church, proceeded towards my mother's grave. The white head-stones, the grassy mounds, the humble wooden rails, and the more imposing monuments, were all bathed in bright moonlight. Amidst them, an old black yew-tree, with outstretched boughs, had a spectral effect. I was just turning the angle of the church, when, to my surprise, I perceived a tall man wrapped in a cloak standing near my mother's resting-place. I could not be mistaken, for I knew the exact situation of the grave, and as the moonlight fell full upon the flat stone, I could almost read its inscription from where I stood. The person I beheld was extremely erect in deportment, and had a military carriage. His cap was removed, and I saw that he was grey-haired and partially bald, with a lofty forehead, but his features being in the shade, I could not clearly distinguish them. So far, however, as they were discernible, they were entirely strange to me. Yet, somehow, I felt that I ought to know him. Who was he? Why should he visit my mother's grave at such an hour? Why display such emotion?

My curiosity being greatly aroused, I stood still to gaze at him. Indeed, I did not like to disturb him, so impressed was I by his appearance.

More than once I saw his lips move as if in prayer. After heaving many deep sighs, and beating his breast, he put on his cap, and thinking he was about to depart, I resolved to address him; but not wishing to take him by surprise, I coughed slightly to announce my approach. He no sooner noticed me than he hurried out of the churchyard, and I watched his tall dark figure speeding rapidly across the fields, until it disappeared from my sight. I felt half disposed to follow him. Yet, to what end? He evidently shunned observation. Wherefore should I intrude upon his grief?

I did not tarry much longer in the churchyard. Kneeling beside my mother's grave, I breathed a hasty prayer, and then proceeded to the village inn, where my horse being in readiness, I mounted him and rode off in the direction of Weverham.

I had fourteen miles to traverse, but what was such a distance as that with a fleet horse on a fine night? A mere question of an hour and a

quarter. Besides, being now well acquainted with the country, I knew how to save a mile or two by taking cross-roads.

The shortest way to Weverham led past Owlarton Grange, and that road I now selected. But the nearest road is sometimes the furthest about, they say; and the proverb was verified in my case.

All went well till I got within a couple of miles of the Grange, when, from some cause or other, my horse fell dead lame. I was obliged to get off and lead him, but the poor animal could hardly hobble after me. What to do with him I scarcely knew, for to take him on to the mill, which was more than four miles off, seemed impossible. My best plan seemed to leave him at the Grange, where I could at all events place him in a shed till the morning. To the Grange accordingly I proceeded, but the horse moved so slowly that midnight had struck before I arrived there.

Being now well acquainted with the premises, I went round to the back, and, opening a gate, soon made my way into the farm-yard. Luckily the door of a cow-house was unfastened, and entering it, I placed my unlucky steed amongst the cattle, took off his saddle and bridle, tossed him a truss of hay, and after making him as comfortable as circumstances would admit, sallied forth with the intention of knocking up Stephen Blackden or one of his hinds.

But my purpose was suddenly changed, for just as I regained the yard, the door of the farm-house was cautiously opened, and two persons issued from it, enveloped in long cloaks, with hats pulled over their brows, and so muffled up that it was impossible to distinguish their features. Notwithstanding this evident attempt at disguise, I felt certain that the pair were no other than Old Hazy and Simon Pownall; and I resolved to watch their movements. After pausing for a moment, to secure the door, they moved off towards the garden, and I stole after them.

On entering the garden the two mysterious individuals plunged into long alley, formed of clipped yew-trees, leading in the direction of the summer-house. I followed, taking care to keep out of sight. The alley once gained, indeed, I was tolerably secure from observation, for it was so dark, owing to the height and thickness of its hedges, that I could scarcely discern the two figures moving on before me.

Arrived at an archway, however, the pair turned off, and when I next beheld them, they were standing together in a retired corner of the lawn. From the preparations they were now making, it was evident that some mysterious rites were about to be enacted. The large white sheet stamped with magical characters, which I had seen, on a previous occasion, in Simon Pownall's room, was spread upon the lawn, and they both seemed occupied in studying its cabalistic signs.

The spot selected for the ceremonial seemed suitable enough. It was a part of the lawn furthest removed from the hall, and screened by a group of shorn trees, which, by a little stretch of imagination, might be taken for men and animals suddenly transformed by the power of enchantment. On the right was a gigantic bear reared on its hind legs, and with outstretched paws prepared to close with a huntsman, who was attacking it with an axe. Behind was a gigantic figure, with a long beard, probably meant to represent a Druid. Then came an evil angel with wide, outspread wings. Then a grotesque figure. Then a Faun playing Pandean pipes, with goats skipping before him; and lastly, a cock crowing on a tree.

Surrounded by these mute witnesses of their doings, the mysterious pair proceeded with their performance. The chief wizard, whom I took to be Simon, produced a wallet from under his cloak, and brought out a human skull and cross bones, the dried skins of toads, lizards, adders, and other reptiles, and disposed them in a circle round the cloth. While he was thus employed, the second wizard produced a little iron trivet with some combustibles; and these he placed outside the mystic ring.

The pair of conjurors then marched thrice round the magic circle, and seemed from their gestures to be muttering spells. This done, they paused, and the second wizard, whom I took for Old Hazy, brought forth a large book bound in black parchment, which I at once recognised as the grimoire he had shown to me in his sanctum.

Opening this magical volume, he pronounced some strange sounding words from it, which might be intended as an incantation, while his companion stepped into the magic circle, and began to trace certain lines upon it with the points of his fingers.

By this time my patience having become exhausted, I determined to put an end to the scene. When, therefore, the second wizard summoned some spirit, with a tremendous name, to appear, I did not wait for the response, but rushing forward, and shouting out, "You have raised a spirit that you did not expect!" I snatched the grimoire from his hands, and with the ponderous volume buffeted his companion soundly on the head and shoulders.

In doing so, however, I knocked off the individual's hat, when to my great surprise and vexation I found it was Old Hazy himself whom I had thus maltreated. At the same time the old gentleman, who had been struck speechless with terror by my sudden appearance, found his voice, and implored me to desist.

Simon Pownall had not waited for me to find out my mistake, but took nimbly to his heels, flying in the direction of the summerhouse. Before, however, he could climb the mound on which it was situated, I was after him, when finding himself hard pressed, the wily fox changed his plan, and ran on till he reached the edge of the moat, into which he unhesitatingly plunged, and swam across to the further side.

I was debating whether to follow him, but by this time Old Hazy having come up, entreated me to let him go; and before I could disengage myself, Simon had disappeared—thus, for the second time, eluding me.

CHAPTER II.

MISS HAZILRIGGE TAKES ME INTO HER CONFIDENCE.

OLD HAZY took my unlucky attack upon him in very good part, but thought I had carried the joke a little too far. He never expected, he said, to be beaten about the head with his beloved grimoire. He accepted my apologies, promising to think no more about the matter, provided I undertook to keep strict silence as to the occurrence; not liking to be made a laughing-stock, as would certainly be the case if the circumstance became known.

Delighted to be let off so easily, I readily agreed to his terms, and we then proceeded to remove all traces of the magical ceremonial from the lawn. After gathering together the mysterious implements, the obnoxious grimoire included, we wrapped them up in the sheet, and carried the bundle between us to the farm-house, depositing it in the room formerly occupied by the soi-disant Dr. Hooker, which communicated, as I had supposed must be the case, by a small private door with the hall. Renewing my apologies to the worthy old gentleman for my maladroit behaviour, I then took leave, and proceeded on foot to the mill, where I arrived without further accident or adventure, at a somewhat late hour.

In a few days my horse having recovered from his lameness, which proved to have been caused by a badly-driven nail, I was able to resume my rides about the country. All my inquiries after Simon Pownall were ineffectual. I could not learn what had become of him after his flight from the garden. Though, of course, in compliance with Old Hazy's injunctions, I made no allusion whatever to Simon's clandestine visit to the Grange, nor to the Der Freischütz scene in the garden, in which he had played the part of Caspar, I thought it right to acquaint Miss Hazilrigge with the rogue's real name and character. She manifested no surprise at the information, but expressed great concern that her brother should be so egregiously duped.

"But it has constantly been the case with him, I can assure you, dear Mr. Clitheroe," she said. "He has been deluded by impostor after impostor for years; and if we get rid of this Dr. Hooker, or Pownall, or whatever his name may be, another cheat will take his place. Decided opposition won't do with my brother. He must be humoured to a certain extent. If thwarted entirely, he would become unmanageable. This you must have perceived is the course I adopt with him, and the course I prescribe to the servants, who are all ordered to indulge their master's whims and peculiarities. You will now understand whatever may have appeared strange in the

B

conduct of Stephen Blackden, the bailiff, and his family. Stephen knows he would lose his place—and a very good place it is—if he didn't humour my brother, and put up with his odd ways, and so does Dame Blackden. So do the whole household, in fact. Ponder makes a complete study of his master's eccentricities, and understands precisely how to treat him. He knows 'the exact length of his foot,' as they say in these parts. But setting aside his fantasies, my brother is so good and kind a master, and so honourable and just in his dealings, that his servants and tenants all regard him and respect him, and though no doubt they occasionally practise upon his credulity, yet on the whole I have no reason to complain. However, a stop must, and *shall* be put to this knavish Pownall's proceedings, and I will take care he no longer infests the premises. Orders shall be given to Stephen Blackden to warn him off."

"Better order Blackden to arrest him, my dear Miss Hazilrigge," I ventured to observe.

"No, I can't consent to that," she rejoined. "I don't choose to have my brother's weaknesses exposed and turned into ridicule, which must be the case if this charlatan is brought to justice. It will be best to get rid of him quietly. Ah! my poor dear brother!" Miss Hazilrigge ejaculated, with a sigh. "What a pity so much goodness as is to be found in his composition should be linked to so much folly. Half his absurdities, I believe, are traceable to the nonsensical stuff with which he crams his brain, and I have more than once resolved to make a grand clearance of his shelves, and commit all the abominable rubbish he has collected to the flames; just as the curate and the housekeeper burnt Don Quixote's books of chivalry. But I have been deterred by fear of the consequences. The proceeding might drive him distracted."

"Upon my word, I believe it would," I rejoined. "Mr. Hazilrigge would never recover the loss of his Frommannus, his Maldonatus, his Psellus, Remigius and Filesacus, and other writers on whom he sets such store. He loves them better than life."

"You are right, Mr. Clitheroe," she said. "It won't do to interfere with him. An oddity he is, and an oddity he must remain to the end of the chapter. His mania is incurable, and must be tolerated—'tis well it's no worse. For my part, I dislike your great bookworms. They're good for little else than an arm-chair in a library with a huge folio before them. I sincerely hope you won't read too much, Mr. Clitheroe."

I replied that I did not think it very likely I should err in that respect.

"I'm glad to hear it," she rejoined. "But now, while we are on the subject of my poor dear brother and his eccentricities, I must make a confidant of you, Mr. Clitheroe, and explain how anxious—how inexpressibly anxious—I shall feel about him—if—if I am compelled to leave him. No, I don't think I ever *can* leave him," she added, applying her handkerchief to her eyes.

Not knowing to what extent her confidence might be given, I

contented myself with inquiring whether she had any immediate idea of leaving her brother.

Her agitation increased as she attempted a response. At last she sobbed out, " It will be a dreadful struggle—a terrible sacrifice, Mr Clitheroe—and I hope Mr. Spring won't exact it from me."

I am sorry to confess, that instead of being moved by this pathetic address, I felt very much inclined to smile; but I managed to preserve my gravity. Though not in entire possession of my friend's sentiments, I thought I might venture to speak for him.

" Mr. Spring, I am convinced, my dear Miss Hazilrigge," I said, " will consent to any arrangement most in accordance with your wishes and comforts."

" Then you think he will allow me to remain at Owlarton Grange —with my dear brother—do you, Mr. Clitheroe ?" she cried, removing the handkerchief from her eyes, and gazing wistfully at me through her tears. " I fancied he was wedded to Cottonborough and the neighbourhood. Now, I have the greatest regard for Mr. Spring, and consider him a most charming person, but even *he* couldn't reconcile me to Cottonborough, or to the sort of society one must be compelled to mix with there. The mere idea of it makes me shudder."

" I have no authority for saying so, of course, my dear Miss Hazilrigge," I replied ; " but I repeat my firm conviction that Mr. Spring will gladly accede to your wishes. Whatever his own inclinations may be, your happiness must necessarily be his first study. Of that be assured. If a certain happy event—to which, I trust, I may without impropriety allude—should occur—I do not see why you should not continue to live here—always supposing the arrangement to be agreeable to Mr. Hazilrigge."

" Oh, there is no difficulty on my dear brother's part," she replied ; " but Mr. Spring objects——"

" You don't say so ?" I cried.

" Decidedly objects," Miss Hazilrigge continued. " He calls this place dull, and declares he should be moped to death if he dwelt here for a month. He doesn't care for hunting, shooting, fishing, or any other country sport. He doesn't like country employments. He doesn't like country gentlemen, or farmers—clodhoppers he calls them. In short, the only place he *does* like appears to be Cottonborough, and the only society he apparently cares for is the society of the Cottonburghers. I pity his taste in the latter particular, I must say. If Mr. Spring has no relish for our pleasant country, I can't abide his filthy town, with its tall, smoky chimneys and its squalid population, and so I have told him. To be frank with you, Mr. Clitheroe, we have joined issue on this point—Town or Country— Cottonborough or Owlarton Grange."

" Country will gain the day," I cried.

" I am not so sure of it," she replied. " Mr. Spring is very obstinate, and clings to Cottonborough as if nothing could tear him from it. But one thing I can promise him—either he must quit that odious, black, smoky place, or he shan't have me. I am not selfish, Mr. Clitheroe, but I am bound to consider my brother, and must not totally disregard my own comforts."

"Certainly not, my dear Miss Hazilrigge," I replied.

Our confidential discourse, which took place in Miss Hazilrigge's boudoir, was here cut short—rather to my relief, I must say—by the entrance of Ora, who, by an arch glance at me, intimated that she could guess what we had been talking about. Her aunt imposed silence upon me by a look, and of course I did not betray the trust reposed in me. But on thinking over what I had heard, I came to the conclusion that the match between the elderly couple was not quite so certain of coming off, as I had previously fancied.

Miss Hazilrigge was sincerely attached to her brother, and I do not think she could have borne a separation from him. Now that it had come to the positive question of leaving Owlarton Grange, she evidently began to feel the strength of the ties that bound her to the place, and to its eccentric but estimable master, and shrank from breaking them. Old Hazy and she had lived together since their early years—how would they get on apart in their latter days? What would become of him when she was gone, and there was no one to take care of him? He would become a prey to every impostor. Would Cuthbert Spring and Cottonborough suffice for the loss of the dear old house, and the dearer old brother? Hardly. The chances seemed against the marriage, unless the perverse old bachelor would give up his residence in the smoky manufacturing town, which Miss Hazilrigge so much abominated, and consent to share the pure delights of the country with her and her brother. But Cuthbert was town-bred, and town-educated, and liked noise and bustle, the busy mart and the crowded street, the dingy warehouse and the stupendous mill, and it was just as difficult to tear him from Cottonborough, as to remove Miss Hazilrigge from the Grange.

Had the case been mine instead of Mr. Spring's, I should have declared for the country, without an instant's hesitation. Owlarton Grange was a delightful residence. Old Hazy was somewhat of a bore, it is true, with his long stories and whimsies; but he had so many redeeming qualities, was so good-natured, so kind and considerate, that it was impossible for any one, much in his society, not to like him. I became very much attached to him; but though willing to listen to his long stories after dinner, over a bottle of claret, I took good care to keep out of his sanctum.

Being now perfectly at home at the Grange, I rambled about the house and garden as much as I listed. No one stood upon any ceremony with me, and I came to be regarded as one of the family by the household. A room was allotted to me in the great gallery, where I retired to read when I pleased, without fear of disturbance. The haunted chamber was always ready for me in case I chose to pass the night at the hall. But I rarely availed myself of the privilege, preferring my snug little bedroom at the mill.

Apropos of the haunted chamber, let me take this opportunity of mentioning that careful investigation of the room enabled me to detect a trap-door, very ingeniously contrived in the planks of the floor near the antique tester-bed. On opening this trap-door, a steep narrow staircase was discovered, on descending which, a long arched passage appeared, built in the inside of the foundation walls of the habitation. After tracking this passage, a second staircase was reached, similar to the first, which landed me, by means of a sliding panel at its summit, in a small room near to the extreme end of the great gallery. From this room, access could be gained through a private door to the farm-house.

The course taken by Pownall in his nocturnal visit to me was therefore revealed. At first I had supposed that the rascal had found his way to the priest's hiding-place, where the murderous deed was committed by Jotham Shocklach; but this proved not to be the case.

Since Pownall's disappearance from the farm-house, no more ghostly noises had been heard, and the awful rapping of the mallet entirely ceased. If things went on in this way, and no new prestigiator appeared on the scene, Old Hazy would lose his character for eccentricity, and Owlarton Grange become little better than an every-day habitation, remarkable only for its antiquity.

But it must not be imagined that the old gentleman neglected his beloved treatises on occult philosophy. On the contrary, he found greater solace in them than ever. Debarred from the society and counsel of the modern Thaumaturgus, as he styled the soi-disant Dr. Hooker, he held constant communion with the departed sages— with Zoroaster, Olaus Magnus, and John Adam Osiander—and if he heated his brain overmuch with their prodigious recitals, he, at all events, committed fewer extravagances.

And where was the bewitching Ora all this while? The bewitching Ora had her own pursuits—I had mine. We were the best friends possible, and if I had encouraged her, I have no doubt she would have been as confidential with me as her aunt had proved. But though we talked together with perfect freedom on most topics, we never renewed the conversation we had had in the garden relative to John Brideoake. Perhaps, she was quite satisfied now that John was in a fair way of regaining his health, and no longer felt any uneasiness about him. Perhaps, his sister was the depositary of her confidences, if she had any to impart. Perhaps, it was not necessary to speak of John at all, since she saw so much of him—rarely a day passing that she did not visit Weverham. Perhaps——but what need of further guessing? I consider it impertinent and unfair to pry into young ladies' secrets.

CHAPTER III.

REVELATIONS.

When not at Owlarton Grange, I was at Weverham; and when not at Weverham, I was at Owlarton Grange. My time was pretty equally divided between my friends. Naturally, the curate's humble dwelling possessed stronger attractions to me than the ancient hall, inasmuch as it contained Apphia; and if I had consulted my own inclinations I should never have been absent from her side. But this might not be; and I was forced to submit to a destiny which for the time seemed unpropitious to my happiness. More than once, when there appeared to be a possibility of my forgetting it, Apphia gently reminded me of the unfortunate promise she had given to her mother, and declaring that no entreaties of mine could cause her to break it, reduced me, in an instant, from a state of rapture to utter despair. Sometimes I thought her unnecessarily cold—and told her so—but I perceived from the expression of her countenance, as well as from the tears starting to her eyes, that my reproaches were unjust, and I hastened to recal them. That she acted from a sense of propriety I knew, and however I might suffer, I felt I had no right to complain.

What the solution of this painful question might be, I did not dare to conjecture. Time only could decide. But though cast down for the moment, I was not without hope for the future.

But I must now proceed to detail an adventure which befel me when returning one evening from a visit to Weverham; and which furnished me, in a strange way, with some rather important information.

The day had been oppressively hot, and as the sun went down there was every appearance of a thunderstorm: heavy masses of leaden-coloured clouds, accompanied by portentous stillness and gloom. The shades of night brought no coolness. Scarce a breath of air was stirring. We sat with open windows, but found little relief, for the scent of the flowers from the garden was almost overpowering.

Still the storm held off, and I thought I should be able to reach the mill before it burst forth. John advised me to wait, and so did Apphia, who seemed more apprehensive of danger than her brother, but I would not listen to their entreaties, and set forth, laughingly assuring them that they need be under no apprehension about me.

Scarcely had I reached the garden-gate, when a flash of forked lightning traversing the sky seemed to rebuke my rashness, while, in another instant, an angry growl of thunder was heard in the distance. Apphia called out to me, imploring me to come back, but I did not heed her, and went on my way.

The mill was distant about two miles, and the nearest road lying

across the fields, I took it of course, walking as fast as I could. But I had not proceeded more than a mile, when the storm broke upon me in all its fury. The rain came down like a waterspout, drenching me in an instant to the skin. Fire and water were commingled, for notwithstanding the deluging showers, the heavens appeared in a blaze. I have never beheld more vivid lightning, nor heard more awful claps of thunder. I should now have been glad to be back again with John and his sister, and regretted that I had turned a deaf ear to Apphia's urgent entreaties to me to stay. But I could not but admit that I was rightly served for my imprudence.

The situation was extremely unpleasant. I was half-drowned, deafened, nearly blinded — wholly confused. I looked around for shelter—none was at hand—for I did not dare to place myself under a tree, knowing well the risk incurred in doing so from the electric fluid.

To turn back was as bad as to go on. So I pursued my course with as much expedition as circumstances would permit. Rapid progress, however, was now out of the question; and indeed it was with difficulty that I got on at all, for the paths were flooded and slippery, and the lightning so dazzling and incessant, that I could scarcely face it.

At length, after crossing a couple more fields, I came to a halt; beginning to fear that I must have got upon a wrong track. In another moment my doubts were converted into certainties. A flash of lightning of extraordinary brilliancy showed me that I was within thirty yards of the high road leading to Owlarton Grange. Instead of proceeding in the direction of the mill, I had therefore been walking away from it for the last quarter of an hour.

Rushing forward to a stile near the high road, I waited for the next flash, hoping it might reveal some dwelling where I might obtain shelter; but though disappointed in this expectation, I caught sight of something, which, under the circumstances, was nearly as welcome —namely, a haystack situated at the further end of the opposite field.

Congratulating myself on the discovery, I at once started towards this place of refuge, and quickly reached it. The haystack proved to be as large as a good-sized farm-house, with widely overhanging eaves and sides sloping down to a somewhat narrow base—promising comfortable shelter at the end not exposed to the weather. I was hastening thither, when the sound of voices arrested me. Something seemed to whisper caution, and well it was that I attended to the monitor. In the intervals between the loud peals of thunder I could distinguish the voices of the speakers more clearly, and they seemed familiar to me, but in order to make sure, I peered cautiously round the corner, and a flash of lightning occurring at the moment, I beheld Simon Pownall conversing with Phaleg and Obed.

Simon seemed ill at ease, and either from fright, or owing to the blue glare of the lightning, looked perfectly livid. But his companions appeared wholly indifferent to the terrors of the storm which agitated him so violently. Reclining against the side of the stack with his brawny arms crossed upon his chest, and one muscular leg twined round the other, gipsy-fashion, Phaleg looked the picture of reckless unconcern; while his son leaned in an equally careless attitude against a donkey, which, with a pair of panniers and a bundle of stakes upon its back, formed a conspicuous feature in the group.

All this I noted at a glance; and I noted, moreover, with some uneasiness, that both gipsies carried their heavy bludgeons with them. It might be the effect of the lightning, as in Pownall's case, but I thought Phaleg's countenance wore an unusually sinister expression. The stack had been cut at this end in steps, and a good deal of loose hay lay scattered about, in the midst of which sat Pownall with his back partly towards me. A ladder reared against the side of the rick showed that the honest husbandman had been recently at work there, not calculating upon such visitors as these.

"Mercy on us!" Simon ejaculated, his teeth chattering with fright—"what an awful peal of thunder! I never recollect such a storm in all my born days. D'ye think we're safe here, my worthy Phaleg?"

"Safe!—ay, to be sure," the elder gipsy rejoined, in a scoffing voice; "just as safe as you'd be in a church—safer, mayhap—for I once seed the tower o' Lymme church struck by a thunderbowt, and some great heavy stones rolled down and broke through the roof, and would ha' killed a score o' godly folk, if they had chanced to be mumbling their prayers at the time."

And the miscreant chuckled at his own pleasantry.

"Don't laugh in that way, I beg of you, my irreverend Phaleg," Pownall rejoined. "It makes the flesh creep on my bones. Powers above! what a flash!—enough to put one's eyes out."

"What, you're afeared o' thunder an' lightnin', are ye?" the caitiff rejoined, scowling at the heavens. "Well, I ain't. I rayther enjoys a storm like this. I account it a pratty sight—a'most as good as fireworks. Some canting folks would fancy that the Dule and all his imps was abroad."

"Have done, Phaleg," Pownall cried, sharply. "This is not a proper season for jesting."

"Well, chant a psalm, if you're so inclined," the ruffian answered, contemptuously. "How long is it since you turned Methoddy parson, eh, Pownall? I thought you were still in the conjuring line."

"Don't be angry, my worthy Phaleg," the other rejoined; "I meant no offence. Let us proceed to business."

"Wi' a' my heart," the other replied. "Go on. I'll listen to you, provided the thunder'll let me."

"I wish I had as much courage as you, my brave Phaleg," Simon replied; "but this storm has robbed me of all mine."

"Robbed you, has it?" the gipsy cried, derisively. "I didn't fancy you had much courage to lose. But if you want to rouse your sperrits, why don't you take a drop o' brandy?"

"An excellent suggestion," Simon said. "Luckily I have my pocket-flask with me. You know whose cellar the liquor comes from, Phaleg," he added, producing a small leather-covered flask, and unscrewing a silver cup from the top, which he proceeded to fill.

"Ay, ay, I know where you got it, and I know also that it be the right sort o' stuff," the gipsy replied. "I wish I were as well varsed i' the black art as you, Pownall. You plays hocuspocus tricks to some purpose."

"That's some of Old Hazy's best Nantz," Simon cried, tossing off the contents of the cup. "Taste it, Phaleg," he said, replenishing the little vessel, and handing it to him.

"I won't say 'No,'" the gipsy rejoined. "Here's success to us all three!" he added, emptying the cup. "A rare cordial, by my soul!" he cried, smacking his lips. "Obed won't object to a drop of it."

"That I won't, father," the younger gipsy replied, with a grin.

"Here you are, then, little Obed," Pownall said, giving him the cup, which he had once more filled to the brim. "Plague on't! how my hand shakes."

"Steady it wi' another cupful," Phaleg rejoined, with a gruff kind of facetiousness. And as Simon acted upon the hint, the gipsy added, "Now we can talk over matters comfortably."

"Ha! ha! so we can," Pownall laughed. "I don't care for the thunder now. It may roar till it's hoarse—ha! ha! And the lightning may burn itself out. But to business," he added, checking his hilarity on the sudden. "You and I are in the same boat, Phaleg, and must pull together, if we want to get along smoothly."

"Well, I'm willing," the elder gipsy said. "You've only to say which way we are to pull."

"Let me first explain how I'm situated," Pownall went on. "The game at Owlarton Grange is up. I could have made a good harvest there, and stayed as long as I liked, if it hadn't been for that meddlesome fool, young Clitheroe."

"Curse him!" Phaleg ejaculated. "He'd better not come across me again. I'd split his skull for two pins."

"'Twas an unlucky day for me that brought him to the Grange," Simon continued, "for he has marred all my schemes. I tried to scare him off the premises by playing the ghost, but he was too wide awake to be so taken in, and I had enough to do to get away from him. T'other night, just as I had enticed Old Hazy into the garden, and was about to play off some conjuring tricks, for which the old fellow would have come down handsomely, my gentleman pops upon us unawares, and not only deprives me of my fee, but forces me to swim across the moat in order to escape."

Simon's description of his misadventures seemed highly diverting to both gipsies, for they broke into a loud fit of laughter.

"I found it no joke, my lively friends, I can promise you," Simon continued, rather testily; "and I don't think that either of you would have liked it. This was my last appearance at the Grange. Old Hazy still sticks to me, and would have me back again if he dared; but owing to this confounded young Clitheroe's interference, Miss Hazilrigge and all the household are against me, and I daren't show my face. Before I bolted, I tried hard to get a good thumping sum out of the old squire, but it was no go. And this brings me to the point, my worthy Phaleg. Since money is not to be had there, it must be got elsewhere—d'ye understand?"

"I shall do so, I dare say, afore you've done," the elder gipsy rejoined.

"Briefly, then," Simon said, "if a certain friend of ours is to come quietly into 2000*l*. a year in a few months' time, he must pay us for permission to obtain it."

"I am quite of your opinion, Mester Pownall," the elder gipsy replied. "If he axes my permission, he shan't have it, unless he *do* pay. But I thought you had got summut already from the young chap."

"So I have, but it's all spent. However, our secret ought to be a mine of wealth to us, Phaleg—a mine of wealth; and I'm content to share it with you, because——"

"You can't help yourself, that's why," the gipsy interrupted, with a coarse laugh. "You're afeared o' me, and *must* stop my mouth, just as Capt'n Sale *must* stop yours. That's the long and short on't, Pownall. Well, I'm willing to act wi' you, so long as you play upon the square. But deal falsely wi' me, and look to yourself, man."

"Trust to my honour, my worthy Phaleg. When we've settled this little affair to our mutual satisfaction with Captain Sale—to our mutual satisfaction, I repeat—I shall make myself scarce—emigrate. I've had enough of a vagabond life, and mean to turn my talents to proper account. America's the land for a sharp fellow like me—or Australia."

"Not a bad plan," Phaleg remarked. "I think I shall go to Horsteraylia myself. What say'st thou, Obed? Wilt go wi' thy father?"

"No," the younger gipsy replied, bluntly. "I shall stick to the owd country. Leave me little Robin," he added, patting the donkey's neck, "and I shall be quite content."

"Well, do as thou wilt, lad," Phaleg said. "Thou shalt have Robin, and welcome—though, mayhap, I shall change my mind afore the time comes for starting. Thy mother and Rue mayn't like to go."

"It'll be your own fault, my worthy Phaleg," Simon remarked, "if you don't get enough to enable you to live comfortably either here or in Australia."

"That's exactly what I should like, Mester Pownall," the gipsy rejoined, dryly; "so I'm quite ready to act wi' you. Where is the capt'n?"

"At Windsor with his regiment, but I mean to write and appoint a meeting with him without delay. I shall take the liberty of informing him that his future fortune as well as the maintenance of his position in society depend upon his keeping that appointment. If he fails, he must take the consequences."

"He'll come then, you think?"

"I'm sure of it. He daren't refuse. And now for the plan——" Here Simon lowered his voice so much that I could not catch what he said.

"How if he should turn rusty?" Phaleg remarked, after a pause.

"In that case, I'll make him feel my power to its full extent," Pownall rejoined. "But, bless you! it'll never come to that. He may stamp and swear—and call me ugly names, as he has often done before—but I know the way to tame him. I shall use an argument not to be resisted. Only let me threaten to produce the rightful will, and he'll agree to my terms pretty quickly—be they what they may. It won't suit him to lose 2000*l.* a year. It won't suit him to be publicly disgraced, which he will be if it comes to be known that he has been acting under a wrong will, with full understanding that it is wrongful. He has to choose between compliance with my demands, and ruin, Phaleg—absolute ruin."

" Poor young gen'l'man!" Phaleg cried, with affected commiseration. " Don't be too hard upon him."

"I don't want to be extortionate, my tender-hearted Phaleg," Pownall rejoined. " But I must take care of myself, you know. Besides, I've got to share the spoil with you. We must have a good round sum. It's our last chance. He'll want to have the will delivered up this time."

" He must be a precious fool if he doesn't," Phaleg said. " It's a wonder to me he didn't bargain for it at first—but he didn't know you so well then as he has done since. You haven't got the will about you now ?—ha!" he added, with a suddenness that made Simon start, and led me to suspect that he had an evil motive for putting the question.

" No, no," Pownall replied, evidently in some trepidation. " Do you think I would carry such a valuable document as that about me? It is lodged in a place of safety—where no one but myself can find it. One can't be too cautious, you know, worthy Phaleg. One never knows into what sort of company one may get."

" Very true," the other replied. " And I wouldn't advise you to take that precious dokiment i' your pocket when you pays Capt'n Sale a visit, or you may chance to return without it. And I think you'd be all the safer at the interview wi' a friend like me at your elbow. But I wish you'd just explain this to me, Pownall. I never could rightly understand how there comed to be two wills; nor how you managed to get the true will into your possession? I suppose you stole it when you broke into the room where the dead man was lying?"

" Hush! Phaleg," Simon cried; " I don't like to speak of the old chap on a night like this. I'll just take another drop of brandy, and then I'll give you the information you desire. Old Mobb, you must know, had two great-nephews—the present Captain Sale and Mervyn Clitheroe. Clitheroe was his favourite, and he meant to leave him his money, but the lad displeased him by shooting a tabby-cat belonging to the old missis, and Mobb changed his mind, making a will in favour of Malpas Sale. That was the first will. Pay attention, Phaleg. By-and-by, however, Clitheroe gets into his uncle's good graces again, the tabby-cat is forgotten, the old missis dies, and a second will is made, by which Mervyn becomes heir. That second will is the true will. Pay particular attention now, Phaleg, and you shall hear how the precious document came into my possession. 'Twas a cleverly-managed affair, as you will admit. On the day of his death old Mobb was burning papers in his bedroom, which was on the ground-floor, with a little window looking in the garden, and he meant to have destroyed the first will—the *first will*, mind, Phaleg—placing it on his bed for that purpose. Now the bed being close to the window, and the window being open, and I chancing to be in the garden at the time—watching the old man's proceedings—I seized the opportunity when Mobb's back was turned, thrust in my hand, and grabbed the will."

"But what were the use of grabbin' it, if it warn't the right will?" Phaleg inquired.

"You shall hear, if you'll let me tell the story in my own way, most respectable Phaleg," Simon replied. "The old man didn't perceive what I had done, but thought he had burnt the will, and soon afterwards took to his bed and died. The right will I knew was locked up in a bureau in the bedroom, but I hoped to get the key, in order to enable me to secure that precious document, and put the wrong will in its place. In this I was disappointed—so I was compelled to break into the room at night to accomplish the job."

"At which time I caught sight of you," Phaleg remarked.

"Unluckily for me, but luckily for yourself, you did so, my crafty Phaleg," Simon went on. "My object in making this change of the will must now be apparent to you, methinks. The second will was found where I had placed it; was read; and Malpas declared heir—heir to 2000*l.* a year. But the true will being in my possession, I could upset him in a moment by its production. And this I took care to let the fortunate youth know. You would have grinned to see how chopfallen he looked when I gave him the information. However, he saw there was nothing for it but to make terms with me, and he did so without hesitation."

"What did you get out of him, may I ask?" the gipsy said.

"That's scarcely a fair question, worthy Phaleg," Simon replied, "and you must excuse my answering it. I dare say you'll learn, though, at our meeting with the captain, for he'll be sure to rake up old scores. Thus you see, Phaleg—and I'll give it you as the moral of my story—a man should never make a second will till he has burnt the first."

At this moment, I bent forward rather incautiously, and, in doing so, made a slight noise, which caught the quick ears of Obed.

I drew back instantly, but it was evident, from the exclamation of the younger gipsy, that he had seen me.

"There's a man round the corner!" he cried. "I saw him draw back his head."

"A listener!" Pownall exclaimed. "If it should be young Clitheroe, we're done for!"

"If it should be young Clitheroe I'll do for *him*," Phaleg roared, with a fearful oath, that left me little doubt he would try to put his threat into execution. "Come along, Obed."

And, as he spoke, he dashed round the corner, brandishing his bludgeon.

They were within an ace of discovering me, and if it had lightened at the time I must infallibly have been detected. But I managed to elude them. Instead of attempting flight, which I knew would be useless, I threw myself on the ground, and crept round the corner of the haystack so expeditiously, that I was actually amongst them before they had moved from the spot. Simon Pownall did not quit his post, and I was therefore compelled to bury myself in the hay, which screened me effectually.

The shouts and oaths of the gipsies as they beat about the haystack reached me where I lay, and told me what I had to expect if my hiding-place should be discovered. Presently they came back, greatly enraged at their failure. Phaleg swore lustily at his son, and told him he must have been dreaming; but Obed stoutly maintained the contrary, declaring that he had seen a man's head as plainly as he now beheld his own father's. Where was he, then? What had become of him? Phaleg demanded. Obed couldn't tell; so, after some wrangling, they both held their peace.

The incident served to break up the conference. Simon Pownall, though concurring in opinion with the elder gipsy that Obed must have been deceived, was evidently rendered uneasy, and declined to talk any more on business. Much to my relief—for I began to find my position almost intolerable—I heard him soon afterwards announce his departure. After exchanging a few words with Phaleg, in too low a tone to reach me, he bade him and his son good night, and set off.

Nothing passed between the gipsies for a minute or two, but when Simon, as I presumed, was fairly out of hearing, the elder ruffian observed to his son, with a laugh,

"I tell thee what it is, Obed—I mean to have that will."

"You do, father?" the younger gipsy replied. "Then you won't work wi' this owd chap?"

"Not unless I'm driven to it, lad," the other replied. "I cannot trust him; and I know he doesn't trust me, but means to throw me over, if he can. All Capt'n Sale wants is the will; and he would liever deal wi' me than wi' a greedy curmudgeon like Simon. We must find out where the will be hidden, Obed."

"You don't think as how th' owd chap had it about him to-night?" the son rejoined.

"I had my doubts," Phaleg returned, "and I thought of knockin' him on the head to see. But if I hadn't found it, it would ha' been awk'ard. I should ha' cracked the nut without gettin' the karnal. So I thought it best to let things bide as they be."

"Lucky for him you did think so, father," Obed laughed. "Well, I've a plan, which, if we can bring it to bear, will enable us to stand in Simon's shoes as regards the capt'n. You shall hear what 'tis when I ha' conned it over."

"Well done, Obed," the elder gipsy cried, approvingly. "Thy wits are sharp enough, lad, if thou chooses to give 'em fair play, and not fancy thou sees a man's head round the corner of a hayrick—ha! ha! But come! the rain's over. Bring along Robin, and let's be jogging."

With this he evidently moved off, and his son was not long in following him.

As soon as I deemed the coast clear I shook off the covering of hay, and congratulated myself on my deliverance. If the miscreants had remained many minutes longer, I must have shifted my position, or **have been stifled.**

Suffering a few minutes more to elapse before quitting the field, I made the best of my way to the mill.

I rose betimes next day, and spent the whole of it in searching for Pownall and the gipsies. But though I scoured the country round for miles, visiting every spot where I thought it likely tidings could be obtained, I learnt nothing. No one answering to Pownall's description had been seen at Weverham, or any of the adjacent hamlets —nor had lodged—so far as I could discover—at any wayside inn, or hovel. I was equally unsuccessful in my quest of the gipsies. The latter, I found, had been encamped on Delamere Forest during the last week, but had struck their tent a few hours before I assisted at their rendezvous with Pownall at the haystack, and in all probability they had removed to some distant spot.

Sorely disappointed, I rode over on the ensuing day to Marston, for the purpose of consulting with Ned Culcheth. Ned advised me to keep quiet, and not give the alarm. Something would soon be heard, he was sure, of Captain Sale, and the moment he arrived at the vicarage I should be apprised. The captain's movements should be closely watched, and, likely enough, we might catch all the birds we wanted with the same net. I was not very sanguine as to the success of Ned's scheme, but having nothing better of my own to suggest, I agreed to it, and the worthy fellow took measures to carry it out.

But while this matter was in abeyance, another event occurred, which I shall relate in the succeeding chapter.

CHAPTER IV.

I GIVE A RUSTIC FÊTE AT THE MILL.

KIND-HEARTED Miss Hazilrigge, ever anxious to promote harmless amusement, and never so happy as when helping to make other people happy—young people especially—persuaded me to give a rustic fête at the mill, promising to take all trouble of the arrangements off my hands.

"You have only to invite your friends," the good lady said. "Leave all the rest to me. Of course you will ask John Brideoake and his sister; and I have no doubt Mr. Cuthbert Spring will come over if you send him word. We have seen nothing of him, by-the-by, for the last week. And now, when shall it be? The sooner the better, I think, for the weather is extremely fine just now, and likely to continue so. To-day is Monday—suppose we say Thursday. That will give plenty of time for preparation. But mind, it is merely to be a rustic fête, and quite simple in character, for if any pretension is attempted, or any fine folks are invited, John Brideoake and his sister will never join it, I'm sure."

"I quite agree with you there, Miss Hazilrigge," I replied; "and as far as I myself am concerned I should very much prefer a little outdoor entertainment at which my humbler friends can assist—and I will therefore invite Ned Culcheth and his wife. I dare say we shall be able to get up a dance on the green sward near the mill-pool."

"Delightful!" Miss Hazilrigge cried. "I hope the Culcheths will come. To make sure, you had better say that I will send some conveyance for them—and they shall be taken back next day. Don't omit to mention that."

"You are kindness itself, dear Miss Hazilrigge," I rejoined, "and leave nothing undone to contribute to the happiness of your friends and dependents."

The fête was therefore fixed for the following Thursday, and I despatched an invitation without delay to Cuthbert Spring. I did not hear from him till the Wednesday morning, when I received a letter to say that he had just returned from London, whither he had been summoned by important business. He would be extremely happy to assist at my rural festivities, he said, and would bring with him his old friend Major Atherton, who had returned with him from town; desiring me to mention to Mr. Hazilrigge that he should claim his hospitality for the night for himself and his friend at the Grange.

"I shall be very glad to see Cuthbert and his friend, of course," Old Hazy said, when I delivered the message. "But who is Major Atherton? I don't recollect him."

I could afford no information, the major being equally a stranger to me, and the old gentleman contented himself with remarking that he had no doubt he must be an agreeable man, or Cuthbert would not have volunteered to bring him.

"Apropos!" he cried. "I dreamed last night of a swan, and that, according to Artemidorus, signifies joy and the revealing of secrets. And the night before, I dreamed that my teeth were whiter, firmer, and more comely than ordinary, denoting, according to Anselmus Julianus, prosperity, good news, and friendship among relations. I have no doubt I shall learn some curious intelligence from Major Atherton, as well as experience much pleasure in his society."

I acquiesced with him in opinion, and here the matter dropped.

My invitation to Ned Culcheth and Sissy was delivered in person. On learning that a light cart would be sent for them early on the morning of the day of the fête, and that the same conveyance would bring them back next day, the only obstacle to their prompt acceptance was removed; and they joyfully promised to come. Sissy said she should look forward with delight to seeing her kind friends at the mill again, and she hoped to be able to bring back little Grace with her, if Dame Mavis would only spare the sweet child for a month. Sissy loved little Grace, she said, as dearly as if she were her own daughter.

Nothing had been heard of Malpas. Ned had caused inquiries to be made at the vicarage, but no letter had been received from him, neither did it appear that he was expected.

The appointed day arrived, and the weather proving highly propitious, I had reason to hope that the fête would go off well. A large level patch of green sward in front of the miller's picturesque abode had been carefully rolled and mown till it resembled a bowling-green, and on this turf the amusements were to take place. Here a marquee was pitched, which had been sent from Owlarton Grange, and, adjoining it, stood a long table, covered with all the essentials of an excellent cold collation: a roast sirloin of beef, roast lamb, pigeon pies, roast fowls, hams, tongues, and other good things too numerous to particularise. Covers were laid for thirty persons, and benches were placed on either side of the table capable of comfortably accommodating that number.

But after all, though good viands and stout ale are not to be despised, a fête would be nothing—in female eyes, at least—without music and dancing. Accordingly, by the kind prevision of Miss Hazilrigge, the Weverham band of musicians was engaged, consisting of a couple of fiddles, a flute, hautboy, and bassoon. A little stage was erected on the right of the lawn, opposite the marquee, on which chairs and stands were placed; and this constituted the orchestra.

A pretty picture altogether; with a background formed by the mill, and the old-fashioned timber-and-plaster habitation contiguous to it. The latter, with its grey thatched roof, its black-and-white chequer-work, and its transom windows, was quite as pleasing an object as the mill itself. On the right of the green was a small but prettily laid-out garden, screened off by a low privet hedge; and on the left lay the orchard, which I have heretofore had occasion to describe. A couple of gaily-decorated boats were moored to the margin of the mill-pool, and hard by the wooden steps, serving as a landing-place, grew a beautiful weeping willow, its pendent branches dipping into the water.

Such was the scene presented to my gaze as I contemplated it with Mr. Ponder, shortly before the arrival of the company.

But pleasing as I then thought it, it was nothing to what it afterwards became, when the green was thronged by merry groups, when every seat at the long table was occupied, and the viands were in a state of active demolition, when laugh and jest went round, when the butler and his assistants were in full employ, when the musicians struck up their liveliest strains, and good-looking lads and buxom lasses footed it blithely in the country dance and the jig.

But lo! an arrival. It is Miss Hazilrigge. Three o'clock is the hour appointed for the fête, but she comes a little earlier, wishing to be satisfied that her directions have been properly carried out. After looking round, and examining all the preparations with a critical eye, the good lady claps her hands with delight, declaring that all had been done to admiration. Mr. Ponder appropriates the compliment to himself, and bows respectfully. Mr. Hazilrigge comes next with Ora, who is charmingly attired, and looks more bewitching than ever in her pretty straw hat. The old gentleman seizes my arm, and tells me, with a comical look, which I scarcely know how to interpret, that he has invited two persons to my fête—a gipsy woman and her daughter. Seeing me stare at him, he hastens to add, "but they're both very decent, well-mannered people, and won't offend anybody. The daughter is one of the prettiest creatures you ever beheld—with such a pair of black eyes—such supple limbs—and such a little foot. She dances like a Spanish gitana. Doesn't she, Ora?"

"She is exceedingly pretty, indeed, and dances with inimitable grace," his niece replied. "Her raven tresses and superb black eyes are enough to make one turn pale with envy. I am very glad my uncle has bidden her to your fête, Mervyn, for she will be quite an attraction to it. The only misfortune is, she will turn the heads of all the men, and make them indifferent to their homely partners. Her mother tells fortunes capitally, and will afford amusement to the younger damsels and their admirers. She wanted to give me a peep into the future this morning—but I declined."

"She told my fortune, though," Old Hazy cried, "and told it remarkably well. I'm not going to let you into my secrets, you saucy minx," he added to Ora, "so you needn't expect it. But as I was saying, this gipsy woman told me a great deal that *has* happened to me, and that is only known to myself and to one other person—and a great deal that *will* happen to me. She seems as well versed in chiromancy as Dr. Hooker himself."

"I shouldn't be surprised if she has derived some of her information concerning previous events in your history from that respectable individual," I observed. But, seeing the old gentleman look rather blank, I added, "Well, I am very glad you have invited the gipsy pair. Ora's description of the daughter makes me curious to see her, and the mother's skill in soothsaying shall be put to the test."

Soon after this, Apphia and her brother arrived, and I flew to bid them welcome. They told me I might expect a large attendance, for the glen was thronged with young folks of both sexes on their way from Weverham. I may here mention that I had left the Weverham invitations to John, as his acquaintance with the village folk enabled him to make a better selection than I could do. I had not given him a very agreeable office, he said, for when a rumour of the fête got abroad everybody wanted to go to it, and numbers were of course disappointed.

But here they come! A large party of lads and lasses, in holiday attire, step upon the green, preceded by Mr. Mavis, who, arrayed in his Sunday habiliments, and having a large bunch of white ribands stuck on his breast, performs the part of usher, takes tickets, and presents the company to me. The young men look rather sheepish at first, and the damsels somewhat bashful, but, encouraged by the bland and friendly manner of Miss Hazilrigge, by the smiles and kind addresses of the younger ladies, and I may venture to say by my own not uncourteous reception, they speedily regain their confidence, and appear quite at ease. By this time, also, the band of musicians have arrived, and taking their places on the orchestra, after a brief preliminary tuning of their instruments, strike up a lively air, and on the instant every countenance becomes animated, and every tongue is unloosed.

After a short interval, more guests arrive—a second detachment of village lads and lasses, more numerous than the first. Mr. Mavis has enough to do to get them all forward, and laughs heartily at their uncouth bows and scrapes, and their funny curtseys. Then come the miller's men—such of them as are married, with their wives and children. Then more villagers, until at last the green is quite thronged. At last—just when I have begun to give them up—to my great satisfaction, I descry Ned Culcheth and Sissy. They are accompanied by Dame Mavis and her little daughter. The crowd draw aside to afford them passage as they advance towards me. Sissy comes first, holding Grace by the hand, looking more like her former self than I have seen her of late. If anything, improved, for, while she has quite recovered her bloom and beauty, her manner is sedate and wholly free from levity. For manly bearing, not one in that assemblage can compare with Ned Culcheth; and yet there are some stout, well-looking lads amidst it too. Ned is a first-rate specimen of a stalwart English yeoman. I feel quite proud of him. His heart beams out in his honest countenance, and makes itself felt in his warm grasp. Giving him and his wife a cordial welcome, I tell Sissy I am glad to perceive that she has returned to her primitive Welsh hat, as a bonnet does not suit her half so well. She colours a little, and turns to her husband, who informs me, with a laugh, that his missis has put on the hat thinking to please me. Well, she *has* succeeded, if such was her intention. Unbidden thoughts cross me. As I look at Sissy and contrast her present cheerful expression and composed manner with her recent woful condition as exhibited on this very spot, I can scarcely believe in the reality of the change. The past now only appears like a troubled dream. Some thoughts of a like nature probably occur to Sissy, for I observe her lip quiver, and a tear start to her eye. Her husband notices her emotion too, and, guessing the cause, catches little Grace in his arms, and holds her up to his wife to receive a kiss. But this does not improve matters, but rather makes them worse, for as Sissy strains her little pet to her bosom, her tears can no longer be repressed, and she rushes away until her emotion quite subsides. But this is the only occasion on which she gives way, and as Dame Mavis kindly says, "it be quite excusable." For my own part, I think all the better of her for the display of feeling. "I do believe Sissy loves my child as well as I do myself," Dame Mavis chatters on; "and I be quite sure the child be as fond of her as she be of her own mother. Therefore, I can't find i' my heart to deny 'em both since Sissy wants to take Grace home wi' her for a month—and I shall e'en let the child go."

Behold a grave and respectable-looking personage, in a blue coat and white waistcoat, with a stately, not to say majestic, deportment! Mr. Ponder comes to tell me that the benches at the table are fully occupied, and the guests eager to fall to—so I accompany the stately butler, and by our joint exertions, aided by those of Mr. Hazilrigge and John Brideoake, every plate is speedily filled, and nearly as speedily emptied. My guests, I must say, whether male or female, have no lack of appetite, and do ample justice to the good things set before them. Luckily, the supply is equal to the demand. Mr. Ponder smiles in his grave manner as he sees the havoc I am making with the noble sirloin of beef—very little of which now remains—and tells me, in an under tone, not to be alarmed, for he has famous cold roast "ribs" in the tent. "I don't think they will eat us quite out, sir," the butler adds. Old Hazy seems enchanted with the scene; declaring that it does him good to see such real, hearty, unsophisticated enjoyment. "I would rather witness a simple feast of this kind," he says, "than a grand civic banquet, with my Lord Mayor at its head." Jugs of stout ale are handed round by old Finch and Rivers, and their contents liberally dispensed.

At length the fire begins to slacken, and it becomes evident that the majority of the party have had enough. Ponder seizes this opportunity of handing round the wine, and having served each of the guests with a glass of fine old sherry, which makes the lads smack their lips with satisfaction, and brightens the eyes of the lasses, the butler informs the company, with a politeness that is generally appreciated, that he is extremely sorry to disturb them, but they must excuse him for intimating that their places were required by the next party. On this they all rise in high glee, tender their thanks to me, and the squire, and madam (meaning Miss Hazilrigge), and the young parson (meaning John), and the young ladies. The benches they have vacated are then instantly reoccupied.

The same scene is acted over again, and the second batch of guests display just as good appetites as the first, and keep us all actively employed. A third party succeeding, evidently possessing as vigorous powers of demolition as those who had gone before, I am fain to resign my post of carver-general to Old Hazy, who very kindly undertakes it for me, and discharges it to the entire satisfaction of the guests.

Meanwhile, other amusements have been going on. The boats have been put in requisition. Ned Culcheth, who plies a famous oar, having had plenty of practice on Marston Mere, has taken his wife and little Grace on a trip to the upper end of the pool, while the second boat has been manned by two of the miller's men, and filled with young village folk of either sex, whose songs and merry laughter can be heard during the whole of their passage across the sheet of water. Ned happens to bring back his party at the very moment of my quitting my post at the refreshment-table, and I am just in time, therefore, to assist Sissy to land.

A hubbub at the further end of the green now informs me of the arrival of the pair of fortune-tellers. Disengaging themselves, as well as they can, from the crowd, by whom they are instantly surrounded, the two gipsy women make towards me. As they approach, I have no difficulty in recognising my old acquaintance, Peninnah, while her companion must certainly be Rue. The charms of the latter have not been exaggerated, either by Old Hazy or his niece. Look at her as she comes along. If that is not a pretty girl, I don't know one when I see her. What with her singular personal attractions, and her characteristic and picturesque attire, she offers quite a study for you, if you are a painter. Slight in figure, and pliant of limb, her movements are as easy and agile as those of a fawn. Her features are cast in a delicate mould; nose fine and straight; lips ripe and full, and as vivid as carnation; teeth like a casket of pearls. You must expect her complexion to be dark, but there is a rich glow beneath the skin that gives it inexpressible warmth and beauty. Her eyes are large,

T 2

black, and full of fire, yet veiled by long silken eyelashes, that mitigate their radiance. Her brows are dark as night, and her jetty tresses are coifed by a coloured Valencian handkerchief, which she wears, coquettishly tied, over the back of her head. Her dress is somewhat showy in point of colour, and fanciful in make, but it suits her perfectly. There, I have done. You ought to have her before you.

Gipsy women wear well, or possess some secret for the preservation of their charms. Old age comes upon them at once, and not by degrees. Peninnah's hair is as raven black as ever, and her eyes as bright; but her cheek-bones are higher than they used to be, and her features generally sharper and more prominent. Still, she may be reckoned a handsome woman. Her countenance has an expression of greater cunning than I remember noticing in it before, and her glances are restless and suspicious. She marches boldly up to me, but notwithstanding her confident air, I can see that she rather doubts the reception she may meet with. She addresses me in the usual formula—asking leave to tell my fortune. I refuse.

"Nay, let me see your hand, my handsome young gentleman," she says; "it ben't the first time I have looked at it. I told you your fortune truly then, and I'll tell it as truly now. Ask him to let me look at his hand, my pretty young lady," she added to Ora. "I know he won't refuse you."

"Oh! you are quite mistaken if you suppose I have any influence over Mr. Clitheroe, my good woman," Ora rejoined. "He won't mind what I say."

"Try," Peninnah cried. "I warrant you'll succeed."

Ora looked at me, and unwilling to disoblige her, I held out my hand to the gipsy woman's inspection.

"Give me a piece of silver," Peninnah said; "gold would be better, if you have it."

"Silver must suffice," I replied, giving her a half-crown. "What do you discover?" I added, as she gazed into the palm of my hand, and attentively perused its lines.

"A good deal," she replied—"a good deal, that you will be glad to know. But you must step aside with me to hear it, for it won't do to speak before all the world."

"Oh! you needn't be under any apprehension, my good woman," Ora said. "Mr. Clitheroe won't mind our hearing what you have to tell. Will you, Mervyn?"

"I am sure he will," Peninnah rejoined, "and therefore I daren't speak. But I will tell you thus much, my pretty young lady, that he's a young gentleman as is born to good luck, though his troubles ben't yet entirely over."

"No, I should think not," Ora cried, with a laugh.

"Why don't you let the woman see your hand, Miss Doveton?" I said.

"Because I'm afraid," she replied.

"Don't be afraid of me," Peninnah exclaimed, in a coaxing voice. "I will tell you nothing disagreeable—that I promise you."

"On that condition, I am willing to try your skill," Ora returned,

taking off her glove, and resigning her white little hand to the gipsy woman.

Peninnah studied its lines attentively for a few minutes, and then looked up perplexed.

"Mind! you are only to tell me what is agreeable," Ora cried "I am almost as superstitious as my uncle, and if misfortune were predicted, I should be miserable."

"Don't be uneasy, my sweet young lady," Peninnah said. "Your path is a path of flowers, as far as I can see. But I thought there was an early marriage, and something that I can't make out seems to hinder it. I should like to look at that gentleman's hand," she added, pointing to John Brideoake, who was standing at a little distance, watching what was going forward.

"Why at *his* hand?" Ora demanded, colouring.

"Oh! be sure I have good reason for making the request, my sweet young lady," Peninnah said. "Will you allow the poor gipsy woman to see your hand, sir?" she added to John.

But he coldly and decidedly refused, crossing his arms upon his breast.

"Never for such a purpose," he said. "I have no faith in your practices, and will never encourage them."

"As you please, sir," Peninnah replied, fixing her dark eyes upon him, "but if I were to tell you all I have just learnt, you would own there is some truth in the art I practise. Let me look at your hand, young lady," she added, turning to Apphia, who was standing near her brother.

"On no account," Apphia rejoined, uneasily, and clinging to John.

"What! you are also afraid of me?—ha!" Peninnah exclaimed, with a half contemptuous laugh. "Have you no curiosity to peer into the future—no wish to know what will befal you? Your brother despises my art, and thinks me a cheat. Show me your hand, and you shall see whether I deserve to be so accounted."

"Yes do, Apphia," Ora cried, rushing up to her. "I want to hear what she will say."

"Well, since you desire it, I will not oppose your wishes," Apphia said, "though I am quite as incredulous as John." And as she spoke, she surrendered her hand to Peninnah, who rapidly traced its lines.

"Ah! what is this I see?" the gipsy woman exclaimed. "You say you are incredulous. Now mark my words. You will be suddenly summoned from this place, and will go—shall I tell you where?"

"No, I don't care to learn," Apphia said, with evident uneasiness.

"I can tell you whither you will go, and what will occur to you," Peninnah pursued. "Strange things are in store for you, and great surprises—some risk, perhaps, of which I can give you a warning, if you will listen to me."

"Desist, woman," John Brideoake interposed. "I will not allow you to listen to her longer, Apphia." And taking his sister's arm, he drew her away.

A sudden cry startled me at this juncture, and turning, I found it had proceeded from Sissy Culcheth. After disembarking from the boat, Sissy had seated herself on the bank near the weeping willow with little Grace, and was so much occupied in playing and chatting with the child, that she had not noticed the arrival of the gipsy pair. Grace at last perceived them, calling Sissy's attention to Peninnah, who was now close at hand. On beholding her, Sissy started to her feet with the half scream I have described. Ned Culcheth heard the cry as well as myself, and was instantly by her side, anxiously inquiring what was the matter?

"There she is!" Sissy exclaimed, in accents of alarm. "That's the black gipsy 'oomans who told me my fortunes, and said you would kill me. How she looks at us! I wish she would go away. She frightens me."

"Shake off your fear, Sissy," Ned cried. "She shan't meddle with you. Away with you, woman!" he added, with a menacing look at Peninnah.

"I don't want to meddle with her," the gipsy woman replied. "I bear her no ill-will. But my words came true, and she knows it. Let her think over what I *did* say, and she'll find I was right. She has had a narrow escape—but the danger is past now, and the rest of her days will be free from trouble."

"Well, there's comfort in that, at all events," Ned said.

"Ay, but I have yet more comfort for her," Peninnah went on. "The dearest wish of her heart will be gratified."

"What's that you tell me?" Sissy cried, gazing eagerly at her.

"The wish nearest your heart is to possess a child like this—ben't it?" Peninnah said. "Let me look at your hand, and I will tell you whether you will have your wish." And as Sissy extended her hand—not without some misgiving—towards her, she added, "Ere three years are flown you will be the mother of two children."

"You promise me this, my good 'oomans?" Sissy exclaimed, joyfully.

"Soh! I am a good woman now," Peninnah cried. "But no matter! good or bad, my words will come to pass."

While Peninnah was thus occupied, Rue, who was standing a few paces off, signed to me to follow her, and moved towards the edge of the mill-pool. Struck by her manner, which seemed to indicate that she had something to communicate to me, I complied, and soon drew near her. Without appearing to notice my approach, or even looking at me, she said, in a low tone, "Be cautious where you go! you are in danger."

"From whom?" I demanded.

"I dare not give you further explanation now," she replied; "but I will try to have a word with you before I leave."

Here we were interrupted by Peninnah, who, calling sharply to her daughter, bade her to come back to her at once.

As soon as I could get an opportunity, I took Ned Culcheth aside, and told him to keep an eye upon the gipsy pair. "But be careful not to alarm them," I said. "When they take their departure, follow them, and find out where they go. I am concerned to give you all this trouble, Ned. But I know you are willing—nay, anxious to serve me."

"'Anxious' is the word, sir," the honest fellow replied. "I was thinkin' of doin' it of my own accord ; and I trust to bring you tidinge before many hours of the whereabouts of Phaleg and his hopeful son —perhaps of the sly old fox, Pownall himself. That gipsy girl is woundy pratty—pity she comes of such a bad stock! I'll just give Sissy a hint of my plans, that she mayn't be uneasy when I go."

Another interruption. Busy Miss Hazilrigge comes up, and tells me she has been looking for me everywhere. She urges me to call for a country dance, and acting upon her suggestion, I at once engage Ora, and then clapping my hands to attract general attention, bid the musicians strike up their merriest tune. The signal causes an immediate stir amidst the assemblage, and in another moment some twenty or thirty young couples stand opposite to each other on the green. Ropes of flowers are then distributed to the dancers by Miss Hazilrigge, who is followed by Rivers, with a large basketful of these wreaths, and the mode of using them is explained by the kind lady. All the damsels are greatly pleased with the garlands, and of course their partners cannot be behind them in admiration. In an instant we are all in our places—Ora, who is full of animation and delight, standing opposite to me. Mr. Mavis and Sissy Culcheth form the second couple—and Ned and little Grace, who is perfectly wild with pleasure, the third. All being in order, the dance commences—and in right earnest. If mistakes are now and then made in the figure, and the ropes of flowers get occasionally entangled, and bring somebody to the ground, or knock off a hat or a bonnet, our enjoyment is not diminished by these incidents. On the contrary, they add zest to the dance. After a little practice, and with Ora's directions, the lads and lasses manage the ropes of flowers extremely well, and, when several couples are dancing, the effect is uncommonly good. Instead of hands across, the ends of the garlands merely are taken, and when going down the middle, the lads not unfrequently twine the flowery ropes round their partners' waists, or hold them above their heads. Ora is enchanted, for the idea of the garlands has originated with her. Though flushed with exertion, she declares she is not in the slightest degree fatigued, but will go down the dance again. The tune is changed, at her request, and we are just about to set off, when I become suddenly transfixed.

The musicians play on, but I heed them not. Mr. Mavis vociferates, "Now, sir, push it!"—the worthy man means poussette. Sissy stares, and Ora playfully chides me. But I do not stir.

I was transfixed in the manner I have described by the arrival of a tall, gentlemanlike, military-looking personage, attired in black, whom I instantly recognised as the stranger I had seen near the grave in Marston churchyard. He was standing near Cuthbert Spring, who was evidently pointing me out to him—and unless I was mistaken, the stranger regarded me with peculiar interest. At all events, I felt an interest in him for which I could in no way account. Who could he be ? and how came he to be with Cuthbert Spring ? Suddenly it occurred to me that he must be Major Atherton. Yet why should Major Atherton take an interest in me, or I in Major Atherton ? That remained to be seen.

How long I should have continued in this state, if Ora had not roused me, I cannot tell. But at last she succeeded in diverting my attention from the stranger, and dragged me into the dance.

"Why, Mervyn," she cried, "what on earth is the matter with you? Don't you see we are all waiting? Pick up your garland, and come down the middle with me at once. How slow you are, to be sure! You seem to have lost all your spirits."

I did my best, but my interest in the dance was gone, and I proved so dull a partner, that Ora began to scold once more, and again inquired what had produced such an extraordinary change?

"I can't account for it myself," I replied, "but a person has just arrived, whose looks seem to exercise an unaccountable influence over me. You can see him. He is there—standing near Cuthbert Spring."

"I can see nothing extraordinary about him," Ora replied, "except that he is very tall—and for a person of his years tolerably good-looking. Who is he?"

"I should think he must be Major Atherton, whom Cuthbert Spring proposed to bring with him."

"Oh, no doubt!" Ora cried. "I hope he will prove an agreeable acquaintance. But come! Exert yourself, do sir! Major Atherton, I perceive, is watching us! Let us show him that we can execute the dance with spirit."

Stimulated by her remarks, I shook off the sort of lethargy into which I had fallen, and acquitted myself so well, that I soon regained my merry partner's good opinion. At last the dance was over, and Ora then said, "Now let us go and take a nearer view of this mysterious individual. Upon my word," she whispered, as we approached him, "for an elderly gentleman he is remarkably good-looking. He has a distinguished bearing, and a very fine countenance."

Here we were greeted by Cuthbert Spring, who left his friend, and came towards us. After shaking hands with us, and paying Ora a few compliments in his usual gallant style, he congratulated me on the success of the fête—saying that the arrangements were excellent, and everybody looked happy.

"My friend, Major Atherton, is greatly pleased with the entertainment," he went on. "You must allow me to present the major to you, Mervyn, and to you, also, Miss Doveton."

I expressed the pleasure I should feel at the introduction in fitting terms, but inquired of Cuthbert whether he had known Major Atherton long, as I did not remember to have heard him mention him before.

"Perhaps not," Cuthbert rejoined, with an odd smile. "Atherton is one of my oldest friends, and I have a very great regard for him. He has been abroad for some years. But he shall speak for himself." So saying, he called to his friend, who immediately complied with the summons, and, stepping towards us, was formally presented to Ora and myself. He certainly did seem very proud—this Major Atherton—excessively proud, for he merely bowed—rather stiffly, too, I thought—on his introduction to me, and directed his conversation chiefly to Ora. But though annoyed by his haughtiness, I was resolved to make him talk to me, and I therefore remarked,

"I think I have seen you before, Major Atherton?"

"Indeed, sir! where?" he exclaimed, quickly.

"In Marston churchyard," I replied, "and under somewhat singular circumstances."

"No more of this now, I entreat you, sir," he cried, with sudden emotion. "I know to what you refer. But I did not suppose you had been there. I now recollect that some one came upon me unawares. You were the person I suppose. I will give you an explanation of the circumstance on a more fitting occasion."

"What is this?" Cuthbert Spring cried, quickly.

"Oh! nothing—nothing," I replied, not willing to press my inquiries further.

"Though you are unacquainted with Major Atherton, Mervyn," Mr. Spring said, after consulting his friend by a look, "I ought to tell you that he is an old friend of your family, and knew your mother extremely well."

"Did he?" I cried. "Then I understand it all, and require no further explanation. We must know each other better, since this is the case, Major Atherton."

"We must, sir," he answered. "Your mother was a most amiable person—far too good for him she married."

"Hold! major," I cried. "Praise one parent as much as you please, but say nothing against the other."

"I merely meant to imply that your father was not worthy of so much goodness," Major Atherton replied, with a grave smile, "and it is perfectly true. Nobody knows his unworthiness better than I do."

"Unworthiness is a term I do not like," I said, rather sharply; "neither do I quite recognise your right to judge of my father's conduct."

"I admire the feeling you exhibit," Major Atherton returned, with perfect calmness; "but, if I am correctly informed, you do not know your father. I do. I know him as well as I know myself; and I am satisfied that his first wife was far above his deserts. He thinks so himself—says so."

"That may be your opinion, and you are, of course, entitled to it," I rejoined; "but it is not necessary to depreciate my father in order to exalt my mother, and I really cannot allow such a course to be pursued."

"On my soul, you are a warm-hearted young fellow," Major Atherton cried. "I should not have thought you could entertain so much regard for a father whom you have never beheld, and who, by all accounts, doesn't appear to have done too much for you—eh, Cuthbert?"

"No," Mr. Spring replied, with a singular smile, "I can't say that I think my friend Colonel Clitheroe has done overmuch for his son."

"I have no complaint to make against him," I returned, "and you will allow that I am the person principally interested."

"No; I will do you the justice to say, Mervyn, that I never heard you utter a word against your father," Cuthbert Spring remarked.

"It is much to your credit, sir," Major Atherton said, addressing me. "Under such circumstances. I don't think I should have been equally contented. But Colonel Clitheroe has not been quite so much to blame as might appear——"

"I don't think he has been to blame at all," I interrupted; "and I must again observe, that these comments on my father's character are anything but agreeable to me."

"Whom are you talking of, gentlemen?" Old Hazy inquired, joining the group.

"Of Colonel Clitheroe, Mervyn's father," Mr. Spring answered. "The colonel, I must say, has a warm advocate in his son. It would afford him great pleasure, I am sure, if he knew how prompt Mervyn is to take his part."

"I am sure it would," Major Atherton rejoined. "Thus much I can say for Colonel Clitheroe—and I say it from personal knowledge—he takes great interest in his son. He fancied all was going smoothly with him, and that he had been adopted by Mrs. Mervyn."

"I have not troubled my father much with my affairs of late," I observed.

"There you were wrong—excuse my freedom in saying so," Major Atherton cried. "It was your duty to let your father know exactly how you were circumstanced. How can a father advise his son, or assist him, if kept in entire ignorance of his proceedings? It was your bounden duty, I repeat, to acquaint Colonel Clitheroe with all that has happened to you."

"Well, major, I admit the force of what you say," I replied, "but such remarks do not seem to come with entire propriety from a stranger."

"I am a stranger to you, sir," Major Atherton said; "but my intimacy with your father warrants me in speaking freely. Possessed, as I am, of his opinions—more than any one else—I may almost be considered as his representative here."

"In that light, I am willing to concede you perfect freedom of speech," I rejoined, "and I promise not to take offence at anything you may say."

A seasonable interruption was here offered, by Mr. Ponder coming up to announce that refreshments were ready, if we chose to partake of them, and we all proceeded to the table. On the way, Major Atherton was introduced to John Brideoake and Apphia, and soon fell into conversation with both of them. He seemed especially pleased with the latter, and took a place on the bench beside her, on sitting down to the collation. While we were engaged in discussing the good things, Peninnah and her daughter approached the table, and addressed themselves to Old Hazy.

"What an uncommonly pretty girl!" Cuthbert Spring cried, pointing to Rue. "Does she tell fortunes as well as her mother? If so, I should like to try her skill. Come hither, my dear," he cried. "Can you give me a glimpse into futurity?"

"To be sure I can, sir," she replied, stepping towards him. "You are a gay and a lucky gentleman, I can see. Love will never break your heart, sir."

"I should think not, indeed," Miss Hazilrigge exclaimed, glancing at her elderly admirer.

"Let me look at your hand, my merry gentleman," Rue continued, "and I'll tell you all about it." And as Cuthbert surrendered his palm to her inspection, she added, "You have been a gay deceiver in your time, as I said just now, sir, and have given many a fair lady a heartache."

"What's that I hear?" Miss Hazilrigge cried, turning scarlet.

"Take care!" Cuthbert Spring muttered. "Don't make mischief. You're on tender ground—hum!"

"The poor ladies themselves were to blame, and not you, sir," Rue went on. "You couldn't help it, you know, if they chose to pull caps for you."

"But you said he was a deceiver, young woman?" Miss Hazilrigge cried.

"I ought to have said, that it was the ladies that took him too much at his word, ma'am," Rue rejoined, "and thought he meant more than he really did—poor deluded creatures!—but the merry gentleman himself was too artful to be caught."

"I am afraid you give him a very bad character," Miss Hazilrigge remarked.

"Lor' bless you, no, ma'am. The merry gentleman has been a great admirer of our sex in his time, but he's less of a rover than he used to be, and will soon settle down quietly enough. He has fixed his affections on some one who will make him a vast deal happier than he has ever yet been as a bachelor. A country life will be his portion——"

"What's that I hear?" Miss Hazilrigge cried, eagerly.

"I was observing, ma'am, that a country life will be the merry gentleman's portion," Rue rejoined; "and fortunate it is for him that it will be so, for his days will be prolonged thereby."

"Dear heart a day!" Miss Hazilrigge exclaimed. "How very, very surprising, to be sure!"

"Bravo!" Cuthbert Spring exclaimed. "Never was truer fortune told. You deserve a piece of gold, my dear, for the talent you have displayed," he added, taking out his purse, and giving her a sovereign. "Now try your skill on the lady."

"Permit me, ma'am," Rue said, taking Miss Hazilrigge's plump hand. "You have had your trials, I see, ma'am. Things have gone counter more than once, and a match has been broken off only two days before it ought to have taken place."

"Dear me! aunt, is this true?" Ora cried. "I never heard of any such match."

"Nor I!" Cuthbert Spring added.

"The lady doesn't contradict me," Rue proceeded. "But it's very well the marriage didn't take place, for she would have been a widow now with ten children."

"A lucky escape, indeed!" Cuthbert Spring cried, with a forced laugh.

"Well, this is very extraordinary, I must say," Old Hazy cried, laughing heartily. (I half suspect he had given Rue a few hints in private.) "I won't mention names, but the gentleman to whom my sister was engaged is dead, and his widow has ten children."

General laughter followed this piece of information, and the merriment was not diminished when Rue said, "You won't die single, ma'am, that I can promise you. Ere six months are over, you'll have a wedding-ring on your finger."

"There, aunt!" Ora cried to the blushing spinster, "I hope you're satisfied now."

"Come, Atherton," Cuthbert Spring said to the major, "it is your turn. Display your hand to the girl, and let us see whether she can read your past and future life from its lines."

"I can read either," Rue rejoined. "The gentleman has only to choose."

"Keep to the past, then," Major Atherton said. "I don't desire to know the future."

Upon this the girl took his hand, and studied it carefully for a short space. At last, her features assumed an air of perplexity, and she called to Peninnah, "Look here, mother! Something puzzles me about this cross-line."

"It's not often you are puzzled," the elder gipsy replied, bending forward to examine the Major's palm. "Why, it's plain enough, that cross-line denotes a death. The gentleman has lost his wife. And look! here's another cross-line——"

"Enough! enough!" Major Atherton cried, snatching his hand hastily away. "I don't want to hear any more of this idle nonsense. You make a guess, and pretend you have hit upon the truth."

"At all events, you must admit that I have made a shrewd guess," Peninnah said.

"I admit nothing," Major Atherton cried, sternly. "The girl confessed her ignorance, and you are no better informed."

"I didn't choose to speak out," Rue said—"that was why I consulted my mother. But if you wish me to tell all I read," she added, with marked emphasis, "I will do so. But don't blame me afterwards."

"Poh! poh! you can tell nothing that I should care to have concealed," the major said, with affected indifference. But I could see that he was not altogether free from uneasiness.

"Let me whisper a word to you," Rue rejoined, bringing her lips close to the major's ear, and saying something to him in a low tone.

He started on hearing her remark, and could not conceal his annoyance. Cuthbert Spring seemed greatly surprised, and made a sign to his friend, which I could not understand.

"Do you wish me to tell the company what I have told you, sir?" Rue cried, with an air of triumph.

"On no account," Major Atherton rejoined, hastily; "not that there is anything in it—but—in short, I don't desire it—so here's a piece of gold," he added, taking out his purse, "to seal your lips."

"It will seal them effectually," she rejoined, dropping him a very graceful curtsey.

"Well, major," Old Hazy exclaimed, with a laugh, "you must own after this that there's more in chiromancy than you suspected. I myself am a firm believer in the art, and have a large collection of writers on the subject. I dare say this pretty lass never heard of Jean Indagine, Taisner, Cocles, or Romphiles."

"Never of one of them," Rue replied. "My mother was my sole instructress in the art of palmistry. She knows all the secrets of our people."

Meanwhile, dancing has been going on almost without interruption, and a fresh country dance being now about to be formed, Cuthbert Spring proposes that we shall all join it, and by way of setting us a good example, offers his hand to Miss Hazilrigge. The elderly spinster simpers a little, but she does not refuse him, and is led forth in triumph. Major Atherton prefers a similar request to Ora, and is equally successful. Apphia naturally falls to my share. Old Hazy has not danced for years, he says, but he won't remain idle on an occasion like the present, so he looks about for the prettiest partner he can find, and chooses Rue, who appears much flattered. John Bridecake looks on with a kindly smile—pleased that we all seem so happy. A right merry dance we have, for the performances of Cuthbert Spring and Miss Hazilrigge afford us infinite diversion. As they go down the middle and come back enchained in a rope of flowers, their appearance is so comical that it is next to impossible to help laughing. Ora puts no restraint upon her mirth, and even Major Atherton's stern features relax into a smile. Poor Miss Hazilrigge, who is rather stout, and wholly unaccustomed to such violent exercise, finds it a little too much for her, and as soon as she gets to the bottom of the dance, withdraws with her partner, to cool herself and recover her breath. Old Hazy astonishes everybody by his display of activity; and Mr. Ponder lifts up his hands in perfect amazement as he watches his master capering about—clapping his hands, calling out to the rustic lads and lasses by name, and bidding them bestir themselves, laughing, shouting, even singing. Rue dances exquisitely—it is quite a treat to behold her. As she takes my hand in the course of the dance, she slightly presses it, and whispers something, but I cannot catch what she says. From the direction of her glances I perceive that her mother's eye is upon her—and I am careful. The old woman watches her like a lynx. Encouraged by Old Hazy's example, and incited by his shouts and gesticulations, the various couples he comes near do their best to please him, and many are the vagaries in consequence. By the time, however, that the old gentleman gets to the bottom of the dance he has had enough of it, and, like his sister, retires to recruit. The dance, however, continues for some time longer, for the rustic couples have strong limbs and are not easily tired, but at last the musicians cease to play—being unable or unwilling to go on—and we come to a sudden stop. The lads and lasses then disperse about the green, and separating from the throng, I walk with Apphia towards the margin of the pool. Here we stand together for a few moments in silence. Words of tenderness rise to my lips, but I dare not give utterance to them. I cannot help, however, fixing an impassioned glance upon her, which proclaims my meaning as plainly as words could do. She makes no response, except a sigh. But what is this? John Bridecake comes towards us, bearing a letter, and, judging by his looks, he brings disagreeable intelligence.

"A special messenger has just arrived with a post-chaise, bringing this despatch from our mother," he said, giving Apphia the letter.

Scarcely able to repress her agitation, she hurriedly broke the seal, and after glancing at the contents of the missive, returned it to John.

"Dear Mrs. Mervyn has become suddenly worse," she said to me, "and desires to see me. My mother enjoins me to start without an instant's delay, if I hope to see her alive, and has sent a post-chaise for me. Oh! who would have expected this!" she exclaimed, bursting into tears.

"It is indeed sad and startling intelligence," I cried. "Mrs. Mervyn dying!—then all my hopes are at an end."

"What is this I hear?" Cuthbert Spring cried, hurrying up to us. "Did you not say that Mrs. Mervyn is dying?"

"A letter, this moment received from Mrs. Brideoake, announces the sad intelligence," I replied.

"The attack must be very sudden, then," Cuthbert Spring rejoined. "I saw Dr. Foam yesterday, and in reply to my inquiries about the poor lady, he told me she was going on tolerably well."

"I cannot refuse credit to my mother's statement," John Brideoake said. "Her words are these: 'A sudden and dangerous change has taken place in the dear invalid, and I fear she may not last many days—perhaps not many hours. She speaks much of you, and earnestly desires to behold you once again, ere her eyes are closed for ever; and if you have any affection left for her or for me, you will come to her on receipt of this, without a moment's delay. The messenger to whose care I entrust this note will bring a post-chaise for you. I confidently expect you ere night. Farewell!'"

"What if it be a device to get Apphia once more into her power?" I cried.

"It looks suspicious, I must own," Cuthbert Spring said. "And yet we may be wrong. Miss Brideoake cannot refuse to go."

"Certainly not," John replied.

"But she must not go unattended," I cried. "Some one must accompany her. I will ride by the side of the chaise, and escort her safely to the Anchorite's."

"Your kindness is unnecessary, Mervyn," John said. "I myself shall accompany her. We are both grieved to quit your pleasant fête so soon—but it cannot be helped. Come, Apphia, there must be no delay. Mervyn will excuse us, and explain our abrupt departure to our friends."

I promised to do so; and as I conducted Apphia to the post-chaise, I told her I should certainly ride over to Cottonborough that night, and present myself on the morrow at the Anchorite's.

"To what end?" she cried. "You will not be admitted."

"Oh! yes, I shall," I replied. "Comberbach will let me in, if he knows I am coming. Direct him to be at the garden-gate precisely at ten o'clock to-morrow morning. I shall be there. It is of the last importance to me to see my kind relative once more, and I trust, through your assistance, to accomplish the object."

"I will give you all the aid I can, Mervyn," she replied, "but I despair of success. Even if Mrs. Mervyn should be able to see you, my mother will oppose the interview. But come by all means, and I will see you if possible. If not, you will understand that I have failed in my endeavours to help you."

"To-morrow may decide our fate," I said.

"It may," she replied. "Our destiny is in Mrs. Mervyn's hands. A word from her might remove the bar to our happiness. And yet, I fear, the word will never be uttered."

There was a pause, after which Apphia said: "Strange, that gipsy woman told me I should be suddenly summoned hence—and should go! I didn't believe her at the moment—but it has come to pass, you see."

"Strange, indeed!" I replied, thoughtfully.

Little more passed between us, for though I tried to assume a hopeful confidence, I could not help secretly sharing Apphia's misgivings, and almost dreaded lest some fresh calamity might be at hand.

The messenger who had brought the post-chaise proved to be the ill-favoured Fabyan Lowe, and aware that this man was devoted to Mrs. Brideoake, and would report all he heard and saw to her, I was careful in bidding Apphia adieu to make no allusion to my expectation of seeing her again on the morrow. Brother and sister having got into the post-chaise, it drove off, the postilion being ordered to proceed in the first instance to Weverham, Apphia having some few preparations to make for the sudden journey.

I then returned to the green, but the fête no longer afforded me any amusement, and it was mainly owing to the untiring exertions of Miss Hazilrigge and her niece that it was brought to a satisfactory close. The gipsy women were still there, but I strove in vain to obtain a word in private with Rue. Her mother's vigilance was not to be baffled.

An hour before the fête broke up, I looked round for the pair again, and not seeing them, ascertained that they had just left. Ned Culcheth had also disappeared.

The fête concluded at eight o'clock. Many of my rustic guests of either sex would have liked it to be prolonged, I make no doubt, but I did not care to gratify their inclinations, and as soon as the more important guests had taken their departure, I withdrew, leaving it to Mr. Ponder to announce the close of the festivities. On a hint from him, delivered with his customary politeness, the company began to disperse immediately, and in less than an hour the green was as quiet as it had been on the previous evening, all traces of the entertainment having disappeared.

I must not omit to mention that, in taking leave of me, Major Atherton said very kindly, that he should be delighted to be of service to me, if I would show him how—and he trusted I would consider him in the light of an old friend: "In that character, let me observe," he said, "that I think Apphia Brideoake a very charming girl—worthy of a life's devotion—and I sincerely hope you may obtain her hand."

I thanked him heartily for his friendly offers and good wishes, and we parted.

About nine o'clock on that same night I mounted my horse, and started on my expedition to Cottonborough, where I hoped to arrive by midnight. The few things I took with me were placed in my saddle-bags. Had I been free from anxiety, I should have greatly enjoyed my ride. But black care followed me like a shadow, and would not be dismissed. The night was fine and not dark, for though the moon was invisible, the deep vault was without a cloud, and thickly studded with stars. The roads were in good order, and I trotted on at a brisk pace, and almost without stoppage, until I neared Dunton Park.

Arrived at the foot of the hill which is crowned by those lordly woods, I drew in the rein, and was proceeding leisurely along, when I heard the clatter of horse's hoofs, and soon afterwards perceived a man galloping towards me. Something must have caught the animal's foot, for he suddenly stumbled and threw his rider. Fearing mischief might have occurred, I rode forward, but ere I got to the spot, the man had regained his legs, and remounted his horse. I expressed a hope that he was not hurt, but he answered in a most uncourteous tone, "What is that to you, sir? Go on your way."

It was Malpas Sale. My enemy had already recognised me. After addressing me in the rude manner I have described, he would have ridden off, but I caught hold of his rein, and forcibly detained him.

"Stay!" I thundered. "Chance has brought us together, and we do not part till you have rendered me an account of your villanous proceedings."

"This language to me, sir!" he cried, foaming with rage. "You must be drunk, or mad. Leave go the rein at once—or——"

"You shall not stir, I tell you," I rejoined, in a determined tone, "till you have rendered me an account of your infamous transactions with Simon Pownall. I know the errand on which you are come from Windsor. It is to buy the will from Pownall—the will constituting me heir to our uncle's property."

"Who told you this?" he demanded.

"No matter whence my information is derived," I rejoined—"it is correct. But I will take such steps as will effectually stop your nefarious design."

"Take any steps you please, sir," he rejoined, scornfully. "I defy you."

"You are over-confident, methinks, with such a peril as this hanging over your head," I remarked.

"There is no peril hanging over my head," he replied, with contemptuous audacity. "My position is perfectly secure, and it is not in your power, or in the power of any living person, to shake it. Mark what I say, and ponder upon it. I am beyond dispute—beyond dispute, I repeat, sir—heir to our uncle Mobberley's property."

And he again laughed defiantly.

"Then you would give me to understand that the nefarious transaction has been completed," I cried—"that you have obtained possession of the will which was fraudulently purloined by Simon Pownall. Is it so? Speak out, without equivocation."

"I *will* speak—if only to annihilate your hopes," he rejoined. "No witnesses are present, so it matters not what passes between us. Learn then, to your confusion, that the precious document, on which your castles in the air have been built, is destroyed—destroyed, I say. All evidence is for ever removed. How say you now, sir? Will the property be yours or mine?—ha! ha!"

My hold of the rein involuntarily relaxed, and, finding himself free, he awaited no reply, but striking his horse sharply with the whip, galloped off, leaving me utterly confounded.

CHAPTER V.

IN WHICH I APPEAR IN A NEW CHARACTER.

SOME minutes elapsed before I recovered from the stupefaction into which I had been thrown by Malpas's startling declaration; and by this time the sound of his horse's hoofs had died away in the distance. I did not attempt to follow him, but while pursuing my journey towards Cottonborough, I set myself deliberately to examine the probability of his astounding statement. Little inclined as I was to credit it, I could not but fear that it might be correct. A falsehood of such magnitude could scarcely have been advanced without premeditation, and with such unparalleled audacity. Neither, unless he had felt perfectly secure, would he have ventured to defy me so insolently. No, no! he must have obtained possession of the will, and have destroyed it, as he had affirmed.

And yet, on the other hand, it was difficult to conceive how the bargain had been so expeditiously concluded between him and the rapacious scoundrels with whom he must have had to deal. How had their demands been satisfied? Pownall had declared in my hearing that he was resolved to have a large sum, and his confederates would be little less extortionate. Malpas was not overstocked with money. Rather the reverse, I fancied. How, at a moment's notice, on his arrival from Windsor, had he managed to raise the funds necessary to complete the iniquitous transaction? Promises to pay, written or otherwise, were not likely to serve his turn with crafty rascals like Pownall and his associates. It must be cash down with them. Since this was certain, how was the money procured?

There was another view of the case. The robber might himself have been plundered. Pownall might have been tricked out of his expected gains. Phaleg and his son had plotted to steal the will, and might have succeeded in their design. But admitting this latter supposition to be the true one, the difficulty of the purchase-money was not removed. Sold the will must have been by Pownall or the gipsies: in either case it must have been well paid for. Again, the question arose—where did the money come from?

The answer must be given by Malpas. His enforced reply must needs throw some light upon the mysterious affair, and lead very probably to his detection. If it could be proved that he had borrowed a large sum at this particular juncture, he must either produce the money, or show that it had been lawfully expended. Again, his accomplices would find it difficult to conceal their spoil. Through them the dark plot might be unravelled. Pownall's meditated flight to America must be prevented, and the gipsies be placed under the surveillance of the police.

Meditations, such as these, occupied me during my ride to Cottonborough. Five miles off, the town became distinguishable through the darkness by its many-twinkling lights. As I advanced, these lights increased in number and brilliancy, until I began to fancy there must be a general illumination in the town. But it was only the cotton-mills lighted up for night-work. Where toil ceases not during the twenty-four hours, gas cannot be stinted, and it is largely consumed in the Cottonborough factories. The huge, ugly fabrics glistened like fairy palaces. But it was with more sorrow than admiration that I regarded them as I rode past.

I put up at the Palace Inn that night, as was my wont.

Next morning, at ten o'clock precisely, as I had appointed with Apphia, I was in waiting near the garden-gate of the Anchorite's. I did not ring the bell, or give any intimation of my arrival, but patiently awaited the appearance of Mr. Comberbach. At last he came. The gate was partly opened, and the butler, peeping out, beckoned me to him. My first inquiries were whether any improvement had taken place in Mrs. Mervyn's health.

"She is rayther better, thankee, sir, but still dangerously ill," Mr. Comberbach replied. "Yesterday, we all of us thought the poor dear lady was going to pop off the shelf altogether; but she has rallied a little since then. The sight of dear Miss Apphia did her a world of good, and she slept tolerably well last night, and awoke somewhat easier this morning."

"I must see her, Comberbach," I cried. "I know you can manage to get me into her room, if you choose."

"You give me credit for a great deal more power than I possess," he replied. "It would have been an easy matter once, but now your humble servant is of small account at the Anchorite's. However, a plan has occurred to me, or rayther, I should say, it was suggested by Molly Bailey—for accomplishing the desired object. But it's very hazardous—very hazardous, indeed, sir."

"I care not. I will adopt it," I exclaimed.

"You mistake me, sir," he replied. "I mean that the plan is hazardous to me and Molly Bailey, and may occasion the loss of our places."

"I should be truly sorry for such a result as that," I said. "But you must not run so great a risk for nothing. Divide that with Molly Bailey." And I placed a five pound note in his hands.

"Excessively obleeged to you, sir, I'm sure," he replied, bowing. "Molly and I always say you are a very generous young gentleman, and deserve support. I'll try and get you into the room. But you must be extremely cautious, and not say a word, if you can help it, while Mrs. B. is by. Molly Bailey will use her best endeavours to get her out of the room for a short time, so as to give you an opportunity of saying a word to our poor dear lady."

"That is all I require, Comberbach," I cried. "And you and Molly may depend upon my gratitude if I can set matters right."

"Well, I hope you may, sir; but I'm not remarkably sanguine," he replied, shaking his head. "Mind, if you're discovered, Mrs. B. must never learn who let you in."

"She shan't learn it from me, you may depend, Comberbach," I replied.

Satisfied with this assurance, he allowed me to pass through the gate, and directed me to make my way through a side walk, which was screened by a shrubbery, to the back of the house; begging me not to leave the covert of the trees until I heard him cough. I complied with his instructions, and was soon summoned from my place of concealment by the signal, when I perceived him standing at an open door. In another moment I was in his pantry.

"And now the plan, Comberbach!" I cried. "What is it?"

"I don't know that you'll altogether approve of it, sir," he replied. "It's Molly Bailey's idea, not mine. You will have to personate Captain Sale."

"Personate him!" I exclaimed, in disgust. "Ridiculous! I shall do nothing of the sort."

"I knew you would object, sir," he replied; "but there's no help. The part must be adopted, or your errand here will be fruitless. Mrs. B. has received a letter from the captain—so Molly Bailey tells me—announcing that he will be here to-day. Consequently Mrs. B. won't be surprised by your appearance."

"Nonsense, man, she will instantly recognise me," I cried, hastily.

"I don't think so, sir," he answered. "My poor dear lady's chamber is darkened, and Mrs. B. generally sits at the further side of the bed—so if you are careful you won't be detected. Luckily, Captain Sale left a suit of clothes behind when he was last here. If you will condescend to put them on, you'll look just like him."

And as he spoke, he opened a press, and took out a braided, military-looking frock-coat, and some other habiliments, which I recognised as belonging to Malpas.

"Here you are, sir!" he cried. "Put on this coat and you'll be the captain himself. Doctor Sale wouldn't know the difference —though he might think his son improved. I'll remain outside while you make the change. Call me when you're ready."

With this he left me, closing the door after him.

My dislike to the part I was about to assume was overcome by the results that might possibly ensue from the scheme; and I felt that if I missed this opportunity of gaining admittance to Mrs. Mervyn, another might not occur. Hastily throwing off my attire, I proceeded to put on the dress laid out for me, and in a few minutes the metamorphosis was complete. Malpas being about my height, and nearly of the same make, his apparel fitted me exactly, and when Mr. Comberbach shortly afterwards came in, he exclaimed, with a laugh, "You'll do, sir! If I had met you as you are now, I should have thought you were Captain Sale. Now you must take the trouble to go back to the garden-gate by the same way you came here—then ring the bell—and I'll be with you in a trice. This will prevent any suspicion on the part of Fabyan Lowe, or of Mrs. B. herself, if she should happen to see you. Here, take the captain's foraging cap, sir, and keep your handkerchief to your face as you come towards the house."

Obeying his instructions to the letter, I returned to the garden-gate, and rang a lusty peal, as if I had just arrived. Mr. Comberbach almost instantly answered the summons, and smiled approval. As he preceded me along the broad gravel-walk, I kept my handkerchief to my face, and adopted, as nearly as I could, the airy gait of Malpas. As we approached the house, Fabyan Lowe presented himself, but, without giving the prying rascal time to address me, the butler hurried forward, and bade him take word to Mrs. Mervyn that Captain Sale had arrived. The ill-favoured man-servant, evidently suspecting nothing, departed on his errand without delay, and Mr. Comberbach ushered me up-stairs to the library, where he left me. I was under great apprehension lest Mrs. Bridcoake might come forth to speak to me; and my relief was proportionate when, as the inner door opened, instead of the Gorgon visage I apprehended, I beheld the good-humoured countenance of Molly Bailey.

"Please to step this way, Captain Sale," Molly said, smiling significantly at me. "Mrs. Mervyn will see you, sir. Thank goodness, she is better this morning—much better! Mrs. Bridcoake is with her, and Miss Apphia. This way, captain."

Summoning up all my resolution, I followed her with gentle tread. Crossing a passage, she paused before a partly-open door, which I knew to be that of Mrs. Mervyn's chamber, and said, in a tone calculated to be heard by those within, "Make as little noise as you can, captain, and speak very low. My missis is easily disturbed."

With this she pushed the door gently open, and I stepped softly into the sick lady's chamber.

CHAPTER VI.

SHOWING WHAT SUCCESS ATTENDED THE STRATAGEM.

As I had been apprised by the butler, the apartment was so much darkened that the chances were against my immediate detection. The window-curtains were closely drawn, and the only light afforded was from a small shaded lamp, placed on the table in a remote corner of the room, near to which Mrs. Bridcoake was seated.

Keeping out of the influence of this lamp, I gently approached the poor sufferer, who was propped up on her couch by pillows. She looked very feeble and attenuated, but held out her hand kindly as I drew near. I bent over her, as well to hide my emotion as to conceal my features from Mrs. Brideoake, and in a low tone expressed my satisfaction at finding her somewhat better. Apphia had been seated near her, but moved away on my entrance, supposing me to be Malpas.

"I am thankful you are come, Malpas," she said, feebly. "I much desired to speak with you relative to your engagement with this dear girl."

"What of it, madam?" I inquired, in a low tone, trembling with emotion.

"Answer me, Malpas," she said. "Are you still in the same mind? Do you really wish the contract to be fulfilled?"

"Why make these strange inquiries, dear Mrs. Mervyn?" Mrs. Brideoake said, rising from her seat, and approaching the foot of the bed. "No change, I am convinced, can have taken place in Malpas's sentiments towards my daughter; neither can he desire to break the solemn engagement into which he has entered with her. Why should you suppose so?"

"Do not be cross with me," Mrs. Mervyn returned. "I only want an assurance from the young people that they continue attached to each other."

"Take the assurance from me, dear madam," Mrs. Brideoake said. "They do."

Apphia uttered an exclamation of dissent, which caught the ears of the sick lady.

"What is that you say, child?" she cried, quickly. "Have you any objection to make? If so, speak! You know how anxious I am for your happiness."

"She has none, madam—she has none," Mrs. Brideoake rejoined, glancing menacingly at her daughter.

"Come hither, my dear," Mrs. Mervyn cried. And as Apphia timidly approached, she turned towards her, and said, "I may not be long spared to you, and indeed I had begun to fear I should never behold you again; but my prayers have been granted, and I have you beside me once more. During my illness something has whispered to me that you are unhappy, and repent of your engagement with Malpas. If it be so, it is not too late to retreat. Do not let any consideration prevent you from avowing the truth."

"You distress me, and you distress Apphia by these doubts, my dear Mrs. Mervyn," Mrs. Brideoake hastily interposed. "My daughter is not so fickle as you imagine her; and as to retreating from her engagement, you may rest perfectly satisfied she will never do anything of the sort. She will not venture to contradict me, I am sure," she added, gazing steadfastly at Apphia.

"But speak, my dear child—speak!" Mrs. Mervyn cried. "Let me have the answer I require from your own lips. Do you really love this young man?"

Thus exhorted, Apphia might have confessed the real nature of her sentiments in regard to Malpas; but, as I looked up at the moment, our eyes met, and she recognised me.

"Yes, madam, I really do love him," she said.

Mrs. Brideoake, who had doubtless expected a very different response, appeared surprised and greatly relieved.

"I hope you are convinced now, my dear Mrs. Mervyn," she said, "though I do not see why my assertion should have been doubted."

"But what says the young gentleman?" Mrs. Mervyn cried. "Surely, there is no drawing back on his part?"

"None whatever, dear Mrs. Mervyn," Apphia exclaimed, eagerly. "I will answer for him."

Mrs. Brideoake looked still more astonished, and smiled approvingly on her daughter.

"Well, my dears," Mrs. Mervyn said, "I am truly glad to find that my misgivings have been groundless. Had it been otherwise, I meant to——but it is scarcely worth while now to state what my intentions were."

"Not in the least necessary, my dear madam," Mrs. Brideoake said.

"Oh! do pray let me hear them?" Apphia cried.

Her mother looked at her, and slightly frowned.

"Well, then, since you desire it so much, I will tell you," Mrs. Mervyn said: "I had fully determined to revoke a certain deed of settlement which I had made in your favour, but which ties you to marry one particular person—namely, him to whom you are engaged, Malpas Sale. The condition was made at your mother's request, and I had begun to fear, as I have just stated, that I had done wrong in making it; but you have now set my mind entirely at rest on that score."

"And you had resolved to set me free, my dear Mrs. Mervyn?" she exclaimed, joyfully. "How shall I thank you?"

"But you do not want to be set free, my dear?" Mrs. Mervyn cried, in surprise. "If you retain your regard for Malpas, and mean to fulfil your engagement with him, what need of any change in the conditions? I would not fetter your inclinations, but since your choice is made, where can be the harm of allowing the restriction to continue?"

"It is a very proper restriction," Mrs. Brideoake cried, "and I would not have it removed on any account."

"I am perfectly aware of your feeling on the subject, my dear madam," Mrs. Mervyn said, "and I yielded to it at the time, as you know, though I thought the condition imposed upon your daughter rather hard. You are quite content with what I have done, my dear?" she added to Apphia.

I could not have helped giving utterance to the feelings that overpowered me, if Apphia had not spoken.

"Quite content, dear madam," she replied, in a low tone.

"And you?" Mrs. Mervyn said, addressing me.

"How can he be otherwise than content with you, madam, since you have secured him a rich wife?" Mrs. Brideoake said.

At this moment Molly Bailey gently entered the room, and signified to Mrs. Brideoake that she was wanted. After delivering this message, she retired, directing an expressive glance at me. Mrs. Brideoake followed her almost immediately, recommending the dear invalid to our attention during her absence.

Apphia and I were thus left alone with Mrs. Mervyn. The moment I had so anxiously desired was come. Yet how to profit by it? The utmost caution was necessary, for I knew that a sudden shock might be fatal to the poor lady.

"Have you anything further to say to me, my love?" Mrs. Mervyn inquired kindly of Apphia.

"Yes, madam, I have something of importance to say to you," Apphia replied, "which I did not like to mention while my mother was by. I am sure you will pardon me when you know all—but I wish that deed of settlement, which you referred to just now, could be burnt."

"You wish it burnt, my dear!—why so, pray?" Mrs. Mervyn demanded.

"Because — oh! forgive me, dear Mrs. Mervyn," Apphia exclaimed—"because I never can comply with its conditions. I never can marry Malpas Sale."

"I am lost in astonishment! You say this to his face? What must he think of you?"

"Compose yourself, my dear madam, and you shall know all," Apphia rejoined. "A deception has been practised upon you, but I trust you will think it venial. Whom do you imagine is near you?"

"Is it not Malpas Sale?" Mrs. Mervyn cried, trembling.

"It is Mervyn Clitheroe, who has put on this disguise in order to approach you," Apphia said. "It is on his account that I wish the settlement to be committed to the flames."

"I see it all now," Mrs. Mervyn rejoined, faintly. "I thought his conduct strange. Give me the scent-bottle quickly, or I shall faint."

"You forgive me, my dear Mrs. Mervyn, for the stratagem I have practised, but I had no other means of gaining access to you," I cried.

"Yes—yes—I forgive you," she answered, pressing my hand gently.

A crisis in my fate had arrived. Oh! how I dreaded lest Mrs. Brideoake should return before the needful explanation could take place. Mrs. Mervyn herself seemed to feel equal uneasiness, for she said in a low tone to Apphia, "My dear, is your mother coming back soon? I hope not—I hope not."

"Are you able to listen to me, dear Mrs. Mervyn?" I asked. Again she pressed my hand gently, and I went on : " Before saying aught of myself, let me tell you how entirely deceived you are in regard to Malpas Sale. He is not what you suppose him. I will not characterise him as strongly as I ought for fear of shocking you;

neither will I pain you by a detail of his evil doings—but let me say in a word that he is utterly unworthy of Apphia."

"Then he shall never have her," Mrs. Mervyn cried. "It will be a difficult task to persuade Mrs. Brideoake that he is as bad as you represent him, and in my present state I cannot attempt it. But at any rate, the match shall not take place."

"Oh! thank you, madam, for that promise!" Apphia cried, with a look of inexpressible gratitude.

"Why did you not appeal to me before, my dear?" Mrs. Mervyn replied, in a tone of tender reproach. "You know that my chief desire is to contribute to your future happiness."

"I did not dare to do so, madam."

"Alas! alas!" the poor lady exclaimed, with a look of great distress, mingled with self-reproach, "I have been much to blame. I ought to have seen with my own eyes, and not with the eyes of others. But you forgive me I am sure. And you too, my dear Mervyn," she added to me, "I fear I have done you great injustice."

"You have done me injustice only if you have supposed me wanting in gratitude and affection to you, madam," I replied. "But you make ample amends by your present kindness."

"I will make all the amends I can for the error I have unintentionally committed," she said. "Tell me what you would have me do, my dear," she added to Apphia.

"The greatest favour you can confer upon me, dear Mrs. Mervyn, will be to destroy that deed of settlement," Apphia said.

"I will do something better than that," the kind lady replied. "I won't destroy it, but I will substitute another name for that of Malpas Sale, and make it imperative upon you to marry the person I shall designate. You understand me, I see. Nay, no thanks. I don't know what your mother will say to me. But I must bear the brunt of her displeasure as well as I can. It shall be done at once. The deed is in yonder closet. Fetch it me, Apphia, and I will make the needful alteration before Mrs. Brideoake returns."

"Why should you heed her, dear Mrs. Mervyn?" I cried. "If you have resolved to perform this generous action, she cannot prevent you, and she must be made aware of it sooner or later."

"That's true," the kind lady replied; "but I would rather she didn't know it just now. We should have a frightful scene. But we are losing time in talking. Where have I put my keys?"

"They are usually placed under your pillow," Apphia observed, searching for them as she spoke. "Yes, here is the black silk bag containing them."

"And here is the key of the closet," Mrs. Mervyn said, giving it to her. "You will find the deed in the little case of drawers with some other papers—the third drawer from the top, I think." And as Apphia flew to execute her orders, the good lady said to me, "There are writing materials on that table, Mervyn—bring me a pen. And draw back the curtains and let some light into the room, that we may see what we are about."

I hastened to obey her, praying internally that Mrs. Brideoake might not arrive to interrupt us. After drawing back the window-curtains as directed, I was proceeding to take up the other articles she required, when Apphia called out from the closet that she had opened all the drawers, but could not discover the deed.

"Not discover it!" Mrs. Mervyn cried. "It must be there. Search more carefully, child. I am sure I put it in the third drawer."

"Perhaps this may be it," Apphia cried, coming forth with a packet tied with red tape in her hand. "But it does not seem to relate to me."

"Yes, yes—that's it!" Mrs. Mervyn cried, eagerly. "Give it me directly, my dear. There's no occasion for you to read it."

And so eager was she to obtain possession of the packet, that she leaned forward and almost snatched it from Apphia. She then proceeded to untie the tape, and, taking out the deed, motioned us to stand aside, while she examined it in order to find out the place where the alteration in the name ought to be made. Having succeeded in her object, she bade me give her the pen, and she had scarcely taken it from me, when the door was gently opened, and Mrs. Brideoake entered, followed by Dr. Foam. The pen dropped from the poor lady's grasp, and she sank back, swooning, upon the pillow.

CHAPTER VII.

I AM WORSTED, AND DRIVEN INGLORIOUSLY FROM THE FIELD.

FULL light being now admitted into the room, Mrs. Brideoake at once recognised me. Her surprise and consternation were so great that she started back, and nearly upset Doctor Foam, who was close behind her. The spectacle, however, presented by poor Mrs. Mervyn in her fainting condition saved me from the torrent of her wrath which must otherwise have fallen upon my devoted head.

"What has happened?" Mrs. Brideoake cried, rushing towards the bed. "You have killed the poor lady between you. Ha!" she exclaimed, noticing the deed of settlement, as it had fallen from Mrs. Mervyn's grasp, "I see what you have been about. Cunning dissemblers as you both are, you have failed in accomplishing your artful design. Henceforth, this shall remain in my keeping."

And she snatched up the deed as she spoke.

By this time Doctor Foam had come up to the bed, and looking at Mrs. Brideoake in a manner that showed he would not be disobeyed, he said, "I insist upon your giving up that document to me, madam——"

"But, doctor——" she cried, as if disposed to resist him.

"I will have it," he continued; "and as opposition will be useless, you had better yield with a good grace, and not force me to take it from you. Nay, madam," he added, as he picked up the deed, which she tossed towards him, and put it into his pocket, "your anger is wasted on me. I am simply discharging my duty to my dear patient. It is evident that she intended to make some alteration in this document; but sudden faintness must have prevented the execution of her design."

"It is fortunate that it did so," Mrs. Brideoake returned. "Advantage has been taken of my poor friend's enfeebled state to endeavour to make her annul her own deliberate act; but luckily the scheme, however well contrived, has failed."

"That may be so, or it may not, for I won't stop to discuss the matter with you now, madam," Doctor Foam rejoined. "On my dear patient's restoration to sensibility I shall deliver the deed to her, and it will then be for her to do with it as she pleases."

"Very proper indeed, doctor," Mrs. Brideoake sneered; "but you will find that while I am by to counsel her, dear Mrs. Mervyn will never commit such an error as to introduce Mr. Mervyn Clitheroe's name into that deed of settlement. For that was the object aimed at I am persuaded," she continued, glancing irefully at me— "that was what brought Mr. Clitheroe here—in this disguise. What must the nature of the design be when such artifices as this are resorted to? What must Mr. Clitheroe's notions of gentlemanlike conduct be when he can put on the very attire of the person whom he is seeking clandestinely to supersede? I blush to think that my daughter should have abetted his base scheme—but it is enough that it has failed."

"No more of this intemperate language, madam," Doctor Foam said; "whether Mr. Clitheroe is to blame or not—whether your daughter has acted properly or the reverse—cannot be discussed now. If you have the regard you profess for Mrs. Mervyn, you will hold your tongue, and assist me to revive her, but if you attempt any further violence, I tell you plainly, madam, I shall order you out of the room."

"This to me, Doctor Foam?" the incensed lady cried.

"Bah!" cried the doctor, snapping his fingers. "Sit down on that chair and calm yourself. Throw the window wide open, Mervyn, and let us have plenty of fresh air. And do you, Apphia, let our patient inhale the spirits of hartshorn while I bathe her temples. We shall bring her round presently. I knew it!" he exclaimed, after a short interval, during which he and Apphia continued unremitting in their efforts, "she revives."

Heaving a deep sigh, Mrs. Mervyn opened her eyes, and looking at Apphia, said, in a low tone, "Where is he?—where is my boy?"

"I am here, madam," I replied, advancing towards the bed.

"Ah! yes, I see you, my dear," she cried, in the kindest tone imaginable. "You shall both be made happy. I shall never live to see you united, but united you shall be. I have done all you desire, have I not? I have changed the name in the deed of settlement. It only now remains to obtain your mother's consent to the marriage, and I am sure she will not refuse."

"You are mistaken, Mrs. Mervyn," Mrs. Brideoake said, rising from her seat. "I *do* refuse—peremptorily refuse my consent. You are mistaken, also, in supposing that you have made any change in the settlement. Happily, you have not done Malpas Sale the great injustice of superseding him for an unworthy rival. Neither, if I have any influence with you, will you do so. Do not listen to the false representations of this designing young man, but attend to me. Naturally I must have my daughter's welfare and happiness at heart, but I should consult neither the one nor the other if I gave her to Mervyn Clitheroe. If after this Apphia marries him, she will marry in opposition to my wishes and injunctions, and will violate her solemn promise to me."

"What is this I hear?" Mrs. Mervyn cried. "Have you given a promise to your mother not to marry without her consent, Apphia?"

"Alas! madam, I have," she replied.

"Oh! this is truly unfortunate!—truly unfortunate!" the poor lady groaned, sinking back upon the pillow.

Her looks frightened Doctor Foam so much that he hurried to the table for some fresh restoratives, saying to Mrs. Brideoake, as he passed her, "You see what mischief you have done, madam. Will nothing keep you quiet? You will compel me to put my threats into execution."

"Do as you please, Doctor Foam," she rejoined. "On you will rest the responsibility of any outrage. Force only shall make me leave the room while this young man remains in it."

"Zounds, madam! you are enough to make one forget the respect due to your sex and your station," Doctor Foam cried. "I won't answer for the consequences if my dear patient is further excited. There is no help for it, Mervyn," he added to me, "go you must." And as he led me towards the door, he whispered, "But don't leave the house. Stay in the library. I will join you there anon."

I glanced towards the bed, and saw Mrs. Mervyn still almost inanimate, with Apphia tending her. I glanced towards Mrs. Brideoake, who had resumed her seat with a look of exultation at my defeat. She pointed to the door, and I felt half inclined to mortify her by remaining, but an impatient gesture from Doctor Foam changed my design, and made me quit the room.

Never, alas! to see my dear friend and benefactress again.

CHAPTER VIII.

MR. COMBERBACH HAS GLOOMY FOREBODINGS.

ANXIOUS to get rid of the hateful attire in which I was disguised without a moment's loss of time, on entering the library I rang the bell, and the summons being answered by Comberbach, I explained my wishes to him, and he conducted me to a dressing-room, where he said he had placed my apparel. The change of habiliments was speedily effected, and as I issued from the dressing-room, very much more at my ease, I encountered the butler, who now inquired how I had prospered in my interview with his mistress.

"I trust Mrs. B. didn't find you out, sir?" he said. "If so, there'll be a pretty kettle of fish!"

I was obliged to confess that the stratagem had been discovered, but I consoled the terrified butler by saying that I felt sure Mrs. Brideoake would not visit her anger upon him, as she had too much upon her mind just now.

"I hope it may prove so," he rejoined; "but you don't know what Mrs. B. is like when she's really put out of temper. Oh! Mr. Mervyn," he added, with a groan, "what a change there is in this house to be sure, sir. It hasn't been like the same place since that woman set foot in it; and instead of getting better, things are likely to get worse. We shan't have our dear missis long, and when she's gone, what's to become of me and Molly Bailey? We can't live with Mrs. B., you know. But it will be a sore trial to both of us to leave the old place where we have dwelt so long."

"Most sincerely do I hope, on all accounts, that you won't be obliged to leave it, Comberbach," I said.

"It will be a sad day, indeed, for us, when Mrs. B. is undisputed missis of this house, Mr. Mervyn," the butler continued, sighing dismally.

"Why do you entertain that notion, Comberbach?" I asked. "Even if you should unhappily lose your dear mistress, it doesn't follow that she will be succeeded by Mrs. Brideoake."

"It follows as naturally as night follows day," he rejoined. "However much things may be kept secret, servants generally have an inkling as to what's going on; and I have tolerably correct information, that if Mrs. B. survives my dear missis, the Anchorite's, and all belonging to it, will be hers."

"You don't say so, Comberbach?" I cried, staring at him.

"Yes I do say it, sir, and I'll stand by it," he replied, confidently.

"Not before Mrs. Brideoake," I rejoined. "What can be the cause of the extraordinary influence that this lady has acquired over your mistress, Comberbach?"

"Don't question me on that subject, sir," he rejoined, in alarm. "I daren't answer you. I wish with all my heart she had never come near the place! It would have been better for my missis—better for you—better for me and Molly Bailey—better for everybody—except herself. Stay, sir! You are not going back to the library?" he added, noticing that I was proceeding in that direction.

"Yes I am," I replied. "No further harm can be done by my staying here, since Mrs. Brideoake is aware that I am in the house."

The butler evidently would have preferred my immediate departure, but he raised no further objection, and I entered the library and sat down. Nearly half an hour elapsed before Dr. Foam made his appearance, and I drew an unfavourable augury from his extremely serious looks.

"Mrs. Mervyn is worse, I fear, doctor?" I said.

"I am sorry to tell you she is," he replied. "I have only quitted her for a moment to speak to you. Go to my house, and remain there till I return. I have no time now to enter upon a subject which I desire to mention to you."

"Can I not see Mrs. Mervyn again?"

"Not to-day," he replied. "It will be useless to wait here with any such expectation. To-morrow, perhaps——but I can answer for nothing. I have sent for Mrs. Mervyn's professional adviser, Mr. Tester. The poor lady contemplates some new arrangements in regard to the disposition of her property, and they must be made without delay."

"Then you think danger is imminent?" I said.

"Nothing must be neglected," he replied, equivocally. "As to your seeing Mrs. Mervyn again to-day, it is out of the question. Until this matter of business is settled I do not wish her to be disturbed. Besides, the Sales are expected here immediately, and it may be disagreeable to you to meet them. You will find a friend at my house whom you will be pleased to meet, and I shall expect to see you both on my return. Good-by, for the present."

With this he left me, and as it appeared certain that I should gain nothing by remaining longer where I was, but in all probability might expose myself to annoyance, I acted upon his advice, and went down stairs at once, with the intention of quitting the house.

I found Mr. Comberbach in the hall, in a very despondent state indeed. Molly Bailey had brought word that his mistress was worse. Fabyan Lowe had been sent off in haste for Mr. Tester—a proof to Comberbach that the doctor thought her end approaching. "Heaven grant she means to make a change in her will!" the butler cried; "and if so, I hope the lawyer won't be too late. I wish I was permitted to advise her. I know who should have the largest share of her property—and who the least." In taking leave of him, I told him I should be there again on the morrow; on which he answered, in a very doleful tone, "All will be over before that, I fear, sir."

On arriving at Cottonborough, I repaired at once to Dr. Foam's residence, which was in the centre of the town. After explaining my business to the servant, he told me that another gentleman was waiting for the doctor, and ushering me into the room where this person was, I found, to my great surprise, that it was no other than John Brideoake.

CHAPTER IX.

IN WHICH JOHN BRIDEOAKE IS MADE ACQUAINTED WITH HIS FAMILY HISTORY BY DOCTOR FOAM.

JOHN informed me that he had seen Doctor Foam on the previous evening, after taking Apphia to the Anchorite's, and the worthy physician had urged him so strongly to remain over the following day, alleging that he had an important communication to make to him, that he could not refuse; and he had now come to keep his appointment with the doctor.

"I am glad you stayed, on all accounts, John," I said. "Mrs. Mervyn is in an exceedingly critical state, and it may be necessary for you to consider what must be done, under such such circumstances, with Apphia."

And I then proceeded to relate to him all that had occurred at the Anchorite's that morning. He listened to me with great attention, and expressed infinite concern that Mrs. Mervyn had been unable to carry out her kind intentions.

We were still occupied with this subject when Doctor Foam made his appearance. He at once relieved my anxiety respecting Mrs. Mervyn, by stating that she was somewhat better, and hoped that all immediate danger was over. However, he should see her again in a few hours, he said, and should then be better able to judge Then turning to John Brideoake, he observed,

"I will now explain my object in begging you to come to me this morning. I am glad that Mervyn Clitheroe is also present, as it is desirable he should hear what I have to communicate. Be seated, I beg of you, for I have much to say. You are little acquainted with your family history, I think?—indeed, I know you are not."

"You are right, sir, I am entirely unacquainted with it," John replied. "My mother has kept me completely in the dark both as to my father's position in the world and her own. As I have heretofore intimated to Mervyn, I am by no means satisfied that I am really entitled to the very name I bear."

Dr. Foam smiled.

"The time is come when you must be let into the secret," he said; "and though I have no authority from your mother for making the disclosure, I am in no way bound to withhold it. It will doubtless surprise you to hear that you are of the same family as the mistress of the Anchorite's, and consequently a connexion of your friend, Mervyn Clitheroe."

"This is gratifying intelligence indeed!" I exclaimed.

"I must request your particular attention to my recital, or it may not be comprehensible," Dr. Foam pursued. "Stuart Mervyn, who suffered for his participation in the unfortunate Rising of '45, had two children. Fulke, father of the present Mrs. Mervyn, and Honoria. The latter was secretly married to a young nobleman devoted to the Jacobite cause, and who, as well as Stuart Mervyn, perished on the scaffold."

"You refer to the unfortunate Lord Wilburton, I conclude, doctor?" I remarked. "I always understood that Honoria Mervyn's connexion with that nobleman was not particularly creditable to her. I am glad to learn from you that her reputation is unsullied."

"Indisputable proof of her marriage with Lord Wilburton exists," Dr. Foam said.

"In what way does this concern me?" John inquired.

"You will perceive anon," the doctor rejoined. "At the time of Lord Wilburton's arraignment and condemnation, his unhappy lady expected to become a mother, and she died on the very day, and I believe on the very hour, that her lord's head fell upon the block. She died in giving birth to a son, who subsequently bore the name of Gerard Wilburton. Attainted of high treason, Lord Wilburton's honours were necessarily forfeited, and his marriage with Honoria Mervyn never having been acknowledged, nothing was done for his supposed illegitimate offspring. I shall not pause to trace the history of Gerard Wilburton, but will merely state that he married and had one son, Scrope—a remarkably handsome fellow, who, although he had neither wealth nor title to recommend him—won the affections of the youngest daughter of a noble house—the Lady Amicia Leyland, fourth daughter of the Earl of Rossendale. This young lady eloped with him, and they were married on the borders of Scotland, and the marriage was so displeasing to the proud earl her father, that he refused to see her again, and left the pair to starve. And well-nigh starve they did; for having little means of support, they were reduced to absolute penury. Six years after this marriage, the grandson of the unfortunate Lord Wilburton died, leaving a widow and two children wholly unprovided for. But destitute as was Lady Amicia's condition, she would have died rather than apply to her family for assistance. They had disowned her, she said, and unless recalled she would never go near them. Fancy a lady who inherited all the pride of one of the loftiest peers of the realm reduced to such a miserable state as I have described! But Lady Amicia Wilburton would never drag her title through the mire, she declared, and took the humbler designation of Mrs. Brideoake. Now, sir," the doctor continued, addressing John, "the last Lord Wilburton was your great-grandsire, and if the title were restored you would bear it."

John made no reply, but seemed lost in thought.

"You must not forget that your great-grandame, Honoria, Lady Wilburton, was Mrs. Mervyn's aunt, and this fact will explain to you why the mistress of the Anchorite's (when made aware by me of the real circumstances of the case) should have taken so much interest in the so-called Mrs. Brideoake. I found all particulars of the secret marriage between Lord Wilburton and Honoria Mervyn detailed in the Jacobite correspondence entrusted to me some years ago by Mrs.

Mervyn; and I have just succeeded in obtaining positive proofs of it, together with indubitable evidences of the lineal descent of Scrope Wilburton, your father, from the unfortunate Jacobite peer."

"I well recollect the circumstance you have mentioned, doctor," I said. "I felt certain at the time that you had made some singular discovery in that Jacobite correspondence. But I suppose Mrs. Brideoake, or, as I ought now to call her, Lady Amicia Wilburton, prevailed upon you to keep it a secret."

"You are right—she did," he replied.

During the progress of this narrative, I had narrowly watched John Brideoake's countenance, but though deeply interested, he manifested no elation. When Dr. Foam finished, he rose from his seat, and taking a turn or two about the room, as if weighing over what he had heard, approached the doctor, and pausing before him, said,

"You have made all clear as regards my family history, sir. But my mother's conduct appears wholly unaccountable."

"Her conduct is intelligible enough," Dr. Foam rejoined, "if the peculiarities of her character are taken into consideration. Pride—unyielding pride—has been the mainspring of all her actions—except in the case of her marriage. Her father, the old Earl of Rossendale, is as proud as Lucifer, and so is her brother, Lord Leyland—so are all the house. Their reproaches on Lady Amicia's ill-assorted marriage, as they termed it, galled her deeply. The first few years of her wedded life were passed abroad. She then returned with her husband to England, and for some time lived in great distress in the neighbourhood of London; but no pressure of circumstances could induce Lady Amicia to apply to her father. After the birth of Apphia, the unfortunate pair removed to Hull, with the intention of proceeding to Edinburgh, but they never reached the latter place, for the seeds of consumption, long sown in Scrope Wilburton, now declared themselves, and in a few weeks he was gone. Then it was that, with the scantiest resources possible, poor Lady Amicia had to provide for herself and her children. But even though thus reduced she never for a moment thought of humbling herself to her father. Her hopes of reinstatement rested on her son——"

"I see it all now!" John cried. "Go on, sir."

"Her hopes of reinstatement, as I have said, rested on her son. Even as a child he gave evidences of ability that led her to expect great subsequent distinction in him. After some debate she came to this town, where she knew there is an excellent free-school—rich in exhibitions and scholarships to both universities—one or more of which the youth might obtain, and so the door to future eminence would be opened to him."

"I feel for her disappointment," John cried, vainly striving to repress his emotion.

"Do not repine," Dr. Foam said. "You did all your strength enabled you to do—too much, in fact. It was about this time, if you remember, that, in attending you at Dr. Lonsdale's request, I saw your mother. I at once recognised her, for I had often seen her before at Lord Rossendale's seat, Buckrose, in Yorkshire, when she was the admired and haughty beauty, Lady Amicia Leyland. You may imagine my surprise at meeting her again under such strangely-altered circumstances. She imposed silence upon me by a look, and sympathising with her misfortunes, I obeyed the injunction. Subsequently, on imparting to her the discovery I had made in the Jacobite correspondence, I offered to introduce her to her connexion, Mrs. Mervyn. But her pride stood in her way, and she at first haughtily declined my well-meant proposal. In the end, however, as you know, her scruples were overruled, and she consented to become an inmate of the house. Then apparently new schemes of ambition dawned upon her. Disappointed in her son, upon whom her hopes of restoration to dignity and power had been fixed, she turned to her daughter. Doting upon Apphia, Mrs. Mervyn promised to give her half her property if she married according to her inclinations. You, Mervyn Clitheroe, were out of the way—you had given offence to Lady Amicia, and had made her your enemy—and you had been supplanted by Malpas Sale. By what arts Malpas had contrived to get into her ladyship's good graces I cannot say; but that he was successful, you have seen. The marriage was agreed upon—all was settled—when you returned, and it was broken off. But Lady Amicia still holds to Malpas, and will not give him up."

"A strange and most deplorable infatuation," John said.

"Strange indeed, and deplorable as strange!" Dr. Foam cried; "but her ladyship is as wilful and determined as she is haughty. She is a warm partisan, as Malpas has found; but a bitter enemy, as you, Mervyn, have discovered to your cost. Her dislike to you has become a rooted antipathy."

"How have I offended her?" I cried. "I cannot tax myself with showing her any disrespect."

"No doubt it was unintentional on your part," Dr. Foam replied; "but some offence must have been given, and she has keenly resented it. She also conceives that her children have been guilty of gross disobedience to her."

"Never, I solemnly declare, save when she has passed the limits of parental rule, have either of her children resisted her authority," John rejoined.

"Well, sir, you now know the precise position in which you stand," Dr. Foam said, after a short pause. "Let me state in addition, that I am firmly persuaded that your grandfather, Lord Rossendale, and your uncle, Lord Leyland, have influence enough to procure the restoration of your title."

"But at this moment, I suppose, neither of their lordships are aware of my existence," John said ; "and I am not likely to remind them of it. Honours have no attraction for me, doctor, and if offered, I should reject them. I love a simple and retired life, and covet no distinction."

"Then you have no pride—no ambition, like your mother?" Dr. Foam said.

"None whatever," he replied—"surprising as it may appear to you."

x

"Still, though you look down with philosophic contempt on dignities and honours, you may desire to be placed in an easy position," Dr. Foam said. "I must now put your scruples to the test. Learn then, that it is good Mrs. Mervyn's intention to make a will in your favour; this will be done on my assurance that the old Jacobite title shall be revived in your person."

John shook his head, and was about to speak, but Dr. Foam interrupted him.

"Hear me out," he said. "This is no fanciful notion. I am confident that if this property comes to you, a reversal of the attainder can be procured, and that you will regain the honours of your ancestors."

"I should not wear them well," John replied, firmly. "I want nothing. If you have any influence with Mrs. Mervyn, urge her to pass me over altogether, and leave the property to my sister and Mervyn."

"This must not be, John," I said. "You owe it to the noble race from whom you are descended, and whose escutcheon has been thrown down, to restore their name to its original eminence."

"You fail to convince me," he rejoined, shaking his head.

"But there is one argument which I can employ," I said, drawing near to him, and speaking in a low tone, "and which ought to weigh with you. Once Lord Wilburton, Ora is yours."

A deep flush overspread his pallid features. A severe struggle was evidently going on in his breast.

"Possessed of this property, you can make an adequate provision for your mother, and above all, for your sister," Dr. Foam said; "and can bestow the hand of the latter on whomsoever you please."

"In the event now contemplated, that deed of settlement will not be acted upon, I presume, doctor?" I said.

"It will not be acted upon," he replied; "and for the best possible reason—because it is no longer in existence. Mr. Tester recommended its destruction; and destroyed it was accordingly, in Mrs. Mervyn's presence. Now, sir," he added to John, "I await your decision?"

"I consent," he replied. "I feel that I have no right to refuse an offer which may be advantageous to others, though it may entail discomfort upon myself."

"Wisely resolved," Doctor Foam cried. "Dear Mrs. Mervyn's last moments will be cheered by the conviction that an old title, lost in the Jacobite cause, may through her instrumentality be revived in the person of her relative. Poor lady! she is as much devoted to the good cause as ever. She has been brought up in Jacobite principles, and has maintained them through life; and in Jacobite principles she will die. And now as to the completion of the proposed arrangement. Mr. Tester is at present occupied in preparing the will for which he has received Mrs. Mervyn's instructions. It will be ready this afternoon, and at six o'clock he and I shall proceed to the Anchorite's. It will be proper for you to accompany us," he added to John; "Mrs. Mervyn may desire to see you. Till then, adieu! Having other matters to attend to, I must perforce dismiss you."

CHAPTER X.

JOHN AND I REVISIT OUR OLD SCHOOL, AND PASS A FEW HOURS IN THE CHETHAM LIBRARY.—ILL TIDINGS.

As we emerged from Doctor Foam's house, the din and confusion of the crowded street almost distracted John, who was in a state of great nervous excitement.

"Let us get out of this dreadful turmoil," he cried. "I am quite bewildered by what has just passed, and seem to be in a troubled dream."

"From which you will wake to wealth and rank," I replied. "Come with me, and I will take you where you will find the quiet you need."

And lending him the support of my arm, which he really needed, we walked on together, passing through St. Ann's-square and the market-place, and never halting till we reached the precincts of the noble old Collegiate Church. Without bestowing more than a momentary glance at this reverend structure, we crossed the churchyard, entered Long Mill-gate, and soon stood before the old school. Yes! there it was—there was the dear old F. G. S.—unchanged to all outward appearance since the days of our boyhood. How many recollections did the sight of this simple edifice—simple it was not in our eyes—conjure up! I saw John once more—a pale, sickly, shabbily-attired lad—and heard unfeeling gibes and taunts addressed to him. Little did those who jeered him for his mean habiliments and his half-starved looks reck that he was of far more exalted birth than themselves! I saw myself—full of health, spirit, energy—hopeful of the future, contented with the present—and I felt that I could not, with entire regard to truth, say as much for myself now that I had become a man.

After gazing for some minutes at the exterior of the school, we passed through the gate, and stepped into the little court-yard—once so familiar to us, and so often trodden by our juvenile feet. From the open doors of the school came the buzz and hum of youthful voices, and I would fain have taken a peep inside; but John urged me to come away, and we proceeded to the Chetham Hospital, which I have already described as closely adjoining the Free Grammar School.

A wicket in the ancient stone gateway admitted us to the large quadrangular court used as a playground by Blue-coat Boys; and as we slowly crossed the wide area, my companion began to feel more at ease. The monastic and college-like air of the buildings around us delighted him. It was like coming home, he said. The happiest

x 2

hours of his early life had been spent in the library we were about to visit. Entering at the low-browed door of the ancient hospital, snatching a glimpse at its huge kitchen, and passing the refectory, we ascended an oaken staircase, and gained a long gallery, with railed enclosures containing shelves full of venerable tomes.

In one of these nooks we found the librarian, a grave, elderly personage, attired in a rusty suit of sable, and John having obtained from him two folio volumes of the "*Patres Apostolici*," in Greek and Latin, while I contented myself with old Izaac Walton, we repaired to the reading-room, and finding it totally untenanted, seated ourselves at an ancient oak desk placed in the depths of an oriel window—John's favourite place of study in bygone days. Here we remained during the whole of the afternoon—sometimes reading—sometimes conversing in a low tone—but never interrupted, for we were the sole occupants of the chamber. In this calm retreat John gradually regained his tranquillity, and when the deep bell of the old church struck four, warning us to depart, it was not without a pang that he quitted the place.

Our next step was to proceed to my hotel, where we partook of a little dinner, and our slender meal over, we went to Dr. Foam's residence. Afflicting news awaited us. Dr. Foam, it appeared, had been again hastily summoned to the Anchorite's by Mr. Comberbach, who had declared his conviction that his mistress would not live through the night. Before setting out, the doctor had left a few lines for John, begging him to await his return, and of course I bore my friend company.

For several hours we were kept in a state of most painful suspense, and it was past nine o'clock ere the doctor returned. He came into the room where we were at once, and, alarmed by his looks, I rushed towards him, entreating him to relieve my anxiety by a single word.

"Tell me she lives, doctor—that will suffice!" I exclaimed.

He shook his head mournfully.

"I am the bearer of ill tidings," he said.

"Shall I never behold her again?" I cried, in a voice of anguish.

"Not in this world," he rejoined, solemnly. "Dear Mrs. Mervyn has passed away from amongst us."

I sank backwards, and buried my face in my hands. I am not ashamed to own that I wept bitterly, for I had lost the best friend I had ever possessed—and one whom I dearly loved.

At last the worthy doctor came to me, and, after addressing a few consolatory remarks to me, said,

"Bear up manfully against this affliction. All your firmness is needed. I have not yet exhausted my stock of bad news."

"What more remains?" I cried, looking inquiringly at him.

"You are chiefly concerned in what I have to tell," the doctor said, addressing John, who was nearly as profoundly affected as myself. "Mrs. Mervyn has not made the will I desired."

"All seems to go wrong at present!" I exclaimed, in a tone of deep disappointment.

"Compose yourself, my good young friend, and hear me out," Dr. Foam said, kindly. "Mr. Tester and I were too late. The will prepared to-day could not be executed, and a will, previously made, must, therefore, be acted upon. Lady Amicia Wilburton is now absolute and uncontrolled mistress of the Anchorite's and all belonging to it."

"Nothing left to Apphia?—nothing to John?" I cried.

"Nothing to any one—except to the lady I have named," Dr. Foam rejoined.

"Heaven be praised!" John exclaimed. "I have escaped this snare. Apphia shall return with me at once to Weverham."

"Do nothing rashly, I implore of you," Dr. Foam returned. "Weigh it well over, before you remove her entirely from her mother. You are now too well acquainted with Lady Amicia's character not to be aware of the consequences of such a step."

"I shall return to-night," I cried. "My business here is ended. Farewell, doctor!"

Dr. Foam made no attempt to detain me, but when John also rose to depart, he begged him to stay, saying he wished to have some further conversation with him.

CHAPTER XI.

DELAMERE FOREST.

I HELD to my resolution, and notwithstanding the lateness of the hour, rode back that night to the mill. The exercise did me good. If I had retired to rest at Cottonborough, I should not have slept a wink. Mrs. Mervyn's death was a great shock to me, and the circumstances attending it made it doubly distressing. What might be in store for me I could not tell, but at present nothing but ill-luck attended me, and it seemed as if I was doomed to disappointment.

Next day, during the afternoon, I walked over to Weverham, to inquire after John and his sister, but nothing had been heard of them. I did not extend my walk to Owlarton Grange, for I was in no mood for society, and it would have been extremely painful to me to enter into a detail of the distressing events that had just occurred. Kind as friends may be, there are times when we shun them; and at this juncture I grieve to say that I felt like a misanthropist. But I did not indulge the feeling long.

On my return from Weverham, I found that a country lad had brought me a note from Ned Culcheth. The missive was rather strangely expressed and somewhat difficult to decipher, for Ned was not much skilled in penmanship, but I made out that he wished me to meet him at nine o'clock that night, at the Headless Cross, in Delamere Forest. He entered into no explanation as to the object of the meeting; but I felt sure that it was not for any trifling cause that he would summon me. It is needless to say that I at once decided to go; and the many conjectures which the note gave rise to offered a reasonable distraction to my harassing thoughts.

Shortly after eight o'clock that evening I mounted my horse, and proceeded along the Tarporley road, in the direction of Delamere Forest. Though a general highway, the Tarporley road was little frequented at this hour, and I do not think, in the course of five or six miles which I traversed, that I encountered as many individuals.

The district I was approaching had a solitary character at all times. The well-cultivated land about Weverham, with its orchards, its rich pastures and large corn-fields, its thick hedgerows graced with numberless detached trees, its beautiful copses, its deep cloughs full of hazels, its homesteads and larger habitations, had given place to a sterile heathy tract, only partially reclaimed and but thinly inhabited. For the last mile I had not discerned a single cottage. Plantations of Scotch firs and pines had succeeded the beech-trees, the oaks, and the elms, to be seen so frequently, and of such luxuriant growth, in the more favoured locality I had left behind, while the hedges had given place to rough palings or stone walls.

As I advanced, the country became even more dark and dreary-looking, being, in fact, little more than a black, boggy waste—perilous to any one who should attempt to cross it at night, from its numerous pitfals, and treacherous quagmires and morasses. Whoso incautiously approached too near one of the latter would be infallibly engulphed in its oozy bed.

This black and sterile waste, which of the vast woods that had once covered it could only now boast a few stunted trees, was, in fact, the famous Delamere Forest. To me it had a special attraction, as being the scene of many of the strangely-fulfilled prophecies of Robert Nixon. Weird traditions of all kinds were attached to it. In its coverts and thickets in olden days the royal hart had often been unharboured by the huntsman, and the wild boar speared; but all beasts of venery had long since vanished, and the only creature left, indigenous to the soil, was the rabbit that burrowed in the sand-banks. For centuries neglected and undrained, the mighty forest had become a pestilent marsh, and such of its ancient trees as had been spared by the woodman's axe had sunk into the pools and mosses, whence huge blocks were occasionally recovered, looking as if charred by fire.

A change, however, came at last. Many hundred acres of the waste had been enclosed and cultivated, and it was evident that in due time the whole would be reclaimed. Meanwhile, that part of the heath at which I had arrived was left very nearly in its pristine wild state, and furnished little occupation save to the turf-cutter. About half a mile off, in the midst of the moor, lay a little lake, or tarn, called Oak Mere, whose inky waters were much resorted to by wild-fowl. Further on was a curious group of small hills, known in the district as the Seven Lowes, and not far from these mounds was another pool.

In this direction the heath was bounded by a long and high ridge running on towards the beautiful village of Kelsal, and the summit of the furthest point of this mountainous barrier was crowned by an ancient British camp, popularly known as Kelsborrow Castle, whence a magnificent view might be obtained. Beyond Oak Mere were several morasses, designated respectively, from persons or circumstances connected with them, Riley Moss, Thieves' Moss, Relicts' Moss, Crap Moss, and Blakeford Moss. Further on there were two more morasses—Pinney Moss and Midgel Moss. Between these two last-named marshes was a large dismal-looking swamp—for pool it scarcely deserved to be called—full of sedges and reeds, known as Great Blake Mere; and not far from it was another piece of water, called Hatchew Mere. There were four wells in the forest, each with a legend attached to it, the most noteworthy being Hind's Well and Swan's Well, and two ancient crosses, both referred to in the prophetic rhymes of Nixon, namely, the Headless Cross and the Maiden's Cross. On the side of the forest opposite to Kelsborrow Castle rose two eminences, respectively known as Castle Cob and Glead Hill Cob; and when I have mentioned the two large enclosures called the Old Pale and the New Pale, the chief features of this singular district will have been specified. Beautiful heaths of various kinds bloomed in the forest, and among the plants that grew there were the bilberry and cranberry, the asphodel, the bog myrtle, and the marsh-cistus.

The night was fine, but cloudy, with a soft southerly breeze, and generally speaking no very great extent of the forest was discernible. All distant objects on the black heathy tract were plunged in obscurity, while even those near at hand could hardly be distinguished. But when light was suddenly thrown on the scene by an outburst of the moon, the waste was revealed in all its gloomy grandeur. The predominant colour of the moor was a rich dark purple, caused by the heath covering its boggy soil; but here and there streaks of white glistening sand crossed it, while patches black as jet told where the turf had been cut. The surface of the moor was irregular and uneven—now swelling into heathy uplands, now sinking into little dells and valleys, in the midst of which lay the tarns.

The sky was overcast as I approached the place of rendezvous, and when within a hundred yards of the Headless Cross, I strained my eyes through the gloom in the vain hope of descrying Ned's stalwart figure. The darkness was too great to allow any object to be discerned at that distance. All at once the clouds drifted past, and, the welcome radiance streaming down, showed me Ned seated on the ancient stone. On the same instant I became visible to him, though my horse's hoofs must have long since admonished him of my approach.

Springing up at once, he advanced to meet me, and, on nearing him, I cried out,

"Well, here I am, Ned, punctual to the appointment. On what sort of errand have I come?"

"It isn't from me that you'll gain an answer to that question, sir," he replied, "but from the pretty gipsy girl. Rue. She it was who commissioned me to bring you, between nine and ten o'clock to-night, to a secluded spot in the midst of the heath, which I dare say you know, called the Chamber of the Forest; promising to meet you there, and give you some important information. If you failed to keep the appointment, she said, you would ever after regret it; and she impressed caution so strongly on me, that I judged it safest only to write a few words to you, feeling sure you would guess my meaning."

"You did quite right, Ned," I replied. "But let us haste to the Chamber of the Forest. I am all impatience to learn what Rue has to communicate. She won't disappoint me, you think?"

"No fear of that, sir," he rejoined. "Her manner showed she was in right earnest. She seemed to be roused by some strong passion—revenge, mayhap."

"Revenge against whom, Ned?" I asked.

"Nay, that is more than I can tell, sir," he replied. "She didn't take me into her confidence. I only judge from her looks."

Our brief colloquy over, we left the high road, and, entering upon the heath, proceeded towards the spot mentioned by the keeper. Our shortest way of reaching it would have been to pass by Oak Mere, and cross the marshy tract adjoining it; but this part of the forest was much too dangerous to traverse at such an hour, and we were therefore obliged to diverge considerably to the right, to make sure of firm ground. This devious route brought us within a short distance of an old pit, where some victims of the Great Pestilence had been buried, and which is known as the Plague Hole. After this we pushed on in silence, not without risk, but fortunately without further hindrance than was caused by the necessity of making an occasional détour in order to avoid a quagmire, until at last we were within a bowshot of the place we sought.

The Chamber of the Forest, once the centre of the vast woods of Mara or Delamere, was now nothing more than a scanty group of venerable trees, looking like the remains of an ancient Druidical grove. On beholding these scathed and hoary denizens of the wood, I jumped from my horse, and consigning the bridle to Ned, walked forward alone towards the grove. I did not observe Rue at first, but, as I advanced, a female figure, wrapped in a cloak, detached itself from the trunk of one of the largest of the trees, and stood before me.

"So you are come," Rue said. "An eventful night this may prove to you."

I inquired in what way.

"Have you no guess?" she rejoined. "But I won't keep you in suspense. Do as I bid you, and you may chance to recover the property of which you have been unjustly deprived."

"You promise me this?" I exclaimed, joyfully.

"Hush! not so loud!" she replied. "I don't promise it. How can I? I can only point out the way to you. What you want you must win. If you fail, it will be from lack of prudence and courage."

"Then I hope I shall not fail," I replied. "How can I reward you for the service you are about to render me?"

"I claim no reward," Rue returned. "All I require is, that two persons whom I shall presently name to you, shall be exempted from harm. Will you promise this—on the word of a gentleman? I have little reason to place faith in a gentleman's word—nevertheless, I will take yours."

I reflected for a moment before making an answer.

"You hesitate!" she cried, angrily. "Then my lips are closed. Depart as you came."

"Nay," I replied, "I was bound to consider your proposal before acceding to it. I will give the promise you require, and keep it faithfully. I do not mean to imply any doubt as to the sincerity of your intentions towards me, but I would fain learn the motives that induce you to render me this great service?"

"My motives are mixed," she rejoined—"partly, the desire of vengeance; partly, anxiety to prevent the perpetration of a crime. You may not give me entire credit for the latter feeling, but it is so. He who has wronged you has also wronged me, and I know that by foiling his present purpose, I shall inflict the severest punishment on him, while I shall prevent those I love from committing a great offence. Do you apprehend me, or shall I speak yet more plainly?"

"I think I understand you," I replied. "Have you, then, been ensnared by the arts of Malpas Sale?"

"Ay," she cried; "I will make no secret of my shame. I was foolish enough to listen to him, and to believe that he loved me. But I soon found out that I had been deceived, and bitterly repented my error. When the charms he feigned to perceive in me no longer pleased him, he slighted me, and, at last, abandoned me altogether. I might have expected as much, but I did not, for, blinded by passion, I placed confidence in his protestations of lasting regard. Lasting regard, forsooth!" she repeated, with bitter scorn—"regard, that barely endured for a month. He soon tired of me, cast me aside, and sought a new object of diversion. Sissy Culcheth's turn came then. You know what happened to her. My mother strove to save her from the net spread for her, but in vain. She was caught as easily as I had been, and would have shared my fate, if chance had not befriended her. But for me there was nothing left except revenge. I am not of a nature to brook such treatment as I have experienced. With the same degree of fervour that I loved Malpas once, I hate him now. It is to revenge myself on him that I serve you. It is through you that I mean to strike the blow that shall crush him. Have I made myself clear now?"

"Perfectly so," I replied. "You have cause enough to justify your vindictive feeling; and yet——"

"You would advise me to spare him," she cried, with a fierce and scornful laugh. "Were I to do so, how would you be righted? Have you now no sense of injury? Do you not know what an outraged woman becomes? If I listened only to the promptings of my heart, I should stab him. But I prefer the mode of vengeance I have adopted."

Feeling it would be in vain to argue with her, I did not attempt it. She went on:

"I have said that in serving you I am not entirely actuated by feelings of vengeance. I would not have those I love become my betrayer's accomplices in villany. I would save my father and brother from the commission of a crime. I would shield them from harm. It is on their behalf that I require the promise you have given me."

"Fear nothing," I replied. "They are safe so far as I am concerned. But in what way do you propose to right me? Malpas himself told me that the will is destroyed."

"He lied," Rue rejoined. "Falsehood is ever on his tongue. The will is still in existence. He affirmed the contrary, because he imagines it can never be produced against him. But he is in error. I will help you to find it."

"You will for ever make me your debtor," I cried.

"Spare your thanks till you have gained the prize," she said. "You shall now hear how matters now stand in regard to Simon Pownall. He is in great jeopardy. He expected to make a good bargain with Malpas for the surrender of that will, but he was indiscreet enough to impart his design to my father and brother. Their cupidity was excited, and a plan, contrived by Obed, was put in execution, by which they hoped to gain possession of the document, and make their own terms with Malpas. They managed to drug Pownall's drink, and while in a state of stupor they conveyed him to a place of security, and shut him up within it. When he came to himself, they demanded the will, threatening, if he refused, to make away with him. But he proved more obstinate than they expected. He told them they might find the will, if they could, but they never should do so with his aid—adding, that if they harmed him they would get the worst of it. My father said that a few days' confinement would make him alter his tone, and so they shut him up again."

"And he is still in their hands?" I inquired.

"He is still a prisoner," she replied, "and as impracticable as ever. My father and Obed have entered into a negotiation with Malpas. What terms they have made with him I know not, for they have kept the transaction secret from me, but to-night the business will be brought to an end. A last effort will be made to shake Pownall's resolution, and, unless he yields, fatal consequences may ensue. This my father has sworn, and I much fear he will keep his oath. The crime must be prevented."

"It shall be prevented, if you will take me to the place where Pownall is held captive," I said.

"The place is not far off," she rejoined; "when I have brought you to it, you will act according to circumstances—but I rely upon your promise to do no injury to those dear to me. Tell my father that I have sent you—and *why* I have sent you. It may check his wrath. Have you no other arms except that hunting-whip?"

"No," I replied; "if I had been aware that I was about to embark on a service of danger, I would have come better prepared. But this hunting-whip will suffice. The handle is as heavy as a hammer. And Ned Culcheth is provided with a stout cudgel."

"Enough!" she cried. "Bid Ned follow us. You will need his assistance. I will show you where to leave your horse."

With this she started off in the direction of the marshy tract adjoining Great Blake Mere, skimming over the ground so lightly that her footsteps seemed scarcely to make any impression on the heath, and moving so fleetly that Ned and I had enough to do to keep up with her.

CHAPTER XII.

THE TURF-CUTTER'S HUT.

ERE long, a black boggy tract opened upon us, intersected by deep dykes, cut in order to drain the morass, and giving abundant evidences, from its shaven surface and its pits, that the turf-cutter had been at work upon it.

On gaining this sombre region, Rue stopped near a couple of shattered and almost branchless trees, and waiting till Ned Culcheth came up with the horse, bade him to tie the animal to one of them. Her order obeyed, the gipsy girl bade us stay where we were for a moment, and keep behind the trunks of the trees. She then almost instantly disappeared.

Of late, the clouds had thickened in the sky, and it had become totally dark. But at this juncture the moon suddenly burst forth and revealed the whole scene. As I have said, we were now on a black bog, hardened by deep drainage, but yielding nothing at present except turf, stacks of which, cut and dried for fuel, were grouped around us in various fantastical shapes; while low walls of the same combustible substance, in various stages of preparation, were reared on all sides. Beyond us was a dismal-looking swamp, which I knew to be Great Blake Mere.

My attention, however, was chiefly directed, during this momentary illumination of the moorland, to the gipsy girl. Catching sight of her figure as it reappeared from amidst the turf-stacks, I discovered that she was hastening towards a low hovel, situated at the edge of the bog on which we were standing, and within a stone's throw of the mere. No other habitation was visible except this lone hut. Stealing cautiously towards the little hovel, Rue paused close to it, listened for a moment, and then, apparently satisfied with her scrutiny, flew back towards us.

"Our business lies in yonder hut, I suppose, sir?" Ned inquired. Like myself, he had been watching Rue's proceedings.

"It does," I replied. "From what I have learnt, the four scoundrels we have so long sought are there. But I have given my word to this gipsy girl not to meddle with two of them—namely, her father and brother."

"Well, it's nat'ral she should wish to save 'em," Ned rejoined.

"It's a pity two such rascals should get off—but better them than t'other two."

I then briefly related Rue's story to him, and had scarcely done, when she again stood before us.

"They are there," she said, pointing to the hut. "Are you ready? Have you cautioned Ned Culcheth?"

"Ay, ay," Ned replied. "Your kin shall come to no harm from me."

"Follow me, then," she replied.

Hastily making our way through the stacks of turf, and stepping over a plank thrown across a wide and deep dyke, we soon approached the hut. By this time the moon was again hidden, and all around had become dark and blank as before. Rue led us on with so much caution, that, had any one looked out, our approach would hardly have been perceived. When close to the hut, she stopped, and pointing towards it, said, "Your adversary is there. I heard his voice. Go and revenge yourself—and revenge me."

As she hissed this stern injunction in my ear, I could perceive, even by that imperfect light, that her beautiful features were so distorted by passion that they scarcely looked human. Without another word, she darted back, and disappeared on the instant.

The hut was a small clay-built tenement, with a grey thatched roof. There was a still smaller out-building, or shed, attached to it. Even where we stood voices could be heard proceeding from the dwelling, and amongst them I had no difficulty in distinguishing the tones of Malpas Sale. Stepping cautiously forward, I approached the hut, desirous, if possible, to ascertain what was passing inside it. A little broken window, placed at a very convenient height from the ground, would have served my purpose perfectly, but I did not venture to avail myself of it, for, if I had done so, my presence must have been instantly detected. I was saved further search for means of investigation by Ned Culcheth, who pointed out a crack in the clay wall, and placing my eye to this crevice, I found that I commanded the whole interior of the cabin.

It was a wretched-looking place, and the only piece of furniture it afforded—a rude three-legged stool—was appropriated by Malpas, who sat with his back towards me, smoking a cigar. He was habited in a dark riding-dress and boots. Opposite him, on a block of wood, sat Simon Pownall, in the most miserable plight imaginable, his apparel torn and disordered, his visage blackened and begrimed, beard unshorn and grizzly, hair unkempt, and looks betokening abject terror, spiced with malignity. So changed was he by the treatment he had experienced, that I scarcely recognised him. Between the prisoner and the principal personage of the party was an old tub, turned upside down, serving the purpose of a table; and on this lay Malpas's cigar-case, and a pocket-flask containing spirit.

Light was afforded by a peat fire burning on the hearthstone, which Obed, at the moment I looked in, was fanning into a flame with his cap. Its light fell upon the swarthy and savage lineaments of Phaleg, who was seated upon a heap of turf, in close proximity to Pownall. Both gipsies had short pipes in their mouths, and puffed away at them

with as much composure and unconcern as Malpas himself. I did not fail to remark that they had their bludgeons with them as usual, and I also noticed that Malpas was armed, for I saw the butt-ends of a brace of bull-dogs peeping out of his coat pockets, and it struck me that the weapons were rather ostentatiously displayed.

"Well, Pownall," Malpas said, "you must have found out by this time that your obstinacy is useless. You will be obliged to give in in the end, and may as well do so now as later on. Act like a man of sense, and tell us, without more ado, where to find the will."

"But what am I to have if I do tell you?" Pownall rejoined.

"Ask your friends here," Malpas returned, with a laugh. "My bargain is with them. They have engaged either to produce the will, or keep you out of the way. I don't deny that I should prefer the former arrangement, but so long as you are in safe custody I am perfectly easy."

"You hear what the capt'n says, Pownall," Phaleg remarked. "He knows you're safe in our hands. If he saw your place of confinement, he wouldn't think you had much chance of getting out of it without our permission."

"What is it like, Pownall?" Malpas inquired.

"The capt'n asks you a question," Phaleg said. "Describe your underground lodging, man."

"It's a dark, damp, unwholesome vault, lying under the shed adjoining this hovel," Pownall cried. "The place is unfit for the vilest criminal—let alone a decent, well-behaved man like me. Look at it yourself, Captain Sale, and it will make your heart sick. I will never believe you could authorise such cruelty as is practised upon me."

"Who's to blame for the cruelty but yourself?" Phaleg roared. "I'll set you free in a moment if you'll only tell where that will is hidden."

"Come, don't be obstinate, Pownall," Malpas said. "You'll gain nothing by standing out. Your chance is gone by. The document can be of no use to you now."

"I don't know that, Captain Sale," Pownall rejoined, sullenly. "Perhaps it may."

"Don't you heed him, capt'n," Phaleg cried. "It never shall be of any use to him. Sooner than that, I'll tie a stone round his neck like a dog, and drown him in one of these black meres."

"Nay, that would be going a trifle too far, Phaleg," Malpas remarked. "I only want him kept out of the way."

"All right, capt'n," the ruffian rejoined. "He shan't trouble you again, I'll warrant him."

"You will do well to listen to what I have to say, Captain Sale," Pownall cried, in a half-menacing tone. "I am not about to beg my life of these men, for I know I am in their power, and it appears they will show me no mercy. But understand this, if I am put out of the way as I am threatened by this villain—or even if I am detained a prisoner much longer—that document will be taken to Mervyn Clitheroe."

Malpas sprang to his feet, and clapped his hands to his pistols.

"Poh! poh! this is mere idle talk," Phaleg cried. "I should like to know how that can be done?"

"You will find out the truth of what I assert if you proceed to extremities with me," Pownall continued, evidently trying to heighten the impression he had produced; "and so will Captain Sale. I took these precautions in case of some such mischance as has befallen me. You are now warned, Captain Sale, and will know what to expect."

"Curse the fellow!" Malpas exclaimed. "If this should be so! —but no! I cannot believe him," he added, sitting down again.

"A mere trumped-up story, capt'n," Obed remarked. "He never said a word of the sort afore."

"Because the occasion never arose before," Pownall said. "I address myself to Captain Sale—not to you. He knows what the consequences will be to himself if the will is produced."

Malpas only gave utterance to a deep oath, but his troubled countenance showed what was passing within. Pownall contemplated him with a malignant grin. The cunning knave began to feel secure.

"Harkee! Phaleg," Malpas cried, at length, "this rascal is too much for us. We had better make terms with him."

"If you don't, you'll never have that property," Pownall said, doggedly. "Detain me a prisoner, or put me out of the way altogether, and as sure as I stand here, that will will be taken to Mervyn Clitheroe."

Both gipsies laughed incredulously.

"Don't mind him, capt'n," Phaleg cried. "It's merely an artful device to get out of our clutches. We've got him safe enough, and mean to keep him. He accounts himself a rare conjuror, but with all his tricks he won't get out of our black-hole."

"After the warning I have given him, Captain Sale, I am sure, will never be so blind to his own interests as to allow me to be sent thither again," Pownall said.

Malpas looked perplexed.

"I tell you what it is, Pownall," he cried, at length. "I don't attach much faith to what you say, but it's best to be on the safe side. Just talk over the matter with your friends there, and when you've agreed together, I'll see whether I can meet you."

"I'm agreeable," Phaleg said.

"But I am not," Pownall cried. "I will have nothing more to do with these men, Captain Sale. They have both played me false, and, so far as I can help it, they shan't derive any benefit from their treachery. They can't produce what you require. Why should they be parties to any bargain between you and me?"

"What game is t' owd fox tryin' to play now, I wonder, father?" Obed remarked to the elder gipsy.

"I can't tell what he be after," Phaleg rejoined, with a tremendous oath; "but this I know—he never sees daylight again unless the will be forthcoming."

"Captain Sale, I appeal to you," Pownall cried. "You are a gentleman, and will protect me. You won't suffer me to be murdered by these ruffians."

And as he spoke, he made an effort to rush towards Malpas, but he was forcibly held back by the iron grasp of Phaleg.

"A word will procure your liberation, Pownall," Malpas observed, in an impassive tone. "You have only to thank yourself if any harm befals you. But since you refuse to listen to me, I must wish you good night. Perhaps you may be more reasonable when I see you next."

And he proceeded deliberately to light another cigar, as if preparing for departure.

"Captain Sale! Captain Sale!" Pownall cried, in extremity of terror. "You won't leave me to these merciless ruffians. I shall never survive it, if I am thrown into that black, stifling hole again, and my death will lie at your door. Save me! save me!"

"Speak the word, then," Malpas rejoined. "The will! where is it?"

"Take me with you, and I will find it for you."

"Don't trust him, capt'n," Phaleg said, still maintaining his hold of the trembling caitiff. "Besides, he shan't go, unless we go with him."

"Another night's confinement won't do you any great harm, Pownall," Malpas replied, with a savage laugh.

"It'll bring him to his senses," Phaleg roared.

"It'll kill me!" Pownall shrieked. "You won't find me alive when you come back, Captain Sale."

"Oh! yes, I shall," Malpas rejoined, indifferently. "And I've no doubt by that time you'll have settled your differences with honest Phaleg and his son. Good night!" And he rose as if to depart.

"I beseech you, Captain Sale, do not abandon me!" Pownall cried. "As I live, I have told you the truth."

"We'll talk more about it to-morrow night," Malpas rejoined.

"But I won't be left here," Pownall cried, struggling ineffectually with Phaleg. "Help! help!"

"Shout till you're hoarse," the gipsy said. "No one will hear you."

The poor wretch continued his outcries.

"Better thrust him into the vault, Phaleg," Malpas said. "He may give the alarm."

"No fear of that, capt'n," the gipsy rejoined. "Hold your tongue! will you, you cursed warmint," he added, with a fearful imprecation.

Meanwhile, I had whispered some directions to Ned, and now, judging the fitting moment come, I gave him the word of attack. Ned, begged me, in a whisper, to let him go in first, and without tarrying for my consent, dashed himself with all his force against the door, bursting it at once from its hinges, and before the occupants of the hut could recover from the surprise caused by his unexpected intrusion, I had sprung over the tub, and forced Pownall from Phaleg's grasp. The miserable caitiff instantly saw that there was a chance of his liberation, and eagerly caught at it. He dexterously tripped up Obed's heels, as the latter rushed forward to intercept his flight, and would have made a prompt exit from the hut, if the doorway had not been blocked up by Ned Culcheth, who had seized and pinioned Malpas. All this was the work of a moment, but in that space of time I had got clear of Phaleg. My hunting-whip enabled me to ward off a desperate blow which he aimed at my head, but I forbore to strike him in return, though I could have brained him, if I had pleased, with the handle, but shouted out—"Hold your hand, Phaleg! I don't want to harm you or your son. I am sent here by Rue."

"What! has she sent you here?" he cried, taken completely aback. "Has she sold her own father? Curses upon her!"

"Turn your wrath against him who deserves it, and not upon her," I cried. "You are not so lost to shame that you will aid the man who has ruined and abandoned your daughter."

"Abandoned Rue!" Phaleg vociferated. "Whom do you mean?"

"There stands the betrayer," I rejoined, pointing to Malpas, who was ineffectually struggling to free himself from Ned. "Let him deny what I say if he can."

"Speak, capt'n," Phaleg roared, "and give him the lie."

"He can't speak," Ned rejoined. "The words would choke him if he tried."

"He now feels the effects of an injured woman's vengeance," I said. "Rue's hand strikes this blow."

"This may be true, father," Obed cried; "and we will settle the account with the capt'n by-and-by. But, meanwhile, we mustn't let these chaps take Pownall away."

"If I had only known this sooner, I'd have strangled the false-hearted villain rather than have had anything to do wi' him," Phaleg cried.

"Take him, and deal with him as you see fit," Ned Culcheth cried, hurling Malpas with such force against the elder gipsy that they both fell to the ground, and following me as I rushed out of the hut with Pownall.

"Take me away from them, Mr. Clitheroe!—take me away!" the miserable wretch cried. "Promise not to deliver me to justice, and you shall have the will. I will show you where it is hidden."

"I can make no promise now," I replied. "Come along!"

By this time we had reached the deep dyke already described, and after we had all crossed it, in order to check pursuit I kicked the plank into the chasm. Scarcely had I done so, when Malpas rushed out of the hut, and on seeing us he gave vent to ejaculations of rage. Fancying himself now in security, Pownall could not help gratifying his malicious feelings, and called out,

"You have lost the will, captain. I shall now deliver it to him for whom it was rightfully intended."

"Ha! say you so, rascal?" Malpas cried. "That shall be prevented, at all events."

And as the words were pronounced he drew a pistol, levelled it at Pownall, and fired with such good effect that the unfortunate man uttered a sharp cry, threw up his arms, and fell backwards into the dyke.

"Lie there with your secret!" Malpas cried, hurrying back to the hut.

CHAPTER XIII.

THE CHASE ACROSS THE MORASS.

On seeing Pownall drop into the dyke, my first impulse was to jump across the chasm and endeavour to arrest his murderer; but as I ran back a few paces in order to give impetus to the spring, Ned Culcheth caught me by the arm, and strove to dissuade me from the rash attempt.

While I was struggling to free myself from his friendly grasp, Malpas again burst from the hut, followed by the gipsies. I could not make out at first whether the intentions of the two latter were hostile to him or the reverse; but I was not long left in doubt, for in another minute all three stopped near a stack of turf, from behind which Obed brought a horse, while Malpas placed what appeared to me to be a pocket-book in the hands of the elder gipsy. This done, Captain Sale mounted and rode off.

"By Heaven, he shall not escape in this manner!" I exclaimed.

And I flew to the spot where my own steed was secured, unloosed him, and was on his back in a moment.

Ned made another effort to detain me, but I was too much excited to heed his remonstrances, and dashed off instantly after the fugitive, whom I could just descry scouring across the waste in the direction of the most perilous morasses. But this did not deter me from the pursuit, but rather encouraged me, as I felt the more certain of his capture. Clearing the dyke, I put my horse to the top of his speed, and was glad to perceive that the distance between me and my flying foe began rapidly to diminish.

Very soon Malpas was scarcely a hundred yards in advance of me. Wherever he went I unhesitatingly followed; and it was a marvel that either escaped the many pitfalls by which the way was beset.

A region was now at hand where the utmost caution was necessary. Yet Malpas did not slacken his pace, or deviate in the slightest degree from a direct course. I expected every moment to see him disappear in the bog, but, astonishing to say, the ground still continued firm beneath his horse's feet, and he must either have known where to find the narrow causeway across this part of the morass, or have accidentally hit it off. By following in his track, I came off equally well.

But bad as this place was, we had greater risks to encounter. We had leaped a brook issuing from Relict's Moss, and were passing between Crap Moss and Blakeford Moss. In front was a small reedy tarn, called Shipley Mere. The whole place, in fact, was a marsh. The ground quaked beneath our horses' feet as we splashed on. Still through all these difficulties and dangers Malpas held on, and I followed.

Shipley Mere was passed in safety. But another dangerous morass was at hand, Thieves' Moss. I never expected Malpas would reach it, or, if he did, that he would be able to proceed further. To my surprise he went on, and though he occasionally floundered, he did not stop. I also got on without material hindrance. We were now close upon the high road across the forest between Northwich and Chester, and before Captain Sale could clear the palings that skirted it, I was within twenty yards of him.

Finding himself hard pressed, he did not attempt to pursue this road, but leaping the fence on the further side, again plunged into the heath, taking the direction of Oak Mere. I after him, of course.

Once more we were on a shaking bog—once in fearful proximity to treacherous quagmires. Immediately on our right was Riley Moss: on the left mere a smaller, but yet more perilous marsh. The swampy nature of the ground no longer allowed Malpas to keep up the headlong pace he had hitherto maintained. It was with difficulty he got on at all. His horse sank in the oozy bog at every step. I was in equal jeopardy, and at last had the mortification of seeing Malpas reach a firm piece of ground, while my horse stuck quite fast.

All danger was now over with Captain Sale. After carefully considering the course to be pursued, he rode off, laughing derisively at my situation, and I soon lost sight of him.

My efforts to free myself from the quagmire in which I was caught only made matters worse. My horse got more and more inextricably involved at every plunge, and at length seemed to be sinking altogether. In order, therefore, to save myself from inevitable destruction, I was compelled to abandon him. The poor animal seemed conscious of the terrible fate awaiting him, and struggled violently to free himself, but his efforts only hastened his doom. Each moment he sank deeper and deeper—until at last, with a shrill cry—he entirely disappeared.

My own position was fraught with too much peril to allow time for reflection on this disastrous event. Grieved as I was to lose my horse, preservation of my own life was the main point to consider. With great difficulty I managed to extricate myself from the morass, and this accomplished, I soon reached a part of the heath where the sod was firm, and there was no longer any risk. I was shaping my course towards the Tarporley road, which was not very far off, when I heard shouts in the distance, and descried Ned Culcheth running towards me. I waited till the honest fellow came up. He had been searching for me, and had been greatly alarmed at my disappearance. After I had explained to him what had happened, he said,

"You've had a lucky escape, sir, I can tell you. These bogs are like quicksands, and when once man or beast gets involved in them, they are never seen again. I wish that confounded Captain Sale were beside your poor horse. But his day of reckoning can't be far off, and he may meet with a worse fate than being smothered in a bog."

We then made the best of our way to the mill, where my companion tarried with me during the few hours left of the night.

CHAPTER XIV.

THE SEARCH FOR THE BODY.

NEXT morning Ned set off betimes for Marston. He had instructions from me to lay all particulars of the dark deed that had occurred overnight before Mr. Mapletoft, a neighbouring magistrate, and to obtain from that gentleman a warrant for Malpas's immediate arrest. I proposed to be at Marston myself in the afternoon, when the accusation against Malpas could be heard by Mr. Mapletoft, but the morning must be devoted to a search for the murdered man. Charged with these instructions, Ned departed.

I should now have been badly off for a steed, but luckily, Mr. Mavis had a stout young horse which he kept for his own use, so I was able at once to supply the place of the unfortunate animal I had lost in the bog.

An impulse not to be resisted drew me in the first place to Weverham. On reaching John's cottage, I found that he had returned from Cottonborough at a late hour on the night before—much to my chagrin, also, I learnt that he had returned alone. I sat down to wait for him in his little parlour. He soon made his appearance, and in a few words made me acquainted with what had occurred since I had left him with Dr. Foam. The doctor, he said, whose goodness of heart and excellence of judgment could not be doubted, had strongly advised him not to remove Apphia from her mother for the present, and had given such good reasons for his counsel, that in the end he had yielded.

By taking away your sister at once, Dr. Foam had said to my friend, you will naturally offend your mother, with whom further disagreement ought sedulously to be avoided. You cannot foresee how Lady Amicia may act. Very probably her character may be softened by her improved circumstances. At all events, give her a fair trial. Consider the importance of a wealthy and titled mother's protection to Apphia, and do not rashly deprive her of such great advantages.

"I could not deny the force of much that the worthy doctor advanced," John said, "and I felt that it would be selfish in me to desire to have my sister with me, since it was so much more to her own interest to remain with our mother. Whether I have done right, time will show. I shall have this consolation at least, that I have acted for the best. Before leaving Cottonborough, I made a point of seeing Apphia in order to ascertain her sentiments. As you may imagine—for you know how devotedly attached my sister was to dear Mrs. Mervyn—I found her plunged in deep affliction, but she herself thought it would not be right to leave our mother at a time like the present. Prudential motives may have swayed her, for all particulars of our family history had been imparted to her by Lady Amicia, but she must have been mainly influenced by the change in our mother's manner. Subsequently I had an interview with Lady Amicia, and am bound to say that she produced a very favourable impression upon me—so favourable, indeed, as almost to warrant me in hoping that the improvement in her character may be permanent. In all respects, indeed, the interview was satisfactory."

Whatever opinion I might entertain as to the probable duration of Lady Amicia's present amiable frame of mind, I made no remark to my friend, but proceeded to recount to him the fearful occurrences of the previous night. He heard me with profound attention, and seemed greatly shocked by the details of Malpas's criminality.

"Badly as I had thought of him," he said, "this far exceeds any notion I had formed of his villany. His base conduct towards that young gipsy girl would suffice to stamp him as an unprincipled profligate—and now he has dyed his hands in blood. What would have been Apphia's fate if she had been united to such a wretch! We may, indeed, congratulate ourselves on her escape."

Soon after this I took leave of my friend, and rode on to Owlarton Grange.

Tidings of Mrs. Mervyn's demise had preceded me. Intelligence of the sad event had been communicated by Dr. Foam to Cuthbert Spring, who, with Major Atherton, was still staying at the Grange. The doctor had imparted full particulars of the poor lady's disposition of her property, mentioning, of course, that the so-called Mrs. Brideoake had assumed her real name and title of Lady Amicia Wilburton. Aware of all this, Miss Hazilrigge and Ora overwhelmed me with inquiries about Apphia and John. Ora was in despair that the property had not been left to the latter, and could scarcely find words strong enough to express her vexation at Lady Amicia's success. "I hope John will get the title, in spite of her," she cried. "I'm sure if we have any means of helping him to do so, they shan't be wanting." Good-natured Mrs. Hazilrigge was nearly as much annoyed by the untoward event as her niece, though she did not exhibit her disappointment with so much vivacity. I was obliged to tell them that the object of their sympathy was quite indifferent to the loss he had sustained, and that when the title had been offered him, he had been most reluctant to accept it.

"Ah, indeed! he has less selfishness than any one I ever met with," Miss Hazilrigge exclaimed. "I have always declared that he is too good for this world."

"Don't you recollect the discussion we had upon this subject some time ago, Mervyn?" Ora said to me. "It now appears that Mr.

Spring was in the secret all the time, and knew that by good right John ought to be Lord Wilburton."

"Yes, I must own that Dr. Foam had taken me into his confidence," Cuthbert replied; "but then I was bound to secrecy."

"Do you think Apphia will remain with her mother?" Miss Hazilrigge inquired.

"Impossible to say," I replied; "but there seems every probability of her doing so."

"What will become of John?" Miss Hazilrigge cried. "Positively, we must have him here."

"Call him Lord Wilburton, aunt, if you please," Ora said. "He must have the title, and we may as well, therefore, give it him at once."

Not wishing to disturb the ladies by any allusion to the errand on which I was bound, I begged a word in private with Mr. Hazilrigge and my two friends, upon which they at once adjourned with me to another room. My relation astonished them all, and no one more than Old Hazy, who could not help expressing great concern for the fate of the luckless Thaumaturgus.

All three immediately volunteered to accompany me to Delamere Forest; and professed their anxiety to assist in the needful inquisition there, and then go on with me to Marston. I gladly embraced the offer, whereupon Old Hazy ordered the carriage to be got ready with the utmost expedition, telling Ponder, at my suggestion, that Stephen Blackden must go with us, and be provided with an eel-spear, a couple of long poles, and a coil of rope. These arrangements made, Major Atherton and I went round to the stables, and, mounting our horses, rode off, leaving the others to follow. As we proceeded on our way, the major fell into discourse with me, and assumed a far more kindly and confidential manner towards me than he had hitherto adopted; expressing great concern at my disappointment in my expectations in regard to Mrs. Mervyn, but hoping that I might still recover my uncle Mobberley's will, which would make amends for all. As to my chance of obtaining Apphia's hand, he thought that the difficulties were certainly increased by the present perplexed state of affairs, but if the young lady remained constant, all must come right in the end.

We had reached the confines of Delamere Forest before the carriage overtook us. Instead of proceeding to the Headless Cross as I had done on the night before, we turned off about half a mile short of it, at a point where the Tarporley road is crossed by the road from Northwich to Chester, and, pursuing the latter, soon got into the heart of the forest.

Here we were compelled to take to the turf, and as the carriage could proceed no further, Old Hazy and Cuthbert Spring alighted, and followed by Stephen Blackden, bearing the eel-spear, rope, and poles, we proceeded towards the hut, which was about a mile distant. A couple of poorly-clad men, with spades over their shoulders, who proved to be turf-cutters, were standing near the little tenement, but noticing our approach, they hastened to meet us. We had no difficulty in crossing the dyke, for the plank had been restored to its original position. On explaining our errand to the turf-cutters, they appeared extremely surprised, but readily promised to aid us in our search, declaring at the same time that they had seen nothing except the plank in the dyke. "To be sure we never expected to see a murdered man there," one of them remarked.

"Whom does the hut belong to?" I asked.

"It was built by one Dick Hornby," the turf-cutter replied; "but he has been dead more than a year, and latterly the hovel has only been used by vagrants. I have seen a couple of gipsies hanging about it for the last three or four days, and I thought they might have taken up their quarters in there, and so I told Tom Tarvin."

"Ay, so you did, Will Duddon," the other replied. "You said you were quite sure the gipsies lodged in old Hornby's hut."

Meanwhile, we had approached the edge of the dyke, and the two turf-cutters, quickly divesting themselves of their shoes and stockings, let themselves drop into the channel, which in this place was about two feet deep in water. The depth of the dyke was about twelve or fourteen feet. The eel-spear and a pole were then handed down to the men, and we watched their proceedings from the brink. I indicated the exact spot where Pownall had fallen, and the turf-cutters carefully searched the channel at the point, but made no discovery. There was a slight—very slight—current in the inky water, and it was possible that the body of the unfortunate man might have been carried on, so they waded along for at least a hundred yards, using pole and spear as they went, but without finding anything —we watching them all the time from above—until they came to a spot which it was impossible the body could have passed. This was a small pool, into which the water flowing along the dyke emptied itself. Beyond, there was another outlet, but it was protected by stakes planted closely together. Here, then, the body must be, if at all, and here a most careful search was made by the two men; but nothing was found, and after some time spent in useless exertion, they were obliged to give up the job.

"He's not here, masters, that's sartin," Will Duddon cried. "We'll hark back, and see whether he be further up; though he must have come down the stream if no life were left in him."

With this they retraced their steps, and proceeded to a considerable distance beyond the place where Pownall had been shot, until they reached another pool, somewhat larger than the one they had just explored. There seemed little likelihood that the body would be found here, but this was the last chance, and accordingly the men set to work again, splashing about, plying spear and pole as actively as before, and leaving not a hole or corner unvisited, but with no better success than heretofore. At last, they both came out.

"Well, we've done our best to find him for you, masters," Will Duddon said; "and if he had been in the dyke, or in either of these pools, we couldn't have missed him. But the man has either got out himself, or been taken out—that's clear."

We could not contradict the assertion. Further search seemed hopeless.

At this juncture Tom Tarvin shouted out, "What's that?" and ran towards a sloping bank through which the dyke was cut in its junction with the pool.

We all thought that the object of our scrutiny was at last discovered, but it proved to be only an old shoe which was left sticking in the soft boggy soil. On examination of this shoe, I felt almost sure that it had belonged to Pownall. If the supposition were correct, how came it there? Had Pownall only been severely wounded, and had he managed to creep out of the dyke at this point? or had the shoe been dropped by those who bore away the body? The former conjecture seemed the more probable, for it was evident that the shoe had been plucked from the foot of the wearer by the tenacious soil of the bog. Further search resulted in our finding an old coloured neckerchief, which I identified as belonging to Pownall, for I had seen him wear it on the previous night. We continued our investigations around and about the place for some time longer, but without further result.

We next proceeded to examine the hut. The interior was left in precisely the same state as I had seen it on the night before. The peat fire was still smouldering on the hearthstone. In searching the shed we made a singular discovery. After removing a quantity of dry fern and gorse, with which the little out-building was filled, we found that the floor was paved, and it presently appeared that one of the flags had an iron ring fixed in it by which it could be lifted, as well as a bar to fasten it down. Raising this flag, which moved on hinges like a trap-door, a dark, damp vault was disclosed. On descending into this subterranean chamber by a short ladder, reared just underneath the opening, we found that it was entirely constructed of stone, and was evidently of great antiquity. Most probably the vault had been an underground cell used by a recluse in old times, and might have belonged to the Monastery of Saint Mary in Vale Royal. A light was kindled, and we were then enabled to examine the spot more carefully. The roof was arched and groined, and the masonry was but slightly dilapidated, but as may be supposed, the place was excessively damp from the constant moisture dripping through the stones. The floor was an inch or two deep in black ooze. Nothing could be more wretched than the aspect of the vault, and the austerest penitent would have shrunk aghast if enjoined to occupy it. And yet Pownall had been thrust into this dismal hole by his confederates! A few trusses of straw were thrown in one corner, on which he had found refuge from the damp floor. The chamber must have been perfectly dark when occupied by the captive, but air was admitted by a small grated aperture at one end of the roof. If this aperture had been choked up, the poor wretch must inevitably have perished. Indeed, it was a marvel that he had survived his confinement. A broken pitcher set on the ground near the trusses of straw was the only memento left of him. We were glad to get out of the place, and breathe the fresh air once more.

"Poor wretch!" Major Atherton exclaimed, "if he was immured in that vault for three or four days, he must have suffered enough for his offences, be they what they may."

"It is very odd we can find no traces of the body," Cuthbert Spring remarked. "The man may have only been wounded after all, and have crept out of the dyke."

"I begin to think so," I said.

"I tell you what, my young friend," Old Hazy observed, gravely. "You need not go so far to find a solution of the mystery. You have been beguiled by evil spirits, and the whole scene you have witnessed has been merely a phantasm conjured up to perplex you. Delamere Forest is notoriously infested by elves, sprites, and fairies, and these mischievous beings have made you their sport. When we get back to the Grange, I will find you several instances of similar delusions in Thiræus and Robert de Triez."

Serious as the subject was on which we were engaged, I could scarcely help smiling at this singular view of the case, and I saw that Major Atherton's gravity was a good deal disturbed, while Cuthbert Spring was at no pains to repress his laughter.

"So then, sir," I said, "your opinion is that evil spirits assumed the forms of Malpas Sale, the two gipsies, and Simon Pownall?"

"I have no doubt of it whatever," he replied. "I will cite you a passage presently in confirmation of my opinion from Père Jacques D'Autum's '*Learned Incredulity.*'"

"I wish I could think so," I said, "but unluckily I cannot help believing in the reality of the scene; and I feel as certain as I do of my existence that I saw Pownall shot by Malpas Sale, and fall—lifeless, it seemed to me—into that dyke."

"If that had been the case, we should find his body," the old gentleman cried. "But we can't, sir—we can't. No; it is evidently a delusion. Read Père Jacques, and be convinced."

No more could be said in refutation of such an argument, so having rewarded the poor turf-cutters for the assistance they had rendered, we returned to the carriage.

It was then decided that we should proceed to Marston by the most direct road, which from this point was by Northwich, and not by Weverham. Old Hazy would fain have had us call at the Grange, saying he was sure we must stand in need of refreshment after our exertions, but this we declined, as we suspected him of a design of producing Père Jacques. Stephen Blackden, however, was dismissed with the implements we had used in the search, and enjoined to make the ladies easy in case of our non-appearance.

CHAPTER XV.

THE EXAMINATION BEFORE THE MAGISTRATES.

WE halted for half an hour at Northwich, and the afternoon was advancing ere we reached Marston. Major Atherton and I had ridden on before the carriage, and we dismounted at the Nag's Head.

"Please to step into the parlour, gentlemen," Mr. Hale, the landlord, said, opening the door of a small room, and ushering us into it. "You'll like to be private, I make no doubt. Mat, the ostler, will see to your horses. Ned Culcheth has only just stepped out, and will be back presently."

"I suppose you know what has happened, Mr. Hale?" I said.

"I do, sir," he replied; "Ned has told me all about it. But you'll excuse me for saying that in the present stage of proceedings I would rather not give an opinion on the subject. There are two sides to every question, you know, sir, and I like to be on the right side."

"Very prudent, Mr. Hale. Can you inform me whether Captain Sale has been arrested?"

"Oh! yes, sir, he's in custody of Bryan Peover, the constable," the landlord replied. "The examination is fixed for five o'clock, for Ned said you were sure to be here by that time, and will take place in the justice-room at the vicarage. It's half-past four now. So you fancy you can bring the matter home to the captain, eh, sir?"

"I'm sure of it, Mr. Hale," I replied.

"Well, they think differently at the vicarage. They say it's a trumped affair. Excuse me, sir—but that's their opinion—not mine. *I* have no opinion at present. Anything more to say to me, sir? If not, I'll go and send a messenger to Mr. Twemlow, the magistrate's clerk, to let him know you are come."

With this he went out, but almost instantly returned to say that a young woman wanted to speak to me outside. On hearing this, I accompanied him to the outer door, where, to my great satisfaction —for I felt how important her testimony might be in the examination—I beheld Rue.

"I thought you would want me," she said, "so I have come. I have seen Ned Culcheth, and have heard all that has happened. You managed the affair badly last night—but you mustn't fail to-day."

"I don't intend to fail, if I can help it," I replied. "But your evidence is material, and must be given."

"It shall," she answered.

At this moment the carriage drove up to the door of the little inn, and as Old Hazy and Cuthbert Spring alighted, she retired.

Shortly afterwards, Ned Culcheth made his appearance, and we set out in a body for the vicarage. The whole village was astir. Women and children stood at the doors of the cottages to see us pass, and a crowd followed in our train. Amongst those who attended us thus, and whom I recognised, were Job Greaseby, the smith; Farmer Shakeshaft; William Weever, from Nethercrofts; and Chetham Quick. Loud and angry discussion was going on amongst these personages as to the probable result of the examination, and I could hear Chetham Quick roundly declare that he was confident the charge would fall to the ground.

The vicarage, as I have already mentioned, closely adjoined the church. It was a large, comfortable old house, surrounded by a grove of fine trees, with a delightful garden at the back, having a smooth-shaven lawn sloping down to the mere. As we turned up the little lane leading to this ordinarily quiet residence, our numbers had greatly increased, and we must have been at the head of a troop of thirty or forty people, all curious to hear the inquiry. Of course, we could not dismiss them, but it was evident that so many persons could not be admitted, and a stoppage took place at the garden-gates, where Ben Tintwisle, the fat old beadle, was stationed. Ben looked very big and portentous, being arrayed in his scarlet cloak, and having his laced cocked-hat on his head, and his rod of office in hand. Twelve persons were only allowed to pass him. Ned Culcheth tarried at the gate for Rue, who had not yet come up, and I went on with the others. A footman was standing at the door, who ushered us into the dining-room, begging us to be seated, and saying he would let us know when all was ready. We took the seats assigned us, and had not occupied them more than a few minutes when the man returned, and requested us to follow him.

The justice-room, whither we were now conducted, was situated at the rear of the house. It was a large, plainly-furnished apartment, with a desk at the upper end, at which the doctor sat when he heard complaints, signed warrants, arranged disputes, or otherwise exercised his functions as a magistrate. On either side of the old-fashioned chimney-piece were bookcases, and facing it was a large bow-window, commanding a beautiful view of the mere. Portraits of some of the Vernon family—Mrs. Sale, it will be recollected, was a Vernon—hung against the walls, and there was also a portrait of my uncle Mobberley, which, though painted after the good old man's death, and copied from a miniature, was exceedingly like him. No attempt had been made to flatter the unpretending old farmer. There he was as I had known him, in his simply-cut blue coat, with his prominent nose and chin, his right eye covered with a great black patch, and his left orb blazing fiercely. Beneath this portrait was suspended a plan of Nethercrofts and the property thereunto appertaining, and I could not help thinking there was a kind of dramatic propriety in the circumstance of this portrait and plan being brought in juxtaposition on the present occasion. Who so fitting to be a silent witness of the scene about to be enacted—a scene arising out of the disappearance of his own will—as John Mobberley? What accessory so appropriate as a plan of the property in dispute?

Ned Culcheth and I were the last to enter the justice-room. Casting my eyes around, I saw that all the rest of the assemblage had taken their places. In the chair usually occupied by Dr. Sale sat Mr. Mapletoft, of Birkinfield Hall, an elderly gentleman, with a quick grey eye, and a keen expression of countenance. He was tall, rather high-shouldered, and of a spare frame, and his silvery white hair contrasted with his ruddy complexion. Mr. Mapletoft's invariable attire in a morning was a green Newmarket coat, buckskins, and top-boots. On the right of the senior magistrate sat Mr. Vernon, of Fitton Park (Dr. Sale's brother-in-law)—a very aristocratic-looking personage, with fine, though rather prominent, features and a very stately deportment. Like Mr. Mapletoft, Mr. Vernon wore a riding-dress and boots. Mr. Hazilrigge, who was in the commission of the Peace, had a place assigned him on the left of the principal magistrate, and next to him—though with a little interval between them—sat Dr. Sale. On the other side of the seat of justice, and close to Mr. Vernon, was placed a small table, at which sat the magistrate's clerk, Mr. Twemlow—a bald-headed man, attired in black—with pens, ink, and paper, and a few law-books before him. Behind the magistrates sat Cuthbert Spring, and a few paces behind Mr. Spring, and in a corner of the room, to which he had retired as if to avoid observation, stood Major Atherton.

One feature in the arrangements of the room did not fail to attract my attention. In the vicinity of Dr. Sale a large Indian screen was placed, so disposed as to conceal the person who sat behind it, and who was no other than Mrs. Sale, from general observation, but revealing her presence to the magistrates, and to all those who, like myself, were stationed near them. After glancing at her for a moment, I did not dare to look at her again, for the sight of her distress quite unmanned me. At the lower end of the room, on the right, were grouped together some ten or a dozen yeomen, amongst whom were Farmer Shakeshaft, William Weever, and old Job Greaseby. A clear space in front of the magistrates was preserved by the fat beadle, who kept continually knocking upon the floor with his wand.

Such were the general arrangements of the room. I ought to mention that there were three doors: one on the right of the chimney-piece, near which sat Mrs. Sale, partially hidden, as I have described, by the screen; and two others at the lower end of the room. One of the latter communicated with the offices, and the other with a little passage leading to the back staircase, and it was through the last of these that Malpas was introduced, as I shall now proceed to relate.

After the senior magistrate and Mr. Vernon had conferred together for a few minutes in a low tone, the former signified to Mr. Twemlow that they were ready to hear the case; whereupon silence having been authoritatively imposed upon the group of talkative yeomen in the corner by the fat beadle, who thumped his wand upon the floor, the magistrate's clerk rose and directed that Captain Sale should be introduced. Upon this, Tintwisle marched to the door I have described, and opening it, delivered the summons in a loud voice.

In the profound silence that ensued, steps could be distinctly heard outside, and in another moment Malpas entered into the room, closely attended by Bryan Peover, the constable, a stout-built, hard-featured man. Stepping lightly forward into the centre of the open space reserved in front of the magistrates, Malpas entered, bowed gracefully and deferentially to Mr. Mapletoft, and those on either side, and then, drawing up his fine figure to its full height, fixed his gaze sternly and steadily on me. He looked extremely pale, but determined. Though it was quite evident from his manner that he did not underrate the peril in which he stood, yet it was equally clear that he was not in the slightest degree cast down by it, but felt confident of acquittal. There was nothing of insolence or bravado in his manner, but he appeared as if deeply hurt and indignant at the charge brought against him, and eager to justify himself. His attire was studiously elegant, and nothing had been neglected likely to heighten the effect he desired to produce. As he entered the room, poor Mrs. Sale started up with a faint cry, and leaned forward from behind the screen to look at him, but Dr. Sale took her hand, and induced her to resume her seat. Major Atherton, also, who had hitherto kept in the background, came forward, as if moved by curiosity. Bryan Peover thought it behoved him to stand close by his charge, but at a sign from Twemlow he now moved back, and Malpas stood alone in the midst of the assemblage.

After the customary oath had been administered to me by the magistrate's clerk, I commenced my narration; but as the reader is already familiar with the particulars of the case, it will be unnecessary to recapitulate them. When I had concluded, Malpas emphatically denied the charge, which he characterised as utterly false and malicious, and declared he should be able completely to disprove it. The first witness whom I called in support of my statement was Ned Culcheth, and he confirmed it in every particular, but the weight which might have been attached to his testimony was a good deal shaken, when Malpas, addressing himself to the bench, said, "You have heard, gentlemen, what this man has stated. Have I your permission to ask him a question, which will throw some light on the motive by which he has been actuated in coming forward against me in this manner?" Permission being granted, he then turned sharply to Ned, and said, " Now, fellow, will you declare upon your oath that you have not sworn to be revenged upon me for some imaginary wrong?"

"It was no imaginary wrong," Ned rejoined.

"That is not an answer to the question," Mr. Mapletoft said. "We do not want to know the nature of the provocation you have received, nor whether it be real or imaginary. But we desire to be

informed whether you have ever nourished ill-will towards Captain Sale, and uttered threats against him? In a word, have you borne him a grudge?"

"I can't deny it, your worship," Ned replied.

Mr. Mapletoft lifted up his eyebrows, and glanced at Mr. Vernon.

"May I ask you, gentlemen," Malpas continued, "to call William Weever, Thomas Shakeshaft, and Job Greaseby, all persons of undoubted veracity, and here present, and inquire from them whether they have not heard Culcheth openly threaten my life?"

"You can call them presently for the defence, if you think it advisable," Mr. Mapletoft replied; "but it is scarcely necessary, since the man admits the fact."

"I admit that I dislike him, your worship," Ned cried, "and I won't deny that at one time I should have thought it no great crime to send a bullet through his head. But when I hated him worst I would never have brought a false charge against him, or against any man. I have told nothing but the simple truth."

"Mere assertion," Malpas cried. "I will presently demonstrate to you, gentlemen, not only the improbability, but the impossibility of the charge brought against me. It is a tissue of lies which I shall rend in pieces without difficulty. I will show you that I am the victim of a conspiracy between Mr. Mervyn Clitheroe and this man Culcheth, both of whom are my avowed enemies, and are seeking in this manner to blast my character and injure me. Mr. Clitheroe has declared that he obtained information from a gipsy girl of the supposed meeting at a turf-cutter's hut in Delamere Forest. Where is the girl? Can she be produced to corroborate his assertion?"

"She can," I replied. "She is without."

"Call her," the senior magistrate said.

At this announcement, for which he seemed wholly unprepared, a great change took place in Malpas. His limbs trembled, and he took out his handkerchief to wipe his brow. As Tintwisle proceeded to summon the witness, he gazed anxiously at the door, and when, after a short interval, Rue entered, he addressed a supplicating glance at her, which she answered by an inexorable look. Malpas's discomposure was too evident not to attract the attention of the whole assemblage. The magistrates regarded him with anxiety, and Dr. Sale could not conceal his uneasiness. As to poor Mrs. Sale, she again leaned forward from behind the screen, shuddered, and could scarcely repress a cry of terror as she beheld the fiercely-vindictive look which the gipsy girl fixed upon her son. Every one appeared instinctively to feel that on Rue's testimony Malpas's fate depended; while no one doubted—not even Malpas himself, I am sure—that her testimony would be adverse to him.

"What questions have you to put to the witness?" Mr. Mapletoft said to me, after Rue had been duly cautioned by Twemlow.

"Let me speak wi' her first, your worship," Ned Culcheth interposed, "seein' as how the matter began wi' me. Did you not meet me," he added to Rue, " on the afternoon of the day before yesterday, at Hob's Hillocks, near Garland Hall?"

" Yes, I saw you there," Rue replied.

" And you told me to convey a message to Mr. Mervyn Clitheroe ?"

" I told you to bid him meet me at a certain spot in Delamere Forest, between nine and ten o'clock on the following night," Rue answered.

" For what purpose?" I demanded.

" Stop! stop! not so fast," Mr. Mapletoft cried, checking me.

" I did not mention any purpose," Rue observed; " but I told Ned to say to you, that if you failed to keep the appointment, you would ever after regret it."

" Then you led Culcheth to suppose it was on a matter of importance that you wished to see Mr. Clitheroe?" Mr. Mapletoft asked.

" The matter was important—to me," Rue replied.

" I have no more questions to ask the young woman, gentlemen," Ned observed. " I undertook to convey her message, and I performed my promise. We both went together to the place of meeting she had fixed—the Chamber of the Forest—at the hour appointed. She was there, and had some discourse with Mr. Clitheroe."

" Did you hear what passed between them ?" Mr. Mapletoft inquired.

" I did not, your worship," Ned replied. " I was too far off. I could only catch a word here and there; but the young woman seemed wild and angered."

" Angry with Mr. Clitheroe ?" the senior magistrate demanded.

" No, not wi' him—wi' Captain Sale," Ned rejoined.

" How do you know that, fellow, if you did not hear what was said ?" Mr. Mapletoft cried, sharply.

" I judged so, your worship," Ned returned.

During the progress of the investigation, Rue's gaze never for a moment quitted Malpas, and, judging from the fierce smile that curled her beautiful lip, she revelled in the torture he endured, and would willingly have prolonged it. He still addressed a supplicating look to her, but her glance was unpitying.

" Now, young woman, attend to me," Mr. Mapletoft cried. " What took place during your interview with Mr. Clitheroe ? What did you say to him ?"

" Much that I cannot relate," she replied.

" That won't do. I must have a direct answer. Ned Culcheth has declared that you appeared angry. Against whom was your anger evinced ?"

" Against one who has done me an injury," she returned.

" But you must name the person," Mr. Mapletoft cried.

" I decline to do so," she answered. " It is a matter which relates only to myself."

Malpas was visibly relieved. But his suddenly-awakened hopes were crushed by her looks, which seemed to say, "I have not done yet."

"Harkee, young woman," Mr. Mapletoft called out. "Do you not see, that by leaving the matter in doubt, you create a prejudice against Mr. Clitheroe? You lead us to suppose you were reproaching him, and we may put an entirely erroneous construction on the object of the meeting."

"You may put what construction you please upon it, sir," she rejoined. "He who has injured me stands before you, but I won't name him."

"Come, woman! speak! Is it Mr. Clitheroe, or Captain Sale?" the magistrate demanded.

"You will get nothing from me on that head," Rue returned.

"Take care, or I will commit you," Mr. Mapletoft cried, angrily.

I now thought proper to interpose. "Allow me," I said to the senior magistrate, "to ask this young woman whether, after our interview, she did not take me and Culcheth to a turf-cutter's hut in the forest?"

"I pointed out the hovel to you," Rue replied, "but I left before you entered it."

"True," I rejoined. "You had previously told me whom I should find there, and the business on which he was engaged; but in order to make sure, you went forward to listen, and returned with the intelligence that he was within."

"I said, 'They were there'—those were my exact words. Ned Culcheth heard me," she rejoined.

"I did," Ned cried. "And I understood you to mean——"

"Never mind what you understood, fellow," Mr. Mapletoft interrupted. "Keep to facts."

Seeing that Rue was unwilling to answer, and attributing her reluctance to a natural desire not to utter anything to criminate her father and brother, I said,

"I will betray no confidence you have reposed in me, and will ask no question that you may not desire to answer, but on one point you must speak out plainly—Did you not take me to that hut to revenge yourself on Captain Sale?"

As I put this question, there was a profound silence, broken only by a half-suppressed sob from Mrs. Sale. Looking in the direction whence this sound had proceeded, Rue was made aware of the poor lady's presence, and became violently agitated. A sudden revulsion seemed to take place in her feelings.

"It is his mother!" she exclaimed, distractedly. "What have I said?—what have I done?"

"You have said nothing, my poor girl," Mrs. Sale cried. "You will not join in this conspiracy against my son—you will not harm him?"

"For your sake, I will not," Rue rejoined. "Let me go. You will get nothing more from me."

"We will see that anon," Mr. Mapletoft cried. "Madam," he

continued, addressing Mrs. Sale, "this interruption is highly improper, and I am obliged to request you to leave the room. Dr. Sale, you will be good enough to take your lady hence." The vicar complied, and opened the door for Mrs. Sale, but ere the poor lady disappeared she threw a look of inexpressible gratitude at the gipsy girl.

In vain after this were interrogations addressed to Rue by the magistrates and myself. She continued obstinately silent, and Mr. Mapletoft's threats to commit her for contumacy were productive of no effect. At last she was removed, but was ordered to be kept in custody by one of the constable's assistants until the examination had concluded.

This peril over, Malpas entirely recovered his courage. Addressing himself to the magistrates, he said it must be sufficiently evident to them that the accusation brought against him was utterly baseless, and made with malicious intent. I had asserted that he was at a hovel on Delamere Forest on the previous night, but I had been unable to prove it, and he could show that the statement was an entire fabrication. He then called John Baguley, Doctor Sale's butler, who declared that to the best of his belief the captain was in his own room between nine and ten o'clock on the night before. Baguley had not seen the captain—but he had seen a light in his room. Moreover, he had not seen the captain leave the house at all overnight, or heard him return at a late hour. Jem Millington, Malpas's groom, was the next witness, and he swore positively that his master's horse had never been out of the stable on the night before, and he didn't believe his master had gone out at all.

"Now, gentlemen," Malpas said, when the groom had given his evidence, "I have proved, I trust to your satisfaction, that I could not have been out on horseback last night at the time mentioned by my accusers, unless I were possessed of a principle of ubiquity, but what will you say when I venture to affirm that the man I am reported to have shot—Simon Pownall—is alive and unhurt at this moment?"

At this assertion, which was made with surprising audacity, and which perfectly confounded Ned Culcheth and myself, great sensation was created amongst the assemblage.

"Prove that, and there is an end of the matter," Mr. Mapletoft said.

"I will prove it," Malpas cried. "Call Chetham Quick," he added, to the beadle.

Tintwisle went to the door, summoned the witness, and the next moment Chetham stepped into the room. After bowing to the bench, the impudent rascal looked at me and Ned as much as to say that he would speedily extinguish us. And so he did; for he swore most positively that Pownall was alive, and to the best of his belief uninjured. "I have received a letter from him this very day," Chetham said, "and he makes no mention of an accident of any kind having happened to him, and certainly does not write like a man who had received a mortal wound. He has reasons for keeping out of the way, or I could produce him at this moment."

"What say you to this, sir?" Mr. Mapletoft called out to me.

"I don't believe a word of it," I cried. "No such letter as described could have been written by Simon Pownall. I am quite sure that the shot fired at him by Captain Sale took effect, and both myself and Ned Culcheth saw him drop into the dyke."

"Where you found him, no doubt, this morning?" Malpas rejoined. "You accuse me of assassination, where is the proof that any crime has been committed?—where is the body of the man I am said to have murdered?"

"Has the body been found?" Mr. Mapletoft inquired.

"It has not, sir," I replied. "We carefully searched the dyke this morning, but were unable to discover any traces of the unfortunate man we had seen fall into it—except two articles which probably belonged to him. But these relics were found at some distance from the spot where the crime was committed. The body may have been removed—or Pownall may only have been wounded, and crept out of the dyke—that is possible."

"Pownall is alive, and fully able, I repeat, to contradict this report of his murder," Chetham Quick cried. "There can be no difficulty in producing him if their worships think it necessary, and this inquiry should be adjourned."

"Well, really, gentlemen, I do not think that any case has been made out," Mr. Vernon said. "An *alibi* has clearly been established by Captain Sale, and the man said to be shot proves to be alive, and most likely unhurt. I will not make any comment on Mr. Clitheroe's conduct, or impute motives to him which may not exist, but certainly he has made a charge which he cannot sustain."

"My opinion is, Mr. Vernon," Mr. Hazilrigge remarked, "that both my young friend Mervyn Clitheroe and Ned Culcheth have been beguiled by evil spirits. You may smile, gentlemen, but I could adduce many instances of similar delusions as related by learned writers—notably, by Thiræus and Robert de Triez. I was present when the dyke was searched this morning, and I came to this conclusion at the time. My opinion is confirmed by what has since occurred. How otherwise, let me ask, can you account for Mr. Clitheroe's conduct? I know him to be utterly incapable of making any false statement—far less of bringing forward a charge like the present, knowing it to be false. Take my word for it, that both he and Ned Culcheth have been deluded. I am glad to find that the individual supposed to be shot is safe and sound, and I hope to see him again."

Old Hazy's observations elicited a smile from the magistrates, but neither of them made a remark. After a few minutes' conference in an under tone, with Mr. Vernon, the senior magistrate said, "We are of opinion that no case whatever has been made out against Captain Sale, and we dismiss the inquiry."

Upon this, the magistrates rose and left the room by the side door,

z

shaking hands with Dr. Sale, and congratulating him as they passed by. The beadle threw open one of the doors at the lower end of the room, and the yeomen went out by it. Old Hazy and Cuthbert Spring had followed the magistrates, and only Major Atherton and myself were left. By this time the vicar had joined his son, and after shaking hands with him, said in a low tone, glancing at me as he spoke,

"If you will follow my advice, Malpas, you will indict your accusers for conspiracy and perjury."

Stung by the remark, and unable to contain myself, I rejoined with some warmth, "Do not imagine that the matter will be allowed to rest here, Dr. Sale. But the next examination must be in a public court."

"It must," Major Atherton cried, coming quickly back from the door, through which he was just about to make an exit—"it must; and I will venture to predict, if the matter is thoroughly sifted, and careful investigations are made in the interim, that if any parties have to be indicted for perjury and conspiracy, it will not be Mr. Mervyn Clitheroe and Ned Culcheth. On the next occasion there must be no suborned hirelings for witnesses. Of Captain Sale's guilt—notwithstanding all that has been alleged to the contrary—I do not entertain the slightest doubt, and I am sure he will not eventually succeed in evading justice."

To this address, which was uttered with stern composure, Malpas seemed disposed at first to make an indignant rejoinder, but he manifestly quailed beneath the major's eagle eye.

"Who are you, sir, that venture to interfere in this matter?" Captain Sale demanded.

"Inquire from your father who I am," the major rejoined, regarding him scornfully. "He will tell you, and will tell you also by what right I interfere. I am a soldier, sir, and have ever borne myself with honour in my profession. No stain attaches to my name. It would be well for you if you could say as much."

"You may be all you assert, sir," Malpas cried, "though as your honour has not been called in question there seems no need to vaunt of it. But whoever you are, you shall answer with your life for the imputations you have thrown out against me."

"You must first clear your character before you are entitled to demand satisfaction from any man," the major replied. "I should refuse to go out with you."

So saying, Major Atherton turned upon his heel, and was about to leave the room, when Dr. Sale hurried after him and arrested him.

"Stay a moment, sir," he cried—"I did not know you were present. I had not heard of your return." And he then added, in a lower tone, but which, however, reached my ear, "I wish you would come to me. Perhaps this unpleasant matter may be adjusted. Nay, I am sure it can, if we only meet to talk it over. There shall be no difficulty on my part. Even if a great sacrifice is required, it shall be made. Anything is better than the scandal which an inquiry like this must occasion. I am sure you will agree with me, on reflection, that on all accounts—*on all accounts*," he repeated, "this affair had better be hushed up. You would not, I am sure, wish to blast my son's prospects in life."

"The affair cannot be hushed up, sir," the major rejoined, in an inflexible tone—" it has gone too far. But were it in my power to stay further inquiry, I would not. Have you exhibited such generosity yourself as to be entitled to ask for consideration towards your son? I will show him none. Come, sir," he added to me. And taking my arm, we left the justice-room together.

CHAPTER XVI.

THE THAUMATURGUS AGAIN APPEARS ON THE SCENE.

I MUST now press on with my story. Momentous events await me. Nearly a month must therefore be passed over, with a rapid glance at what has occurred during the interval.

Poor Mrs. Mervyn had been laid in her family vault at the Collegiate Church. Though not invited to the funeral, I, nevertheless, attended it, wishing to pay the last mark of respect to one who for years had almost supplied to me the place of a mother. Many sincere mourners were there besides myself—many who had benefited largely by the good lady's generosity and charity, and who deeply deplored her loss, fearing that little was to be expected from her successor. All her old servants and dependents followed her to the grave, and bade a tearful adieu to the best and kindest of mistresses. Poor Molly Bailey wept bitterly, and Mr. Comberbach was quite as much affected.

The butler's apprehensions, however, that he and Molly Bailey would be summarily dismissed, were soon dispelled. On the day after the funeral, Lady Amicia announced that she meant to make no change whatever at present in the establishment, but should maintain the house on precisely the same footing as heretofore. The arrangements, therefore, of the Anchorite's remained entirely undisturbed; and whatever might be its new mistress's future plans, she allowed no intimation of them to escape her. No increase of servants was made—no carriage ordered—no display of pomp or state attempted. Lady Amicia and her daughter led a life of strict privacy; and during the short period I have mentioned, there were no visitors to the house that I heard of, except Dr. Foam and Mr. Barton Lever.

But what was most agreeable to Apphia, and reconciled her more than anything else to her new position was, that all intimacy had ceased between her mother and the Sales. Malpas waited until Mrs.

Mervyn's funeral had taken place before presenting himself at the Anchorite's, but when he did come, Mr. Comberbach (as the butler subsequently informed me) had the pleasure of saying that her ladyship was not at home to him, and of adding that he needn't give himself the trouble to call again, for her ladyship never would be at home to him—neither would Miss Apphia. Deeply mortified, as may be supposed, Malpas retired, but he attributed the rebuff he had met with, no doubt, to the scandal occasioned by the charge which I had brought against him. On the next day, Dr. and Mrs. Sale drove over to try and explain matters, but with very indifferent success. Lady Amicia gave them at once to understand that a person on whom such grave suspicions rested, as was the case with their son, was wholly unsuited to her daughter, and the match must be peremptorily broken off. Dr. Sale vainly employed all the specious arguments in his power—and Mrs. Sale used true maternal pleadings—Lady Amicia continued inflexible. But though my opponent was thus removed, my own cause did not seem to be materially advanced by his defeat.

Poor John's love affairs were in a more desperate state than mine. Ora's disappointment was excessive when she found that he would not stretch out his hand to grasp the prize offered him. She could not believe in such absurdity and nonsense, and tried to rally him out of his determination. In vain. Then she pouted, grew piqued, and at last fairly quarrelled with him. As to kind-hearted Miss Hazilrigge, she sided in this instance with her niece. She was sorry for John, but provoked at his stupidity. And I did not wonder at her being so. I felt provoked with him myself. And if he should lose Ora altogether for his folly, I am sure not one young lady in a hundred would sympathise with him. Not be a nobleman when he might, but prefer remaining a poor curate, besides giving up a beautiful heiress! Was there ever such a crazy being?

Since the Anchorite's had passed into Lady Amicia's hands I had never been near the place, neither had I heard directly from Apphia, but I had received many kind messages from her, conveyed through John, to whom she wrote constantly. During the whole of the period I am thus hastily surveying, I had remained in the country, in accordance with the advice of Major Atherton and Cuthbert Spring. After Malpas's examination before the magistrates, we all returned to Owlarton Grange, and on the following day the two gentlemen I have mentioned were closeted with me for some time, and at last the major said, in reply to some rather too hasty remark of mine,

"You must have a little patience, my young friend. Mr. Spring and I have thought the matter well over, and I trust that in a short time we may be able to settle everything satisfactorily for you."

"Say in a month, major," Cuthbert Spring cried. "I am pretty sure that by that time all may be accomplished. And with the conviction that his friends are at work for him, I think this eager young gentleman may be well content to keep quiet for so short a period, and get into no fresh scrapes—if he can help it," he added, with a laugh.

"Well, gentlemen," I replied, "I can only say that I am infinitely obliged to you. Act as you please. You shall have no interference from me; and I will do my best not to get into any fresh scrape."

"Enough!" the major cried. "In a month's time we hope to have a good account to render you. Remember, you are to be perfectly quiet, or you may mar our projects."

I gave them a fresh assurance on this head, and our colloquy then ended. Later on in the same day the two gentlemen left Owlarton Grange for Cottonborough, where the major told me he should take up his quarters with his friend. While taking leave of me, Cuthbert Spring recommended me to pass as much of my time as I could at the Grange.

"You are always welcome, I know," he said, "and you will find the society here agreeable. I do not wish you to play the spy upon our worthy but eccentric host, but if you observe anything very unusual about him, drop me a line."

I promised compliance with the request.

Major Atherton also took leave of me very kindly, but he rather surprised me by requesting, almost in the same terms as Cuthbert Spring, that if Old Hazy indulged in any unusual eccentricities, I would let him know.

I again promised compliance, though I wondered what they wanted, and began to fancy they must apprehend that the old gentleman was going out of his mind.

And here it may be asked whether the matrimonial arrangement between Cuthbert Spring and Miss Hazilrigge had approached any nearer to a conclusion? Apparently not. Soon after the old bachelor's departure, I happened to be left alone with Miss Hazilrigge, and took the opportunity of inquiring whether Mr. Spring had made up his mind to leave Cottonborough.

"I really can't tell," she replied. "Whenever I press the question, he returns an evasive answer, but he has promised to come to a positive decision within a month. I have given him clearly to understand that I will never leave the country; so the affair will then be settled, one way or the other."

"Everything, it appears, will be settled in a month," I thought, struck with the coincidence of the time.

As counselled by the two friends to whom I had confided the management of my affairs, I passed the greater part of my time at the Grange. I endeavoured to accommodate matters between Ora and John, but did not find the task very easy of accomplishment. She could not be made to understand that John's reluctance to move out of his present sphere arose partly from extreme humility of character, and partly from a delicate state of health, which made him shrink from mixing with society. Whatever his own feelings might be, she declared, he was bound to sacrifice them for her. He might prefer to remain a poor curate, and if such were his choice, he might continue in a state of single-blessedness so far as she was concerned, for a poor curate she did not intend to marry. She would give him a month to decide. And if at the end of that time he retained his present opinions, she would think no more of him.

So John's fate was to be decided in a month—a term, it seemed, assigned to us all.

Poor John's cottage was no longer the cheerful abode that it had been before his sister's departure. It was brightened by no female presence—and there was no ministering angel at hand to watch over and nurse him. Yet he uttered no murmur, but discharged his duties zealously as ever. He now and then walked over with me to the Grange, but as Ora now received him with great coldness he derived little pleasure from these visits.

And how was Malpas going on all this while? Did he seem affected by the critical position in which he stood? Not in the least, —so far as I could learn. But, in truth, I knew very little about him. An occasional rumour of his proceedings reached the Grange, and the last thing I heard of him was that he had made a match for five hundred guineas with a certain Captain Brereton, a young gentleman quite as much addicted to sporting pursuits as himself, and that they were to ride a steeple-chase together between Ashley and Nethercrofts. This match, which had excited great interest among the gentry of the neighbourhood, was on the eve of coming off. I rode over to Marston on the very day before it was to take place, and found everybody talking about it.

But before explaining what took me to Marston, it will be necessary to make some mention of Old Hazy, whose proceedings had begun to attract my attention.

The old gentleman often expressed regret at the loss of the Thaumaturgus. No one had ever suited him so well. Despite the many proofs he had received of the rascal's mal-practices, he still clung to him, and made excuses for him. According to Old Hazy's showing, Dr. Hooker was an injured man; and so infatuated was the credulous old gentleman, that I felt that the rogue would be able to impose upon him again if he only got the opportunity.

Rather to my surprise, Major Atherton did not write to me at all, the correspondence from Cottonborough being conducted by Cuthbert Spring. One day there came a letter from Mr. Spring, stating that though the police had now been actively employed for more than three weeks, they had failed in discovering Simon Pownall's retreat. On reading this letter to Old Hazy, I observed a singular smile cross his countenance, and he remarked—"Ah! they'll never catch Dr. Hooker."

"I shouldn't care if the rascal did get off," I said, "provided he left the will behind him."

"Give yourself no concern about that," he observed. "The will will turn up soon. I am sure of it. There are more ways than one of discovering lost treasure," he added, significantly. "And I flatter myself that I am quite as likely to hit upon the right plan as Cuthbert Spring or Major Atherton."

On that same day another circumstance occurred, which confirmed the suspicions aroused within me by the old gentleman's observations. For a long period—ever since the disappearance of the Thaumaturgus, in fact—no nocturnal disturbance had occurred at Owlarton Grange; but Mr. Ponder now imparted to me in confidence that he had heard mysterious sounds in the haunted chamber, and he was afraid Jotham Shocklach was about to resume his midnight knockings. At this time, though I passed the greater part of the day at the Grange, I invariably slept at the mill; but after what I had just heard from Ponder, I thought I would try the effect upon Old Hazy of a proposal to occupy the haunted room that night. As I expected, he did not like it at all, made several absurd excuses, and ended by saying that I could have the room to-morrow—but not that night. I felt sure then that my suspicions were correct, but determined to satisfy myself before taking any decided steps.

I took leave of the old gentleman at the usual hour in the evening, but, instead of starting for the mill, I remained in the garden, and concealing myself in the yew-tree alley, did not issue from this retreat till I judged that the inmates of the house had retired to rest. I then came out upon the lawn, and took up a position commanding the large bay-window of the haunted chamber. The night was perfectly dark, so it was not likely I should be perceived. All the lights in the house seemed to be extinguished, and apparently no one was astir.

This state of things continued for more than half an hour, until I heard a clock strike the hour of midnight. Scarcely had the sound ceased, than the window at which I was gazing became suddenly illuminated. Unluckily, the thick curtains, which I have already mentioned in my description of the room, were partially drawn across the deep embrasure, so I could not distinguish what was passing inside. But careful watching soon convinced me that there were two persons in the chamber. One of them, unquestionably, was Old Hazy; and the other, or I was greatly mistaken, was the Thaumaturgus.

But as I could not leave the matter in doubt, I considered how I could ascertain the point without giving the alarm. There was no ladder at hand to aid my investigation as on a former occasion, but I soon found that, by taking advantage of the branches of a large pear-tree which had been trained against the wall, I could reach the window, and I at once put the idea into execution. Proceeding with great caution, I quickly ascended so high that, by grasping a branch of the pear-tree with my right hand, and planting the point of my foot on the window-sill, I was enabled to peep into the room. Still the thick curtain defied my scrutiny. But though I could not see, I could hear; and the voice which reached me was that of Pownall. The rascal was evidently concluding some arrangement with his dupe.

"Well, then," he said, "I am to have the money to-morrow night, provided I put you in possession of all my magical treasures——"

"Not forgetting the will," Old Hazy interrupted. "You mustn't omit that."

"Oh! yes, you may count upon the will," Simon rejoined. "I shan't be sorry to be rid of it. But mind! you are not to deliver it to young Clitheroe until a month after I am gone. You will pledge your word to that effect?"

"I will," the old gentleman rejoined. "To-morrow night, at the same hour, we will meet again for the last time—but not here—in the summer-house. If you are ready to fulfil your part of the bargain, I will fulfil mine."

"Oh! you needn't be afraid of me," Simon rejoined. "I'm sure to be ready. I'm only too anxious to be off. Though I oughtn't to say so, for you have afforded me a secure asylum."

"Yes, yes, they never thought of looking for you here," the old gentleman replied, with a laugh. "I am not quite sure that I am right in affording you a hiding-place, but I couldn't betray a professor of the occult sciences."

"Of course not," Simon rejoined. "But as I was saying, I want to be off. The wound in my side caused by the pistol-shot is quite healed, and I feel strong enough for the voyage I contemplate to the New World. Ah! if that ball hadn't glanced off my ribs, all would have been up with me. Captain Sale thought he had laid me low, and fancied he had buried his secret in the dyke; but it will rise up against him, when he least expects it. Even now he persuades himself that I will make terms with him, but I will never do so. That will shall never come into his hands. Money shan't buy it him. I will only use it as an instrument of revenge. It will hit more sharply than his pistol-shot. He tried to take my life, and though I won't take his life in return, I'll ruin him."

There was a short pause, during which he no doubt perceived that he had gone too far, and that this injudicious manifestation of his vindictive feelings had startled his companion, for he added, by way of mollifying the old gentleman—"But such sentiments as these are unworthy of a philosopher, and must be repressed. I will strive to bear no man malice—not even Captain Sale."

"I am glad to hear you say so," Old Hazy replied. "But you have never explained to me how you escaped that night. How did you contrive to get out of the dyke?"

"It was a wonderful escape to be sure, sir," Pownall replied; "indeed, it would almost appear that I was born neither to be shot nor drowned. Luckily for me when I fell into the dyke my head remained above water, for I couldn't stir for some minutes. When I could use my limbs once more, I crawled slowly along the bottom of the trench, until at last I reached a pool, where I crept out, and in doing so lost one of my shoes——"

"Which we found, together with your neckerchief," Old Hazy remarked. "Pray go on."

"After resting myself for some time upon the bank, I mustered up strength enough to carry me across the moor, staggering on till I reached the Chester road, where, as good luck would have it, a waggon chanced to be passing at the time on its way to Cottonborough, through Northwich. I told the waggoner I had missed my way across the forest and had got into a bog, and, my appearance confirming the statement the man believed me, took compassion upon me, and allowed me to get into the back of his wain, and rest myself amidst the straw. He left me at a little roadside inn about a mile from Marston, whence I despatched a messenger with a note to Chetham Quick, who came to me at once."

"Chetham Quick could safely swear, then—as he did in giving his evidence—that he knew you were alive," Old Hazy remarked; "but he declared you were unhurt."

"Chetham would swear black is white if he thought anybody would believe him," Pownall replied. "The double-dealing rascal is in Captain Sale's pay. However, I won't say anything against him, for he behaved kindly enough to me on that occasion—concealed me in a place of security—dressed my wound—gave me restoratives—supplied me with clothes—money—and whatever else I required. In return, he wanted me to give up the will to Captain Sale. But that wouldn't do. So I took French leave of him a few nights ago, and came to you. And now, sir, I think we had better separate. I am fearful of being discovered. To-morrow at midnight—in the summer-house—all shall be concluded. Then I'll trouble you no longer." And I could tell from the sound that he was moving off.

"You can find your way in the dark?" Old Hazy demanded.

"As easily as a cat," the Thaumaturgus replied.

Listening attentively, I then heard the trap-door let down, and knew which way he had gone. I waited for a moment or two longer, until the closing of the door told me that the chamber was deserted, and then descended.

This was the business that took me to Marston.

CHAPTER XVII.

FORTUNE AT LAST FAVOURS ME.

NEXT morning I rode to Marston, as I have stated, and despatched Ned Culcheth to Cottonborough with a letter to Major Atherton, acquainting him with the discovery I had made, and begging him to come over that evening with Cuthbert Spring. I requested them to meet me at the mill at ten o'clock, and to bring an officer with them. I felt sure they would not disappoint me.

Before starting for Marston I had taken the precaution of making such arrangements with Ponder and Stephen Blackden that Pownall could not escape; though indeed I had little uneasiness on that score, for I felt sure the rascal would keep his appointment with Old Hazy. No doubt we could have discovered his hiding-place, but the grand object was to secure the will, and this might have been defeated by any precipitate measures.

On my return, I thought it best to prepare Miss Hazilrigge and Ora for what might occur at night, and very much surprised they both were by my relation. Many odd and unaccountable things as her brother had done, Miss Hazilrigge said, this was the oddest and most unaccountable of all. This juggling Pownall had bewitched him. "However," she said, "I am rejoiced that the rascal is likely to be caught at last, and I sincerely hope that the ridiculous position in which my brother will find himself placed will serve him as a lesson for the rest of his life."

The kind lady then expressed her willingness to act in any way that I might direct her, and I recommended that nothing whatever should be done to excite the old gentleman's suspicions. She promised to keep watch over the household. Ponder, old Finch, and Stephen Blackden had already been taken into my confidence, and could be safely relied upon, but none of the others were to be let into the secret.

In the course of the afternoon I took an opportunity of examining the summer-house. It was a pretty octagonal structure, situated, as I have already mentioned, on the top of a small mount, and had large windows looking in every direction over the gardens. Internally, this pleasant little structure had a coved ceiling, moulded and painted with frescoes, and the spaces between the windows were decorated in a similar manner. Its sole furniture consisted of some half-dozen rustic chairs and a table; and the latter being covered with a piece of old tapestry which hung down nearly to the ground, immediately suggested a place of concealment to me. The summit of the mound outside the summer-house was flagged, the sides being covered with shrubs, and access was gained to the building by a flight of stone steps.

The rest of the day seemed to pass very slowly, and I wandered about the garden, longing for the arrival of night. Old Hazy did not show himself till dinner-time. He was in particularly good spirits, and while we were sitting together over our wine, after the departure of the ladies, he told me, with a very mysterious look, that he felt sure he should soon have good news for me.

"A month hence, I prognosticate you will be a rich man, Mervyn," he remarked, with a laugh.

"Why do you fix that precise time, sir?" I demanded.

"Because I have been casting a horoscope," he replied; "and I find from the configuration of the planets that your uncle's will will be certainly recovered at that time."

"If recovered at all, it will be so before then," I rejoined.

"No it won't!" he cried, with great emphasis. "Mark my words, it will be found this day month—not a day—not an hour sooner. My calculations never err. If you get it before the period I have named, write me down an ignorant pretender."

"If I *should* chance find it before," I ventured to reply, with a certain significance, "I hope you will never place faith in impudent pretenders again, sir."

"Ha! what's that?" he exclaimed, quickly. "But I know you look upon all professors of occult philosophy as impostors."

"Not without good reason, sir," I rejoined. And here the conversation dropped.

Everything was favourable for the scheme. The night was dark but fine, so the ladies could venture forth into the garden, without any kind of discomfort. Before ten o'clock I went away, having previously arranged with Miss Hazilrigge that a little before midnight she and Ora, accompanied by the three men-servants, should repair to the *allée verte*, where they would find Cuthbert Spring and Major Atherton. As soon as I gave the signal, which I had agreed to do by sounding a dog-whistle, the whole party were to hurry up to the summer-house, where I doubted not all would be accomplished.

I made haste to the mill, and found that my friends had already arrived, and had brought an officer with them. In anticipation of a successful result, they had given Ned Culcheth orders how to act on the morrow. If the gipsies could be found they were to be secured, and a warrant was to be obtained for Malpas's arrest, but not to be put in execution until our arrival.

As the night was now advancing, and I was anxious to be at my post, I soon set off back again to the Grange, leaving the others to follow more leisurely. Avoiding the stone bridge in front of the house, I pursued a circuitous route to the stables, where I found Stephen Blackden, and committed my horse to his care. In another moment

I was in the garden, and speeding through the dark alley in the direction of the summer-house.

The night was pitch dark. Not a star shone down upon me, but I wanted no guidance, for I knew every inch of the ground, and very soon gained the top of the mount, and entered the little building. It was almost too dark to discern any object in the interior, but after stepping quickly round the room to make sure that no one was there, I proceeded to ensconce myself under the table.

If time had passed slowly before, it now seemed not to move at all, and I do not recollect in the whole course of my life a half-hour so long as that passed under the table in the summer-house.

At length, to my indescribable delight, I heard the stable clock strike twelve. In another moment footsteps were audible outside, and then the door was opened. One of them was come. My heart beat so violently that I had to hold my hand against my side to still it.

After entering the room, the new-comer stood still for a moment, and called out, "Are you here, Dr. Hooker?" Receiving no answer of course, the old gentleman uncovered a dark lantern which he had brought with him, and which he must have hitherto carried under his cloak, and suddenly lighted up the place. I was afraid he might be tempted to look under the table, and so detect my presence, but no such thought crossed him. Having surveyed the room for a moment, and muttered something to himself, he closed the cover of the lantern, and all became dark again. Then I heard him approach the table, and sit down upon one of the chairs beside it.

For a minute or two he remained perfectly quiet, but after that he began to manifest his impatience in various ways, drummed upon the table over my head, and exclaimed, "Why doesn't he come? It is past the hour. What can have detained him?" Two or three minutes more elapsed, and my neighbour's impatience seemed to increase, while mine most undoubtedly did not diminish. At last a noise was heard outside, and Old Hazy started up, exclaiming, "Ah! here he comes at last!"

Oh! how overjoyed I felt when Pownall's quick step resounded in the room, and I distinguished his voice. My first impulse was to spring from my concealment and seize him, but anxiety to ascertain that he had brought the will with him restrained me.

"Are you there, sir?" he inquired.

"Yes, here I am," Old Hazy replied; "and here I have been for the last quarter of an hour. You're behind time."

"I'm sorry to have kept you waiting, sir," Pownall rejoined; "but I couldn't come sooner. However, I'm quite ready for you."

"I'm glad to hear it," the old gentleman rejoined. "I'm quite ready too. Let me hear what you have got."

"Open wide your ears then, worthy sir, while I particularise the marvellous contents of this wallet," the other replied. "In it you will find a scroll drawn up by the great Cornelius Agrippa himself; another scroll covered with magical characters for raising spirits, in the handwriting of Dr. Dee. Also Dr. Dee's wondrous piece of crystal."

"Are you sure it is Dr. Dee's crystal?" Old Hazy cried. "I have seen an extraordinary stone belonging to the illustrious doctor in the possession of a learned friend of mine—the President of the Chetham Society—but I never met with the crystal."

"Here you will find it, then," Pownall replied; "you will also find Pope Leo's magical speculum, and the original compact between Dr. Faustus and the Prince of Darkness, with the doctor's signature traced in his own blood, and the sign-manual of Satan, with which you are sufficiently familiar, I know, to be able to identify it."

"But how did you obtain the latter remarkable document?" Old Hazy inquired.

"It is a long story, and I have not time to relate it now," the other rejoined. "But you may rely upon its authenticity. Then there are curious secrets by Albertus Magnus—secrets never yet revealed to the world; undiscovered treasures by the Lesser Albert; treatises, that have never yet seen the light, by Paracelsus, Cardan, and Michael Scott."

"Amazement!" the old gentleman exclaimed. "What a wonderful collection you have got together!—and all in that wallet!"

"I have not enumerated half—not a third," Simon replied; "there is an original treatise on Judicial Astrology by Joseph de Tertiis; and another most remarkable discourse on the interpretation of dreams by the great Artemidorus."

"You don't say so?—an unpublished work by Artemidorus!" Old Hazy exclaimed. "Oh! if you had anything unknown to the world by Psellus, or my favourite Robert de Triez!"

"You will find short treatises by both of them," Pownall replied.

"I am eager to inspect them," the credulous old gentleman cried. "Dear me! to think that such treasures should exist!"

"You will possess some of the greatest curiosities in the world," Pownall returned. "Necessity alone compels me to part with the collection."

"No doubt of it," Old Hazy said. "Well, I have brought a pocket-book with me containing the sum you require — namely, 500*l*.,—but there is one thing more which you have not yet mentioned, but which I shall require before the money is paid—the will."

"Old Mobberley's rightful will, constituting Mervyn Clitheroe his heir," Pownall cried. "It is here."

And he clapped the parchment upon the table with a report that made every fibre in my frame quiver.

Was the will really there? or did it only belong to the string of fables with which he had been deluding Old Hazy? My misgivings were soon dispelled.

"I must look at that will," the old gentleman said, uncovering the dark lantern, and once more throwing a light upon the scene.

"Yes, look at it, sir!—satisfy yourself that it is all right," Pownall cried; "but pray be quick! The light may betray us."

"I won't be long," Old Hazy rejoined. "Yes, yes, there is no doubt about it. This is the document we have been in quest of so long. This is old Mobberley's rightful will."

Scarcely were the words uttered than I sprang from beneath the table, and stood before the startled pair. The lantern had not been darkened, and the first object that met my view was the will lying partly open upon the table. I instantly seized it, and having secured it, placed the whistle to my lips, and blew a loud call.

Hitherto, not a word had been spoken. Both Pownall and Old Hazy were stupified by my unexpected appearance; but the sound of the whistle recalled Pownall to a consciousness of danger, and he made an effort to fly. In vain. Instantly seizing him, I forced him into a chair. At the same moment lights could be seen without, and several figures appeared at the windows.

"What does all this mean?" Old Hazy cried.

"It means that I am betrayed by you," Pownall cried, in a rage. "I see through it all. I took you for an old idiot—but you have wit enough, it seems, to circumvent me."

Before the old gentleman could make any answer, the door of the summer-house was thrown open, and the interior of the little building was filled by the party I had summoned. The first to enter were Major Atherton, Cuthbert Spring, and the officer.

"Here is your prisoner," I said, consigning Pownall to the latter. "Don't let him slip through your fingers."

"No fear of that, sir," the officer rejoined, putting a pair of handcuffs over Pownall's wrists. "I'll forgive him if he gets away from me."

"Have you got the will?" Major Atherton eagerly demanded.

"Yes, here it is," I answered, producing it. "I am righted at last. Here is my title to my uncle Mobberley's property."

"Huzza!" Cuthbert Spring exclaimed. And the joyful shout was repeated by Ponder and the others, while the two ladies clapped their hands.

"Most sincerely do I congratulate you, my dear boy," Major Atherton said. "And I trust that fortune, who has so long regarded you with frowns, will henceforth only smile upon you."

"Let me look at the will for a moment," Cuthbert Spring said. "Yes, I see it's all right. Well, you are a lucky fellow, Mervyn. Two thousand a year—that's your income."

Old Hazy did not say a word, but seemed overwhelmed with confusion. Miss Hazilrigge now addressed him.

"Brother, brother!" she cried, "are you not ashamed of yourself to have been so long the dupe of such a miserable juggler as this?"

The old gentleman made no reply, but hung his head.

"Are you not ashamed of yourself, I say?" his sister repeated.

"I'm not quite such a miserable juggler as you suppose, madam,"

Pownall cried: the rascal had by this time recovered his assurance. "Your brother is not the only person who has taken me for a conjuror, though I must say," he added, with a laugh, "that he is the most credulous gull I ever met with."

"You hear that, brother?" Miss Hazilrigge cried. "You hear what the impudent rascal calls you?"

"Yes, I hear it," the old gentleman groaned.

"I could make him swallow anything," Pownall cried, chuckling. "He believes that yonder wallet contains Dr. Dee's crystal, Pope Leo's speculum, Dr. Faustus's compact with Satan, together with unpublished treatises by all his favourite writers on occult philosophy —ha! ha! ha!"

"What! you have told me a pack of lies, eh?" Old Hazy cried. "There are no magic scrolls—no crystal—no speculum—no diabolic compact—no treatises by Artemidorus, Psellus, Robert de Triez, and the others?"

"You had better look for them," Pownall rejoined, coolly.

"Oh! you prodigious villain! Oh! you arch deceiver! I'll strangle you!" the old gentleman cried, with an explosion of rage. And he might have executed his threat if we had not stopped him. "Oh, sister!" he added, "how egregiously I have been duped. Well may this rascal call me an old idiot. I merit the appellation."

"You will be a wiser man in future, I am quite certain, brother," Miss Hazilrigge replied, kindly. "I have hopes of you now."

"If my good friend will only forswear his books of magic, witchcraft, and judicial astrology, and avoid such society as he has here formed, his cure will be complete," Cuthbert Spring remarked.

"I'll do it!" Old Hazy exclaimed. "I'll burn all my books to-morrow. I won't keep one of them."

"Not even Robert de Triez?" I asked, with a smile.

"Not even Robert," he answered, firmly.

"I shall hold you to your promise, brother," Miss Hazilrigge said. "You hear what your master says, Ponder. ALL the books in his study are to be burnt." And she gave him some private directions in an under tone.

"I shall be very glad to do it, ma'am," the butler replied; "and to clear the house of all such vermin as have so long infested it," he added, with a glance at Pownall.

"Since things have taken this turn," Cuthbert Spring remarked, "any objections I might have had to a country life are removed. I shall give up Cottonborough."

"And come to Owlarton Grange. Delighted to hear you say so!" Old Hazy exclaimed. "I hope soon to call you brother-in-law."

"Oh! pray don't talk in that way?" Miss Hazilrigge cried.

"You can't expect my uncle to spare your blushes, aunt," Ora said, "after taking him to task so sharply as you have just done."

"Hold your tongue, you saucy minx!" the elderly spinster rejoined.

"Well, gentlemen," Old Hazy said to the major and Mr. Spring, "you have taken me a little by surprise, but you shall have the best accommodation I can offer you. You will sleep at the Grange, of course?"

"Of course they will, brother," Miss Hazilrigge interposed. "I expected them, and have provided accordingly."

"Yes, we must trespass upon your hospitality to-night, Mr. Hazilrigge," Major Atherton observed. "Our work is not ended. We have more to do to-morrow."

"I hope you won't let Captain Sale and the two gipsies escape, gentlemen," Pownall cried. "Only confront me with them, and you shall hear what nice disclosures I will make."

"You shall have an opportunity of speaking out, depend upon it," Major Atherton rejoined. "Mr. Hazilrigge, I must beg your permission to keep this rascal here to-night in custody of the officer. By this time to-morrow, he will be lodged, I trust, with his three accomplices, in Chester gaol."

"Stephen Blackden shall put him in the farm-house, and keep watch over him with the officer," the old gentleman replied. "And now, since we have nothing more to detain us here, suppose we adjourn to the house."

"You will find supper ready for you," Miss Hazilrigge said. "I am sure dear Mr. Spring will be all the better after his journey for a slice of cold chicken and a glass of champagne—and so will the major."

"Upon my word, you are very considerate, my dear Miss Hazilrigge," the old bachelor rejoined, gallantly offering her his arm.

We had a very merry supper that night, and my health was drunk in foaming bumpers of champagne by all the party.

I slept that night in the haunted chamber—and haunted I was, not by Jotham Shocklach, but by my uncle Mobberley. Before retiring to rest, I had read over the will and placed it for better security under my pillow—so no wonder I dreamed of him who made it.

CHAPTER XVIII.

THE STEEPLE-CHASE.

I AWOKE next morning in a very strange state of mind. For a few moments I could not believe in the occurrences of the previous night. Had I indeed become suddenly wealthy? Was I really possessed of two thousand a year? Was Nethercrofts mine at last? The will might have disappeared like a fairy favour. To satisfy myself, I thrust my hand beneath the pillow, and brought it forth. Yes, there it was beyond all question. I opened it and began to read it again, though by this time I was perfectly familiar with its contents. Blessings on him! my dear old uncle Mobberley had constituted me his heir. In all other respects the will corresponded with that which had been acted upon—the various bequests made in both instruments being identical, with one material exception. I hugged the precious parchment to my bosom, and thought I would never let it out of my possession. I am ashamed to relate the follies I committed. I sang, laughed—even wept—with delight. Springing out of bed, I began to caper about the room, and was still exercising my limbs in this manner when the door suddenly opened and Ponder entered. As I did not immediately desist from my saltatory performance, but even bounded about with increased vigour, the sedate butler gazed at me in perfect bewilderment, showing by his countenance that he thought I must have taken leave of my senses.

"Give me joy, Ponder!" I exclaimed—"give me joy! I am just come into two thousand a year."

"I am quite aware of it, sir," the butler replied; "and the fortunate circumstance may account for your exhilaration."

"I mean to make everybody about me happy and comfortable," I continued. "I have a great regard for you, Ponder—a particular regard—and shall evince it by making you a handsome present."

"Very much obleeged to you, I'm sure, sir," he replied, bowing respectfully. "But excuse me for saying, that I hope now you've come into your property that you'll take care of it."

"I mean to do so, Ponder," I replied. "But I thank you for your excellent advice, and will double the gratuity I intended to make you."

The butler again bowed, and I executed a pirouette before him.

"Shall I open the window, sir?" he asked, beginning to be slightly alarmed.

"By all means, Ponder," I replied. "A little fresh air will be agreeable. By-the-by, has he escaped?"

"Who, sir—the prisoner?" he exclaimed. "Oh, no! we have him safe enough."

"I'm sorry for it," I rejoined.

"What! sorry he has not escaped, sir?" he cried, staring at me.

"Well, it is odd, Ponder," I said, rather more calmly; "but I feel so uncommonly happy just now, that I can't bear to think of anybody being miserable. I wish Pownall had got off."

"That would never do, sir," he replied, gravely. "Such a rascal mustn't be allowed to go at large. He doesn't seem to be much concerned at his position, and his main anxiety appears to be that Captain Sale and the gipsies should be taken. He talks of all he has done with great freedom to the officer, and says he means to make a clean breast of it. By-the-by, you'll be glad to hear, sir, that all my master's books of magic and witchcraft are burnt."

"What, *all* his treasures, Ponder?" I cried, becoming suddenly tranquil.

"Every one of 'em, sir," he replied. "Not a single volume has been spared. Miss Hazilrigge was fearful he might change his mind, and bade me set to work the first thing, so I called up the men at four o'clock this morning—long before the old gentleman opened his eyes—and we made a great bonfire in the yard, and threw all the abominable rubbish into it. A precious lot of musty old books there was, sir. We filled a large clothes-basket choke full wi' 'em more than a dozen times. One of the last we threw into the fire was that big black book, which he used to call the Devil's Grammar" (Mr. Ponder meant the Grimoire), "and you should have seen how it hissed and crackled. You'd ha' thought it had got into its natural element. You may smell the smoke of the bonfire even here. My master will never behold his treasures again—and a good job too!—but Pownall saw the last of 'em, for the window of the room in which he is confined looks out into the yard, and he and the officer perceiving the blaze, came forward to ascertain what we were doing. You should have seen how the old rascal grinned as we cast basketful after basketful of books into the fire."

"Well, I hope your master won't be angry, Ponder," I said.

"No fear of that, sir," he replied. "When I went into his room just now I told him what I had done, and he said it was all right. He would never have had the heart to give the order for the execution himself, he declared, but he was glad it was over. I do verily believe, sir, that henceforth my master will be a very different person. His eyes seem fairly opened at last, and if he gets rid of his eccentricities and oddities, he will be one of the best and kindest men breathing."

"He is that already, Ponder," I replied. "But I am delighted with what you tell me about him."

Shortly afterwards, the butler left me, and as soon as my toilet was completed I came down stairs, having by this time regained my customary composure. I could not make up my mind to part with the will, but kept it in a place of safety about my person.

When we met at breakfast I received the warmest congratulations from the whole party, and little else was talked about except my good luck. Miss Hazilrigge and Ora laid out the most delightful plans for my future life, in which, as a matter of course, Apphia was included, and I was so intoxicated with success, that I began to fancy that everything would turn out exactly as they arranged it.

"I despair of nothing now, my dear Miss Hazilrigge," I said. "Still there is a great difficulty to be overcome in the person of Lady Amicia Wilburton."

I observed Major Atherton and Cuthbert Spring exchange significant looks when I made this observation, and the latter remarked, with a smile,

"I don't think your case quite so hopeless now as heretofore, Mervyn. As possessor of Nethercrofts, Lady Amicia may be more favourably disposed towards you. Let us get over the business of to-day, and we will then turn our attention to that important point."

Old Hazy was in excellent spirits. I had never seen him more cheerful—so it was evident that the destruction of his once-beloved books did not weigh upon his mind. I should not have ventured to say anything to him on the subject, but he referred to it himself, declaring that he would never again read a treatise on the occult sciences. And I may add that he has kept his word.

This being the day appointed for the steeple-chase, we knew where to find Malpas. The race was to be run at three o'clock, and before that hour we meant to be upon the ground. From what Ned Culcheth had stated to my two friends there was little doubt that Phaleg and his son would be captured at the same time.

At noon we started for Marston—Old Hazy in his antiquated barouche, with Major Atherton and Cuthbert Spring; Pownall and the officer in the post-chaise, which had been retained for the purpose. I rode on before the others, wishing to call at Weverham, and acquaint John with the good news. He was equally surprised and delighted by my relation.

"You are, indeed, most fortunate, Mervyn," he said, "and I pray that you may live long to enjoy your newly-acquired property."

I thanked him heartily, and said that I only required one thing now to make me entirely happy—his sister's hand.

"If that is all you lack to complete your felicity," he replied, with a kindly smile, "I do not think it will be wanting. Do not question me further. I may not speak."

I left my friend full of joyous anticipations—the only drawback to which was my incertitude as to the conclusion of his own love affair. I had not ventured to introduce the topic, having nothing satisfactory to communicate.

As I returned to the highway, on quitting the village of Weverham, I came upon the barouche and post-chaise, and after chatting for a short time with the occupants of the former vehicle, galloped on in advance.

Oh! how I enjoyed that ride! Everything took a colour from

the sunshine in my breast. The landscape brightened and revealed beauties and picturesque combinations which I had not hitherto discerned in it. Not a sound—not an object but yielded me delight. All seemed in harmony with my own blissful feelings. Even the consideration of the unpleasant task on which I was bound did not obtrude itself upon me, until I came within half a mile of Marston, when I was reminded of it by seeing Ned Culcheth.

The trusty fellow was seated on a bench in front of a little wayside inn, and as I came in sight, he started up and ran towards me. On learning that I had got the will, he took off his cap, and waved it over his head with a prolonged and joyous shout. After this demonstration of delight, he held out his honest hand to me, and I grasped it cordially. He then tried another shout, but this time his voice failed him, and he was obliged to brush the moisture from his eyes.

"Hang it!" he exclaimed, "I don't know how it be. I never felt so glad in all my life, and yet I must needs be snivelling. This will be rare news for Sissy, and for all Marston, when they come to hear it."

"I dare say they can give us a glass of good ale yonder, Ned?" I said, pointing to the little inn.

"As good as any in Cheshire," he responded.

"We'll try it, then," I said. "You must drink my health."

Upon this we repaired to the inn, where I alighted, and Ned emptied a glass of the nut-brown beverage to my health and happiness. When the honest fellow's enthusiastic delight had somewhat abated, I questioned him as to the steeple-chase. He told me that no change had taken place in the arrangements, but that the match was to be run at three o'clock, as appointed, and that Captain Sale was expected to win it.

"He may win the race, Ned," I remarked, "but he will lose all else—honour and liberty. What of the gipsies?"

"Captured by this time I make no doubt, sir," he replied. "They have been seen this morning, and the officers are after 'em."

"And Malpas has no suspicions, you think, Ned, that a warrant has been obtained for his arrest?"

"None whatever, sir," he rejoined. "I wouldn't trust Bryan Peover, so I placed it in the hands of Mike Heron, the Knutsford constable. Mike won't hesitate to do the business. Captain Sale has been stayin' for the last week wi' his uncle Squire Vernon, at Fitton Park, and not half an hour ago I met one of the squire's keepers, who told me the captain is in wonderful spirits, and makes sure of winnin' 1000*l.* by the match."

While we were thus conversing, the barouche came up, and was brought to a halt, as was the post-chaise that followed it containing the prisoner. Pownall was at once recognised by the keeper of the wayside inn, which proved to be the house where the caitiff had been left by the waggoner on the night of his escape from the dyke.

A brief consultation was then held as to the course to be pursued. Major Atherton and Cuthbert Spring were for arresting Malpas at once, but Old Hazy pleaded hard that he should be allowed to run the race.

"Don't deprive him of the amusement," he said. "It may be the last race he will ever run."

The last race he would ever run! Little did the old gentleman deem how prophetic were the words he uttered.

After a short halt, we went on, Ned getting up in front of the post-chaise. Very few persons noticed us as we passed through Marston. The village was almost deserted, the majority of the inhabitants having gone to witness the race. Simon Pownall, who was anxious to elude observation, leaned as far back as he could in the chaise, but he was recognised notwithstanding by more than one old acquaintance.

Our road took us past Nethercrofts. As we passed by the old farm-house, I saw Hannah standing at the orchard gate, and could not help stopping to tell her of the extraordinary changes that had taken place. When she heard that my uncle Mobberley's rightful will had been found, and that I was now incontestable heir to the property, she held up her hands and screamed with delight, calling out, "Well, to be sure! Who'd ha' thought it?" Her husband, William Weever, she told me, was gone to see the race, and I should most likely meet him on the ground. She would answer for it he would be rarely pleased with the news.

After bestowing a glance at the dear old farm-house, enchanted to think that I could now call it my own, I hastened after the others, and overtook them at the bottom of a gentle descent which had brought them within a short distance of the mere. My breast swelled, for all I saw was mine—those rich meads and pleasant pasture-land, and that picturesque coppice, running down to the borders of the lake, all belonged to me.

We went on for nearly a quarter of a mile further, and I was still on my own ground, when we came to the locality of the steeple-chase.

On the summit of a gentle eminence on the right, about half a mile off, which eminence commanded a complete view of the whole line of country marked out for the race, a stand had been erected. Close to it were three or four booths. The entire crown of the hill and part of the sides were occupied, as at a regular race, by a throng of spectators on horseback or on foot, mixed up with vehicles of various kinds, from the landau and phaeton to the gig and taxed-cart. Of horsemen there could not have been fewer than three or four hundred, while of persons on foot there must have been double that number. Plenty of witnesses, I could not help thinking, of Malpas's approaching disgrace.

The stand was filled with spectators—chiefly ladies, most of them, no doubt, wives and daughters of the neighbouring gentry—and above it floated a large flag. The course to be taken by the riders in the race was indicated by tall flagstaffs planted at various points, and seemed to have been skilfully planned, as it offered many difficulties, while at the same time there were plenty of open spaces left, over which the horses could stretch well out, and make good trial of their speed. As we came in sight of the hill loud shouting was heard, and great commotion was perceptible among the horsemen, several of whom were riding to and fro, proving that the race was just about to begin.

Both vehicles were at once brought to a halt, and while the others were alighting I dashed through a gate into a large field on the right, at the bottom of which flowed a brook, forming the boundary of the Nethercrofts estate. This brook, as was shown by the flag-staff on the opposite bank, had to be crossed by the riders, and at a place of great hazard. Not only was the stream upwards of thirty feet wide at this point, but its banks were broken, while there were several old pollard-willows that seemed to stand right in the way, and great caution would be required to avoid these trees while making a jump. Altogether it was a most awkward spot, as I saw at a glance. Indeed, I knew the place well, having often angled in the brook. In anticipation of mischief, a number of lookers-on had collected on the further side of the brook, while some adventurous country bumpkins and lads had clambered up the pollard-trees in hopes of obtaining a better view. I was about to ride down the field, when my attention was directed to a group consisting of some half-dozen men, with a woman near them. In the latter I at once recognised Rue, and I knew who the others must be.

As I advanced, I descried Phaleg and his son with an officer on either side of them. Both gipsies were handcuffed. Poor Rue, who was evidently much cast down, looked reproachfully at me, but did not speak. I could not but feel compassion for her. The constables told me, with a laugh, that they had pounced upon the ruffians the moment they entered the field. Mike Heron, the Knutsford constable, now came forward, and touching his hat, asked if I had any orders to give him. I told him to go up to the stand, near which the winning-post was situated, and as soon as the race was over, to arrest Captain Sale. Mike departed on his errand forthwith.

By this time Major Atherton and the others had come up, bringing Pownall with them in charge of the officer. On finding that his accomplices were captured, Pownall testified his extreme satisfaction, and commenced jeering them bitterly. The gipsies scowled at him, but made no reply to his taunts.

After a moment's debate, it was decided that we should station ourselves near the pollards, so I dismounted, and leaving my horse in charge of a farming lad, we moved down in a body towards the brook, the officers following us with the three prisoners.

Scarcely had we taken up a position, when a bell was rung, informing us that the riders had started, and we presently caught a glimpse of them speeding across the clear space on the near side of the mill. At this moment Captain Brereton took the lead, though Malpas was not far behind him. Both were in jockey-dresses, Malpas wearing a blue cap, with a white jacket crossed by a broad sky-blue stripe, and his opponent a white cap and pink jacket. As far as could be judged, they

seemed pretty well matched in regard to horses, and both rode remarkably well. Two flights of hurdles were cleared in no time, and then we lost sight of them both for a few moments. Over a stiff fence they both came at last, doing their work in gallant style, but Malpas was now ahead, and kept his place as they flew across the open. On—on—on. They were now within a hundred yards of the brook, and were greeted by the cheers of the spectators. Malpas's name was chiefly coupled with the shouts. He still led, and the cries were that he would win.

Despite the peculiar circumstances in which I stood in reference to one of the riders, it was impossible not to be interested in so well-contested a race. I approached the side of the stream the better to observe them, and my example was followed by Major Atherton and Cuthbert Spring. In this position I think I must have caught the eye of Malpas, though I cannot be sure, but it seemed to me that he noticed me, and slightly swerved. Be this as it may, a sudden flush overspread his countenance, which had hitherto been pale with excitement. However, he held on unfalteringly. He was now full twenty yards in advance of Captain Brereton, and the crowd of spectators collected at this point cheered him as winner. With these shouts ringing in his ears he charged the brook.

From the style in which his horse jumped I thought the animal would have landed him in safety—but I was mistaken. A terrible crash told me that an accident had happened. But I scarcely saw it, for all passed like a vision before my swimming eyes. The horse was down, and Malpas was lying, stunned and bleeding, and with fast-approaching death written in unmistakable characters on his countenance, at the foot of one of the pollard-trees, against which he had been dashed. A moment before he had been full of power, pride, triumph—now he lay there helpless as a crushed worm—dying!

In the midst of the fearful outcries occasioned by this disastrous occurrence, Captain Brereton, who could not, of course, check himself, leaped the brook, and with better luck than Malpas, landing upon a firm spot on the bank, and, avoiding the pollards, went on, shouting that he would bring medical aid directly. But it would be of no use. All the surgeons in Cheshire, or in England, could not help Malpas now.

As soon as Captain Brereton was out of the way, we rushed to Malpas, but he besought us not to move him, for his agony was excruciating. At this moment, a piercing shriek arose, and Rue rushed forward. Her wrongs were forgotten, and all the tenderness she had once felt for her betrayer returned to her breast. Kneeling beside him, she took his head gently upon her lap, and strove by every means in her power to alleviate his sufferings. Aware who was near him, the dying man thanked her by his looks.

The scene, which produced an ineffaceable impression upon me, now rises before me with its minutest details. I see Malpas stretched upon the bank, at the foot of the pollard-willow, groaning with agony—with no power of movement in his well-shaped limbs. What a contrast does his gay attire offer to his ghastly looks! He is supported by the poor gipsy girl whom he has wronged, who watches him with intense anxiety, and would lay down her life to save him. Behind. stands his groom, holding his unlucky steed, which is but slightly injured. Amongst the spectators of the accident are many who have known the dying man, and are. affected in various ways. Cuthbert Spring and Old Hazy, who are standing near the sufferer, seem quite horrified by the dreadful occurrence, and so does Ned Culcheth, but Major Atherton looks grimly on. He has seen death too often on the battle-field to be moved. But there is another group on which the spectacle might be expected to produce a powerful effect —a group consisting of the reckless young man's evil associates, Simon Pownall and the gipsies. How are they affected? Phaleg and his son look on with sullen unconcern, and the vice-hardened countenance of the elder gipsy displays no emotion whatever. Obed is not quite so stoical, but even he has a callous look. But Pownall, who is seated on the ground, averts his gaze, and tries to stop his ears with his manacled hands. All his cynicism is gone.

Such was the aspect presented by the various groups gathered around the dying man. For myself, I can affirm that I was dreadfully shocked, and that feelings of commiseration were paramount to all others in my breast.

Malpas at last made me out, and fixing his glazing eyes upon me, faltered forth:

"Have you got it?—the will!"

"It is here!" I cried, exhibiting the document to his failing gaze. His looks expressed satisfaction, and he said faintly,

"It is well. I shall die easier for your forgiveness, Mervyn."

"You have it, Malpas," I rejoined, taking his helpless hand in mine. "I forgive you from the bottom of my heart."

He thanked me by a look, for his stiffening fingers could not return my pressure.

"Let me have yours too, Rue?" he said, with a last effort.

She gave it him at once, and with a passionate outburst of grief that attested the depth of her affection.

Unwilling to behold this heart-rending spectacle, I looked away for a moment, when a piercing cry smote my ears, and told me what had occurred. Malpas was gone to his account.

Shriek after shriek followed from the unfortunate gipsy girl— each more harrowing than that which had gone before it. At last she flung herself despairingly upon the lifeless body of her lover.

Even the rugged breast of Phaleg was touched by his daughter's affliction, and he implored the officers to let him go to her. As to Obed, he was so violently excited that he broke from the constable who held him, and rushed towards Rue, when he was again seized. It was a frightful scene, and I felt so heart-sickened that I rushed away.

Seeing how painfully I was affected, Major Atherton immediately followed me, and by the kindest solicitude tried to restore me. He remarked that, distressing as the occurrence might be, it was better for himself—better for all connected with him—that Malpas had died thus. The major then recommended me to go to Nethercrofts.

"Go and take possession of the old house at once," he said. "Stay there to-night. Your tenants will make you up a bed—and they must manage to make up a bed for me as well, for I intend to claim your hospitality. Don't remain any longer here. I will take all disagreeable business that remains to be done off your hands, and will explain to Mr. Hazilrigge and Cuthbert Spring that I have sent you away."

"But I shall see you again soon?" I said.

"You shall see me to-night," he replied. "You remember where you first beheld me?"

"Perfectly. At my mother's grave in Marston churchyard."

"Come to that hallowed spot at nine o'clock this evening," he replied. "You will find me there. I have a secret to reveal to you." And without another word, he turned away and rejoined our friends.

I had just mounted my horse, and was about to ride off to Nethercrofts as I had been enjoined by this singular man, who exercised such an extraordinary influence over me, when Ned Culcheth came up, and after a few remarks, said,

"What a strange thing it be, sir, that Captain Sale should meet his death at yonder spot."

"Why stranger there than elsewhere, Ned?" I asked.

"Because the Nethercrofts estate begins at that point," he rejoined. "No sooner does he touch the land he has coveted, and has striven to wrest from the rightful owner, than his horse dashes him against a tree, and he dies at the foot of the man he has wronged. It looks like a judgment."

I made no reply, but the words sank deep into my breast.

CHAPTER XIX.

ONCE MORE AT THE GRAVE.

WHILE crossing the fields that night from Nethercrofts to keep my appointment with Major Atherton, I was strangely agitated. What was the nature of the revelation to be made to me? Certain notions had sometimes crossed me in regard to this inscrutable personage, but they seemed so wild and extravagant that I did not dare to indulge them. Accordingly, I had dismissed them as soon as formed. But now they came back upon me with greater force than ever. The truth seemed suddenly to flash upon me. And I hurried on, eager to turn my conjectures into certainties.

Full of hope, and with a breast beating with new-born emotions, I passed through the little gate opening upon the churchyard. A wan moon, struggling through passing clouds, feebly illumined the place. By this scanty light I could distinguish that he was standing near the grave, and I flew towards him.

He did not keep me a moment in suspense, but held out his arms as I approached.

"My son! my dear son!" he exclaimed.

"My father! my dear father!" I rejoined, rushing into his embrace.

Profound emotion kept us silent for some minutes. He then spoke:

"When you beheld me that night—though I little thought you were present at the time—I registered a vow on this spot that the rest of my life should be devoted to my son. Since then you have been the sole object of my thoughts. But wishing to study your character and disposition from a point of view which circumstances enabled me to take, I presented myself to you as a stranger; and I continued the part I had commenced, because I desired to see how you would act at a critical conjuncture—contenting myself with looking passively on, but ever ready to come to your assistance in case of need. Had not your mind been greatly engrossed by other matters, you must have discovered me. More than once I have been on the point of acknowledging myself to you, but I have checked myself, because I had determined that the disclosure—which has been, perhaps, too long delayed—should be made on this spot—that here, in your dear mother's presence, as it were, I would avow myself your father, and give you my benediction. Take it, my son," he added, spreading his arms over me, " and if a blessed spirit can be permitted to hover unseen over the living, be assured that your mother is near us now. Kneel down, my son—kneel down—and let us pray!"

On this we both bent the knee reverentially, and continued for some time occupied in fervent devotion. Perchance a gentle spirit *did* look down upon us the while.

My father was the first to rise. When I quitted my kneeling posture, and gazed into his countenance, its habitual sternness had given way to an expression of mildness and benevolence. He again embraced me, and with increased affection. We remained for some time longer near the grave. He had much to say, and wished to say it there. For it seemed to both of us that there was an unseen listener to our converse.

My father told me what had brought him back to England. Death had been busy around him in the burning land he had quitted. Wife and children had all perished from one of those dire scourges that in India decimate a city. He was away from them at the time, and when he returned to Lahore, where he had left them, all were gone. His thoughts then naturally reverted to his son in England, and feelings of affection, hitherto repressed or diverted into other channels, sprang up at once in his bosom. Of his son's precise position he was almost ignorant, for of late the young man had failed to write; while the accounts he received from his ever-active correspondent, Cuthbert Spring, were neither very clear nor very satisfactory. He would go to England. Why should he stay longer in India? He had wealth enough, and had seen service enough. He would retire from the army. His resolution was acted upon; and as soon as the necessary arrangements for his departure could be completed—and they were got through with all possible despatch—he returned to his native land. He had given no intimation of his return to any one—not even to Cuthbert Spring; but on his arrival in London he wrote to his friend, begging him to come up to him. From Cuthbert he learnt all particulars of his son, and what he heard brought him quickly to Cottonborough with his friend. His first visit had been paid to the grave in Marston churchyard, where I had seen him. The rest I knew.

Such was the recital made to me by my father as we stood together on that hallowed spot.

At its close, he knelt down again, pressed his lips to the monumental stone, and walked slowly away, motioning me to follow him. He did not proceed towards the little gate by which I had entered the churchyard, but moved in the opposite direction, until at last we stood opposite the vicarage.

"There is the house of mourning," he said; "and if you could enter it, you would find a mother wailing for her only son—a father prostrated by affliction. I have little commiseration for the worldly vicar whose pride has been thus humbled, but I sincerely pity Mrs. Sale. A worse calamity might, however, have befallen her. If she knew all, she might not deplore her son's death. I saw the lifeless body borne home upon a hurdle, and heard the mother's cry of anguish on beholding it. It wrang my heart as much as that poor gipsy girl's frantic ejaculations had wrung it before to-day, and I was glad to get away."

What he said conjured up such a painful scene to my imagination, that I involuntarily made a movement to depart, and he withdrew with me at once.

On our way to Nethercrofts, where we were both to pass the night, my father informed me that Pownall and the gipsies had been taken to Chester. And I may add, as this will be the last time of mentioning them, that all three met the punishment due to their offences. The gipsies got two years of imprisonment with hard labour; while the Thaumaturgus had an opportunity offered him of visiting Australia—free of expense.

CHAPTER XX.

AT HOME AT THE ANCHORITE'S.

ABOUT a week after the events last recorded, between two and three o'clock in the afternoon, my father and myself drove from the hotel at which we were staying in Cottonborough to the Anchorite's. We made rather a gay turn out, for we occupied a stylish chariot which Colonel Clitheroe had just received from town, with a footman on the box in a dark undress livery, and with a cockade in his hat. A pair of spanking greys, driven by a smart-looking postilion in a scarlet jacket and irreproachable leathers, soon made their way through the crowded streets, rattled across the iron bridge over the Ater, bowled along the Broughton road at the rate of ten miles an hour, and almost before we had time to think of it, brought us to our destination.

There were two other carriages under the trees at a little distance from the entrance to the Anchorite's, one of which I recognised as Dr. Foam's old-fashioned yellow chariot, but the other was a very handsome equipage indeed, with a remarkably stout, consequential-looking coachman, and a powdered footman, both in rich liveries, seated on the hammercloth. I noticed that this carriage had an earl's coronet on the panels.

Meantime, our footman had rung the bell, and the summons was answered by Mr. Comberbach, arrayed in a handsome suit of sables, with aiguillettes on his shoulder, and having an important and almost majestic air. The butler was attended by two other men-servants, likewise attired in black, but I was glad to perceive that the inauspicious-looking Fabyan Lowe was not one of them. Mr. Comberbach advanced towards my father as he alighted, and having respectfully saluted him, accorded me a most smiling welcome.

Ah! how different were my feelings as I now entered the gate of the old house from those I had experienced when passing through it last! Now all looked bright and smiling. As Mr. Comberbach marched with more than his usual pomp along the broad gravel-walk, he ever and anon cast a bland and benign look at me, and just before reaching the porch, he stayed his stately step, and said,

"Her ladyship is on the garden terrace near the river, Colonel Clitheroe, and if you please, sir, I will conduct you to her at once. But perhaps," he added, with a glance at me—" perhaps it may be agreeable to you, Mr. Mervyn, to see Miss Apphia first."

"By all means, Comberbach," I replied, eagerly. "You anticipate my wishes."

"Have the goodness to come up-stairs with me to the library, then," he said. "No necessity for disguise now," he added, in a low tone.

"I will wait here for you, Mervyn," my father remarked, with a smile. "You can dispense with my company, I am sure. Go, my boy. Success attend you!"

I thanked him with a smile, and while he walked into the dining-room, I followed the butler up-stairs, and was ushered by him into the library. As soon as we had entered the room, Mr. Comberbach unbosomed himself in this wise:

"Well, sir, things have turned out much better than I expected. Her ladyship makes a very good missis—a little overbearing at times, but nothin' to complain of. We've got rid of that prying rascal, Fabyan Lowe. Molly still keeps her place, and is likely to keep it, for she has got used to her ladyship's ways, and knows how to please her. We shall never have such another missis as dear Mrs. Mervyn—but it's no use grievin'. We must make ourselves as comfortable as we can in this Vale of Tears. And talkin' o' that, sir, I have at last made up my mind to marry——"

"Molly Bailey," I suggested.

"Right, sir," he replied—"right. Miss Apphia has kindly obtained her ladyship's consent to our espousals—so as there is now no impediment we shall soon be man and wife. We have been already asked at the Old Church. Ours has been a longish engagement, Mr. Mervyn,—well-nigh thirty years. I wouldn't recommend you to wait so long, sir," he added, with a knowing look.

"I don't mean to do so, Comberbach," I replied. "You must look quick, or I shall be married before you. But tell me!—who is with her ladyship in the garden?"

"Lord bless me, sir! don't you know? I thought Colonel Clitheroe would have told you. Didn't you see the carriage at the gate? It's her ladyship's father, the old Earl of Rossendale, and her brother, Lord Leyland. They've been staying in Cottonborough for the last three days. Dr. Foam is with them in the garden. Other company are expected, and a cold collation is laid out in the dining-room. The Rev. Mr. Wilburton is here, sir."

What else he might have informed me I know not, for at this moment the inner door opened, and as Apphia and her brother entered from it, the loquacious butler took flight.

She was dressed in deep mourning, which seemed to suit her somewhat serious style of countenance and sedate deportment better than gayer apparel would have done. When I say serious, I am almost afraid of conveying a wrong impression of her looks, which wore a gentle pensiveness, very far removed from gravity, and still further from gloom. Nothing, indeed, could be sweeter than the smile with which she greeted me—nothing more affectionate than her manner.

For a few moments I saw only her. John seemed to vanish from my sight. I told her I was come to claim her as my bride, and that if I were refused, I was resolved to carry her off in spite of all opposition. She answered, with a smile, that happily such extreme measures, which she herself might feel compelled to resist, did not need to be resorted to, for she thought, if a formal claim for her hand were now made to her mother, that it would not be rejected.

"Then there is no longer any impediment," I exclaimed, joyfully. "You are mine, dearest Apphia—mine for ever!"

"Yes, yours for ever, dearest Mervyn," she rejoined, with inexpressible tenderness—"yours for ever!"

I drew her towards me as the words were uttered, strained her to my bosom, and sealed our marriage-compact on her lips.

"Heaven bless you both!" John ejaculated, fervently. "My dearest wish on earth is gratified."

"We must join the party in the garden," Apphia said, gently extricating herself from my embrace. "Recollect, dear Mervyn, you have my mother's consent to obtain. You know the promise I gave her?" she added, with a smile.

"A most unfortunate promise I thought it," I cried.

"You need not mind it now," she replied. "Come! I long to hear what you think of my new relations—though I am sure you will like them."

We then went down stairs, and ere we had reached the hall, my father, hearing our voices, came out of the dining-room to meet us. Apphia sprang affectionately towards him.

"Is it as I hope? Am I to call you daughter, my dear child?" he inquired.

She answered gently in the affirmative, and the colonel, enchanted, pressed his lips to her forehead.

We then went forth into the garden. My father offered Apphia his arm, and I did not dispute the privilege with him, but contented myself with walking on her other side.

At an earlier period of my history, I have mentioned that a long, sheltered walk through the garden conducted to the banks of the Ater, where the green slopes, shaded by fine old beech-trees, growing on a dry sandy soil, formed a delightful place of promenade in warm weather. Towards this spot we now shaped our course, as we understood that Lady Amicia was there with her guests.

We found the party seated beneath the trees. The Earl of Rossendale was a venerable-looking man, with snow-white hair, and a truly noble cast of countenance. Years ago he must have had a very stately presence; even now there was an air of infinite dignity about him. Though turned eighty, he bore his years well, and looked as if able to sustain the load for some time longer.

What the old earl had been his son now was—a person of most commanding appearance, lofty in stature, well-built, and with features not merely handsome, but proclaiming his high birth. His carriage was erect, and his deportment ordinarily extremely haughty, though on this occasion I am bound to say that his manner was remarkably affable. In point of age, Lord Leyland was between fifty and sixty, but though he had led a very active political life, and had filled very important offices both at home and abroad, there was still some of the fire of youth in his glance, and no lack of vigour in his frame. In fact, he might have passed for a younger man by ten years than he was in reality. There was a strong family likeness between Lady Amicia and her relatives, and a remarkable expression of pride, which time had not effaced in the lineaments of the venerable earl, could be distinctly traced in the features of his son and daughter.

Lady Amicia was dressed in deep mourning, and her attire became her exceedingly. Never before had I seen her appear to such great advantage. She was seated between her father and brother, while Dr. Foam occupied a place near the old earl. On seeing us, Lord Leyland immediately arose, and advancing to meet us, shook hands with great cordiality with my father.

"You must make me known to your son, Colonel Clitheroe," he said, with a very encouraging look at me. "I ought to know him, since he is to have my niece. Upon my word, colonel, you have no reason to be ashamed of him—nor have we."

"None of us, I trust, will have reason to blush for him, my dear lord," my father answered, proudly.

"Come with me, young sir," Lord Leyland cried, taking my arm with great good-humour; "I will introduce you to my father myself."

And he led me towards the old earl, who got up at my approach, and offered me his hand. I never beheld anything finer than his manner. A monarch could not have exhibited greater dignity. I almost felt abashed as I took the hand proffered me.

"Here is your grandson—that is to be—my lord," Lord Leyland cried, "and I think you will approve of him as much as I do."

"I am very glad to see him, and I *do* like his looks," the earl said, glancing kindly at me. "Emulate your father, young man," he added to me, "and we shall all be proud of you."

Having made as suitable a reply as I could, I next addressed myself to Lady Amicia, who received me with a kindness of manner as unexpected as gratifying.

"I will frankly own that I have done you great injustice, Mervyn," she said. "I have suffered myself to be prejudiced against you, and have believed assertions which I ought to have treated as calumnies. But I will make every reparation in my power. I know what you would ask of me, and will anticipate the request. My daughter's hand shall be yours—her heart has been yours long ago. I will say more—I feel certain that she could not find a worthier husband."

My feelings so completely overpowered me that I was unable to make an adequate reply. I attempted to speak; but my emotion was too great, and checked my utterance.

"I will thank you for Mervyn, dear mother," John said, stepping forward. "And let me add, that you have doubled the favour by the manner of conferring it. Never have I loved and honoured you more than at this moment."

"Well, then, this important matter is settled," Lord Leyland cried, coming to my rescue. "We are all agreed that the marriage *is* to take place, and the only thing remaining to be done is to fix the day."

"The sooner the better," I cried.

"Suppose we say this day month?" Lord Leyland said. "Will that do, Apphia?"

"Nay, don't appeal to me, uncle," she replied. "However, I shall raise no objection."

"And I am sure Mervyn will not," my father interposed. "With Lady Amicia's permission, the wedding shall take place on this day month."

Her ladyship graciously signified her assent, and my happiness was complete.

"Can we not manage to find John a wife at the same time," Lord Leyland cried. "I think I *have* heard of a certain young lady—possessed of great personal attractions—amiable as beautiful—and an heiress, if I am not misinformed—who might, perhaps, be prevailed upon to give her hand, if properly solicited."

"The experiment may be made at once," I said, "for here she comes."

While Lord Leyland had been speaking, I had descried Comberbach advancing with a party consisting of Old Hazy and his sister, Ora and Cuthbert Spring.

The new-comers, it appeared, had been invited to meet my father and myself, and experienced a most friendly reception from Lady Amicia—so friendly that Old Hazy was quite overwhelmed by it. Could this affable lady be the domineering, disagreeable personage he had heard of? Impossible! Miss Hazilrigge was equally surprised, but greatly pleased, as was Ora, to whom Lady Amicia paid the most marked attention.

Apphia, of course, was delighted to see her friends, and the party from the Grange at once found themselves at home. Indeed, with the exception of Lady Amicia's two noble relatives, they were among old friends, for Dr. Foam was well known to Mr. Hazilrigge, and had often experienced his hospitality at Owlarton Grange.

But even from the "great folks," as Miss Hazilrigge termed them in private to me, they met the same friendly welcome. The old Earl of Rossendale quite unbent, and, as is always the case when a proud man *does* unbend, was infinitely more agreeable than a person of habitually easy manners. He seemed quite to appreciate Old Hazy, who, with all his peculiarities, was a perfect gentleman of the old school, and this Lord Rossendale did not fail to discover. So the venerable and courtly peer and the worthy old commoner got on remarkably well together. Old Hazy and the ladies were invited to the earl's seat, Buckrose, in Yorkshire; and in his turn Lord Rossendale promised to pay his new friend a visit at Owlarton Grange. These invitations were not matters of form, but were heartily given on both sides, and what is more, both visits were paid.

Courteous and pleasant to all, Lord Leyland devoted himself chiefly to the ladies. I saw in a moment that he was greatly struck by Ora, as indeed he could not fail to be, for she was looking her very best, was exquisitely attired, and in high spirits. I also quickly perceived that he was determined to set matters right between his nephew and the young heiress.

"Why the girl is a perfect angel," I heard him exclaim to John; " I never beheld a more charming creature—magnificent eyes—and the figure and step of an Andalusian! What could any man wish for more? You mustn't let such a prize slip through your fingers."

"I am afraid he will, unless your lordship comes to his assistance," I observed, *sotto voce.*

The hint was not lost upon Lord Leyland. He at once set to work, and very soon contrived to settle the little lovers' quarrel. By gently fanning the rising flame, he soon caused it to burn as strongly as ever. When this reconciliation was effected, and John was safely caught in the toils of his fair enslaver, Lord Leyland announced that he had obtained a promise that the dormant title would be restored, and his nephew might therefore be considered, to all intents and purposes, Lord Wilburton.

A fair opportunity was here afforded Lady Amicia for a display of generosity, and I am happy to say she did not allow it to pass. She at once declared that her son should have half her property—even more, if he needed it—to support his title.

And what answer did John make? Did he coldly and philosophically put aside his good fortune? Could he disoblige his noble relatives, and disappoint his mother? Could he resist all our friendly importunities? Above all, could he withstand the bewitching glances of her he loved? He yielded, and with a good grace. In fact, his noble kinsmen, and the language they held, had awakened a proper pride in his bosom, and he began to perceive that he might do more good in the exalted position that awaited him than in the lowly station which he had previously chosen. Heretofore his mother had made him shrink with alarm from the chance of contact with the great world. But recent experiences led him to believe that he should benefit by mixing with it. And he was right. As Lord Wilburton—for he soon afterwards obtained the title — his character was strengthened and refined, his delightful social qualities were brought into play, and his power of doing good increased twenty-fold.

While general conversation was going on, Cuthbert Spring drew me aside.

"A word with you, my young friend," he said. "I suppose you understand it all now?"

"I understand that I am completely happy," I replied; "but how these extraordinary changes have been brought about passes my comprehension. My father has kept me quite in the dark."

"Your father is fond of surprises, as you must have seen," Cuthbert rejoined. "He won't unmask his batteries till all is ready for action. During the whole of the month that you were enjoined to keep quiet—for he was afraid of your meddling with his plans——"

"Not having any great opinion of my capacity, I suppose——"

"He and I were hard at work for you," Cuthbert proceeded. "It was rather a difficult job," he added, lowering his voice, "to accommodate matters with Lady Amicia, but with Dr. Foam's help, who has been of immense use to us, we accomplished it at last. You never suspected that your father was a daily visitor here, eh?"

"Never," I replied. "I didn't dream of such a thing. Apphia never mentioned him in her letters to her brother."

"Not in those he showed you, I dare say. But John has been let into the plot for the last three weeks. But I haven't told you all. As soon as matters were adjusted in this quarter, and her ladyship's consent to the marriage was *all but* obtained—we all three—that is, your father, Dr. Foam, and myself—went over to Buckrose, where we were extremely well received by the old earl and his son. Full explanations were given by the colonel of his intentions in regard to you, which are very handsome I need scarcely say, and the treaty of alliance was speedily concluded so far as Lord Rossendale was concerned. His lordship was pleased to say, that as he took it for granted you must resemble your father, he should unhesitatingly give his sanction to your union with his granddaughter. Before this, I ought to tell you, a complete reconciliation had taken place between Lady Amicia and her noble relatives, but they had not met. This matrimonial arrangement induced Lord Rossendale to expedite the visit he intended to pay his daughter, and Lord Leyland accompanied him, as you see. Your crowning piece of good-luck, however, was the recovery of the will, which came in the very nick of time, and at once turned the scale in your favour with Lady Amicia. We gave ourselves no trouble about Simon Pownall, for we felt certain he would go back to the Grange and get entrapped there. Now you know all. Ah! colonel," he added, as my father and Dr. Foam came towards us, "I have been telling Mervyn of your plot."

"I have plotted for his happiness," my father replied, "and I hope have succeeded. Mervyn, you are greatly indebted to these two kind friends—but especially to Dr. Foam, without whose assistance you would not be here at this moment. He smoothed the way for us."

"Tut! tut! say no more about it, colonel," the worthy physician cried. "All's well that ends well! Things went very cross with Mervyn for a long time, but they have got straight at last. I think he will now admit that I did well in counselling Apphia to remain with her mother."

I took both his hands, shook them, and thanked him from the bottom of my heart.

After passing some time pleasantly under the trees, we were summoned to a collation by Mr. Comberbach, and adjourned to the house. It was an excellent repast, and greatly enjoyed, but I shall not pause to describe it, contenting myself with mentioning three toasts given on the occasion. The first of these proceeded from the Earl of Rossendale, and had reference to the marriage which had that day been fixed between myself and his granddaughter. This toast was remarkably well received. Lord Leyland then called upon us to drink health and happiness to another couple, whom he was delighted to say were to be shortly united—his nephew, whom he would venture to style Lord Wilburton, and Miss Ora Doveton. The cheers which followed this toast had scarcely subsided, when Dr. Foam proposed a third couple—his old and esteemed friend Cuthbert Spring and Miss Hazilrigge. The last toast was drunk amidst great cheering and laughter.

On that day month the three marriages were solemnised at the Collegiate Church.

A word ere bidding the friendly reader farewell.

I am now living at the Anchorite's, which Lady Amicia has resigned to us. My father, I am happy to say, is our constant guest. It is almost needless to say that Mr. and Mrs. Comberbach retain their situations. But with me Mrs. Comberbach will always be Molly Bailey.

Lord and Lady Wilburton reside in Yorkshire, at no great distance from the Earl of Rossendale's seat, Buckrose. Lady Amicia has taken up her abode in the same county, but passes the greatest part of her time with her father, with whom she has become an extraordinary favourite.

Old Hazy with Cuthbert Spring and his wife are joint occupants of Owlarton Grange, and the hospitality of the house is by no means diminished. My wife and myself are ever-welcome visitors, and have always the haunted room assigned to us. When business brings Cuthbert Spring to Cottonborough, as is not unfrequently the case, he takes up his abode at the Anchorite's.

I am often at Nethercrofts to look after my property, and derive great assistance in its management from trusty Ned Culcheth, whom I have appointed my bailiff. I have given Ned a comfortable farm-house, where he is as happy as a prince—a great deal happier, indeed, than many princes—for when he returns home at eventide, after a day's work, he has not only a fond wife to welcome him, but three blooming children to climb round his knees "the envied kiss to share."

THE END.

LONDON:
WHITING AND CO., 30 & 32, SARDINIA STREET, LINCOLN'S INN FIELDS.

www.ingramcontent.com/pod-product-compliance
Lightning Source LLC
Chambersburg PA
CBHW020543300426
44111CB00008B/771